Members of the Steering Committee

William L. Cary
Dwight Professor of Law,
Columbia University

Benjamin V. Cohen
Lawyer, Washington, D.C.

Roger F. Murray
former S. Sloan Colt Professor of
Banking and Finance, Columbia University;
Chairman, The Common Fund for Non-Profit Organizations

M. J. Rossant
Director, The Twentieth Century Fund

William Stott
William Stott Associates

Roy A. Schotland, Chairman
Professor of Law, Georgetown University

ABUSE ON
WALL STREET

ABUSE ON WALL STREET

Conflicts of Interest in the Securities Markets

Report to the Twentieth Century Fund
Steering Committee on Conflicts of Interest
in the Securities Markets

A Twentieth Century Fund Report

Q

QUORUM BOOKS Westport, Connecticut ● London, England

Library of Congress Cataloging in Publication Data

Main entry under title:

Abuse on Wall Street.

   "A Twentieth Century Fund report."
   Includes bibliographical references and index.
   1.   Brokers—United States—Addresses, essays,
lectures. 2. Conflict of interests (Agency)—United
States—Addresses, essays, lectures. I. Twentieth
Century Fund. Steering Committee on Conflicts of
Interest in the Securities Markets.
KF1071.A75A2   346'.73'092   79-8295
ISBN 0-89930-001-4

Library of Congress Catalog Card Number: 79-8295
ISBN: 0-89930-001-4

First Published in 1980 by Quorum Books

Greenwood Press
A division of Congressional Information Service, Inc.
51 Riverside Avenue, Westport, Connecticut 06880

Printed in the United States of America

10 9 8 7 6 5 4 3 2 1

Contents

Illustrations

Tables

Foreword

We are, to paraphrase Chesterton, all conflicted now. Anyone who is at all active in our society is confronted by conflicts of some sort, but most of us have little difficulty in resolving them in a responsible fashion. Certainly, the securities industry, where conflicts abound, has long had a heightened awareness of the problems it poses. Because the industry is dealing largely with other people's money, it has been the most scrutinized and the most supervised in terms of conflicts, real and potential. Yet there has been little in the way of sound and systematic research on the current state of conflicts in the securities markets—what they are, why they matter, and how to deal with them.

The Twentieth Century Fund, which almost from its beginnings took an active interest in the proper functioning of the securities markets, decided that this gap in our knowledge ought to be filled. In doing so the Fund was not motivated by a desire to engage in scandalmongering or headline hunting; neither was it concerned about theoretical or potential conflicts where the opportunity for exercising self-interest could conceivably be damaging to others. Rather, its main objective was to concentrate on situations in which actual and practical difficulties exist.

In carrying out this examination, the Fund established a steering committee, headed by Roy A. Schotland, professor of law at Georgetown University Law School; the committee, in turn, selected an experienced group of independent investigators to deal with specific areas of the securities markets. Each of the investigators had freedom to report on the situation as he found it, while the steering committee, after deliberating over the evidence, sought to provide a balanced perspective on conflicts and what ought to be done to mitigate them.

The findings of the investigators and the conclusions of the steering committee make clear that no pervasive problem of conflicts exists today. This should prove reassuring to all investors, including the millions who have an indirect stake through corporate or union pension funds. But if there is no need for radical reform, the fact is that the big increase in indirect investment and the expansion of financial firms have brought an increase in conflict situations and in their complexity that call for new protective measures. The most significant contribution made by the investigators was identifying actual conflicts—a prerequisite to establishing reasonable and effective safeguards against them.

Because the financial industry is so used to living with conflicts and so accustomed to observing rules that guide the exercise of fiduciary responsibility, the steering committee in its recommendations for reform strongly favored new voluntary measures for self-policing. Self-policing of course has not always worked as well as it should, but it remains preferable as a means of guiding ethical or responsible behavior than attempting to regulate such behavior through legislation or administrative fiat. Perhaps the main value of the entire examination is that it alerts both the financial industry and the public to the principal areas where abuses exist and suggests the kind of preventive medicine for them that, if administered in time, can help to maintain confidence in the integrity of the marketplace.

At a time when the financial industry is plagued with a great variety of problems and challenges, conflict situations may not appear to be of critical importance. But abuses in the handling of conflicts tend to engender distrust and suspicion more widely than other weaknesses or shortcomings. What is more, as the various reports demonstrate, conflicts are manageable, provided they are recognized and the will to manage them exists.

The Fund is grateful to each of the investigators—to Richard Blodgett, author of the *New York Times Book of Money*, who reported on union pension funds; to John Brooks, of *The New Yorker*, author of *The Go-Go Years* and other books on the securities markets, who reported on corporate pension funds; to Edward S. Herman, professor of finance at the University of Pennsylvania's Wharton School, who reported on commercial bank trust departments; to Louis M. Kohlmeier, a Pulitzer Prize-winning journalist, who reported on state and local public employee pension funds; to Martin Mayer, author of *The Bankers*, who reported on broker-dealer firms; to Chris Welles, author of *The Last Days of the Club*, who reported on nonprofit institutions; and to Nicholas Wolfson, of the University of Connecticut Law School, co-author of *Regulation of Brokers, Dealers, and Securities Markets*, who wrote on investment banking. Some of their reports were researched and written in the mid-1970s, and although they have been subject to some updating, they have not taken detailed account of more recent developments, most of which, partially as a result of their work, have been positive.

I want to pay a personal tribute to the members of the steering committee—William L. Cary, Dwight Professor of Law at Columbia University Law School and a former chairman of the Securities and Exchange Commission; Benjamin V. Cohen, the architect of most of the original legislation affecting the securities markets and a trustee of the Fund; Roger F. Murray, former S. Sloan Colt Professor of Banking and Finance at Columbia University; and William Stott, formerly vice-president in charge of investment at Morgan Guaranty Trust Company; and Roy A. Schotland. As one privileged to serve with the committee, I can attest to the thoughtfulness and conscientiousness of its members.

I want to offer special thanks to Roy A. Schotland, who was responsible for drafting the introduction and conclusions of the steering committee and also prepared the investigation of real estate investment trusts. He was unflagging in his industry and levelheaded in recognizing that, although conflicts cannot be eliminated, they can—and should—be reduced.

M. J. Rossant,
Director
The Twentieth Century Fund

May 1979

ABUSE ON
WALL STREET

Introduction
by Roy A. Schotland
for the Steering Committee

I • INTRODUCTION

Many forms of conduct permissible in a workday world for those acting at arm's length are forbidden to those bound by fiduciary ties. A trustee is held to something stricter than the morals of the market place. Not honesty alone, but the punctilio of an honor the most sensitive, is then the standard of behavior. As to this there has developed a tradition that is unbending and inveterate. Uncompromising rigidity has been the attitude of courts of equity when petitioned to undermine the rule of undivided loyalty by the "disintegrating erosion" of particular exceptions. . . .Only thus has the level of conduct for fiduciaries been kept at a level higher than that trodden by the crowd.[1]

Half a century has passed since Benjamin Cardozo, then chief judge of New York, set forth his now classic description of the obligation of the fiduciary to act fairly in the interests of his clients. A year later came the stock market crash of 1929, which led to the Securities Act of 1933 and the Securities Exchange Act of 1934, the most important and comprehensive securities market legislation in history.
   Commenting on those events in 1934, Justice Harlan Fiske Stone said:

I venture to assert that when the history of the financial era which has just drawn to a close comes to be written, most of its mistakes and its major faults will be ascribed to the failure to observe the fiduciary principle, the precept as old as Holy Writ, that "a man cannot serve two masters."[2]

Since those days the securities markets have operated reasonably efficiently and remained relatively free of scandal. Yet it is by no means clear that they have functioned as well as they might. In discussions at the Twentieth Century Fund in the early 1970s, a number of people with a great variety of involvements in the securities markets concluded that the "departure of the small investor, perhaps some of the volatility of the market, and certainly much of the prevailing cynicism about Wall Street might be traced to a widespread, though generally not perceived, concern over conflicts of interest within the financial community." The Fund sponsored this study in an attempt to assess the pervasiveness of such conflicts of interest, to evaluate their significance, and to recommend realistic procedures for their resolution.

II • WHAT IS A CONFLICT OF INTEREST?

The researchers and the members of the steering committee that the Fund established to examine this subject shared the problem of defining the term *conflict of interest*.[1] We found clarity of definition important because mere mention of the phrase opens, as did Pandora's box, a burst of problems and reactions that hinder analysis.

Yet the term *conflict of interest* is not obscure; it denotes a situation in which two or more interests are legitimately present and competing or conflicting. The individual (or firm) making a decision that will affect those interests may have a larger stake in one of them than in the other(s), but he is expected—in fact, obligated—to serve each as if it were his own, regardless of his own actual stake.

Conflicts are occasionally described as "the problem of wearing two hats," but as the pages that follow suggest, many conflict situations might be more accurately characterized as "hydra-hatted." Self-interest is always one of the elements in a conflict. (Of course, even self-interest may be divided—as between a desire to preserve reputation or self-image and a desire for gain—but conflicts within the self go beyond the scope of these studies.) In many conflicts self-interest clashes with fiduciary obligations.

Conflict situations become *hydra-hatted* when conflict arises among professional obligations. For example, a fiduciary may have two long-standing clients between whom, unforeseeably, an event or transaction creates a conflict that involves the fiduciary. Or a bank officer with fiduciary obligations to his bank may become a director of a borrower corporation, thus assuming obligations to that corporation and its stockholders that may—and are likely to—conflict with his obligations to further the bank's interests.

The institutions we have studied operate primarily as fiduciaries; as such, they are under *legal* obligations to act in the interests of their customers. A trustee or investment advisor, merely by opening the door to do business, undertakes legal obligations to do business as a fiduciary. A fiduciary's responsibility to his client—for example, that of a guardian to a ward—is to promote and protect the interests of the client to such an extent that the client may be justified in trusting that his interests are the only ones being considered in matters affecting him, unless and until he is told otherwise.[2] Even when the client is told otherwise, as in the setting of fees, the fiduciary is not free to seek what the traffic will bear; rather, he is supposed to use not only honest but disinterested judgment in determining what is reasonable compensation. The conflicts of interest confronted by fiduciaries, especially institutions handling large amounts of other people's money, are cause for special concern and have important implications for public policy.

It is important to distinguish the relationship between fiduciary and client from that between ordinary buyer and seller. A used car salesman has much narrower obligations to his customers than a fiduciary has to his client. Of course, sellers have obligations of truthfulness—for example, the used car dealer has a duty not to set back the odometer—and in some situations sellers may have special duties, such as when a buyer relies upon a seller to select an article for a particular use. But except for such limited duties, neither party is obligated to serve the other's interests. Buyers make marketplace decisions about products or sellers, and sellers make similar decisions about how much they want the sale and how much they want goodwill. Despite the difficulty purchasers may have in buying an automobile, selecting a bottle of wine, or having a television set repaired, the commercial marketplace generally does an efficient and effective job of resolving conflicts of interest between buyer and seller; at worst, a buyer may lose a few dollars and switch to another seller. For the sale of certain commodities, such as legal drugs, in which the consequences of bad selection or advice may be more severe, government maintains elaborate licensing and related regulatory systems.

But the marketplace for professional services, such as medical treatment, legal advice, and investment management, poses more complex problems. First, the need or wish for confidentiality makes marketplace-type shopping unfeasible. Second, the importance of the service rendered makes the cost of a mistake too high to justify reliance on the trial-and-error approach that a consumer may use in the commercial marketplace. Finally, the buyer is simply unable to evaluate not only the worth of the services but even what services are required. Even after a transaction is completed, it is difficult for the buyer to determine whether the service was appropriate and the fee reasonable.

Along with the power and right to make decisions about his property, health, or legal affairs, the buyer of professional services cannot avoid conferring on the seller the *power* to exploit his trust to serve the seller's own ends instead of the buyer's. The buyer of professional services has no choice but to put aside *caveat emptor* and to repose trust in the seller. To compensate for the buyer's vulnerability, certain standards of behavior on the part of sellers in whom such trust is reposed have become law.

In the financial field, legislation defines the fiduciary obligations of brokers, dealers, pension fund officials, trustees, underwriters, and other professionals. Of course, legislating a principle does not guarantee a result; there are unprofessional professionals and faithless fiduciaries. But the law both reflects and supports the expectation of special conduct that is set forth in the fiduciary's unique responsibilities.

A century ago our law treated the mere presence of a conflict of interest as reason to void a transaction. Although, in time, we abandoned that procrustean prophylactic, we may have failed to develop doctrines and devices adequate to safeguard against the abuses to which the blanket prohibition was addressed.

Since this study began, public concern about conflicts of interest—especially, although not exclusively, in public service—has risen dramatically. Concern about some of the financial institutions we studied, such as pension funds, also has risen sharply, as has awareness of the significance of conflicts of interest in all financial institutions. For example:

- In 1977 the Federal Deposit Insurance Corporation (FDIC) found that fifty-eight of the ninety-nine bank failures between 1960 and May 1977 occurred because "insiders" engaged in self-dealing. In 1976 the FDIC promulgated a more stringent set of rules for bank insiders' dealings.
- At the same time, the Federal Home Loan Bank Board issued significant new guidelines on conflicts of interest in savings and loan associations.
- In 1978 the Federal Reserve Board and Comptroller of the Currency issued unprecedentedly specific guidelines regarding conflicts in bank trust departments.
- In 1974 Congress passed the most important legislation of the 1970s affecting financial institutions, the Employee Retirement Income Security Act (ERISA). It includes an unusually full treatment of fiduciary obligations. The implementation of this legislation, resolving old problems and creating some much-debated new ones, has brought new visibility to fiduciary obligations.
- Since ERISA's enactment, congressional committees have begun an unprecedented exploration of state and local pension funds. (We are gratified to learn that these committees used our work on this subject as a guide in selecting the focus of their inquiries into fiduciary questions.)

III • CONFLICTS IN FINANCIAL INSTITUTIONS

Conflicts of interest in financial institutions have special importance. Bank trust departments, which are the largest institutional investors, manage over $500 billion of assets. Private pension funds hold approximately $300 billion and are the largest category of institutional accounts (about 60 percent of such funds are managed by bank trust departments); state and local pension funds hold another $140 billion. Such institutions constitute the bulk of both our primary capital markets, buying the new issues of the nation's corporate borrowers, and our secondary capital markets, trading and pricing corporate securities that are already outstanding. The performance of these institutions has vast and immediate consequences for the entire private sector.

These institutions perform such a wide variety of functions that they are inescapably enmeshed in a maze of conflicting obligations. Financial institutions face more complex conflicts than, for example, the "one-dimensional" tension between a lawyer's self-interest in receiving reasonable compensation and his obligation to honor a client's reliance upon him in deciding what compensation is reasonable.

Even a financial institution with only a single function faces a "second dimension" of conflicts in its obligations to its various customers. An investment advisory firm whose sole function is to provide investment advice on a retainer basis must decide how much attention each of its numerous accounts is to receive, in what sequence they are to receive new advice, and how limited-supply investments, such as "hot" new issues or participation in a private placement, shall be allocated. Unless clients have previously agreed to differences in fees or other terms, it is an abuse to favor the accounts that matter most to the advisor—who thus indirectly serves himself, at the expense of his less sophisticated but equally well-entitled accounts.

But most financial institutions perform more than one function. Broker-dealers, banks, and bank trust departments perform a multiplicity of functions. For example, most large broker-dealers: (1) execute orders to buy and sell stocks; (2) execute orders for bonds and other investments, for which the commissions or other compensation will be higher than on stocks; (3) execute orders—sometimes as brokers acting strictly as customers' agents and sometimes as dealers acting as principals for themselves and selling to or buying from their customers; (4) provide investment advice, usually free of charge and thus potentially with an interest in generating orders (hence, many in the industry now favor a separate charge for this service); (5) perform the foregoing functions not only for a large number of generally small individual customers but also for a smaller number of institutional investors, not all of which are huge but almost all of which are much more valuable customers, in dollar terms, than most individual investors; (6) underwrite new issues, in which capacity the firm is obligated both to the corporation selling the securities and to the customers to whom they are being sold; in addition, in "hot" markets underwriting involves acute problems of allocating securities among customers, and in all markets it involves considerable "after-market" problems; and (7) serve as a depository for customers' funds and securities, with the right to use such assets for the benefit of other customers or of the firm itself.

IV • CLARIFYING CONFLICTS

Three aspects of conflicts need special clarification and emphasis. First, it should be recognized that the self-serving opportunities present in conflict situations usually are not exploited. If exploitation of such opportunities were more common, fiduciary relationships would seldom have survived, reputations would rarely have been intact, and the law would have had to intervene far more than it has. A *conflict* is a situation that may—but need not—result in self-serving abuse or the betrayal of one client's trust to benefit oneself. Throughout these studies conflicts in which improper favoritism or self-serving *might* occur have been kept distinct from actual abuses.

Unfortunately, the phrase *conflict of interest* has a negative connotation, due to the widespread and cynical notion that conflict leads inevitably to abuse. Hence, many people say "I have no conflict" when they mean they have committed no abuse. When individuals who obviously do have conflicts use that form of denial, it usually serves to raise rather than to allay suspicion.

Second, conflicts are frequent, indeed nearly ubiquitous, because valuable efficiencies result from having one individual (or firm) perform a variety of functions. Some conflicts, such as interlocking directorships, are easily avoidable. But stockbrokers serve also as dealers to be able to meet orders in a full range of securities without unnecessary transaction costs. Are higher costs worth paying to avoid the conflicts inherent in the broker-dealer's dual functions? Or if a bank in a small community cannot offer trust services because combining the banking and trust functions generates conflicts, then that community may be unable to support any local investment advisory service. Is the cost of foregoing such service—hard to measure but real—greater than the cost of the problems inherent in living with the conflict?

Third, abuses of conflicts of interest must be distinguished from conduct that is simply criminal. Most conflict abuses incur merely civil sanctions, criminal sanctions being inappropriate in most cases of conflict between—by definition—two interests *legitimately* present. The legitimate presence of these interests makes it difficult to know (let alone to know "beyond a reasonable doubt") whether the conflict was abused or the same transaction would have occurred—and on the same terms—even if no conflict had been present. For example, when a corporate officer appropriates to his own use funds or property that he controls but does not own, he cannot claim any legitimate interest in personal use of that property and he is simply guilty of embezzlement. But when a corporate officer responsible for purchasing supplies has a brother who is one of the main sellers of an item the officer must purchase, he has a conflict because it is legitimate for him—in fact, incumbent upon him—to consider whether to purchase from his brother among other suppliers. Of course, the officer involved should arrange for his superior officers to make the decision. But whoever decides, if the brother is chosen to supply the item, it will not be clear whether an abuse has or has not occurred—whether the brother was selected properly or at unnecessary expense to the purchasing corporation—unless the price and terms can be readily compared with those of alternative suppliers. Even if the price is high, whether it is unfairly high depends on considerations such as whether the item is sometimes in short supply or often needs servicing; under these conditions a reliable supplier may be well worth a higher price. In contrast, a purchasing officer who receives gifts from a seller in return for the corporation's business has no legitimate interest in the gift, and the value of the gift need not be assessed (assuming that it is above whatever is deemed the *de minimis* level) in determining the costs and benefits of the officer's choice. Such an arrangement is nothing more than a criminal kickback or bribe.[1]

V • WHY DO CONFLICTS MATTER?

The main concern of the steering committee has been to explore the occurrence of actual abuses and the adequacy of safeguards against future abuse. Actual abuses, even if infrequent, are important primarily because they inflict injuries and arouse fears. When someone in a position of trust takes an improper economic advantage, he or she deprives some individuals of what is rightfully theirs and hurts others by lowering the operating efficiency of both firms, or causing inefficient allocation of resources, or both.

When abuses of conflicts occur, they cause injuries falling into one—or more—of five different categories:

1. The fiduciary may, directly, take from a beneficiary more than is fair. (*Fairness* involves the degree of disclosure; what a disinterested person would have done; and apart from those criteria, a range, or gray area, in which reasonable persons might disagree.) A simple example is taking advantage of a client's trust by setting excessive fees or performing unnecessary services. Slightly masked, this abuse assumes forms such as the broker-dealer's *churning* of an account, described in our broker-dealer study; " 'Churning,' says a young enforcement officer of the New York Stock Exchange, 'is really theft.' There are truly amazing cases on record.'' Individual firms have set up monitoring programs or even employed special "compliance officers" to prevent churning. And both industry self-regulatory bodies and the Securities and Exchange Commission (SEC) also have undertaken similarly elaborate and impressive efforts for the same purpose.

Churning, however, is the infrequent extreme, an outright abuse that is possible because of the presence in securities markets of fiduciaries whose advice is peculiarly difficult to fashion, equally difficult to evaluate, and in many situations made yet more problematic by the omnipresence of incentives to shape the advice for the fiduciary's benefit. Such incentives may arise from the ways in which persons giving advice are compensated, or from the bundling of such advice with other services, or from the fact that the client who is used to relying on "his" broker or investment banker is unlikely to feel less reliance when that firm acts not as the client's agent but instead as a principal selling to the client. Thus, improper shaping of advice may occur when a broker-dealer recommends a purchase or sale not sincerely on the merits but because he wants to generate some commissions; this abuse occurs more frequently as an occasional slippage than in its extreme form—churning. Or as in a case that our broker-dealer study cited, an investment banking firm may advise purchase of a security even though simultaneously its own investment judgment is causing it to liquidate its own holding of that security.

In some situations the fiduciary may take small amounts from each of its beneficiaries; for example, a trust department, without disclosure, may place uninvested cash from all its trust accounts in non interest-bearing deposits in its own commercial banking department. Our trust department study makes clear that this practice once pervaded the industry[2] and that the Federal Reserve and the Comptroller of the Currency not merely allowed but even encouraged it by recognizing a non interest-bearing time deposit—an instrument for which it is hard to imagine any economic justification—for uninvested trust cash. We are pleased to note that, with high interest rates leading to increased concern about cash management and with computer capabilities lowering the cost of making idle cash productive, trust departments have been altering their practices over the past several years.

2. The fiduciary may, indirectly, take from a beneficiary what belongs to the beneficiary, often by diverting to its own use assets belonging to its beneficiaries. For example, a corporation may use its pension account funds to pursue a corporate purpose, such as an acquisition, even though that use may be unsound from the investment perspective of the pension beneficiaries. The tax code has recognized this problem (although some corporate pension plan assets might not be technically the property of the beneficiaries) by providing for revocation of a plan's tax exemption if the assets were used for any purpose other than the beneficiaries' benefit. Our study of corporate pension funds notes that one small company had its pension fund buy the company's office building, at a price that was a bargain for the pension fund according to an appraisal secured by the company but was 15 percent higher than fair market value according to the Internal Revenue Service (IRS). One major company, F.W. Woolworth, had 27 percent of its assets in company real estate and mortgages, in addition to some holdings of Woolworth common stock. Such investments are unsound, even if fairly priced, because they make the beneficiaries unduly dependent on Woolworth's continued success, which, given the fate of W.T. Grant, cannot be taken for granted. Two other major companies, Georgia-Pacific and Genesco, not only used their pension fund assets to buy their own common stock but did so in such volume and at such times as to manipulate their stock's price illegally, thereby obtaining the means to acquire other companies on falsely favorable terms. Today, the SEC and ERISA have reduced the opportunities for such abuses.

Similarly, a state or local pension fund may invest in tax-exempt local securities, diverting assets into an investment that makes little sense for an account that is itself tax-exempt. This practice is so obviously unsound that it was vanishing throughout the United States until New York City's financial crisis caused its municipal union pension funds to invest such large proportions of their assets in local tax-exempt securities that the state had to pass special legislation protecting the trustees from liability; this deviation from the trend in pension fund management became a *cause célèbre*. In the private sector, multiemployer or "union" pension funds have invested assets in ventures selected to serve the union's interests rather than to further retirement security.

Indirect taking also may involve capturing for the fiduciary's own benefit what would have belonged to the beneficiary if the fiduciary had adequately discharged his obligations. For example, a firm active in real estate investment for its own account and also sponsoring a real estate investment trust owned by diverse public stockholders constantly faces the problem of deciding which account shall participate in attractive investment opportunities. Thus, Chase Manhattan's prospectus for its real estate investment trust (REIT) declared:

The real estate investment activities of the Advisor and certain of its affiliates engaged in the mortgage banking business will parallel those of the [REIT] in many types of investment, and therefore to a certain extent the Advisor and such of its affiliates will be engaged in competition with the [REIT] for investment opportunities.

Exacerbating that competition the first chairman of the REIT also was the Chase Bank's executive vice president in charge of its real estate and mortgage department, the normal pattern in bank-sponsored REITs. Another major bank-sponsored REIT held a second mortgage loan junior to a first mortgage held by the bank advisor. Although such practices cannot, without more information, be declared improper, they raise considerable concern. The bank REITs' handling of this problem compares unfavorably with the standard operating procedure of insurance company-sponsored REITs, which provide for *joint* investments by sponsor and REIT to minimize the likelihood that unduly weak investments might be shunted to the REIT. These are examples of an old problem of general corporate law, known as "diversion of corporate opportunity," that arises with particular complexity in large, multifunction firms managing accounts for different ownership interests.

A different form of diversion of corporate or trust property, not always recognized as such, is stock trading on "inside information." A banker or corporate officer receives such information for job-related purposes, not for personal profit. In the same vein, a banker receives inside information from borrowers to secure and service loans, not so he can make incidental use of that information for his own benefit or that of other accounts.

3. A fiduciary rarely has only one client, and although differences in treatment are inevitable and largely proper, some differences amount to unfair discrimination. For example, an investment manager with large pension accounts is answerable for their management to what are usually highly sophisticated corporate managements, in contrast to the usually strikingly lower sophistication, and perhaps less close attention, of personal trust account beneficiaries. Although often the investment manager will be a full, formal trustee for the personal trusts and only an agent—with lesser legal responsi-

bility, and less reliance reposed—for many of the pension accounts, he may give the latter fuller attention, faster action, possibly better talent, and sometimes even preferential allocation of investments. The purpose of such preferential treatment is to prevent the more sophisticated pension account principals, who closely monitor performance, from taking their accounts elsewhere (or, as is more common, merely shifting new inflows of cash to other managers). If disclosed and fee-rated, such discrimination is proper; if not, it mocks the formal trust obligation.

Very few trust departments and broker-dealer firms managing accounts have developed procedures to prevent improper preferential treatment. Some investment managers pool personal trust assets in common funds and give these funds first-rank treatment. But for various reasons, substantial amounts of assets cannot be pooled and must remain sitting separately in personal trust accounts.

4. An abuse of a conflict also may hurt the fiduciary's competitors. For example, an investment manager that also competes for private placements can give better-than-market terms to private-placement customers by "dumping" the private placements into its "captive" investment management accounts. A major bank managing a very large teachers' pension acount apparently did just that in one instance reported in both our study of state and local pension funds and our study of trust departments. Such dumping, of course, hurts the account, but this possible harm is not the inhibiting factor it should be if the bank can benefit significantly from ignoring its fiduciary obligations. It is more likely to benefit in this way if the account's principals are not sophisticated or are, for political reasons, unlikely to go elsewhere. Any such abuse of essentially captive accounts places other firms that compete for private placements or other banks competing for general banking relationships at a competitive disadvantage in regard to the terms they can offer unless they too have captive accounts and a readiness to abuse them.

5. Some conflict abuses may harm third persons entirely unrelated to the fiduciary or the beneficiary. If some firms secure business because of abuses of conflicts (or other nonmarket factors) rather than because of their efficiency, not only do more efficient competitors suffer, but the overall efficiency of the particular market also declines. Such declines cause economic losses to customers as well as harm to other participants in those markets—and their employees and stockholders—who are entitled to operate on the assumption that their success or failure will depend on their ability, effort, and related performance and not on improper or illegal preferences.

For example, Merrill Lynch acting as underwriter for McDonnell Douglas disclosed material information about that company to selected institutional customers before the information became public, enabling those customers to trade at predisclosure prices but leaving out other Merrill Lynch customers, even those to whom the firm was obligated. If the conduct had remained undiscovered, it also would presumably have given Merrill Lynch an advantage with the favored customers vis-à-vis other broker-dealers. And it also placed anyone who happened to be trading McDonnell Douglas stock at that time under an information disadvantage that is not merely unfair but illegal: the law recognizes our need to preserve fair and open public securities markets lest we lose public confidence in those markets, thereby losing public readiness to participate and weakening or destroying the effectiveness of those markets in capital formation.

Such injuries occur with sufficient frequency and seriousness to justify business and government in taking corrective measures, although these measures are not without their own costs.

In addition, conflicts of interest matter because of appearances. As Louis Kohlmeier demonstrates in his study of state and municipal pension funds, when a banker not only sits on the board of a public pension fund but also manages that fund's equity investments, outsiders have reason to doubt that the fund is being administered in the best interests of its beneficiaries, no matter how selflessly the banker may in fact be fulfilling his responsibilities. Or as John Brooks suggests in his study, even if a corporate pension fund purchasing the stock of the sponsoring corporation sincerely believes those securities are a wise investment, the conflict of interest is so obvious that many corporations strictly prohibit this practice and federal law now limits it. To the extent that major firms in the securities industry fail to provide the appearance as well as the reality of abuse-free behavior, the entire industry becomes suspect and legal intervention becomes more likely.

VI • WHY DO CONFLICT ABUSES OCCUR?

The failures of fiduciaries to meet their obligations are occasionally due to greed but may also result from limitations on market forces, weaknesses in the structure of firms, or simple failure to focus on conflict problems. For example, market competition to render investment management services is limited because most states allow only banks to serve as corporate trustees. Competition in a particular community may be limited by that community's inability to support two investment advisory firms and the reluctance of local purchasers of such services to deal with nonlocal firms. Competition in these services also is limited by the fact that they are, for many purchasers, less important than other services—such as banking—rendered by the same seller. Thus, a completely informal "tying"—motivated by nothing more sinister than convenience and custom—has made competition in the investment management market less vigorous than, say, in banking or brokerage. Commercial banking is so much more competitive than most other services rendered by banks, such as trust management, that these other services have been priced to win and hold banking relationships. This structure often results in excellent treatment for important banking customers but potential problems for many smaller or less sophisticated customers.

In the past decade, the growth of pension funds (and an increasing number of individuals with substantial wealth) has vastly increased competition in investment management. And the small investor has benefited from a proliferation of vehicles for indirect investment that are highly competitive. Heightened competition has noticeably reduced abuses of conflicts, such as those in the management of uninvested cash.

But a good deal of abuse stems simply from inadequate attention to conflicts. Recently, conflicts have become more visible, in part because of a few scandals, and in part, as Martin Mayer observed in our report on broker-dealers, because as open fraud has become less common, the next step forward in the morality of the marketplace has been to attend to conflicts.

The previous lack of concern for conflicts stemmed largely from a surprisingly widespread failure of people charged with the management of money that did not belong to them to recognize that they were under fiduciary obligations and/or to understand what those obligations entailed.[1]

Failure to recognize that one has assumed fiduciary obligations is memorably exemplified by J. Howard Pew, head of the family controlling Sun Oil, who had put over one-fifth of the shares of Sun, worth about $400 million, into a tax-exempt foundation run by a board of seven people, six of whom were Pew family members. The foundation enjoyed tax-sheltered income, gave away little of it (let alone the principal), and made no public reports of any kind until the tax law was changed to require reporting. Pew commented: "I'm not telling anybody anything. It's my money, isn't it?"[2]

In fact, it was not. The tax laws had given Pew the choice of paying taxes to government or using somewhat larger sums, through the medium of a foundation, for some tax-exempt (because publicly beneficial) purpose.

Similarly, the officials of pension funds—corporate or union, state or local—have failed to see that the assets they were managing under special tax exemption were not their own or their organizations' but other people's. Congress well understood that pension and nonprofit organization officials might tend to think of these massive funds as their own money. Hence, the tax exemption for pensions expressly requires that they be operated for "the exclusive benefit of employees or their beneficiaries"; the Taft-Hartley Act authorizing multiemployer pension funds repeats that requirement; and the tax code exempts a variety of nonprofit and eleemosynary organizations from taxes with the provision in each case, like a legislative litany, that "no part of the net earnings inures to the benefit of any private shareholder or individual."

The general principle is clear and sweeping, but the showing in our studies that pension, foundation, and endowment assets have been used improperly for private benefit is not news. Our contribution has been merely to report on these diversions more fully and more cohesively than have previous commentators.

Our examination of different industries reveals not only the recurrence or pervasiveness of some problems, such as using pension assets for investments that further the pension officials' interests rather than the beneficiaries, but also the historical evolution of such problems. Only within the last decade at most has fiduciary status come to be taken seriously throughout the pension sphere. As Louis Kohlmeier wrote,

A basic attitude, long taken by both private and public employers and acquiesced to by employees and often by their unions, was that pensions were gratuities, awarded with gold watches at age sixty-five for many years of loyal service.

Although Congress had long ago decreed that tax exemption was available for pension assets only if they were used for the "exclusive benefit" of beneficiaries, Congress did not fully elaborate the implications of that decision until the 1974 passage of ERISA. Similarly, with respect to foundations, it was not until the 1969 tax code amendments that the public obligations of foundation officials were not merely decreed but spelled out specifically enough to matter.

It can be argued that anyone managing other people's money had every reason to be aware that in so doing he incurred special obligations. The obligations of fiduciaries are as old as the existence of such arrangements; they are recorded in several centuries of Anglo-American trust law. But for many of the new arrangements, such as pension funds, trust law provided only analogies. Moreover, the nature of beneficiaries has changed. In the early trust situations, beneficiaries were relatively few in number and frequently were individuals of relatively substantial means, thus presumed able to protect themselves. As pension plans and eleemosynary institutions grew, their "beneficiaries" become more numerous and varied but were deemed neither sophisticated enough nor entitled to participate significantly in making decisions about the institutions or their assets. More recently, participation by affected persons has become a general norm, and specific legal changes have increased the entitlement of many beneficiaries. Thus, arrangements that may have been adequate earlier have come to need adjustment.

VII • THE CHALLENGE CONFLICTS PRESENT

It is easy to urge that all conflict-of-interest situations be eliminated. Some authorities argue, for example, that broker-dealers should not be permitted to be underwriters as well. But in his study of investment bankers, Nicholas Wolfson points out that segregating underwriters would be an extremely costly solution and, worse, would probably not even achieve the benefits that its advocates claim. As Martin Mayer puts the problem in his study:

Many conflicts are unavoidable: like thermal pollution from a power plant, they are the externalities of productive behavior. The question is whether institutional arrangements enlarge or diminish the uninvited harm done by such conflicts, and whether the costs of changing the arrangements exceed the benefits derived.

The challenge presented by conflicts of interest, then, is not simply to eliminate all or suffer all, but rather to analyze several questions in each kind of conflict situation:

- How likely is the conflict to lead to abuse?
- If abuse occurs, how severe will the injuries be?
- If protective measures are warranted (to prevent the abuse, to limit its harmfulness, or to facilitate redress), can the costs of such measures be kept lower than the costs of risking the injuries?
- In light of these considerations, is the conflict worth eliminating or should it be endured?

These questions may, in some situations, be answerable in precise cost-benefit terms, but in most situations the sensible course is to apply the questions to the particular facts and reach a considered answer.

The Fund's studies show that even some firms that are among the leaders of their industries have taken inadequate care to surround serious conflicts with safeguards. Some particularly respected regulatory bodies, as well as Congress, have demonstrated a lack of sophistication or even of concern about minimizing the likelihood of conflict abuses. Too many avoidable abuses have occurred and too many apparent abuses have been left without exculpatory explanation. Accordingly, these studies conclude with specific recommendations of the steering committee.

Our studies concentrate on the large firms, in part because of their financial significance and in part because information about large firms is easier to obtain than information about small firms. In addition, large firms have more resources than small firms with which to erect safeguards against abuses. Proposed solutions to conflicts problems, whether legislation or trade association ''models,'' that do not take variations in firm size into account may overburden small firms. For example, a trust department officer from a small bank, after hearing of the elaborate, thorough safeguards that one of America's biggest banks had established to prevent misuse of ''inside'' information, said, ''My bank can't afford two dining rooms. We don't have even one dining room.'' Small firms are likely to have a great deal of personalized contact with customers and beneficiaries, and such contact is often a valuable safeguard. On the other hand, small enterprises, such as the only bank trust department in a small community, often function amidst a web of intimate, interlocking relationships far more challenging to fiduciary integrity than the situations faced by major firms dealing almost exclusively with large, highly visible corporations. A small firm or, say, a small college, that seeks to recruit someone with financial experience for its board, may be limited in its choice to a handful of persons who may have other conflicting relationships with the firm or college. In contrast, a large firm or organization has sufficient drawing power to secure the services of persons who have no conflicting entanglements.

Large firms are no more subject to conflicts than small firms, but their problems command more attention, as has been illustrated most recently by the concern over the conflicts that occur when major financial institutions participate in the corporate warfare that breaks out when Company A seeks to take over an unwilling Company B. ''Reprehensible and indefensible breach of the most primitive concepts of business decency and honor'' is typical of the charges leveled by target companies. Moreover, there have been lawsuits reversed against leading investment bankers such as Morgan Stanley and Lehman Brothers; banks such as Chemical, Continental Illinois, Irving Trust, and Morgan Guaranty; and top corporate takeover lawyers such as Joseph Flom. Contested takeovers generate hyperbole and litigation. But as is typical in conflict-of-interest problems, not even the leading firms thought through matters enough to be able to answer press inquiries, let alone to have prepared any guidelines to help avoid abuses and such appearances of abuses as will assure lawsuits.[1]

VIII • OUR STUDIES

This volume contains eight chapters, each focusing on the conflicts in a particular sector of the securities markets: corporate pension funds, broker-dealers, state and local pension funds, commercial bank trust departments, investment bankers, ''union'' (multiemployer) pension funds, nonprofit institutions, and real estate investment trusts.[1] The last of these studies has not been released previously. The other seven have been updated for publication in this volume. The studies were prepared under the general direction of the Twentieth Century Fund Steering Committee on Conflicts of Interest in the Securities Markets. But each researcher worked independently and arrived at his own conclusions about the importance of conflict-of-interest problems in the financial institution he examined. Using a variety of approaches, all endeavored to identify the major conflict situations, the conditions in which they arise, the evidence (if any) of abuse, and the procedures—both self-imposed and legally required—that are followed to limit abuse. Some authors also considered the need for corrective steps and the form they might take; the steering committee itself addresses these questions in the last chapter of this volume.

The methods and limits of this study should be noted. Each chapter rests on extensive interviewing and use of extensive published and unpublished documentary sources. No questionnaires or other widespread survey devices were used. To verify the accuracy of information, the authors made many follow-up inquiries. The steering committee debated the sensitive issue of confidential interviews and unattributed quotations; in the end the committee members agreed that judicious use of such statements was preferable to a blanket bar.

As Edward S. Herman said in opening his trust department study:

The interview proved an effective means of eliciting both fresh information and many nuances not obtainable by more impersonal methods. Nevertheless, the author doubts that interviews were capable of yielding adequate information on matters of extreme delicacy, such as those involving either violations of the law or the use of power in ways contrary to official policy.

Although fully aware of these and other limitations on interviews, as well as on news stories, court papers, and similar sources even after verification, the steering committee concludes the project confident about the soundness of its information base, at least for the purpose of the conclusions and recommendations set forth here.

The very nature of conflicts of interest sharply limits the availability of exhaustive information or data that could support precise statements about, for example, the frequency or severity of injuries that are feasible in some fields. The kinds of records that exist on loan defaults, pollution levels, and auto accidents are inconceivable on stock frauds, let alone on the far subtler, far less clear categories of conflict abuses. Thus, although our information is necessarily episodic and suggestive, it is, as Learned Hand said, "the kind of evidence on which responsible persons are accustomed to rely in serious affairs." [2] All of the authors, as well as the steering committee members, have enjoyed intensive familiarity with financial institutions over long periods and from a variety of perspectives. This project and the closing chapter of conclusions and recommendations reflect collegial care and shared conviction. Of course, others' judgments may differ from ours, but we will have succeeded if the judgments expressed in this book are subsequently refined and advanced by continuing dialogue as a result of this project.

The project's largest study, by Edward S. Herman, professor of finance at the University of Pennsylvania's Wharton School, is of commercial bank trust departments, which are part of an important industry with enormous—some would say excessive—economic power. How does the trust department vote proxies, especially if the stock is in a corporation that is a significant customer of the bank's commercial department? How does a bank regulate the flow of information it secures in its capacity as creditor about customers whose stock may be held in the trust department? How does a trust department allocate its information and attention among its hundred or even thousands of accounts, some vastly larger and belonging to more "important" clients than others? These are among the difficult problems Herman examines.

Like trust departments, many broker-dealer firms must accommodate obligations to a large, varied group of investment management clients, handle both the invested cash and the securities of their customers fairly and efficiently, and prevent the use for investment purposes of any information that their principals may have if they serve on corporate boards. The report by Martin Mayer (author of *Wall Street: Men and Money* and *The Bankers*, among many other books) examines how broker-dealers deal with these problems. Mayer gives special attention to several unique conflicts of broker-dealers, such as the inherent tension between their advisory roles and the brokerage compensation system, which has depended on the amount of trading, and the inherent conflict in the firm's roles as broker or agent in some transactions and as dealer or principal in others. The latter conflict becomes particularly complex in the familiar, much examined, and much regulated setting of "block trading" firms.

In his chapter Nicholas Wolfson, professor of law at the University of Connecticut School of Law, writes that underwriting raises unique—and perhaps uniquely acute—conflicts between obligations to the issuing corporation and to the public investors. More complex conflicts arise from the differences in the interests of the issuing corporation's stockholders, management, and the various classes of public investors. Wolfson follows these problems through the underwriting sequence, from selecting the underwriter and preparing the offering through pricing the issue, determining the underwriter's compensation, and providing an orderly trading market.

Pension funds are the largest category of investment portfolios; some are managed by trust departments, others by insurance companies, broker-dealers or investment advisors, or the sponsoring employer itself. The study of corporate pension funds is by John Brooks of *The New Yorker* magazine, author of *The Go-Go Years* and *Business Adventures*, among other books. State and local government pension funds are treated by Louis Kohlmeier, syndicated columnist and author of *Regulators: Watchdog Agencies and the Public Interest* and *God Save This Honorable Court: The Supreme Court Crisis*. Although Brooks and Kohlmeier consider some of the same questions that the other studies address, they also analyze problems such as the selection of investment management and the pressure to allocate brokerage commissions and custodian services to regional firms, which particularly characterize public pension funds. With the substantial increase in fiduciary protections provided by ERISA, the impact of which is just beginning to be felt, it is timely to examine what problems pension funds have experienced and what new protections this legislation offers them. It is especially timely to consider such questions in the public fund setting, which is untouched by the new federal law.

Like the studies of corporate and state and local pension funds, our examination of "union" pension funds is an unprecedented effort to go beyond what had been only a scattering of headlines, episodes, and lore. The author, Richard Blodgett, also has written the *New York Times Book of Money* and is editor of *The Corporate Communications Report*. What we commonly refer to as "union" pension funds are, more precisely, "multiemployer" or jointly administered funds structured according to the provisions of the Labor Management Relations Act of 1947 (the Taft-Hartley Act). Management representatives generally have been less active than union representatives in the joint administration of these funds—hence, the familiar but somewhat imprecise label. Union funds have achieved general notoriety not so much for conflict of interest abuses as for actual criminal behavior, involving, in particular, a *few* of the several Teamsters' funds. Like other institutional investors, union pension funds have conflicts in areas such as the selection of investment management and the choice of investments. But they also have some unique conflicts as a result of the joint labor-management administrative structure and the funding provisions of the Taft-Hartley Act. These provisions, intended to prevent unions from using pension funds for institutional self-aggrandizement at the expense of the workers, have left management representatives without any incentive to participate actively in the administration of the funds or to counterbalance union representatives. Recent judicial decisions may be creating such incentives, but in the meantime, of all the institutions covered by ERISA, union pension funds may pose the most controversial and difficult challenges to the implementation of the act.

Unlike trust departments or broker-dealers, which are general participants in securities markets, or pension funds, which hold general portfolios of investments, real estate investment trusts (REITs) are an investment vehicle. In recent years the sudden, sharp growth of REITs has switched to severe decline, a common reversal in real estate and in investment vehicles that become faddish. Because these vehicles were created by statute, they might easily have been "conflict-proofed," but they were not.

Roy A. Schotland, professor of law at Georgetown University (and chairman of the steering committee on conflicts of interest), has studied the role of conflicts in the decline of REITs, the response of REIT managements to the problems the conflicts presented, and the lessons that the fate of the REITs suggests for legislators dealing with conflicts in complex financial institutions and instruments.

Because the steering committee's study was entirely sponsored by a foundation, the report on nonprofit institutions by Chris Welles, a contributing editor of *Institutional Investor* and author of *The Last Days of the Club*, is especially appropriate. Focusing almost entirely on foundations and educational endowments, Welles finds that:

The basic problem is that all nonprofit institutions . . .depend on benefactors from the business world. . . .These individuals are generally well intentioned. But they sometimes have difficulty separating their philanthropic and fiduciary activities from their personal business interests. When they permit the latter to take precedence over the former, the conflict of interest inherent in their situation degenerates into abuse.

Our Goal

Some who read these studies and the steering committee's recommendations may be disappointed that more radical changes have not been recommended. Others may be disappointed that the investment professions are not viewed as favorably as they perhaps would like. The book will, we hope, draw comments, perhaps even controversy. We believe such a response will enhance comprehension and resolution of these problems.

As Justice Felix Frankfurter wrote some thirty years ago: "To say that a man is a fiduciary only begins analysis."[3] The Twentieth Century Fund study of conflicts of interests in the securities markets is dedicated to the continuing analysis of fiduciary responsibilities.

NOTES

I. Introduction

1   *Meinhard v. Salmon*, 249 N.Y. 458, 464, 164 N.E. 545, 546 (1928).
2   "The Public Influence of the Bar," *Harvard Law Review*, 48 (1934), p. 8.

II. What Is a Conflict of Interest?

1   Most of the few available studies of conflicts of interest focus on the conflict between a public official's governmental responsibilities and his private economic interests. One such study opens with the statement that for seventy-five years officials, scholars, and others have attempted to define a

vague, nebulous thing called "conflict of interest." Interestingly, The Dictionary of American Politics, Black's Law Dictionary, and The Encyclopedia of Social Sciences fail to list the phrase among their many thousands of entries.

> —David A. Frier, *Conflict of Interest in the Eisenhower Administration*, (Gretna, La.: Pelican, 1970), p. 3.

Webster's Third New International Dictionary defines the term as "a conflict between the private interests and the official responsibilities of a person in a position of trust (as a government official)."

2 A *fiduciary* is simply an individual who has agreed to undertake the legal obligations inherent in a status such as formal trusteeship or guardianship. Fiduciary obligations exist in a variety of relationships, with varying degrees of intensity; for example, the formal trustee is under more intense, and more precisely spelled out, obligations to his beneficiary than is a corporate director to the body of stockholders. See Scott on Trusts (1967), 3rd ed., p. 39, and Scott, "The Fiduciary Principle," *California Law Review* 37 (1949), p. 539.

IV. Clarifying Conflicts

1   The actual treatment of "securities law fraud," rather than its mere legal wording, supports the distinction between crimes on the one hand and conflicts on the other. For example, the use of inside information about issuers is a conflict problem recurrent in many multifunction financial firms. The law on that problem and on some conflicts within operating corporations has grown under Securities Exchange Act Rule 10b-5, where "fraud," an old *malum in se* concept, is described and criminal sanctions are available. "Securities law fraud" is far broader than common law fraud, and although criminal prosecutions are possible as a matter of law, the criminal armory is rarely if ever brought to bear in that lively, interesting area of 10b-5 that goes beyond classic common law fraud.

2   There were impressive exceptions. For example, the Hartford National Bank's trust department maintained thousands of passbook savings accounts at unaffiliated thrift institutions. Similarly, the Citizens & Southern Bank trust department publicized its practice of placing uninvested cash in special income-producing investments and invited beneficiaries—or potential customers—to contrast this practice with that of other bank trust departments.

VI. Why Do Conflict Abuses Occur?

1   This spread of the fiduciary "status" has been fueled probably more by ERISA than by any other single force, but the act's imposition of obligations is consistent with broader current trends.

The surprise many pension officials have felt in learning how substantial are a fiduciary's obligations caused one organization of pension specialists to distribute a bumper sticker saying: "Cheer Up! You could be a FIDUCIARY!"

[2]Chris Welles, "Nonprofit Institutions," p. 496, this volume, quoting Waldemar A. Nielson, *The Big Foundations*, A Twentieth Century Fund Study (New York: Columbia University Press, 1972), pp. 121-23.

VII. The Challenge Conflicts Present

[1] Certainly the problem cannot be dismissed out of hand, as a bank counsel from a leading firm did recently with unlawyer-like rashness: "sheer nonsense . . .I personally would never advise anyone not to finance a transaction they would ordinarily finance, even though the target company may be one of their customers." Richard S. Simmons, in panel on "Financing and other Aspects of Cash Tender Offers," *The Business Lawyer*, 32, no. 4, (1977), pp. 1415, 1419, 1421.

The most striking instance of unresponsiveness in the face of substantial public interest involves Morgan Stanley's role in a contest to acquire Olinkraft. A second, competing offer for Olinkraft stock was made by Johns-Manville at the end of September 1978. Johns-Manville's public SEC-filed offering document included Olinkraft's own projections of earnings for 1979-81, which had been obtained from that company in late 1977 by an unnamed "financial adviser." Even when *The Wall Street Journal* reported that "Wall Street sources [are] wondering whether Morgan Stanley may have compromised its integrity," that firm and Johns-Manville refused to say whether the "financial adviser" was indeed Morgan Stanley, let alone to provide any explanation of the conduct under attack. *The Wall Street Journal*, October 26, 1978, p. 14.

But a few days after that refusal, Morgan Stanley sought to present the allegedly exonerating facts (see p. 563, below) in a letter to the editor of *The Wall Street Journal*. But the editor said that the information was merely a belated answer to the reporter's questions, and they had to buy an advertisement to print their letter. *The Wall Street Journal*, October 3, 1978, pp. 12, 18.

VIII. Our Studies

[1] We did not study investment companies because the literature on them already is extensive. See, for example, "The Mutual Fund Industry: A Legal Survey," *Notre Dame Lawyer* 44 (1969), p. 732; William J. Nutt, "A Study of Mutual Fund Independent Directors," *University of Pennsylvania Law Review* 120 (1971), p. 179; Alan Rosenblatt and Martin E. Lybecker, "Some Thoughts on the Federal Securities Laws Regulating External Investment Management Arrangements and the ALI Federal Securities Code Project," *University of Pennsylvania Law Review* 124 (1976), pp. 629-654. For similar reasons we did not study savings and loan associations. See Edward Herman, "Conflict of Interest in the Savings and Loan Industry," *Home Loan Bank Board* (Washington, D.C.: U.S. Government Printing Office, 1969), vol. II, pp. 763-969. We were unable to cover insurance companies, although we had hoped to do so. They, and commercial banking, are probably well worth study. Other Fund studies, such as a pending one on art museums, explore similar issues in nonfinancial areas. Further studies will, we hope, be stimulated by this project, even in areas not often thought of in connection with such problems. For example:

[C]onsider that Larry King, husband of Billie Jean King, is president of W.T.T. team she plays for, the New York Apples, that he also has pieces of two other clubs and that he is director of the league's endorsements division. "It's not as if Larry is taking the money from both ends and hurting people," contends a friend. "It's just that he's protecting his interests from both ends."

> Gerald Eskenazi, "Conflict of Interest Questions Confront Sports," *The New York Times*, January 8, 1977, p. 120.

[2] *NLRB* v. *Remington Rand*, 94 F. 2d 862, 873 (2d Cir. 1938).

[3] *SEC* v. *Chenery Corp.*, 318 U.S. 80, 85-6 (1943).

Commercial Bank Trust Departments
by Edward S. Herman

AUTHOR'S PREFACE

As is suggested by its title, this monograph focuses almost exclusively on conflicts of interest associated with the trustee-investment advisory and management function of commercial banks. This is itself a large and complex subject area, and although it has been treated at length here, this effort is neither exhaustive nor final. The numerous other areas of linkage between banks and securities markets that involve potential conflicts of interest are virtually ignored. Thus, only passing mention is made of conflicts associated with the simultaneous roles of banks as underwriters and buyers of municipal securities and of those connected with the banks serving simultaneously as lenders to customers and as trustees of their bond issues, among other matters.

Much of the material for this study was gathered by the author and two associates in the course of more than three hundred interviews with past and present personnel from trust and other bank departments and brokerage houses. Almost all of these interviews, which were conducted between 1969 and mid-1974, were granted on a promise of confidentiality to both the individual and the institution. Approximately seventy banks were covered, in most cases by interviews with more than one individual; and a deliberate attempt was made to examine a selection of small- and medium-sized trust institutions, as well as large metropolitan banks.

The interview proved an effective means of eliciting both fresh information and many nuances not obtainable by more impersonal methods.[1] Nevertheless, the author doubts that interviews are capable of yielding adequate information on matters of extreme delicacy, such as those involving either violations of the law or the use of power in ways contrary to official policy. In these cases definitive knowledge may be confined to confidential documents or perhaps only to the minds of the top officers. This problem is especially relevant in the sensitive areas in Section II dealing with customer accommodation practices and the control or influence exercised by banks over portfolio companies. These doubts are strengthened by the fact that in the one medium-sized and the one large bank where the author's personal relationships encouraged frank responses, evidence of the exercise and abuse of power, although not extensive, was distinctly more abundant than in other banks. Furthermore, the author was unable to arrive at any firm conclusions in a number of cases involving allegations of abuse because of an inability to gain access to reliable data. The conclusions reached in Section II are therefore tentative and qualified, because the information needed for definitive judgments could be obtained only by a determined application of subpoena power.

Because banks, bank trust departments, and the markets in which they operate have been in the process of rapid change in recent years, scholars are threatened by rapid obsolescence. Although this monograph cannot be said to have fully escaped this danger, an attempt has been made to cast the issues in a historical and problem-oriented perspective, which may lengthen its life and expand its relevance.

The author wishes to thank Carole K. Edelstein and Carl F. Safanda for their invaluable efforts as interviewers and for other assistance. M. J. Rossant, director of the Twentieth Century Fund, Roy A. Schotland, chairman of the Fund Steering Committee on Conficts of Interest in the Securities Markets, and the members of the Steering Committee have all contributed a great many valuable suggestions for improving this chapter. Thanks are also owed to the Center for the Study of Financial Institutions of the University of Pennsylvania Law School, and its director, Robert H. Mundheim, for financial and other assistance in an earlier phase of this research effort. Among the many other individuals who contributed to this study with criticisms, ideas, information, and encouragement, special mention should be made of J. Richard Boylan, chief operating officer of Provident National Bank's trust department; James S. Byrne, editor of *Tax Notes*, formerly with *The American Banker*; Benet D. Gellman, counsel of the House Committee on Banking and Currency; and Reese Harris, formerly head of the trust department of Manufacturers Hanover Bank. Carl F. Safanda and the editors of various journals have allowed the author to use a number of paragraphs from jointly produced articles covering matters treated in this chapter, namely, ''Proxy Voting by Commercial Bank Trust Departments,'' *The Banking Law Journal* (February 1973), pp. 91-115; ''The Commercial Bank Trust Department and the 'Wall,' '' *Boston College Industrial and Commercial Law Review* (November 1972), pp. 21-44; ''Allocating Investment Information,'' *Financial Analysts Journal* (January-February 1973), pp. 1-10.

Minor additional alterations and a few updatings of fact in areas where notable changes had occurred were made by the author in January 1977, in connection with the preparation of this chapter for the present volume.

I • INTRODUCTION

''Conflict of interest'' is an ambiguous and difficult concept, in part because it is used in both the potential (*ex ante*) sense and in an actual or realized (*ex post*) conflict. In the first sense, attention is focused on what might be expected to develop out of a given set of relationships or structure; in the second sense, it centers on active conflict choices in the process of being made or already completed. A potential conflict may be said to exist when a bank does an extensive business in investing money for clients as fiduciary, but at the same time has other divisions that could benefit or suffer from the decisions of the fiduciary arm. The disposition of brokerage commissions, for example, might be used to attract broker deposits to banks. If the brokerage commissions could also be used to benefit the fiduciary accounts instead of the bank, a potential conflict of interest would arise out of the structural arrangements and relationships of the institution. Even if there were no way in which the brokerage commissions could be used in the interest of the fiduciary accounts, a potential conflict would exist, based on the value of the brokerage to the institution and its cost to the trust accounts.

Potential conflicts may or may not be realized. Realization is sometimes prevented by legal and regulatory constraints, ethical considerations, self-imposed rules, and lack of opportunity. Self-imposed constraints, for example, may include: (1) rules that exclude all other bank personnel from trust affairs; (2) requirements that the fiduciary arm not deal in the assets of customers of other divisions of the large entity; or (3) granting the fiduciary arm automatic rights of ''first refusal'' of all assets bought and sold by both the bank and an affiliate (a rule for some of the bank real estate investment trusts [REITs]).

Ethical contraints on the realization of potential conflicts of interest are real, but they often bend before the winds of competitive pressure and profit opportunity. In the 1920s the abuses of the bank security affiliate[1] and, until the late 1960s, the almost universal practice of using trust department commissions for the acquisition of deposits from brokers, to the principal advantage of the commercial department and the bank as a whole, were examples of such bending of constraints.

When potential conflicts of interest materialize into real conflict choices, the decision may or may not be damaging to the party with an interest different from that of the fiduciary. The natural expectation is that the fiduciary will prefer itself where conflicting choices have to be made or that it will choose in favor of the better informed and larger customer, thus indirectly favoring its own interests. But self-imposed rules and moral codes, efforts to lean over backward to avoid discrimination in favor of itself, or fear of law violations and adverse publicity, may reduce or eliminate entirely any adverse effects of conflict of interest. The extent to which potential conflicts result in abuse is likely to depend on a complex of changing factors, including public knowledge and exposure, law and enforcement traditions and practices, and the nature of the customers and their tolerance of and capacity to resist such abuse.

Conflict of interest arises naturally out of many profit-seeking endeavors. As firms attempt to grow, they are attracted to activities that are ''closely related'' to those in which they are already engaged. These may be either complementary or similar to existing activities, and they often require similar facilities. In consequence these additional activities frequently can be undertaken with relatively low marginal costs of production and/or distribution, and they afford not only potential economies of scale but the greater appeal of a fuller line. A bank that buys bonds for its own account can, at no great added expense and with a number of advantages, underwrite and retail bonds,[2] advise on bond purchases, and manage bond portfolios in a fiduciary capacity. But the addition of each of these supplemental activities presents a potential for conflict, for each involves the bank in a role in which its interests may vary by function and client.

Diversification thus enlarges the possibilities for conflict of interest. "Related" activities often involve conflict, as the added functions frequently enlarge the number of choices an institution must make between its interests and those to whom the institution has some fiduciary obligation.[3] If an organization expands into a related activity solely to provide for its own needs, it does not involve itself in overlapping interests or obligations, and conflict does not arise. Backward or forward integration into ore supply or steel fabrication by a steel producer does not involve the creation of conflict of interest, although it may conceivably increase the monopoly power of the producer. Similarly, a computer-servicing facility of a financial institution used solely to meet its internal needs would not create conflict.

When, however, the institution establishes and obtains control of the management contract of a publicly owned REIT, a potential conflict of interest is automatically created, because the bank is interested in mortgages for its own portfolio (and perhaps also for advisory clients other than the REIT) and has a smaller financial stake in the REIT portfolio than its own. Under these conditions conflict of interest has been "built-in."

Commercial Bank Involvement in Securities Markets

A great many conflict-of-interest problems of commercial banks are connected with their various kinds of involvements in securities markets. These involvements and conflicts are not new; they date back to the earliest operations of banks. The entire history of bank diversification, in fact, may be looked upon as a process of additions of activities with a potential for conflict, creating economic, moral, and legal problems and tensions, some never resolved, others settled by changes in practice, still others resolved by outside intervention.

BANK "OWN-ACCOUNT" TRANSACTIONS IN SECURITIES

In the traditional theory of banking, whose impact extended well into the present century, the business of banks was short-term lending, reflecting a liability structure dominated by demand and short maturity time deposits. But the traditional theory never corresponded very closely to reality. Industrial and utility interests, eager to provide themselves with credit, frequently long-term credit, established many banks in the nineteenth century. These satellite institutions, so-called improvement banks,[4] were heavy lenders of long-term capital. Numerous banks in the eighteenth and early nineteenth century were given charters conditional on agreements to engage in long-term financing of the federal or state government or to help finance canal or turnpike enterprises. Under many Free Banking Acts, and then under the National Banking Act of 1863-64, the investment of some part of bank capital in government securities was required by law, and note issuance called for the acquisition of government securities eligible as collateral.

Thus, own-account holdings of government securities were significant from the earliest years. In 1870, for example, 25 percent of the resources of national banks were held in the form of U.S. government obligations. Subsequently, there was a decline in bank holdings of U.S. government obligations but a rise in other types of long-term investment securities. In 1972 the category "investments" accounted for 30.7 percent of commercial bank resources, only 11.2 percent U.S. obligations, the balance mainly municipal securities.[5] Still more long-term credit is hidden within the "loan" category. In recent decades bank loans with a maturity of one year or more have been placed in a special category called "term loans," which fall somewhere between traditional loans and long-term investments. In mid-1973 term loans amounted to 36.5 percent of the commercial and industrial loans of the one hundred sixty large banks reporting weekly data to the Federal Reserve.[6] But many long-term bank loans are still classified as ordinary loans, although they are subject to regular renewal and are long-term in fact as well as by understanding between bank and customer.

Banks have always been significant investors in long-term securities for their own account; they employ personnel to evaluate, buy, and sell such securities. In addition, banks have always had prestige, a conservative image, and easy access to wealthy individuals and correspondent banks, who were already customers interested in security market services. Hence, it was easy for them to move into advising customers on, and supplying them with, investment securities.

LENDER TO THE SECURITIES INDUSTRY AND ITS PARTICIPANTS

For many years banks also have been lenders on securities collateral, usually to customers dealing in the bond or stock markets but sometimes for commercial and personal credit.[7] They also extend credit to broker-dealers and bond houses to finance inventories and to investment bankers to finance unsold new securities.[8] The financing of speculative purchases of securities by demand or time loans goes back at least to the 1820s.[9] By 1910 it was estimated that some $14 billion in credit was being extended in the New York call-loan market, and one-third of the loans extended by New York City banks were estimated to be brokers' loans.[10]

The relative importance of loans on security collateral has declined markedly, the great fall-off following the 1929 crash. In 1972 commercial bank loans for carrying securities amounted to only $15.8 billion, or 4.7 percent of total bank loans (with approximately the same percentage applicable to the large commercial banks).[11] But despite this decline, the absolute volume of bank loans for carrying securities is still large; and the banks are as important as ever to brokers as lenders,[12] deposit administrators, custodians, buyers and sellers of securities for bank-managed portfolios, sources of referrals, and suppliers and purchasers of a wide and proliferating variety of services. Banks and brokers participate in a customer relationship that provides mutual services, with varying degrees of strength on each side of the equation. But by and large the bank is the stronger party, less dependent on the business of the individual broker or on brokers in general.

COMMERCIAL BANKS AS SECURITIES UNDERWRITERS

In addition to serving as key lenders to investment banking firms, commercial banks have at times been important participants in investment banking operations, either directly or through affiliates. Investment banking became a regular line of business for some banks in the 1830s and 1840s, developing out of their own portfolio activities, demands on them to buy the securities of governments and improvement corporations, and the profitability of investment banking operations. Banks had found that as investment bankers they were in a position to gain a special deposit windfall, supplementing the direct yield on securities, if borrowers to whom they had sold securities did not draw upon their deposit credits immediately. Banks also found that investment banking functions could bring in fiscal agency deposit business—with a bank serving as paying agent for dividends and customer interest obligations—as well as ordinary deposit business.[13]

Despite these potential gains, the banks' early move into investment banking proved abortive, and in the depression of the 1840s, a number of the more important investment banking commercial banks failed (most notably, Biddle's Bank of the United States of Pennsylvania). The field then came to be occupied largely by private bankers.[14] By narrowly defining banking functions, the National Banking System also contributed to the separation of commercial and investment banking. But in the late nineteenth and early twentieth century, with the investment banking opportunities that arose from industrial growth, the acceleration of merger activity, and the related surge of new security issues and stock market activity, banks again became involved in investment banking through the vehicles of their own bond departments, the trust company, or the security affiliate. By 1900 national as well as state banks—especially the larger ones in New York City, Boston, and Chicago—were directly engaged in substantial investment banking activities.

In 1902 the Comptroller of the Currency put forward a new interpretation of the National Banking Act, which severely restricted securities activities of national banks; but the banks quickly circumvented these restrictions by means of the "Chicago Plan," whereby the national banks established security affiliates, with common management and ownership, incorporated under less restrictive state legislation. Refusing to penetrate behind a singularly transparent corporate veil, the comptroller found that the national banks were "not interested in them [these security affiliates] at all. The line of cleavage [was] clear and distinct."[15] Given this regulatory sanction, the affiliate device enlarged the possibilities for bank participation in investment banking. Stimulated by World War I and then by the further expansion of public interest and participation in securities activity in the 1920s, the banks greatly increased their investment banking activities. The most important single step in this process was the 1916 acquisition of the investment business of N.W. Halsey and Company by the National City Company, the security affiliate of the National City Bank.[16] Other banks soon followed, and by 1922 the rush was on. By 1929 an estimated 600 banks were engaged in the securities business as dealers and distributors, including 132 banks operating through securities affiliates. The banks had achieved a position of approximate equality with private bankers "both from the standpoint of investment banking machinery and from the standpoint of the volume of securities underwritten and distributed by the two groups of institutions."[17]

The stock market crash, depression, and revelations of abuses in the sale of new securities (only a few of them related to the linkage of banks and investment banking affiliates) resulted in the passage of the Glass-Steagall Act of 1933, which forced banks to curtail their investment banking activities sharply and to withdraw completely from important sectors of the investment banking business. But commercial banks retained the right to underwrite U.S. government and municipal general obligation bonds, which became relatively more important in the total volume of investment securities after 1933. In these fields the great commercial banks have assumed a dominant position: in the first half of 1973, six of the ten largest underwriters of municipal general obligation bonds were commercial banks, accounting for 35 percent of the total underwritten.[18] For their own accounts, in mid-1972 commercial banks held about $86 billion in municipals, or about 50 percent of all such debt outstanding.[19]

During the past decade, the larger banks have been endeavoring, with some limited success, to break out of the Glass-Steagall framework of restrictions on their securities activities. They have tried, unsuccessfully thus far, to get their underwriting powers in the municipal bond field extended to revenue as well as general obligations. They have attempted to gain the right to issue and distribute the securities of investment funds they would organize and manage (including commingled fund participations sold to the general public). But in a 1971 decision, *Investment Company Institute* v. *Camp*,[20] the Supreme Court refused to allow bank sponsorship and distribution of open-ended commingled funds on the ground that such activities would violate the Glass-Steagall Act. The Court pointed to a wide variety of potential abuses that might tempt commercial banks engaged in general investment banking functions, stressing that the aggressive merchandising necessary to the continuing solvency of open-ended funds made them particularly susceptible to practices that could weaken confidence in the sponsoring bank as a whole. But since the decision in *Camp* concentrated on open-ended funds, several banks decided to organize closed-end funds, which issued limited amounts of stock infrequently and were thus, it was argued, exempt from the separation of investment banking mandated by the Glass-Steagall Act. The Investment Company Institute (ICI), the trade association of the mutual fund industry, thereupon sued again,[21] alleging violation of the act and arguing that Congress meant to segregate the entire securities industry from commercial banking, not merely the underwriting function of investment banking. In support of this argument, the ICI asserted that the ''vast majority'' of investment companies in existence when the Glass-Steagall Act was passed were closed-end companies and that substantial potential for abuse was present *whenever* a bank sponsored or acted as investment advisor to a fund.

Another bank–securities industry confrontation arose when, in the words of Securities and Exchange Commission (SEC) Chairman Ray Garrett, Jr., ''the First National City Bank, again . . . decided to test the boundaries of the bank exemptions in the federal securities laws, [and] joined with Merrill Lynch to create a special investment advisory service for investors who could invest at least $25,000.''[22] This effort was challenged by the SEC and settled by a consent decree that involved abandonment of the advisory service but did not admit the validity of the SEC's principle. Meanwhile, the banks were aggressively pressing into nonadvisory brokerage-type activities, including dividend reinvestment plans and stock purchase programs involving automatic deposit deductions and monthly bank investments by contract for customers.[23] They have also moved aggressively into longer term private placements, leasing, project financing, the arrangement of mergers and acquisitions, and general financial advising, to the dismay of the investment banking fraternity.[24] The banks succeeded in getting the Board of Governors of the Federal Reserve System to find their sponsorship and management of closed-end investment companies appropriate under the Bank Holding Company Act Amendments of 1970, but, as noted above, that ruling is under court challenge.

The main conflict-of-interest problems associated with bank sponsorship of investment companies flow from potentially competing fiduciary obligations and from unsound banking practices that might occur if commercial banks sought to prop up faltering funds that they sponsor or manage. A primary Glass-Steagall type of conflict problem, the dumping of bank-underwritten securities into controlled portfolios, would still seem to be potentially applicable to bank underwriting of government issues.[25]

ADVISORY AND ASSET MANAGEMENT

A major connection between banks and the securities markets—the one with which this study is mainly concerned—arises out of bank investment advisory and fiduciary management activities. Although these activities can also be traced to the early years of banking history, they have become quantitatively significant only in this century. Although they provided a great deal of advice on an *ad hoc* basis to their customers, especially correspondent banks, until 1913 national banks were forbidden by law from serving as trustees under deeds of trust, with the result that before World War I ''practically all of the trust business handled by corporate fiduciaries was in the hands of trust companies.''[26]

Trust companies and their role. Trust companies were the premier ''growth companies'' among the financial institutions of the post-Civil War era.[27] Although trust companies had a number of distinguishing features, they were first and foremost commercial banks, [28] entering the field either through the back door of special legislative charter or through ''free banking'' laws. As Comptroller of the Currency W.B. Ridgely noted in 1904, ''a very large portion of the new organizations are merely commercial banks, having trust company privileges perhaps, but in reality doing comparatively little strictly trust company business.''[29] The New York trust companies did a substantial trust business, but they did a huge ordinary deposit business as well. In 1904 $216 million of their deposits were designated trust deposits, but $591 million were called ''general deposits.''[30] In Massachusetts ''no state banks have been chartered for many years, and a very large part of the trust companies do only a banking business. Of the 48 trust companies engaged in business in that State on November 16, 1909, only 26 trust departments. . . .''[31] And in Alabama in 1904, ''we have no trust company doing only a trust business, nor one in which the execution of trusts is the leading department of its business. . . . ''[32] In those states where the law was stringent, excluding trust companies from banking, their development was slight. In brief, ''preference for organization under the trust company law is not due to the desire to carry on a trust business, but to the greater liberality of the trust company law in its regulation of the banking business.''[33]

Trust companies were also distinctive in their provision of a safe, liquid, and interest-bearing savings outlet for depositors, especially large depositors, a service that was unique in the late nineteenth century and met a real need of the affluent and the business community.[34] As a result the trust companies injected a new and powerful element of price competition into banking, with these aggressive, growth-oriented outsiders upsetting a broad system of monopolistic price-making that yielded exorbitant returns to established firms.[35] Price competition was extended under this influence not merely to the larger time accounts but to smaller savings accounts and active demand deposits as well.[36]

Trust company charters, which often ''contained provisions such as might suggest themselves to the parties seeking them,'' [37] allowed the companies to take advantage of new profit opportunities from which national banks were legally precluded. For example, large profits were derived by trust companies ''from the skill of their officers in financing important combinations and aiding in the creation of new enterprises.''[38] The trust company often evolved out of firms engaged in specialized nonbanking functions, such as life insurance, safe deposit, and real estate title business. In the words of banking historian George Barnett, "the elimination of the insurance powers of the trust company and the addition of banking powers . . .has gradually standardized the powers of the trust company, until at the present time [1911] the trust company . . .may be fairly well defined as a bank which has power to act in the capacity of trustee, administrator, guardian, or executor."[39]

If national banks wanted to enter the trust business, as many did before 1913, they had to do it indirectly by switching to a state bank or trust company charter or by affiliatĭng in some manner with a state bank or trust company.[40] Affiliations assumed many forms: *de novo* organization of a trust company, the acquisition of control of operating state banks and trust companies by national bank interests, or alliances based on interlocks and stock ownership that were frequently a prelude to merger.[41] In 1900 all thirty trust companies in New York City were interlocked with national banks, and half of them were interlocked with six or more national banks.[42] By 1913, when national banks were finally allowed by law to enter the trustee business, the law was merely confirming a *fait accompli*.

By 1900 trust companies held 26 percent of the banking assets in New York City, and their growth was so spectacular that they were being formed by investment bankers and brokers as speculative stock ventures. A great many of the affiliated trust companies were taken into the national banks after 1913, with the trust business forming the nucleus of a trust department, and the other business redistributed among the other departments. Those trust companies that retained their trust identity became less and less distinguishable from ordinary commercial banks, for as the latter expanded their fiduciary business, the former aggressively diversified into regular commercial business.

Growth of the trust business.   Corporate trust business, which predominated in the earliest years, appears to have been of modest importance until the 1890s, when the spurt of new security issues and mergers increased the volume of work such as executions of deeds of trust, certification of bonds, registration of ownership, keeping accounts of ownership transfers, payment of interest and dividends, and the management of sinking funds. From its inception corporate trust business was regarded by bankers not only as a direct source of profits but also as a source of other loan and deposit business. Bank pre-eminence in the corporate trust field has been maintained up to the present day by a combination of experience, legal requirements that banks act as trustee,[43] and the pulling power of banks' relationships with the corporate community. The conflict of interest built into this process of selecting corporate trustees was noted more than half a century ago:

The peculiarity of the trustee's situation is that it is chosen by the promoters, founders or conductors of an enterprise to represent bondholders or the holders of other securities whose interests, in fact, are antagonistic to those who choose it. At the very beginning of the business, when the trustee evinces too great anxiety to protect the interests of bondholders, it is apt to disconcert, and perhaps repulse, the parties who bring it business, because it is undeniable that some promoters or managers of business are too apt to resent too much interference with the plans which they had prepared for the protection of those from whom they expect or hope to borrow money.[44]

Conflict of interest between the bank as protector of bondholders and as trustee by grace of a bond-issuing customer is well recognized by trust people today. Some banks are uncomfortable at the possibility of having to press for bankruptcy and liquidation in the bondholders' interest while struggling to keep the company afloat to salvage both short- and long-term credits. Banks may even enter a conflict situation where (as in the case of more than one trust institution today) two customers, with bonds trusteed in the corporate trust department, both go into bankruptcy and assert plausible bondholder claims against one another. Some trust departments refuse corporate trust business from any but strong customers, and others seek the transfer of such business upon the onset of serious weakness; but conflicts nonetheless continue to arise in the context of solicitation heavily oriented toward bank customers.[45]

Information on personal trust business in its early phase of growth is sparse, but personal trusts had reached impressive size by World War I, at which time executorships and personal trust business "constituted the greater part of trust activities."[46] Bank and trust company personal trust assets, totaling perhaps $7 billion in 1912, rose to $30 billion in the late 1920s, receded in the 1930s, and, as may be seen on Figure 1, made a steady advance thereafter. The ratio

Figure 1: Growth of Personal Trust and Pension Fund Assets of Commercial Banks and Trust Companies, 1900-72 (Ratio Scale)

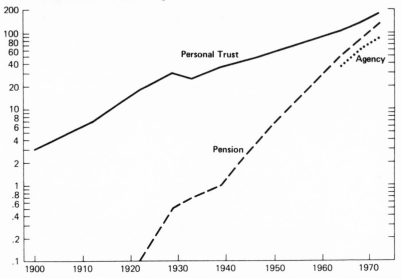

Sources: Edna Ehrlich, "Functions and Investment Policies of Personal Trust Departments," *Monthly Review* (New York, Federal Reserve Bank of New York), October, 1972, p. 259; R. W. Goldsmith, *Financial Intermediaries in the American Economy Since 1900* (New York: National Bureau of Economic Research, 1958), Appendix A; Board of Governors—FDIC—Comptroller, *Trust Assets of Insured Commercial Banks*, 1971 and 1972.

chart indicates that the really rapid surge of personal trust business occurred in the period 1912-29, while bank employee benefit plan and pension business[47] went through an even more rapid growth phase after 1945, rising from perhaps $5 billion in 1950 to $134.5 billion in 1972 ($140.7 billion in 1975). Although total personal trust and estate assets of bank trust departments were still larger, amounting to $183.1 billion in 1972 (only $164.9 billion in 1975), pension fund assets for the ten largest trust banks exceeded personal trust and estate assets by more than two to one.[48]

Immediately after World War II, banks were about on a par with insurance companies, as measured by pension fund assets managed. Insurance companies, however, were severely hamstrung in subsequent years by tax disabilities, legal limitations on their ability to invest in equities, and the inflexibility of their traditional and legally obligatory commitment to group deferred annuity contracts.[49] Their long-term liabilities were commonly met by investments in long-term debt instruments, and the experience rates they could offer to pension plans were based—in the late 1940s and early 1950s—on interest rates that were just starting to rise. The insurance companies attempted to offer accounts separate from their own portfolios for funding pension business, but they met with obstacles in state laws and SEC interpretations of separate accounts as investment companies requiring registration under federal authority. These legal obstacles were not cleared up until 1962-64, after which insurance company competition in the pension fund area became more formidable. But as late as 1969, pension reserves funded in separate accounts of insurance companies amounted to only $3.5 billion.[50] By the end of 1972, separate accounts amounted to $10.1 billion, as compared with a bank pension fund total of $134.5 billion. One recent survey of corporations with pension fund assets of $10 million or more revealed that a ''very large majority'' were still unaware that insurance companies had developed machinery to handle pension accounts.[51]

In competing for pension funds, as in personal trusts, banks have enjoyed a number of strategic advantages over their main rivals: (1) the aura of conservatism, permanence, and solidity that has been important to the directors of many companies seeking pension management;[52] (2) the legal power to serve as trustee, which has been decisive in many cases;[53] (3) the ability to provide a number of related services in a single package—trustee, investment management, and custodial; (4) the special derivative advantages of asset management, particularly the associated trust deposits and float, and the preservation and strengthening of customer relationships, which have increased bank incentives to get business and permitted the offering of lower prices; and (5) a preferred marketing position arising out of business relationships with many companies looking for pension fund management. The banks also have had fewer legal and tax encumbrances to their move into equity investment than some of their rivals (notably the insurance companies).[54]

During the first great surge of pension fund business, from 1950 to the mid-1960s, banks were virtually able to sweep the field, controlling three-quarters of corporate pension plans and probably a comparable or slightly larger fraction of pension fund assets.[55] After 1965 competition stiffened somewhat, and the banks lost a little ground to their main rivals—insurance companies, investment counseling firms, mutual fund complexes, and brokerage houses—mainly in number of accounts managed, rather than total assets. Investment counseling firms in particular increased their importance as fund managers, but bank asset dominance continued at about its old level, because the banks retained the bulk of the very largest funds.[56] Given the sheer rapidity of the growth of pension funds, the limited extent of the encroachment of nonbank managers and smaller banks is remarkable, perhaps even worrisome in terms of concentration of economic power. It is possible that correctives will yet come out of "natural" developments. The enormous volume of pension money in some banks has raised the question: "How can $15 billion be run to do better than the averages?" It may be that the averages are an appropriate standard, but many pension fund sponsors take the view that more can be expected. A great many companies also take the view that diversified investment management of their pension funds is desirable, as a stimulus to performance competition.

Corporate managers have become increasingly performance-oriented and are quicker to drop poor performers and take on new ones.[57] And they are even more prone to alter the direction of flow of money among existing managers according to relative performance.[58] But there are counterfactors: the low bank fees, the desire to stay on the right side of powerful lenders, the preference or need for a manager with fiduciary powers, and the security of the great name. Thus, the tendency has been to diversify by parceling out new funds to the unrepresented large banks. It may be that a reduced expectation of performance will actually enhance the power of the dominant giant banks, as their other advantages may then outweigh their undramatic potential performance as investment managers.[59] Today, the relative position of the large banks seems less threatened by excessive bulk, public and legislative fears of the concentration of bank power, and competition from nonbank and lesser-bank rivals than it did in the late 1960s.

Economies of scale in the trust function have not been mentioned as a factor explaining either the competitive superiority of banks or large bank preeminence. In fact, economies in the trust business appear to be related mainly to size of account rather than number of accounts. In Neil B. Murphy's study, a 10 percent increase in account size (measured by revenue produced) resulted in a 7.2 percent increase in trust department costs; a 10 percent increase in number of accounts, but with size of account held constant, was associated with a cost increase of 9.7 percent, a difference that is not statistically significant.[60] Murphy concluded that the trust function may permit some economies of scale,[61] but their magnitude, by implication, would appear to be small. Small trust departments are often unprofitable, and size bears a positive relationship to profitability in bank trust operations. This would seem to be evidence for economies related to trust department size. But apart from vagaries of accounting practice that should give pause, the smaller departments are characterized by a larger proportion of small and relatively unprofitable individual accounts, so scale factor measurement is distorted by the noncomparability of output units. Just as with business loans, as trust account size increases, gross revenue per dollar of trust account does not decline in proportion to the decline in costs per dollar of account; thus, both large loans and large trust accounts tend to be more profitable than small accounts.[62] Because only large banks can make large loans and obtain large pension fund and other substantial trust accounts, economies of scale are more a *result* of size and pulling power than a *cause* of competitive advantage.

Although 3,999 banks had trust departments at the end of 1974, the bulk of trust business was in the hands of a relatively small number of major institutions. Table 1 shows that the 60 banks with trust assets of $1 billion or more, only 1.5 percent of bank trustees by number, managed $216 billion in trust assets, 66.3 percent of the aggregate. The 3,223 banks with trust assets under $25 million, 80.5 percent of trustee banks, managed only 3.7 percent of trust assets. Table 1 also shows a steady increase in average size of account, paralleling the increase in trust asset size class, with the average size of the top class exceeding that of the smallest by a factor of 13. This relationship reflects both the larger size of accounts and the greater proportion of advisory and employee benefit fund accounts associated with larger trust departments. The latter types of accounts tend to be larger than personal trusts, but the size of the accounts in each class is positively related to trust department asset size. Bank trust business is clearly highly concentrated, although the volume of business is so huge that a large absolute number of trustee banks have a substantial volume of trust assets.

The evolution of trust department structure.   Trust department structure and policy was long dominated by the personal trust function. The large number of relatively small personal trust accounts and the special legal obligations associated with the trust relationship created a huge burden of detail, as "each trust is a separate account, requires a separate portfolio and must be administered according to varying circumstances, such as legal requirements, type of property contained in the inventory, duration, the needs of beneficiaries and economic conditions."[63] From these obligations also followed a conservative investment philosophy, reinforced by court interpretation of the trustee function,[64] which stressed preservation of principal and risk avoidance for the trusts (and trustee).[65] As noted by one trust banker:

The overriding fear of committee members is the always present possibility of a surcharge action, whether justified or not, by a beneficiary against the trust institution for an alleged act of improper management.... Numerous court decisions over the years have confirmed the historic belief that the trustee risked surcharge if speculation took the place of investment, while ultraconservatism on the part of the trustee was a riskless pattern of conduct.[66]

Table 1: Size Distribution of Commercial Bank Trust Departments, December 1974

SIZE ($ ASSETS)	NUMBER OF TRUST DEPTS.	PERCENTAGE[a] OF NUMBER	ASSETS ($ MILLIONS)	PERCENTAGE OF TRUST DEPT. ASSETS	NUMBER OF TRUST DEPT. ACCOUNTS	PERCENTAGE OF TRUST DEPT. ACCOUNTS	AVERAGE SIZE OF ACCOUNTS
Under 10 million	2,805	70.1	5,272	1.6	127,381	9.5	41.4
10 to 25 million	418	10.4	6,748	2.1	105,063	7.9	64.2
25 to 100 million	454	11.4	22,846	7.0	244,475	18.3	93.5
100 to 500 million	222	5.6	47,419	14.6	327,207	24.5	144.9
500 million to 1 billion	40	1.0	27,460	8.4	122,196	9.1	224.7
1 billion and over	60	1.5	215,582	66.3	410,989	30.7	524.5
All trust departments	3,999	100.0	325,328	100.0	1,337,311	100.0	243.3

[a]Rounded to nearest tenth.

Source: Compiled from Board of Governors—FDIC—Comptroller, *Trust Assets of Insured Commercial Banks*, 1974.

The detail and the threat of surcharge had several structural manifestations. First, in most banks each account was (and still is) handled in tandem fashion by an administrator and an investment officer. The former would handle the paperwork and customer contact functions; the latter would make the specific investment decisions under the supervision of higher authorities in the department. Second, there emerged a multilayered committee system in which decisions were made and reviewed at progressive stages and on a collective rather than an individual basis. This system was reinforced after 1936 by Regulation F of the Board of Governors of the Federal Reserve System, which made a trust investment committee mandatory and required that it approve all investments and review accounts at least once a year.[67] The underlying purpose of this regulation was "to provide that collective, rather than individual, judgment should govern the investment of trust funds."[68] This reliance on collective judgment by a layered committee system contributed further to a bureaucratization of trust department decision-making, with the result that in many cases "the details receive the first attention and demand time far beyond their importance, and relegate policy matters to second place and limited time."[69] And the details that could command high level attention have been numerous. An officer of one New York trust institution noted that his trust department held thirty-five thousand different issues of securities. And another trust officer claimed that, in the recent past, "committees seriously considered questions such as 'Shall we pave Mrs. Jones's driveway?' There were many of these questions since [the bank] holds $5 million in real estate. Another serious question is the sale, in a probate account, of a car."

These traditional arrangements and attitudes, along with the widespread insensitivity of customers to the details of trust department practices and performance, contributed to sluggish responses, a downgrading of investment skills and effort, and conflict of interest.[70] Changes in these traditions were greatly stimulated as the possibilities of superior investment decision-making for enhancing values and for reducing pension fund costs were brought home to investors and corporations financing pension funds, especially by the great attention and publicity given to performance differentials in the "go-go" era of the mid-1960s. Mutual funds especially opened new vistas associated with aggressive investment management, including heavy trading, the energetic pursuit of information, the payment of substantial sums for high-grade personnel, and organizational arrangements conducive to rapid decision-making and action. With the great increase in the importance of performance-oriented accounts, especially in the 1960s, the committee system and its underlying conservative philosophy of investment came under attack and underwent various kinds of modification. The first Annual Institutional Investor Conference panel of 1968, on "Improving Bank Trust Investment Results," opened with a statement that "the pressures of performance have been felt by bank trustees everywhere."[71] With this pressure came the realization, voiced by First National City's Hulbert W. Tripp, that "over a long period of time, banks have not distinguished themselves by a spectacular investment record.''[72] But the banks were trying: they gave more autonomy to managers of performance-oriented accounts and more resources and influence over investment choices to researchers. They organized and deployed special teams to meet the demands of aggressive accounts and set up ''special situations'' funds in which pension fund accounts of the bank could invest under the direction of one or more highly rated analysts.

An even more important attempt to change was manifest in a powerful centralizing tendency, which saw the multilayered committee system bypassed, with one or a few individuals achieving substantial control over trust departments and imposing their investment vision on portfolio managers. As stated by one leading trust department official:

Essentially what we have done in our bank is to come down frankly to one committee which consists of myself, my boss, and the heads of the portfolio and research departments. We review securities before they go on our approved list or off. I usually go over some of these beforehand, and then it goes to this committee which meets every two weeks on investment policy and selection of securities. This is practically the only committee that we have. Now, if you read some of our literature, you will find that all the brass in the bank is on another committee. But we just report to them. Some don't take it too seriously.[73]

Centralization reflected the belief of many banks that they could attract and hold only so many first-rate portfolio managers, plus the fact that variations in account performance could be embarrassing to the bank. At one large bank:

The [bank] found that during the go-go era things got very messy in the EBF area with performance between accounts varying drastically. Therefore, it has instituted ''mirror portfolios'' in the pension area, with the managers having no more than 30 accounts with a maximum market value of $250 million; all accounts are in the same issues, within reason, and the number of issues per account has been cut down—no more than 40 names.

The discretion of portfolio managers was narrowed in the centralizing banks by a more rigorous confinement to the ''approved lists,''[74] by the use of ''bogeys,''[75] and by other kinds of pressure that assured a substantial mirroring of all accounts in a particular class. Informal pressures were often brought to bear in the review process, and the portfolio manager was instructed on his limited range of discretion.

Efforts to revitalize the structure of a bank trust department sometimes led to the decision to circumvent it altogether. In the early 1970s, a number of banks decided to spin off their investment function, or parts of it—usually the research and investment advisory arms—into separate subsidiaries, often leaving only the personal trusts in the bank.[76] Such a step permitted higher salaries to be paid than were possible within the bank's salary structure and thus allowed more talented personnel to be hired and retained. In some cases there was an opportunity to receive equity in the new organization. It was hoped that the new organizations would convey an aggressive image that would generate new business for the banks' investment research arms and thus spread overhead and increase income. It was also hoped that the new organizations might be better adapted to the differences in investment needs and performance goals that divide personal trust from pension management. Thus, it was planned that Chase Manhattan's new subsidiary would manage its $9 billion or more in institutional, endowment, and pension funds, while some $3 billion in personal trust would remain in the bank.[77] In another spin-off, " 'the least investment-sensitive types of account' will continue to be managed from the trust department."[78]

As has been seen, the responses of the banks, especially the largest institutions, in adapting their trust departments to changing conditions have certainly been proved adequate by the test of remarkable business success. The following sections may shed some light on whether the potential conflicts of interest built into these complex organizational arrangements and relationships can be resolved within this kind of structural reorganization.

II • THE CUSTOMER RELATIONSHIP AND THE BANK TRUST DEPARTMENT

With the enforced exit of banks from the underwriting of corporate securities under the Banking Act of 1933, trust departments remained as the bank area of contact with securities markets holding forth the greatest potential for conflict of interest. Many of these conflicts arose from the role and status of the trust department in the commercial bank.

Most banks initally undertook to provide trust services mainly to preserve and strengthen existing customer relationships, in the belief that the trust department "serves to tie-in the customer more closely to the bank. Such service alone is sufficient to justify the existence and development of the department."[1] With few exceptions, making trust department operations profitable in and of themselves was secondary. According to one well-known trust banker of the formative period:

It is . . .my impression that in many instances the trust department was very frankly organized simply as a service department, and that it was not the intention to put it on a sound profit and loss basis, the theory being that the expenses of the department would be more than compensated for by further strengthening of the relation of the customer with various other divisions of the commercial bank . . .[and] many an institution has put in a trust department without any very definite idea or even hope—that it can be made independently profitable.[2]

This rationale for the development of fiduciary services by banks fits Donald Hodgman's conception of the form taken by the competition, in lieu of price cutting, with new and complementary services added to strengthen the links between banks and their deposit customers and improve the banks' ability to preserve and enlarge their deposit base.[3] Of course, banks strive for direct earnings from new peripheral services, but the role of these services in supporting the deposit-customer/bank relationship and the banks' deposit base is often the first consideration. In the case of bank trust departments, change in these priorities has proceeded at varying rates and in many cases is incomplete. As recently as 1962, a bankers' association survey reported that "in determining what objectives of the trust department were most important to their bank the heaviest votes were for: 1. Serve as a device to hold and increase commercial bank business."[4] And many more recent interviews by the author have indicated that the service function orientation is still widely prevalent and the push for autonomy far from complete, especially in banks below the top score or so in trust volume.

A main reason for the secondary status and power of the trust department has been its relatively small contribution to bank earnings. The deposit and loan activites carried out by the commercial department have always brought in a much larger fraction of bank income, and despite the great increase in volume in recent decades, the importance of bank trust business is still relatively small;[5] in 1972 the median proportion of total bank operating income represented by trust income for the one hundred largest trust banks (measured by trust income) was 6.7 percent and the mean value, which gives greater weight to the larger trust institutions, was only 5.3 percent.[6] Only in sixteen of the hundred largest trust banks did trust departments account for 15 percent or more of the gross operating revenue. The real contribution of trust departments to bank earnings may be greater than these figures suggest,[7] but much of the business of the trust department may be attributable to its commercial bank connection. A bank is more likely to receive invitations to serve as corporate trustee, registrar, transfer agent, or custodian or manager of employee benefit plans for its commercial customers than from strangers, and new business activities in the trust department have focused heavily on soliciting the bank's commercial customers.[8] Some part of the solicitation effort in the personal trust and agency area also has been devoted to attracting the individual business of executives of commercial customer companies.[9]

The trust arm's potential for contributing to the customer relationship, and hence for conflict of interest, would seem immense. In the absence of any constraints—which do exist in fact and sharply limit conflict abuse in practice —trust assets might be employed to acquire control or influence over commercial customers or potential customers. Banking customers could be accommodated and the resources of the commercial department relieved, at the expense of trust accounts, by trust investment in customer bonds, notes, and other assets.[10] Trust departments might also assist commercial customers by buying or not selling their securities in declining markets,[11] by purchasing or financing in support of acquisition efforts, by refusing to sell to outsiders in takeover bids threatening customer managements, and by supporting customer management groups in proxy contests and in the disposition of proxies in general.

In many cases corporate business has been obtained by trust departments as part of a reciprocal relationship in which bank and customer build up credits with one another by giving and taking business offered and sought by the other. This relationship may lend itself to a subtle form of coercion, as doing business with the other party becomes "the better part of valor." In half a dozen cases, the author has been told that a particular piece of corporate business was obtained by bank "muscle," with the customer (in each case a modest-sized business) accepting the bank's trust department service out of fear of displeasing a powerful creditor. Several trust department officers, past and present, have told the author that the commercial relationship not only attracts but holds trust business on the bank's books; one of them asserting that in the mid- and late 1960s a major bank with which he was associated "couldn't lose" two-thirds of its corporate pension business.

Trust department clients include those who do business with the commercial arm and those who do not, those with no leverage in other parts of the bank, and those with a great deal of leverage. This extensive and deliberately incurred overlap of customers reduces effective separation of the different divisions of the bank. Preservation of trust department autonomy and a wholly objective treatment of security purchases and sales, or of controversial questions of proxy disposition, are likely to be more difficult when the securities and proxies are those of powerful and sensitive customers of the bank.

Although trust departments are still secondary income producers and have yet to throw off completely their service and support role, there has been a clear and discernible trend, especially among the larger institutions, toward greater autonomy and power in the advisory-investment management function. The trust department has been a separate division and profit center in a number of major institutions for a great many years, but even within sizable banks, its autonomy has increased with the growth in its size, bureaucratization, emphasis on investment performance, and publicity given to success in this area, which has added to the importance of the advisory-management function as an income producer.

Another important factor making for autonomy has been the emergence of legal problems associated with commercial-trust coordination—particularly those relating to inside information and broker-deposit reciprocity. Size, bureaucratization, and the performance phenomena by themselves had never sufficed to cause Morgan Guaranty Trust Company, the leading trust institution, to separate its banking and trust department research efforts; this separation did not occur until 1969, with the critical impetus coming from the threatening legal environment. This new set of legal problems was a key factor enabling trust departments to overcome their traditional subordinate position in the politics and power structure of the bank and to achieve a degree of independence not previously available to them.

In the smaller trust institutions, the same trends are discernible, but with weaker effects. Small trust department size and overlapping personnel still make for commercial bank domination and a lack of autonomy, and the impact of increased interest in performance and the legal threats associated with the misuse of inside information and brokerage have been modest. For the clientele of smaller banks, performance, hard to evaluate in any case, may be outweighed by conservatism, convenience, and personal and business reciprocity. The result is that "good commercial relationships" have remained a factor in the decision-making of many small trust departments.

In the balance of Section II, attention is directed to five conflict issues associated with the customer relationship, including its potential: (1) as an inducement to banks to attempt to establish positions of influence or control over portfolio companies; (2) as a source of customer accommodation; (3) as a source of constraint in trust department purchases and sales of securities; (4) as a basis of preferential treatment in investment management; and (5) as a source of influence over trust department use of voting proxies.

Customer Control Through Security Acquisitions

That banks might use trust department assets as a means of acquiring influence or even control over customers, or potential customers, was suggested with considerable force in the Patman Report of 1968,[12] which showed that not only did trust banks manage a huge volume of assets (about $250 billion at the time), but also that many individual banks held significant stock positions in a number of portfolio companies. The report found that the forty-nine leading trust banks had as many as 5,270 separate holdings of 5 percent or more of the stock of portfolio companies, often with director interlocks supplementing the stock ownership.

These and other Patman Report findings suggest that banks have greater power than had been known. But whether or not these findings can be interpreted as proving extensive bank control or substantial influence over portfolio companies is debatable. The statistics themselves require some clarification. The 5,270 holdings of 5 percent or more include preferred stock positions, usually without voting power. Moreover, bank trust departments often do not have the exclusive power to vote common stock in their portfolios. Many of the large holdings are family personal trust holdings for which the bank serves as administrative and contingent trustee, with control remaining in the hands of dominant family members.

In many cases the stock of a single company is divided into several units, or trusts, each with different allocations of voting powers. Thus, for some companies part of the stock is held by the bank with sole power to vote, part is voted by the bank together with a cofiduciary, and part is voted entirely by outsiders. With the 1967 data for six major trust banks made available by the Patman Committee, the author has compiled in Table 2 a distribution of 956 trust department holdings of 5 percent or more, classified by percentage size of holding and by distribution of voting power. Column 5 separates from the combination cases (given in column 4) those where the bank's sole voting rights still extend to 5 percent or more of the stock.[13]

The table shows that the six trust banks have the sole power to vote 24.4 percent of their large holdings and that for an additional 12.8 percent of their large holdings they retain sole voting rights over 5 percent or more of the stock, although they do not have sole voting powers over all of this stock in their portfolios. Interestingly, sole voting power is most prevalent where the bank has majority ownership (29.0 percent versus 24.4 percent overall), although the additional sole voting right power in the associated combination cases is less than overall (only 3.9 percent, for a grand sole voting right total of 32.9 percent of the majority ownership cases).

Two of the six banks whose holdings are included in Table 2 submitted to the Patman Committee a classification of their large holdings broken down between closely held companies and others. For the two taken together, only 15 of the 216 portfolio company holdings of 10 percent or more were in publicly owned securities; the other 201 were classed as closely held corporations. Of the portfolio companies majority-owned by the 2 trust departments, 133 of 134 were closely held. In the single case of a majority-owned portfolio company that was *publicly* held, the bank in question had no voting rights. The bank had sole voting rights in 45 of the 133 closely held companies, but as is noted in the table, 34 of them were "corporations organized for the exclusive purpose of holding title to property, collecting income therefrom . . .[and disbursing the proceeds] to tax exempt pension and profit-sharing trusts." Apart from these artificial creations, in only 11 of 100 majority-owned entities did these two banks have sole voting powers,[14] and the six banks in Table 2 held sole voting rights in not 29 percent but 19 percent of the portfolio companies in which they had majority ownership.[15]

These data indicate that a large proportion of the sizable holdings of trust banks are in very small, closely held companies that have come into the banks in their trust executor function. This situation poses a number of conflict-of-interest problems that may have been neglected in the overriding concern over banks' use of trust department assets to acquire control. One such problem is the extent to which the banks may use their power as lender to acquire the estate and pension business of small and dependent proprietors and companies in the first place. A second problem is the banks' disposition or liquidation of the assets of closely held companies where the banks have an interest in preserving a customer relationship or where other customers may be interested in acquiring the company. (These matters are considered briefly in the section on Customer Accommodation.)

Even with the major qualifications in the data just discussed, the great trust banks have large stock positions in many listed companies and may have used, or may in the future choose to use, their enormous assets to acquire influence or control. Or they may have had influence and/or control inadvertently thrust

Table 2: Voting Rights of Six Major Trust Banks in Their Trust Department Holdings of 5 Percent or More (1967)

						Distribution of Voting Rights						
		(1)		(2)		(3)		(4)		(5) WHEN		(6)
PERCENT OWNED BY BANK	NUMBER OF COMPANIES	SOLE POWER OF BANK		NO BANK RIGHTS		PARTIAL BANK RIGHTS		COMBINATION, CASE IN GIVEN STOCK[a]		COMBINATION, BANK RETAINS 5 PERCENT SOLE		TOTAL BANK SOLE POWER [EQUALS (1) + (5)]
		NUMBER	PERCENT	NUMBER	PERCENT	NUMBER	PERCENT	NUMBER	PERCENT	NUMBER	PERCENT	NUMBER	PERCENT
5 to 10	275	52	18.9	23	8.4	48	17.5	152	55.3	75	27.3	127	46.2
10 to 20	170	41	24.2	15	8.8	79	46.5	35	20.6	24	14.1	65	38.2
20 to 50	201	50	24.9	24	11.9	100	49.8	27	13.4	11	5.5	61	30.3
50 to 100	310	90[b]	29.0	36	11.6	164	52.9	20	6.5	12	3.9	102	32.9
	956	233	24.4	98	10.3	391	40.9	234	24.5	122	12.8	355	37.1

[a]*Combination case* means that the voting rights in bank-held stock are not uniform and fall into two or all three of the categories enumerated.

[b]Thirty-four of these ninety cases, all occurring within a single bank, were "corporations organized for the exclusive purpose of holding title to property, collecting income therefrom [and disbursing the proceeds] to tax exempt pension and profit-sharing trusts."

Source: Compiled from original data by the House Committee on Banking and Currency.

upon them by the sheer magnitude of their investment activities. Table 16 of the Patman Report shows that the 49 largest trust banks held more than 5 percent of the voting stock of 145 of the 500 largest industrial corporations in 1967. But in 32 of the 145 cases, the bank had sole voting rights over less than 1 percent of the portfolio company's stock. In only 71 of the 145 cases did the banks have sole voting rights over 5 percent or more of the common stock. In 5 of these 71 cases, the banks held still larger amounts of the same stock in accounts over which the banks had no voting rights; and in 13 more, the over 5 percent holding was distributed among 2 or more banks. But individual banks still had sole voting right holdings in excess of 5 percent in the common stock of 53 large industrial corporations.

Table 3:   Interlocking Relations Between Morgan Guaranty Trust Company and Firms Engaged in the Smelting and Refining of Nonferrous Metals, Mid-1967

| | | | PERCENTAGE OF OUTSTANDING STOCK HELD BY BANK | | |
PORTFOLIO COMPANY	INTER- LOCKING DIRECTORS	EMPLOYEE BENEFIT PLAN MANAGED BY MORGAN	PREFERRED	COMMON	COMMON W/SOLE MORGAN VOTE
Kaiser Aluminum and Chemical Corp.	—	—	5.7	6.6	5.7
Kennecott Copper	—	3	—	17.5	10.5
American Smelting and Refining	—	1	—	15.5	9.8
American Metal Climax	—	—	—	8.7	6.3
Phelps Dodge Corp.	1	1	—	6.0	2.4
General Cable Corp.	1	—	—	—	—
Revere Copper and Brass	—	—	—	7.9	4.9
Scovill Manufacturing	1	3	—	11.5	6.8
St. Joseph Lead	1	2	—	7.4	3.6
International Nickel Co. of Canada	3	—	—	—	—
Alcan Aluminum, Ltd.	—	—	—	5.1	4.4

Source: Committee on Banking and Currency, *Commercial Banks and their Trust Activities: Emerging Influence on the American Economy* (Washington, D.C., 1968), vol. 1. pp. 694-701

The Patman Report showed, for example, that in 1967 the Morgan Guaranty Trust held over 5 percent of the stock of a number of important corporations in nonferrous metals and had other relationships with them, suggesting potential influence or control. These relationships are summarized in Table 3, with separate columns for total voting rights of Morgan-held stock and sole voting rights in that stock by the bank. The figures indicate that sole voting right stockholdings of Morgan were substantially lower than total stockholdings (averaging about 64 percent of total voting rights). But Morgan's sole voting right power still exceeded 5 percent in five of the nine stock-ownership cases, raising questions about the bank's potential control of the individual companies involved. And the multiplicity of Morgan holdings and links between competitive companies suggest even more serious potentialities for an industry-wide constraint based on this unifying influence. The Patman data show that Morgan and other large trust institutions had similar large holdings and interlocking relationships in such other fields as paper and paper products, book publishing, textiles, industrial chemicals, steel, mining, trucking, air transportation, insurance, cosmetics, and cement.[16] The Morgan spectrum of trust related interests, by industry group, as of 1967 is shown on Figure 2. These were supplemented in a great majority of cases by banking relationships between Morgan and the trust portfolio companies.

In quite a few industries, a number of bank trust departments held multiple and overlapping large equity holdings along with substantial creditor positions, often supplemented by interlocks. These holdings raise questions of possible collective banker domination over major companies and even major industries, resulting from common interests and viewpoints, with or without coordination. The airlines are a case in point. The Patman data show heavy and overlapping trust department stock investments, commercial loans, and interlocks by many of the major New York banks in 1967.[17] In the case of Pan Am, the Chase Manhattan Bank held 6.7 percent of the common, had an $8.5 million loan outstanding, and was a pension trustee; the First National City Bank had a director interlock, managed two Pan Am pension plans, and had a $7 million loan outstanding; Morgan had a loan to Pan Am of $20.5 million. All three banks were interlocked with major insurance companies that had large lending relationships with Pan Am.[18]

Do these large holdings and other relationships add up to positions of domination by the trust banks? The question has two aspects: whether banks have *tried* to obtain control or influence via trust department investment, and whether they have in fact *obtained* such power.[19]

It may be argued that intent is not especially relevant, because power may be thrust upon the banks by the sheer magnitude of their holdings. The largest trust institutions, those with trust assets ranging up to $24 billion, encounter difficulty in building up a significant equity position for their major accounts in any but the very largest companies without acquiring a substantial percentage of stock. Morgan, for example, had eighty-one holdings with a market value of $50 million or more at the end of 1972; a 1 percent shift in its aggregate portfolio would have involved a purchase (and sale) amounting to $274 million.[20] Nonetheless, intent is important. An investment rather than control orientation will lead to a greater concern with marketability and thus a deliberate and necessary effort at diversification as well as a preference for blue chip companies with large capitalizations. Intent will also affect the manner in which stock power and proxies are used.

Figure 2: Interlocks and Trust Department Stockholdings of Morgan Guaranty Trust Company by Industry Group, 1967

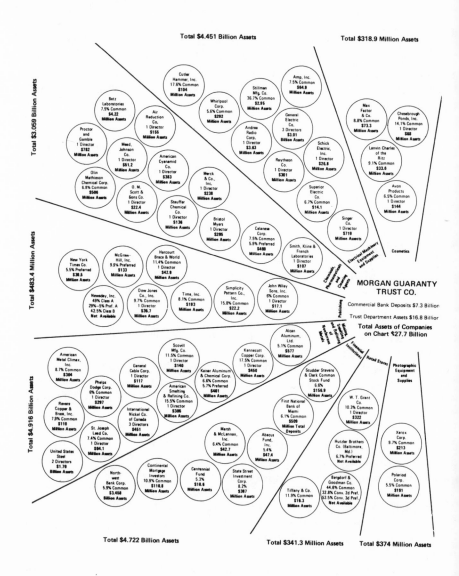

Source: Committee on Banking and Currency, *Commercial Banks and Their Trust Activities: Emerging Influence on the American Economy* (Washington, D.C., 1968), vol. 1, pp. 700-701.

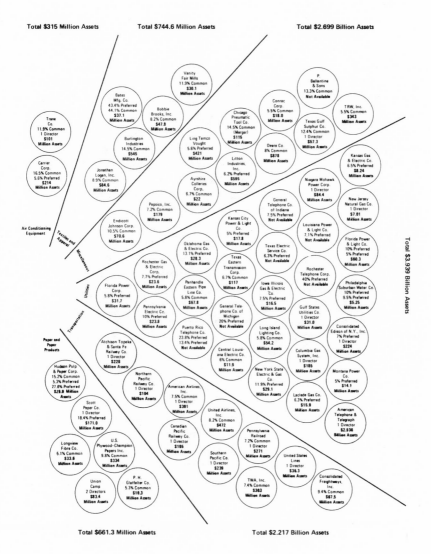

Total $315 Million Assets   Total $744.6 Million Assets   Total $2.699 Billion Assets

Total $3.939 Billion Assets

Total $661.3 Million Assets   Total $2.217 Billion Assets

Banks might try to obtain control for several reasons. They might want to assure competent management—either by installing their own personnel or by controlling the choice of personnel—to protect their investment. In the case of small and closely held companies, the assumption of control may be a necessary corollary of "prudent" fiduciary behavior. It is conceivable that some trust bankers, like the great investment bankers at the turn of the century, see themselves as the forces of law and order in the business community, bringing excessive competition under control, assuring that management is in competent and reliable hands, and simultaneously enhancing their own positions as creditors and owners. Banks might also seek control to capture for themselves the company's banking business and any additional custom obtainable via company reciprocity.[21] They might even seek (unneeded) business at the expense of the captive portfolio company.

But many factors tend to discourage banks from using trust department assets to acquire control, factors sufficiently potent so banks have, I believe, seldom attempted to do so. One negative factor is bank organization. In the larger banks, trust departments are separate bureaucracies with increasing autonomy, whose function is managing and servicing trust accounts and other investor clients. Their personnel are not qualified by training or experience to manage operating companies, or even to select qualified people. Their expertise lies in evaluating securities. In this role trust departments compete with other professional investing groups and are under strong competitive and moral pressure to adhere to professional performance standards. Although they may be interfered with occasionally for the higher strategic interests of the bank,[22] the bigger the bank and trust department the more these intrusions are resented and tend to become exceptional. This bureaucratic structure does not preclude investment for control, but it makes it more cumbersome and costly.

A second and related constraint on bank investment for control is pressure from clients who have left their funds with the bank to be managed. As we have seen, such clients have increasingly sought good investment performance. "Bank control" theorists tend to overlook the fact that the only beneficiaries of bank control are the bank and its stockholders, and that those whose assets are managed have potential conflicting interests with the banks.[23] Especially in the pension fund area, competition has become acute, and the larger firms that allocate pension fund resources among investment managers are knowledgeable about investment management quality,[24] which affects their own costs and thus their profitability. Any bank whose investment policy was dominated by a desire to control would probably do badly as an investment performer and would soon lose trust department (and other) business as a consequence.[25]

One analyst suggests that banks interested in control would display this in relatively stable holdings, which they would tend not to allow to fall below levels that might threaten their control positions.[26] Evidence on this point is not abundant, but case histories of major trust department divestments point rather clearly toward investment, not control criteria. The most notable in-

Table 4:   Decline in Morgan Common Stock Holdings of Firms Engaged in the Smelting and Refining of Nonferrous Metals, 1967 and 1973

	PERCENTAGE OF COMMON STOCK HELD IN	
	1967	1973
COMPANY	(from Table 3)	
Kaiser Aluminum and Chemical Corp. (and K. Industries)[a]	6.6	1.7
Kennecott Copper	17.5	6.2
American Smelting and Refining	15.5	0.2
American Metal Climax	8.7	b
Phelps Dodge Corp.	6.0	2.5
General Cable Corp.	(under 5.0)	b
Revere Copper and Brass	7.9	b
Scovill Manufacturing	11.5	2.4
St. Joseph Lead	7.4	b
International Nickel Co. of Canada	(under 5.0)	b
Alcan Aluminum, Ltd.	5.1	b

[a]In 1967 Morgan held 6.6 percent of the stock of Kaiser Aluminum and Chemical, whereas in 1973 the 1.7 percent was a holding of Kaiser Industries, which is, however, a large minority holder of the stock of the former (amounting in 1972 to approximately 39 percent of the common).

[b]Indicates less than $1 million in 1973, the cutoff point in the Morgan report for that year.

Sources: Table 3, based on the Patman Report of 1968; *Report III of the Trust and Investment Division, Morgan Guaranty Trust Company*, April 1974.

stance involves the airline stocks, where the numerous "control" level holdings of the early and mid-1960s were widely sold off by bank trust departments as the financial positions of the airlines deteriorated. As of July 21, 1967, Morgan Guaranty, for example, held 7.5 percent of the common stock of American Airlines, 7.4 percent of the common stock of TWA, and 8.2 percent of the common stock of United Airlines. By December 31, 1968, however, these holdings had fallen to 0.3 percent, 0.6 percent, and 0.5 percent, respectively.[27] The Morgan trust department report for 1973 shows that at the end of the year Morgan held $7.1 million of American Airlines stock, 2.9 percent of the total outstanding, but not so much as $1 million of either TWA or United Airlines. The huge Morgan investments in the nonferrous metals area, shown above in Table 3, also have been largely disposed of since 1967. Table 4 shows the comparative figures for Morgan nonferrous metals common stockholdings in 1967 and 1973. It is clear that major divestment of these stocks took place, with only Kennecott left as a holding in excess of 2.5 percent of the total outstanding. The Morgan report also shows that between 1968 and 1973 the common stockholdings of employee benefit plan (EBP) accounts in the "metals and minerals" field was reduced from $640 million to $69 million, or from 9.5 percent to 0.7 percent of EBP holdings.[28] These figures suggest that a change in assessment of the desirability of these stocks was Morgan's primary and perhaps exclusive consideration in acquiring and disposing of them.[29]

A third major constraint on bank use of trust department resources for control is the law. Bank control over corporate customers through stock ownership is still barred under the antitrust laws as an illegal form of vertical integration.[30] When a bank establishes a strong position in several competitors via stock ownership or interlocks, it leaves itself open to attack for reducing competition. In March 1970 the Justice Department filed a civil antitrust suit against Cleveland Trust, seeking a divestment of its stock in and termination of its interlocking directorships with three of four allegedly competitive companies.[31] The bank had acquired substantial stockholdings and voting power in four companies with significant market shares in the sale of automatic screw machines and had bank officers on the boards of each of these companies. A consent settlement entered into in 1975 restricted Cleveland Trust's allowable interlocks with a number of machine tool industry members with whom the bank had had long and close relationships. Although this suit is unique, many bank investment managers regard it as a warning.

At least as important a legal constraint is the bank's obligation as a fiduciary to its trust accounts. If a trust department had invested heavily enough in Penn Central stock to establish control, and if it were possible to show that this drive for control had been at all influential in its investment policy, the bank's violations of its fiduciary obligations as trustee would be so flagrant that it would be a sitting duck for massive recovery and punitive suits.[32] Banks have proven to be increasingly vulnerable on matters involving deviations from trust department autonomy and pursuit of trust interests, but a systematic use of trust department assets to gain control would put them in a truly perilous legal position.

A fourth constraint is the fact that the management groups controlling corporations would not relish being displaced, or even sharing control with external interests, and could be counted upon to resist any such threats to their own domination. Bank trust departments have acquired most of their sizable discretionary holdings during the past two decades, and one would expect to be able to identify a number of cases of management resistance to such takeovers if they involved the capture of control by banks.[33] The lack of evidence of such resistance suggests that banker control via the trust department investment route may be of marginal importance.

In reality, corporations are nearly always pleased when the trust departments of banks with whom they do business invest in their stock, even in sizable blocks. In addition to helping push up prices, stock acquisitions are regarded by the portfolio company as a vote of confidence and an act of loyalty on the part of an ally. They help to consolidate a reciprocal business relationship, tying the bank and its customer more closely together. That the bank will support the control group is an unstated but obvious premise.[34]

It may be argued that bank control is obtained so gradually and exercised so subtly that management scarcely notices the change. This argument raises the question of the mechanics of control and whether a minority stock interest with or without an associated directorship is likely to enable bankers to control companies, discreetly or otherwise. It is not possible here to discuss in detail the nature and bases of corporate control. I can only state my own conclusion,[35] which is that for sizable, publicly owned companies with diffused stock ownership the acquisition of under 10 percent of the stock by an outsider is not likely to dent the strategic position of an entrenched management group.[36] Control of the proxy machinery by management makes such a modest investment innocuous from a control standpoint, barring a prearranged deal or a full-fledged proxy contest.[37]

In addition to its stockholdings, of course, the bank may also have director links with a portfolio company. In 1967 the 49 largest trust banks had 8,019 director interlocks with 6,591 companies, including 768 interlocks with 286 of the 500 largest industrial firms and 146 interlocks with 29 of the 50 largest life insurance companies.[38] The exact significance of these relationships—far more extensive for banks than for other institutional investors[39]—has yet to be assessed adequately. They surely add to bank weight in decision-making and its business pulling power. They are known to be related in a statistically significant way to bank management of pension funds, ownership of a company's stock (percentages of both outstanding issues and the bank portfolio), loans, and fraction of company deposits held with the bank.[40] None of the other types of financial institutions with interlocking directorates shows statistically significant relationships between interlocks and these other variables, with the exception of loans.[41]

Nevertheless, a director interlock is still unsatisfactory evidence of control or even substantial influence, even where accompanied by a stockholding of 6 to 8 percent. Boards of directors are generally dependent bodies, chosen by the chief executive or by a very small group of inside officers who are themselves typically the true locus of control.[42] Despite their dominant legal position, boards of directors generally do not set overall corporate policies, nor do they even choose the top officers of the corporation (except in crises, such as upon the unexpected death of a controlling officer). It is tacitly understood by outside directors that they do not share in corporate control but are serving essentially in an advisory capacity for the purpose of providing expertise, an outside vantage point, and an honorific name and title, and that in return they obtain information and preserve and cultivate a business relationship. Typically, if board members come to question the direction of policy or doubt the capacity or integrity of the controlling officer, they may keep their reservations to themselves, resign voluntarily (and thus follow what amounts to a ''Wall Street Rule'' with regard to directorships), or, upon an open manifestation of disagreement, are asked to resign.

The large banks uniformly deny a desire or capacity to control portfolio companies in which they invest, with the exception of closely held estate assignments. Many of them have established formal or informally enforced ceilings on aggregate percentage holdings in portfolio companies, based, according to the banks, almost exclusively on marketability considerations. Of twenty-one respondents to Senator Bentsen's 1973 questionnaire requesting data on holdings and policies for large trust departments, two-thirds reported formal limits on their aggregate permissible holdings in discretionary accounts, none exceeding 10 percent.[43] Of the three respondent banks with assets managed in excess of $10 billion, Manufacturers Hanover Trust and First National City Bank had 10 percent general limit rules; Morgan, the largest, had no such rule.[44]

Despite these denials and limiting rules, large stockholdings, director interlocks, and frequent substantial creditor positions with companies heavily invested in by trust departments must still give the banks some degree of power vis-à-vis these companies. Some of the largest trust banks in cities like Cleveland, Baltimore, and Pittsburgh are so important in the local economy and society, with such extensive links throughout the community via interlocks and trust stockholdings, that allegations of virtual hegemony, or at least that they serve as a key body in integrating and stabilizing a dominant local interest group, are believable even if not easily proved.[45] Through their trust department investment activities banks control many closely held companies, and even in publicly owned companies control is surely acquired or thrust upon the banks on occasion by their financial and legal position—as, for example, when a company runs into management difficulties, and the bank has board membership, large credits outstanding, and common stock in its investment portfolios.[46] What is even more general is that the banks' position is strengthened in their relationships with customers, adding to the banks' weight and influence and enabling them to exact a somewhat larger average toll in a system of reciprocal benefits.

Although bank trust departments have apparently not sought or obtained control very often (closely held, estate-derived companies, as usual, excepted), they have frequently attempted to exercise some *influence* over corporate managements. Manufacturers Hanover, for example, in its reply to the Bentsen questionnaire, while denying any interest in control, did maintain that ''it is sometimes desirable for such holdings to be sufficiently large so that executors' and trustees' views will carry more than normal weight when presented to company management, i.e., with respect to mergers and acquisitions, corporate policies relating to product safety, employment practices, etc.''[47] Only rarely do trust banks seem to use this ''more than normal weight'' to help determine who runs the company. That kind of decision-making interest and power more often arises out of commercial department lending activities and rights under credit agreements involving troubled borrowers. Trust departments are often prepared to exercise whatever influence they can muster where mergers involving portfolio companies are proposed, but here, too, creditor positions frequently give the bank more leverage than equity holdings. Notes and other debt instruments that require creditor approval are sometimes held by trust departments, but much more common is a creditor veto power in the commercial department of the bank.

Banks may play an important role as financiers and advisors in merger programs of acquisition-minded companies, but again, it is the creditor role, the willingness to finance mergers with bank credit, that is critical here; trust department participation has been of marginal importance.[48] Commercial bank involvement in mergers is part of a now fairly standard financing service to customers, the bank sometimes getting special benefits in the form of deposit balances transferred from displaced banks of the acquired companies.[49] Banks are also important engineers and brokers of mergers, but again, mainly through commercial bank interest and resources. In the flurry of takeover bidding in the late 1960s, acquisition-minded companies and brokerage firms were more important than commercial banks as merger organizers. The institutional investor, including the bank trust department, was brought in, not as a planner or initiator but as a buyer or seller of stock, "interested only in alleviating [its] own problem (e.g., locked-in stock) or in capitalizing on the profit potential of a takeover bid. . . . "[50] In facilitating transfers by purchase and subsequent tendering, the trading-oriented investment companies were very much more important in the 1960s (and worrisome to corporations fearful of takeover bids) than commercial bank trust departments.[51]

Many bank trust departments communicate their disapproval of those merger proposals[52] or financing plans that they feel are inappropriate or damaging to trust interests.[53] Occasionally, they offer advice on other matters, such as marketing strategies, especially when the department not only has a substantial position in the portfolio company but also feels competent to advise. But most of them either do not believe they have the expertise to participate in most managerial decisions made by portfolio companies or feel it is incompatible with their specialized function as investment managers. Trust department officials also claim their *power* to influence (let alone control) is sharply limited, even where their stockholdings are substantial, especially with the larger companies. Several of the banks claim that with 6 percent of a company's stock, if they feel strongly about a merger proposal or new financing plan, they can get a respectful hearing from the management of a large company, but in such cases their influence is based more on reasoning than power.[54] But if other banks and institutional investors stress the same points, however, it is admitted that the possible consequences to the portfolio company (a decline in stock price, a poor reception for its new issue) may have substantial weight in the company's decision.

The power of the large investor in these matters tends to vary inversely with portfolio company size. Rarely does one hear of a successful effort to alter a decision taken by a large company. But quite a few trust officers describe incidents in which they informed the managements of medium- or small-sized companies in which they held major investments (over 1 percent but under 10 percent) of their displeasure at a proposal, sometimes indicating their intention of selling if the plan were carried through. The response, according to trust officials, was often postponement, cancellation, or alteration of the character and terms of the new financing or merger proposal. The threat of dumping the stock or selling it to unfriendly outsiders appears to be the prime source of influence of trust departments over portfolio companies. This influence, effectively employed mainly within a narrow range of financial decisions and for price-sensitive small companies and conglomerates, is wielded by a direct contact with management, not by use of trust department voting power.[55]

In several cases with which the author is familiar, the exercise of influence by trust departments was constructive, and the institutional investor served as an effective and informed proxy for other investors.[56] But in other instances trust departments have wielded their influence in a manner more consistent with the larger strategic interests of the bank, accommodating a customer interest in conflict with that of fiduciary accounts and company shareholder interests. Some of these conflicts and abuses are discussed and evaluated in the sections that follow.

Customer Accommodation

The phrase *customer accommodation* is employed here to describe the use of trust department resources to service the demands and needs of commercial customers. This service might be at the bank's initiative in order to relieve pressure on its commerical lending capacity by trust acquisition of customer debt, or it might result from customer initiatives—for example, in response to the expectation of certain customers that a "loyal" bank would demonstrate its allegiance by purchasing part of the customer's newly issued securities.

At one time it was considered an advantage of having a trust arm that the bank could sell to the trusts "securities from the company's own bond or mortgage department."[57] But from very early times, it was also recognized that the bank took special risks in transferring assets in which it had some special interest.[58] Thus, accommodation practices have always been constrained by the fear of potential legal liability. Their scope also has been related to the degree of autonomy of the trust department and, conversely, the extent to which it has been integrated into the larger entity as a service vehicle.

Over the past decade, accommodation practices in trust departments have persisted more conspicuously in the handling of estates and closed corporations than in trust portfolio investment, partly because of less publicity and partly because more acute conflicts arise there. A great variety of assets flow into the bank for disposition as estate executors—personal property, real estate, and control holdings in small corporations—which the bank usually tries to dispose of fairly quickly. In a number of substantial trust banks, new probate holdings are brought to the attention of a corporate financial services branch of the commerical division, which deals with mergers and acquisitions. The bank's customers frequently have an interest in the disposition of this property. For example, a memo was circulated within a trust department by a commercial officer indicating that an important customer executive

. . .asked me to make the bank aware of two interests he presently has:

1. He is a very avid coin collector, and apparently owns a valuable private collection. He wishes to have the opportunity to make an offer to purchase rare coins which might turn up in our estates. . . .

2. One of [X's] companies is anxious to make acquisitions. They presently have no specific criteria as to size or type; however, I would guess he is talking about fairly small closely held firms. He would appreciate being advised whenever we are aware of businesses which are or might be for sale.

The potential conflicts of interest here would not result in abuse if the bank was scrupulous in getting reliable valuations and competitive bids or if the customer on the other side of the transaction were of equal importance to the bank. But it is obvious that the "wall" between the trust and commercial departments was permeable in this case,[59] and that the same power factor that led to its breach could lead to abuse.

In many instances real property or controlling blocks of stock in closely held companies come into the bank with customers in eager pursuit. In one recent case described to the author, a number of trust department officers were alerted to the fact that a good customer was assembling farm properties. This bank eventually established its own farm management division, which led it into another conflict situation: it had an interest in selling off farm properties to buyers who would leave the management in the hands of the bank. The bank also may sometimes want real estate property for itself—for example, as a location for a facility of its own.[60]

When controlling interests in closely held companies come into the trust department, a crucial conflict hinges on the bank's interest in keeping control in the hands of a management that will remain a "friend of the bank." The same problem arises when a takeover from the outside threatens a customer whose stock is held by the trust department. The bank has an interest conflicting with that of the fiduciary department beneficiaries and may seek to thwart the takeover by pushing for arrangements less advantageous to the fiduciary interest.[61] The present management of a small company whose control is at stake is often interested in buying the controlling shares. And the bank may face a conflict in that a tough stance on valuation might impair its relationship with the successor management. The problem is, of course, greatly accentuated when the customer is not only deeply interested in acquiring trust-held shares but also has a special power position in the bank, such as a directorship,[62] or when there is a long-standing business and personal relationship with bank officers and directors.[63]

In some cases the interested customer is correspondent bank whose management may want to acquire the controlling shares. In the late 1960s, several large trust banks had policies of notifying the correspondent banking arm before the probate department sold any stock in local banks and offering the stock of a correspondent bank to its principal officers before it was made available to others. One large trust institution routinely asked local bank officers to assist in the valuation of the stock in the bank, which they knew they might later be offered for purchase. Because probate assets can be used to cement customer relationships, the pressures on banks to compromise fiduciary obligations may be severe. The author was told about many cases of banks resisting or ignoring such pressures, sometimes at cost to themselves. Although the number of instances of banks compromising the interests of their fiduciary clients in disposing of probate property is probably small, in the unpublicized environment in which these dealings occur, these conflicts must certainly result in a significant number of realized abuses.[64]

Accommodation via investments of regular accounts of the trust department has undoubtedly diminished since the mid-1960s. In the 1950s and the early 1960s, private placements were a major vehicle of trust department fixed income investment, and a substantial fraction of these were made to customers. The conflict potential here is enormous, as the banks may not only use the trust department as a lending supplement to the commercial arm[65] but might also make credit available on favorable terms. Several important trust department officers claim that a few New York City banks were definitely using cheap private placements as a vehicle for attracting commercial business in the 1950s, and a number of insurance company veterans stated that they thought the entire structure of bank private placement rates suspiciously low. In the only known study of the yield on private placements accepted by a major trust institution in its fiduciary capacity, it was found that the Mellon Bank, in its heavy private placement commitments for the Pennsylvania Public School Employees' Retirement Fund for the period 1960-71, had a yield differential over comparable public offerings of about ¼ percent compared with ½ percent for the life insurance companies, and "did not do as well on its private placements as it should have done."[66]

The banks' reply to these allegations is that private placements were good investments, taken largely from prime customers, and appeared at the time to be the best available options. Although these private placements were usually of high quality, whether they were generally the best available options at the highest possible prices is questionable. According to quite a few trust veterans, private placements were often taken by the trust departments grudgingly and under pressure. From 1958 to 1963, at least a dozen major private placements were described by the analysts or officers as "inappropriate," which suggests that the best available options were not only sacrificed in individual cases but might not have been pursued in general.[67]

Still, it is important to recognize that trust department officials did generally manage to hold the line on quality.[68] It was recognized in many banks that trust department investments linked to commercial interests might well make the bank the guarantor for particular trust department investments. In several banks an explicit rule was adopted that dual loans would be made (short-term in the bank, long-term in the trust department) only for those companies of above-average quality. Despite these rules, in the low publicity and minimal regulatory environment of that period, trust departments bent to a greater or lesser degree, depending on the pressures on the banks, the attitudes of top management toward involving the fiduciary arm in conflict, and the degree of autonomy of the trust department. In the best of situations, where customers had substantial deposit relationships with the bank, there was, at a minimum, occasional pressure on the trust arm to "take a very long look" at customer private placements. Sporadic deployments of trust resources in the strategic interests of the commercial arm occurred widely. It is not at all clear that these involved significant direct losses to the trust clients of banks, but the banks were not well regarded as investment managers before the latter 1960s and early 1970s. One cannot but suspect that the factors that caused such pressures and occasional deviations from trust department autonomy and dedicated fiduciary interest may have contributed to deficient performance and reputation.

Customer accommodation has often been a product of customer pressure, with the banks and trust departments frequently going along reluctantly, indeed, sometimes only after a struggle. Companies with pension plans, for example, often desire access to, or some degree of control over, the resources in their own pension funds. They may want the fund to buy shares in the company to help support the price of the stock or perhaps to help maintain management control. The Patman Report indicated that 734 of 13,500 employee benefit funds managed by the large trust banks in 1967 had invested to some degree in their own companies' securities. In some cases loans were extended to the companies, or other arrangements were found to make pension fund assets available to the company. In a number of instances, trust banks have been induced to enter into sale-leaseback contracts with franchised dealers of the founder company.

Although on rare occasions employee benefit plans permit a company to direct the purchase of its own stock, more often the manager is instructed or permitted to invest up to 5 or 10 percent of fund assets in the company's own shares. The large banks do not like such arrangements, partly because of the constraint on their freedom of action, partly because of the diplomatic difficulties in selling the securities when appropriate, and partly because of the general conflict of interest involved in allowing noninvestment considerations to enter into their decisions.[69] A number of the larger banks will not accept the management of pension and profit-sharing plans involving such constraints.

Sometimes there is customer pressure to buy a new issue of common stock or bonds. Some banks do, but increasing numbers do not, and those that do may make only a token purchase. A great number of trust officers have acknowledged this kind of pressure, but they almost invariably deny that they are affected by it (although conceding its occasional impact elsewhere). Some have described incidents where a failure of the bank to "come through" led to a discontinued or weakened relationship, but these cases appear to be of diminishing frequency.

In the case of one major trust bank, the bank trust department was asked by the customer and its investment banker to take a part of a new bond issue.

Although the trust department did not like the bonds, it agreed to take some if the price was right. The yield was below the ceiling fixed by the department, however, and it refused to buy. The investment banker was furious, especially because the bonds were doing badly, and threatened the withdrawal of the customer's demand deposit. An order to buy came from above, and the trust investment committee, under pressure, voted to do so. But the two top officers of the trust department protested further, arguing that if the securities were bought they should be acquired for the bank's own account—and they were; in the end the trust department did not buy any bonds.

In another recent episode, because a major industrial company had several times changed the provisions of its private placement with two banks, the banks wanted to dispose of their holdings. The company did not want these bonds traded on any financial market because of a soon-to-be-issued affiliated credit company bond; so not being able to buy its own bonds, it loaned a brokerage house the sum necessary to acquire the bond, pending relocation. The company then approached a large trust bank with which it had a director interlock and a major customer relationship and asked it to take some or all of the bonds. According to two employees of the bond department, the customer applied pressure on the commercial arm, including a threat of withdrawal of deposits and shift of other business. Pressure was then put on the trust department, which had not been interested in private placements and ordinarily only bought bonds of a higher quality. After some resistance the trust department succumbed, and after some haggling over the price, it eventually absorbed half of this large private placement.

Accommodation may also be expected by a customer threatened with a takeover or in need of assistance in connection with its own takeover efforts. In the former case, the customer may press the bank to refuse to tender its stock and even to acquire more stock to head off the merger attempt; and on a number of occasions, the banks have complied. One major trust bank, which managed the pension funds and held about 5 percent of the stock of a good commercial customer, was faced with the attempt of a conglomerate to take over the customer. The bank bought the customer's stock for the customer's own pension fund accounts, even though the trust department did not like the stock. In several cases described to the author, trust department tenderings of large blocks of stock were "sweetened" by making the bank the exchange offer agent in the transaction. In its discussion of National General Corporation's (NGC) acquisition of Great American Holding Corporation (GAH), the Institutional Investor Study notes that a bank (Girard Trust) holding 5 percent of GAH shares for its discretionary accounts "was named exchange offer agent, although NGC had no previous connections with the bank. The bank subsequently tendered half of these shares to NGC and sold the balance in the market near the termination of the NGC exchange offer when it was reasonably certain that such shares would be tendered to NGC because of the activity of arbitrageurs."[70]

In the 1969 effort of Electronic Data Systems (EDS) to acquire Collins Radio Company, two large New York City trust banks (Chase and Morgan) were in an unenviable conflict position, both being major creditors of Collins and together owning 23 percent of Collins's outstanding shares in their fiduciary capacity. If the tender offer had been advantageous to the trust accounts, as it often has to be to elicit the necessary response from shareholders, the simultaneous threat to the commercial relationships would place the banks in a severe conflict situation. The two banks cooperated with the Collins management in defeating the takeover bid by refusing to tender and changing the credit agreements so the outstanding loans became due immediately upon the acquisition of control of 30 percent of Collins's stock by a single owner.[71] The banks claim that the commercial and trust departments operated in total isolation from one another in arriving at their decisions in this case, and that the trust decisions to reject the offer were based on the disparity in size and price-earnings ratios of the two companies.[72] Insofar as these important decisions were made by the ultimately responsible top officers and board, however, it is evident that a dichotomy of mind would have been necessary for these individuals. Moreover, one former officer of Morgan, while claiming that the investment management department had no knowledge of the restructuring of loans to Collins, stated privately that "this action was to the detriment of the investment department, because it made it nearly impossible for an acquirer to take over Collins—thus, the holders of Collins stock lost this takeover increment in the value of their stock.''

Similar conflicts may arise when a customer wishes to take over another company. Suppose, as has happened, that the trust department holds a significant block of the customer's stock and considers the merger proposal a mistake. The commercial department may also consider the merger dubious, but it may be even more concerned over possible deposit losses. When one trust department expressed strong and threatening disapproval of a customer's prospective merger in 1965, according to a high-ranking officer involved, it took only two hours for the repercussions to be felt by the commercial arm, the highest officers in the bank, and then the trust department. This merger was eventually called off for other reasons, but the pressures on this trust department from other parts of the bank were so intense that trust officers considered it unlikely that the department would have been able to dispose of the customer's stock if this had been deemed a proper response to the prospective merger.

Further complications may arise when the trust department owns stock in the target company sought by a customer. In one episode described in detail to the author by an analyst at a large trust bank, the bank trust department held about two thousand of the six hundred thousand outstanding shares of Bank A, 20 percent of which was owned by a customer of the trust bank. Bank B, 50 percent of which was owned by a more important customer of the trust bank, attempted to acquire Bank A via a tender offer. The first customer opposed the sale, and the trust bank's holdings became important because of the need of a two-thirds vote of approval. The bank analyst advised against tendering on the ground that the terms of the merger were unsatisfactory from the standpoint of Bank A. According to the analyst, this conclusion caused consternation in the commercial department of the trust bank, and pressures were applied to persuade him to change his view. He refused and was supported by the head of the trust department. Because the beneficiary of the trust expressed strong opposition to the proposed deal, the responsibility for noncooperation with the substantial customer could, in this case, be passed off on the beneficiary.

It is impossible to measure the extent to which banks accommodate customers in the sense used here. A trust department normally acquires securities of many large firms that happen to be customers of the bank, so separating out the ''customer effect'' requires more than identifying customer securities in the trust department. The Institutional Investor Study (IIS) attempted an analysis of this problem on the basis of data collected from 288 portfolio companies, but even their valuable effort was able to deal with only a limited range of information. For example, the study did not include debt instruments held by trust departments, an especially suitable mechanism for customer accommodation.[73] The IIS found that there is an exceptional opportunity for accommodation practices by banks, based on the extent of their dealings with portfolio companies. ''The banks, on average, 'know'[74] 41.5 percent (or 120) of the sample companies. Other institutional types 'know' a considerably smaller number of sample companies—between 11.8 percent and 15 percent or between 34 and 43 companies.''[75]

The author attempted to gain some insight into the accommodation practices and possibilities of trust banks by examining the specific holding of both stocks and debt instruments of one major trust bank as of June 30, 1967.[76] On the basis of an imperfect and incomplete customer list for that bank,[77] the stocks, bonds, and special notes of fourteen portfolios were classified according to the percentage of customer issues in each. Overall, on average, 30 percent of the number of stocks in the fourteen portfolios were issues of customers of the bank.[78] And overall, an average of 29 percent of the bonds in these portfolios, measured by par value, were bonds of bank customers. Eleven of the fourteen portfolios contained special notes, in six cases consisting exclusively of customer notes. Recent statistics compiled by the Continental Illinois National Bank show that of the fifty companies in which that trust department has its largest equity investments, 75 percent are commercial borrowing customers of the bank, and 37 percent have outstanding loans or lines of credit in excess of $5 million each.[79]

Nothing in these data proves that any securities are held to accommodate customers, and the Continental Illinois data were compiled by the audit department over what was claimed to be a firm ''wall.''[80] But these data show an opportunity for accommodation that has been realized in the past and still retains its potential for abuse.[81] In the case of the 1967 single bank data discussed above, the percentage of customer issues in the portfolios is substantially greater (and statistically significantly greater) than would be expected on the basis of random portfolio selection. It may still be argued that the bank knows its customers and that disproportionate investing in customer securities is therefore defensible on solid investment grounds such as superior knowledge and confidence in management. This argument, however, assumes a flow of information between departments that is incompatible with the alleged total independence of the trust department and its investment decision-making.

Considering common stockholdings alone, the IIS found a significant statistical relationship between bank trust stockholdings and each of the independent variables used in the analysis: personnel ties, employee benefits plan management, loans, and deposits. However, the total effect was found to be small:

> Combining all of these hypothetical assumptions for a company and bank of average size from the sample . . .produces a rather small expected fractional holding in the bank's stock portfolio. While the average bank would be expected to have shares in an average company it "knew" amounting to .33 percent of the bank's portfolio, the existence of all of these relationships would be expected to result in a holding comprising about 1.15 percent of the bank's portfolio.
>
> Since the average market value of these banks' shareholdings is $2.6 billion, this would amount to $30 million.[82]

It is important to remember that the IIS data are incomplete for measuring the customer relationship, and debt holdings of trust departments—most relevant for accommodation—were excluded. Nevertheless, these findings do suggest that in the contemporary legal, organizational, and competitive context, the customer relationship does not appear to have major effects on the composition and quality of discretionary trust portfolios.

The Problem of Selling Customers' Securities

In virtually every trust bank, it is acknowledged that at one time or another, a decision to sell off substantial amounts of the securities of a good commercial customer "created a lot of flak," and that the fear or reality of unfavorable customer reactions restrained sales on occasion, with potentially adverse effects on trust department investment performance. In recent years banks have been protected against this kind of pressure by increased trust department autonomy and by the banks' own legal liabilities for interdepartmental communication. Banks also have benefited from increased customer sophistication on these matters, although some bank customers still doubt the reality of the wall.

In a number of cases, sales have not taken place because of specific business being done with the customer that was thought to require reciprocal and friendly behavior by the bank. In one recent instance, for example, when a large new offering of customer's stock threatened to depress its price, investment officers of the bank proposed selling the stock, buying warrants, and waiting for a lower price. The top management decided that the stock would not be sold as a matter of "policy." Some of the investment officers thought that one reason for this decision was that the bank was an agent in the offering and therefore would gain a substantial daily inflow of balances. In another instance, where an officer of a bank was a director of a customer company and the bank carried out a range of services for the customer, the pension fund managers of the bank were prevented from unloading a part of their holdings because of the "explaining" that the officer would have to do as a director of the customer.

Constraint in selling not only may be related to the sensitivity of commercial customers but also may be a function of a more direct bank interest. The bank as creditor may have a stake in the successful outcome of a new stock issue or in the maintenance of a market for the customer's outstanding securities, creating a sharp conflict of interest between the bank's obligations as fiduciary and as creditor. In one case the commercial department, concerned over how a sharp drop in the price of customer's stock might affect the payoff of a large loan, prevailed upon the trust department to delay a desired sale and then to spread it out over a longer period.

In its case against Continental Illinois begun in 1973, the Air Line Pilots Association (ALPA) emphasized the fact that Continental bought for its fiduciary accounts substantial equity interests in a number of companies (Penn Central, Management Assistance, Inc., Lum's, TWA, and U.S. Freight) with whom Continental had a creditor relationship. In each instance Continental either sold off the stocks only after their prices fell sharply, or was still holding them, despite severe declines, at the time the suit was initiated. For example, Continental invested $488,250 in Management Assistance, Inc. (MAI), in 1965 and 1966, and still held the same number of shares at the end of 1971, when their value had sunk to $32,881.[83] Continental was the principal creditor of MAI during the period of decline in its stock and by explicit agreement had access to all confidential information about its operations.[84] A number of issues are raised by this situation: whether the trust department's acquisition of this stock was linked to the bank's interest in the company; whether information on the quality and status of the company was communicated from the commercial department to the trust department; and whether the bank was inhibited in selling off the stock either by its own stake in the company or out of fear of "inside trade" violations of the securities laws.[85] Whatever the merits of the ALPA case, the potential conflict and basis of a selling constraint are clear.

The belated sales of large quantities of Penn Central stock by major bank trust departments just before June 21, 1970, raise similar conflict-of-interest questions. Chase, Morgan, and Continental Illinois together sold 1,160,075 shares of Penn Central between April 1 and June 19, 1970.[86] A great deal of attention has been directed to whether these sales were based on "inside information.'' The question of why such sophisticated investors stayed so long with so risky, ill-managed, and deteriorating an enterprise is more interesting. Some of the author's bank informants have stressed the difficulty of selling in volume, the belief in the government's inevitable bailing out of the railroad, reluctance to admit a serious error in judgment, and simple ignorance of the facts. Other such informants, however, have suggested the importance of large ''background'' considerations: (1) the unwillingness to disaffect the management of the ailing giant and risk losing substantial deposits; (2) the large debt positions of some of the institutions, which would be damaged by a collapse in the price of Penn Central stock; and (3) a tacit understanding among the banks that they were ''in this together''and had a joint interest (and perhaps ''social responsibility'') in standing by the railroad and not starting a panic exit. Insofar as these considerations influenced the disposition of trust holdings of Penn Central, fiduciary principles were clearly violated. It is not yet possible to make a definite assessment of the importance of these constraints, but their total irrelevance would suggest a degree of ineptitude that is perhaps even more difficult to accept.

Customer resentment at sales of their securities has often been expressed by verbal protests, but on occasion has gone to the point of withdrawal of balances and other terminations of business. As a result of such experiences, many banks make it a policy to notify customers of prospective sales.[87] One rationale given for a notification policy is that the customer might want to try to arrange for the placement of the securities with other investors to avoid disturbing the market.

Apart from advance notice, banks use a number of other means to reduce any damaging effects of trust security sales on their customer relationship. They can assure the customer of their continued regard for the stock while explaining the sale strictly in terms of a temporarily excessive price; and they can avoid public and written announcements of sales. This latter policy is especially important for banks offering a correspondent bank investment advisory service. The decline in the investment status of an important customer may be communicated relatively easily within the bank. But there may be strong constraints against putting this negative view in writing for external distribution. It has sometimes been difficult to get a customer removed from the approved list, in part because approved-list status may be a requisite for acquiring bonds and notes of an issuer under the investment rules of some trust departments.

Another policy option is to avoid buying customers' securities in the first place. Several medium-sized trust departments maintained such a policy into the 1970s. In one such case, the policy was installed after a sale was made over the objections of a major customer and the commercial department. This in turn led the customer to withdraw accounts from both the commercial and trust departments. None of the giant trust institutions have a policy of avoidance, in part, of course, because it would unduly restrict their investment opportunities, given the large number of major companies who are commercial clients. They also may be in less need of such a self-imposed constraint, given the national status and sophistication of many of their customers, the ready marketability of their customers' securities, and the prestige and power of the banks, which may make them more independent. In recent years constraints on selling because of customer sensitivity and power seem to have been significantly greater among small and medium-sized banks, where the power of major local customers has sometimes been relatively high and where the trust department has been too small to have much autonomy.

The intrusion of the commercial relationship into the investment decision-making process has rarely been a result of settled policy. Within a bank where episodes of unwarranted constraints on sales have been recounted, one is often regaled with stories in which the trust department or top bank management resists customer pressure or freely sells out holdings of a company with a representative on the bank's own board. A customer constraint on selling is hard to distinguish from mere conservatism and bureaucratic inertia. The stock may continue to be held for a complex of reasons, with the customer relationship only one and perhaps a subordinate factor. The relationship has sometimes meant only that additional soul-searching is required to assess the risk incurred by those recommending a sale.

The scope and significance of customer constraints on the sale of trust department securities is impossible to estimate. But the judgment of many participants is that customer constraints were never of more than modest importance and have declined under the same kinds of pressures that have reshaped the business in general over the past decade—publicity, legal threats, performance competition, and increased trust department size and autonomy. The decline in importance of this constraint is most evident in the case of the very large trust institutions. But even these institutions occasionally feel its impact.

Preferential Treatment in Investment Management

Banks have potentially severe conflicts of interest in their handling of the accounts of different clients, who vary greatly in importance to the bank and in sophistication, sensitivity to performance, and willingness to apply pressure (including moving their accounts elsewhere). By enlarging their ''related'' business, banks have brought in new layers of customers and further potential problems of conflict.

Differential treatment among accounts may arise out of basic economic and structural arrangements built into the growing trust department as well as out of explicit responses to customers. Before discussing customer pressures, brief attention will be given to account load differentials, variation in the quality of portfolio managers, and other organizational factors that result in differential investment management.

ACCOUNT LOAD DIFFERENTIALS

Table 5 shows the breakdown of account loads for portfolio managers in 1970 for one large trust institution.

Table 5: Account Loads of Portfolio Managers at a Major Trust Bank, 1970

	NO. OF ACCOUNTS	NO. OF MANAGERS	NO. OF ACCOUNTS PER MANAGER[a]	AVERAGE ASSETS PER ACCOUNT	AVERAGE ASSETS PER MANAGER
				[THOUSANDS OF DOLLARS]	
Employee benefit funds	533	5	53	$3,500	$175,000
Personal trust	3,198	9	201	550	110,550
Estates	277	2	139	700	97,300
Investment advisory	575	6	96	1,000	96,000

[a]Not including accounts in pooled funds or common trust funds.

Source: An internal computation made available by a large trust bank.

It is obvious that in this institution, as in most, account loads were heaviest in the personal trust area. Personal trust portfolio managers may be responsible for from two hundred to one thousand separate portfolios in the larger banks— even more on average in smaller institutions. This is a result of the small size of these accounts, which are difficult or impossible to manage both attentively *and* with a profit to the bank. The banks try to combine as many of these accounts as possible into common trust funds, but even today trust department salesmen sell the personal service that banks offer, which makes a subsequent shunting into a common trust fund awkward. Heavy account loads make it difficult for the average personal trust manager to respond quickly to new information, and typically, these accounts appear to be reviewed rather than actively managed.[88] As one portfolio manager stated to the author: ''Most personal trusts hit the portfolio manager's desk only a month before the account is due for review.'' Turnover figures developed in the Institutional Investor Study show that the typical personal trust account is subject to very little investment activity.[89]

In the employee benefit area, many banks have deliberately reduced account loads to permit portfolio managers to do more than just review accounts. One bank executive described his institution's approach as follows: ''Pension fund managers have no more than thirty accounts with a maximum market value of $250 million in total assets; all pension fund accounts are in the same issues, within reason, and the number of issuers per account has been cut down. No more than forty names would be used at any one time.'' In contrast, the number of personal trusts handled by a single portfolio manager does not seem to be changing. This can have performance consequences. In the words of one personal trust portfolio manager, a number of whose accounts held Penn

Central stock beyond the bankruptcy date, ''The only explanation of the failure to sell, as well as the lag in the whole personal trust area, was the burden of overwork; I intended to sell, but didn't get around to it.''

The personal trust manager is also handicapped in responding quickly by the variety of tax considerations and investment restrictions and objectives as well as a cumbersome review process. The need to secure outside approval increases response time for the nondiscretionary accounts. The efforts of one personal trust portfolio manager responsible for six hundred accounts were allocated as follows: ''What happened when I received investment information was that I took care of the bigger accounts and the ones that were more alert, calling in frequently to discuss investment matters, and despite my goodwill, I neglected the mass of small accounts.'' Another with seven hundred accounts claimed that ''I couldn't find out who held what, and as a result, the larger accounts got the benefit of information.'' At this portfolio manager's bank, however, computerization was about to be extended to include personal trust accounts, and he was optimistic that this would reduce preferential treatment.

VARIATIONS IN THE QUALITY OF TRUST PERSONNEL

In the larger trust banks, personal trust portfolio managers have had relatively low status. With some exceptions this group tends to consist of relatively unproved and unseasoned individuals plus an older group of veterans harking back to pre-performance days and oriented to customer contact. Their lesser status is manifested in relatively low salaries, heavier work loads, and responsibility for accounts that involve more paperwork than intellectual challenge. A common in-bank ranking of portfolio managers is that ''the pension fund managers are more aggressive, smarter and are able to get the jump on other portfolio managers. On the average, the investment advisory account managers are next in order of competence and aggressiveness, and the personal trust portfolio managers follow in the rear.'' According to one former head of research, the effect of this perception of competence and aggressiveness is that ''the personal trust department is generally last informed on any new developments. This is only logical, because the personal trust department does not contain the best minds of the bank, and as a consequence research has to spell out any moves it was recommending in a way that can be understood by these portfolio managers. Even after making recommendations to the personal trust department, research has to hold their hand while they make a decision to buy or sell a hundred shares. These people are last on the list, because it would be a complete waste of knowledge to make them first.''

The more aggressive portfolio managers (mainly pension trust and investment advisory) often develop informal contacts and rapport with research analysts, based on mutual interest. The analysts know what these managers are investing in, that they want to be kept informed, and that information given to them will be appreciated and used. Mutual interest appears to be highest when portfolio managers are able to invest in smaller companies, glamour stocks, and special situations, because these companies are more interesting to analysts than the ''blue chips.''

Personnel differences thus help give rise to *ad hoc*, informal networks of information that can operate to the advantage of pension funds and other more aggressively managed accounts.

OTHER ORGANIZATIONAL AND STRUCTURAL FACTORS

Other organizational and structural differences also affect the information distribution process. For example, during the late 1960s, many banks felt the need to establish a reputation as ''performance-oriented'' money managers and moved to set up pooled employee benefit funds, sometimes labeled ''special situations'' funds, to invest in the ''hot stocks'' of the day. The typical procedure was designed to give the pooled fund portfolio manager the best available information and the ability to respond quickly to that information. To this end the pooled fund manager was often located physically in the research department, and the sole control over his decisions was an *ex post facto* committee review of transactions in the account. In addition, all research analysts were encouraged to suggest possible investments for the fund, and the pooled fund portfolio manager was given extra commission dollars to direct to his own information sources. Because this type of account was a ''showcase'' used to display the bank's skills to prospective customers, no organizational pressures limited time and effort, and as one analyst noted: ''With regard to the special situations fund, there was an inordinate amount of time spent on analyzing the stocks for the account.'' According to another analyst, there was little concern about conflicts of interest: ''The analysts collectively ran a pool of pension fund money and could place securities in this account without any restrictions as to competing with other accounts for stock or for information.'' In short, the research department served these large-account-oriented funds on a preferential basis.

Correspondent investment services set up to supply correspondent banks and other subscribers with the investment information produced by the research department further complicate information sequences.[90] Operating a large research department is expensive, and reselling the research output to other clients may permit a reduction in the unit cost of the research product. Typically, the supplier bank's printed memoranda will be mailed to subscribers simultaneously with internal distribution, but subscribers receive the memoranda several days later than the supplier bank's internal accounts. To improve the salability of the correspondent service, banks offer a variety of ''extras,'' including the right to call the research department to get its current opinion on a security or—better still—the benefit of being called by the research department when its opinion of a security changes. Some subscribers may, consequently, regularly receive information before all the supplier bank's internal accounts have received it. As one bank officer in charge of its service indicated to the author: ''I will tell the correspondents what the bank is buying and selling in detail and keep them right up-to-date, even though this may hurt us.'' Others relying on the mail may get their information after price movements based on actions by earlier recipients.

In the areas discussed above, information dissemination has developed with little apparent thought about possible conflict of interest.

PERFORMANCE AND CUSTOMER PRESSURE

Many banks have moved toward centralized, mirrored accounts, but mainly in the pension fund area and under the pressure of comparisons and complaints by the larger and more sophisticated customers. It would, of course, be difficult to have mirrored accounts for the variety of constrained smaller portfolios managed by banks, but this practice results in a great deal of differential treatment for accounts of varied size and power.

Most of the internal accounts receiving and using information on a priority basis can be termed ''sensitive'' accounts, in that either the management contract is tied to investment performance or the customer is important or sophisticated, so there may be repercussions if the account does not perform. Pooled funds, common trust funds, and closed-end funds may also be sensitive, because the investment results are usually disclosed to customers and the public. Typically, the most sensitive accounts are in the pension fund area; investment advisory accounts are less sensitive, and personal trust accounts are less sensitive still because of both the immobility of these accounts and the lesser interest and sophistication of the customers.

The power of certain customers sometimes enables them to bargain with trust departments for a priority position in the information allocation sequence. For example, the largest and most important commercial customer of one bank did not want its pension fund participating in a pooled fund, but did want a portion of its investment portfolio in the same kind of ''hot'' issues. An officer of the bank described the situation as follows: ''When the research department came up with an idea that would be useful for the pooled fund, there was a problem with regard to allocating investment opportunities between the pooled fund and the customer's account. Although pro rata division between these two accounts was not the general rule, there were some exceptions. On occasion we could favor the customer's account, because it was the bank's largest customer and had tough investment people who were very performance oriented.''

Another type of bargaining involves commercial department pressure to get a more experienced portfolio manager assigned to a powerful customer's pension fund account. Said one banker: ''Sometimes a company's treasurer will call the commercial department and say: 'Do you really think those guys in your investment department know what they are doing?' The head of the commercial department will then call the head of the trust department and say: 'Since we are the primary corporate contact, we were questioned by the treasurer of Company X. Was the fund handled by one of your stronger people? Maybe there should be a review of objectives; do you understand the client?' ''

In this fashion a customer can exert pressure on a bank that sometimes results in better treatment for its account. The pressure does not by itself bring better investment performance, but it may force the bank to give an account preferential treatment until the customer is placated.

One key issue is the extent to which preferential allocation of information to favored accounts may *create* "performance" at the expense of other accounts.[91] For example, where a bank-wide recommendation is made to purchase an issue with relatively small capitalization or float, an upward price movement will almost certainly follow. Accounts that are able to move first will share in more of the appreciation. Occasionally, perhaps with innocent intent, the bank may not put a recommendation on all buy (or sell) lists simultaneously. For example, in one bank several stocks with small floats were moved to the pension fund "buy list," but then were explicitly postponed from elevation to the personal trust list "pending forthcoming management calls," presumably to confirm the validity of the positive appraisals already received. Although some trust department officials recognize that a problem exists, the absence of any systematic disclosure of information allocation policies or investment performance figures has made impossible any assessment of the extent to which information sequence has created "performance" for favored accounts.[92]

Another conflict problem relates to the allocation of securities. First, there is the question of which accounts get newly acquired securities and at what price, especially where the trust department is buying large quantities over time at different prices. When several large blocks are acquired, many of the large institutions allocate among the pooled orders at an average prorated price. Small accounts may do well, sometimes getting their modest allotments first, and at a good (large block) price. But small accounts requiring cofiduciary approval for purchase may pay a higher price because of slow responses, through no fault of the banks, who may have asked for discretionary control to permit them to move fast and participate in block acquisitions.

A second and less familiar conflict is related to the accommodation purchases of customer securities discussed earlier. If the trust department buys securities to accommodate customers, they have to be placed somewhere, and they may tend to gravitate toward the less sensitive accounts. For example, one bank trust department a few years ago bought a large block of bonds of a director-interlocked customer, whose common stock was not on the trust department's approved list. The bond specialist of the bank informed the author that this purchase of bonds was "expected of the bank" as a *quid pro quo* for the board directorship, the bank's award of the role of collection agent on the bond issue, and the generally good customer relationship. A large fraction of these bonds was put into one of the bank's common trust funds and into a nonprofit trust account managed by the bank; that is, into relatively weak and insensitive accounts. An examination made by the author of fourteen trust portfolios held in this bank in mid-1967 revealed that "special notes" of the bank's own customers tended to show up regularly in the common trust fund and in nine of ten randomly selected portfolios of small nonprofit accounts, but in only one of three portfolios of major companies. Although these data are incomplete, the findings suggest the need for a rigorous test of the possibility that customer securities may end up more frequently in "weak" portfolios than in "strong" ones.[93]

Where a bank is placed under pressure by a strong customer to get it out of a security expected to decline in price, further abuses become possible. In the extreme case, these abuses may include stuffing the portfolios of uninformed or exceptionally weak customers to facilitate the exit of the stronger customer in a particularly disorderly, or thin market. In one such case described to the author by an investment banker, one customer, highly dependent on credit from a powerful trust institution, was virtually forced to place its pension fund with the bank. Approximately 10 percent of the assets of this fund were shortly thereafter placed in the stock of a financially stricken customer with whom the bank was deeply involved and whose stock was of less than investment grade. Almost immediately after acquisition, this issue fell to a small fraction of its original price. The investment banker believes that a very strong and alert pension fund customer of the bank learned of the coming debacle and insisted that the shares of the sagging company be removed from its portfolio. Because the market was thin, the shares were placed in weaker portfolios. The investment banker claims that the customer knew this but was too dependent on bank credit to withdraw, sue, or even complain.

This last case is without doubt exceptional, but the placement of accommodation securities in weaker portfolios appears to be more common, although information permitting a final judgment is not available.

Proxy Voting and the Customer Relationship

INTRODUCTION

Potential conflicts of interest in bank trust department disposition of proxies have been frequent and have led to an unknown but probably substantial number of abuses. Institutions traditionally have tended to vote shares almost uniformly in favor of incumbent managements, and customers have come to expect these pro-management votes as part of a reciprocal relationship with banks. The force of publicity and legal challenges has not yet broken down this long-standing practice of accommodation.

The pressures on banks from customers concerned over the voting of proxies are strong, if not irresistible. Banks are often requested to send in their proxies in the interest of meeting quorums. In most cases customers can be accommodated with little strain, because the issues do not typically involve the interests of the bank's fiduciary accounts. But when they do, the bank has a dilemma. If the customer is sensitive to bank "disloyalty," the costs of opposition can be serious—loss of deposits, corporate trust appointments, and other business.

Banks may also confront a dilemma when their holdings of a stock are substantial, in which case votes in support of management (or for acquisition by outsiders) may be interpreted as evidence of an intent to use power to dominate.[94] This may be one reason why some of the larger banks have begun to show an interest in getting rid of their voting rights.[95]

The larger the bank, the greater the likelihood that its portfolio securities will include those issued by customers. But customer influence does not necessarily have a greater impact on the proxy policy of large rather than small trust banks. Great size and numerous customers of large banks reduce the relative importance of each customer, whereas in small banks the estates of single families and the pension, corporate trust, and banking business of one or a few powerful local firms may bulk large in the affairs of the bank. The local bank may not be able to treat proxies "objectively" in such situations, and the bank's absolute discretion in voting may be more formal than real.

Larger banks claim that their customers do business with them on substantive grounds that are not likely to be affected by their voting of trust-held stock. They can, moreover, stress to the customer the autonomy of the trust department and its decision-making processes. The trust departments, for their part, emphasize their legal obligations to beneficiaries and the high risks in deviating from these obligations. These dangers are not only legal; the trust function has a moral and ideological component that influences those implementing it. Hidden costs to internal morale and external reputation may well be associated with violations of this "morality."

The balance of forces at work shaping bank disposition of proxies is not easy to disentangle, especially because it has been changing over the past dozen years. Before the 1968 Patman Report and the corporate reform movement of the late 1960s and early 1970s, the public and the legislatures knew very little about trust departments and their proxy behavior. Ignorance and lack of any strong countervailing pressures generally contributed to blanket proxy support of customer managements. This policy was a logical outcome of "competition," because the important competition was for commercial customers, not for trust department clients. Of course, trust banks did not invariably support the managements of customers in their voting of discretionary proxies, but the pressures against an antimanagement stance were powerful, were weakly opposed, and therefore prevailed in a large proportion of contested cases. In the words of one experienced trust officer of a medium-sized trust bank:

We never voted no on a proxy. At the most we abstained. You always checked with the commercial officer. The proxy decision was based on the bank's own stake in the matter, not the trust department shareholder's stake.

The Patman Report and the modest increase in publicity that followed it have altered the picture somewhat, but not greatly. As late as 1970,[96] approximately one-fifth of the largest trust banks had an official policy of consistently supporting management; and in interviews at a number of banks in the period 1969-74, official policy statements were shown in which "stocks of local companies known to be bank customers'' were especially mentioned as calling for regular support in handling discretionary proxies.[97] In several smaller trust banks, the policy has been to vote uniformly with the managements of national companies (where no influence is believed possible) and to exercise rather more discretion on local company proxy solicitation. But the great majority of trust banks studied from 1969 to 1974 consistently gave proxy support to the management of customer companies (and to a slightly lesser extent, portfolio companies in general).[98] Even the larger trust institutions, which show a greater willingness to oppose customer management than smaller ones, do not do so very often. Some make it explicit policy "to vote with management on all of its proposals in all companies where the trust department has substantial holdings." Some of their opposition is tokenism. Executive officers of the trust departments of two large banks acknowledged to the author that in their institutions a number of anti-management votes are now established each year "for the record," as evidence of responsible stockholder behavior. (Presumably, in most of these cases, the bank would be inclined to vote against management on substantive grounds but might not have gone to the bother—or have been willing to incur the costs involved—in the absence of the newly felt need for establishing a record of "independence.") These banks may say officially that they reserve the right to vote against management, and in very exceptional circumstances they may, but their actual policies may differ very little from those of banks with official pro-management policies.

The Institutional Investor Study finding that nine of the fifty largest trust banks acknowledged an official proxy policy of automatic management support is somewhat surprising, given their potential liabilities as trustees for any losses that result from "a failure to use reasonable care in deciding how to vote the stock and in voting it."[99] One would expect a rational *official* policy to be independent, even if *de facto* policy is wholly or essentially passive and pro-management.

BANK HANDLING OF PROXIES

The larger trust departments typically have an officer and clerks who process all proxy requests, categorizing the requests as routine and nonroutine and the banks' voting power as sole or shared with outside cofiduciaries. An additional variable may be the number of shares held or dollar value of holdings. Proxies of portfolio companies held in nominal amounts are most often classed as "routine." When the bank has full authority and when matters are considered routine, individuals in charge of the proxy operation are authorized to execute the proxy and send it to the company. Nonroutine matters are usually referred to the investment research department for recommendations, and the ultimate decision in voting is made by a trust department committee that is either specially organized to carry out this activity or more often a regular standing committee with other administrative functions. In very exceptional cases, the issues may be of such importance that they are referred to the board trust committee or to the top officers of the bank.

The bulk of proxy requests are treated as routine. Director selection at portfolio companies, for example, is almost always a routine matter in the absence of a proxy contest. Nonroutine matters are often those proxy proposals that have a direct and obvious bearing on the value of the security, such as a merger or a major new financing. There are, however, no hard and fast rules for determining in advance what matters will be deemed routine. The status of the portfolio company may influence the designation—a proxy proposal by a company that is also a highly valued commercial customer of the bank may receive a quasi-routine treatment on matters otherwise nonroutine. A commercial bank official may suggest ''nonroutine'' treatment for a proxy when a commercial customer wants an expedited disposition or when the bank as a whole may gain from a formal committee stamp of approval on an issuer's proposal.

In recent years the most common basis for trust department opposition to portfolio company management proposals appears to have been management's desire to reduce or abolish the preemptive rights of stockholders to participate in new share offerings, thereby diluting the value of the stock of existing shareholders in the interest of giving management greater flexibility in its financing efforts.[100] Other management proposals to alter the capital structure via new issues of common stock, preferred stock, the issuance of warrants, or the granting of stock options to management personnel also have been relatively important sources of opposition by bank trust departments.[101]

Mergers have elicited relatively significant opposition to proposed management actions. Changes in an issuer's articles of incorporation or by-laws designed to make acquisitions by outsiders more difficult have also been opposed frequently by trust departments as contrary to the interests of their fiduciary accounts. Overall, bank trust department behavior with respect to takeovers and proxy contests has been too complex to permit any ready generalization. Powerful customers may be trying to take over a portfolio company, or they may be resisting a takeover. The trust department may find itself in the middle of a struggle between two customers, and their relative importance may be influential or decisive in the trust department's evaluation of a merger proposal or bid for control via a proxy fight.[102] The weight of the customer relationship in such decisions is discussed below.

On social issues, bank voting has been essentially supportive of management. No bank except First Pennsylvania Bank and Trust Company appears to have sided with Campaign GM on any proposal by means of an actual vote of shares (although a number of banks wrote letters to GM spelling out their own views on certain of the issues). Campaign GM raised the difficult issue[103] of the extent to which an investment manager and trustee should work for more responsible social policies on the part of portfolio companies. Sometimes more rapid social responses might be in the stockholders' direct interest; for example, early constructive actions might enable companies to avoid costly catch-up hiring of minority group and women executives under legal compulsion. But responsible actions also may be at the expense of the corporation's stockholders.[104]

TRADITIONAL RATIONALES FOR BANK PROXY POLICIES

The traditional rationales for passivity and a pro-management disposition of proxies have been variations on three themes: cost, impact, and the general appropriateness and desirability of giving regular support to portfolio company managements. In regard to cost, the handling of proxies involves expense, and a proper appraisal of the issues raised in each proxy proposal requires a substantial investigative effort. These costs clearly would be unduly burdensome when the bank holds only a few shares of an issue, and even in the case of large holdings, they can be relatively substantial. Smaller trust departments with many personal trusts and numerous small-sized holdings are therefore not likely to be inclined to take proxies very seriously on sheer cost grounds, except in cases of large blocks of stock, which are often in closely held local companies. This is probably an important reason why a large fraction of the smaller—as well as some of the larger—trust departments have followed a policy of either voting proxies for management in all cases or throwing them into the wastebasket (again, except for large blocks and holdings of local customers).

Another reason is the belief on the part of many bank officers that proxy activism is ineffectual. Especially where the bank has relatively small holdings, but even with substantial blocks of stock, many trust officers believe the entrenched managements of large companies are not capable of being defeated or even influenced on an issue by proxy votes. They regard small companies as more responsive, either because the blocks of institutional investors are relatively large (e.g., bank holdings in closely held companies) or because the smaller companies are more fearful of takeovers or concerned about the price and financing effects of negative reactions by institutional investors. Partly for these reasons, banks tend to use proxies with serious intent and effect more often with smaller companies than with larger ones.

A number of trust officers believe that portfolio company policy, especially in the case of large firms, can be influenced only, if at all, by persuasion before the management has committed itself to a position, or by an overwhelming groundswell of investor dissatisfaction.[105] A number of trust department officials argue that proxy voting is *ex post facto*—that is, management has already made a decision by the time a matter is submitted to the shareholders for approval and is not likely to be moved at that late date. The time to influence management, therefore, is before the decision is made, and it is argued that a private and reasoned communication with management by an informed and substantial investor, *ex ante*, is the most effective way to exercise influence.

These arguments are not unreasonable, but they raise a number of questions. For one thing the institutional investor may not know of an action until after the management is committed. Moreover, public opposition (as opposed to a strictly private communication) by a well-regarded investor may be influential precisely because of its potential effect on others. To some degree, also, these arguments appear to be rationalizations of a desire to avoid ruffling the feathers of the managements of portfolio companies. Institutional investors clearly believe, however, that isolated shareholder proxy actions are ineffective, and this belief has an impact on their proxy behavior.

Many institutional investors who give complete proxy support to management claim to do so on a quasi-philosophical principle—that they have invested in a company largely because of its management, which they should then aid and support as long as that management commands their broad loyalty. If the company falters seriously enough to deserve open expressions of dissatisfaction through the proxy vehicle, the stock should be sold.[106] This policy may be designated the "Wall Street Proxy Rule," as it is really a subcategory of the familiar "Wall Street Rule," which rationalizes selling a stock rather than attempting to influence management. The argument that "because it is the management we buy, that management should be given uncritical support" is not especially persuasive, but in one form or another it receives wide support in the institutional investor community. In many cases the rule seems to be a rationalization of an unwillingness to go to the trouble of dealing with proxies on an issue-by-issue basis, which may rest in part on a belief in the futility of such an exercise, or on an unwillingness to antagonize the managements of portfolio companies. The Wall Street Proxy Rule also reflects the traditional conservatism and "play-it-safe" attitude of many trust officers, well expressed in the statement of one of them that "If I don't vote, I can't be hurt; and if I do vote, I don't know whether I'll be hurt or not."[107]

The Wall Street Proxy Rule appears to be a simple solution to the question of proxy policy, but if adherence to such a policy in a particular case were followed by a decline and perhaps even failure of the portfolio company, the threat of liability for irresponsible fiduciary behavior might well be strengthened. A failure to sell, *plus* a failure to act for improvement within the corporate legal forms, could make the fiduciary quite vulnerable. And the rule will clearly not do when the corporate trustee has such a substantial position in an issue that it cannot sell the stock without causing a serious depression of the market price.

ACCESS TO INFORMATION AND PROXY POLICY

The desire of institutional investors for investment information contributes to their passive and pro-management proxy policy. The investment research departments of the large trust banks produce "original research," which often involves fairly continuous communication with companies in which the trust departments have active investment interests. A number of high trust department officials say they will not invest in a company if they cannot get on the phone and talk about company affairs to people they know there. Others place great weight on personally "knowing management," partly because it provides access to information but also because it allows them to maintain firsthand knowledge of the general direction of the company and the capacity of the management team.[108]

The cultivation of personal relationships with the portfolio company's officials and the maintenance of general goodwill are a part of gathering information. The failure of the institutional investor to give the management support on proxy issues could damage these relationships and impair, or even cut off, direct access to information. This might seriously hamper the investment analysis activities of the trust department, and a policy of "cooperation with management on which we rely for successful investment" thus may be regarded as a necessary element of trust department research and investment policy.[109] In several instances, when trust departments voted with management on issues in violation of established departmental principles (for example, 80 percent vote requirements for shareholder approval of mergers), this has been explained by analysts as the product of fear of information cutoffs by issuers when the department held large amounts of stock or when the holdings were in small companies that made very little information available publicly.

Access to information can also be looked upon as a value provided to the bank for reciprocal benefits. Support of portfolio company managements in the disposition of proxies is one form of reciprocity. It has the merit of low direct cost, although not so low as a policy of total disregard of proxies. It can also be reconciled with the interests of trust department beneficiaries, because information access can presumably contribute to better investment performance. The desirability of the trade-off in particular instances, however, may be open to question.

THE CUSTOMER RELATIONSHIP AND MANAGEMENT DEFENSES AGAINST TAKEOVERS

The interests of trust department beneficiaries often come into conflict with those of portfolio company managements regarding proposals for article and by-law changes to increase the percentage of stock needed to vote approval of a merger or sale of assets. In recent years many management groups have sought such amendments to help stop threats of takeovers. But because takeovers almost invariably push up the prices of stock, amendments that discourage takeover bids would appear to be detrimental to the interests of shareholders[110] and thus are frequently voted against by many trust departments.[111] Sometimes, however, trust departments vote to sustain the management's desire for protection from "raiders." Unfortunately, it is impossible to ascertain either the frequency of the support votes or the basis on which they are decided.

In a number of votes on this issue by one large trust bank, the customer relationship appears to have been critical in several decisions to support the management proposals. As an official policy, the trust investment committee of this particular bank had established that increases in the number of shareholder votes required to approve an amendment to the by-laws or articles of incorporation involved "relinquishing important stockholder powers and rights, particularly with regard to determining the desirability of any potential merger or purchase propositions." It was felt that when management wanted protection beyond the requirement of a two-thirds vote of shareholders, the matter should be given the closest scrutiny, and in a number of instances in 1969 and 1970, the trust department voted against such proposals. A proxy proposal was then circulated by the management of a major company—a customer, with whom the bank had a director interlock—for a by-law change to require an 80 percent approval by shareholders. The research analyst who followed this company recommended voting against the proposal. The first trust department committee to evaluate the proposal unanimously recommended a negative vote, citing the official policy as its basis. The next higher committee to pass upon the matter met two days later and decided to defer any action:

Committee discussed proposals and was concerned with the changes, particularly the proposal that would make quite difficult certain changes in the future. In view of the present excellent management of the company, the committee wanted to support it, but was reluctant to approve arrangements that would insulate all future management groups.

In this instance, after a period of indecision lasting about two weeks and despite the previously established principle and negative recommendation by the analyst, six days before the annual meeting the trust investment committee concluded as follows:

In view of high regard for the present management of this company, and recognizing that common stock would be sold if this element did not prevail in the future, it was decided that management should be supported. Accordingly, committee approved voting proxy in favor of management's proposals.

In this case adherence to the Wall Street Rule, that is, selling the stock, would have been difficult, because the bank held close to 10 percent of the outstanding stock of this issuer, equal to approximately 30 percent of the preceding year's trading in the security. The bank was locked in by the large size of its holding as well as by a close customer relationship that added to the difficulty of selling. And this same customer relationship also appears to have influenced the decision to accommodate management by a proxy vote for an 80 percent rule that was contrary to the interests of the fiduciary accounts, according to the principles established by the trust department itself.[112]

III • BANK TRUST DEPARTMENT ACCESS TO INSIDE INFORMATION

A widely discussed potential conflict of interest for bank trust departments stems from their possible access to privileged information obtained in other parts of the bank, especially the commercial arm. Banks often have director representation on the boards of companies who may also be trust department portfolio companies, and these directors may have access to inside information relevant to investment management. An even more important information source is the customer financial data that flow to the bank as creditor, along with the incidental knowledge gathered by loan officers in their regular contacts with officers of the customer. Some of this information finds its way into the commercial bank's credit files, but much of it is in confidential loan officer files or is merely in the heads of these individuals.

Inside Information and Its Value to the Trust Department

Bank trust department investment personnel disagree concerning the value of both commercial credit files and loan officer-director "inside" facts for their own operations. Of twenty-two analysts who expressed a definite judgment to the author on the value of credit files, fifteen regarded them as virtually useless and used them sparingly or not at all, even when freely available. This negative view of credit files rested mainly on the narrowness of their information—commercial officers, they claim, ask questions and obtain data pertaining more to the liquidation value of a company than to the dynamic factors that are of interest to a securities analyst. Some analysts, particularly in the lesser trust institutions, point out that these files are confined to local companies that are of little interest to the trust department. The seven analysts who found the files helpful stressed the value of their earnings reports and their detail on those local companies that were in trust accounts.

On the other hand, of the same group of trust department analysts and other personnel, sixteen spoke favorably of commercial officers as a source of information. They stressed the continuous contact of the loan officers, the great stability of personnel in the lending function (in contrast with the high turnover of investment analysts), and their ability to convey insights into such key variables of the company as managerial quality and change "that make a stock worth looking into or reconsidering." The six analysts (including two in large New York City banks) who were critical of loan officers emphasized the subjectivity of their judgments, the different questions that interested them, and the tendency of some loan people to be overly protective and virtual salesmen of customer managements.

This charge is leveled even more frequently against bank directors on customer boards who, it is claimed, frequently know (and learn) very little about the business and tend to be moved easily to whatever view the management wishes to convey. Half a dozen different analysts spelled out to the author cases where judgments by a director regarding the prospects of a customer portfolio company were overly sanguine and led to errors in investment decision-making. Of course, analysts tend to report on those cases in which their methods and judgments proved superior to those of higher authorities, but the cases themselves point up the fact that access to insiders and information and judgments from privileged sources are not consistently reliable bases of decision.[1]

Despite these caveats the customer relationship can sometimes put the bank in possession of nonpublic information that has investment significance: notably, data on unexpected changes in earnings; new technological, product, and marketing developments; and mergers.[2] In the past when a bank could freely use this information, it was helpful,[3] but even then its positive effects on investment performance did not necessarily outweigh the possible negative effect of the customer relationship on the institution's ability to buy and sell freely. With the rise of legal liabilities for the misuse of inside information, moreover, such information may not only be unusable but it may even constrain actions based on *nonpublic* information because of the mere *appearance* of potential illegality.[4] Obviously, the banks that have chosen to avoid customer securities completely in their fiduciary investment portfolios concluded that the insider advantage was offset by other considerations. It is impossible to measure these relative effects, but the assessment of many industry members and the record of bank performance suggest that the negative effects of constraints arising out of the customer relationship may have at least offset any positive effects on performance resulting from access to inside information.

The Law and Interbank Information Flows

TRADITIONAL LAW AND PRACTICE

Before the rise of the "insider" problem and the liabilities associated with the possession and use of privileged information, it was established practice for banks to use the personnel and knowledge available from all the activities in which the bank was engaged in the interest of the institution as a whole. One of the original arguments for association of trust and commercial banking functions, in fact, was "better investment facilities and a stronger group of directors, and the valuable information and help which can be obtained from other departments of a bank."[5] In justification for the absorption of Equitable Trust and Interstate Trust by Chase in 1930, for example, it was emphasized that "the extensive information and wide experience of the bank as a whole will be available to the executive officers of the trust department. . . ."[6] Interlocking directors were long recognized as helpful not only in "cementing entirely harmonious and profitable relations" between institutions but also because "the knowledge which a director acquires from one institution is useful in his capacity as director for another."[7]

Early trust law assumed that the special skills, knowledge, and contacts of the professional trustee would be put to use for trust beneficiaries. Solicitation of information from "insiders" and reliance on judgments of people close to the "insiders" were therefore regarded as material evidence of the trustee's care and prudence.[8] In one New York case, the Fulton Trust Company's accounting was questioned by beneficiaries who sought to surcharge the trustee for retention of Cuban American Sugar stock and Guantanamo Sugar stock.[9] The decedent's will authorized continuation of investments "without any personal liability for so doing," and the trustee could be held liable only if the plaintiffs presented evidence of "lack of reasonable care." The court noted, among other things, that the trustee's directors "consulted Henry Clark, a brother of the testator, and first vice president of the Cuban American Sugar Company, and it was his advice, given as late as 1928, not to sell. They consulted Horace O. Havemeyer and William O. Havemeyer, well known figures in the sugar trade, and received the same advice."[10]

The trustee with access to pertinent information was considered to have a duty to gather and use it, and the more responsible and aggressive ones did so, at least until the concept of "insider liability" began to complicate matters. "Material inside information"[11] is the very type of information that, if available, a prudent trustee was under a duty to consider in making an informed judgment.

INSIDER AND TRUSTEE OBLIGATIONS AND THE "WALL"

The series of "insider" liability cases beginning with *Cady, Roberts*,[12] and continuing to the recent *Investors Management* case,[13] seriously disrupted the traditional relationships and information flows within commercial banks. With these decisions trading on material inside information became contrary to public policy, so knowledge transfers between the trust and commercial departments became permissible only if they did not involve material inside information.

It is in this context that commercial banks have claimed the existence of, and tried in many instances to erect, a "wall,"[14] a barrier to the flow of any material or privileged information between the trust department and the bank directors and commercial arm. The wall concept suggests that the trust department acts autonomously and on the basis of its own internally generated information or on the basis of information received from independent outside sources. Thus, in a bank with a demonstrably effective wall, the trust department could not be successfully charged with trading on material inside information that may have been available to the commercial department.

Much of the information received by various departments of a bank, however, is not material inside information. The total walling off of departments would therefore impede the flow of information that is not barred from use by "insider" prohibitions. The concept of material inside information is also imprecise, and information that was formerly thought to be privileged may prove to be otherwise in the view of a court. In such a case, the failure of a trust department to obtain and use this information may not be justifiable on the simple defense of a paramount duty to obey SEC Rule 10b-5. Fear of such a dilemma has been partially allayed in the 1970 *Investors Management* decision, where the SEC asserted that:

...there is no basis for the stated concern that a fiduciary who refrains from acting because he has received what he believes to be restricted information would be held derelict if it should later develop that the information could in fact have been acted upon legally. If that belief is reasonable, his non-action could not be held improper.[15]

But the logic of this holding does not extend to a case where, because a wall is unable to discriminate between different kinds of information, the trust department fails to receive clearly unrestricted information from the commercial department. And the difficulty of defining the "reasonableness" of a bank's belief that particular information is privileged is not reassuring to a trustee who may find this question being determined initially by a lower court. Finally, the courts have not yet spoken on this question. Thus, despite the language of the opinion, it cannot be assumed that the failure of a trust department to receive or to use certain information can be successfully defended simply on the basis of the bank's obligation to obey Rule 10b-5.[16]

Another problem is the bank's credibility and ability to prove effective separation in a 10b-5 action. After all, bank departments separated by a wall are still part of a single legal entity with a common interest. The passing of crucial information between departments is simple. Thus, when a trust department trades in a stock in a manner consistent with access to inside information actually in the possession of the commercial department, proving the effectiveness of an interdepartmental wall would not be an enviable task. The bank acting in a manner consistent with the possession of such information may be held to be a "tippee"[17]—the "tip" having been passed to the trust department by the commercial department or by a bank director. Chase, Morgan, Citibank, and other creditors who were also trustee investors in the stock of the dying Penn Central Company in 1969-70 have confronted precisely this problem. Selling trust stock around the time of receipt of adverse information as creditor put the banks in the awkward position of having to prove a negative— namely, that information did *not* flow from the commercial to the trust arm. Although that proposition may have been true, the proof offered was not compelling.[18] In the *Investors Management* case, several of the defendants failed to convince the SEC that they had traded on the basis of *nonprivileged* information. A footnote by the commission contains the following language:

We consider it appropriate to observe that in future cases we would view as suspect and subject to close scrutiny a defense that there was no internal communication of material non-public information and its source by a member of a broker-dealer firm or other investment organization who received it, where a transaction of the kind indicated by it was effected by his organization immediately or closely thereafter. A showing of such receipt and transaction prior to the time the information became public should in itself constitute strong evidence of knowledge by the one who effected the transaction and by the firm. [19]

The legal problems facing bank trustees are further manifested by the recent decision of the Southern District Court of New York in *Slade* v. *Shearson, Hammill and Co.* [20] Part of the *Investors Management* case settlement involved a commitment by Merrill Lynch to establish a wall between its underwriting and other departments that would prevent inside information from passing from the underwriting division to retail brokerage customers. [21] Shearson, Hammill was sued by brokerage customers for its *failure* to receive from retail salesmen inside information obtained by the underwriting department. Shearson, Hammill sought a summary judgment, partly on the ground that it could not legally transmit such information. The brokerage house acknowledged that it continued to sell the security and that its retail sales force solicited business using obsolete information. In denying summary judgment, the court cited the *Texas Gulf Sulphur* ruling, mentioned earlier, that "anyone in possession of material inside information must either disclose it to the investing public, or . . .abstain from trading in or recommending the securities concerned while such inside information remains undisclosed." The integration of operations of a brokerage-investment banking house is very likely greater than that of a large trust bank, but it is still of great interest that the court refused to treat the departments as separate entities, choosing instead to ascribe certain obligations to the overall organization.

Slade v. *Shearson, Hammill and Co.* also points up the continuing possibility that a wall that prevents *any* information from being transmitted to or used by the trust department may open a bank to a suit by trust beneficiaries, alleging that the bank's failure to use nonprivileged information to protect the trust or to advance its investment objectives was a breach of duty. [22] A policy of withholding information from the trust department in the interest of avoiding transmission of material inside information would not excuse obstructing the flow of all pertinent but nonprivileged data. Some wall rules explicitly state that "these instructions . . .in no way alter the duty of those charged with the trust investment decisions to obtain all relevant information which they can properly receive and use." [23] The banks benefit from the belief, which they have cultivated in the past and still do not discourage, that association with a bank gives a trust department a knowledge advantage. [24] Thus, a failure to transmit relevant information that is not "inside" reflects a defect in the wall, not an acceptable consequence of its effectiveness. If the problems of establishing an adequate wall are formidable (as they are), and if the trust banks seem to be left in an intolerably ambiguous legal position as a result, it may be recalled that an important admonitory principle of trust law is that the trustee must not put himself in a conflict situation in the first place.[25] Perhaps the bank trustee should not have put itself in a position where its interest in the maintenance of normal commercial relationships and the avoidance of 10b-5 suits might conflict with its duty to act in the best interests of the trusts. The widespread construction of walls in banks itself points up the fact that a potential conflict—and thus possible liability for having taken a conflicting position—has been built into the very structure of banks with trust departments.[26]

Business and Structural Impediments to a Solid Wall

Even before the inside information issue arose, bank trust department growth had led to greater departmental autonomy paralleling increased size and specialized function. But the degree of separateness varied greatly, and for good business reasons was never complete. Despite the natural growth in trust department autonomy, therefore, the pressure for a wall has been mainly external and has threatened to carry the banks to a degree of separateness that would be disadvantageous to their overall business interests. The advantages of association were key elements in the long process of integration of trust and commercial operations.[27] The value of knowledge-sharing and the usefulness of information flows have already been mentioned. Also discussed earlier was the role of an affiliated trust department as a so-called feeder, facilitating the expansion of the commercial department and aiding in the retention of existing bank customers by permitting the bank to offer a full line of banking services.

Other parts of the bank, especially the commercial department, have provided important sources of business for the trust department. A rule quoted to the author by more than one individual involved in pension fund marketing is that "pensions follow corporate banking business." Even in banks with walls, the trust and commercial departments engage in information exchanges and some degree of coordinated activity to generate new business. These cooperative efforts go beyond mere *ad hoc* referrals of specific prospects, often including: (1) systematic transmission of credit information as a basis for contacts;[28] (2) programs teaming new business officers in the trust department with certain commercial officers; (3) quota and reward systems for referrals; (4) joint presentations to prospective customers; and (5) formal educational sessions.[29] In at least two sizable banks with official walls, the administrator of pension fund accounts is employed by the commercial arm of the bank, while the fiduciary arm handles the investment of pension assets.

The bank-customer relationship extends across departmental lines in other areas where separation would be artificial and is often bypassed. In the age of deposit reciprocity, the bypassing was massive, with trust department brokerage commissions allocated mainly according to deposits from brokers. Even today the broker-bank relation remains one in which the pressures for a single-entity perspective are continuous. In 1973 one brokerage firm official told the author, "We think in terms of an integrated array of services and responses." The expectation of an entity response leads to a steady stream of requests for interdepartmental credits and rewards. A commercial officer responsible for a brokerage house account will often be asked to help obtain trust department commissions that would compensate for the services rendered to the commercial department. Many loan officers acknowledge that they will intercede on behalf of brokers, not to get them rewards but to "get them a hearing" on the legitimate services they have to offer by introducing them to the appropriate individuals in the trust department. Loan officers deny that this intercession involves any reciprocity, because the brokers will have to earn their commissions by performing services for the trust department. This assertion seems valid for a number of banks large enough to ignore broker pressures, but not for all banks.

The walls between bank departments have often been and still are breached by customers who want to use credits in one division to compensate for services obtained elsewhere in the bank. For example, a customer may request that payment for a trust department service be made by credit for a demand deposit held by the customer in the commercial department.[30] An illustration is provided in the Investigation of Conglomerate Corporations: an executive of Gulf and Western, a customer of the walled Chase Manhattan Bank, expressed a desire to pay for a trust department service with an additional commercial balance rather than a larger fee. An internal office memorandum of Chase, dated October 3, 1967, states:

During a discussion with Roy Abbott [the G and W officer] yesterday, Roy asked me whether or not the transfer agency relationships we have from Gulf and Western are profitable to us. Roy felt that because of the high volume, these may not be showing the profit that we would like. If this is the case, he would prefer that we make our adjustment in balances rather than by increasing fees. Bill Adams is looking into this.[31]

It is interesting to see that trust department compensation in the form of payment to the commercial arm of the bank was not automatically ruled out as impermissible, but was in fact suggested by Abbott, who, as it happened, was himself a former Chase officer. Compensation to the "other side" of the wall is a convenience that some commercial customers desire, and even a walled bank finds it difficult to avoid making this kind of accommodation to good customers. Some communication and mutual adjustment across the wall has to take place to implement such a compensation arrangement.

Banks also inevitably take a cross-department, total-bank view in planning operations for individual departments. In deciding where to deploy its capital and work force in the future, the bank must evaluate the returns to the bank from each subdivision. To this day many bankers explain the low rates charged by banks on trust accounts not only by legal ceilings but also as a result of the banks' "looking at the total picture and charging on the basis of a total relationship." Other bankers acknowledge that pricing strategy on corporate trust and investment accounts involves giving weight to float or trust deposit balances held in the commercial department of the bank. And this kind of entity-view pricing strategy frequently has made such trust department subdivisions as registrarships and transfer agencies unprofitable. Sometimes even the already low rates of segments of the corporate trust department are breached when the commercial arm asks corporate trust to accept at less than standard rates a client with substantial balances, sometimes with interdepartmental credit adjustments. In some cases the trust department resists, as in one instance when a good corporate customer of one large bank with a relatively solid wall refused to pay the higher charges levied on custodial accounts, on the ground that his bank deposit was sufficiently large to exempt him from such an increase. The matter was taken to the chief executive officer of the bank. He ruled in favor of permitting the customer to escape the higher rates. No credit was given the trust department for the deposit covering this discriminatorily low rate, although the department was permitted to note this arrangement and concession in its internal reports to top management.

The solidity of the wall between the commercial and trust departments must also be affected by certain inherent characteristics of banks and bank trust departments. The board of directors of a bank is legally responsible for bank profits *and* for the proper performance of fiduciary obligations in all cases where the bank is a trustee.[32] It is the stockholder's capital fund that protects the trust beneficiaries, and any surcharge for a failure of responsibility by the directors will be levied upon that fund.[33] Thus, the board and the chief executive officers of the bank have a responsibility to both the commercial *and* trust departments, and maintaining an effective wall between them would require a dichotomy of mind that may be difficult or impossible to attain.[34]

The same structural problem is evident where the bank's investment policies are said to depend in large measure on its knowing and evaluating corporate management. An officer of the United States Trust Company of New York, for example, has said that his company makes about 80 percent of its investment judgment on the basis of management.[35] Another officer of the same company stated: "At U.S. Trust we very seldom invest a substantial amount in a company whose management we've never met." He indicated that management could best be appraised when the corporation is a customer of the bank's commercial operation.[36] Once officers have made an appraisal of management from their standpoint as lender, they may find it difficult to change their appraisal when new information flows into the commercial department without simultaneously altering the judgment of that management as an investment for trust accounts.

The board and executive officers, in attempting to establish an effective wall, may delegate responsibility to lower echelon personnel and create separate units between which few if any interchanges of information occur. But ultimate responsibility nonetheless remains with those charged with legal obligations to the bank's shareholders. Thus, even where divisional separation and delegation of authority are relatively great, strategic cases or crisis situations will be brought before the board or principal executives for action, and the wall may suddenly disintegrate as information from all departments is pooled in the interest of the larger entity. A case in which a crisis situation generated a sudden flow of information from the trust department was the tender offer made in 1969 by Leasco Data Processing Equipment Corporation for Chemical Bank of New York. In responding to this threat, the top management of Chemical Bank, which had an official wall between the commercial and trust departments, very quickly got a detailed breakdown of the amount of Leasco stock held in the various trust accounts of the Chemical Bank trust department.[37]

Within the formal organization of most banks, a directors' committee generally deals with trust affairs. This committee is sometimes comprised solely of outside directors, but more commonly it includes both outside and inside directors, at least one of whom is an executive officer of the bank. In some banks the board trust committee is essentially inactive, functioning only as a formal body to fulfill a legal requirement—a "rubber stamp." In others it may be designed mainly to evaluate top trust personnel and department procedures. In still others the board trust committee sets trust department policy, plans investment strategies, or evaluates trust department security holdings.

Officer-director participation in trust department decision-making varies from bank to bank and is hard to measure. In the present study, the author found that in about twenty-three banks—approximately one-third of those examined—commercial officers were currently serving or had recently served on active decision-making committees within the trust department. A review of more detailed data available for twelve medium-sized and large trust departments revealed that in five cases the board trust committee or individual high-level commercial officers serving on trust committees played an "active" role in trust department decision-making.[38] In three cases the board was clearly inactive. In four banks the evidence was unclear, partly because of recent changes in structure and policy. In brief, the still frequent direct involvement of high bank officials in trust department decision-making remains a structural obstacle to an effective wall.

Another set of obstacles to an effective wall may be described as associational. The smaller the bank and trust department, the more likely that trust and commercial people will be in close physical proximity. In some cases they may even be the same people. Even in large institutions, dining facilities, for example, are usually shared by all bank departments. The movement of personnel between trust and commercial departments in some banks also makes close personal relationships likely.

Under these circumstances information available to the commercial department and relevant to the trust department may well be either known to the trust officer, because he also occupies a commercial banking position, or accessible to him, because it is in the possession of personal friends or acquaintances who work under the same roof, for the same management and corporate ends. In short, only an extremely strong wall could overcome the forces of common interest, close physical proximity, and ties of personal loyalty.

THE CURRENT STATE OF BANK WALLS

The wall is not a physical barrier between departments, although it may provide for their physical separation; it is essentially a body of rules and procedures designed to control the interdepartmental flow of information. Most walls are not intended to prevent the passage of all information or to terminate all forms of contact between departments. The typical wall is much more limited in scope—a result, in large part, of the major structural and legal impediments to complete separation just described.

The essential—in fact, usually the sole—component of the wall is an official policy statement or rule prohibiting the transfer of confidential information between departments, or limiting other departments' access to commercial department credit files. A typical policy statement and wall rule, that of the Chase Manhattan Bank, states:

In view of the *Texas Gulf* case, the *Merrill Lynch* case, [and] the New York Stock Exchange policies, (1) inside information gained by the Bank or employee regarding the Bank or any other corporation should not be used by the Bank or any employees in purchasing or selling securities or recommending to others the purchase or sale of securities, and (2) such inside information should not be disclosed to persons outside the Bank. . . . As a matter of Bank policy material factual information (as distinguished from the opinions of persons who are not insiders or such analyses as the Bank or other "outsiders" may make) regarding a corporation which has not been made generally available to the investing public is to be treated as inside information irrespective of the immediate source. . . . To insure the proper use and control of information received by the Bank in its several capacities there is to be *no* flow, or incidental communication, of inside information regarding other companies from the commercial departments or divisions of the Bank to the Fiduciary Investment Department. Similarly, there is to be *no* flow, or incidental communication of inside information regarding other companies [from fiduciary to other departments]. . . . In addition, trust and fiduciary investment personnel, when interviewing corporate officers or representatives of brokerage houses, should make it clear that they are not seeking inside information.

These instructions, however, in no way alter the duty of those charged with trust investment decisions to obtain all relevant information which they can properly receive and use. The proscription relates solely to "inside information" which is "material." To be "material," the information must be such that, if generally known, it would be likely to affect investment decisions or the market value of the security involved. To be "inside," the information must not have been publicly disclosed. . . .[39]

It may be noted that this policy statement (rule) does not describe the existence of any machinery for enforcement;[40] it merely orders that inside information not flow between departments. When David Rockefeller of Chase told the House Banking and Currency Committee that "there is no flow, or incidental communication of inside information, from the commercial departments or divisions of the bank to the fiduciary investment department" at Chase, he presumed that self-enforcement was totally effective.[41] But a number of trust department officials have stressed to the author that, intent and seriousness of a wall rule aside, confusion and occasional ineptitude within a large organization can easily result in privileged information moving between divisions of a bank or nonprivileged information failing to move. On several occasions the author was told, with some indignation, of cases in which commercial officers knew of impending debacles to customers and failed unintentionally to communicate this information to the trust arm, which held substantial investments in the customers' securities.

In many cases the wall rule itself, and even more often its practical application, pertains to trust department access to commercial credit files. Many walls consist merely of a denial of access, sometimes paper only ("for the record"), sometimes taken quite seriously. In many smaller institutions, where trust and commercial personnel may well overlap, no walls of any kind have yet been established. Small institutions, of course, have relatively few commercial customers whose securities are likely to be of interest to the trust department. But as late as 1971-72, several banks with trust assets in excess of $1 billion had still not established an official rule on transfers of information between departments.

Of thirty-three banks examined for this purpose, it was reported that in thirteen banks credit files were currently available to the trust department (1969-74). In eight of these thirteen, files were available to trust department personnel directly, and in five, by roundabout procedures. In ten banks it was reported that credit files were accessible in the recent past (1965-68); and in ten, credit files were reportedly entirely closed off. These numbers require some qualification, however. Banks in which continued access was reported before 1974 may well have changed their policies since then. On the other hand, in seven of the ten banks with official policies of keeping credit files inaccessible to the trust department, no information was obtained from lower echelon personnel or outsiders either confirming or denying implementation of these policies.

Of the banks that have closed off or sharply restricted trust department access to commercial credit files, few, if any, have terminated all communication between analysts, portfolio managers, and loan officers in the various departments. In most cases the official walls apply only to confidential information. As noted above, at Chase Manhattan Bank, one of the first banks to concern itself with this problem, the official policy guide not only confines its wall prohibitions to "inside information" but states explicitly that "these instructions . . . in no way alter the duty of those charged with trust investment decisions to obtain all relevant information which they can properly receive and use. The proscription relates solely to 'inside information' which is 'material.' "[42]

Verbal communication still goes on between departments in most large banks with official walls,[43] and access of commercial personnel to trust department files and analysts is often unrestricted, even when the flow the other way is limited.[44] A trust department officer in a walled bank is generally still permitted to contact a loan officer for nonprivileged information such as a generalized judgment on the quality of the management of a corporate customer; and a loan officer will sometimes consult with a knowledgeable trust department analyst on matters such as interpretation of complex facts in the prospectus for a security offering.

The available data indicate that both decisions about what constitutes "privileged" information and enforcement of wall rules are generally left to the individuals subject to the rules. The Chase memorandum cited above, one of the few that attempts to define the difficult terms involved, states: "To be 'material,' the information must be such that, if generally known, it would be likely to affect investment decisions or the market value of the security involved. To be 'inside,' the information must not have been publicly disclosed."[45] These definitions clearly leave a great deal to be resolved by the enforcing individual or group. The frequent absence of *any* official definition of inside information, and the even more general failure to produce rules for identifying different classes of information, suggest that some walls may be only "for the record" and that others may be extremely crude in application. Unless the cutoff of information is comprehensive—and the data reveal that it generally is not—a serious effort at sorting out privileged and nonprivileged information, involving considerable thought, operational definitions, and enforcement machinery, would be required if walls were to accomplish their objectives.

In some banks individuals are advised to consult their department head or the bank's legal counsel in cases where there is doubt about the confidentiality of information and the appropriateness of interdepartmental communications. In other banks communication between trust department and commercial department personnel can be carried out only with the approval of the head of the department.[46] Apart from these procedural arrangements, the present study found no instance where special enforcement machinery had been established to supervise interdepartmental information flows on a continuing basis. As the author was informed by a high officer of one large bank, "the effectiveness of our wall rule depends on the integrity and good sense of the personnel involved."

Regulation has contributed little to the solution of the problem of bank handling of inside information. This issue attracted minimal regulatory attention until banks showed signs of serious legal vulnerability to attacks for which the wall was proving an imperfect solution. After a four-year debate, in March 1978, an amendment to Regulation 9 was put into effect by the Comptroller, which permitted joint use of facilities and interchange of personnel between bank departments, but required that the trust department establish appropriate policies and procedures to insure that investment decisions of the trust department are not based on nonpublic information. The large banks had pressed for a more forthright requirement of separation; the smaller banks, on the other hand, wanted official sanction of their commercial-trust overlap.[47] The amendment straddled this fence, adding little of substance as regards procedures and mechanisms, which are left to the banks and call for no changes in existing arrangements for the large institutions. It may at best add some small modicum of legal protection to trust banks in the problematical cases that their underlying conflict position occasionally thrusts upon them.

It may be concluded, then, that the major institutions at least have built walls that substantially reduce the contacts between the trust and commercial departments. But even the large banks have neither eliminated integrated decision-making encompassing the trust department nor severed all direct interdepartmental links. Proximity, long-standing personal and business relationships, new business referrals and other joint or complementary business connections, and a common top management and corporate objective continue to tie the bank and all its employees together. The constraints of the wall rule, moreover, are not generally extended to nonprivileged information and frequently apply only to credit file access, not to personal communications. The wall is therefore commonly and regularly breached, although to a lesser degree than in the past and perhaps to a much smaller degree for truly inside information. This point, however, is necessarily hard to establish. The incompleteness of the barrier and the lack of machinery for filtering out inside information from all other information pose a serious problem for the trust banks. The interpretation and enforcement of wall rules must be carried out on an individual basis by the hundreds of employees in the credit and investment departments. That the wall will hold back "material inside information," but that all other relevant data will pass through under these conditions, is doubtful.[48]

It is also doubtful, however, that the availability of inside information to the banks, and any flows over or through the walls, will be of net advantage to them, given their potential liabilities for its use and the immobilizing effect of its mere possession.[49]

IV • BANKER-BROKER RECIPROCITY

The disposition of brokerage commissions attributable to bank fiduciary accounts has been the most publicized of all conflicts of interest between banks and their fiduciary clients. The volume of brokerage commissions increased greatly in the 1950s and 1960s as a result of the rapid expansion of total fiduciary assets, the shift toward equities, the more rapid turnover of portfolios,[1] and the fixed commission rates on the stock exchanges, which were artificially high on large transactions. Although antirebate rules protected the large brokerage surpluses produced by this system from price concessions, many indirect forms of competition were developed.[2] Brokerage surpluses were also subject to direct attrition in the late 1960s and early 1970s by the continued expansion of off-the-exchange trading and the gradual introduction of negotiated rates.

According to standard legal principles applicable to a fiduciary, the banks were obligated to try to recapture these surpluses for the benefit of their fiduciary accounts.[3] With rare exceptions they did not begin to do this until subject to external pressure in the late 1960s and early 1970s. Instead, they used the bulk of these commission surpluses to enlarge or protect the bank's deposit base. The character and rationale of the traditional reciprocity system and the forces inducing the banks to move away from it during the past decade will be examined below.

Directed and Free Brokerage

Banks do not have the right to dispose of all brokerage commissions generated by trust department investment activity. Their customers have been increasingly aware that brokerage arising from activity in their accounts is valuable, and many of them have insisted on reserving the right to direct brokerage to reward friends and relatives or for their own business advantage. Many large companies use part of the brokerage arising from activity in their pension fund accounts to compensate other members of the brokerage community—especially investment bankers—who perform important services for them and can be rewarded in this way.[4]

Thus, the net brokerage available to bank trust departments (and banks) is gross brokerage less that part of the total subject to outside direction. In 1968 forty-six of the largest trust departments produced a gross sum of about $222 million in brokerage commissions, but $83 million, or 37 percent, was directed from outside the bank; only $139 million was "free brokerage" to be allocated by the banks.[5] Because the forty-six large banks accounted for somewhere between 65 and 70 percent of the assets of all trust departments, but a relatively larger proportion of trading activity, trust departments in the aggregate produced perhaps $250 to $275 million in gross brokerage and about $150 to $175 million in free brokerage. Although the extent of outside direction among banks varies considerably, on the average it seems to have been greater in large rather than in small institutions. The Institutional Investor Study survey of forty-six large trust banks showed that ten of them had outside direction of 50 percent or more of trust department brokerage, and only two of the forty-six had less than 10 percent of their brokerage directed from the outside.[6] There are no equally reliable figures for smaller institutions; nevertheless, although the variation among the estimates obtained from fifteen small bank interviews was considerable,[7] the median value for outside direction was only 15 percent, compared with 30 to 40 percent for the forty-six large institutions.

Direction of brokerage has been an area of bank-customer bargaining and negotiation for many years. Trust institutions have tried to get as much of the brokerage as possible and, for the portion they relinquish, to limit outside direction of commissions to cases compatible with "best execution." In addition to wanting the brokerage because of its value, the banks dislike the extra work and the inefficiency of trade execution associated with outside direction.[8] They argue for the primacy of best execution even for directed accounts on grounds of their fiduciary obligation to the beneficiaries of the trust.

The extent to which banks accept directed brokerage has varied directly with their eagerness to enlarge their trust business[9] and inversely with the power and prestige of the bank, which may enable it to insist on bank direction as a condition for taking accounts. Power and prestige, although generally associated with size, are often offset by other factors, such as eagerness to expand. In several instances successful expansion and enhanced prestige have been accompanied by a gradual diminution of emphasis on growth and a simultaneous stiffening of rules on the amount of brokerage that may be directed.[10] The size and power of the *customer* are also positively related to bank size, but work in the opposite direction from *bank* size and power. Large companies that allocate the management of pension funds know the value of brokerage and tend to regard it as part of the package of valuables that may be used to bargain with bank managers. For example, if the company believes the bank's fee plus custodianship of the fund's assets plus, say, 30 percent of the brokerage generated is adequate to compensate the bank, it may insist on the right to dispose of 70 percent of the brokerage.

Of the "free brokerage" left to the banks after netting out that part of the gross subject to outside direction, some must be used to pay brokers for the necessary costs of execution; the balance is a surplus. The "give-up" system in use during the past several decades sheds some light on the potential magnitude of brokerage surpluses available—at least in the recent past—to large institutional investors. This system was employed most extensively by mutual funds, which seem to have generated the largest volume of surpluses and had a strong incentive to redistribute commissions within the brokerage community. Although they manage a much smaller volume of securities than bank trust departments,[11] mutual fund managements have produced comparable or larger volumes of total commissions[12] based on a higher proportion of common stock to total assets,[13] a higher turnover rate,[14] and an average transaction size substantially greater than that of the banks.[15] Given the failure of the commission rate structure to reflect economies of size of order, profits per order increased with size.[16] Brokers were therefore willing to concede (or give up) a substantial fraction of big order business, which could be bargained away by the funds' managements.

Competition among brokers in the give-up era was sufficient to establish a norm of 60 percent as the fraction of a substantial order available for use by institutional customers, although deviations from that figure occurred frequently.[17] In 1968 give-ups by check for New York Stock Exchange (NYSE) members accounted for 38 percent of the $243 million of investment company commissions they received—and such commissions are not the only form of give-up.[18] Nor are they the only way of disposing of surpluses; a significant fraction, for example, may be given to the executing broker for services rendered. Mutual fund management groups made extensive use of the commission give-up system as an incentive to brokers to sell shares of their funds.[19] Other institutional investors had difficulty using brokerage surpluses, because they had little need for any other services that brokerage firms could render.[20] This was not true of banks.

Although not quite so large as those of mutual funds in 1968, the brokerage surpluses of banks have generally been of comparable size. But the banks have made only slight use of the give-up; it amounted to only $6.4 million of the $222 million in commissions paid by the large banks in 1968.[21] But the brokerage generated by the banks has been an important resource to the brokerage community, accounting for more than a third of total institutional business,[22] and it has been less volatile than the commission business of the investment companies.

Trust Department Brokerage Allocations before the Patman Report

In the decade before the Patman Report of 1968, a large proportion of bank-directed trust department brokerage was used to enlarge bank demand deposits. Veteran trust department officers, while disagreeing to some extent on the reasons, concede that most of the free brokerage of banks was used in this way. Of fourteen trust banks providing the author with fairly firm estimates of brokerage allocations for the period 1958-64, in only one case was the allocation for broker deposits thought to have been under 50 percent; in eleven cases it was estimated to have been in excess of 90 percent.

In one major trust institution, the first explicit but small allocation of brokerage for research assistance was made in 1961. Thereafter it was increased gradually until 1968, when reciprocity was abandoned as a formal policy. In another major trust institution, brokerage allocated to services for the trust department (mainly execution and research) amounted to approximately 8 percent in 1958, 14 percent in 1962, and 20 percent in 1970, after which an official policy change eliminated reciprocity for deposits. In bank after bank, the same story is repeated: domination of brokerage allocations for commanding brokers' deposits began to weaken slowly in the early 1960s and more rapidly after 1965 and was officially abandoned on a large scale between 1969 and 1972.

During the "recip era," a great many banks allocated brokerage among their broker-clients on the basis of fairly exact formulas. Broker deposits would be computed regularly, and brokerage would be distributed insofar as feasible in the same proportion as the broker's share of aggregate broker deposits. Almost all of the banks kept traders aware of the deposit position of members of the brokerage community, usually on a monthly basis, sometimes in the form of memos suggesting brokers to be used, others going so far as to list in schedule form the dollar amounts or percentages of free commissions to be allocated to each broker-dealer. The Institutional Investor Study, reporting on the situation in 1969, describes a case involving one of the fifty largest trust institutions in which an officer was made responsible for seeing that deposits and commissions were "in ratio" for all broker-dealers by the fifteenth of the following month.[23] The process more often was a less formal "spreading around" of brokerage among deposit-maintaining brokers.

Even in the "recip era," though, a number of banks did not necessarily give brokers their "fair share" if this did not produce efficient execution. Some trust department officers would explain the deficiency to the broker, sometimes adding an exhortation on "shaping up" their execution capability. On the other hand, at least some banks regularly and knowingly sacrificed efficiency in execution to reward brokers with good balances but poor execution. The officers of the bank mentioned above, where all broker-dealers were put into "equal ratio" by mid-month, acknowledged rejecting large blocks if the commissions would go to nondepositing brokers or would disrupt the ratio.[24] And a number of interviewees described arrangements and policies that systematically impaired execution efficiency. One trust officer described a lengthy conflict with the commercial department, which kept pressuring him to stop using a large house that gave best prices for certain securities of great interest to the trust department, but which "does not do any business with us" (i.e., hold deposits in the bank). This officer refused to desist without a written letter from the bank's top officers ordering him to stop doing business with the nondepositing firm. Eventually, he persuaded the firm to place a $25,000 dormant deposit in the bank to alleviate the pressure on him. In other cases trust officers described regular sacrifices of a half point or more in order to do business with the numerous small local brokers who kept their deposits in the bank.

Possibly even more important, but hard to demonstrate, is the lack of incentive for efficient execution (e.g., cultivating block business within and without the trust department) that was built into the recip system. Large and efficient block trades must bypass small brokers, and major efforts in this direction would have been incompatible with the system of deposit rewards. The recip system is analogous to that of "fair trade," where manufacturers and retailers cooperate in a mutually satisfactory arrangement that gives price protection to the retailers, who then reciprocate with friendly treatment of the fair trading manufacturers' products. Although this system produces too many retailers, participating manufacturers have a vested interest in its preservation. The deposit reciprocity system likewise produces too many brokers, but the banks, if not the fiduciary accounts, had a vested interest in preserving this system.

A selected sample of 96 institutionally oriented broker-dealers in 1968-69 showed that they maintained about 8,500 deposit relationships, an average of 88 per firm, with 4,754, or more than half of them, inactive deposit accounts[25] —and correspondingly large numbers of brokers executing trades for the banks. One of the most telling indices of the inefficiency of these large numbers, and their dependence on the deposit-based recip system, was the radical decline in numbers of brokers used by banks as recip was abandoned in the late 1960s and early 1970s. The axe applied to the brokerage community was described to the author with obvious relish by trust department personnel, because reciprocity had been a bone of contention between commercial and trust interests for many years. A great many of the brokers receiving commissions from the trust department in the recip era were strictly customers of the commercial arm. With the shift in control of trust department brokerage, many of these commercial customers were quickly dropped.[26]

During the "recip era," banks competed actively for broker deposits. Some aggressive banks raised their offering price of commissions/deposits to enlarge their deposits, and others responded in kind to avoid a broker deposit outflow. To do any business with many banks, brokers had to establish a commercial deposit account; the bigger the account, the more commissions they got. The normal practice for a broker dealing with a bank was a system of chargebacks, or paybacks, to the institutional sales personnel assigned to the bank: the salesmen would have deducted from their share of commissions from the bank a charge equal to the going rate of interest that the brokers would have to pay for the money kept in this account.[27] With rising interest, more pressure would be applied to the bank for commissions that would justify the high expense. Broker complaints and threats were continual, and bank personnel spent considerable time explaining and negotiating. Sometimes, having overcommitted themselves, they would suggest that brokers withdraw deposits, or brokers did this of their own accord for more profitable use elsewhere.

Brokers often would "shop" banks, soliciting the largest commission return for their deposit dollars. Even relatively unaggressive brokers would shift their deposit accounts from commission-stingy banks to more generous ones. In the 1969-70 period of tight money, commission payments for deposits tended to range between 7 and 10 percent of collected balances, which worked out to between 15 and 25 percent of deposits as seen from the viewpoint of the broker.[28] Banks took some account of whether the deposit was active or dormant and in periods of relatively easy money gave some weight to broker loans in addition to deposits.

In 1968, when the reciprocity system was already in decline, the Institutional Investor Study's statistical analysis of deposit-commission relationships still indicated that approximately 43 percent of brokers' deposits in thirty-two large banks could be explained by the distribution of brokerage among those depositors.[29] The IIS analysis also indicated that an increase of $1.00 in commissions paid by the bank was associated, on the average, with a $4.26 increase in brokers' deposits at that bank.[30] On the assumption of a 9 percent rate of interest imputed by the brokers to their additional deposits, a $0.38 cost would yield an added gross sum of $1.00. With a profit margin on an average-sized trust department transaction estimated at only about 33 percent in 1968, this would not be a very attractive proposition taken by itself. As an application of an active balance, however, it would look good, and it might be the entry factor that would open up doors to satisfactory rewards for other broker services.

Rationale of the Reciprocity System

Few trust department officials defend the deposit-reciprocity system of past years; most explain it simply (and sometimes a bit shamefacedly) in terms of the overriding dominance of commercial bank interests and a resulting institutionalization of a morally and legally dubious practice. Those who do defend the system rest their case mainly on the alleged absence of alternative uses of brokerage. In this rationale the brokerage community was offering little or no research that would have been worth acquiring and executions were not yet important—only later did the increasing ability of brokers to execute large block trades alter this picture. Besides, fixed commission rates and antirebate rules precluded the direct capture of brokerage surpluses.

The defense contains some elements of truth, but it is essentially misleading. What it neglects is the cash value of the recip system to the bank, and the preeminence of the commercial department in fixing the allocation of brokerage. The recip system brought to the bank deposits and other benefits from brokers, whereas the use of ''soft'' brokerage commission dollars to buy services useful to the banks' fiduciary accounts would have benefited the banks only indirectly, if at all. The conflict between bank and fiduciary interests in the allocation of brokerage was clear, and its relevance to bank decision-making cannot be ignored.

The use made by banks of brokerage services for their fiduciary clients in the 1950s and 1960s sheds some light on this issue. A majority of trust department officials interviewed by the author in 1969-74 described the reciprocity issue as one of intermittent conflict between the bank and its commercial arm on the one hand and the trust department on the other. In bank after bank, the story is told of a fight for a small and then larger share of brokerage allocations for the use of the trust department—advances sometimes interrupted by regression.[31] One institution, eager to improve its trust department, was able to obtain the services of a widely respected trust officer only by offering him, among other things, full control over the allocation of trust department brokerage. Before the 1970s, in most banks, control over brokerage allocations was a matter of political power within the organizational structure as well as simple profit interest of the bank.

Many trust department veterans recall with some bitterness their dependent position, hat-in-hand, appealing to the higher authorities for access to enough of their own brokerage to reward outsiders for services they deemed important. In one sizable California institution, the commitments of brokerage allocations to deposits became so overextended in the late 1960s that the trust department had to use hard dollars to purchase outside advisory services. More often they simply had to forego such outside services. On the other hand, in a few instances where smaller banks had substantial deposits with big city banks, these deposits might contribute in some measure to paying for research and other services required by the trust department. But this situation was not common, because the bank's deposits were usually kept to the minimum necessary to provide services to itself, and the trust department was required to be self-financing. In one case, however, the head of a medium-sized trust department decided it would be helpful to buy a research service offered by a New York City bank. This service would require a $200,000 deposit, so top management reluctantly agreed that if the trust department could obtain $200,000 in additional deposits from its brokers, the department could use these new deposits to purchase the research service. The trust department obtained these deposits by promising the brokers a 10 percent commission return on their deposit accounts, with the commissions coming from a slight squeeze on brokers getting a free ride.

Another important body of evidence on the "lack of alternative uses" rationale for reciprocity is the comparative allocations of brokerage by banks and other investment managers. The Institutional Investor Study found that in 1968 insurance companies and other self-administered institutions used a much higher fraction of their brokerage for research services than investment companies and banks did. An even more interesting comparison, however, is between banks and investment companies, because in contrast with insurance companies, both had profitable uses for brokerage other than acquiring services for fiduciary accounts, and both had large brokerage surpluses. In 1968 the forty-six large banks examined by the Institutional Investor Study allocated only 12.2 percent of their free brokerage for research, in contrast with 23.1 percent allocated by forty-nine investment company complexes.[32] Banks used a median of 13.3 percent of their free commissions for research, as opposed to the 27.3 percent used in investment company groups. Thirty-five of the forty-six banks paid out less than $500,000 in research commissions, as compared with eighteen of forty-nine investment company complexes; and ten of forty-six banks paid less than 10 percent of free commissions for research, while only six of the forty-nine investment company groups paid that small a fraction of the total.[33]

These differentials could conceivably be explained as a consequence of a greater internal research effort by banks that reduced the need for research from brokers' analysts. But the Institutional Investor Study's raw numbers show that major investment companies had a larger percentage of total personnel serving in economic and investment research staff functions than did bank trust departments.[34] And trust departments apparently have had little difficulty in putting a substantial part of their enlarged free brokerage into the purchase of externally produced research.

Other explanations for the differentials seem more persuasive. One is that competition seems to have been more intense among mutual funds than among bank trust departments in the 1960s. Emphasis on performance was taking hold in the banks only slowly in the later 1960s, and demand for research services may have reflected this lag, at least in part. A second factor may well have been the adverse publicity on investment company use of give-ups to reward sellers of shares, which had already subjected them to legislative and regulatory pressures by the early 1960s. The banks escaped comparable publicity and threats for almost another decade. A third factor, and the one that probably deserves the greatest weight, was the dominant commercial arm's ability to maintain its historic vested interests almost intact until a real threat of legal liability came along.

Before the 1970s the banks did not consistently strive for best prices on trades. Good executions often were compatible with deposit reciprocity; and when they were not, some banks would typically sacrifice the immediate recip payoff for the advantage of a superior trade. But in other cases, even execution was systematically sacrificed to rigid recip formulas. With heavy attention to recip, one might hypothesize a tendency on the part of both investment companies and banks to neglect the over-the-counter market in favor of more expensive trades on the exchanges. An Institutional Investor Study sample of trading by institutions in 1968-69 revealed that in their trading in NYSE securities, insurance companies used the over-the-counter market twice as frequently as banks (in percentage of trading volume) and four times as frequently as investment companies.[35] Unfortunately, not too much weight can be given to this finding without a fuller examination of the trading interests and needs of these institutions.[36]

The banks were remarkably unenterprising during the recip era in seeking ways of recapturing the brokerage surpluses theoretically belonging to their fiduciary clients. The mutual funds were protesting excessive commission rates from at least the early 1960s, and by 1966 at least four of them had arranged for subsidiaries to gain membership on regional exchanges as a device for recapturing brokerage surpluses (in several cases using them to reduce advisory fees).[37] A vigorous bank effort to obtain a readjustment in exchange commission rates on large transactions might have carried considerable weight. But at that time, the banks were fully committed to a reciprocity system with the brokerage community, profitable to both.

Factors Underlying the Decline of Deposit Reciprocity

The major reasons for the movement away from deposit reciprocity were competition, publicity, and the law. These factors are closely interrelated, as publicity may activate the law and can even be regarded as an important ingredient of competition. Before the spurt in pension fund business during the 1960s and the parallel increase in emphasis on performance, competition among bank trust departments was very modest and nonbank competition was slight. There was little customer sensitivity to performance, fees, execution, and brokerage allocations. Conservatively oriented and influenced by personal and other banking relationships, the personal trust tradition dominated bank trust business. Many pension and profit-sharing plans solicited from customers were also bank-related and not performance-oriented. Just as the trust department was a service arm of the commercial bank, with the commercial department the prime source of profit and focus of interest, so trust department service was secondary to the lending relationship with the bank and was of less concern to the pension fund customer.

This situation changed markedly during the 1960s. Customer interest became more acute, especially among the larger pension funds that realized the importance of performance to their own profits and paid much closer attention to all aspects of management fees, costs, and revenues. In periodic conferences with institutional clients, more and more managers were obliged to explain the uses to which they put brokerage and to bargain about it. Firms increasingly studied the relative performance of pension fund managers; an informal association of large companies came into existence to compare findings on evaluating and dealing with investment managers,[38] and specialty firms were established to meet the demand for appraisal of performance.[39]

In the 1960s, under the pressure of improved knowledge and greater interest and power on the side of buying clients, competition intensified both among banks and between other investment managers and banks. The rapid growth of pension funds and economies of size in their management made them very attractive to banks, and a great many began to pursue such funds aggressively. Both insurance companies and investment counseling firms also increased their efforts to get pension and investment advisory accounts and in the late 1960s and early 1970s penetrated this market with some success.[40]

Publicity about bank reciprocity practices was very slow to materialize, despite this intensifying competiton. As early as 1963, SEC Chairman William Cary pointed out before a congressional committee that ''we have learned that at present brokerage is often distributed by banks according to a formula which rewards those brokers who keep balances in the bank or have other business relations with the bank,''[41] and the SEC's Special Study of the same year discussed the practice more fully.[42] But it was not until the publication of Heidi Fiske's article, ''How Banks Pass Out Commissions,'' in *The Institutional Investor* of December 1969, that bank reciprocity practices became the subject of serious discussion and criticism, leading to legal and regulatory actions that affected bank behavior.

In the early summer of 1970, an official of the Antitrust Division of the Department of Justice warned the banking community that the department regarded reciprocity involving brokerage exchanged for deposit balances as illegal, and that continuation of the practice would result in suits for injunctive relief.[43] This was followed by the filing of class action suits against Morgan Guaranty Trust and Chemical Bank by Abraham Pomerantz and associates, in which the courts were asked to give injunctive relief restraining the banks from deposit reciprocity and to require the banks to pay treble damages by reason of the antitrust violations involved in the practice.[44] The bank authorities responsible for trust department examination and supervision also began to respond to new revelations and to apply their own pressures on the banks to discontinue these practices.[45]

These new legal and regulatory threats rapidly accelerated what had been a slowly moving trend, and bank after bank told brokers that commissions would no longer be paid for deposit balances and the trust department would no longer be made aware of the identity of those brokers that held deposits with the bank.

Another important factor in the decline of reciprocity was the growing importance of execution as an element of good performance. This was largely a function of the rapid growth of institutional block transactions, the increasing awareness of the possibilities of savings via efficient trading, and the competitive market that made this service more available. The stress on execution was also given impetus by the initiation and progress of negotiated rates on NYSE transactions, beginning in 1969. The share volume of institutional investors rose by 548 percent between 1960 and 1969, in contrast with a 133 percent increase for individual investors, and the average share size of institutional orders rose during the same period by 197 percent for banks and 577 percent for mutual funds.[46]

The increase in demand for large block service led brokers to invest more capital in block positioning and in skilled trading personnel and facilities. Firms offering this function were able to attract business and establish valuable relationships with institutions' traders and other dispensers of institutional brokerage. With the rise of the large order and block trading as significant factors in the market, executions became an important competitive variable.

Many institutional investors recognized that differences in execution, especially in a world of large volumes, could significantly affect performance. During the late 1960s, the value of Wall Street research also began to be questioned, reinforcing the belief of institutional investors that execution deserved first priority in contrast with the more debatable benefits of "research." The legal challenge to reciprocity also pressed the institutions more surely toward emphasizing execution. There was no question that best execution was in the interest of fiduciary accounts.[47]

Recent Developments in Bank Trust Department Brokerage Allocations

In a great majority of trust banks, the recip system remained essentially intact until the threat of antitrust and civil legal actions became urgent. The system began its decline about 1965, was widely abandoned in 1969-70, and declined slowly thereafter in the remaining trust banks.

The threat of legal liability became acute in 1969-70 and altered the conditions of debate and the balance of power within the banks. Previously, trust department demands for control over brokerage were couched in terms of department objectives, which conflicted with the needs of the commercial arm. The legal issue, which was always in the background, moved to the forefront in 1969-70, immeasurably strengthening the bargaining position of the trust department in brokerage allocations.[48] The banks no longer could admit that commissions generated by fiduciary accounts were not regularly available to the trust department to use for the benefit of those accounts.

An official abandonment of deposit-based reciprocity does not necessarily mean an abandonment in fact. But a purely nominal departure would have left the major banks almost as vulnerable as if they had openly retained the earlier arrangements, because traditional recip practices involved many people and effects that could not be kept fully hidden.[49] There is little question that deposit-based reciprocity has suffered a major decline in importance, especially among the larger and more visible trust institutions. A substantial number of banks claim that broker deposits no longer exercise *any* influence on brokerage allocations; a contention that may be true but is hard to verify. Because deposit-based allocations have now taken on an aura of illegality, information has become less accessible, and official pronouncements cannot suffice to establish the true state of affairs. It also seems likely that continuation of traditional recip allocations, even on a sharply contracted scale, would tend to be more informal, with knowledge confined to a smaller group within the bank. Loose and informal rewards to substantial broker-depositors may not be easily discerned, especially when the bank may be receiving other services from the broker.

Bank methods of rewarding brokers have always been imprecise—with the exception of deposit recip—and subject to a complex of forces and judgment decisions because of the difficulties in assessing broker contributions and the influence of power and personality factors in the bureaucratic decision-making process. To some extent this uncertainty is deliberately imposed to elicit services from brokers that might not be forthcoming if the brokers knew where they stood in the bank's allocation schedule. But this has also made brokerage allocations open to personal influence and abuse. Banks have alternated between centralization plus complex formula-based systems of allocation to maintain control, on the one hand, and individual participation in allocation decisions to allow flexibility and rewards for aid given to specific analysts and portfolio managers, on the other. Brokers attempt to locate the source of bank brokerage decisions in order to focus their attention, blandishments, pressure, and services where they will count; and brokers have often felt that it was important to have a "friend" in the bank to help see that their interests were attended to. A Wall Street division commercial officer could (and still can) be the brokers' friend, introducing them to strategic trust department people and putting in a good word for the customer.

When one bank president announced to assembled officers the abandonment of deposit reciprocity on grounds of legal liability (about 1966-67), the hope was expressed that the trust department would continue to recognize the value to the bank of large broker-depositors. If trust department officers and traders are broadly aware of substantial broker deposits, recip on this traditional basis can be maintained on a lower and informal level, paralleling reciprocity on other services. In 1972-74, although a majority of large banks denied that any commissions were allocated on the basis of deposits, several acknowledged that deposits were a minor basis of allocations, not by deliberate bank choice but as a result of residual patterns and broker preferences by bank traders. One large trust bank in late 1973 volunteered the figure of 5 to 10 percent as the allocation based on broker deposits. A few other substantial institutions and a relatively larger fraction of smaller and medium-sized trust banks acknowledge that "friend of the bank" considerations, including deposit holdings, play a continuing role that varies from substantial to merely marginal holdovers from the past.

A great variety of opinion and considerable confusion prevail in the brokerage community as to the factors that now elicit bank commissions. A number of brokers deny that deposits are a factor, but an equal number still regard them as relevant, although less so. Several broker representatives assert that they would "not want to be the ones to pull out" a deposit from banks with which they do business. In mid-1973 the partner of one major brokerage house informed the author that his firm still moves deposits around on the basis of commissions and other business received from banks. Several analysts also have observed that institutional salespeople for brokerage houses continue to ask: "What do we have to do to get some business from you? Shall we send you something?" These salespeople apparently still believe that deposits produce commissions and that some form of minimal "research" may be required to rationalize a commission flow.

The rapid decline of reciprocity after 1968 increased the volume of free brokerage available to bank trust departments. This factor was offset in part by the development of negotiated rates on large transactions, which tended to reduce total commission volume. But the release of brokerage from recip, combined with the continued growth in the aggregate volume of bank trust assets, left trust departments with great increases in available brokerage.[50]

With this massive growth in resources, many trust departments found their situation changed from one of scarcity and rationing to one of affluence. In most banks execution received much higher priority, with the trading function upgraded both internally and externally. Block trading houses, such as Salomon Brothers and Goldman Sachs, obtained a great influx of business, as their execution capability became something for which the affluent trust departments were prepared to pay. Research specialty firms, such as Baker Weeks and William Witter, also obtained a windfall from a clientele anxious to buy the best research and often prepared to pay heavily for top account status.[51] Firms with high-level research plus execution capability, such as Oppenheimer, were especially well situated to profit from the new brokerage dispensation.

Diversification into services potentially attractive to trust departments became a high priority for brokerage houses, under pressure from negotiated rates, a decline in total commission volume, and the fall in recip. The large number of brokers used by trust banks in the recip era had always been objectionable to the more aggressive, investment-management-oriented officers of trust departments, and the shift in power over brokerage allocations to them often led to a decimation of the ranks of brokers receiving bank commission business. But many small brokers remained in the fold, either because of some real service rendered or as a result of personal and traditional relationships.

Their new riches also led trust departments into efforts to innovate in putting their surpluses to the best possible use. Most notable was the outcropping of "games" established to allocate commissions to brokers for measurable research performance. According to the Chase game, established in March 1970, brokers were invited to participate in managing hypothetical portfolios in accordance with certain rules relevant to bank decision-making.[52] The participating brokers would be given a minimum value of commissions as participants and a significantly larger volume as winners. The Security Pacific Bank of Los Angeles established a similar competition, using computerized evaluation of broker portfolio choices, based on a fairly elaborate system of rules. Other banks have also experimented with game systems.

Banks with games and those without have paid much closer attention to establishing principles for rewarding brokers. More or less elaborate formulas have been developed, using inputs from analysts and portfolio managers as well as the results of "games" and other measures of research impact on trust portfolios to arrive at schedules for research payments to brokers. Sometimes a portion of research-based allocations are reserved for individual rewards by analysts and portfolio managers. These research allocations must then be integrated with efforts to achieve "best execution." They also must be reconciled with the uncertainty of total commissions to be allocated. The execution function requires discretion on the part of traders, and *de facto* allocations will depend to a considerable extent on trader skills, biases, and bank pressures.

In some cases the bank trust department may be prepared to commit itself in advance to brokers for a certain volume of commissions, with the hope that this will get them execution and other services that will more than equal the value of the promised commissions.[53] This type of arrangement assumes that brokers will provide adequate execution to fulfill the bank's commitment without more than occasional sacrifice of "best price." This system is also justified on the grounds of the interest of fiduciary accounts in preserving Wall Street brokerage firms, whose survival has been threatened in recent years by factors such as price bargaining by institutional investors, including the banks themselves.

Trust departments are interested in other services provided by brokers besides execution and research, such as opportunities to participate in new securities issues at favorable offering prices. Representatives of one major trust institution informed the author that approximately 20 percent of its total commission business in 1972, a sum equal to that allocated for both research and execution, was employed to reward firms that provided the trust department with valuable new issues opportunities. With the great increase in bond investment management and trading over the past few years, bond investment information has been of great interest to the larger banks.

More debatable uses of brokerage surpluses still occur, reflected in the existence of firms that specialize in "soft dollar " programs, which provide a variety of services—including investment letters, directories, conference fees—to trust banks who will channel brokerage to participating brokers, who in their turn pay the sponsoring firm for this listing service. The best known of these soft dollar programming firms, Investment Information, Inc., reported having over seventy-five banks as soft dollar customers in 1976.[54] An SEC release of March 1976, which attacked fiduciary use of brokerage for the procurement of services "readily and customarily available to the general public on a commercial basis," was a response to the proliferation of this kind of brokerage disposition by banks and other fiduciaries. Many of the services acquired with soft dollars meet the overall needs of the trust department operation, but if anything used by the trust arm can be acquired via brokerage allocations there is an obvious potential conflict of interest—the banks might choose this route to reduce expenses formerly met by trust fees, in lieu of taking lower prices on the brokerage itself by diligent shopping around.

The elimination of fixed commission rates on the stock exchanges on May 1, 1975, raised new questions about the legality of fiduciary soft dollar payments even for such a traditional service as specialized brokerage research. Previously, fixed rates permitted the allocation of brokerage for execution plus research, with no penalty to execution (unless off-the-exchange or larger block purchases could be arranged). With fully negotiated rates, however, it was often difficult to pay for research via brokerage allocations without paying more than the minimum available for execution alone. It might be thought that paying higher-than-minimum commissions for a service like research would be clearly acceptable for a trust fiduciary, but several problems make for complications. One is the possibility that research might provide a cover for other bases of allocations and reciprocity. Another problem is that trust fiduciaries take on accounts as experts in investment, and buying facts and judgments on investments from the outside might be regarded as violating this advertised in-house capacity to evaluate securities. A third awkwardness is that payments for research via higher prices to brokers does not yield services clearly allocable to the fiduciary accounts paying for those services. Broker research goes to enhance the department's overall investment capacity, and benefits a variety of accounts, but to different degrees.

Whatever the merits of these doubts, the matter was sufficiently uncertain that, in June 1975, a section [28(e)] was added to the Securities Exchange Act of 1934, specifically to allow brokerage payments above the minimum available by a fiduciary who has "determined in good faith that such amount of commission was reasonable in relation to the value of the brokerage and research services provided . . . viewed in terms of either that particular transaction or his overall responsibilities with respect to the accounts as to which he exercises investment discretion.'' There remains a question about whether Congress can constitutionally allow overpayments for one account of a fiduciary when the benefits will possibly go elsewhere; and there are more immediate issues about how far a fiduciary can go in buying services with brokerage commissions that are available for cash and that the fiduciary might have been expected to provide internally or acquire out of trust fees.[55] But it would appear that explicit brokerage payments in excess of the minimum are allowable for research services that can be defended as carried out in good faith.

In sum, bank trust department reciprocity practices in commission allocations appear, at least for the larger trust institutions, to be broadly compatible with the interests of the bank's fiduciary customers. Apart from some relatively small deployments of trust department brokerage for reciprocal compensation, the broad conflict problem that persists is whether or not abuses can be kept out of such a complex area, where soft dollars are paying for execution plus, and where judgment and evaluation by analysts, portfolio managers, and traders are inescapable and hard to police.

V • UNINVESTED TRUST CASH

A long-standing conflict between bank and trust interests arises out of the fact that trust accounts hold cash, which may be kept in the bank itself. Estates coming into the bank may already contain cash, and additional cash is often produced when the estate is liquidated or its assets diversified. Funds flow in and out of personal trusts, agency accounts, and pension funds as dividends and interest are received, paid out, and reinvested, and securities are sold pending required outlays to beneficiaries or the purchase of other securities.

It is to the bank's advantage to hold trust cash,[1] and, *ceteris paribus*, the larger the amounts of uninvested cash, the better off the bank.[2] But it is usually to the trust's interest to minimize cash holdings. Conflict arises only if the cash is held in the bank itself or if the trustee is permitted to make a profit on this self-dealing with the trust. An uncompromising application of basic fiduciary principles would have prevented this conflict from arising in the first place. The trustee's duty requires that he ''not deal with himself or put himself in a position where his interest might be in conflict with his duty'';[3] a duty ''sufficiently broad to embrace transactions with trust funds resulting in indirect profit to the trustee, such as commissions or compensation as brokers or bankers or for other professional or business services.''[4] Other common language describing the duty of the trustee holds that the law ''does not tolerate personal dealing with the trust estate nor permit the making of a penny's profit. The rule is grounded in sound morals and is reflected in the supplicating words of the Lord's prayer, 'Lead us not into temptation.'''[5]

Exempting trustee banks from the loyalty rule by allowing them to deposit trust funds with themselves has not come easily to the legal fraternity. In their authoritative *The Law of Trusts and Trustees*, Bogert and Bogert note that ''In the original Restatement of Trusts by a close vote of the annual meeting the rule was stated that it was improper for the corporate trustee to deposit trust funds with its own commercial department, and this rule is continued in the Second edition of the Restatement.''[6] But some cases held that trustee holding of cash was legal if customary rates of interest were paid on the accounts, and in fact the Bogerts say that ''the weight of authority at common law sanctioned this practice. . . .''[7] Many state laws have been enacted making deposits in the bank's own commercial department lawful, often with the requirement that securities be pledged covering the value of the trust deposits,[8] but making no distinctions between in-bank deposits that bear interest and those that do not.[9] The Uniform Trusts Act of 1937, adopted in five states, permits trustee holdings of trust cash where the trustee is subject to government supervision, pays the same rate of interest on trust funds as on other deposits, and maintains a securities reserve covering the uninsured market value of the trust deposits.[10]

In effect, then, fiduciary rules against self-dealing have been set aside in the case of trustee holding of trust cash, and this important exception has long been institutionalized by practice, statute, and regulatory accommodation. There have always been conscientious bankers and regulators very much concerned about the potential for abuse in this direct form of self-dealing. R. L. Taylor, a Philadelphia trust banker, speaking before the American Bankers Association in 1907, told the body that ''the bank account [of the trust department] should be separate and apart from all other funds, and *good practice usually demands that it be kept elsewhere than in the banking department of one's own company.*''[11] Despite this admonition bank self-interest prevailed over ''good practice,'' and although there are notable exceptions, it has been an almost universal rule among trust departments to hold some or all trust cash in the trustee bank.

The Importance of Trust Cash

As may be seen in Table 6, at the end of December 1975, the 4,049 insured commercial banks with trust departments had aggregate trust assets of $397.2 billion. Of this total the $16.7 billion sum of lines 8 through 12 would appear to correspond most closely to a concept of cash assets, defined as money proper plus assets held in a highly liquid form pending distribution or investment. This total is incomplete, as some fraction of transitional holdings is placed in short-term government or private paper. But even on a narrow definition, the cash assets of trust departments are large: $16.7 billion, or 4.2 percent of aggregate trust assets. Of this $16.7 billion, $10.9 billion, or 2.8 percent of total assets (65.3 percent of cash assets), was held as deposits in the trustee bank itself, the balance in other institutions, including savings and loan associations.

Table 6: Trust Assets of Insured Commercial Banks, December 1975

TYPE OF ASSET	LINE	$ VOLUME (THOUSANDS OF DOLLARS)	PERCENTAGE OF TOTAL
U.S. govt. & agency obligations	1	36,050,998	9.0
State, county, & municipal obligations	2	23,908,001	6.0
Other obligations	3	71,360,412	18.0
Common stocks	4	214,457,811	54.0
Preferred stocks	5	5,391,792	1.4
Real estate mortgages	6	7,137,930	1.8
Real estate	7	13,410,630	3.4
Savings & loan accts.	8	927,669	0.2
Time deposits own bank	9	8,305,358	2.1
Time deposits other banks	10	4,771,015	1.2
Demand deposits own bank	11	2,577,001	0.7
Demand deposits other banks	12	135,524	0.0
Miscellaneous	13	8,784,053	2.2
Total Assets	14	397,217,631	100.0

Source: Board of Governors-FDIC-Comptroller, *Trust Assets of Insured Commercial Banks, 1975.*

For a great many trust banks, probably more than a majority of the top one thousand, the trust department is the largest depositor in the bank. At Morgan Guaranty, for example, although in-bank trust department cash was only 0.30 percent of total trust assets at the end of 1973, it amounted to $70 million. [12] Quite a few sizable trust institutions have in-bank trust deposits of $10 million or more, and even for the large institutions, the trust department's deposits often make the difference between marginal and substantial earnings. From 1968 to 1971, New York City's ten largest banks showed net operating losses before account was taken of trust deposits. In 1972 these ten trust departments showed only a $5.2 million net operating profit on gross revenues of $361.2 million, but trust department earnings become significant when the $105.9 million of earnings credits on trust deposits is allocated to these trust departments. [13] For 1969 the Institutional Investor Study estimated that the value of trust cash to the banks, exclusive of "float," [14] was 26.6 percent of direct trust department revenues. [15] New York Federal Reserve Bank data for the ten largest New York City trust departments in 1969 showed $137.1 million in deposit credits, $307.2 million in direct revenues, or a 45 percent ratio exclusive of float. [16] For the smaller trust departments, their balances may not assure profitability, but they are important in keeping losses down, thus making this marginal operation worth preserving.

In-bank cash holdings as a percentage of trust assets decline as trust department size increases (Table 7). This is a result, in large part, of the small average size of accounts in the smaller trust departments and the lesser ability of the small departments to use sophisticated methods for making money market investments for accounts in transition. It is also likely that more conflict-of-interest abuses in trust cash management occur in smaller departments, partly because of the lesser sophistication of their customers and personnel, and partly because their unprofitability may induce them to be overgenerous to themselves where feasible.[17]

Table 7:   Trust Cash Held as Deposits within the Trustee Bank,
by Size of Trust Assets, 1974

TOTAL BANK TRUST ASSETS ($ ASSETS)	RATIO OF BANK-HELD TRUST CASH TO TRUST ASSETS (PERCENT)
Under 10 million	13.2
10-25 million	8.5
25-100 million	5.6
100-500 million	3.5
500 million-1 billion	2.5
Over 1 billion	2.3
All banks	3.0

Source: Computed from Board of Governors-FDIC-Comptroller, *Trust Assets of Insured Commercial Banks*, 1974.

Trust cash has become more important to banks and trust clients both as a result of an expansion in trust asset volume and because of the increase in interest rates over the past decade. With higher rates the opportunity cost of idle cash to trust clients has risen accordingly, and the benefits to the banks of acquiring and holding trust cash have increased. Potential conflict has also been enhanced by technological progress, which in the form of computerization has made it possible for banks to handle trust cash more efficiently than in the past. The avoidance of conflict abuses thus has become incompatible with static, traditional trust cash management; it has required positive action adapting to the changing technical environment.

Bank Handling of Trust Cash

Trust departments can hold trust cash in their own banks as either demand or time deposits. About $10.9 billion of trust cash was held in these forms as of December 1975. The division between time and demand deposits (shown in Table 6) is misleading, however, as it suggests that the $8.3 billion of in-bank time money bears interest as do conventional time deposits. For several decades, however, the Federal Reserve authorities and the comptroller have allowed and even encouraged trust banks to reclassify a portion of general trust deposits into a non interest-bearing time category for the purpose of reducing the banks' reserve requirements.[18] As expressed in the Comptroller's Manual, under the heading ''Time Deposits'':

Occasionally it will be found that a bank is carrying a substantial portion of its trust department funds as a time deposit in the commercial department without interest for the purpose of reducing the amount of reserve required to be carried. This practice is permissible, but the bank is required to make a periodic analysis of the individual accounts involved in order to determine the total amount which may be deposited. The deposit must be subject to a written agreement between the trust department and the banking department providing for at least 30 days notice or a maturity of not less than 30 days after the date of deposit.[19]

The banks can meet the nonwithdrawal requirement by keeping that fraction of these transitory accounts in the time category that will not be called for during the relevant period. For example, if the bank finds that the general trust department deposit has not declined by more than 30 percent at any time in recent years, it might set 60 percent as the fraction safely classified as non interest-bearing time. Individual account cash demands can still be readily met, because the classification is applicable to totals, not the placement of individual account cash. Trust department reports to the federal banking agencies are not required to include a breakdown of "time deposits—own bank" as between real, interest-bearing deposits and those put into the time category by the bookkeeping adjustment just described. But it would appear that well over 50 percent of the category "time deposits—own bank" is of this non interest-bearing variety, and for the large banks, between about 50 percent and over 90 percent of all in-bank trust deposits seem to be classified as non interest-bearing time.

The comptroller warns the banks that "it is a breach of trust" to build up in-bank deposits by deliberately or negligently withholding investments or distributions at the expense of the bank's clients,[20] and examinations pay explicit attention to the size of bank holdings of cash in their fiduciary accounts. The law and court decisions have also established that interest must be paid on trust deposits in some cases[21] and that general fiduciary standards of "reasonableness" must limit the volume and duration of bank holdings of trust cash. But legal and regulatory standards have been vague, and their effectiveness as a constraint on bank cash management practices has probably been modest.[22] As noted by one court:

It is conceded that a trustee owes a duty to invest trust funds within a reasonable time after they are received, but what is a reasonable time depends upon circumstances. Measured by this standard, periods of three months, six months and one year have been held to be reasonable.[23]

Bank procedure in handling trust cash has also been affected by the distinction made in law and practice between *income cash*—interest and dividends received regularly and normally paid out to beneficiaries of personal trust accounts on a fixed schedule—and *principal cash*, which is a part of the trust corpus temporarily in non income-bearing form. Income cash is regarded as a transitory holding that will be paid out shortly and that is subject to immediate demand by the beneficiary, although this right is rarely exercised. Because of these characteristics, plus their typical small size, income cash holdings have traditionally been maintained as in-bank cash, at least for personal trust accounts. Because pension fund payouts are not closely geared to income received by the fund, a great many bankers do not ordinarily apply the distinction between income and principal to such accounts.[24] The law and regulatory rules may require that a distinction be made between income and principal for personal trust accounts, and bank procedures frequently involve the setting up of separate income and investment accounts for each trust, with only investment account cash normally invested in short-term interest-bearing assets. There is also some uncertainty in the minds of trust officers about whether income cash may be ''invested'' legally, even to the extent of placement in quality short-term paper.[25] At the suggestion of the banks, trust agreements often are written to make explicit provision for the investing of income cash in liquid assets to eliminate any legal uncertainties that might constrain the trustee. But although some banks have striven to minimize the distinction between income and principal cash and to incorporate both into their new and advanced systems of cash management, most have been content to keep income cash separate and hold it on deposit in the trustee bank.

The *principal* cash of personal trust accounts is thought of in a different way, on the ground that it is a permanent holding, part of the trust corpus for which earnings must be sought. If principal cash is to be held for some time before investment, there is little doubt that it should be put into some income-bearing short-term instruments, unless the sums are very small or the period of idleness extremely brief. State law may actually stipulate payment of interest for such idle funds. Indiana trust law requires a 3 percent payment after six months of idleness (unless settlor or court provide otherwise), and New York requires that court-appointed trustees pay interest on balances of $1,000 or more held as trust principal for more than sixty days.[26] Although principal cash may be held in interest-bearing deposits (including certificates of deposit) of the trustee bank, a number of trust banks adhere to the rule that it should be placed outside the bank[27]—in savings and loan associations, savings banks, or money market instruments.

Some institutions have no explicit rules governing the handling of trust cash. Others have rules that consist merely of a general admonition to keep uninvested cash at a minimum. For most banks there is also an informal absolute or percentage ceiling on uninvested cash, at which point the portfolio manager is expected to act. This ceiling can range from 1 to 10 percent of account assets; more often it is expressed in absolute sums, most frequently $1,000, but sometimes $3,000 to $5,000, usually applicable to principal cash, but in a few banks applied to all cash. In a minority of banks, it is claimed that even principal cash below the ceiling is put to work, perhaps in a savings account, and sums above the ceiling may be invested in variable notes[28] and other liquid market instruments. When cash is to be paid out of principal, as in the liquidation of an estate, some bank rules require them to move quickly into in-bank deposits.[29] Rules frequently provide for systematic review of uninvested cash by more senior management, a procedure urged upon the banks by regulatory authorities.

Banks differ markedly in the speed with which information is provided to portfolio managers on levels of uninvested cash in their accounts. In some institutions information is available every day, or every other day; in others it is provided only weekly, monthly, or even less frequently. Often the information goes directly to the administrator of the account instead of the trust investment officer, who receives it later. In the case of a very few advanced computerized systems, the information on uninvested cash is not only provided daily but is also used—that is, the cash above certain minimum levels is invested—without the necessity of discretionary action.

The banks also differ in the short-term options they give their portfolio managers. Most of the larger trust banks have developed variable note, or so-called Master Note, plans—arrangements with large issuers of commercial paper for the daily purchase of their paper by the trust departments. In a number of banks, these plans were originally suggested by large customers, who sometimes provided the computer programs for the variable note operation. More recently a number of banks have started short-term securities funds of their own,[30] consisting of a pool of commercial paper, certificates of deposit, and short-term U.S. government instruments in which eligible portfolios within the trust department can participate on a highly flexible basis. These liquidity funds permit greater diversification,[31] reduce the inefficiency of buying numerous issues with adjustments necessary on a daily basis for each,[32] and bypass the difficulties caused by an occasional shortage of Master Notes in times of monetary ease.[33] They have tended to displace Master Notes, which have also fallen into mild disfavor as a corporate borrowing vehicle and have run afoul of a regulatory judgment that they should be subject to a 10 percent of capital and surplus limit paralleling that applied to the commercial arm.[34]

Smaller banks have not had the resources or volume of business to permit the provision of special outlets for uninvested cash. Many of them have relied heavily on deposits in their own banks as their vehicle for handling uninvested cash, although some have conscientiously sought interest-bearing obligations on the outside. Provident National Bank of Philadelphia attempted to fill this gap with a short-term fund explicitly designed as a vehicle to service the short-term investment needs of smaller trust departments.[35] This was followed by a rapid expansion of the use of such external money market funds by small trust departments interested in putting idle cash to use and unable to support such funds internally. Some $600 million was invested by trust departments in external money market funds by the end of 1976. This promising development was slowed up by a December 1975 ruling by the Comptroller, precipitated by the spreading trust department use of money market funds, that mutual fund purchases by a trust department were unlawful delegations of investment power, although usable under certain special conditions. This negative regulatory response, slightly relaxed in September 1976,[36] seems to have been based on a narrowly literal interpretation of the prohibition of a "delegation of investment powers" by a fiduciary.[37]

There are different degrees of accessibility of individual acounts to variable note plans and internal short-term investment pools. In a few banks, the variable notes are available only to pension funds and agency accounts or to large accounts. More often they are open to all accounts, but in units of $1,000 or $5,000. Amounts below the variable note ceiling may be put into alternative short-term investments within the limits of bank policy[38] and the discretion of the portfolio manager. The short-term liquidity fund is used only by a small minority of banks and is usually available only to pension accounts. In its initial survey of the "Collective Funds of 50 Largest Trust Departments," *The American Banker* (May 23, 1974) found that only thirteen of the fifty largest departments have such funds, and eleven of the thirteen were available for the principal or exclusive use of pension funds. Only the First National Bank of Chicago reported separate liquidity funds for pension *and* ordinary trust accounts. Their Common Trust Fund G, a liquidity fund open to personal trusts, had assets of $62.5 million at the end of 1972, with 2,776 participants. In the handful of cases where personal trusts now have access to liquidity pools, only one regularly placed income cash in the fund. In all of them, cash can be placed in the fund for one day, in each case with a $1,000 minimum for entry. Several claim to be engaged in serious study of the feasibility of reducing the minimum. In a few banks, computerization permits automatic investment in the liquidity fund of cash that would otherwise be uninvested for one day.

There is great variation in the assiduity with which banks attempt to minimize uninvested trust cash. A number of trust department heads and top bank officials speak fervently on the subject and take actions that make their words believable. John McIntyre of Citizens and Southern National Bank of Atlanta is said to be "one of a very few trying to figure out an economical way to invest all those balances instantaneously so that the bank gets no use whatsoever from them."[39] But others are less enthusiastic. When McIntyre suggested such a system to participants at a trust convention, he was not well received. " 'You would have thought I was a Benedict Arnold, or something,' he says."[40] In a few banks, the banks' own auditors are reported to be more severe in criticizing uninvested cash balances than the regulatory authority. Some institutions have gone to great pains to provide options for trust cash, even at a net cost to themselves. The Northern Trust system, in effect since October 1971, was not only expensive to develop but resulted in a decline of about one-third in trust deposits held at the bank, despite a substantial increase in trust assets under management. The trust department's in-bank cash at Citizens and Southern has fallen by an even greater proportion over the last few years, and John McIntyre claims that the greatest economies and corresponding decline in cash holdings

(50 percent or more) have been found possible in the personal trust area.[41] As a less familiar illustration, a number of small- and medium-sized trust banks in Pennsylvania for many years provided mortgage pools with fixed prices and no entry or exit charge for the temporary investment of personal trust funds and with participation units as small as ten dollars. Especially in the case of accounts restricted by court or trust agreement to investment in first lien mortgages, cash accumulations of income up to mortgage investment size could involve substantial deposit windfalls to the banks (and sacrifices to the trust accounts). Mortgage pools for investment of such accumulations, with small participation units, represent an impressive case of "utmost fidelity."[42]

Conflicts in Trust Cash Management

Conflict-of-interest abuses in the handling of trust cash may be classed under three headings: (1) the holding of excessive cash in the trust bank; (2) the failure to credit the trust accounts properly for benefits derived from directly held trust cash; and (3) reciprocity gains taken by the bank for itself for trust cash placed outside. The first type is the most obvious and most commonly discussed and the one to which regulation has directed primary attention. It is also the most difficult to evaluate, as adequate criteria of "excess" do not exist, and differences in size of account, account objectives, investment opportunities at any given moment, and money market options for particular banks and accounts make generalization hazardous. The author has heard of numerous episodes of excess cash in particular banks or individual accounts, but their overall significance is impossible to establish or judge. There are also numerous cases of what appear to be policy bias toward holding cash or letting it sit without energetic attention; several of these are described in the previous section, but again they are hard to quantify or evaluate on an overall basis.

Most telling, perhaps, is the slowness with which banks have developed and improved machinery for keeping trust cash to a minimum, and even within banks the application of these improvements has lagged. Master Note plans spread rather slowly in the 1950s and 1960s, and more sophisticated vehicles for investing trust cash in bank-managed pools of money market instruments have developed even more slowly. Computerization has made it possible for the large trust banks to keep their trust accounts pretty close to fully invested. Although progress along these lines was significant after the mid-1960s, some billion dollar trust banks did not even have Master Note plans in 1973. The tendency to apply the most sophisticated cash management techniques (such as liquidity pools) to pension funds, while preserving the distinction beween income and principal cash for personal trusts, can be explained in part by the smaller size and more complex demands of trust accounts, by statutory limits on personal trust fees, and by legal obstacles to a more efficient handling of their cash. But is also evident that trust founders and beneficiaries are weaker bargainers, less well informed, and less aggressively pursued by the banks, and that the banks have a stake in preserving such distinctions as that between income and principal. A truly "undivided loyalty" to beneficiaries would have resulted in a more rapid advance in the cash management of personal trust accounts.[43]

The development of methods of reducing uninvested trust cash is analogous to the banks' pre-1969 interest in finding ways to use brokerage for the benefit of trust accounts. The banks did not push very hard to break out of the reciprocity system, and they have not struggled to devise and apply sophisticated methods to reduce uninvested cash for the same reason—because the status quo was profitable.[44] As advances do occur in the management of trust cash, they are almost invariably applied first to aggressive customers of great importance to the bank, then to lesser customers.[45]

A second conflict issue, which is less frequently discussed, is the failure of the trust banks to credit the trust accounts for returns derived from the use of trust assets. It may be argued, of course, that without this kind of windfall benefit, the banks would have to charge higher fees,[46] and that as a consequence the matter is trivial. But this misses an important point. When there is a built-in conflict of interest, as there is in bank holding of trust cash, an open and explicit fee would be preferable to an indirect and implicit mode of reward that puts the bank in the position of being able to enhance its gains by violating its fiduciary duty. (The people who now get lower fee rates are also not necessarily the same as those with relatively substantial cash balances; in fact, on bargaining-power logic there is likely to be a *positive* correlation between relative size of fees and cash balances.) As noted earlier basic fiduciary rules have been suspended in this area by long-established practice, statute, and regulation. As a result, although a bank may not use trust brokerage to acquire broker deposits for the advantage of the bank alone, it may use trust deposits *directly* for its own advantage.

An important defense of existing practice rests on the contention that it would be illegal to credit trust accounts for the value of demand deposits, given the prohibition of interest payments on this form of deposit. But existing practice dates back to a period before the prohibition of interest on demand deposits. And even today there is no prohibition against the use of interest-bearing deposits for that part of trust deposits not subject to withdrawal for thirty days. Bankers point out, of course, that at present, when general trust deposits are classified as time accounts, this calculation is based on probabilities and is not applicable to individual deposits. But at the larger banks at least, computerization now makes quite easy an allocation on the basis of average balances per period in individual accounts. But it must be acknowledged that for the smaller institutions such calculations would be impractical. It is interesting to note that the authorities permit crediting the *trust department* with earnings on trust deposits,[47] even if the matter of crediting the individual accounts either has not arisen[48] or has been regarded as illegal or impractical. Exceptions do not seem to be made easily where the fiduciary accounts are the sole beneficiary.[49]

Several banks deploy trust cash on a reciprocity basis, placing some or a large part of it in other institutions,[50] but allocating it on the basis of deposits held in the trust bank. This practice is neither common nor of great quantitative importance, but it has considerable interest because of the principles involved. This use of trust deposits is very closely analogous to the now condemned employment of trust brokerage commissions to buy bank deposits. Properties (deposits rather than commissions) belonging to the trusts are used by the trust department for the advantage of the bank—to build up commercial deposits—rather than to benefit the trust accounts themselves. But this use of trust cash is hardly more detrimental to trust interests than keeping all the cash in the bank itself in the first place, without any compensation of the trust accounts.

The Consequences of Trustee Bank Holding of Uninvested Cash

The conflict-of-interest abuses that arise from trustee bank holding of the uninvested cash balances of trust accounts have been brought under increased constraint, but not eliminated. Hard information on the extent of past and present abuses is difficult to obtain, and the lack of standards on the subject compound the problem. Abuses appear to have declined in quantitative importance and persist in grosser forms mainly in some of the smaller trust banks; but as discussed earlier, standard practice and rules and the lagged diffusion of maximizing techniques to lesser accounts involve what appears to be significant conflict abuses persisting even among the larger institutions, applicable primarily to "weaker" accounts.

Another possible consequence of trust bank holding of the uninvested cash of fiduciary accounts may be a reinforcement of the competitive edge held by the larger trust institutions over other asset managers. It may allow the banks to offer lower fees or extra services or to engage in more intensive marketing efforts, which may add to the other factors making for bank predominance in this market. The Institutional Investor Study found that bank fees were similar to those of investment advisors for large pension fund accounts but lower for those under $25 million.[51] Similarly, bank rates for personal agency accounts under $5 million were lower than those charged by investment advisors to their individual accounts.[52] A 1973 study by the financial research firm Technimetrics found that the average annual fees for managing a $5 million portfolio were as follows: (1) bank trust departments, $12,050; (2) brokerage firms, $16,300; (3) insurance companies, $20,390; (4) affiliates of mutual fund companies, $24,600; and (5) large investment counselors, $24,000.[53] Of course, the lower fee rate is only one advantage possessed by banks in competing for advisory accounts, and it is very probably not one of the more decisive considerations.[54] It also is in the client's interest, although it has been argued above that it is not desirable that the advantage be taken through the back door. Yet better through the back door than no door at all. Through this imperfect mechanism, prices to fiduciary clients may be brought to a somewhat lower level.

One school of thought contends that the aggressive pursuit of trust accounts by banks is an artificial product of the prohibition of interest payments on demand deposits.[55] Given the noncompetitive differential between payments on demand deposits (zero) and returns on deposits (rates on loan funds), the banks have been induced to expand in areas where deposits can be captured. Trust accounts have provided a large deposit windfall, with direct trust deposits, float, deposits acquired in the past via the use of commissions allocated to brokers and through the general strengthening of the customer relationship. According to this argument, if the prohibition of demand deposit interest were eliminated, the interest of banks in trust accounts would dwindle and with it their competitive advantage and power.

This hypothesis is plausible and probably has some explanatory value, but freeing deposit competition would probably not reduce bank advantages in the fiduciary management area substantially. Indeed, banks might push into trust activities even more aggressively to compensate for reduced profit margins.[56]

Moreover, this theory tends to ignore the complexity of the customer relationship, which makes a tie-in effect and the marketing of a "full line" profitable. The theory also assumes that peripheral services are necessarily unprofitable and fails to take into account the changes that have already tended to shrink the volume of uninvested cash. Finally, the theory presupposes an effect of the freeing of deposit competition on the profitability of demand deposits and on the willingness of banks to diversify and to subsidize peripheral services that is not supported by the record before the Banking Act of 1933. In the 1920s and earlier, competition never succeeded in reducing profit margins on demand deposits to the point where banks lost interest in them or slowed down the long and steady process of bank diversification.[57] Complaints about trust and other service department unprofitability in the interests of the commercial arm were as common before 1933 as after.[58] It may be argued that institutional changes, including the more vigorous application of antitrust in the financial sector, make competition more acute today than before 1933, but this point is debatable.

Protections Against Abuse in Trust Cash Management

A number of factors already limit abuse in the handling of trust cash. Fiduciary responsibilities are strongly felt in many departments, and where these operate in a setting of substantial departmental autonomy, they provide a real protection of fiduciary interest. Intrabank protections are least effective where the trust department is small and unprofitable, where its officers have little independence, and where their power to make key decisions is restricted. But in all cases, trust department officials must deal with a real conflict between bank and fiduciary interest. Furthermore, full pursuit of the fiduciary interest requires the dismantling of practices and rules inherited from an era when conflicts could be more readily ignored and before computerization and efficient money market systems made it easier to reduce uninvested cash. As with brokerage allocations, some cash handling and crediting rules immediately impress the outsider as involving conflict abuses. But in many banks, these have become established routine, still to be shaken loose either by moral repugnance from within or by attacks from the outside.

Changes are in process, however, partly as a result of internal forces, but mainly because of the pressure of competition and the demands of powerful customers. In soliciting important pension clients, the large banks must not only show performance but also explain exactly how resources, including cash, are employed for the client's advantage. Effective procedures for minimizing uninvested cash have become a regular part of the package used in the solicitation and preservation of major pension fund accounts. As competition enforces such procedures for large and informed customers, pressures build up for their diffusion downward to clients with less bargaining power.

Regulation also affords some protection against abuse in the holding of cash. The Comptroller's Manual, as noted earlier, specifically condemns the deliberate holding of excess cash for the bank's interest as a serious violation of fiduciary obligations.[59] It is sometimes alleged that regulation has addressed itself to this conflict with energy and effect,[60] and it is probable that really gross abuses in trust cash management would be attended to by the regulators. But a number of caveats are in order. Perhaps the most important is that the interests of the regulatory authorities and the fiduciary accounts may be in conflict. The primary interest of the regulatory authorities is in the solvency of the banks; the function of regulation is often acknowledged to be "keeping the banks open"[61] by seeing that they do not leave themselves vulnerable to solvency-threatening surcharges. The lesser interest of the regulators in the fiduciary clients is evident in their long disregard of brokerage allocations for the acquisition of bank deposits. When the federal authorities finally did get around in 1969 to instructing examiners "to enquire into bank policies relating to the allocation of brokerage business," they quickly found that "it appears that the practice, while perhaps used in past years,[62] is no longer a factor in placing brokerage."[63] Similarly, in the area of cash handling, the sanctioning by the regulatory authorities of the placement of trust cash in non interest-bearing time deposits is clearly to the advantage of the bank, not to the fiduciary clients of the trust departments. This preoccupation with the welfare of the bankers in these instances has probably been encouraged by the unprofitability of so many trust departments,[64] which may have added to the normal quota of regulatory protectiveness.

Regulatory protection against abuses in the area of cash management suffers further from the difficulty of establishing standards, and regulators have tended to fall back on insisting that the *banks* install review practices and apply internally established standards.[65] Asking questions and imposing self-reviews may well have curbed some of the more serious potential excesses. But very few cases of abuses in the holding of trust cash have been carried up to the comptroller's office,[66] and in one district, the author was informed that over the period of a decade no trust examiner had claimed that any bank held too much trust cash. Perhaps this complete absence of apparent regulatory conflict with the banks on the issue of uninvested cash reflects total purity, but it is more likely that it reflects superficial regulation.

VI • CONCLUSIONS

As banks have expanded their operations from traditional banking functions to other activities, they have established more and more situations in which they may have to choose between their own interests and those of fiduciary clients or among clients of varying importance. Conflict has also been built into the fiduciary function as a consequence of the role envisaged for the fiduciary arm in earlier years, which implied subordination of the trust department and its functions to the interests of the bank as a whole.

The potential for serious conflict would seem on its face to be considerable. And there is scattered but convincing evidence of bank abuses in past years in accommodation loans and dispositions of estate property, holdings of trust cash in excess or at less than competitive rates, discriminatory treatment of customers of different status and power, and improprieties in the allocation of trust-generated brokerage. But these abuses do not appear ever to have reached massive proportions. Probably more damaging to fiduciary accounts than conflict abuses as such were the conservatism and relative neglect of the trust function and its secondary status in terms of the allocation of bank talent, which may well have been a complex reflection of a basic conflict of interest.[1]

Conflict abuses have always been constrained by the legal rules applicable to fiduciaries and the fear of surcharge and adverse publicity. And banks have an interest in doing well for those trust clients who are purchasers of other bank services, an interest that has become much more compelling with growth in importance of more sophisticated and better informed pension fund and agency accounts. In response to the pressures and publicity associated with the competition for these performance-oriented accounts, banks have devoted many more resources to the fiduciary investment function. The demands of the aggressive accounts may have created new conflict potentials by virtue of their preferred status relative to less informed and less powerful fiduciary clients,[2] but by and large, the greater competition and more visible results have probably tended to reduce conflict abuses overall. The increased autonomy of the trust arm, a result of greater trust department size, the special demands of an increasingly competitive environment, and the pressures of the law, has also worked to lessen conflict.[3] The Employee Retirement Income Security Act of 1974 (ERISA) set forth and prohibited by law a variety of self-dealing transactions among parties-in-interest involved in pension funds. This law, still untested in the courts, is widely believed to have injected a new note of caution into fiduciary dealings with conflict potential.

Generally, conflict tends to be more important in smaller trust institutions that have not established a more or less autonomous fiduciary arm or abandoned the tradition of the trust department as a service vehicle. But these smaller units are of slight quantitative importance in the total trust business. Within the larger institutions, the disposition of estate property and closely held companies and the handling of personal trusts and the less performance-oriented funds of smaller companies and nonprofit organizations remain the areas where potential and realized conflicts are most severe.[4] The frequency of conflicts over estates and closely held companies is a result of acute bank and customer interest in these properties, the absence of a strong countervailing bargaining force, and limited disclosure or other forms of control. Abuses involving small personal trusts and the smaller pension and advisory accounts are, similarly, a result of lack of client knowledge, an imbalance of bargaining power, and a lack of publicity. Measures of investment management "performance" are most often applied to the handling of preferred and "showcase" accounts rather than to the disposition of estate properties, closely held companies, and "insensitive" accounts in the personal trust and pension and advisory area.[5] Admittedly, monitoring results here would be difficult, but it is precisely in these areas that conflict abuses are most likely to impair investment performance.

Publicity and disclosure have been helpful in containing conflict-of-interest abuses in bank fiduciary activities. In a way their effectiveness reflects unfavorably on the efficacy of law and bank regulation, which moved with glacial speed on such matters as deposit-commission reciprocity before extensive media publicity. The difficulty with privately generated publicity as a protective mechanism is that it assumes an interest, knowledge, willingness, and power on the part of bank clients to carry out suits,[6] and of media enterprises and researchers to initiate, obtain information, and publish critical investigations on bank abuses that may be unrealistic. Thus, publicity and disclosure have been of limited value in dealing with estate and "insensitive" account conflicts, although the background threat of publicity may well have exercised a constraining influence on the realization of conflict even in this sphere. Disclosure that would put on the public record transactions and relationships that involve potential conflicts of interest can be of service in mitigating conflict, but its usefulness is easy to overestimate. Disclosure is a passive form of control that does not directly require anything but the requisite production of facts. The record of disclosure under the securities legislation also suggests that the difficulty of defining and eliciting *relevant* facts and the absence of context can seriously reduce its value. This is an area in which constructive action is possible, but the reform potential of required disclosure should be recognized as modest.[7]

Regulation also has been of somewhat limited value in controlling conflict of interest. For a long period, examinations in the trust area were undernourished and unintensive, implementing what was at best an auditing function.[8] Regulation has also been more concerned with bank liability[9] than with the interests of the banks' fiduciary clients.[10] With this tradition regulatory action cannot be expected to be adequate where conflicts change or new ones emerge, but it may still serve to police rules imposed from the outside.[11]

More fundamental solutions to conflict-of-interest problems would involve some structural revamping of trust banks, most notably a more complete separation of the trust investment management functions from that of commercial lender and depository. Such changes are sometimes urged strictly on the basis of the insider advantage accruing to the trust arm and the difficulty of controlling it without total separation. This advantage, especially under existing legal conditions, is of limited value to the banks and their trust departments and would seem to be of insufficient importance to sustain any case for major structural alteration. Deserving more weight is the overall set of conflicts of interest arising from the association of commercial and trust banking. Although these problems are probably of declining importance under the force of trust department growth and external competitive and legal pressures, they are still significant. But where these conflicts appear to be most acute—in personal trusts, estates, and closely held companies—spin-offs and divestments would seem of limited feasibility and value for reasons discussed shortly.

Also argued as a basis for structural change is the immense size of the great trust institutions. A large and powerful commercial department facilitates getting trust business, and a large trust department adds to the power and leverage of the commercial bank. Although the direct control powers accruing to trust banks from their large security holdings probably have been exaggerated,[12] the power that banks derive from their control over fiduciary assets seems indisputable. What is more, the total spectrum of advantages of the large trust banks, including their ability to use trust-generated cash directly, helps them to maintain their domination of the rapidly growing pension fund business, suggesting continued increases in size and power. Some positive public policy response seems worthy of serious consideration on grounds of sheer concentration of economic and social power, if not on the grounds of conflict of interest (the primary concern of this chapter).

A total separation of trust and commercial activities into completely unaffiliated entities would clearly resolve the problems of inside information and other conflicts associated with the commercial-trust relationship and would serve to diminish the power of the large trust banks. The establishment of the "wall" and the increases in trust department autonomy make such "surgery" seem cleaner and less disruptive.

Arguing against separation is, first, the absence of evidence of extensive and demonstrably costly abuses that would readily justify an action as drastic as an "unscrambling of eggs." A second difficulty with separation is the apparent decline of those abuses that remain. A third difficulty is that a large number of existing trust relationships are based upon the financial power and responsibility of the commercial bank, so severing the relationship would present thorny legal problems.[13] A fourth difficulty arises from the service nature and relatively low cost of bank-supplied trust services. The advantages that banks derive from providing these services, and certain efficiencies in marketing, have almost certainly kept the costs of trust services to public buyers below those that would prevail in a bank-free trust service market.[14] It is not easy to recommend, and would be difficult for legislatures to require, structural changes that are likely to injure the consumers of these services, unless the evil to be eliminated can be shown to be of great and pressing urgency. In short, legally enforced total separation of trust and commercial banking could not now be based on the level of present abuses and anticipated benefits to consumers of trust or commercial banking services. It would have to be based on the belief that the tie-in gives the banks an advantage in competing for trust business and that the power flowing from this linkage poses a threat to a democratic and decentralized capitalist system.

Spin-offs into holding companies would be a halfway solution that would seem to get at few, if any, conflict-of-interest and power issues. The same may be said of the recommendations of the Hunt Commission, which proposed the enactment of a federal ''prudent man rule,'' the filing of reports on large trust department holdings and related interlocks, and regulatory surveillance over reciprocity, executions, trust cash management, and the effectiveness of prohibitions against bank and bank personnel use of inside information.[15] These proposals go only slightly beyond the point to which regulators and the banks have already moved voluntarily. The proposal for a federal ''prudent man rule'' has little relevance to real conflict-of-interest issues and amounts to a call for a *federal* platitude to supplement those of the states. The proposal for disclosure of information about large trust holdings (5 percent or more) adds little to that already disseminated voluntarily by the large banks, and the practical implications of disclosing those holdings are slight. The proposal for regulatory surveillance to see that brokerage allocations are not employed to attract deposits is hardly a bold innovation, given the already widespread official abandonment of deposit-based reciprocity by the major banks. The least defensible proposal of the Hunt Commission, however, was that the regulators see that ''each corporate fiduciary achieves the best executions'' and also establish that the banks have effectively prevented trust department personnel from having access to inside information. These tasks would be entirely beyond the capabilities of the regulatory process, and their enactment would violate a fundamental rule against legislating the inherently unenforceable.

Specific Proposals

Short of total legal separation of trust and commercial departments—the pros and cons of which were discussed above—there are a number of changes of more modest scope that might alleviate conflict overall or provide net benefits in specific areas of conflict of interest.

1. *Constraints on further combinations involving major trust banks.* A good case can be made for imposing severe constraints on the acquisition of other trust institutions—especially large ones—by existing sizable trust banks. A grievous error in public policy was made in allowing the numerous mergers among large trust banks after World War II, but even at this late date, it may still be useful to bar any future merger growth by trust banks with banking and trust assets each in excess of, say, $1 billion. A major justification for such a limitation would be to constrain sheer accretion of power. But this limitation would also help prevent any further reductions in the number of bank trust competitors and any increase in the concentration of trust assets via acquisition.

2. *Enlarging potential competition by easing entry into the trust business.* Insurance companies and investment counseling firms suffer a competitive disadvantage in not being able to serve as legal trustees under formal deeds of trust. Pension funds as well as personal trusts normally require a legal trustee, and banks have a significant initial advantage in offering both trustee *and* investment management services.[16] With suitable capital requirements and other protections, there is no reason why bank competitors should not be able to serve as trustees. Entry into the field of trustee service could be extended to encompass the formation of new trust companies, which, especially as affiliates of other financial entities, might serve to invigorate competition in the fiduciary sector.[17]

3. *Ceilings on portfolio company holdings of bank trust departments.* As a precautionary attempt to prevent bank control or excessive influence via stockholdings, it may be desirable to impose ownership ceilings, with some account taken of bank voting rights in a particular stock and some weight given to the existence of a customer relationship with the portfolio company. For example, in the absence of a lending relationship, a 10 percent ceiling might be imposed on bank ownership of the common stock of publicly held companies where the voting rights are held by the bank; where the voting rights are held by the bank with a lending relationship, a 5 percent ceiling could be imposed. This kind of rule would have the further benefit of constraining the growth of the largest trust banks. It might also induce them to search more aggressively beyond the top tier of blue chip investment opportunities.

4. *Limits on direct self-dealing in trust property.* In handling estates and closely held companies, publicity and competition have not provided the protection they have afforded elsewhere. It would be salutary to establish a rule that banks cannot acquire trust property for their own use without open competitive bidding or valuation by a court of competent jurisdiction.

5. *Limits on other forms of conflict involving trust properties.* Constraints on the sale of trust property are also desirable when the bank has a customer relationship interest in the property or when the property is sought by a customer or affiliated person.[18] As in the previous case, publicity and competition are minimally effective in protecting the integrity of such transactions. A rule forcing competitive bidding or court adjudication in the valuation and selling process might be salutary, and it might even protect a bank under pressure from a powerful customer for a privileged sale.

6. *Limits on the placement of customer securities in weak portfolios.* There may have been a serious problem of accommodation and dumping in the years before 1965, but it has diminished in importance over the past decade. Nonetheless, little knowledge of the true state of these abuses is available either to the public or to regulators. A legal or regulatory rule might be useful, but such a rule would be hard to formulate. It would be needed only for personal trust and other small accounts, as the large customers are able to take care of themselves. The rule could be made applicable only to funds under $25 million in size, and it could take the form of prohibiting new acquisitions of stocks or debt instruments for small accounts where the companies or securities acquired were rated less than A by a standard rating service or were not on the trust department's "approved list" to buy.

7. *Preservation of a legal basis for class action protection of the small fiduciary customer.* The class action suit was widely and effectively used in the late 1960s and early 1970s. Recently, a reaction based on fears of a swamping of courts with nuisance suits and resentment at the development of a virtual "class action bar" has developed. *Forbes* reports that in addition to an increased frequency of judicial dismissals on grounds of unmanageability, "in some 26 states, bills are pending in the legislatures that would more or less sharply limit class-action suits."[19] Federal class actions, previously less encumbered than those under state law,[20] were set back by the Supreme Court's finding of the need for a "minimum jurisdictional amount" of $10,000 an issue for plaintiff access to the federal courts.[21]

The court decision in *Schaffner* v. *Chemical Bank* (1972) dealt a damaging blow to class action suits as protective devices against the abuse of small victims of trustee banks.[22] In principle the trust fiduciary area is one in which the class action suit should be serviceable, given the great number of small accounts, each without the incentive or resources to employ individualized legal processes to obtain remedies[23] and with limited disclosure to the accounts of bank policies and practices impinging on their welfare. Admittedly, the risk of frivolous and harassing suits against the trust banks is real and would be heightened by protecting and/or liberalizing the right to bring class actions; moreover, the class action suit is not an efficient vehicle for protecting the shareholder (let alone a broader public) interest. But it is one of the few potentially effective private sources of remedy for abuse, and its impairment would not seem justified in the light of the historic record of regulatory protection. It should be possible to frame legislation putting reasonable constraints on abuses while retaining a legitimate form of legal protection.

8. *Disclosure of sequences in the disposition and use of information*. To reduce any tendencies to make preferential use of investment information, it might be useful to require bank trust departments to make written disclosures of their policies. This would include statements regarding how information flows to discretionary and nondiscretionary accounts and how accounts rank in the information receiving sequence.[24] It should also include disclosure of the differences that may be anticipated for varying account types as a result of block and/or collective purchases or sales made on the basis of new information or reappraisals. Finally, disclosure should be made of the conditions under which some accounts may be buying while others are simultaneously selling, as well as of policy on crossovers between accounts, whether direct or by arrangement with brokers.

9. *Required public disclosure of holdings, relationships, and trading activity*. The large banks have moved steadily toward public disclosure of various trust matters, and this method of dealing with conflict is likely to be pursued further, partly, unfortunately, because of its relative innocuousness. Required disclosure can have some constructive impact, however, if the matters disclosed are useful to the general public, legislators, and trust clients.[25] The following information, some of which is now provided in the annual trust reports of several major trust banks, is of the type that might be worth including:

a. The number of shares, market value, and percentage of voting stock in all companies in which the trust department holds shares valued at $1 million or more[26]

b. The percentage of voting stock in all other companies in which the trust department has sole voting rights of 5 percent or more of the voting shares

c. For each of the above listed holdings, the percentage of voting stock over which the bank has sole voting authority[27]

d. For each of the above listed holdings, names and primary business affiliations of each common director

e. For each of the above listed companies, the dollar amount of debt held by the trust department

f. For each of the above listed companies, an indication of whether the bank has a commercial relationship with the company, such as a deposit account averaging $50,000 or more over the past year, a line of credit with the bank during the past two years, or a loan outstanding from the bank during the past two years[28]

g. For each of the above listed companies, the number of transactions, the dollar volume of purchases, and the dollar volume of sales of the stock during the previous twelve months[29]

h. For each of the above listed companies the number of trustee appointments held by the bank for debt instruments issued by that company

10. *Disclosure and other reforms in the practice and regulation of bank handling of uninvested trust cash*. Potential conflicts of interest in trust bank holding of fiduciary account's cash are so direct that the heritage of practice and regulation from a conflict-insensitive past requires a careful reexamination. The most complete and direct solution to abuse here, short of total separation of the trust arm from the bank, would be forcing banks to hold trust cash elsewhere, thus reducing bank incentives to maintain excessive trust cash balances and putting banks on a par with competitive fiduciaries. One argument against this proposal is that the banks would simply resort to reciprocity deals with those banks chosen as depositories.[30] Although this is indeed likely, the circuitousness of using external balances would somewhat reduce the likelihood of abuse. Furthermore, dealings with the outside banks would tend to be in the hands of trust department personnel, which would increase the weight given trust interests. Those who use the argument that the banks would engage in such reciprocity abuse, to demonstrate that the status quo is preferable, fail to see the critical implications of their argument for the integrity of existing arrangements. If we can blithely assume a resort to reciprocity in the *banks'* interest upon enforced outside cash dealings, by what logic can we assume the predominance of trust account interest in the disposition of trust cash and allocation of credits between banks and fiduciary accounts right now?[31]

The case for allowing trust banks to hold cash of their fiduciary accounts rests on convenience, institutionalized practice, legal limits on personal trust fees, the pressing income needs of many small trust departments, the likely emergence of reciprocal use of cash, the probability that the existing system results in somewhat lower trust fees, and the fact that existing abuses, although real, are not so extensive as to make a compelling case for radical surgery. But if trust banks *are* permitted to continue to hold trust cash, at least the seriousness of the present conflict should be recognized and treated accordingly in law and regulation. This would call for a number of changes, of which the following seem most worthy of prompt consideration:

a. The regulatory sanction of the practice of classifying some trust deposits as non interest-bearing time deposits should be discontinued. This sanction adds an incentive to the banks to hold trust deposits, precisely what ought to be discouraged.

b. Legal and regulatory impediments to temporary income-yielding investments of trust cash, whether income or principal, ought to be done away with.

This includes the recent and misplaced opposition to small bank trust department investment in money market funds on grounds of an unwarranted "delegation of investment authority." These rules impose unreasonable obstacles to minimizing uninvested trust cash and provide built-in excuses for the abuse of fiduciary responsibilities.

c. Regulatory authorities should be induced, perhaps by legislative enactment, to shift the balance of their interest in the trust area from concern with bank solvency to the protection of the interests of the fiduciary clients of the banks. In the matter of bank handling of uninvested trust cash, this should take the form of a serious attempt to develop regulatory criteria of what constitutes an excess balance for individual accounts, account classes, income and principal cash, and trust departments as a whole. Criteria could be based on cost data for various types and sizes of accounts, studies of the availability and costs of various cash options, and the development of comparative information on cash/asset ratios that could be used for overall appraisal.[32]

d. Trust banks should issue an annual report to regulators and clients revealing the amounts of trust cash in dollars and as a percentage of trust assets; the division of trust cash between in-bank and out-of-bank holdings; and the in-bank division between time and demand, with time that bears no interest so designated. The report should also include current rules on the handling of uninvested income and principal cash, including dollar and time limits on investments and access to variable notes and special short-term funds, any distinction made between income and principal cash, and any differentiation of accounts by type, size, or character.

NOTES

Author's Preface

[1]*In the text, when no source is given for a quotation from a trust department official, it may be assumed that the statement was made in the course of an interview.*

I. Introduction

[1]See below, pp. 28-30, and W. Nelson Peach, *The Security Affiliates of National Banks* (Baltimore: Johns Hopkins Press, 1941), Chap. 5, and citations therein.

[2]As dealers in and underwriters of U.S. government securities, banks start from an initial position of advantage in that many of their customers will prefer doing business with them, barring significant price differentials. The Federal Reserve survey of factors determining selection of dealer found that: "Second [to price] in terms of number of votes, both in ranking as of considerable importance and as most important, was 'other banking or financial business with primary dealer or bank'; it was rated as the most important factor by nearly 20 percent of the respondents." The report goes on to say that "this factor may provide a partial shelter for a particular dealer for some portion of the business he transacts." Board of Governors of the

Federal Reserve System, *Joint Treasury-Federal Reserve Study of the U.S. Government Securities Market, Staff Studies—Part 1* (Washington, D.C.: July 1970), p. 61.

[3]See Edward S. Herman and Carl F. Safanda, "Bank Trust Department Investment Services for Correspondent Banks," *Indiana Law Review* (Spring 1973).

[4]Many of the names of these banks reflected their tie-in with specific enterprises or classes of business; for example, the Morris Canal and Banking Company (New Jersey), the Blackstone Canal Bank (Rhode Island), and the Achtafalaya Railroad and Banking Company (Louisiana). See Fritz Redlich, *The Molding of American Banking* (Baltimore: Johnson Reprint Corporation, 1968), vol. II, p. 326.

[5]*Federal Reserve Bulletin* (August 1973), p. A22.

[6]Ibid., p. A29

[7]Redlich, op. cit., I, pp. 11-12; II, p. 349.

[8]Jacob H. Hollander, *Bank Loans and Stock Exchange Speculation,* Sen. Doc. 589, 61st Cong., 2d Sess. (Washington, D.C.:1911), p.4.

[9]Redlich, op. cit., I, p. 149.

[10]Ibid., II, p. 180.

[11]*Federal Reserve Bulletin* (August 1973), p. A22.

[12]*Federal Reserve Bulletin* (December 1970), p. 910; (July 1973), p. A36.

[13]Redlich, op. cit., II, pp. 341, 379.

[14]Ibid., p. 343 ff.

[15]Quoted in Redlich, op. cit., II, p. 394.

[16]N. W. Halsey was a large firm, with two hundred employees, a $100 million a year investment business, and offices in more than ten cities. With its own bond department and as a result of further acquisition and internal growth, National City Company by 1927 had more than fifty branch offices in the United States and Canada, and "was reputed to be the largest agency in the world for the distribution of investment securities." See Peach, op. cit., pp. 18-20, 86-89.

[17]Ibid., p. 20.

[18]Information provided by the Securities Industry Association.

[19]Elizabeth Hobby, "Maturity Distribution of Obligations of States and Political Subdivisions Held by Insured Commercial Banks, June 30, 1972," FDIC (Washington, D.C.: 1973), p. 3.

[20]401 U.S. 617 (1971)

[21]This case was still pending in January 1975.

[22]Speech before the 55th national trust conference of the American Bankers Association, reprinted in *American Banker* (February 27, 1974), p. 6.

[23]Of these, dividend reinvestment plans were quantitatively important by the end of 1976, with almost 2 million participants and assets of $1.2 billion; employee stock purchase plans, by contrast, had asssets of only $120 million, and automatic investment service plans declined to a volume under $5 million in 1976, after a well-publicized bank entrance in 1973. See Securities and Exchange Commision (SEC), *Interim Report on Bank Securities Activities*, (January 3, 1977), pp. 36-37, 62-63. See also Chris Welles, "Are the Big Banks Getting Too Big?" *Institutional Investor* (December 1973), pp. 182, 184.

[24]Chris Welles, "Commercial Banks Move in on Investment Banking," *Institutional Investor* (March 1975), pp. 24-25.

[25]The problem is undoubtedly less severe now than it was in the pre-1933 period. The restriction to government issues greatly reduces the potential for abuse. So does the publicity attaching to fiduciary policies and the increased attention to these matters on the part of bank and regulatory authorities. Both bank and legal rules have become more oriented to the avoidance of conflict abuse, with special restrictions on direct sales from bank underwriting-entities to bank-managed portfolios—rules, incidentally, that point up the continued potential for conflict.

[26]Committee on Costs and Charges, Trust Division, American Bankers Association, *Guide to Trust Fees* (Washington, D.C.: American Bankers Association, 1932), p. 31.

[27]Between 1875 and 1900, New York City trust company assets grew at a compound annual rate of 9.6 percent, versus 4.1 percent for national banks, 5.4 percent for state banks, and 4.2

percent for savings banks. Their deposits grew at a compound annual rate of 10 percent (4.9 percent for national banks, 6.6 percent for state banks, and 4.1 percent for savings banks). These figures are taken from H. Peers Brewer, *The Emergence of the Trust Company in New York City: 1870-1900* (unpublished Ph.D. dissertation, New York University Graduate School of Business Administration: 1974), Chaps. 3-4.

[28]One trust company executive told an audience of bankers in 1904 of the occasion when he learned the "main point" of the "trust company problem": "When I came to New York in 1884 to examine the subject of trust companies in the preparation of the bill which afterwards became the Illinois law, Mr. Stewart, the President of the United States Trust Company, gave me the most kind and useful assistance. In the course of my investigation I questioned him rather closely respecting fees and charges for services in the execution of trusts. After giving me many details, he summed up the subject by saying, 'Don't bother too much about fees and charges—never let them control—get the business. What you want is not fees but deposits!' " Eugene Prussing, "National Banks and the Trust Company Problem," *Proceedings of the American Bankers Association* (1904), p. 136.

[29]"Government Control of Banks and Trust Companies," *The Annals of the American Academy of Political and Social Science* (July -December 1904), p.23.

[30]Frederick D. Kilburn, "Control and Supervision of Trust Companies," in ibid., p. 36.

[31]George Barnett, *State Banks and Trust Companies Since the Passage of the National Bank Act,* National Monetary Commission, Sen. Doc. 639, 61st Cong. 3d Sess. (Washington, D.C.: 1911), p. 243.

[32]According to Chappell Cory, secretary of the Birmingham Trust and Savings Company, quoted in Francis M. Peurifoy, "Growth and Development of Trust Companies," *Banking Law Journal* (1904), p. 604.

[33]Barnett, op.cit., p.234.

[34]In the words of one trust company representative, "As the savings bank has become the depository for the funds of the 'provident poor' so the trust company may be said in a measure to have become the depository for the funds of the provident rich." Clark Williams, "Status of New York City Trust Companies," *Trust Companies* (1906), p. 4.

[35]As one established banker noted in protest, "The banks have been driven into paying interest by the trust companies doing a banking business. . . ." A. S. Frissell, "Trust Companies and Reserves," *Annals of the American Academy of Political and Social Science* (1908), p. 468. The refrain all through this era was of "unfair," "unethical" competition based on special favors granted the intruder (especially taxes and scope of business allowed). It was also felt that "It would be much more dignified to have uniform rates than to have the cut-throat business which many have been engaged in from the unseemly scramble for large deposits. . . ." E. Stanley, "Shall Trust Companies Charge for the Care of Small Accounts?" *Proceedings of American Bankers Association* (1910), p. 462.

[36]"It is in just this class of deposits [subject to withdrawal by check] that competition between banks and trust companies has been fiercest, involving conditions which cause conservative bankers the deepest concern. . . . All sorts of inducements are made to secure deposits, and instances are not rare in which business has been done actually at a loss rather than it should be permitted to pass to a competitor." "Trust Company Recommendations by State Bank Superintendent," *Trust Companies* (1906), p. 23.

[37]In the ironical language of the Superintendent of Banking of New York; in Kilburn, op. cit., p. 39.

[38]Charles A. Conant, "The Growth of Trust Companies," *Review of Reviews* (1902), p. 574.

[39]Barnett, op. cit., p. 18.

[40]The motivations in these affiliations were complex. The severe competition from the trust companies led to various kinds of efforts to ameliorate such behavior, and there is little doubt that the great number of affiliations built up in the decades around the turn of the century were developed with this in mind. In the words of one observer, "The growing tendency to interlink the interests of national banks and of trust companies through the directors of one serving on the board of the other is a most favorable element in cementing entirely harmonious and profitable

relations between both classes of institutions." "Affiliations Between National Bank and Trust Company Interests," *Trust Companies* (December 1906), p. 864.

[41]Control by no means proceeded in one direction only. Trust companies sometimes organized or acquired control of state or national banks. In 1906 W.G. Brown of the Hospital Trust Company of Rhode Island, a state in which trust companies far exceeded the national banks in resources, said: "I think I am safe in saying that with only a few exceptions the control of the national banks in Providence is lodged with the trust companies." *Proceedings of the American Bankers Association, Trust Company Section* (1906), p. 185.

[42]Brewer, op. cit., Chap. V, p. 23.

[43]Under the Trust Indenture Act of 1939, the issue and public sale of debt securities requires, with certain exceptions, the appointment of a trustee or trustees, one of which must be a bank or trust company.

[44]Dimner Beeber, "The Duties and Responsibilities of a Trust Company in Connection with Investments to be Offered to the Public," *Proceedings of the American Bankers Association* (1910), p. 458.

[45]In a recent illustrative case, First National City Bank was trustee under a bond indenture for bonds issued by Equity Funding Corporation and at the same time served as the lead bank in a revolving credit agreement with Equity Funding. A successor trustee, U.S. Trust, has sued First National City over a number of alleged sacrifices of the trust beneficiary interest to that of the bank's interest as lender. For example, the complaint states that "FNCB failed to accelerate the maturity of the debentures until May 1, 1973 in order to take the collection of quarterly interest for the quarter ending on December 31, 1972. . . . Had FNCB accelerated the maturity of the debentures at any time prior to May 1, 1973, FNCB would have been required under Section 613 of the Indenture to set the amount of the December 31, 1972 interest payment apart and hold it in a special account for the benefit of the Debenture-holders. . . ." *Complaint in case of United States Trust Company of New York* v. *First National City Bank,* Sup. Ct., N.Y. (undated), p. 19. Whatever the merits of this and other allegations in the complaint, it makes clear the potential conflict that can arise from simultaneously doing corporate trust and commercial business with a customer.

[46]Committee on Costs and Charges, *Guide to Trust Fees,* p. 31.

[47]"Employee benefit plan" is a large class of which pension plans are a major subcategory. For brevity we shall sometimes use the dominant sector, pension plan (or fund), as synonymous with the broader category.

[48]Computed from material in Board of Governors, FDIC, Comptroller, *Trust Assets of Insured Commercial Banks* (Washington, D.C.:1976).

[49]These matters are discussed in some detail in *Institutional Investor Study Report of the Securities and Exchange Commission,* House Doc. 92-64, 92 Cong., 1st Sess. (Washington, D.C.: March 10, 1971), vol. 2, p. 543 ff. This document is referred to below as "11S," with volume number and page.

[50]Ibid., pp. 548-549.

[51]See Barbara Patocka, "How Insurance Companies Are Fighting for the Pension Dollar," *Institutional Investor* (February 1974), p. 72.

[52]"Indeed, the banks' biggest advantage is the way corporations themselves are structured: If things go badly, the chief financial officer can always tell his board, or the union, 'Look, I gave responsibility to the Chase—how much more careful can you be than that?' " Everett Mattlin, "Prospecting the Hottest Investment Frontier," *Institutional Investor* (August 1971), p. 43.

[53]A 1970 internal memorandum of one major investment counseling firm, on the subject of the disposition of the pension plan of a major corporation, states:

I contacted Mr. [Jones], Treasurer, last week and learned that [corporation X's] Board has chosen two new money managers. We, as well as all other investment counseling firms, were excluded from consideration because we were unable to act as a Fiduciary. [X] chose two banks, each to share one half of the annual cash flow of [Y] million.

[54]The legal lists of securities encumbering the investments of bank trustees did not apply to pension fund accounts or to trust accounts that explicitly gave the banks freedom of action.

[55]Edna E. Ehrlich, "The Functions and Investment Policies of Personal Trust Departments," *Monthly Review*, Federal Reserve Bank of New York (October 1972), p. 265.

[56]Ibid. In 1971 the Bell system added eleven nonbank advisors to the more than fifty banks managing Bell pension money. But according to Julie Rohrer, the eleven new managers only had "well over $100 million"—out of a total of $8 billion. Julie Rohrer, "Everybody Wants to Split—But How Are They Going About It?" *Institutional Investor* (August 1971), p. 66 and passim.

[57]Ibid., pp. 65-71. Several years of inferior performance ranking for Chase Manhattan Bank's investment arm led to a reported loss of over $1 billion in pension fund accounts. See Steve Yahn and Julie Rohrer "Chase Investors Admit Huge Pension Account Loss," *Pensions and Investments* (January 14, 1974), p. 1.

[58]A sample of new accounts (by number, not asset volume) taken on by corporate pension fund managers in 1972 shows that only 24.2 percent were allocated to banks. "The New Pension Fund Managers: A Sampling," *Institutional Investor* (January 1974), pp. 99-100. Further bank losses to insurance companies and investment counseling firms in relative number of accounts seems to have taken place in 1975. See "Who Got the New Pension Accounts in 1975? And Who Lost Them,"*Institutional Investor* (December 1975), pp. 81-90.

[59]This point is stressed in Chris Welles, *The Last Days of the Club* (New York: E. P. Dutton, 1975), Chap. 9. The evidence does not show clear-cut performance differences either between banks and other manager types or by size of bank. A study by William G. Burns and Richard H. Klemm of thirty Bell funds managed by banks for the period 1968-72, plus comparable data for other manager types, concluded:

1. "All groups generally underperformed the market averages for the six-year period."
2. The banks underperformed the market in 1967-68, came close to it in 1969-70, and outperformed the market in 1971-72.
3. "The different characteristics normally attributed to the various classes of managers do not result in significantly different performance results;"
4. There was no substantial difference among the Bell thirty bank managers in performance based on size, although the range of variation in performance was greater for the large banks. William G. Burns and Richard H. Klemm, "Performance of Bank Managers of Trust Funds," Rodney L. White Center for Financial Research, Wharton School (n.d., mimeo), pp. 3-5.

[60]Neil B. Murphy, "A Cross-Sectional Analysis of the Cost of Operations of Trust Departments," *Journal of Money, Credit and Banking* (February 1969), p. 94. This pioneering effort was based on data of 1960-65, which may be obsolete in the light of the extensive computerization of trust department activities over the last decade. It also suffered from an inability or failure to separate out and analyze separately personal trust, employee benefit fund, and corporate trust accounts, even though a mix-of-accounts variable—personal trust accounts/total accounts—was included in Murphy's analysis and found to be statistically insignificant and erratic in sign (suggesting inadequate specification and control).

[61]Ibid., p. 93

[62]On the effect of the analogous variation in business loan size in making it difficult to compare the efficiency of large and small banks, see Jack M. Guttentag and Edward S. Herman, *Banking Structure and Performance* (New York: New York University Institute of Finance, 1967), pp. 109-114, 169-174.

[63]N. Gilbert Riddle, "Trust Investments: Their Extent and Some Related Economic Problems," *Law and Contemporary Problems* (Summer 1938), p. 343.

[64]Under the "prudent man rule" applicable to most bank-administered trusts, "In making investments the trustee is under a duty not only to exercise such care and skill as a man of ordinary prudence would exercise in dealing with his own property, but he must use the caution of one who has primarily in view the preservation of the estate entrusted to him, a caution which may be

greater than that of a prudent man dealing with his own property.'' Austin W. Scott, *The Law of Trusts* (Boston: Little, Brown, 1967), 3rd ed., vol. 2, pp. 1409-1410.

[65]The American Bankers Association's Statement of Principles of Trust Institutions affirmed in 1933 that the "trustee is primarily a conserver . . . ." (Article III, Section 3, and Article IV, Section 2.)

[66]James C. Cox, "Trust Investment Committees: Making Them More Effective," *Trusts and Estates* (August 1969), p. 803.

[67]Sec. 6(c), Regulation F, Revised effective June 1, 1936, *Federal Reserve Bulletin* (May 1936), p. 327.

[68]*Digest of Rulings of the Board of Governors of the Federal Reserve System,* from 1914 to October 1, 1937 (Washington, D.C.: 1938), p. 49.

[69]Richard P. Brown, "Trust Department Organization under Regulation 9," *Trusts and Estates* (December 1963), p. 1180.

[70]The caution engendered by the traditional conservatism militated against conflict, but the lack of incentive and pressure to perform worked in the opposite direction.

[71]"Money Management," transcript of First Annual Institutional Investor Conference, January 31-February 2, 1968 (Institutional Investor Systems, Inc., 1968), p. 151.

[72]Ibid., p. 153.

[73]H. W. Tripp, First National City Bank, in ibid., pp. 168-169.

[74]An approved list is a schedule of securities declared eligible for purchase by portfolio managers by the top officers of the trust department. These securities are usually followed by the research department and rated for quality and prospects on a weekly basis. Discretionary buying may be confined entirely to this list, but exceptions are usually made for experienced portfolio managers handling pension funds and other large accounts.

[75]*Bogeys* are essentially rules or instructions about percentages of particular stocks or (more often) classes of stocks that must be held in certain portfolios. Usually, they define the structure of portfolios for 60 percent or more of their total holdings.

[76]Heidi Fiske, "The Banks Fight Back," *Institutional Investor* (April 1972), pp. 41-48.

[77]H. Erich Heinemann, "Chase Planning New Unit for Investment Business," *The New York Times*, April 20, 1972.

[78]Fiske, op. cit., p. 43.

II. The Customer Relationship and the Bank Trust Department

[1]W. J. Kieferdorf, "Ideal Organization of Trust Department as to Personnel, Operations and Equipment," *Trust Companies* (October 1926), p. 419. The same point has, of course, been made in regard to other service departments. For example, "There is, we admit, little direct profit in the safe deposit department when run on a small scale, but the indirect profit of keeping your customer in the house may be considerable." William Carr, "The Advantages of Operating Safe Deposit Vaults in Connection with the Trust Company," *Proceedings of the American Bankers Association, Trust Company Section* (1900), p. 205. The SEC noted in 1977 that "according to Bank Study interviews some banks have been accepting DRP business from companies . . . [where] these plans are unprofitable for the banks, but the service is provided in an attempt to attract these corporate clients to subscribe to other services offered by the banks." *Initial Report on Bank Securities Activities*, (January 3, 1977), p. 29.

[2]John C. Mechem, "Trust Department Earnings: Adequate Fees and Practical Systems of Cost Accounting and Allocation" *Trust Companies* (July-December 1926), p. 400.

[3]Donald R. Hodgman, *Commercial Bank Loan and Investment Policy* (Champaign-Urbana: University of Illinois, 1963), pp. 97-102.

[4]*Trusts and Estates* (September 1962), p. 817. In a 1967 statement of the "six classical reasons" for the existence of a trust department, five are service functions, the sixth is that "*Sometimes,* it is a source of worthwhile earnings to the bank," Philip F. Searle, "Trust New Business Program," *Trusts and Estates* (December 1967), p. 1136.

[5]It may well be smaller than in the past for trust-oriented banks. The fusion process often reduced the importance of the trust business in total income generation, as specialist trust banks frequently became parts of larger entities that had little or no trust business before merger. A survey of the income sources of twenty-three trust companies in the mid-1920s showed an average of 20 percent of profits coming from the trust function for these institutions, better than double the values shown in the text here for 1972. J. G. Smith, "Survey of Market for Corporate Fiduciary Services," *Trust Companies* (January-June 1927), p. 329.

[6]Figures computed from "Trust Income of 100 Top Banks and Trust Companies," *American Banker* (June 25, 1973), with the blanks filled in on the basis of information obtained from the banks.

[7]There are several ways in which trust department contributions to bank earnings may be understated. First, according to several bank officers, bank accounting procedures may be biased against a division that is relatively unimportant and that provides a great deal of service to other parts of the bank. Capital and other overhead allocations may be too high, and the imputed value of the services provided may be too low. (Joseph Worty, an officer of the New Jersey National Bank, claims that trust department losses are "figments of accountants' imagination," with internal computer service charges per account running from $35 to $222, while available from the outside for $6 per account. ["Computer Overcharges Called Trust Loss Key," *American Banker* (October 19, 1976)].) Second, the trust department has always accepted a certain amount of business at relatively low prices in order to accommodate customers, with the expectation of compensating returns in other parts of the bank. The trust department typically does not receive credit for its share of earnings that show up elsewhere. Trust deposits held in the bank are an exception, although even in this case not all banks credit the trust department for trust deposits, and the rate at which credit is applied is often low.

[8]In nine interviews where the author was given an estimate of new trust business attributable to commercial customers, the range was between 30 and 80 percent, the median 50 percent. See also J. Harvie Wilkinson, "Don't Isolate Your Trust Department," *Trusts and Estates* (June 1960), p. 577.

[9]One important trust institution reported, "In October we instituted a new service known as Plan FOUR, which consists of an overall review and continuing surveillance of the personal financial affairs of groups of top executives of major corporations. Our compensation will be provided by the corporations themselves, which will offer our package of services as a valuable and, we believe, sought-after fringe benefit. We have all of the capabilities for this type of individual counseling within our organization today, and the value to us of the establishment of such working relationships with many of the leaders of American industry cannot be over-estimated." United States Trust Company of New York, *1969 Annual Report*, p. 5.

[10]*Potential* customers might also be attracted by assistance rendered through trust department acquisitions of their securities. One trust officer described to the author in some detail how a willingness of the trust department to take a large share of a big block that a major company was shopping around (to avoid depressing the market) led to the initiation of significant commercial business for the bank.

[11]This might also help the commercial arm of the bank directly if it had loans outstanding to the customer—an illustration of a serious potential conflict involved in a joint commercial and trust department involvement with a customer. This kind of help is not invariably regarded as unacceptable practice; for example, the First National Bank of Chicago in the Declaration of Trust for its Group Fund A for Pension and Profit Sharing Trusts includes the following language:

Section 6.3 Investments. No investment shall be deemed improper or imprudent merely because the Bank has participated in any way in the issuance, underwriting or original sale thereof, or because a part or all of the proceeds received by the issuer or seller are used or to be used to satisfy any obligation to the Bank.

[12]*Commercial Banks and Their Trust Activities: Emerging Influence on the American Economy,* Staff Report for the Subcommittee on Domestic Finance, House Committee on

Banking and Currency, 90th Cong., 2d Sess. (Washington, D.C.: 1968), 2 vols. This document is referred to below as "Patman Report," with volume number and page or chapter.

[13]For example, it can be seen by comparing columns 4 and 5 for the 5 to 10 percent owned row, that in 75 of the 152 combination cases the banks' sole voting holding still exceeded 5 percent.

[14]In two cases they had no voting power at all; in eighty-three cases they shared it with a cofiduciary; and four cases were combinations but with banks retaining sole voting rights over 5 percent or more of the stock.

[15]This percentage might fall further if complete information on closely held versus public companies were available for the other four banks.

[16]Patman Report, I, Chap. 3.

[17]See ibid., pp. 484-485.

[18]Ibid., p. 493. Continuing concern over the power position of the banks vis-à-vis the airlines has caused the Civil Aeronautics Board to announce the launching of a study of airlines' relationships with financial institutions holding "substantial amounts" of airline stock, debt, or leases of aircraft. See "CAB to Launch Lengthy Study of Influence Financial Firms Have Over Airline Policies," *The Wall Street Journal*, January 28, 1974.

[19]There is a fine line between control and influence, but the former clearly implies the power and authority to make the fundamental corporate decisions either directly, through representation in management, or indirectly, via recognized power to displace the management and associated authority to make key decisions whenever desired. *Influence* connotes a more restricted power, that may be confined to certain decision areas (e.g., a result of debt agreements) of a negative, veto character, or a power position less than decisive but sufficient to command attention, capable of constraining management in particular areas, or even constituting a regular part of the input of judgment to which the management gives weight. See A. A. Berle and Gardner Means, *The Modern Corporation and Private Property* (New York: Macmillan, 1932), pp. 69-90; Edward S. Herman, "Do Bankers Control Corporations?" *Monthly Review* (June 1973), p. 13 ff.

[20] *Report II of the Trust and Investment Division of Morgan Guaranty Trust Company* (May 1973), pp. 15-16. Morgan's trust asset total fell to $24 billion in 1973.

[21] In one bank with a large stock position and long-term relationship with a portfolio company, the author was informed that the bank, although not in control, had sufficient influence to get the company to buy its tires for delivery trucks from a particular tire manufacturer, who reciprocated by doing business with the bank.

[22]Despite some occasional rhetoric suggesting the contrary, the famous Chase deal with Resorts International for stock of Pan American does not appear to be a good illustration of commercial bank intervention in trust department affairs. This exchange appears to have been agreed to by officers of the Chase trust department for what they deemed to be a real profit advantage for some of their pension fund accounts. The theory that this deal was carried out for some larger strategic interest of the bank as a whole is not confirmed by any evidence in the Celler Committee hearings on conglomerates, and from the standpoint of these large interests, the deal was a major blunder. Pan American, a more important customer than Resorts International could hardly have been pleased at Chase's role. The companies whose pension fund assets were involved in the proposed transaction were not happy, although much of their displeasure was *ex post facto* and reflected adverse publicity and unforeseeable investment developments. In any event Street reports claimed that the trust department officials involved were called on the carpet precisely for their failure to clear such important transactions through the higher bank authorities.

[23]A good example by a scholarly bank control theorist is Jean-Marie Chevalier's *La structure financière de l'industrie amèricaine* (Paris: Cujas, 1970).

[24]In its investigation of pension funds, the IIS found that in the case of 232 of 253 bank-managed accounts, the employer made an effort to measure the performance of the plan manager. See vol. 3, p. 1008.

[25]Morgan Guaranty Trust, the bank with the largest volume of trust assets and many substantial holdings in individual companies, has an established reputation, exceedingly valuable to the bank, as a superior investment manager.

[26]Chevalier, op. cit., pp. 45, 211-212.

[27]*The Banking Reform Act of 1971*, Hearings before the House Banking and Currency Committee, 92nd Cong., 1st Sess., Pt. 2 (Washington, D.C.: 1971), p. 807.

[28]*Report III of the Trust and Investment Division of Morgan Guaranty Trust Company* (April 1974), p. 29.

[29]The clear primacy of investment considerations here does not rule out a possible marginal influence of control-type concerns, even in this instance. It should also be pointed out that primary or even exclusive emphasis on investment criteria would still not dispose of the control and influence issue: power may exist and be used when the banks possess it only as a side effect of investment-oriented decision-making. And it may add to power derived from other sources (such as creditor status).

[30]This does not, of course, rule out the possibility that control may be exercised in ways that fall outside the orbit of the law. Bank powers to withdraw credit, or to use restrictive covenants in loan agreements, are almost certainly more important control devices than stock investments or interlocks. But they are not questioned in the law as are stock acquisitions for control; they are intertwined with ordinary rights of a property holder to protect his property.

[31]*U.S.* v. *The Cleveland Trust Co.*, Civil No. C-70, 301, N.D. Ohio (March 26, 1970).

[32]The degree of involvement of the banks with Penn Central as creditors and trust department investors, such as it was, left them vulnerable to charges of misusing inside information and allowing commercial relationships to influence investment decision-making. See below, p. 58.

[33]The attempt by the management of Leasco to take over control of the Chemical Bank in 1969 not only created a furor but also produced a vigorous counterattack by the bank's management to ward off the threat. It is unreasonable to suppose that the managements of substantial industrial corporations would succumb more quietly. For a description of a process of active resistance by an industrial company to a real takeover effort by financial institutions, see *Bath Industries, Inc.* v. *Blot*, U.S.D.C. E.D. Wisconsin, No. 69-c-453 (November 3, 1969), CCH Federal Securities Law Reports #92,521.

[34]See below, pp. 72-79.

[35]Spelled out further in a review article of Chevalier, op. cit. above, n.23; *The Antitrust Bulletin* (Spring 1973); and E. S. Herman, "Do Bankers Control Corporations?" pp. 12-29.

[36]It was noted above in the text that in the case of the two large trust banks breaking out their closely held companies, only 15 of their 216 large holdings of over 10 percent were in publicly owned companies.

[37]A classic illustration of a large holding (20 percent) unable to acquire representation on a board, or any substantial influence, may be found in *Detroit Edison Co.* v. *Securities and Exchange Commission*, 119 F.2d 730 (1941), cert. den., 314 U.S. 618. More recently, Alleghany Corporation, with 30 percent of the voting stock of USM Corporation, but without control or dominant influence, decided to make a bid for control. Alleghany was rebuffed by the management of USM, and a flurry of charges, suits, and countercharges was followed by Alleghany's abandonment of its effort. The 30 percent holding had given it two directorships, but clearly nothing approaching control. See "USM Resists Alleghany's Advances," *Business Week* (June 15, 1974), pp. 35-36.

[38]Patman Report, I, p. 3.

[39]IIS, vol. 5, p. 2734.

[40]Ibid., pp. 2728-2729.

[41]Ibid., pp. 2742-2748. Property and liability and life insurance companies showed a statistically significant relationship between interlocks and loans/outstanding. Investment advisors showed no significant relationship (p. 2747).

[42]See Myles L. Mace, *Directors: Myth and Reality* (Boston: Harvard Graduate School of Business, 1971); E. S. Herman, "The Greening of the Board of Directors?" *The Quarterly Review of Economics and Business* (Autumn 1972).

[43]*Financial Markets*, Hearings on the Impact of Institutional Investors in the Stock Market, Subcommittee on Financial Markets, Senate Finance Committee, 93d Cong., 1st Sess. (Washington, D.C.: 1974), Appendix. Some of the limits reported were merely guidelines, not firm ceilings that could not be exceeded. The distribution of ceilings, so interpreted, was: no rule, 7

banks; 10 percent rule, 7 banks; 5 percent rule, 5 banks; 9 percent and 7 percent rules, 1 bank each. Several banks reported ceilings based on percentages of floating supply or trading volume of a security—one, for example, 10 percent of trading volume; another, 6 percent.

[44]Such rules would most obviously affect a trust bank with Morgan's huge asset total. As Morgan chairman, Ellmore C. Patterson, indicated in December 1973, ''a percentage limit on the aggregate holding of a given stock would mean that new customers of a trust department would be unable to have in their accounts any shares of stock in which the department's holding was already up to the limit.'' Speech before the annual meeting of the Savings Bank Association of New York State, quoted in *American Banker* (December 19, 1973), p. 8. This would not be a practical problem for most banks, even large ones, but it may well be for Morgan. Representatives of Morgan argue against ceilings on the ground that aggregates ignore the requirements, objectives, and constraints of individual accounts; that liquidity depends on special characteristics of the security, and so on; and that legal constraints and the competitive and fiduciary pressures on a trustee-manager make the control issue unreal. See *Financial Markets*, pp. 6-7.

[45]On Cleveland see the discussion of the role historically played in that city by the Cleveland Trust in Welles, *The Last Days of the Club*, Chap. 9; also ''When a Bank Holds the Purse Strings,'' *Business Week* (July 25, 1970), p. 54; Patman Report, I, pp. 631-653, 783-785. On Baltimore see the Patman Report, I, pp. 543-557. On Pittsburgh, ''Power and Progress in Pittsburgh—The Social Consequences of Image-Changing and Self-Interest in the Mellon Empire,'' *Transaction* (September-October 1965), p. 15 ff.; Patman Report, I, pp. 753-774.

[46]For a recent illustration apparently based on creditor position only, see Richard Leger, ''Taking Charge? Bank of America Moves to Direct Memorex; Company's Problems Viewed as Still Severe,'' *The Wall Street Journal*, March 27, 1973.

[47]*Financial Markets*, p. 15.

[48]The best-known illustration is the Chase financing of the merger-based growth of Gulf and Western. The information available indicates that this was largely or entirely a commercial bank—customer operation, with the trust department of Chase having little or no role in the process. See *Investigation of Conglomerate Corporations*, Staff Report of the Antitrust Subcommittee, House Committee on the Judiciary, 92d Cong., 2d Sess. (Washington, D.C.: 1971), pp. 166-212.

[49]Ibid., pp. 181-187. See also IIS, vol. 5, p. 2801.

[50]IIS, vol. 5, p. 2828.

[51]Ibid., pp. 2812-2814. See also ''Why the Big Traders Worry Industry,'' *Business Week* (June 25, 1970), p. 55.

[52]According to the IIS Questionnaire returns, 68 percent of bank trust departments participated in no other kind of management decision but that involving acquisitions. IIS, vol. 5, p. 2767.

[53]See the further discussion on this point below, p.76.

[54]Only 34 of 215 institutional investors responding to the IIS claimed to have participated in general corporate matters, and only 10 of the 34 believed that their interventions had some impact. IIS, vol. 5, pp. 2759, 2768. Only 2 of 9 intervening banks reported having an impact on portfolio companies.

[55]It should be noted that influence as described here excludes that which may come *ex ante* and by actual continuous contact with and participation in portfolio company affairs (as with a director representative). Bankers and portfolio company officers claim that this kind of influence is minimal, a claim supported in Mace's *Directors: Myth and Reality*, passim.

[56]For a good illustration, see the discussion of the suit carried out by Provident National Bank to block a bid by Pacific Power and Light to control Telephone Utilities, Inc., ''Pacific P & L Bid for Telephone Utilities, Inc., Is Target of Suit by Big Philadelphia Bank,'' *The Wall Street Journal*, May 7, 1973, p. 10.

Corporate managements also seem to regard institutional involvement as generally constructive. A 1970 study of three hundred listed companies carried out by Louis Harris for the American Stock Exchange disclosed that by a seven to one margin those whose stock was heavily owned by institutions regarded institutional involvement as ''constructive'' rather than ''destructive.'' The findings of this study are further summarized in Welles, *The Last Days of the Club*, Chap. 9.

[57]Harold H. Rockwell, "Ascertaining Cost as Basis of Fair Compensation for Trust Services," *Trust Companies* (September 1927), pp. 283-284.

[58]"[A] trustee, buying securities from its own institution, makes itself a guarantor of these securities." "Helps for Trust Officers," *American Bankers Association Journal* (1928), p. 890.

[59]See below, pp. 89-92.

[60]See *Central National Bank of Cleveland* v. *Mary Elizabeth Brewer et al.*, 220 North Eastern Reporter, 2nd, 846 (Ct. of Common Pleas, Ohio, 1966).

[61]See, for example, "When a Bank Holds the Purse Strings," *Business Week* (July 25, 1970), p. 54.

[62]See *Manchester* v. *Cleveland Trust Company*, 114 North Eastern Reporter, 2nd 242 (Court of Appeals, Ohio, 1953). A special problem arises when the trust department comes into possession of stock in the trust bank itself. In connection with two modest-sized banks, the author was informed by former bank officers that the controlling interest of the bank forced on the trust department a policy of hanging onto the bank's own stock to facilitate control by the dominant individuals.

[63]As in the struggle over the Denver *Post* between Helen Bonfils and others associated with the *Post*, and S. I. Newhouse. See *Rippey* v. *Denver United States National Bank, et al.*, U.S. District Ct., Colorado, Civ. No. 66-C-359, October 16, 1967; Patman Report, I, pp. 779-782.

[64]For property kept in the bank while estates are in process of settlement, and for real and personal property managed by the bank over extended time periods, abuses sometimes occur in the form of special charges or service fees. A former head of a small to medium-sized trust department described to the author a system of regular overcharging used in that department, in the form of service fees paid to the mortgage department of the bank for the collecting of rents and the purchase of mortgages.

[65]It may only be a coincidence, but the sharp increase in the use of private placements in the mid- and late-1950s paralleled a tightening of monetary policy and pressures on the availability of bank credit.

[66]Jack M. Guttentag and Hans R. Stoll, "Performance, Policy and Management of Pennsylvania Public School Employees' Retirement Fund," Fels Center of Government, University of Pennsylvania (February 1973), pp. 3-17. The differential does not appear to be accounted for by risk variations, according to the authors.

[67]Without full autonomy, responsibility, and a recognized obligation to pursue the best investment strategies for fiduciary accounts without any restraint, it is quite easy to conceive of overall investment decision-making being unimaginative and capable of rationalizing actions consistent with those desired by the main power elements in the bank.

[68]Even those trust officials who acknowledged to the author that they had sometimes yielded to pressure and provided accommodation loans at discount prices, almost without exception, claimed that the quality of the investment had to be good.

[69]The pressure in these cases comes from the founder company management, but the beneficiaries in whose interest the investment manager undertakes to manage are the employees covered by the plan. There is a tension here, and a conflict between the fiduciary obligations of the manager and the power of the founder company's management as customer and as organizer of the plan with power of removal.

[70]IIS, vol. 5, p. 2784.

[71]In connection with the abortive 1968 Northwest Industries effort to take over Goodrich, Goodrich's $200 million lines of credit were restructured so all credits would be in default upon a successful Northwest takeover. See Julie Rohrer, "Art Taylor of International Paper: The Investment Banker as Corporate Financial Officer," *Corporate Financing* (March-April 1972), pp. 28-29.

[72]IIS, vol. 5, pp. 2810-2811.

[73]The information employed was essentially deposit balances, lines of credit, loans, and EBP manager-founder relationships as of a single date. This was combined with information on institutions' shareholdings, personnel ties with portfolio companies, and various size and locational indices as a basis for regression analysis. Omitted were: (1) information on relationships at

other points of time than September 30, 1969; (2) measures of durability of relationship; (3) other business relationships than those explicitly included (e.g., foreign, custodial); (4) personal or familial relationships; (5) other qualitative measures of intensities of relationships; and (6) internal bank data (memos, letters) that might throw light on the policy bases of bank actions.

[74]*Know* means to have a relationship with the company of the type included in the analysis (for example, a director interlock or a line of credit).

[75]IIS, vol. 5, p. 2725.

[76]This data was made available to the author by the House Committee on Banking and Currency from their materials that went into the Patman Report.

[77]The customer list was made up from three sources: (1) primary affiliations of directors of the bank; (2) companies whose pension funds were managed by the bank; and (3) customers whose names were volunteered by interviewees associated with the bank.

[78]The data collected for the Patman Report unfortunately did not include the value of stock in portfolios, only the name of issue and number of shares. For bonds, par value figures were available.

[79]Ray F. Meyers, executive vice president of Continental Illinois, "Trust Departments Should be Integrated More Closely Rather than Separated," *American Banker* (February 15, 1974), p. 22.

[80]Mr. Meyers got the audit department to produce statistics without company names, which he says "illustrates how very carefully we preserve the 'wall' between the trust department and commercial department in our bank." Ibid., pp. 20, 22.

[81]Some further light is thrown on this matter in a later subsection where the distribution among these portfolios by client characteristics is discussed. See pp. 62-63.

[82]IIS, vol. 5, p. 2728.

[83]See *Air Line Pilots Association, International* v. *Continental Illinois National Bank and Trust Company* Civ. 73-C-772, Complaint filed in U.S. District Ct., Northern District of Illinois (March 27, 1973), p. 25 ff.

[84]Ibid., p. 33.

[85]The inside information issues raised here are discussed at length in the next chapter. The suit considered in the text is still pending. In May 1974 the District Court, denying a motion to dismiss, ruled that the allegations of nondisclosure of material information in contravention of Section 10b gave rise to a cause of action justifying a trial. The court also ordered that the ALPA suit be consolidated, for discovery purposes only, with similar suits brought against Continental by four other unions. At present jurisdictional aspects of the suit are being appealed to the U.S. Court of Appeals for the Seventh Circuit. Pretrial discovery was expected to begin about October 1974.

[86]*The Penn Central Failure and the Role of Financial Institutions*, Staff Report of House Committee on Banking and Currency, 92nd Cong., 1st Sess. (Washington, D.C.: 1972), p. 322.

[87]A few banks that follow a notification policy also claim to have established a thoroughgoing wall between trust and commercial departments, so the trust department would not even know who the bank's commercial customers are!

[88]The head of one small to medium-sized trust department informed the author that he had "drawers of accounts of $30,000 and under that he *never* looked at." In one sizable institution, the budgeted time for investment management (excluding administration and contacts) in the early 1970s was eight minutes per account per annum. *Active* management implies that the account will be attended to whenever investment facts call for reassessment or action; *review* implies a fixed schedule and usually infrequent reassessment of the components of an account. In some banks personal trust accounts are actively managed, or at least some of them are. In many banks they are actively managed in theory, but not, for the most part, in practice. Overall, for the majority of personal trust accounts a single review seems to be their sole period of systematic investment attention during the course of a year.

[89]IIS, vol. 2, p. 464.

[90]See further, Edward S. Herman and Carl F. Safanda, "Bank Trust Department Investment Services for Correspondent Banks,"*Indiana Law Journal* (Spring 1973), pp. 427-449.

[91]The question has also been raised whether major trust institutions can create performance for their entire set of portfolios by their enormous volume and resultant market price impact. This is an important issue, an extended discussion of which is beyond the scope of the present chapter. This writer's judgement, based on the limited evidence now available, is that the majors clearly can have a short-term impact on price, but they are probably incapable of maintaining price-earnings differentials not vindicated by real developments over the longer term. See Irwin Friend, Marshall Blume, and Jean Crockett, *Mutual Funds and Other Institutional Investors* (New York: McGraw-Hill, 1970), Chap. 5.

[92]There has been a long-standing problem in trust banks of bank *personnel* operating as "favored accounts" in their personal investment activity. A great many investment officers and employees trade and invest for their own accounts, and the temptations to move ahead of clients on the basis of prospective bank action must be severe. The major banks generally have rules barring, or requiring bank approval or at least disclosure of, personal trading in securities that the trust department is actively buying, selling, or in process of reevaluating, but enforcement machinery is lacking, and reports on changes in the holdings of trust employees are not ordinarily required. Serious abuses by bank personnel in their private investment operations are reported by trust officers to have occurred in several major banks in the 1960s, but hard information is unavailable, and the scope of this potentially important problem is obscure.

[93]A "weak" portfolio is one whose founder and/or beneficiaries tend to be less informed and less aggressive in following fund investment performance, and who are in a poorer bargaining position vis-à-vis the investment manager and hence less capable of exerting pressure on the manager.

[94]The complaint of the Department of Justice in the case involving Cleveland Trust cites as evidence that the bank's stockholdings are not solely for investment, the fact that "Cleveland Trust consistently exercises the voting rights to these shares of stock to elect directors, and to influence important management and policy decisions." Op. cit., above, n. 31, § 16.

[95]In early February 1974, Samuel Callaway, head of the Morgan trust department, testified before a Senate Finance subcommittee that he and his associates had been "actively exploring possible ways of divesting ourselves of voting rights with respect to stock we hold as trustee." This desire to get rid of "the burden of voting our trust holdings" was specifically related by Callaway to the desire to contradict the notion that "through our trust holdings, we somehow desire to control corporate managements." Quoted in *American Banker* (February 7, 1974), p. 1.

It may be noted that other large banks do not share Morgan's desire to rid themselves of the voting burden. Manufacturers Hanover Trust, for example, contends that "Since executors and trustees have the duty of safeguarding the investments they make and since voting is an important part of this process, shares should continue to be voted by executors and trustees in the best interests of their accounts." *Financial Markets*, p. 15. First National Bank of Chicago goes further, saying that it would be "improper" and a "questionable practice" to relinquish "an essential power needed for the protection of an investment, particularly where such power may be exercised incident to a proposed merger, acquisition or dissolution." Ibid., p. 18.

[96]IIS, vol. 5, p. 2751.

[97]In one such policy statement shown the author in 1971, it was stated that: "In the case of certain customer companies, maximum effort is given to turning in proxies for the largest number of shares possible."

[98]Official policies of voting uniformly with management are even more prevalent among other institutional investors (IIS, vol. 5, p. 2751), but as noted in the text below, the other investors do not have the legal constraint imposed on a trustee institution requiring it to vote stock in the interest of its fiduciary accounts. Furthermore, the differences in actual voting practices (as opposed to official policies) do not appear to be very great.

[99]Uniform Trusts Act, § 8, as quoted in Austin W. Scott, *The Law of Trusts* (Boston: Little, Brown, 1967), 3rd ed., vol. 3, § 193.3, p. 1603. The duties of a bank trustee in voting shares held in a fiduciary capacity were spelled out by the Committee on Trust Policies of the Trust Division of the American Bankers Association in 1944 as follows:

It should be the general policy of a trust institution to vote rather than not to vote the shares of stock it holds in trust accounts. If it does not vote the shares, it should have a satisfactory, positive reason for not voting . . . . A trust institution should have definite procedures as to voting shares of stock held in trust accounts . . . . A trust institution should not sign a proxy in blank. (Quoted in ibid., p. 1603, n. 4.)

In addition to legal vulnerability based on a failure to vote stock (and perhaps also where the trustee follows undeviating and official pro-management policies), liability would appear to be most likely where the trustee received some direct reward from a portfolio company for voting in accordance with the desires of the company's management. In this case liability could be founded on trust law prohibitions of self-dealing by a trustee, *Cleveland Trust Co.* v. *Eaton,* 11 Ohio Misc. 151, 229 NE2d 850, *rev'd,* 21 Ohio St. 2d 129, 256 NE2d 198 (1967); or on decisions prohibiting the sale of fiduciary office, *Rosenfeld* v. *Black,* 319 F. Supp. 891 (S.D.N.Y. 1970), *rev'd,* 445 F.2d 1337 (2d Cir. 1971). When the trustee receives indirect compensation for its votes, perhaps in the form of increased fees for other services, liability would probably be sustained on similar grounds. *Bryan* v. *Security Trust Co.,* 296 Ky. 95, 176 S.W. 2d 104 (1943).

There appears to be no case, however, that deals with the more important situations where the trustee's reward is not specifically allocable to a proxy vote but is implicit in a system of reciprocal business dealings or is an act necessary for *preserving* a business relationship. In principle this type of voting constitutes an instance of self-dealing by the fiduciary, but in the absence of specific proof of direct or indirect reward associated with a particular transaction (in this case a vote), courts have been reluctant to challenge established business practices on the basis of abstract principles of trust law. For example, courts frequently proclaim that trustees must not place themselves in a conflict-of-interest position, but seldom find liability where they do, in the absence of demonstrable harm. *Epworth Orphanage* v. *Long,* 207 S. Car. 384, 36 S.E. 2d (1945). At best, then, potential conflicts and implicit self-dealing may increase the degree of scrutiny by a court evaluating the ''fairness'' or ''reasonableness'' of a trustee's voting of proxies.

[100]Over a third of the negative votes by institutional investors, as reported in the Institutional Investor Study, were against proposals to abolish, reduce, or remove the preemptive rights of existing shareholders. IIS, vol. 5, p. 2754.

[101]See IIS, vol. 5, pp. 2750-2755. Stock options have fallen in relative importance as a source of institutional investor opposition to management proxy proposals as compared with the pre-1960 period; today, stock option proposals are likely to be opposed only in cases viewed as involving serious overreaching or where the institutional investor has other reasons for dissatisfaction with the management, which it manifests in this way.

[102]See above, pp. 61-62.

[103]More difficult, in fact, than the choices faced in many proxy contests. See, for example, the testimony of Barr, Wolfson, and Young in *Stock Market Study (Corporate Proxy Contests),* Hearings on S. 879 before a Subcommittee of Senate Banking and Currency Committee, 84th Cong., 1st Sess., Pt. 3 (Washington, D.C.: 1956), pp. 1332-1505. See also David Karr, *Fight for Control* (New York: Ballantine Books, 1956), pp. 148-151.

[104]A conservative conclusion might well be inferred from two principles of traditional trust law. First, ''it is the duty of a trustee in voting shares of stock to use proper care to promote the interest of the beneficiary.'' *Restatement of the Law, Trusts* (St. Paul, Minn.: American Law Institute Publishers, 1959), 2nd ed., vol. 1, § 193, p. 427. The ''interest'' of individual private trust beneficiaries would not appear to be enhanced by policies that promote the broad public welfare at the expense of the trust. Second, it is the duty of a trustee to make such investments as a ''prudent man'' would make, having in view the preservation of the estate (ibid., § 227, p. 530). The ''prudent man'' standard does not expressly include or exclude consideration of non-economic factors in making investment decisions. But it may be questioned whether or not a ''prudent man'' would invest—and retaining stock is investing—in a company that was about to

suffer an adverse economic impact and expect to "preserve" the trust fund. An examination of the cases dealing with voting by a fiduciary suggests that a fiduciary considering *only* economic factors in exercising a proxy will face little prospect of surcharge, absent willful default or supine negligence. Proof that a trustee has made an "honest exercise of business judgement" is generally the judicial standard that must be met. *In re Ebbet's Will*, 139 Misc. 250, 248 N.Y.S. 179 (1931); *In re Connor's Estate*, 153 N.Y.S.2d 185 (1956). For a negative view of efforts to stimulate corporate social activism, see Milton Friedman, "The Social Responsibility of Business Is to Increase Its Profits," *The New York Times Magazine*, (September 13, 1970). For a negative view of the practicality and prospects of corporate reformism, see E. S. Herman, "The Greening of the Board of Directors?" *Quarterly Review of Economics and Business* (Autumn, 1972); for a positive view of the corporate reform movement, see Donald E. Schwartz, "Towards New Corporate Goals: Co-Existence with Society," *Georgetown Law Review* (October 1971), pp. 57-109.

[105]For example, the dissatisfaction of large institutional investors was an important factor in the collapse of the Penn Life-National General merger. Manufacturers Hanover Trust reportedly sold 1.1 million shares of Penn Life, worth almost $17 million, in anticipation of an undesired merger with National General, which contributed substantially to a sharp decline in Penn Life's price. See "National General, Penn Life Merger Is Off, But Clouds Now Hang Over Both Companies," *The Wall Street Journal*, September 11, 1972, p. 34.

[106]Some bank trust departments use negative votes or abstentions as an indication of dissatisfaction with a management or engage in such antimanagement acts only when dissatisfied and when, presumably, sale of the stock looks more and more attractive.

[107]Ralph H. Spotts, "Voting Trusteed Stock," *Trusts and Estates* (February 1939), p. 206.

[108]An executive of one large trust institution says the three top officers personally know the top management of each of the principal companies in which the trust department invests heavily. This is an implementation of the bank's philosophy that confidence in and knowledge about management is crucial to sound investment.

[109]The quoted phrase is from a trust department policy statement shown the author in 1971.

[110]The evidence indicates that shareholders of target companies involved in uncontested as well as contested takeovers reap a substantial premium over the normal market price of their shares. As one commentator concluded, "The average premium over market currently being paid in noncontested mergers is approximately 21 percent . . .and there is a 25 percent premium in contested and exchange offers." John S. R. Shad, "The Financial Realities of Mergers," *Harvard Business Review* (November-December 1969), p. 146.

[111]Of 398 votes classified in the Institutional Investor Study, 73 involved proposed changes in an issue's articles of incorporation or by-laws that would increase the percentage of shareholder votes required to approve a merger or a sale of assets. IIS, vol. 5, p. 2754.

[112]An analysis of votes made contemporaneously by this institution on the same proxy issue—an 80 percent vote requirement—reveals:

Company	Approximate Number of Shares Held	Director Interlock	Commercial Customer	Vote
A	600	No	No	No
B	14,000	No	No	No
C	300	No	No	Abstain
D	4,000	No	No	No
E	140,000	Yes	Yes	Yes
F	700,000	Yes	Yes	Yes

III. Bank Trust Department Access to Inside Information

[1]The *Equity Funding* case is a good illustration of this, as a number of large investors friendly with the top management thought—incorrectly—that they had reliable inside information. See

Edward S. Herman, "Equity Funding, Inside Information, and the Regulators," *UCLA Law Review* (October 1973), pp. 4-5.

[2]A memorandum of May 9, 1966, signed by an officer of Chase Manhattan Bank, notes that an official of Gulf and Western, a Chase commercial customer, "agreed to keep us better informed concerning proposed mergers and acquisitions and important investments, i.e., notifying us prior to announcements in the newspapers." *Investigation of Conglomerate Corporations*, Staff Report of the Antitrust Subcommittee of the House Committee on the Judiciary, 92d Cong., 1st Sess. (Washington, D.C.: 1971), p. 198.

[3]In the case of Chase's foreknowledge of Gulf and Western's mergers, for example, a study by the staff of the Antitrust Subcommittee of thirteen mergers indicated that the price of the stock in the acquired companies went up on average about 29 percent during the month before the first press release announcing the merger. Ibid., p. 196.

[4]During the heyday of merger activity in the 1960s, a number of large trust banks were in continual possession of confidential information about active merger negotiations involving commercial customers. Several banks had a policy of suspending trading in these securities by the trust department during such intervals, which had the effect of quite frequently immobilizing the trust arm for some issue that it held.

It was also shown earlier that as the Penn Central debacle approached, the large trust banks were placed in a very awkward position with their sizable holdings of Penn Central stock in fiduciary portfolios, along with creditor relationships that periodically gave the bank privileged information. Proving that trust department sales were based strictly on publicly available information when inside information was flowing into the bank would not have been easy. See above, pp. 53-56.

[5]John W. Remington, "Trust Business of Tomorrow," *Trust Companies* (December 1938), p. 677.

[6]Quoted from a public release of the merging banks, in "Chase National Bank to Provide Superior Type of Trust Service Upon Consummation of Merger," *Trust Companies* (May 1930), p. 765.

[7]Affiliations Between National Bank and Trust Company Interests," *Trust Companies* (December 1906), p. 864.

[8]See, for example, *In re Pate's Estate*, 84 NYS 2d 853 (1948). The beneficiary knew some of the "insiders," and the trustee was justified in taking his opinion into consideration. "Indeed, it was the duty of the trustee to get as much information on the subject as it could." Ibid., p. 857. The test by which fiduciaries were judged was whether or not they had conscientiously taken advantage of all sources of information reasonably available to them. *Matter of McCafferty*, 147 Misc. 179, 208 (1933).

[9]*In re Clark's Will*, 257 N.Y. 132, 177 N.E. 397 (1931).

[10]Ibid., p.399.

[11]Material information is "information which in reasonable and objective contemplation might affect the value of the corporation's stock or securities . . . . It is information which, if known, would clearly affect 'investment judgement' . . .or which directly bears on the intrinsic value of a company's stock." *SEC* v. *Texas Gulf Sulphur Co.*, 258 F. Supp. 262, 280 (S.D.N.Y. 1966). A recent discussion of the "affect investment judgment" test of materiality added: "Among the factors to be considered in determining whether information is material . . .are the degree of its specificity, the extent to which it differs from information previously disseminated, and its reliability in light of its nature and source and the circumstances under which it was received." *Investors Management Co.*, Securities Exchange Act Release No. 9267 (July 29, 1971) CCH Fed. Sec. L. Rep. § 78, 163, p. 80, 519.

[12]*Cady, Roberts and Co.*, 40 SEC 907 (1961).

[13]*Investors Management Co., Inc.*, [Current Binder] CCH Fed. Sec. L. Rep. § 77, 832 (June 26, 1970), aff'd § 78, 163 (July 29, 1971).

[14]Also called the "Chinese wall," in obvious reference to the Great Wall completed by Ch'in Shih Huang Ti about 228 B.C. He built the wall to defend his northern borders, the side from which he was most frequently attacked. "It is the greatest and most monumental expression of the

absolute faith of the Chinese in walls.'' *Encyclopedia Britannica*, 1953 ed., vol. 5, p. 556.

[15]*Investors Management Co.*, above, n. 13, § 80, 522.

[16]The recent case of *Black* v. *Shearson, Hammill and Co.*, 266 Cal. App. 2d 362, 72 Cal. Rpt. 157 (Ct. App. 1968) is notable for its lack of sympathy with someone who has put himself in a conflict-of-interest situation. As the court stated: '' . . .we have been given no sufficient reason for permitting a person to avoid one fiduciary obligation by accepting another which conflicts with it . . . . The officer-director's conflict in duties is the classic problem encountered by one who serves two masters. It should not be resolved by weighing the conflicting duties, it should be avoided in advance . . .or terminated when it appears.'' Ibid., p. 161.

[17]The term *tippee* refers to one who, although unrelated to a corporation, receives inside information concerning it from another who *does* stand in a fiduciary relationship with the corporation. See Alan R. Bromberg, ''Tippee Risks and Liabilities,'' *The Review of Securities Regulation* (September 4, 1970), p. 875.

[18]See below, p. 89, and n. 48.

[19]See above, n. 13, above, p. 80, 522, n. 28.

[20]No.72 Civ. 4779, January 2, 1974; CCH Trade Reg. Service, §94, 329.

[21]*In re Merrill Lynch, Pierce, Fenner and Smith*, SEC Release No. 34-8459 (November 25, 1968).

[22]As indicated above, banks traditionally held out their commercial departments to be a special source of information. Today, trust department advertising continues to call attention to the bank's information-gathering skills in the investment area. A 1971 advertisement for the First National City Bank of New York uses the following language: ''Our research department knows how to harvest the most significant investment information. They keep on top of what's happening in the city. All around the country. In all fields of investment.'' *Institutional Investor* (August 1971), p. 25. Even more recently (1974), in soliciting subscriptions for its publication *Economic Week*, the same bank stated that ''For decades, First National City Bank has based billion-dollar decisions on confidential—and often highly sensitive—information relayed to it directly by its own worldwide financial and economic intelligence network.'' Letter signed by Leif H. Olsen, Senior Vice-President, undated but received in mid-1974, p. 1. Courts may hold an institutional trustee to its representations of superior investment knowledge. See for example, *Liberty Title and Trust Co.* v. *Plews*, 142 N.J. Eq. 493, 60 A.2d 630 (Ct. Ch. 1948). Where a wall obstructs the flow of relevant investment information and the trust beneficiaries have not been notified of this constraint, a court might find that the trustee has not made adequate disclosure.

[23]Quoted from the Chase wall rule, presented more fully in the text below.

[24]See above, no. 22.

[25]See, for example, *Albright* v. *Jefferson County Nat'l Bank*, 292 N.Y. 31, 53 N.E.2d 753 (1944); *In re Ryan's Will*, 291 N.Y. 376, 52 N.E. 2d 909 (1943). An exception to this rule may be made where the creator of the trust has placed the trustee in an obvious conflict-of-interest situation that was recognized and accepted at the time the trust was drawn. *In re Kellogg's Trust*, 35 Misc. 2d 541, 230 N.Y.S. 2d 836 (Sup. Ct. 1962). See also *Black* v. *Shearson, Hammill and Co.* discussed in note 16 above.

The rule suggested by these cases is obviously not predominant, otherwise potential conflicts of corporate trustees could not have become as extensive as they are, but it hovers in the background as a consideration that may be brought to bear in cases where beneficiaries are dissatisfied with the trustee's conduct. Although the rule would probably not be applied where trust beneficiaries could have profited by the use of confidential information that was held in the commercial department but not transmitted to or used by the trust department, it could well be considered pertinent where confidential information fails to pass through a wall constructed to circumvent potential conflicts of interest, or where corporate relationships influence the acquisition, sale, or nonsale of trust securities.

[26]The Comptroller of the Currency indicated recently that he may amend Regulation 9 to deny accesss of trust department personnel to commercial credit files and forbid their basing any decision upon nonpublic information, no matter what the source. Bureau of National Affairs,

News and Comment (February 6, 1974). Perhaps this would help extricate national banks from their legal dilemmas, but it would not guarantee that result. Such a rule would have a Canute-like quality in that it is quite beyond the enforcement capabilities of the comptroller. And as is noted below, the comptroller's own existing rules make the board of directors of a national bank responsible for the trust department as well as the bank as a whole.

[27]See James G. Smith, *The Development of Trust Companies in the United States* (New York: Holt, 1927), pp. 356, 364, 409; Philip F. Searle, "Trust New Business Program," *Trusts and Estates* (December 1967), p. 1133; E. Deane Kanaly, "The Bank Trust Department: Its Purposes and Their Achievement," *Trusts and Estates* (September 1969), p. 883.

[28]See, for example, J. Harvie Wilkinson, "Don't Isolate Your Trust Department," p. 577, in which one bank's program was described as follows: "A copy of every credit memorandum comes to our trust department, so that we are able to pick up the names of those good commercial customers who may otherwise have been overlooked by our lending officers." Officers of seven banks interviewed in the present study reported that credit information and reports of commercial officers are continually transferred to new business trust officers to facilitate contacts with potential clients.

[29]A fairly typical operation in one moderate-sized bank was described to the author as follows: New business officers are assigned to a number of group heads on the commercial side. They work with those heads to get them to stimulate the employees under them to get new business. There is a printed schedule of rewards for referrals that is applicable to either commercial officers or estate-planning officers. The estate-planning officers focus their efforts on establishing rapport with the group heads. There are also monthly sales meetings that bring together both commercial and trust department personnel, at which the estate-planning people get fifteen minutes in which they can report progress, prod, and instruct on the new business effort.

[30]See further, Edward S. Herman and Carl F. Safanda, "Bank Trust Department Investment Services for Correspondent Banks," pp. 435-437.

[31]*Investigation of Conglomerate Corporations*, Staff Report of Antitrust Subcommittee of the House Judiciary Committee, 92 Cong., 1st Sess. (Washington, D.C.: 1971), pp. 182-183.

[32]"All matters pertinent [to the operation and performance of the trust department], including determination of policies, the investment and disposition of property held in a fiduciary capacity, and the direction and review of the actions of all officers, employees and committees utilized by the bank in the exercise of its fiduciary powers, are the responsibility of the Board." Comptroller of the Currency of the United States, *Comptroller's Manual for Representatives in Trust* § 9.7 (n.d.).

[33]See, for example, New York Banking Law § 100-b (McKinney, 1971).

[34]Speaking at a panel discussion dealing with bank-related insider problems, Mr. Phillip Loomis, then General Counsel of the SEC, stated:

I was talking about this point to a banker—and it wasn't too small a bank. He said that he was often consulted by both the trust department and the commercial department, and that what he learned in one capacity he had to "forget" in the other, which struck me as something of a mental feat!

"The Loan Officer and Conflicts of Interest," *Journal of Commercial Bank Lending* (June 1969), p. 10.

[35]Statement of T. Richard Spoor, Vice-President, United States Trust Co., quoted in "Report on New Jersey Trust Conference," *Trusts and Estates* (January 1969), p. 56.

[36]Statement of Charles Buek, in "How the SEC Study Views Bank Trusts—and Vice Versa," *Finance* (May 1971), p. 40.

[37]Hearings on Leasco Data Processing Corp., before the Antitrust Subcommittee of the House Committee on the Judiciary, 91st Cong., 2d Sess., Pt. 2 (Washington, D.C.: 1969), pp. 148, 532.

[38]In one medium to large sized institution, the vice-chairman of the board was on a variety of trust department committees explicitly to "represent the interests of the bank" (according to one high bank official).

[39]*Investigation of Conglomerate Corporations*, op. cit., pp. 198-199. The policy statement quoted here is dated November 4, 1968, but it was still in effect, according to Chase officials, in 1974.

[40] The Conglomerate Study noted that despite the Chase allegations of a strict policy, "No mechanism for control of this information was demonstrated." Ibid., p. 198.

[41]*The Banking Reform Act of 1971*, Hearings before the House Committee on Banking and Currency on H.R. 5700, 92 Cong., 1st Sess., Pt. 2 (Washington, D.C.: 1971), p. 751. Mr. Rockefeller stated further: "I am not personally aware of a single instance where it [the wall rule] has been violated." Ibid. Given this lack of a single instance of violation, and the absence of any formal enforcement machinery, it is difficult to understand what Mr. Rockefeller meant by his statement that "This policy has been strictly enforced. . . ." (Ibid., p. 753.)

[42]Chase Manhattan Bank, Policy Guide, quoted in *Investigation of Conglomerate Corporations*, op. cit., pp. 198-199.

[43]Of 33 banks responding to questions concerning verbal communication between personnel in the commercial and trust departments, only 4 reported that commercial officers are not permitted to talk to trust department people at all. In the remaining 29 banks, although willingness to discuss investment matters varied, 19 reported that commercial officers readily communicate with trust department personnel.

[44]The problem of confidentiality rarely arises in connection with information originating with the trust department, so the flow from that department to the commercial department does not raise serious insider problems.

[45]*Investigation of Conglomerate Corporations*, op. cit., pp. 198-199.

[46]In a recent panel discussion before an audience of bankers, one banker-participant made the following statement:

In our shop the trust department officer can get the credit file only if he gets approval from the manager of the credit department. Just as a matter of interest, with a show of hands, how many people here work in banks where only the commercial banking officers can get to the credit files? In other words, where the trust department officers cannot get those files under any circumstances. [The show of hands was a little less than a majority of the audience.]

Statement of Mr. Duffy, quoted in "The Loan Officer and Conflicts of Interest," *Journal of Commercial Bank Lending* (June 1969), p. 10.

[47]Laura W. Rossman, "Bankers Ask Comptroller Role Defining Trust Access to In-House Information," *American Banker* (December 6, 1976).

[48]According to David Rockefeller, chairman of Chase Manhattan Bank: "To assure the proper use and control of information received by the bank in its several capacities, there is no flow, or incidental communication of inside information, from the commercial departments of divisions of the bank to the fiduciary investment department. . . ." Hearings on H.R. 5700, H.R. 3287, and H.R. 7440 before the House Committee on Banking and Currency, 92nd Cong., 1st Sess., Pt. 2 (Washington, D.C.: 1971), p. 751. In light of the text discussion above, it is submitted that the accuracy of such a statement is not only inherently doubtful but also beyond Mr. Rockefeller's or any similarly situated bank officer's capacity to know.

[49]Connecticut Bank and Trust's holding of 3.27 million shares of W.T. Grant Co. at the time of its bankruptcy, which has led to a suit by some of the beneficiaries, is explained, at least in part, by the fact that the bulk of this holding belonged to the Grant Foundation, which stopped selling "because its inside knowledge of what was happening at Grant made it impossible to continue." See *Business Week* (March 8, 1976), p. 63.

IV. Banker-Broker Reciprocity

[1]The increases in equities and turnover rate were partly a function of the rapid growth of pension fund assets under bank management.

[2]It was not an improper rebate under NYSE rules to require the executing broker to ''give up'' more than half of his commission to other brokers or to hold deposits with a bank as an explicit reward for the allocation of brokerage. A member firm could use its computer to value the customer portfolio in exchange for brokerage, but the member could not make its computer available to the customer for another use, such as preparing a payroll. IIS, vol. 4, p. 2273.

[3]When a fiduciary uses advantages arising out of a trust for its own benefit and profit, such use constitutes fraud and a fiduciary may be called to account for violation of duty. *Lonsdale* v. *Speyer*, 249 App. Div. 133, 291 N.Y.S. 495 (1965). See also, *Albright* v. *Jefferson County National Bank*, 292 N.Y. 31, 53 N.E. 2d 753 (1944); *In re Richardson's Will*, 149 Misc. 192, 266 N.Y.S. 388 (1928); *Osborn* v. *Bankers Trust Co.*, 168 Misc. 392, 5 N.Y.S. 2d 211 (1938); *In re Young's Estate*, 249 App. Div. 495, 293 N.Y.S. 97 (1937); *Wallace* v. *First Trust Co. of Albany*, 251 App. Div. 253, 295 N.Y.S. 769 (1937); *SEC* v. *Chenery Corp.*, 318 U.S. 80, 85-86 (1943).

[4]The direction of brokerage from the outside rarely has a functional relation to the welfare of account beneficiaries. This is true even when it is employed to reward brokers for services rendered the founder company, as distinguished from the pension fund itself, and it is more obvious when brokers are rewarded for handling the personal accounts of the high officers of the founder company. In one illustrative case of corporate direction that appears to be fairly common, a bank was obligated to direct $100,000 of commissions to a broker, a director of a public utility plan-founder company, who performed no services whatsoever to the bank or trust. This may have been a way in which the founder company compensated the director for services rendered to it (or to its officers). In this specific instance, there was evidence that the bank had to sacrifice best execution to meet its $100,000 directed target. In some cases brokerage diversion results from the fact that the director helped the bank land the account and received his brokerage *quid pro quo*.

[5]IIS, vol. 4, pp. 2184-2250.

[6]Ibid., p. 2252.

[7]As noted in the Preface, these interviews extended from 1969 through 1974. Direction of brokerage from the outside seems to have been on the decline during this period.

[8]The existence of outside direction also opens up avenues of abuse based on the lack of central control over brokerage allocations. It becomes possible when adequate controls are lacking for portfolio managers to direct brokerage according to their interests, telling the trader that this piece of brokerage is directed by prior arrangement to X, in fact, the manager's brother-in-law.

[9]For example, they have urged brokers to send them trust business, with an agreement to accept substantial direction to the broker from any referred clients. Or they have asked prospective pension fund customers who their favorite broker is, as part of a new business selling strategy.

[10]One major trust institution, for example, began a program of relative retrenchment after 1965, focusing its new business effort largely on investment advisory and pension accounts, encouraging splitting off parts of large accounts to other managers, and trying to eliminate unprofitable business. In addition, it got much tougher about accepting brokerage direction, insisting on no more than 50 percent direction even on pension fund accounts. Its proportion of directed brokerage declined from about 50 percent in 1967 to 30 percent in 1971.

[11]In 1969 the forty mutual fund complexes studied by the Institutional Investor Study had total assets of $24.9 billion, the entire mutual fund business had assets of $255.2 billion, including common stock amounting to $165.1 billion (over three and one-half times the $44.8 billion in mutual fund common stock). IIS, vol. 2, pp. 130-131, 152-153.

[12]The fifty-seven largest investment company complexes paid more than $275 million in commissions in 1968; the forty-six large trust departments providing the IIS data on this point produced $221 million in brokerage in the same year. IIS, vol. 2, pp. 2250-2252; vol. 4, pp. 2226-2229. The trust banks included here accounted for a little more than two-thirds of all bank

trust assets, probably a smaller proportion of industry assets than was accounted for by the fifty-seven largest fund complexes (37 percent versus 27 percent). IIS, vol. 2, p. 188.

[13]In 1969 the common stock holdings of bank trust departments averaged 65 percent of total assets, registered open end investment companies 82 percent. IIS, vol. 2, pp. 130-131, 150.

[14]The average turnover rates for registered investment companies in fund complexes in 1969 was 62.9 percent. There is no comparable single figure for bank trust departments, but the component with the highest turnover rate, pooled employee benefit funds, was 34.5 percent in 1969. The turnover rate for the largest component of trust assets, personal trusts and estates, was under 6 percent. IIS, vol. 2, pp. 192, 464.

[15]In 1969 the average share size of order executed on the NYSE by mutual funds was 3,726 compared with 493 shares for bank trust departments. The differential between mutual funds and banks actually increased between 1960 and 1969, with fund order size increasing by 577 percent, bank order size by 197 percent. The continued necessity of making many small orders for the numerous personal trusts and estates, of course, pulls down the average value of bank orders. IIS, vol. 4, p. 2169.

[16]A study done for the NYSE in 1970 showed that transactions of one thousand shares or more yielded profits of 42.2 percent and up. NERA, *Stock Brokerage Commissions; The Development and Application of Standards of Reasonableness for Public Rates* (July 1970), quoted in IIS, vol. 4, p. 2179.

[17]"Most NYSE member firms are willing to give up as much as 60 percent of the commissions on institutional orders to other member firms such as the institutional customer directs. And some of them make a special effort to attract such business by letting it be known that they stand ready to surrender 70 percent or even more of their commissions to any NYSE firm or firms designated by the customer." SEC, *Public Policy Implications of Investment Company Growth*, H. Rep. 2337 (Washington, D.C.: 1966), p. 170. See also, IIS, vol. 4, p. 2184.

[18]IIS, vol. 4, p. 2183. What are called "floor give-ups," where the broker executes the order but does not confirm it, are not included in these figures.

[19]See Wharton School, *A Study of Mutual Funds*, H. Rep. 2274 (Washington, D.C.: 1962), pp. 534-537; SEC, *Public Policy Implications of Investment Company Growth*, p. 15; IIS, vol. 4, p. 2283-2285.

[20]In the case of one major insurance company, for example, because of a lack of any alternative uses for brokerage commissions, "In 1968 these firms [providing research services to the insurance company] on the average received between five and six times the commissions they had been budgeted to receive." IIS, vol. 4, p. 2264.

[21]Ibid., p. 2184.

[22]And 21 percent of total share volume on the NYSE in 1969. Ibid., p. 2168. The commission volume of forty-seven large banks as a percentage of total commissions for the top fifty broker-dealers in 1968 was approximately 38.6 percent. Ibid., p. 2232.

[23]Ibid., p. 2280.

[24]Ibid.

[25]Ibid., p. 2281.

[26]In the case of one major bank, the decline in number of brokers from the recip era to 1973 was from 246 to 25; in a medium-sized midwestern institution, the decline reported by a former officer was from 186 to 60, with a further objective of reduction to 30.

[27]The broker's balance might, of course, be a working balance, but the marginal balance was often borrowed, sometimes from the bank in question.

[28]IIS, vol. 4, p. 2280.

[29]Ibid., vol. 2, p. 470.

[30]Ibid.

[31]In one small trust bank, which was persuaded to use 80 percent of trust brokerage for research allocations in the mid-1960s, a retreat to under 50 percent for research and over 50 percent for deposit recip occurred several years later upon the departure of the trust department leadership and a virtual abandonment of a serious trust effort by the bank's top management.

[32]IIS. vol. 4, p. 2263.

[33]Ibid., pp. 2266-2267.

[34]Ibid. vol. 2, pp. 241, 458.

[35]Unpublished memorandum on "Location of Trading by Institutions," dated July 10, 1970.

[36]This examination would constitute a major study in itself. Bankers claim that for really large blocks and for handling extended buy or sell programs running over many months, the OTC firms are not competitive with the large listed block houses—in terms of stock available, willingness to commit capital in positioning, institutional contacts, and even in reliability in handling the trade without generating costly counterspeculation (i.e., anticipatory buying or selling by outsiders aware of the large block interest of the institution). Of course, significant counterspeculation also arises from the responses of the institutions communicated with in the process of assembling large blocks.

[37]SEC, *Public Policy Implications of Investment Company Growth*, pp. 172-173.

[38]A major association, sometimes known as the Pension Group, was established in the late 1950s or early 1960s, and now comprises twenty large companies whose pension officers meet regularly to exchange information and discuss their joint interest and problems in the pension field.

[39]This demand comes more from the buyers of investment management services than from the suppliers. Pension fund founder companies frequently request that brokerage be directed to A. G. Becker or other firms for studies of the performance of this manager relative to its main competitors. The suppliers are less enamored of these comparisons.

[40]See above, pp. 34-35.

[41]*Common Trust Funds, Overlapping Responsibility and Conflict in Regulation*, Hearings before a Subcommittee of the House Committee on Government Operations, 88th Cong., 1st Sess. (Washington, D.C.: 1963), p. 12.

[42]*Report of the Special Study of Securities Markets of the Securities and Exchange Commission*, Part 2 (Washington, D.C.: 1963), pp. 659-661.

[43]Donald I. Baker. "Banking and Bigness—And the Search for a Better Tomorrow," Speech before the Federal Bar Association Convention September 17, 1970. (Mr. Baker was deputy director of Planning, Antitrust Division, Department of Justice.)

[44]These actions, filed in December 1970, were ultimately unsuccessful, not on their merits or demerits of the central arguments but because of judicial findings of an inappropriateness of their character as class action suits. See *Schaffner* v. *Chemical Bank*, No. 70 Civ. 5323 (MP), March 10, 1972, U.S. District Ct., S.D.N.Y.

[45]See further below, pp.118-120, 121-122.

[46]IIS, vol. 4, pp. 2167, 2169.

[47]Research could be used with relative ease as a cover for continued deposit reciprocity; questions could also be raised about why a professional manager with a larger research staff and deliberately undertaken fiduciary obligations to manage should have to rely on outside research support at all.

[48]Several trust department officials described to the author their use of these new developments in their struggle for brokerage control. They maintained clipping files and would send throughout the bank reprints of legal actions and pronouncements by Patman and Pomerantz that pointed to potential liability or legislative action arising out of lack of trust department autonomy.

[49]Some of the individuals involved and records of their transactions with the banks are outside the banks themselves and are not subject to their direct influence; and even within the bank, it would be almost impossible to impose a sufficiently comprehensive set of controls and dual records that would make a full-scale recip system beyond the discovery powers of an assiduous reporter, let alone a legal action that could employ a search of internal records and sworn testimony of witnesses.

[50]If total commission volume fell from $10 million to $5 million, while recip fell from 90 percent to zero, brokerage available to the trust department would have increased from $1 million to $5 million.

[51]This raises a question of how many buyers can simultaneously obtain effective top account status at a few firms. If the new demand is highly concentrated, the effect may be simply to raise the price of effective top status, maintaining a given level of distribution of research and enhancing the incomes of the top supplier firms.

[52]See Heidi S. Fiske, "Chase Manhattan's Paper Portfolio Derby," *Institutional Investor* (March 1970).

[53]The most well-known system of this type, installed by Bankers Trust, makes it explicit that the broker is expected to produce "return service" worth at least one and one-half times the commissions guaranteed. See Joseph Rosenberg, "Heard on the Street," *The Wall Street Journal*, August 24, 1973.

[54]Nancy Martin, "Soft Dollar Practices of Some Trust Departments May Be Reviewed in Light of SEC Warning," *American Banker* (April 20, 1976).

[55]See especially Leo Herzel, " 'Paying Up' on Stock Brokerage Commisssions Under Section 28(e) of the Securities Exchange Act of 1934," *The Business Lawyer* (April 1976), pp. 1479-1488.

V. Uninvested Trust Cash

[1]As expressed by George G. Bogert and George T. Bogert, *The Law of Trusts and Trustees* (St. Paul: West Publishing Co., 1960), 2nd ed., §543 (K), p. 551:

One of the main sources of its income as a bank is the loaning of the balances which are on deposit with it and the resultant receipt of interest. From the point of view of the stockholders of the bank it is desirable to secure the largest possible amount of deposits. As a trustee, on the other hand, the corporation should seek the safest place of deposit and the most advantageous terms (if the payment of interest on checking account balances is allowed). In its desire to maintain its deposits at a high figure, the bank may be tempted to leave trust funds on deposit for an unnecessarily long time or in an unprecedentedly large amount, where its duty as trustee would lead to investment of idle balances.

[2]The *ceteris paribus* encompasses, among other things, the possible adverse secondary effects that may well constrain the bank, such as legal and regulatory rules, customer resentment, and performance demands.

[3]*Albright* v. *Jefferson County National Bank*, 292 N.Y. 31, 53 N.E. 2d 753 (1944); *In re Hubbell's Will*, 302 N.Y. 246, 97 N.E. 2d 888 (1951).

[4]*Byran* v. *Security Trust Co.*, 296 Ky. 95, 176 S.W.. 2d 104 (1943).

[5]*Shanley's Estate* v. *Plews*, 142 N.J. Eq. 493, 60 A. 2d 630 (1948).

[6]Bogert and Bogert, op cit., pp. 551-552.

[7]Ibid., § 598, p. 336.

[8]Ibid., pp. 339-348. For example, in Massachusetts a 1935 statute (G.L. [Ter. Ed.] c. 172, 54A) explicitly allowed trust companies to hold trust assets in cash, if equivalent security collateral was maintained. In *New England Trust Company* v. *Triggs*, the court says that "The statute plainly was designed to qualify the rule . . .that it was a gross breach of duty for a trust company to deposit fiduciary funds in its commercial department. . . ." 135 N.E. 2d 541, 547 (1956).

[9]New York has no law requiring or inhibiting the payment of interest on uninvested cash for the bulk of bank trust accounts. For the minor segment of accounts held pursuant to court appointment, there is a statutory requirement of interest, but even for such accounts, the rule does not apply until the cash has been idle for sixty days. For sums of at least $1,000 held more than 60 days, interest must be paid at a rate of 1 percent per annum less than the discount rate on 90-day commercial paper at the Federal Reserve Bank of New York, but no less than 0.75 percent and no

more than such rate as the State Banking Board may prescribe or, if no rate had been prescribed, the maximum rate payable on savings deposits. New York Banking Law § 100-b (4), as amended June 4, 1974, L. 1974, c.768. The only case law applicable to the main body of trust accounts (non-court-appointed) holds that the trustee is *not* obliged to allow a "fair rate of return" on trust cash balances, but only "the rate of interest customarily paid by banks on similar types of deposit." This provides no criteria for evaluating the type of deposit chosen by the trust institution. If the commercial banks customarily place trust account cash in demand deposits, where no interest is customarily paid, this would appear to meet the legal standard. See *Application of Harris*, 146 N.Y.S.. 2d 730, 735, 286 App. Div. 794, 798 (1st Dept. 1955), *aff'd sub nom Matter of Ferris*, 3 N.Y. 2d 70, 143 N.E. 2d 505 (1957).

In Illinois both a trust officer interviewed and a state reguatory official interpret applicable law (Ill. S.H.A., Chap. 32, § 290) as neither requiring nor inhibiting the payment of interest on uninvested trust cash. Interestingly, although the state's Probate Act makes guardians or conservators chargeable with 5 percent interest on cash that is wrongfully or negligently held uninvested (Ill. S.H.A., Chap. 3 § 258), it contains no comparable sanction against administrators or executors.

[10]See Bogert and Bogert, op. cit., § 7, pp. 25-26. The Uniform Trust Act requires that in the absence of contrary state law, a bank must pay on uninvested trust cash "the same rate of interest it pays on similar non-trust deposits" (Sec. 4.). Two of the five adopting states have deleted the interest provision. In one, Oklahoma, the code simply fails to mention interest; in the second, North Carolina, the code *requires* that uninvested trust funds be "promptly invested, distributed or deposited . . . . as a demand deposit in the commercial department of the bank or another bank or in savings accounts in the bank or another bank . . ." N.C.G.S. § 36-27 (1966), amending § 36-27, c.197, s.4 (1939); 60 Okla. St. Ann. § 175.10 (1971). Until a 1963 amendment to the North Carolina statute, *only* demand deposits were permissible.

New Mexico, Nevada, and South Dakota have adopted the Uniform Act, including the interest requirement, but no cases have arisen under them. A New Mexico trust officer reports that the practice there is to use own-bank savings accounts for uninvested cash, except in cases where the cash is to be held for a short time (no longer than one or two weeks), in which case demand deposits are used as a matter of administrative convenience.

[11]*Proceedings of the American Bankers Association, Trust Company Section* (1907), p. 300. Emphasis added.

[12]*Report III of the Trust and Investment Division of Morgan Guaranty Trust Company* (April 1974), p. 29.

[13]These were based on bank application of an earnings figure to trust department deposits averaging 5.16 percent in 1972. The meaning and significance of these figures depend, of course, on the validity of the accounting principles employed by the bank in allocating overhead, capital, and other costs and revenues that must be imputed to the trust and other departments.

[14]Banks pay for securities only upon delivery, but most of them debit the deposits of accounts purchasing securities at the normal settlement date, which may be before delivery (and payment). The result is resources available to the banks that do not show up in the deposit accounts, so-called float. In the period when "fails" on security delivery were frequent, float balances could be large. This was true for the period studied by the IIS: three banks providing information on this point reported float balances of 10 percent, 10 percent, and 40 percent. IIS, vol. 2, p. 481. But float exists and may be substantial quite apart from "fails," based on ordinary collection lags.

[15]With float included, the IIS estimate was that trust department cash provided a return to the banks of approximately 30 percent of direct trust revenues. Ibid., pp. 481-482.

[16]Federal Reserve Bank of New York, "Survey of Earnings and Expenses of Trust Departments in New York, New Jersey, and Fairfield County, Connecticut in 1969," Table III.

[17]The huge percentage holdings of cash by the small trust departments shown in table 7 are certainly suspiciously high.

[18]See "Time Deposit of Trust Funds in Member Bank's Own Banking Department," *Federal Reserve Bulletin* (January 1950), p. 44. Trust department officers in several small banks

informed the author that this reclassification option had been called to their attention by the regulators and a chief examiner in a major Federal Reserve district acknowledged that encouragement of this practice has been a deliberate policy.

[19]Comptroller of the Currency, *Comptroller's Manual for Representatives in Trust*, (n.d.), p. 33.

[20]"Even though fiduciary funds are deposited in the bank's commercial savings or other department, it is a breach of trust for the bank negligently or otherwise improperly to withhold investment or distribution. If a bank is endeavoring to increase aggregate deposits by this means, it is committing a serious breach of trust and examiners should be alert to the possibility of such practices." Ibid., p. 80.

[21]See above, n.9 and 10.

[22]See further below in this chapter the discussion of regulation of uninvested cash.

[23]*Braman* v. *Central Hanover Bank and Trust Co.*, 47 A. 2d 10, 25 (1946). In Pennsylvania, although case law has established that the trustee must abide by a reasonableness standard, in the two cases that deal explicitly with this issue, in one five-year period and in the other a twenty-year period were deemed to be unreasonable spans of time for corporate trustees to utilize trust funds in their commercial departments without benefit to the trust estate! *Jones Estate*, 400 Pa. 545, 558-9 (1960); *Lare Estate*, 436 Pa. 1, 10 (1969).

[24]Some but not all banks distinguish between "accumulating" personal trust accounts—that is, those in which dividends and interest income are added to the trust corpus rather than being paid out—from other accounts, and treat cash in these in a manner paralleling principal cash.

[25]In addition to legal uncertainties, there are other obstacles to the use of pooled funds containing short-term liquid earning assets for the benefit of personal trust accounts. New York law, for example, places a number of obstructions in the way of bank investment of personal trust cash in common funds, including the requirement of maintenance of a register showing the details of holdings of each trust in the CTF (General Regulation, 22.31), and participations only upon written request with five days notice (22.50).

[26]Bogert and Bogert, op. cit., § 598, p. 344. See further, n. 9, above.

[27]Martin E. Lybecker reports that one trust department was using eight thousand separate passbook savings accounts for its trust customers. "Regulation of Bank Trust Department Investment Activites: Seven Gaps, Eight Remedies," *Banking Law Journal* (January 1974), p. 931.

[28]Variable notes, sometimes called Master Notes, are bought and sold daily from large outside borrowers. They are discussed further in the text below.

[29]"The general rule of the trust committee is, because we can't predict the market, and in order to safeguard the remainder interests in the event of a declining market—that is a reason for converting the assets to cash." Quoted in *New England Trust Company* v. *Triggs*, 135 N.E. 3d 541, 548 (1956). The trust company was surcharged in this case for holding over $100,000 of a $165,000 corpus uninvested, and in the trustee bank's demand deposits, for a longer period than could be warranted by reasonable prudence.

[30]There are some that may be traced back quite a few years, but for most banks using them, they are a recent development. See Lybecker, op cit., pp. 929-931.

[31]A disadvantage of Master Notes cited by Northern Trust Bank of Chicago has been that "in order to achieve diversification, multiple notes had to be purchased for the same account." "Cash Management and the Short Term Investment Fund," Statement for the Comptroller of the Currency (n.d.), p. 2.

[32]By 1968 Northern Trust was using twelve Master Notes, and "the time required to sort out the sell transactions to determine the available capacity, apportion the buy transactions into the available notes, reject excessive buys and find other outlets for them, and confirm loan balances" involved administrative strains. James R. Haring, "A Common Trust Fund for Managing Short-Term Cash," *Trust and Estates* (May 1974), p. 301.

[33]According to the Northern Trust statement to the comptroller, "as money became more available [after the 1969 credit crunch] corporations moved to dress up their balance sheets with

more permanent financing. Two of our issuers terminated their relationship and two others cut back their limits, At the same time our business was growing and demand for this ideal instrument was increasing. We were forced to ration its use by the nature of the cash requirement and place our largest accounts in less desirable fixed maturity instruments.'' Op. cit., n. 31, p.2.

[34]This 10 percent rule was put into the form of a proposal amendment to the regulations, dated December 17, 1976. The proposal has been defended by the deputy comptroller in charge of trusts on grounds of congressional policy, diversification needs, and the possibility that banks may be putting too much of their Master Notes into issues of commercial customers. (''C of C to Limit Size Of Trust Dept. Notes,'' *American Banker* [November 15, 1976].) The congressional limit, however, applies to the use of bank money, whereas Master Note lending is for the account of many fiduciary customers. If bank trust departments are lending excessively on notes of commercial customers, it is a very serious matter that would seem to call for a less oblique attack than a 10 percent of capital ceiling; it would suggest the need for a direct limit on the use of Master Notes with interlocking companies, or ceilings, collateral, or very high-quality requirements applicable to customer notes.

[35]David C. Tyson, ''Money Market Fund Builds $16 Million Assets in First Three Weeks,'' *American Banker* (November 1, 1973).

[36]These conditions included ''specific authority in state statutes or decisions.'' Since in roughly half the states there was no explicit statutory authority to buy investment company securities, merely a ''prudent man'' rule, for half the states investment by small trust departments in money market funds was put under a legal cloud. A clarification issued by the Comptroller in September 1976 relaxed this constraint by suggesting that mutual fund investments might be permissible if implied rather than explicitly stated by state law or judicial opinion. (''Comptroller Relaxes Curb on Mutual Fund Investment by Banks,'' *American Banker* [October 2, 1976].)

[37]The ''investment'' involved here is limited to the disposition of cash assets. The alternative ''investment decision'' might well be simply holding fiduciary assets in the form of bank-held cash. The regulatory authority is making it difficult for small trust departments to compensate for their diseconomies of small scale, but at the same time is giving them a temporary windfall at the expense of the fiduciary accounts.

[38]Which may circumscribe choices to, say, local savings and loan associations, savings deposits in the bank itself, and so on. Or these smaller sums may just enter general trust demand deposits of the bank.

[39]Heidi Fiske, ''John McIntyre: Portrait of the Commercial Banker as a Trust Chief,'' *Institutional Investor* (April 1972), P. 128.

[40]Ibid.

[41]Information provided by interview.

[42]It is a small irony that several of these pools have had to be terminated as a result of a 1972 ruling of the comptroller that required frequent and regular valuations of internal funds with assets in excess of $100,000. This was very difficult in the case of mortgage pools containing several hundred or even thousands of mortgages. Despite the clear service and benefits of such funds to the fiduciary accounts, the comptroller refused to give them an exception from this rule, even where a substantial reserve fund had been established by the bank.

[43]It is an impressive fact that John McIntyre of Citizens and Southern found the greatest opportunities for reductions in trust cash in the personal trust area. Citizens and Southern makes little distinction between income and principal cash as is consistent with trust agreements, and interprets any limitations on ''investing'' income cash as compatible with placing them in short-term quality money market instruments.

[44]The fact that Northern Trust should have pioneered in the development of a sophisticated cash management system is also of interest here. It is not one of the top dozen in trust income or assets, but its trust department is relatively large in the total business of the bank and was even more so in the past. Several bank officers have suggested this is an explanatory factor in Northern Trust's more energetic pursuit of the matter than their own bank.

[45]As noted this is justified in part by the higher cost of bringing such services to smaller accounts.

[46]It is also argued that legal ceilings on fees *necessitate* this indirect form of taking rewards. This neglects the fact that in most cases banks have the legal remedy of resigning from a trust that involves them in true losses to their own stockholders.

[47]In this case, also, the authorities take a rather cavalier attitude toward the "wall," advising the bank on how to improve its reserve position, and in general treating the wall as nonexistent.

[48]One chief examiner, rather indignant at the question of whether or not it would be legal for the bank to pay interest on trust deposits now classed as time but given no interest, replied that "the question has not arisen."

[49]See above, pp.34-36.

[50]The two instances reported to the author in some detail involved reciprocal dealings with savings and loan associations. It should be pointed out that the choice of issuer under Master Note Plans may involve some reciprocity—customer relationships of interest. There has been a definite tendency to choose as Master Note participants issuers having other relationships with the banks. Unfortunately, it has not been possible to deal with this matter here.

[51]IIS, vol. 2, p. 476.

[52]Ibid., pp. 476-77.

[53]Technimetrics, Inc., "Facts on 180 Major Pensions Fund Managers" (n.d.), p. 3.

[54]See above, pp. 34-36.

[55]See "Memorandum Re: Bank Reciprocity and the Prohibition of Interest Payments on Demand Deposits—Institutional Investor Study Report Follow-Up" (unpublished memo, 1971), p. 17.

[56]The rush of the larger banks into bank holding companies and into the nonbanking activities permitted these organizations has sometimes been explained as a consequence of the pressure of rising costs of time money. See, for example, John R. Bunting, Jr., "One-Bank Holding Companies: A Banker's View," *Harvard Business Review* (May-June 1969), p. 100.

[57]See Albert H. Cox, Jr., *Regulation of Interest Rates on Bank Deposits* (Ann Arbor: University of Michigan, 1966), Chaps. 1-2.

[58]In the mid-1920s, for example, it was a common view that:

Even allowing for the patient novitiate stage it is no secret that many trust departments are operated at a loss. Numerous trust companies and banks justify trust departments mainly as "feeders" or as adjuncts to the other departments for competitive reasons. A large volume of trust assets is in fact liability.

Unsigned editorial in *Trust Companies* (July 1925), p. 128.

[59]See above, n. 2.

[60]Lybecker, op. cit., p. 933.

[61]This was the phrase employed by one chief examiner in charge of trust examinations in 1970 to describe the function of examinations. See also below, n. 65.

[62]The "perhaps" suggests that the comptroller's office was still not quite prepared to admit the use of recip in prior years.

[63]In at least a dozen interviews in 1970, the author was told that deposit buying was still a major factor in the allocation of brokerage. One can only assume that the examiners used a familiar and unrewarding procedure of asking high officers of banks whether they were allocating brokerage for deposits and took the negative replies at face value.

[64]The reports by several small banks, mentioned earlier, that regulators had instructed them on the possibilities of reducing reserve requirements via reclassification of some part of general deposits to noninterest-bearing time accounts fits into the same pattern.

[65]The main thrust of examinations of trust departments has been establishing that records, procedures, and lines of authority are "sound and adequate to protect the institution against unusual probable liabilities" (quoting from the Federal Reserve's Trust Department Check List for Examiners). With respect to cash, the main item on the checklist, under Investment

Procedures, is formalistic: "Do procedures provide for appropriate attention to:...(9) Uninvested cash."

Similarly, the FDIC's only formal requirement governing trust departments of nonmember insured banks is that the boards of these banks adopt a "Statement of Principles of Trust Department Management." According to Frank Wille, chairman of the FDIC, "One of the main purposes is to determine if any contingent liabilities, potential losses, or estimated losses have developed from fiduciary activities." Letter to Congressman Wright Patman, November 20, 1972.

[66]Fewer than a dozen in ten years, according to a statement made to the author in 1970 by the deputy comptroller in charge of trusts.

VI. Conclusions

[1]See above, p. 58 and n. 67.

[2]See above, pp. 70-72.

[3]See above, pp. 38-39, 40-43, 65-66, and passim.

[4]See above, pp. 50-52.

[5]See above, pp. 63-66.

[6]In a number of cases, small clients alleging abuse have claimed difficulty in locating qualified legal counsel willing to enter into a contest with a powerful local bank.

[7]See the positive proposals discussed briefly toward the end of this chapter.

[8]According to Dean Miller, deputy comptroller in charge of trusts, "At times, trust department supervision has been in the position of the poor relation, with the priorities for assigning personnel, scheduling examinations, and determining corrective actions in trust departments extremely low and with the incidence of original and innovative thought virtually absent ....[Early examinations] physically verified the assets and checked the accuracy of the book-keeping systems, using forms adapted from the commercial examining function." According to Mr. Miller, new priorities and an orientation toward fiduciary principles in the broader sense have now been adopted, especially since 1962. Speech before the American Bankers Association, July 22, 1970, reprinted in *Annual Report of the Comptroller of the Currency for 1970*, pp. 264-265.

[9]See above, p. 119 and n. 65. In a speech given at the Southeastern Trust School in 1971, the deputy comptroller in charge of trusts noted that examinations "correct matters of criticism in a manner calculated not to jeopardize the confidentiality of the customer's property, or the soundness of the bank." He went on to express opposition to "a system of supervision based principally upon disclosure," consistent with the bank-protective philosophy deeply imbedded in trust regulations. Quoted in *American Banker* (July 7, 1971), p. 4.

[10]In the comptroller's *Annual Report for 1955*, written at a time when regulatory attention to the trust function was mechanical and slight, it is nonetheless stated that "All national banks which are exercising fiduciary powers are endeavoring to supervise and administer their trust departments in full accordance with the provisions of law and sound fiduciary practice. The interests of the various beneficiaries are given prime consideration..." (p. 29). How the comptroller's office knew this to be true for each and every one of the 1,480 national banks serving as fiduciaries is not stated.

[11]See below, pp. 127-128.

[12]See above, pp. 43-56.

[13]In a number of jurisdictions, the trust function is confined to banks because of their apparent financial solidity. Trust agreements are written with a specific bank as trustee and, if that bank can no longer serve, provide that a new trustee will be sought. The legal problems in separation are real, but they are not insoluble.

[14]The existence of forty-nine nondeposit trust companies suggests that splitting off a trust department from a commercial bank would leave the trust department as a viable entity. An

examination of the existing nondeposit trust companies, however, reveals that few are primarily in the business of offering fiduciary services to the public. Some of them are in, or have evolved out of, the business of managing the wealth of one family or operating as custodian to a title insurer or mutual fund. Those independent nondeposit trust companies that are conducting a public fiduciary business find themselves at a competitive disadvantage in vital areas such as generating new business leads and meeting the rates charged by other fiduciaries for comparable services. Few of the trust companies unaffiliated with a commercial bank are prospering. It should be noted, however, that nondeposit trust companies *would* certainly prosper if a bank affiliation to the trust business was generally terminated by law.

[15]*Report of the President's Commission on Financial Structure and Regulation* (Washington, D.C.: December 1971), pp. 101-109.

[16]See above, p. 34 and n. 51.

[17]The competitive value of such entry is suggested by the fact that "Banks have vigorously resisted the granting of even limited trustee powers to nonbank institutions as being inconsistent with the specialized nature and responsibilities of trusteeship." American Bankers Association, *The Commercial Banking Industry* (Englewood Cliffs, N.J.: Prentice-Hall, 1962), p. 313.

[18]See above, pp. 56-57.

[19]"Throwing Out The Baby . . .Is Little David Taking Unfair Advantage of Goliath?" *Forbes* (April 15, 1974), p. 59.

[20]Federal class action suits could be brought in federal courts on the basis of state law, however, only if there is "diversity of [state] citizenship" between the parties, which is to say that a New York beneficiary would not be "diverse" from a bank operating entirely or mainly in New York. There are some potential federal bases for class action suits that would hurdle or reduce jurisdictional obstacles, but, few efforts having been made along this line, the status of actions is uncertain. See 28 U.S.C. § 1337 for a jurisdictional basis in which the "citizenship" of the parties is irrelevant and a minimum jurisdictional amount is not required; see also *Moore's Federal Practice*, vol. 7B, p. JC-517 (1973); *Burns* v. *American National Bank*, 479 F.2d 27 (8th C.A. 1973), allowing a class suit under § 1337 to recover allegedly usurious interest charges on loans, although the ony federal statutory requirement involved was that national banks could not charge more than rates permitted by the relevant state law.

[21]*Snyder* v. *Harris*, 394 U.S. 332 (1969).

[22]*Schaffner* v. *Chemical Bank, et al.*, No. 70 Civ. 5323 (M.P.), March 10, 1972 (USDC, SDNY).

[23]By a strange turn of logic, the court argues in *Schaffner* that a class action on the reciprocity question would have involved "a colossal marshalling of judicial resources," but that "no especial disadvantage to an injured individual from use of traditional means [an individual accounting and suit] seems apparent . . . ." Given the certain economies of scale in marshalling evidence on a collective basis, the relative cost to individual and bank should be even more colossal, and the inducement to the individual to proceed against the bank should be nil. If a class action could not have been sustained on the reciprocity issue, it seems unlikely that it could be employed successfully on other matters relevant to small trust accounts. The *Schaffner* decision may have been affected, however, by the fact that the plaintiff had an account in which the brokerage was entirely directed from outside the bank from the inception of the trust agreement and had no valid interest in the bank reciprocity issue.

[24]For example, where there are different categories of advisory clients receiving mail versus immediate phone notification of changes in ratings, these should be made very explicit. See further, Edward S. Herman and Carl F. Safanda, "Bank Trust Department Investment Services for Correspondent Banks," *Indiana Law Journal* (Spring 1973), pp. 437-449.

[25]An illustration of a meaningless piece of information is the figure given in the 1971 annual reports of several of the larger trust banks on the number of anti-management votes made during the previous year. Morgan did not include such information in its 1972 report, but in its report dated May 1972, Morgan states that "Last year there were eight instances in which we judged the best interests of our clients or beneficiaries to be served by voting against the recommendation of

management; the year before there were 14 such cases.'' But it is nowhere stated how many votes were made by the bank, or how many contested votes, and no other base value was given that would make such figures meaningful. It appears that as recently as 1967 the same bank did not vote against management in any instance. Arthur M. Louis, ''Mutual Funds Have the Votes,'' *Fortune* (My 1967), p. 207. There is the further problem already mentioned of sorting out those anti-management votes established ''for the record,'' which may be made in the case of non-customers, or nonsensitive customers, and where in general the cost to the bank may be slight. Such votes may obscure a continued uncritical proxy accommodation of the managements of substantial and sensitive customers.

[26]Custodial holdings would not be included in this reporting.The 1973 Morgan report does precisely what is called for in (a), with the holdings broken down further as between personal trust, employee benefit plan, and investment advisory. The Citibank 1973 report goes almost as far, listing market values and percentage holdings for the one hundred largest noncustodial holdings of the trust department. Mellon provides market value figures for trust holdings exceeding $20 million, and percentage of market value for holdings in excess of $50 million.

[27]Citibank provides this information in its 1973 trust department report for its top one hundred holdings. For its holdings in excess of $50 million, Mellon's 1973 report provides a breakdown of investment authority rather than voting power.

[28]Restrictive covenants are often imposed on portfolio companies under loan agreements, which may permit lenders to control the future financing activities of borrowers, their payment of dividends, mergers, consolidations, or sales of assets. At a minimum such constraints should be reported systematically to banks' supervisory authorities. Perhaps they also should be made available on the public record on the ground that they are probably more relevant to influence and control than stockholdings. See for example, *Toolco-Northeast Control*, CAB Docket 11620 (1965); *Meteor-Metropolitan Aircraft Agreement*, 26 CAB 596 (1958); *Canadair* v. *Seaboard World Airlines*, 43 Misc. 2d 320, 250 N.Y.S. 2d 723 (Sup. Ct. 1964).

[29]Citibank's 1973 report shows the common stock purchases and sales of director-affiliated companies.

[30]See Lybecker, op. cit., p. 13, n. 27.

[31]For example, on the assumption that a bank is weakening and threatened with failure, would it be reasonable to expect the bank as trustee to remove trust deposits from itself to a safer institution?

[32]A number of banks monitor their own cash performance and that of individual portfolio managers more rigorously than do the regulatory authorities. At least one large bank computes ratios of cash to assets for individual managers and for semi-autonomous area units of a far-flung trust operation, and even monitors the amounts of income cash left uninvested within the system.

Real Estate Investment Trusts
by Roy A. Schotland

I • INTRODUCTION

In 1960 Congress passed tax legislation easing the establishment of real estate investment trusts (REITs). The stated purposes of this legislation were to facilitate capital-raising for real estate investment; to give small- and medium-sized investors the opportunity to participate in large-scale, professionally managed real estate investments that previously had been restricted to wealthy individuals and institutions, such as banks and insurance companies; and to promote the construction of residential units.

Congress did not consider applying to REITs certain safeguards that govern the operations of other investment vehicles and institutions that manage investments. Nor did Congress establish any federal authority, such as that of the Securities and Exchange Commission (SEC) over investment companies or the bank regulators over trust departments, to protect investors and the public interest in REIT operations, beyond requirements applying to all publicly held companies. (Like REITs, insurance companies are regulated only by the states, but state regulation of insurance is generally better than state regulation of REITs if only because the states have been regulating insurance since the early 1900s; whereas REITs are a relatively new phenomenon.)

From 1960 until 1969, REITs grew very slowly. In 1969, responding to conditions in the stock market and the passage of the Housing Act of 1968, the industry's assets increased from $1 billion to $2 billion; in 1970 they more than doubled, and by the end of 1973, they exceeded $20 billion. The equity capital invested by the public had risen 1300 percent in five years, and to each dollar of equity was added three dollars of debt. Some of the debt was long-term; much more of it took the form of short-term borrowing from banks, and most was in even shorter term commercial paper. The REITs, which lent money for longer terms, thus had a precariously heavy debt load and a volatile financial structure.

The meteoric rise of the REITs was not the exclusive responsibility of the REITs themselves. Investment banking firms, including virtually all of the most prestigious houses, found a bonanza in new offerings of REITs; from 1969 to 1972, REIT underwritings were among the leading activities in Wall Street. Banks, entering a period of both easy money and unprecedentedly aggressive banking practices, eagerly provided REITs with more and more credit—ultimately, more than $11 billion. Many—although not all—major banks sponsored their own REITs, and between 1972 and 1974, while industry assets more than doubled, those of bank-sponsored REITs increased almost tenfold, eventually comprising about one-third of the industry's assets.

The average purchaser of REIT shares, according to the only survey done, was an individual of about retirement age. Of the REIT stockholders surveyed, 69 percent were over fifty-five years old, and 49 percent had incomes of over $25,000; almost all had invested in common stocks, and a majority had also invested in mutual funds and bonds.[1] In purchasing REIT shares, these investors acted far more on brokers' advice than they did in purchasing other types of securities.

Association with the large, well-known, and supposedly conservatively managed financial institutions that were their sponsors made many REITs look both attractive and safe. Moreover, at its height, the dividend yield of REIT shares was substantially above that of the average New York Stock Exchange common stock and as high as the yields of AA-rated bonds; and REITs also offered the hope of capital appreciation.

On the other hand, investors—and the broker-dealers legally obligated to consider an investment's suitability for the particular customer—should have been aware that REITs contained elements of substantial risk:

1. Under the tax legislation, REITs qualified for tax advantages only if they invested at least 75 percent of their assets in real estate. (In practice, almost all REITs were 100 percent invested in real estate.) Thus, REITs were much less diversified than even investment companies that concentrated in equities, because such investment companies almost always invested in a number of sectors.

2. Real estate, especially construction, has long been one of the most cyclical sectors of our economy. Therefore, dividends were likely to fluctuate substantially. Because the tax law required REITs to pay out at least 90 percent of net taxable income, they were largely unable to build up retained earnings in good years so as to enlarge the equity cushion to absorb possible losses and to maintain dividend levels in weak years.

3. Within the real estate sector, the riskiest investments are in short-term construction and development loans. Over two-thirds of REIT assets went into financing such loans; many of the largest REITs were wholly or almost wholly so invested.

4. As if risk were a good thing of which there could not be too much, the industry leveraged the equity invested in it by heavy borrowing; such borrowing was heaviest in the already high-risk construction and development REITs. As of late 1974, the five largest REITs, all in construction and development, had debt-equity ratios averaging 5.65 to 1. The ratio for the industry as a whole was 3 to 1. Moreover, although most of this debt was short-term, the REITs themselves made long-term loans.

When the general economic boom of the early 1970s began its decline, real estate, which had been experiencing not mere boom but excess, was a natural early victim of the slowdown. During 1973, while new REIT offerings attracted 15 percent more equity investment, REIT share prices fell steadily. At the end of 1973, the general economic decline was sharply reinforced by the Arab oil boycott and energy price revolution. In 1974 interest rates rose to an unprecedented 12 percent prime rate, and REITs staggered under the burden of over $11 billion in bank loans and commercial paper, almost all at rates several percentage points above prime. From the beginning of 1973 to the end of 1974, stock prices generally fell by about 50 percent; REITs' share prices fell by about 85 percent, and their dividend payouts fell over 60 percent. At their nadir, in mid-1976, the payouts were a mere 20 percent of the peak level. Fortunately, a substantial number of REITs were able to continue dividends without interruption, and some were sound enough to continue with little or no reduction in amount. But in early 1975, about eighty REITs, 40 percent of the industry, seemed on the brink of bankruptcy.

The size of the debt load and the fear of domino effects if REITs were forced either to make their interest payments or to declare bankruptcy caused the banks and REITs to enter a "workout" period. This phase, characterized by an unusually patient treatment of the loans and a steady, difficult shrinkage of REIT assets, probably will last—for a large fraction of the industry including many of the biggest REITs—into the 1980s.

Of course, the REIT disaster was a classic case of economic euphoria, a speculative bubble bound to burst, although the inevitable comedown was worsened by unforeseeable external events. Certainly, the 1974 recession was far more severe than had been anticipated even by able businessmen and economists. And certainly, the recession was most severe in the real estate sector. But just as certainly, conflicts of interest, built into the structure of REITs and compounded in unprecedented ways, increased the REITs' incentive to expand and particularly to expand via borrowing, and thus increased the REITs' riskiness.

The initial conflicts were external to the REITs. The investment bankers had powerful incentives to sell new securities, and for a while REITs were a particularly salable item. The commercial bankers had powerful incentives to lend, and for a while REITs were particularly able to absorb borrowed money. Such conflicts affected, although perhaps to lesser degree, industries other than REITs. But still other conflicts were built into the structure of REITs and compounded through most of the industry by accepted practice.

Although the REITs were apparently independent, and few sponsoring companies held more than nominal amounts of shares in their REITs, the sponsors nonetheless controlled their REITs through the so-called advisor system. Few REITs managed their own investments; most had boards of trustees but no officers or employees. Instead, they contracted for "external management" by "advisors." Most REIT sponsors maintained that unless the trust had external management, it could not qualify as a "passive investor" under the tax requirements for REITs.[2]

Almost invariably, the chosen advisor was the REIT's sponsor or its affiliate or subsidiary. The sponsors not only were represented on REIT boards, they selected the other board members. Before 1974 REIT boards of trustees seem never to have rejected the advice of their advisors.[3]

The use of external management, rather than internal management by an entity's own officers, is unusual but not unprecedented in American business. Mutual funds and closed-end investment companies are managed by external investment advisors that usually have no significant investment in the controlled entity and are compensated through a management contract. But detailed regulatory safeguards protect the interests of investors in such entities.

Indeed, the troublesome interrelationships between REITs and their promoters closely resemble those that prevailed between investment companies and their promoters before the enactment of the Investment Company Act of 1940. That act virtually bars leveraging via borrowing; closely regulates use of the public pool of money in the investment fund; and, since amendment in 1970, requires that advisory fees be reasonable in amount and structure.

Unlike investment companies REITs could and did borrow. Putting aside the question of how much borrowing might be too much, substantial borrowing is clearly more consistent with real estate investment than with the conduct of publicly held investment companies. But when it came to deciding how much borrowing was appropriate, in almost every REIT, the interests of the shareholders conflicted with those of the advisors.

Most REIT advisory fees were scaled to the total assets—including borrowed assets—under management. This system of compensation gave the advisors an incentive to assume more debt. Although shareholders might benefit from this borrowing, their potential gain was much less, proportionately, than that of management. But the risk of the leverage was almost wholly on the shareholders. Thus, the advisors had an incentive to borrow that conflicted with their concern for the stability of the shareholders' investment. It is impossible to say how much of the REITs' actual borrowing was attributable to the advisors' pursuit of fess, how much to economic euphoria, and how much simply to reasonable business judgment. This ambiguity is typical of conflict situations.

Changing the basis for figuring advisory fees would almost certainly reduce the advisors' incentive to borrow excessively. Another key conflict presents a harder problem. The major banks, insurance companies, and real estate-oriented firms that sponsored most of the large REITs also continued to engage in real estate activities for their own accounts. In the course of normal activities, they could expect to find themselves competing for investments against the REIT they were managing on behalf of its public stockholders. Of course the REITs also benefited, presumably, from their sponsors' real estate expertise, which, in the case of preeminent firms such as the Chase Manhattan Bank and Equitable Life, understandably appeared at least as desirable as that of any other managment the REIT might secure. A requirement that REIT advisors be "independent" might have reduced the REITs' access to expertise and thus their attractiveness to investors.

The period of REIT prosperity was less than five years. Problems other than conflicts of interest played a major role in the 1974-75 debacle. But clearly, REIT managements confronted a choice between serving their own interests and serving the best interests of their stockholders. Those who chose not to fulfill their fiduciary responsibilities caused an indeterminate but significant part of the severe losses suffered not only by REIT investors but also by others, including labor as well as investors and management, in the real estate sector. That some REIT managements were exemplary does not alter the fact that the REITs' legal structure and accepted industry practice presented undue invitations to abuse.

The real estate industry has recovered from 1974-75 and some REITs are impressively successful. But neither government nor the private sector has even begun steps to prevent the incentives to overexpansion and the other troublesome conflicts in this industry from producing new injuries.

II • THE REIT INDUSTRY

The 1960 federal legislation responsible for the growth of the REIT industry gives investors in real estate substantially the same tax advantages as investors in mutual funds and closed-end investment companies; that is, the REIT does not pay corporate income taxes on the net income it distributes to shareholders. (The shareholders, of course, pay taxes on what they receive.)

To qualify for these tax advantages,[1] a REIT must:

1. Distribute at least 90 percent of ordinary income to shareholders. (In practice, most of them distribute 100 percent.)
2. Have 100 or more shareholders. No more than 50 percent of its shares may be owned, directly or indirectly, by five or fewer persons.
3. Invest at least 75 percent of its assets in real estate or real estate mortgages and derive at least 75 percent of its income from rents, mortgage interests, and gains from the sale of such interests.
4. Not acquire real estate primarily for resale purposes. Only a limited percentage of the REIT's gross income can come from the sale of real property held less than four years.

Shares of REITS are neither redeemable for cash nor constantly offered. Like the shares of closed-end investment companies, REIT shares are traded in the securities markets so their value is determined by buyers and sellers in these markets. Most REIT shares are listed: as of end-1977, REITs with $5.9 billion of assets (far more, at that time, than the shares' market value) were listed on the New York Stock Exchange (NYSE) and another $1.5 billion on the American Stock Exchange (Amex).[2]

REIT Regulation

Like insurance companies REITs are regulated only by the states, but state regulation of insurance is generally better than state regulation of REITS, if only because insurance companies have been in existence for several hundred years and the states have been regulating them since the early 1900s, whereas REITs are a relatively new phenomenon.   —

In most states REITs that are not listed on major exchanges are subject to state requirements when they make new public offerings. Corporations must obtain clearances in every state in which they wish to offer securities, unless they are exempt from the state regulations. State securities administrators communicate actively with one another, especially on large or controversial offerings; hence, approvals and disapprovals may be uniform. Generally, the states vary in their securities regulation policies. But under the auspices of the Midwest Securities Commissioners Association, state officials have arrived at some significant common policy positions regarding REITs. The members of this association represent twenty-four states, not all of them midwestern,[3] and have reputations as tough regulators.

In 1961 the Midwest Commissioners produced a statement of policy regarding REITs that, amended and updated several times since then, constitutes the essence of state regulation in this field. The statements have been formally enacted in only eight states,[4] and even in the association's member states, many offerings have not complied with the statements. But many states have used the statements as guidelines, and the American Stock Exchange has adopted them as part of its listing requirements and guidelines.[5]

Types of REITs

The objectives of REITs, in terms of investment location, type of property, and precise form of investment, vary widely. *Equity* REITs limit themselves to ownership of real estate properties; others, known as *hybrids* combine such ownership with mortgage holdings. These two categories combined account for under 20 percent of the industry's assets.[6]

Those REITs concentrated (that is, 50-100 percent of their assets) in short-term construction and development mortgages and loans accounted for fully 60 percent of the industry's assets in 1974, although that proportion has since declined because such investments have been the most problem-ridden part of the industry. The largest REITs (ten of the twelve largest, thirty of the fifty largest) were primarily of this type. Other REITs also have substantial investments in construction and development. At the peak of such lending, the industry as a whole had over half of its assets in this form of investment, particularly profitable when the real estate sector prospers but correspondingly vulnerable when the cycle turns down. The remaining 20-plus percent of the REITs are concentrated in long-term and intermediate-term mortgages.

Some trusts are involved in nationwide investments, and others are regionally or locally oriented. About half of all REIT assets are located, in declining order of magnitude, in Florida ($3 billion), Texas ($1.7 billion), California ($1.5 billion), Georgia ($1.1 billion), and New York ($759 million).[7] The sizes and financial structures of REITs also vary considerably, as do the types of investments. Some trusts invest only in, for example, shopping centers or apartment buildings; other have a wider mix.

Diversity also characterizes REIT sponsors. *Independent* REITs—those without substantial sponsors, such as banks—account for about one-third of the industry's assets. Until recently commercial bank-sponsored REITs also held about one-third of the industry assets, invested almost completely in short-term construction and development loans. (Since 1974 the assets of this group have declined more than those of the industry generally.) Life insurance company-sponsored REITs account for under one-eighth of the industry assets and have invested mainly in long-term and intermediate-term mortgages. Those REITs sponsored by mortgage bankers and other kinds of real estate-oriented companies account for somewhat more than one-eighth of industry assets. And a few REITs have been sponsored by conglomerate corporations.

The Investment Picture

In 1961-62, in response to the change in the tax laws, nineteen new REIT issues totaling $170 million were offered to the public. But from 1962 to 1967, only $70 million was raised for new REIT issues. Most of these were "equity" REITs, making direct purchases of real estate and so earning rental payment, rather than lending to real estate ventures.

It was only after 1968 that "mortgage REITs," providing both long-term financing and short-term construction and development financing, came into favor. During the 1969-70 recession, tight money prompted mortgage financiers to tap the public market, and the public was attracted by the yields that REITs offered. The stock market was going through a severe slump, but the equity REITs had held up well during 1966 and 1969 declines. The Housing Act of 1968 committed the government to encourage an unprecedented expansion of residential building—the construction of 26 million housing units by 1978. The result was widespread optimism about the future of real estate in general.

Many people in real estate finance viewed REITs as a device to stabilize the supply of funds for construction, particularly residential construction.[8] It was thought that REITs would provide the real estate industry with both professional management and large amounts of permanent equity capital; REITs would tap a new source of capital—investors who might have wanted to participate in real estate investment but could not or would not do so directly. In spite of their newness, REITs quickly assumed an important role in direct real estate lending, particularly in construction and development; they provided 20 percent of all such lending in the United States and just under 20 percent of lending for residences.[9] Over half of the assets of REITs were in residential properties, especially condominiums and apartments.[10]

In 1969 new offerings more than doubled the industry's total assets. (See Tables 8 and 9.)

Table 8: REIT Assets, Year-End Totals ($ Billion)

	TOTAL	SHAREHOLDERS' EQUITY
1961	0.30 (est.)	N.A.
1965	0.70 (est.)	N.A.
1968	1.03	0.47
1969	2.03	1.24
1970	4.73	2.89
1971	7.72	3.97
1972	14.18	5.11
1973	20.19	5.84
1974	21.02	5.02
1975	19.19	3.48
1976	16.52	2.74

Source: National Association of Real Estate Investment Trusts (NAREITs), *1977 Fact Book.* Copyright © 1978, pp. 24, 28.

Table 9: REIT Public Offerings ($ Million)

	NUMBER	TOTAL AMOUNT
1961	14	$71.9
1965	14	32.6
1968	14	122.4
1969	58	1,256.7
1970	72	1,687.4
1971	79	1,989.8
1972	67	1,223.3
1973	65	867.1
1974	17	23.7
1975	4	0.4
1976	8	87.4

Note: Small Portions of some of these totals were private placements.

Source: NAREITs, *1977 Fact Book.* Copyright © 1978, p. 27.

Starting early in 1970, a host of organizations rushed into the new issue market to take advantage of the demand. The sponsors had names like Chase Manhattan Bank, Bank of America, Bankers Trust Company, First Pennsylvania Bank and Trust Company, Wells Fargo & Co., Equitable Life Assurance Society, Connecticut General Life Insurance Co., Mutual Life Insurance Company of New York, Transamerica Corp., City Investing Co., and Merrill Lynch. They inspired confidence. And the underwriters included almost every well-known brokerage firm. (But one of the largest bank stock firms, Keefe, Bruyette & Woods, out of concern about both the soundness of investment in a sector so crowded and the REITs' inherent conflicts of interests, refused to underwrite any REITs.)

The bank-sponsored REITs led the stampede. In 1970 to 1972, major public offerings—that is, those over $25 million—of bank-sponsored REITs included those shown in Table 10.

Table 10: Bank-Sponsored REITs

1970	BANK	(MILLIONS)
February	Wachovia	$65, equity
April	Barnett	$25, equity
June	Chase Manhattan	$68, equity, $45 debt
June	Wells Fargo	$75, equity
July	Bank America	$51, equity, $26 debt
July	First Pennsylvania	$32, equity
September	Citizens and Southern	$50, equity
October	Bankers Trust	$15, equity, $10 debt
October	First of Denver	$30, equity
November	Tri-South	$27.5, equity
December	Pittsburgh National	$30, equity
1971		
January	Cleveland Trust	$50, equity
May	Chase Manhattan	$100 debt
July	Hamilton	$25, equity
August	First Pennsylvania	$30 debt
November	Hartford National	$15, equity, $15 debt
November	NJB Prime	$15, equity, $15 debt
November	Continental Illinois	$100, equity
December	First Wisconsin	$30, equity
1972		
February	Tri-South	$25 debt
May	U.S. Bancorp	$12.5, equity, $12.5 debt
July	Barnett	$30, equity
October	Citizens and Southern	$30 debt
December	Continental Illinois	$25 debt

Source: Securities and Exchange Commission Economic Staff Paper 75-1, *REITs: A Background Analysis and Recent Industry Developments, 1961-74* (1975), pp. 56-61.

Chase Manhattan's REIT, the largest of all, started with $113 million in June 1970 and made loan commitments of $878 million within the next year and $1.4 billion by 1973.[11] First Wisconsin, starting with $30 million in December 1971, had loaned over $200 million by 1974. The public was enchanted by this kind of "growth." The Chase REIT shares sold as high as 70 (early in 1973), First Wisconsin's as high as 45.

In 1960 REITs were a little industry with total assets of approximately $250 million. At their peak in 1973, the industry's assets amounted to $21 billion. This rate of growth is probably without precedent in the history of American finance.

The new money pouring in went mostly to "mortgage REITs" investing in long-term first mortgages, short-term or subsidiary mortgage loans, and land development or construction. Except for long-term first mortgages, mortgages are considered relatively risky and therefore command a relatively high rate of return. Mortgage REITs are really a kind of financial intermediary, although they are not subject to regulation by banking or insurance authorities. They claim as a virtue freedom to negotiate relatively speculative real estate loans that banks and insurance companies are legally prohibited from making.

The highest return—and corresponding risk—lay in the shortest-term lending, for construction and land development. The major source of construction and development funds was the commercial banks. They invested under 3 percent of their assets in such loans; the REITs invested over 50 percent of theirs.[12] No single large bank so employed more than 10 percent of its domestic loan funds, let alone of its assets. But the Chase REIT invested over 60 percent of its loans in construction and development. And much—perhaps most— of the REITs' construction and development lending was to borrowers that had obtained no permanent financing for their projects. For example, only 23 percent of the Chase REIT's construction and development loan borrowers had permanent financing; and half of that 23 percent had received such financing from the Chase REIT itself.[13] Banks and savings and loan associations rarely made construction and development loans without this safeguard.

Conflicts of interest—although not those of REITs—were present at the very inception of the industry's boom. Investment bankers failed in several ways. First, in their due diligence work, they did not adequately assess the investment management capability of the REITs they underwrote. Of course, REITs were something of a novelty and could not be judged before being brought to the market as a company already operating in an established industry can. The REITs were the first investment vehicle consisting of fully disclosed, widely held portfolios concentrated in real estate and substantially in relatively risky forms. But it should have been obvious that with so much money being raised so fast and with such pressure to put that money to work, competition to find outlets for funds would be intense, standards would be lowered, and not enough experienced and competent professionals would be available to manage this activity.[14] In some instances the management gap probably was hard to see without a crystal ball, but in many REITs, including some with quite distinguished sponsorship, it was not.

Second, in 1969 investment bankers adopted, to enhance the attractiveness of REIT shares, the practice of setting up equity offerings as packages of shares plus warrants. By 1973 they had sold more than $1.5 billion of such packages. The warrants were exercisable to purchase more shares later, in many cases at the same prices as the original share offering. The equity expansion of REITs depended upon further offerings, but the warrants made it harder to raise the prices of subsequent offerings and thus limited the ability of REITs to add equity. Some experts view this form of financing as an improperly motivated imposition on the REITs by the investment banks; others consider it entirely defensible. Exercise of the warrants would bring more equity capital into the REIT without any additional fund-raising costs, including fees for the investment banker. Such fees often approximated 9 percent or even 10 percent of the equity raised; avoiding them thus benefited the REIT shareholders.

Third, although REIT managements were far from opposed to growth, the investment bankers who would underwrite further offerings of equity or longer term debt had a particular interest in growth and pressured REITs accordingly. In early 1975, at the bottom of the REIT decline, a high official of the REIT trade association identified three groups as responsible for what befell the REITs and their investors. He started with the underwriters:

The stock market was dull in 1969 and 1970 with few attractive issues. REITs provided the market sex appeal during this relatively dry period. The selling pitch was earnings—leverage, greater earnings per share—higher stock values. Magically, an income security turned into a growth stock. . . . The way to increase per share earnings was to borrow and increase investments. The Wall Street pressure for this result was tremendous.[15]

The investment bankers' conflict was compounded by that of the broker-dealers who were usually, of course, a different arm of the same firm. Investors who bought REIT shares relied more on their stockbrokers than when buying other securities; and they usually bought REIT shares for income, but many REIT investors also sought capital growth.[16]

In practice, the yield from REIT shares was little, if at all, higher than that from utilities, but the risk—in both yield and price—was incomparably higher. For customers who were retired or preparing for retirement, especially the significant number who needed both income and capital conservation, most REITs—especially construction and development REITs that in fact absorbed the most public investment money—were unsuitable choices.[17]

The REITs were a bonanza for Wall Street. Underwriting is the most profitable of the various activities that comprise the market; in 1969-70 more than one-ninth of all equity capital raised by new companies went into

REITs.[18] In its zealous pursuit of the profits to be gained for underwriting and subsequently handling the trading of REIT shares, Wall Street neglected the interests of its other clients, the investors who bought the shares.

The Expansion of Debt

Another group sharing responsibility for the debacle is the commercial bankers:

[W]hen the trusts found the market less receptive to new share issues, they compensated by increasing their leverage further. Commercial paper became a major source of this capital. . . . accounting for 30% or more of the total debt of short term mortgage trusts. On a dollar-for-dollar basis, commercial paper had to be backed up by bank lines of credit. . . . These lines required compensating balances of 10% and 15%. This was easy money for the banks which were under some earning pressure themselves. In some cases, not many, a few banks urged trusts to take on lines or increase lines to levels beyond immediate needs of the REIT. One of the difficulties in this developing credit picture was that many line banks were not expecting any funding of these lines and credit analysis was minimal.

It is noteworthy that during all this time, only a few long-term loan agreements were made. Most of the credit was provided on a very short-term basis by noncontractual, loosely knit consortiums of line banks with no group responsibility. In retrospect, a most vulnerable situation. The fact that these lines grew so rapidly and so loosely suggests some responsibility for the ensuing problems lies with the banking industry.[19]

In the 1960s the short-term lending REITs increased their assets by borrowing long-term through private placements, primarily with insurance companies. But in 1971 many of these REITs began to turn heavily to short-term borrowing, in particular from the commercial paper market, a source of cheaper money. They had to back up their commercial paper with unused lines of bank credit. The banks issued this credit at the prime rate of interest—that is, the rate at which they charged their best customers—and required the trusts to maintain as compensating balances 10 to 15 percent of the unused amount of a line and 20 percent of the portion of a line drawn down. Still, commercial paper was cheaper for the REITs than direct bank loans, and the REITs made ever-increasing use of it.

At the end of 1973, the REITs had $4 billion outstanding in commercial paper, compared with $1.5 billion of bank term loans and revolving credits in use and less than $4 billion of longer term debt.[20]

The REITs' total debt dwarfed their equity and was overwhelmingly short-term. (See Tables 11 and 12.)

Table 11: REIT Industry Equity and Debt ($ Billion, Year-End Data)

	SHAREHOLDER'S EQUITY	SHORT-TERM DEBT	OTHER DEBT
1968	0.47	0.09	0.47
1969	1.24	0.23	0.56
1970	2.89	0.80	1.04
1971	3.97	2.24	1.51
1972	5.11	6.21	2.86
1973	5.84	10.47	3.88
1974	5.02	11.76	4.24
1975	3.48	11.17	4.54
1976	2.74	9.04	4.74

Source: NAREITs, *1977 Fact Book.* Copyright © 1978, p. 28.

The short-term construction and development REITs did the most leveraging.

Table 12: Distribution of Bank Loans within the REIT Industry (as of End-1975)

REIT CATEGORY	PERCENTAGE OF TOTAL REITS' ASSETS	BANK LOANS AS PERCENTAGE OF CATEGORY'S ASSETS
Equity trusts	7.1	10.8
Intermediate-term mortgages	5.6	57.8
Long-term mortages & equities (hybrids)	18.8	39.1
Short-term mortgages & equities	7.3	42.3
Short-term mtg.—commercial bank	20.2	77.6
Short-term mtg.—independent	15.7	74.6
Short-term mtg.—mortgage banker	12.0	64.0
Short-term mtg.—misc. financial	10.8	64.8
Subordinate land trusts	2.4	43.5

Source: Hearings on REITs before the Senate Banking Committee, 94th Cong. 2d Sess. (Washington, D.C.: May 1976), p. 43; data presented by Professor Brian M. Neuberger of San Diego State University.

The debt-equity ratios of REITs, at their peak, were lower than those of commercial banks, but commercial banks have comparably greater diversification of assets, holding not only more categories of loans and other investments but also large numbers of loans in each category. In addition to less exposure if any one or several ventures cannot pay interest when due, more diversified lenders also enjoy a more reliable cash flow. The "maturities" of REIT assests and liabilities also were ill-matched; borrowing short and lending long lead to trouble if interest rates rise. Most of the commercial paper issued by REITs had maturities of one or two months or, at most, six months, and the bulk of REITs' direct borrowing from banks was for three months or due upon demand. On the other hand, the shortest term loans made by REITs were for one- and two-year terms.

Some industry people maintain that the limits imposed by the independent rating services and the lending banks did serve to prevent excessive borrowing.[21] But the level of risk and the pace of expansion of REIT debt reflect poorly on the effectiveness of those limits and raise questions about the judgment of many allegedly sophisticated financial professionals.

A third group also helped shape the fate of the REITs:

The REIT advisers also played an important role in this growth. While they wished along with REIT shareholders for increases in per share earnings as a mark of their success, the measure of monetary compensation for their efforts was not always consistent with shareholder interests. During this period of rapid growth, most trust advisers were compensated according to the asset size of their REIT. The greater the level of mortgage investments, the greater the fee.[22]

Few if any aspects of REIT structure functioned as a brake on borrowing.

The Decline and Faltering

Although REIT share prices peaked in November 1972 and January 1973, the first warning flags, or at least signs of change, were visible earlier. In 1972 public offerings amounted to $1.223 billion, but they were down over one-third from the record volume of $1.990 billion in 1971. Public offerings by new REITs declined almost 50 percent from 1971 to 1972. As early as November 1971, the managing trustee of one of the largest REITs, Continental Mortgage Investors, told *The New York Times* that newer REITs had "relaxed, if not abandoned conservative underwriting standards" in putting their funds to work.[23]

After January 1973 REIT share prices declined steadily, ending the year 41 percent down.[24] Stocks generally (the S&P 500 index) declined by only 16 percent. A year later, December 1974, the stock market touched "bottom," having fallen by 30 percent in a year—a record drop. That year REIT stocks plummeted 73 percent to their own bottom, 15 percent of the market value of the industry at the beginning of 1973. (Since then REIT stocks have recovered somewhat; as of early 1978, the industry's market value was 29 percent of what it had been in 1973.[25])

Given the financial situation of the typical REIT investor and the way which REITs had been promoted, dividends are a particularly important aspect of performance of this investment vehicle, and in fact, dividend payments fell precipitously. (See Table 13.)

Table 13: Dividends Paid by REITs

PERIOD IN WHICH DIVIDEND CHECK SENT	NO. OF REITS PAYING A DIVIDEND	TOTAL DISTRIBUTED
1972 Jan-Mar	112	$ 99,808,535
Apr-Jun	126	111,830,891
Jul-Sep	131	121,701,426
Oct-Dec	137	136,701,929
1973 Jan-Mar	144	147,808,062
Apr-Jun	148	148,901,500
Jul-Sep	154	152,832,281
Oct-Dec	152	157,018,399
1974 Jan-Mar	147	147,354,632
Apr-Jun	144	134,464,362
Jul-Sep	126	83,222,545
Oct-Dec	101	57,500,206
1975 Jan-Mar	78	42,516,097
Apr-Jun	76	39,593,017
Jul-Sep	71	36,855,536
Oct-Dec	68	32,728,803
1976 Jan-Mar	68	33,621,884
Apr-Jun	68	30,970,465
Jul-Sep	70	30,115,718
Oct-Dec	69	31,591,323
1977 Jan-Mar	70	32,413,943
Apr-Jun	72	32,513,492
Jul-Sep	74	33,616,531
Oct-Dec	74	35,318,205
1978 Jan-Mar	75	38,052,309
Apr-Jun	74	36,061,490e

Note: e = estimated.

Source: NAREITs, *REITs Qurterly, 1977: IV*. Copyright © 1978, p. 3.

The severity of the REITs' decline affected the prices of all REIT stock, but in varying degrees. (See Table 14.) Least affected in their operations were the "equity" REITs, but they accounted for only 7.1 percent of total REIT assets (as of end 1975).

Unsurprisingly, the short-term construction and development loan REITs ran into the most trouble. They had financed plainly excessive building of condominiums, apartments, and office buildings in particular. In 1974, when the economy and the real estate market turned down, these buildings had extremely high vacancy rates. At the same time, interest rates soared to historic highs, so even developers with completed projects that might have been sound in normal times found themselves unable to pay back interest or principal.

Table 14: REIT Categories' Stock Price Declines

CATEGORY	PERCENTAGE OF TOTAL REIT ASSETS (AS OF END-1975)	STOCK PRICE DECLINE, DEC. 1972 TO DEC. 1974
Equity trusts	*7.1*	*51%*
Intermediate-term mortgages	*5.6*	*82%*
Long-term mortgages & equities (hybrids)	*18.8*	*80%*
Short-term mortgages & equities (hybrids)	*7.3*	*78%*
Short-term mtg.—commercial bank	*20.2*	*89%*
Short-term mtg.—independent	*15.7*	*91%*
Short-term mtg.—mortgage banker	*12.0*	*84%*
Short-term mtg.—misc. financial	*10.8*	*86%*
Subordinate land trusts	*2.4*	*77%*

*Source:*Hearings on REITs before the Senate Banking Committee, 94th Cong., 2d Sess. (Washington, D.C.: May 1976), pp. 53, 60-61; data presented by Professor Brian M. Neuberger of San Diego State University.

Although the ills of the construction industry were aggravated by the general, sharp rise in interest rates, they also had other major causes. One was the boom psychology of the early 1970s, which had encouraged vast overbuilding. By 1973 Florida, where the REITs had invested $3 billion, was glutted with condominiums. But many developments in the economy also conspired against the real estate industry. The cost of construction was soaring as a result of almost unprecedented general inflation accompanied, in some cases, by a shortage of construction materials. The Arab oil embargo raised not only energy prices but also the prices of a host of petrochemical-related products used in construction. The deepening recession, and a downturn in real personal income, discouraged many Americans from investing in second homes.

Many REITs renegotiated the loans they had made, granting additional money in cases to avoid foreclosing on the projects. The renegotiated loans were often so large and were granted on such liberal terms as to preclude any chances of a profit for years to come. But any alternative course probably would have been worse.

When it became clear that developers were running into problems, the commercial paper market reacted and some REITs became unable to refinance their commercial paper borrowings. Instead, they had to draw on their lines of bank credit and thus pay higher interest rates. However, a number of major banks that were heavily involved in REITs lent freely rather than let these REITs declare bankruptcy. As a result the REITs' outstanding commercial paper shrank—just during 1974—from $4 billion to $700 million, and their debt to banks rose from $6.5 billion to $11 billion.

The continued survival of many REITs confirms the old maxim that borrowing heavily from banks assures favorable treatment for the borrower in the time of trouble. The banks moved much of the approximately $11 billion REIT bank debt from short- to medium-term credit and drastically lowered their interest rates. Bankers had evidently decided they could gain more by granting more favorable payment terms than by forcing bankruptcies. Moreover, most banks, especially the major ones, shared the fears expressed by the Federal Reserve Board that calling the loans and thereby forcing a number of REITs into bankruptcy might have a domino effect on the rest of the financial system. Consequently, only a few REITs went into bankruptcy proceedings, although many developers did and unemployment in construction soared.

In 1974, just when earnings of REITs were being shrunk by their borrowers' difficulties, payouts to REIT stockholders were further reduced as the managers began, belatedly, to build up loan loss reserves. From the end of 1973 to the end of 1975, the industry's total loss reserves rose from $89 million, only 0.5 percent of industry mortgage investments, to over $2 billion, about 15 percent of mortgage investments.

The failure of REITs to maintain adequate reserves before 1973 was in part an unintended effect of the tax code requirement that trusts distribute at least 90 percent of their net income to shareholders. Theoretically, REITs could retain about 10 percent with which to build up equity and a cushion for loan losses. In fact, however, they paid out virtually all their earnings and maintained very little in the way of loan loss reserves.

Apparently, they were less afraid of losing money on their loans than they were of the Internal Revenue Service (IRS); industry leaders believed that if the IRS calculation of a REIT's net income for a given year was greater than the amount of which the REIT had paid out 90 percent, the REIT could not settle accounts simply by paying out the amount of the shortfall but would be disqualified from REIT status, with all its tax advantages. The IRS was generally disinclined to allow larger loan loss reserves than could be justified by experience. Of course, the REIT industry had little experience, and allegedly, no data acceptable to the IRS on real estate losses in general were available. The REITs also had considerable incentive to distribute as much as they could to stockholders because high yields raised stock prices, increasing the REIT's ability to sell equity and, in turn, borrow. And increases in both equity and borrowing increased the management's advisory fee.

Both before and after the debacle, similar REITs maintained strikingly different ratios of loan loss reserves to total mortgage investments. The differences may have reflected different levels, in either confidence on the part of REIT managements, in the loans they made or aggressiveness about expanding total assets to raise advisory fees, or both. Among trusts reporting no problem investments as of the end of 1972, the Chase REIT had a loan reserve ratio of 0.16 percent, only one-fifth as high as the loan loss reserve ratio of Continental Illinois Realty, 0.78 percent. Long-term REITs, which made much less risky loans, maintained much higher loan loss reserve ratios than the Chase and several other short-term REITs. The ratio of Connecticut General REIT was 0.33 percent, that of Equitable Life 0.21 percent. At the end of 1975, Continental Illinois Realty had raised its reserve ratio to 9.23 percent, but Chase had raised its reserve nearly twice as high, to 17.03 percent. Connecticut General had a peak ratio of only 1.83 percent (1976), and Equitable's peak was only 0.70 percent (1977).

Among the fifty largest REITS, the loan loss reserve data defy correlation with any measure. The sizes of pre-1973 reserves do not correspond either to pre-1973 losses or to post-1973 losses. Nor do they show a correlation — either positive (to compensate for risky investments) or negative (indicating confidence in these investments)—with REIT aggressiveness as measured by debt-equity ratios, or with overall portfolio size.

Why?

Why did REITs fare so poorly? The problems of the construction loan REITs in particular have cost many investors their retirement security. The REITs' conflicts of interest were unusual in type and severity, but conflicts were not the prime cause of the trouble. The industry's leading—and independent—investment analyst describes the REIT "explosion of 1969-72 as another manifestation of the financial madness which had gripped crowds historically."[26] The REITs happened to be at the center of boom-time business at its worst. According to a Wharton study initiated by NAREIT:

[T]here was a very extraordinary slippage in the underwriting of real estate credits during the "easy money" period of the early 1970s, which coincided with the rapid growth in total REIT assets. This comment applies to the standards utilized by all short-term construction and development lenders; commercial banks, savings and loan associations, REITs, and mortgage banking companies. The period might be described as that of a blind euphoria concerning the actual size of the market for new condominiums, motels, and office buildings in many areas of the nation. Scores of REITs began a competitive scramble to put to work the easy money, made primarily possible by the commercial banks, flowing into their coffers.[27]

The boom was based on a strong—even if only cyclical—demand for construction capital, encouraged by national policies favoring residential construction, in which half of the REIT activity occurred. Booms often breed speculative excess. REITs rose and fell so dramatically because, as a REIT executive explained succinctly, of "sloppy banking, dumb loans on our part, and bad investment banking."[28]

If conflicts had been controlled properly, the excesses and decline almost certainly would have been less, perhaps substantially less, severe, but larger forces were at work. Those forces were largely the normal, basically healthy aspects of cyclical behavior in a free economy. Conflicts, without adequate safeguards to prevent abuse, interfere with the discipline and self-correcting tendencies of efficient markets. Conflicts in REITs, although not a major cause of the trouble, added to it and almost surely will do so again if ignored.

III • CONFLICTS OF INTEREST

Real estate investment trusts are riddled with conflicts of interest. Not all of these conflicts call for changes in REIT structure or practices, but all warrant attention to determine why each arises, the degree of harm its presence permits, and the corrective measures that, if justified at all, have the fewest undesirable side effects.

The most important conflicts in REITs are: (1) the externalized management structure; (2) the method of calculating the advisor's fees; (3) competition between REIT and sponsor-advisor for desirable investments; (4) self-dealing; and (5) the representation of both REIT and sponsor-advisor by the same law firm (this practice was universal until after the 1974-75 debacle, when some REITs chose or were required to secure their own counsel).

The "Externalized" Management Structure

In almost all American corporations other than investment companies and REITs, the stockholders elect a board of directors that selects the company's officers, sets their compensation, and makes basic policy within which the officers manage the company.[1] In the abstract such a structure renders management directly accountable to the stockholders; in fact, most managements dominate their boards rather than vice versa,[2] and accountability to shareholders, such as it is, depends less on the election of directors (except in the abnormal, rare instances of proxy contests) than on the shareholders' ability to sell their stock. Presumably, if enough shareholders sell, the shares become so cheap that another company can take over the corporation and replace the management. (Takeover threats, as a device to hold management accountable, need not be examined here.) In practice, in normal corporate structure, stockholders have little influence on policy because most boards are wholly or largely composed of the company's officers rather than outsiders acting as "trustees" and reviewing the officers' performance objectively, although this pattern is changing dramatically.[3] Moreover, even boards that include "outsiders" control the nomination of new directors[4] and the proxy solicitation process, and the vast majority of shares are voted in favor of their nominees or proposals.

The trustees of REITs and the directors of investment companies are even less accountable to their shareholders than are ordinary corporate boards because of the externalized management structure. Like most corporations the typical REIT (or investment company) has a board elected by its shareholders; unlike a corporation it has no officers or employees. Instead, the board hires a separately owned "external" management firm to act as "advisor." Almost invariably, the firm chosen is the REIT's original sponsor, is represented on the REIT board, and selects the "unaffiliated" members of that board. The advisor recommends the REIT's investments, arranges credit for the REIT, and administers all its affairs. For these services the REIT pays the advisor an "advisory fee." As the REIT's advisor, the firm (or its affiliates) also has the opportunity, in a great many cases, to earn other very substantial fees.

Although investment companies also have externalized management,[5] REIT trustees have a greater obligation to their shareholders than do investment company directors. One reason why is that unlike investment company advisors, who are empowered to, and do, make all investment decisions, REIT advisors (in theory) only submit recommendations to the REIT trustees; the trustees have formal decision-making responsibility. Another reason is that the almost universal method of setting REIT advisory fees causes an unusual divergence of interests between advisors and shareholders, not only on the amounts of fees but also on decisions regarding both the REIT's financial structure and its specific investments.

Moreover, unlike an ordinary corporation's managerial personnel, who very often hold substantial and even major portions of their personal wealth in the form of shares of their company, REIT advisory firms and their personnel seldom hold more than nominal stock positions in their REITs.[6] Thus, most REIT managements lack the incentive that owning stock would probably provide to protect the shareholders' interest in the REIT's soundness as an investment. (The sponsor-advisor of General Growth Properties, one of the most successful REITs, and its staff have held about 23 percent of their REIT's shares.[7]) And REIT boards do not confront disclosure requirements strict enough to carry with them effective accountablity to shareholders.

In theory corporate profits belong to the stockholders, and in ordinary corporations that are not too small to fall under SEC requirements, the compensation of management is disclosed to the stockholders. Stockholders can compare officers' salaries and bonuses with those of their counterparts in similar companies and decide whether the cost of management is reasonable. In REITs only the total cost of all management services is disclosed to stockholders. This figure is not broken down into categories such as operating expenses, salaries, or profit. Thus, REIT shareholders cannot evaluate the appropriateness of management compensation. Perhaps even more important, the "independent" members of the REIT board get little or no information about the REIT advisor's expenses. (Investment company directors receive substantially more information, although their stockholders do not.)

To the extent that an ordinary corporation's board does actually select and dominate officers, it negotiates the terms of management's compensation through arm's-length bargaining. (Even in many insider-dominated boards of ordinary corporations, the committee on executive compensation consists of independent directors.) The dominance of advisors' representatives on REIT boards is, of course, incompatible with arm's-length bargaining over advisory contracts. Moreover, because the externalized management is hired as a firm rather than individual by individual, individuals in the management group are accountable not to the REIT board but only to their superiors in the advisory firm.

In conformity with a statement of policy issued by the Midwest Securities Commissioners Association, inspired by an analogous federal statutory requirement for investment companies, a majority of REIT trustees were independent of the advisor.[8] If, in fact, only the independent trustees negotiated the management contract for the REIT, then, to the extent that these trustees were exercising independent judgment, the contract would indeed be the product of arm's-length bargaining and might reasonably be expected to be fair to the REIT. But as a leading attorney who has sued many investment company advisors once observed: "If you really want to have a watchdog watch a man, you don't have the man select the watchdog."[9] The REITs'

"unaffiliated" trustees had basically been invited to join the club... they were there as a pleasant part of their overall business relationship with that banking organization, and... to expect them to exercise any kind of independence in that kind of a setting was just truly out of the question. [This has been referred to as] the fiction that surrounded the independence of the REIT. ... [10]

To the shareholder, the independent trustee is someone who, for compensation ranging up to about $12,000 a year, and a chance to spend a long weekend at a choice resort free of charge three or four times a year, has assumed as an avocation the responsibility for protecting the REIT's shareholders from mismanagement by the adviser. To the adviser, on the other hand, the independent trustee is someone whose experience in a particular geographic area or real estate activity augments the adviser's capability to recommend timely changes in the REIT's investment policies and evaluate investment opportunities as they are generated. There is, of course, a degree of truth in both views.... [11]

Moreover, the criteria for independent trustees of REITs were markedly more permissive than those for independent trustees of investment companies:[12]

[I]f the purpose of the requirement is to insure that the operations of the REIT are subject to the review of trustees whose loyalty is solely to the REIT, [the criterion] may not be adequate. For example, it includes as independent the lawyer or other professional to whom the adviser represents a significant client or a significant source of business, as well as the developer who relies heavily on the adviser or its affiliates for procuring or furnishing financing from sources other than REIT.[13]

In short, the boards of REITs with external management had a unique combination of high obligation and low accountability.

In early years, about forty REITs, representing only a small percentage of the industry's assets, depended on internal personnel for management. During the mid-1970s, a number of REITs that had ceased to be profitable made major changes in their fee arrangement structures. By the end of 1977, ninety REITs, holding 37 percent of the industry assets, had internal management.[14] As they become profitable again, these trusts may or may not return to externalized management; meanwhile, the bulk of the industry has retained the external management structure.

A Uniquely Severe Conflict: REIT Advisors' Fees

''The $100 Million Question'' is the subtitle of the 1975 annual survey of REIT advisory fee plans conducted by Audit Investment Research, a highly regarded investment advisory service and the main independent source of information about REITs. The question is:

[W]hether fees were not $100 or $110 million too high during [the REITS'] halcyon days.

Some Trustee boards have implicitly answered that question in the affirmative by requesting their Advisers to stay on the job with little or no fee. In effect they are asking the Adviser to give back some of the profits it earned in the lush days. . . .

A second group of answers comes in reaction of Trustee boards to the ancillary question of whether Advisers should make profits from their Trusts in these troubled times (when shareholders are seeing red ink and banking no dividends). . . .

A third group of answers has come from the Trustees who have decided to internalize management and operate without an investment adviser. . . .

The industry's trauma has raised this $100 million question forcibly. It will not go away.

[A]bout $170 million. . . is needed to operate the REITs whereas the higher expense ratios in the most profitable heydays of the REITs in early 1973 would produce $280 million in annual expenses.[15]

This 65 percent overcharge was made possible by conflicts and inadequate disclosure: The externalized management structure virtually eliminated the possibility of arm's-length bargaining over fees. And the management compensation arrangement encouraged management to leverage the REIT's assets by borrowing, providing a "reward for mismanagement."[16] These conflicts in REITs operated against sound judgment about both the proper debt-equity ratio overall and the appropriateness of each specific potential investment.

Adequate disclosure might have served to prevent abuse of these conflicts. But the information presented to potential investors was "deceptively simple"[17] and seriously incomplete. Prospectuses and routine reporting for REITs seemed to supply the information necessary for a determination of management costs but did not show what proportions would be or were spent on managing the REIT and what proportions would be profit to the managers; they did not clearly explain the advisory fee formula or describe the fees other than the advisory fee that might accrue to the advisor and its affiliates. Certainly, the information available to investors did not enable them to compare the management expenses of several REITs.[18]

As early as 1961, one authority noted that the yield on REIT shares would probably be insufficient to justify the investment risk unless management kept its costs very low.[19] But REIT managements had conflicting incentives to raise these costs. Few REIT sponsor-advisors owned any stock in their REITs; "the honey that drew the bees to sponsorship of REITs was the hope of high profit margins [on the fees] with minimal investment."[20] Of course, some sponsors, particularly the large banks and insurance companies, may have been motivated less by the fees than by the other benefits, such as those that might flow from the existence of a REIT to complement the sponsor's own real estate activities. In fact, REIT management costs proved to be so much higher than those of other mortgage investments that one commentator recently exhorted other real estate organizations to match the REITs' "generally far superior" level of compensation "to compete with the REITs in attracting comparable management."[21]

Early in the REITs' history, before significant sums were involved, the typical REIT paid advisory fees in the range of 1.0 to 1.2 percent of "total invested assets." But the term *total invested assets* was ambiguous. Starting in 1961 state securities commissioners, particularly the members of the Midwest Securities Commissioners Association, tried to regulate the calculation of advisory fees and other expenses.

In 1961 the Midwest group set three relevant limits:

1. Annual advisor fees should not exceed 0.5 percent of net assets. (The word *net* normally denotes what remains after deduction of all liabilities, but the term seems not to have been so interpreted in this context.[22])

2. Total expenses (excluding interest but including the advisory fee) should not exceed 1.5 percent of "average net assets," calculated on the basis of cost

less depreciation or, in the judgment of the trustees, fair market value of the net assets of the trust, whichever is less. (Thus the definition included no reference to liabilities.)

3. No trustee, officer, independent contractor, or investment advisor should "receive a commission or other renumeration, directly or indirectly, in connection with the disposal or acquisition of trust assets."

The implementation of the Midwest provisions was extremely uneven.[23] Moreover, when REITs began to proliferate, in 1970, the Midwest group greatly relaxed its treatment of advisors' income. They changed the formulas and the base for calculating both fees and total expenses. They retained the ceiling on total annual expenses—including the advisory fee—at 1.5 percent of "total invested assets." But they increased the maximum advisory fee, which had previously been limited to 0.5 percent of assets without reduction for liabilities, to the greater of either 1.5 percent of true net assets (assets reduced by liabilities) *or* 25 percent of the REIT's net income before deduction of the advisory fee itself (and certain other specified expenses).[24]

For example, if REIT ABC had $100 million in total invested assets, $50 million in liabilities, and $2 million in net income, then 1.5 percent of total invested assets would be $1.5 million; 1.5 percent of average net assets (assuming no change during the year) would be $750,000; and 25 percent of net income would be $500,000. The advisory fees would be limited to $750,000, and total expenses, including the advisory fee, would be limited to $1.5 million.

The actual calculation of the fee was a highly complex operation[25] that reportedly "requires about three hours of concentrated staff time each month, involving among other things some estimation of expenses which may be chargeable to the trust during the month."[26]

A particularly important aspect of the advisory fee formula was its treatment of assets attributable to borrowing by the REIT. Although, in addition to jeopardizing the stockholders' position, leveraging could endanger the longer term flow of fees to the advisor; in the meantime it increased the advisors' fees far more, proportionally, than the stockholders' earnings. As a leading banking securities analysis firm observed:

by proceeding from an all-equity position to a 5 to 1 debt leverage position, the REIT was able to increase earnings 50% . . .[while the advisor] recorded a 500% increase in [its] gross earnings . . . .at higher levels of the prime [interest rate], the earnings from leveraged funds could actually be negative after consideration of the adviser's fee. Thus, the theoretical situation exists where the [stockholder] receives no benefit (or a negative benefit) from the incorporation of higher risk. . . .[27]

Shifting the base calculations for gross assets to true net assets (unless 25 percent of net income provided a larger fee) might have been expected to discourage excessive leveraging. But the 1970 regulations increased the lever-age a REIT could assume and the amount of nonfee income an advisor and its affiliates could capture.

From 1961 to 1970, the regulations had set maximums of 66.66 percent of the REIT property's fair market value for secured borrowing and 8 percent of its net assets for unsecured borrowing. These limits permitted about a three-to-one debt-equity ratio. In 1970 they were replaced by a provision that aggregate borrowings "shall not be unreasonable in relation to the net assets," the ceiling to be stated in the prospectus. Thus, before 1970 a REIT with equity of $50 million could not have borrowed more than approximately $150 million and could not have incurred total expenses of more than $3 million, including an advisory fee of about $1 million. After 1970, when the debt-equity ratios of a number of major REITs approached six to one, a REIT with $50 million in equity could have total assets of about $350 million and total expenses of $5.25 million. Its advisory fee might be lower than under the pre-1970 treatment, unless 25 percent of net income provided more. The new limit on the advisory fee was apparently effective in curtailing borrowing in a number of REITs, particularly the most highly leveraged ones. But in others advisors were able to end-run the limit because of another feature of the 1970 guidelines.

Before 1970 the statements of policy flatly barred any trustee, investment advisor, or officer of a REIT from receiving "a commission or other remunera-tion, directly or indirectly, in connection with the disposal or acquisition of trust assets." After 1970 only receipts in connection with a self-dealing transaction were barred, in the sense that such receipts would count against the advisory fee. Because the guidelines allowed REITs to incur total expenses of up to 1.5 percent of gross assets, REIT managers could enhance their incomes by earning nonadvisory fees up to a ceiling that could be raised infinitely high by leveraging. And in fact, many REITs derived less income from advisory fees than from related fees and commissions.

Apart from the substantive requirements imposed by the states, the SEC required REITs to disclose the dollar amounts of advisory fees, the formulas used to calculate these fees (although the form used for disclosure might be "deceptively simple"), and the formulas for any other fees or commissions the advisor and its affiliates might enjoy.

Although *nonadvisory fees*—fees paid by the REIT for mortgage origination and servicing or for property management, or fees paid by the REIT's bor-rowers for loan commitment, placement, brokerage, or some other service—often totaled more than the advisory fee, REIT reporting almost always simply lumped such payments together as "other expenses" without indication of how much went to the advisor and affiliates and how much (if any) to indepen-dent outsiders. A few REITs did voluntarily disclose to their stockholders how much the advisor and affiliates received from the REIT in nonadvisory fees; fewer also disclosed receipts from their borrowers.

But except in a few situations, the portion of the advisory fee that went into operating the REIT and the portion that represented profit for the advisor were undisclosed not only to the REIT stockholders but even to the unaffiliated trustees who were theoretically responsible for both hiring the advisor and setting the fee level and structure. "No one will ever know if trusts would have fared better in the real estate recession if advisory fees had been used to provide the quality and scope of loan underwriting and monitoring services trustees thought they were buying."[28] Probably, the SEC refrained from requiring disclosure of information necessary for "unaffiliated" REIT trustees to judge the advisory contract because it was not until 1970 that legislation enacted at the SEC's request explicitly obligated the "disinterested directors" of investment companies to secure "such information as may reasonably be necessary to evaluate the terms of any advisory contract. . . . "[29] This improvement in the regulation of investment companies, which are far older and, in terms of SEC attention, far more important than REITs, simply has not yet caught up with REITs.

The best data available to a diligent and knowledgeable investor who wishes to evaluate a given REIT as a prospective investment are the identity of its sponsor-advisor, the kinds of investment it makes, its financial structure, and its track record, if any. But the past investment performance of a REIT is much harder to evaluate than that of an investment company. Investment companies disclose fully the contents of their portfolios, including both the names of the issuers and the number of shares of each security held. The availability of this information makes it possible to evaluate the performance of an investment company portfolio and to measure its riskiness in general terms or with mathematical precision. Such information is incomparably more useful than the best investment data that a REIT can provide. Even elaborate descriptions of particular real estate investments, especially in construction and development, can never be as informative as routine reporting about the kinds of securities held by investment companies.

The potential investor might try to compensate for his difficulties in evaluating investment performance by comparing total management costs, the distribution of these costs between expenses and profits, or the respective ability (or inclination) of the sponsor-advisors to reimburse their REITs if necessary.

Unhappily, very few REITs are reporting to *their* shareholders on a regular basis the results of operations of their adviser. When this is done, it is usually contained in proxy statements supporting expense-only fees. Thus the REIT shareholder remains largely in the dark about how the dollars of advisory fees are actually being spent. Perhaps it will take some evolution toward greater maturity among REIT trustees to elevate disclosure standards in this area.[30]

To the extent it can be determined, advisory fee income was often extremely profitable—profitable enough to raise "The $100 Million Question." The 1975 survey of fees by Audit Investment Research concluded, "Frankly we know of no other business in the country that is or was so profitable."[31] (See Table 15.)

Table 15: REIT Advisory Fee Profit Margins (Pretax Income of Advisors from This Fee, as Percent of This Fee; No Other Fees Included)

	1969	1970	1971	1972	1973	1974	1975	5-YEAR OR 6-YEAR COMPOSITE
Lomas & Nettleton								
a. Percent			66.3	68.6	68.6	69.1	64.5	57.9
b. Total year-end invested assets (millions)			$180	$321	$378	$335	$339	
Great American Mortgage								
a. Percent				22.5	21.8	25.2	8.0	
b. Total year-end invested assets (millions)				$246	$426	$466	$390	
Diversified Mortgage								
a. Percent	38.7	40.1	38.0	37.2	36.8	6.3		
b. Total year-end invested assets (millions)				$288	$343	$381		
NJB Prime								
a. Percent					59.1	23.9a		
b. Total year-end invested assets (millions)					$ 94	$109		
Beneficial Standard								
a. Percent					29.8	13.2		
b. Total year-end invested assets (millions)					$ 95	$101		
GREIT								
a. Percent			1.9	8.2	7.4			
b. Total year-end invested assets (millions)			$ 37	$ 47	$ 60			

Note: Profitability data for ten other trusts are available but not included in the table for two reasons:

1. Gulf, HNC, and Wells Fargo are omitted because their advisors derived income from sources other than the REIT and do not report REIT-related profits separately. In the cases of Gulf and Wells Fargo, the advisors' profits actually exceeded their gross REIT advisory fees; HNC showed a loss.

2. Other REITs are omitted because data are available only for a single year or not available when there were any profits but only when severe losses were occuring. These are American Century (31.4% profit margin in 1973); Northwestern Financial (35.3% profit margin in 1973); First Pennsylvania (losses of $553,000 in 1974 and $62,000 in 1975); IDS (losses of $8.1 million in 1974 and $32.7 million in 1975); Cameron-Brown (loss of

$7.5 million in 1974); Tri-South (loss of $739,127 in 1974); and Northern States (operating without fee in 1973-74, suffered losses of $254,018 and $276,118 in those years).

[a]The advisor drew a fee only until April 30, 1974. In 1975 the advisor lost $234,400. AIR-1975, pp. 16, 34.

Source: Compiled from AIR-1973, p. 12; 1974, pp. 50-51; 1975, pp. 34-38; and 1976, pp. 37-40. Copyright by Audit Investment Research, Inc., and reprinted by permission. All other rights reserved.

CALCULATING FEES

The methods used to calculate REIT advisory fees varied considerably, but certain basic practices were widespread. About three-fourths of the 112 REITs that Audit Investment Research surveyed in 1974 paid their advisors 1.0 to 1.2 percent of total invested assets, without any "volume discount" as the total amount of assets rose.[32] About two-thirds[33] included in the "assets" base on which they calculated their advisory fees and total expenses unfunded portions of loans that had been closed, even though the unfunded portions were not then part of the actual assets and actually never would be, at least in the case of the bulk of the industry assets, construction and development loans. Such loans are usually drawn upon by the builder in stages over the whole construction period, as the money is needed. Construction and development lenders assume that only an average of 50 percent of such a loan will be outstanding at any one time. The rationale for basing the advisory fee on the total amount of such a loan—including even funds that had not yet been borrowed by the REIT to meet the commitment—was that the advisor had to arrange the entire loan. (The REIT would not disclose the actual amounts of such unfunded portions,[34] but a careful reading of the fee formula might make clear that such sums could be included in calculating the fee.) By 1974 this treatment of unfunded portions was losing significance simply because new commitments were coming to a halt.

In addition, and apart from nonadvisory fees, over three-fourths of the REITs paid incentive fees based upon return of equity: one-third to one-half paid additional incentive fees based upon percentages of capital gains, and many paid both, although the importance of this practice also has declined, with capital gains, since 1974. A handful of REITs paid only incentive fees.[35]

Almost three-fourths of REIT advisors were permitted to receive fees for nonadvisory services.[36] The total income from several different kinds of fees was apparently very large. The Midwest Commissioners called for some of these receipts to be deducted from advisory fees, but confusion or outright inconsistency evidently prevailed, and few REITs made such deductions. The most common forms of nonadvisory income were "forfeited commitment and standby fees" and "servicing and supervisory fees."[37] But many REIT advisors also received fees directly from the REIT's borrowers, for services variously "styled as commitment, placement, origination or brokerage."[38] Such fees were a major part of the REIT-related revenues of some advisors. Few REITs disclosed to their stockholders (except as a possibility in the description of the fee formula) fees paid to the advisors by the borrowers, and still fewer included borrower payments in the advisory fee or expense limits. Some of these fees went entirely to the advisor or an affiliate; some were shared with the REIT. Despite the sketchiness of information about such fees, they clearly represented a substantial amount of money, at least some of which may have been what lawyers call ''corporate opportunities,'' improperly diverted from the REITs themselves.

For example, IDS Realty, advised by a subsidiary of Investor Diversified Services, manager of the nation's largest mutual fund complex, generated the following for the advisor and its affiliates:[39]

	1972	1973	1974
Advisory Fee		$ 928,000	$1,926,000
Incentive Fee		2,000	350,000
Less: refund because of limit		—	(388,000)
Advisory Fee Paid		$ 930,000	$1,888,000
Nonadvisory Fees:			
Origination, appraisal, and other fees from borrowers	$ 898,000	$1,456,000	$1,872,000
Servicing fees	—	77,000	417,000
Distribution of subordinated debentures[a]			2,248,000
Debenture registrar fee[a]			26,000

[a]Paid to an affiliate of the advisor.

Not counting the income from services in connection with the subordinated debentures, total fees in 1973 came to $2,463,000, when total operating income for the REIT before payment of fees and expenses was $5,940,000; in 1974 total fees were $4,176,000, when REIT total income was $7,500,000.[40] The REIT generating those fees for its sponsor-advisor had about $50 million in total assets at the beginning of 1972 , averaged about $180 million during 1973, and averaged about $300 million during 1974.

Another REIT, Justice Mortgage Investors of Dallas, produced $754,406 in origination fees from the borrowers—almost double the additional advisory fee paid by the REIT, which had total assets of under $15 million at the beginning and $42.5 million at the end of 1972. In 1973, with Justice's assets averaging $70 million, origination fees from borrowers rose to $809,000, but by then the advisory fee was $951,000.[41] In addition to those fees—and another $36,000 each year in ''incentive'' advisory fees—Justice Mortgage's advisor had an insurance affiliate that earned premiums from the REIT's borrowers in connection with loans by the REIT, totaling $46,000 in 1973 and $133,000 in 1973. The total income to Justice's advisor and affiliate in 1972 was about 4 percent of rough average net assets; in 1973 it was almost 3 percent.

In 1974 Audit Investment Research reported nonadvisory fee income amounts for 10 of the 112 mortgage REITs surveyed, including IDS Realty and Justice Mortgage. For the other 8, the disclosed nonadvisory fee income was almost as large as the advisory fees in four instances, over half as large in one instance, and over one-fifth as large in three instances. [42]

A particularly problem-ridden form of nonadvisory fee income generated by REITs was payments to trustees and trustees' affiliates for services to REIT borrowers and prospective borrowers. For example, the chairman of the advisor to Associated Mortgage Investors owned a firm that prepared and reviewed cost projections on projects to be financed by that REIT; this firm received $215,000 from borrowers or prospective borrowers in 1972. Another trustee headed a firm that received $97,000 from borrowers and prospective borrowers for "brokerage appraisal." Three officers of Alison Mortgage were partners or associates in the law firm that acted as counsel to the REIT in many loan closings; in 1973 the law firm received $103,703 from borrowers from that REIT. The firm of the chairman of the advisor to Dominion Mortgage received legal fees, totaling $146,700 in 1972 and $278,087 in 1973, from borrowers from the REIT. In 1973 the firm of a trustee of North American Mortgage received $259,000 in legal fees, and the firm of two officers of the advisor to Republic Mortgage received $242,426.

Of course, these sums were not gifts but payments for services. And it is standard practice for borrowers to pay, for example, the lender's counsel's fees. If the lender had to pay these fees, he would simply charge the borrower more. Although the borrower pays this fee, the lender's counsel is not therefore expected to represent the borrower's interests. The conflict implicit in the availability of such fees to the lender's counsel arises only when counsel is also an officer or trustee of the lender. An officer or trustee has an obligation to the REIT's stockholders to make sure that a given loan will benefit the REIT. Counsel, on the other hand, has an interest in seeing that the loan goes forward so as to produce a closing fee, whether or not it will benefit the REIT.

Two justifications might be offered for the fee picture. First, the advisory contracts were renewable each year and REIT boards could cancel them on short notice. Second, REIT activity involved a high level of risk, and therefore REIT managers might have been entitled to a rich flow of fees in good years. But the relationship between REIT boards and advisors discouraged a critical approach to contract terms, and in fact, no REITs canceled or failed to renew their advisory contracts until the debacle was well under way. Indeed, in the much longer history of investment companies, only three or four have severed relations with their external advisors. Going to a new advisor would be even harder for a REIT than for an ordinary investment company because the REIT's advisor would have hard-to-transfer knowledge of the real estate investments in the REIT's portfolio. Moreover, if anticipation of lean times were what prompted advisors to keep their fees and profits high in the good years, it should also have prompted other precautions such as contractual provisions for periods of little or no earnings, reduction of aggressive leveraging, or expansion of loan loss reserves.

Even when economic disaster did strike and most REITs entered an era of low profits, no profits, or even sharp losses, the REIT structure and operation allowed some advisors to continue enjoying ample compensation. For example, Continental Mortgage (CMI) filed for bankruptcy in March 1976, with 90 percent of its loans no longer accruing interest; in fiscal 1975 it had paid its advisor company—a partnership largely owned by two brothers, Monte J. and Neil W. Wallace—almost $88 million in fees. In earlier years the fee had been approximately $10 million, about 60 percent of which appears to have been pure profit. An SEC complaint filed in January 1978 charged that the advisor had concealed the REIT's "true' financial condition in 1974 and 1975, a condition that would not have justified such high fees.

Even more striking, in September 1975 the SEC filed a civil action charging First Mortgage (FMI), its advisor, and certain principals—including Jack R. Courshon, a founder of the REIT and chairman of its board—with violations of disclosure rules. An article in *Forbes* in February of that year[43] had described many of the alleged violations, apparently designed to conceal defaults and other serious problems so FMI could continue to appear to show growth in earnings from quarter to quarter. This growth also meant a growth in the fees of the advisor, of which Jack R. Courshon and his brother Arthur, also an FMI trustee, owned 37.4 percent. The SEC charged FMI with creating a shell corporation that would buy out developments in default with new loans from FMI, arranging for developers to take over troubled properties—sometimes at what appeared to be a profit for FMI in return for large loan commitments at bargain interest rates, and engaging appraisers who would inflate the value of a project that FMI was financing. These subterfuges could not work forever, but in 1974, when half the trust's loans were in default, the advisor was paid fees of more than $5 million.

The SEC's complaint was settled without prosecutions or reimbursement. Under a consent decree, FMI became internally managed; the board agreed to elect five new unaffiliated trustees and to form an executive committee consisting of a majority of unaffiliated trustees operating under set controls and guidelines.

At other REITs revolts by REIT boards, stockholder class action suits (against more than twenty-five REITs), pressure from lenders, concern for the sponsor's reputation, and doubtless simple integrity have drowned advisors in red ink. Extensive changes have been made in advisory fee arrangements.

Starting in mid-1974, REITs began abandoning the Midwest Commissioners guidelines, which had been designed in such an optimistic spirit that when the REITs' income flows and shareholders' equity began to run down, their advisors could not even cover expenses, let alone receive profits. In setting up new arrangements for management compensation, some REITs wholly ignored the Midwest limits; most came up with formulas that at least purported to be in compliance with the guidelines. For purposes of enforcement, the Midwest guidelines were primarily applicable to new offerings, but no new offerings were made in 1974-76. Even when the guidelines were continually applicable as part of the American Stock Exchange (Amex) listing requirements, at least two Amex-listed REITs "effectively abrogate[d]" the limits.[44]

Changes in management compensation followed three main routes. About fifty REITs[45] internalized management. Some REITs took this route when their trustees found it necessary to terminate relations with the advisor. For example, the Cabot Cabot & Forbes REIT internalized managment when its sponsor, the real estate developer of the same name, became delinquent on $12 million in investments held by the REIT. San Francisco Real Estate Investors became independent when its advisor's parent imposed budget restrictions that threatened to reduce services just when more services were needed.[46] In other instances advisors preferred not to serve for little or no profit, or the trustees' new cost-consciousness led to internalization. Some equity REITs internalized because of an IRS ruling subsequently reversed in the 1976 amendments.[47]

About ten REITs—all but one of them sponsored by publicly held financial institutions with major reputations—took a second route: that is, to operate entirely without reimbursing the advisor even from actual advisory expenses.[48] The group serving without fees includes Chase Manhattan, Manufacturers Hanover, First Wisconsin, City Investing, and State Mutual Life Assurance.[49] Some REITs established these unusual arrangements, apparently, at the behest of bank creditors and in connection with new agreements. For example, in 1975 the IDS REIT's advisor agreed to serve without any fee while $128 million in a new credit agreement remained outstanding. Earlier, the IDS advisor had waived fees on nonearning assets and on loans to the advisor's affiliate; in 1974 the *advisor's* loss amounted to $8,107,844; in 1975 it was $32,706,904.

About fifty REIT advisors are serving for expenses only or reduced flat fees. The variations of those arrangements, and changes as the picture has evolved, are legion.[50] The REIT management fee picture leaves large questions open. Apart from the estimated overcharge of $100 million, it is impossible to determine how much of the overleveraging was due to advisors' efforts to increase their advisory fees, how much less money REIT stockholders would have lost if advisors had had no financial incentive to overleverage, how much lower advisory fees might have been given arm's-length bargaining—or even disclosure, and how much of the fees should have gone—but in the absence of arm's-length bargaining or disclosure did not go—into financing care in investment selection and other management tasks that might, in turn, have benefited the stockholders. Performance was indeed poor, and the evidence of excessive profits substantial, but of course the inadequacies of performance are not clearly traceable to inadequate effort by management. Nor can the fee formulas be *proved* to have caused the excessive leveraging, although the likelihood that the fee structure would encourage leveraging seems strong.

Publicly Held Sponsor-Advisors and Sponsors and Trustees Engaged in Their Own Real Estate Activities

During the boom a number of major banks saw REITs as "banking's new profit partner,"[51] and bank-sponsored REITs accounted for one-third of REIT industry assets. But most major banks, although lending heavily to REITs, avoided REIT sponsorship, for whatever reasons. Citicorp, for example, is particularly innovative and expansionary, but it did not sponsor a REIT. Nor did Morgan, Mellon, First Chicago or First of Boston become REIT sponsors. In one case, according to an unidentified top bank officer quoted by the *Los Angeles Times*,

> There were several reasons, but the conflict of interest question was certainly a big one. We saw that we would be working with two sets of shareholders—one for the bank and one for the REIT. Is the trust advisor supposed to earn money for the REIT shareholders or for the bank shareholders? This conflict bothered us.[52]

The determination of the fee for advisory or related services was a manifestation of this conflict. Apart from paying the interest on its loans, a REIT's only significant expenses were advisory and related fees. The evidence of extraordinarily high profit margins in REIT advisory fees suggests that this conflict was resolved in favor of the sponsor's stockholders and against the REIT's stockholders.

Some forty banks, as well as insurance companies, real estate-oriented firms and conglomerates, virtually all of which were publicly held (some of the real estate-oriented firms were partnerships or privately held), managed two-thirds of REIT industry assets. In the case of over half the industry's assets, therefore, the conflict between the REIT stockholders and the sponsor's stockholders went beyond advisory fees. Sponsorship by firms also engaged in their own real estate activities obviously had its benefits.[53] A recent SEC statistical report (which does not deal with conflict-of-interest questions) states:

> There are a number of possible investment advantages of investment in affiliated trusts, particularly the REITs sponsored by enterprises or institutions active in real estate and finance. Such benefits include the availability of investments, cost savings due to economies of scale and the elimination of start-up costs and the availability and cost of credit.[54]

Many REITs attracted public investors precisely because they offered such benefits. And the name and reputation of the sponsor eased the sale of REIT shares, long-term debt, and borrowing in the commercial paper market.

Connecticut General Insurance, for example, was particularly able to aid in selling shares of its REIT:

> Some 1,200 of our insurance agents and brokers are registered representatives of CG Equity Sales Company. The company is the broker dealer affiliate of Connecticut General. . . .
> . . . CG Equity Sales Company representatives sold a significant portion of the total underwriting and could have sold more if additional units had been available.[55]

All of the insurance company-sponsored REITs and twenty-nine of the thirty-nine bank-sponsored REITs incorporated the name of the sponsor in the REIT's name, as Chase Manhattan Mortgage and Realty Trust, or MassMutual Mortgage and Realty Investors.[56]

> Stockholder reaction . . . was typified by the observation of a Milwaukee attorney who invested in the trust's stock when all signs pointed up. "I got in," he said, "because this was being run by First Wisconsin and I felt they were a good orderly investor-minded organization."[57]

The thirty-nine bank-sponsored REITs were all among the one hundred largest REITs. Their interaction with their sponsor involved especially acute conflicts and led to avoidable injuries not only for the REIT stockholders but also for the stockholders of many of the sponsoring banks.

Although the advisory fee was the source of one of these conflicts, banks did not embark on REIT sponsorship primarily to obtain such fees. The sponsors were actually not the banks themselves but the bank holding companies. Banks are always the largest component of their holding companies, usually contributing well over 90 percent of the holding company's earning. Despite the overcharges, REIT advisory fees tended to get lost in the bigger bank holding company picture. In 1972 and 1973 (its best years), the Chase Manhattan REIT, which was the biggest REIT of all, accounted for 0.31 percent of the Chase Manhattan holding company's total income and only 7 percent of its nonbank income.[58] In a smaller bank, the REIT fees might have mattered more but probably would not have amounted to enough, by themselves, to motivate sponsoring a REIT.

The main reason why banks became interested in REIT sponsorship was well explained, only a few months after Chase Manhattan set up its REIT, by a Chase officer:

> Looking into the future we saw before us enormous capital needs in the area of new construction which commercial banks will not be able to meet even in periods of easy money. Chase's Real Estate and Mortgage Loan Department, as the largest construction lender in the United States, began receiving evidence of this problem in a rather dramatic way.
> [1969] was real evidence of things to come regarding the future, when without curtailing any of our Real Estate and Mortgage Loan Department lending activities, we

had to turn down over one billion dollars in prime construction and development loan opportunities because the funds were not available.

Becoming an advisor to Chase Manhattan Mortgage and Realty Trust was the logical extension of our current activities. Chase . . .had considerable experience in making equity real estate investments.[59]

The rise of the REITs coincided—because of general economic expansion and rising availability of credit—with the banks' movement into holding companies and bank-related activities, of which the REIT industry was only one. The banks had their own mortgage loan departments; many bank holding companies also owned mortgage banking subsidiaries. They had real estate expertise that could be "leveraged."[60] Banks and their REITs often shared offices, staff, and facilities—as well as clientele and ventures. In short, in many situations the only genuine distinction between the REIT and the bank itself (or one of its wholly owned affiliates) was that the REIT's stockholder family was different from the bank's.

Loans that might be too risky for the bank, or blocked because the bank had already reached its loan limit to that borrower, or forbidden by certain regulations, could be passed along to the REIT. (Indeed, Congress may have intended REITs specifically to make land loans, subordinated loans, and other loans that would have been considered too risky for banks and insurance companies.) The bank would realize some income through advisory and/or mortgage placement fees and keep its borrowing customer happy. Bank and REIT loan facilities could complement each other; for example, the REIT might advance a construction loan while the bank arranged long-term financing, or vice versa. The REIT itself could borrow from its sponsor, on current market terms. Such loans to the REIT earned the bank interest, produced compensating balance deposits in the bank, and expanded the asset base used to calculate the advisory fee.

On the other hand, a bank could give its REIT an advantage over nonbank-sponsored REITs by waiving or lowering the compensating balances—even though such generosity reduced the bank's income and might not be in the best interests, at least in the short run, of the bank's stockholders. The Chase Manhattan Bank has at times relieved its REIT of any compensating balance requirement. BankAmerica Realty Investors also has at times operated with such low compensating balances that observers have assumed that the sponsor, BankAmerica Corporation, was favoring its trust.

Banks have been accused of other so-called sweetheart arrangements, such as reducing the rate of interest faster—and perhaps to lower levels—for their own REITs than for others during periods of declining interest rates or simply giving their REITs more favorable rates or access to credit than they could secure elsewhere. (After the 1974-75 decline, several major bank sponsors seemed to be massively favoring their own REITs because of the terms on which they engaged in "asset swaps.") If the bank or its real estate department was "loaned up," the REIT could borrow from other banks or tap public funds, and its long-term debt or commercial paper would expand the sponsoring bank's deposits. Perhaps the most important benefit that banks derived from advising a REIT, according to *The Wall Street Journal*, was that

...if a trust was lending $20 million to a contractor, and a check was issued by the adviser's bank on Friday, the check mightn't clear until the following Wednesday, giving the bank six days of interest on the check's "float."

With trusts that lent hundreds of millions of dollars, the interest on the float was sizeable.[61]

The advantages that flow to the REIT from the sponsor's expertise, contacts, and resources, weighed against the disadvantages created by conflicts, create a dilemma for regulation. For example, the Equitable Life Mortgage and Realty Investors is now the second biggest REIT, and it has never suffered more than minor reductions of earnings or dividends. If it were separated from its advisor, Equitable Life Assurance Society, this REIT would lose a nationwide network of loan originators, advantages in raising money, experienced personnel, and other benefits that have made it successful. In the very different situation of the formerly biggest, now in bankruptcy, Chase Manhattan REIT, bankruptcy was long avoided in large part because of its link with its sponsor:

Adam Heck, president of Chase Trust, is keenly aware of [his] possible ace in the hole. "I have their name, which I'm sure they must consider in any meditations they have," he says.

Concurring in this view is William Bateman, an executive vice president of Chase Bank. "We're not anxious to see anything with the name Chase Manhattan in bankruptcy anywhere," he says.[62]

But sponsorship by a firm that is, to some extent, in the same business as its REIT poses problems such as the fair allocation of potentially attractive investments between REIT and sponsor and protection of the REIT's portfolio against investments dumped by the sponsor in the expectation of obtaining related business benefits.

Such conflicts of interest were not kept secret. The prospectus for the initial offering of the Chase Manhattan REIT stated:

The real estate investment activities of the Advisor and certain of its affiliates [i.e., the bank or another real estate affiliate] engaged in the mortgage banking business will parallel those of the Trust in many types of investments, and therefore to a certain extent the Advisor and such of its affiliates will be engaged in competition with the Trust for investment opportunities.

The first chairman of the Chase REIT was Raymond T. O'Keefe, who, as executive vice president of the Chase Bank, continued in charge of its real estate and mortgage loan department (until his retirement in 1973). This dual role was characteristic of the bank REITs. In addition, usually many or most of the REIT advisor's staff came from the sponsor's real estate department.

Bank sponsors and insurance company sponsors developed different practices, fairly uniform in their groups, for investment allocation.[63] Many bank sponsors retained rights of first refusal, leaving themselves vulnerable to the charge that they were skimming off the better deals and even using REITs as ''dumping grounds'' for deals they considered marginal or worthwhile only because of tangential benefits.

Such charges would be difficult to prove—or disprove. Although the REITs and their advisors might compete for specific investments, in general, they played different economic roles. Whether the REITs borrowed from banks or in the commercial paper market, they paid higher interest rates than more established lenders and therefore had to lend at higher rates. Those real estate developers that had a choice would borrow at lower rates, such as those available from banks or insurance companies; those developers who were willing to pay the REITs' higher rates did so precisely because the projects for which they sought financing were riskier. It is difficult to distinguish between ''dumping'' and simply adopting a policy of higher risk at a higher rate of return. It was natural for borrowers from a REIT to give business to the REIT's sponsor because so many of the contacts between REITs and their borrowers originated with the sponsor. The bank sponsors charged their REITs finder's fees and other fees for services outside the routine advisory arrangement. So if a borrower from a REIT subsequently became a customer of the sponsoring bank, neither having had a prior relationship with the bank nor having been directed to the REIT by the bank for that initial loan, the REIT might have seemed entitled to some compensation or portion of the benefit to the banks. Yet at least in the case of the Chase Manhattan REIT, the prospectus was plain: ''It is not contemplated that the Trust will benefit from any such banking relationships or compensating balances.''

Giving REITs a right of first refusal would not, in any case, have eliminated the allocation conflict because the advisor that made the REIT's investment decisions was an affiliate or subsidiary of the sponsor. Even if responsibility for these decisions had been assigned to the ''unaffiliated'' trustees, in the majority of cases, these trustees' conflicting relationships would have limited their effective independence. And even sincerely independent and diligent unaffiliated trustees can hardly be expected to take the time to review all relevant investments the sponsor is considering for itself. But if the REITs had been able to exercise a right of first refusal independently and effectively, the shareholders of the sponsor would have suffered the loss of investments that otherwise would have been secured for their firm.

Insurance companies did give their REITs rights of first refusal, and a number of them, to avoid ''dumping ground'' charges, participated regularly in their REITs' commitments. Usually, they took 10 to 20 percent of each loan made by the REIT. For example, under a self-imposed requirement intended to protect its REIT, the Mutual Life Insurance Company of New York invested 10 percent of the total of each loan it generated for MONY Mortgage Investors, with neither part of the loan junior to the other. Such a requirement, if the sponsor-advisor's participation is substantial enough, encourages selection of prudent loans for the REIT: if the loans prove unsound, the advisor, too, will be hurt.[64]

No bank sponsor is known to have imposed such requirements on itself in its REIT's charter. Banks and their REITs often took portions of the same loan at the discretion of the advisors and trustees,[65] but the REIT's investment might be subordinated to the bank's, or priced differently, or made on terms otherwise different from the bank's participation. These arrangements were by no means unnecessarily unfair to the REIT; part of the purpose of sponsorship was to enable a bank or insurance company to provide a customer with not merely dollars but also complementary forms of financing. A short-term REIT could finance construction and its sponsor bank or mortgage banking affiliate could guarantee permanent financing, or conversely, the bank might give the construction loan, relying on its REIT for long-term participation. For example, Citizens and Southern Realty Investors, sponsored by Georgia's largest bank, had a loan "secured by a wrap-around second mortgage which is junior to a first mortgage held by the adviser."[66]

In projects for which a bank was financing construction and its REIT undertaking long-term financing, if the construction costs ran higher than original projections, the REIT was legally entitled to withdraw from its commitment. But such a withdrawl would have been detrimental to the bank's interest. If the same officials worked for both the bank and the REIT, they would have been hard put to arrive at a decision that would be fair to each master under such conditions.[67]

Self-Dealing

The "unlimited potentialities"[68] of REITs for self-dealing present problems whether or not the sponsor is publicly held and whether or not it conducts its own real estate activities as well as advising its REIT. The Investment Company Act of 1940 flatly bars self-dealing between investment companies and their externalized advisory firms (or affiliated persons or firms)—unless specific advance approval is secured from the SEC. Investment companies and their advisors have little legitimate reason to engage in sales of property. Hence, a flat prohibition imposes little constraint on their legitimate operations.[69] But the availability of bank sponsors, for example, as lenders or depositories for their REITs, permits huge efficiencies that probably outweigh the costs of the accompanying conflicts.[70] Instead of imposing a flat bar, therefore, the various bodies of law relevant to REITs required that conflict transactions be fair to the REIT and, when such transactions were attacked in court, were held to impose on the affiliated firm or person dealing with the REIT the burden of proving fairness. But court challenges of self-dealing transactions are rarely successful. Neither general law nor specific REIT legislation provided REIT shareholders with any significant protection against abusive self-dealing.[71]

Ironically, one of the most widespread and potentially abusive kinds of self-dealing arose from the legal requirement in some states—perhaps the most important is New York—that when a REIT filed its initial prospectus, it had to indicate how the money would be invested. The purpose of this provision, of course, was to protect investors. But because of it, sponsors seeking to come to market ahead of other institutions also eager to sponsor REITs did not wait patiently for good investments to come along but scrambled to find what they could. The most readily available investments were insider deals. For example, the initial prospectus (May 1972) for U.S. Bancorp Realty and Mortgage Trust, sponsored by Oregon's largest bank, informed prospective investors that the Trust's first properties would be purchased from the Dan Davis Corporation, 97 percent of whose outstanding capital stock was owned by Dan Davis and his wife. Davis, a Portland, Oregon, developer, was nominated and served as a trustee of the REIT. (He eventually resigned.) The REIT purchased a group of industrial facilities and office and commercial buildings from Davis's company for $14,139,340, a price "determined by arm's length negotiations between the Trust and Dan Davis and . . . based upon an expected return to the Trust on its investment" as well as upon independent appraisal. Davis's company, the prospectus stated, "will realize a gross profit for tax purposes on this transaction of approximately $6.36 million before deducting expenses." The purchase price may have been fair, but the transaction committed to an "insider" fully 56 percent of the REIT's $25 million in initial total assets.

A REIT's declaration of trust and prospectus usually set limitations on self-dealing. Many trusts, for example, prohibit their trustees, officers, and employees, as well as those of the advisor and its affiliates, from engaging in purchases, sales, or loans with the trust, but expressly allowed such transactions with the advisory firm itself, subject to certain conditions, such as [72] approval of the transaction by a majority of trustees and members of the investment committeee who are not affiliated with the other party to the transaction; a determination by the trustees that the transaction is fair and reasonable; and an independent appraisal of property to supplement the appraisal contained in mortgages.

A representative example of self-dealing between REITs and their advisors, and advance disclosure, is the February 1973 prospectus issued by Justice Mortgage Investors in connection with an offering of $20 million of debentures. The REIT had begun operations in 1972, with an equity offering of $21 million; later, its total assets passed $80 million, at which size it was a little above the median for the industry. The advisor was a wholly owned subsidiary of Glenn Justice Morgage Company, Inc. (the "mortgage company"), a large mortgage banking firm active in loan origination and administration, located like its REIT, in Dallas. The REIT invested primarily in first-mortgage construction and development loans and planned to continue to do so.

During 1972 the advisor received some $440,000 in advisory fees, representing about 1 percent of Justice Mortgage Investors' total assets and about 2 percent of its net assets for that year. The net earnings of the trust for 1972, after advisory fees and other expenses, were about $1.7 million.

The prospectus carefully disclosed that four of the nine REIT trustees, who held the four highest operating offices of the REIT, were also executives of the mortgage company.

The declaration of trust and the prospectus imposed restrictions on self-dealings. For example, they required that contracts with trustees of affiliated persons be subject to approval, after disclosure of the relationship, by a majority of the unaffiliated trustees, and that the terms of such transactions be at least as favorable to the REIT as those obtainable from unaffiliated persons.

The declaration and prospectus prohibited loans by the trust to the advisor, trustees, and officers or employees of the trust *in their individual capacities* as well as property transactions with entities controlling or controlled by the prohibited persons. Thus, the prohibitions did not apply to the mortgage company or to companies doing business with affiliated persons, for example, borrowers paying origination fees to the mortgage company.

The very purpose of the REIT, of course, was to make loans referred to it by the mortgage company. The mortgage company and the advisor were to present loan opportunities to the REIT resulting from the active mortgage banking business of the mortgage company. The advisor and mortgage company would be compensated by the REIT and the borrowers (through origination fees).

The prospectus also noted that the REIT could make long-term loans (none had been made at the time) and that, under a nonexclusive servicing agreement, the mortgage company would service such loans for the REIT for stated fees that were "as advantageous to the Trust as those obtainable from unaffiliated sources." The REIT also retained the right to make servicing arrangements with unaffiliated mortgage bankers.

With respect to competition for investments, the advisor and the mortgage company gave the REIT a right of first refusal on first-mortgage construction and development loans that were not prohibited by the declaration of trust. The first refusal rights did not cover longer term mortgages or other investments, although the sponsor's mortgage banking business spanned nearly the entire spectrum of real estate finance.

Nearly all of the REIT's loans were to borrowers in the five-state area in which the mortgage company did its business. In the REIT's first year of operation, according to the 1973 prospectus, the mortgage company originated most of its loans and received in origination fees $754,406—almost 175 percent of the advisory fee—from the borrowers. The prospectus also revealed that "certain affiliates" of the REIT owned insurance agencies and that during 1972 these agencies received $57,000 in insurance premiums paid by borrowers in connection with loans made by the REIT. Neither the origination fees nor the insurance premiums were deducted from the advisory fee.

Another picture of self-dealing appears in the 1974 prospectus of Flatley Realty Investors, a relatively small equity REIT (assets of over $20 million now, formerly around $30 million). This REIT was organized in 1972 by Thomas J. Flatley, a Boston real estate developer, who became the REIT's president and treasurer and a trustee. He also was the sole stockholder, president, treasurer, and director of Gibbs Management Corporation, which the REIT retained to operate certain of its properties. During the fiscal year ending June 30, 1973, the REIT paid a fee of $130,709 to its advisor and a fee of $18,700 to the management company. The Flatley prospectus noted that Mr. Flatley was engaged in the acquisition and development of real estate, that the REIT also was engaged in these activites, that Mr. Flatley and the REIT therefore might compete for opportunities, and that the REIT did not have first refusal on investments. The prospectus even noted that: "it may . . .be more profitable to Mr. Flatley to take an investment opportunity for his own account or the account of the Operating Company rather than presenting it to the Trust." The REIT could purchase property from, sell property to, or make loans to Mr. Flatley and the operating company and other organizations with which trustees, officers, or employees of the advisory management or operating company were affiliated. The unaffiliated trustees, too, "in their individual capacities are also permitted to engage in business activites of the kinds conducted by the Trust, and therefore, it is possible that situations may arise involving a conflict of interest." The possibilities were clearly enumerated:

Conflicts of interest may also arise if the Trust, as permitted by the declaration of Trust, with the approval of a majority of the independent Trustees, (a) makes or participates in loans to Mr. Flatley or the Operating Company or the Management Company, (b) pays servicing fees to Mr. Flatley or the Operating Company or the Management Company, (c) makes loans on which Mr. Flatley or the Operating Company received commitment, brokerage or placement fees, (d) borrows on recommendation of the advisor to increase the Trust's invested assets on which the Advisor's compensation is based . . ., (e) issues long-term commitments to refund short-term loans made by or through Mr. Flatley or the Operating Company, or makes or participates in construction or other loans on property as to which Mr. Flatley or the Operating Company has a commitment to provide or subsequently provides the long-term financing, or (f) pays Mr. Flatley, the Operating Company, the Management Company or any of their affiliates to manage the real estate interests in which the Trust participates. The Trust has retained the Management Company as an independent contractor to manage certain real estate of the Trust.

The prospectus stated that, in 1972, the REIT had acquired its initial investment from Mr. Flatley for $3,081,000 in REIT shares and warrants. Mr. Flatley reported a taxable gain of $344,485 on the transfer of properties; the prospectus supplied the financial details:

The Trust's tax basis for the properties is . . . approximately $1,969,000 compared with their purchase price of $3,108,000. Thus, even though, for financial reporting purposes, each of the properties is being carried by the Trust at its appreciated value, the tax on such appreciation, with the exception of the tax on the taxable gain of $344,485, is not being paid by Mr. Flatley but is being deferred until such time as the Trust may dispose of the respective properties. . . . Any such tax will, therefore, fall in the trust or its shareholders, indirectly diluting the interests of the shareholders.

The prospectus reported that in 1972 the REIT had purchased land underlying an apartment complex in Taunton, Massachusetts, from the P. F. O'Connor Realty Trust. The following year the REIT sold the land back to the P. F. O'Connor Realty Trust, which then turned around and sold the Flatley Company the land and the apartment units on the land.

The REIT also made loans to Mr. Flatley and companies in which he had an interest. In 1972 the REIT took a $1 million participation, with a commercial bank, in a construction loan to Mr. Flatley. In 1973 the REIT made two construction loans to Mark Development Corporation; Mr. Flatley was the principal shareholder of Mark Development, the remaining share being owned by employees of the Flatley Company. In the same year, the REIT loaned $160,000 to a limited partnership in which Mark Development was the general partner.

The prospectus reported that all of the above transactions were approved by a majority of the REIT's unaffiliated trustees "and are considered by those Trustees to be on terms fair and reasonable to the Trust and in no event less favorable to the Trust than terms available for comparable investments with parties not so affiliated."

GREIT Realty Trust

In October 1970 Remico, Inc., was organized to serve as the investment advisor of GREIT Realty Trust. Two of the seven shareholders of Remico were trustees of GREIT, and Remico and GREIT shared common office space.

A prospectus for an offering of shares in the REIT, dated July 1971, stated that some of the trustees, some of the directors, and some of the affiliates of the trustees and directors "are engaged in real estate investment activities which may give rise to possible conflicts of interest." In fact, the prospectus reported that approximately 30 percent of the trust's real estate investments involved affiliated persons.

One of the trustees, for example, was Gustave G. Amsterdam, who controlled Bankers Securities Corporation, a real estate company. The prospectus listed several transactions between the REIT and subsidiaries of Bankers Securities Corporation:

One such subsidiary has a 50 percent interest in the partnership which sold the Mohawk Mall property to the trust and is the lessee under a lease-back. . . . Another such subsidiary held a two-thirds interest in the Sussex Square Apartments purchased by the Trust and leased back to the seller. . . . Another such subsidiary sold the Jamestown Village Apartments to Stanley R. Fimberg (who subsequently became a director and shareholder of Remico), who simultaneously sold to the Trust and leased back the land underlying the Apartments.

In addition, Albert M. Greenfield & Co., Inc., "which is under the control of Mr. Amsterdam," received a total of $304,299 for management and advisory services to the trust during the five years ended October 31, 1970.

During the same five years, Albert M. Greenfield & Co., Inc., also received commissions from various insurance companies for insurance on behalf of the trust, "the annual premiums for which amounted to $55,999, $56,680, $64,065, $48,325 and $115.836. . . ." Albert M. Greenfield & Co., Inc., also received commissions of $107,000 from sellers of property purchased by the trust.

Another trustee of GREIT was Robert K. Greenfield, a limited partner in Queen Properties. In 1970 the trust purchased from Queen Properties a 24 percent interest in the lease of a motor inn and the ground under it for $1 million and then leased this property back to Queen Properties. Robert K. Greenfield also was a partner in a law firm that was general counsel to the trust; "Among the costs of the project paid by the seller out of the proceeds of the sale were legal fees and expenses of the law firm in which Mr. Greenfield is a partner, in the amount of $173,280." In addition, Mr. Greenfield's law firm received a total of $260,768 in fees for services from the trust during the five years ending October 31,1970. The firm also represented the trust in its public offering, for fees of about $65,000. "It will also receive fees estimated at $9,000 for legal services to Remico."

In 1975 the trust's special counsel reported that GREIT might have claims against Gustave Amsterdam and Robert Greenfield and suggested that they both resign as trustees. Then in November 1975 and March 1976, shareholders filed suits against the trust, alleging that it had not fully disclosed transactions with the two men and that its board should not have let such transactions occur. In April 1976 the board voted on whether to renominate Greenfield, whose term as trustee was expiring. The vote was split; Amsterdam and Greenfield voted for retention of Greenfield as a trustee. Without a majority vote, Greenfield's name was retained. Then one trustee resigned, and at the trust's June 3 annual meeting, Greenfield was reelected in spite of the opposition of a small group of shareholders.

Investors who read the prospectuses had explicit warning of self-dealing. But such investors presumably believed that the benefits of the demonstrable real estate expertise of the sponsors would outweigh the hypothetical costs of self-dealing.

Ironically, when the economy declined and the REITs were at the cutting edge of one of the worst real estate depressions in the history of the United States, self-dealing between some REITs and their sponsors may have benefited REIT stockholders at the expense of the stockholders of the sponsor-advisors. Although of course the extent of the losses was not remotely foreseen, the possibility that the advisors would come to the rescue became clear very early. The 1973 Justice Mortgage prospectus revealed that one loan, on which $137,000 had been advanced and an additional $168,000 committed, had already been foreclosed. The mortgage company, which had agreed to protect the trust against any losses on that loan, took over responsibility for the loan. (The prospectus warned that neither the advisor nor the mortgage company had an obligation to make rescues on other loans.) Given the risks that characterized REIT lending, such situtations should have been anticipated, although the sponsors of REITs expected the enterprises to be generally profitable. The stockholders of a publicly held sponsor, particularly a financial institution with so much at stake in its name and reputation for soundness and responsibility, may have had a legitimate complaint that they had never bargained for "what is tantamount to an open-end liability to 'bail out' their troubled REITs if they were at all responsible for the original placement of the asset in the REIT."[73]

Most bank sponsors were major lenders to their own REITs. Such self-dealing carried a substantial risk of injury to the REIT or the bank or both, to the extent that a lack of arm's-length bargaining for credit led to undue optimism about the REIT's prospects. For example, BT Mortgage Investors received 55 percent of its loans from its sponsor, Bankers Trust. But a big bank like Bankers Trust incurred less risk than, for example, First Virginia Corp. This bank holding company advanced $17.5 million to its REIT, First Virginia Mortgage and Real Estate Investment Trust. At the end of 1974, that sum represented 29.9 percent of consolidated stockholders' equity in the bank holding company. The First Virginia Bank itself was limited by law to a maximum $7.5 million exposure to one borrower. Its holding company and affiliates were not similarly limited, but in fact, the risk rested on the bank. The purpose of some of the complex self-dealing between REITs and their bank sponsors was to end-run such legal lending limits. For example, First Pennsylvania's holding company purchased $10 million of First Penn REIT's commercial paper, and in addition, the REIT had a $20 million line of credit from the bank, on which it had already drawn a $9.4 million loan:

On September 9, 1974 this loan was $14,985,000 after reductions of $6,925,000 and a $12,500,000 increase used to reduce a $25,000,000 loan owed to a foreign bank which extended the due date of the remaining $12,500,000 to October 24, 1974.

Coincident with the extension but as a totally independent transaction, the bank affiliated with the Adviser deposited an additional $7,500,000 with the foreign bank, making a total of $12,500,000 on deposit. This deposit bears interest at the London interbank rate and also matures October 24, 1974. No right of offset against the Trust's debt exists.[74]

When REITs began to proliferate, many observers of the securities markets assumed that banks' loans to their own REITs would prove advantageous mainly to the banks. Wright Patman, who had been a foe of banks throughout his long career as chariman of the House Banking and Currency Committee, was the *sole* voice in Washington that predicted problems with REITs. In mid-1970 he noted, in addition to other conflicts, that: "[F]or every dollar that a bank lends its affiliated trust, it makes a management fee of 1 percent or more per annum, in addition to earning interest."[75]

But when trouble came, banks incurred substantial costs in their efforts to help their floundering REITs. Banks took over troubled loans, softened the terms of their own loans to their REITs, and made huge "swaps" with their

REITs—that is, canceled debts in exchange for items from the REIT portfolios, including loans that were not paying interest. Between March 1975 and March 1976, REITs and their sponsor banks made about $200 million worth of swaps. The Chase was the prime example. The Chase bank had a loan limit of about $200 million to any single customer; by early 1975 the bank had committed $150 million (the largest single part of a $700 million revolving-loan agreement involving forty-one banks) to its own REIT. Thereafter:

In October and November, 1975, the Chase Bank, not the holding company, agreed to purchase from the Chase Manhattan Mortgage & Realty Trust, the REIT advised by the Bank, over $160 million of the REIT's outstanding loans.

The loans are mostly short-term mortgages where the borrowers need and are entitled to draw an additional $30 million, which Chase Bank will supply. The purchase was connected with a new credit agreement for the REIT by the REIT's 41 lending banks . . . .

There is no disclosure of how the loans purchased by the Chase Bank were selected or whether independent appraisal had been used to determine their value. If the Chase Bank realizes more on the loans purchased than its investment plus an undisclosed fee, the REIT would receive additional sums. The other creditor banks each had a first-refusal right on the loans purchased; the other creditor banks must agree that the purchase price is fair to the REIT.

There is no mention of what steps, if any, assure that the purchase is fair to the Bank. I understand that David Rockefeller, asked in a public meeting whether any of the loans purchased were not accruing interest, answered ''Some.'' Since that meeting it has become known that of the total purchase of $160.6 million, $85.9 million was non-income producing and, according to the REIT's own SEC filing, ''there was no ready market for these loans and the terms and prices obtained are fair and could not necessarily have been obtained if such loans had been sold on a liquidation basis.'' Although most of the acquired loans are on non-accrual, the bank is paying interest to the trust at the bank's 90-day CD rate on the balances owed for the loans. This is being disbursed to the trust according to its cash needs. At year-end, $145 million of the purchase price was owed to the trust.

In short, the Chase Bank has a loan exposure to its REIT of $150 million, and an exposure of an additional $160 million—with yet $30 million more to be added—by the purchase of loans which nobody else would buy on the terms the Chase Bank gave. I don't know whether the Chase Bank participated with its REIT in some other loans, which would take the exposure to this venture even beyond the $340 million we know of. While it is true that the exposure involves a variety of ventures, and while a judgment of the size of the eventual losses cannot be formed without vastly more information plus a crystal ball, a sense of the enormity of the risk the Chase Bank has taken because of its REIT can be formed.

This exposure is 140 percent as large as the Bank's reserve for all loan losses. Previous instances of purchases of this size are not known. [76]

Other REITs and their sponsors found themselves similarly situated. The First Wisconsin Bank and its REIT have received the widest publicity because the REIT itself sued its advisor and the bank holding company parent; the litigation is still pending. In June 1974 the bank, having been lead lender for loans totaling $130 million or 78 percent of the REIT's portfolio, bought some loans from its REIT and agreed to reimburse the REIT for losses on other loans costing the bank (holding company) $10 million, or after-tax earnings of $1.20 per share in 1974. The REIT's portfolio subsequently became even more troubled.

In another situation characterized by a leading bank securities firm as "a virtual open-ended liability," Citizens and Southern Bank accepted liability for up to $30 million for its REIT's loans as part of the terms of a revolving credit secured for the REIT from other banks.[77]

Clearly, these practices have benefited neither the banks' nor the REITs' shareholders. When such sponsors as banks created REITs and managed them, their interests were so interwoven and the conflicts so many and complex that the most honest officials could not possibly make decisions that would serve all parties fairly.

Use of the Same Law Firm by the REIT and the Advisor

The same law firm usually represents a REIT, its advisor, its advisory personnel, and the unaffiliated trustees. The practice does not violate the Code of Professional Responsibility of the American Bar Association, although the interests of the different parties are likely to conflict.

A single independent certified public accounting firm may, of course, audit the statements of both the advisor and a REIT. Indeed, current accounting practices favor the hiring of one accounting firm to audit all members of an affiliated group so the firm can carefully examine the details of member relationships.

But the accountant's role differs from that of the attorney; the accountant's duty is primarily to encourage full and fair disclosure. Although the attorney also participates in the disclosure process, he is primarily a confidential advocate, negotiator, and fiduciary advisor who is responsible for unearthing problems—especially those involving fairness—and suggesting solutions for them. When negotiating a contract with an unrelated party, the lawyer will argue for the warranties, representations, and other contractual arrangements most favorable to his client and will have considerable knowledge of un-affiliated experts who can make independent verifications. If a lawyer represents both the REIT *and* its advisor, his independence is obviously compromised when he has to try to obtain the best terms for each client.

When the management of a business entity is sued in a derivative action (an action initiated by a shareholder on behalf of the entity), the regular counsel for the entity cannot represent both the entity and the management. Usually, the regular counsel chooses to represent management, and a special counsel represents the entity. Thus, in a derivative action initiated by a REIT share-holder on the REIT's behalf against the advisor and the REIT's trustees, the REIT's counsel could not represent both the REIT and the trustees, even if he did not also represent the advisor. Because of the manifold, continuing conflicts in the operation of externally managed REITs, dual representation is as serious a problem during the REITs' formation and ordinary operations as it is during litigation.

Disciplinary Rule 5-105 of the American Bar Association's Code of Professional Responsibility prohibits dual representation of clients with conflicting interests unless:

1. "It is obvious that [the lawyer] can adequately represent the interest of each [client]"; and
2. "If each [client] consents to the representation after full disclosure of the possible effect of such representation on the exercise of [the lawyer's] independent professional judgment on behalf of each [client]."

Adequate disclosure is not at issue because both the advisor and the independent trustees know of the dual representation and its possible effects. In addition, prospectuses often note the dual representation. The issue is whether "it is obvious that [the lawyer] can adequately represent the interest of each [client]." The ABA, the SEC, and state blue-sky authorities have apparently assumed that the interests of both the REIT and the advisor could be fairly represented by a single law firm. In fact, however, such dual representation poses an unusual number of problems for the attorney involved. The relationships between most REITs and their advisors are intricate and complex. The contracts and legal arrangements covering these relationships are determined by counsel, and the variety of possible safeguards for the REIT is almost limitless. Statutory guidance is lacking; hence, almost every action of the lawyer in the dealings between advisor and the REIT involves discretionary decisions in drafting, negotiation, or advice.

Separate counsel for the REIT and for the advisor would not eliminate conflicts, but it would facilitate the resolution of conflicts and help to safeguard the interests of the REIT's security holders. Admittedly, the REIT's counsel would know that the advisor controlled the REIT and, thereby, the lawyer's continued employment. But even if the lawyer feared that certain actions might cost him the REIT as a client, he would be concerned about the loss of only one account: the REIT. If the same law firm represented both advisor and the REIT, actions interpreted as unwarranted solicitude for the REIT's interests could lead to the loss of both accounts. The use of separate counsel, therefore, would considerably strengthen the independence of the REIT's lawyer and, in turn, the independence of the unaffiliated trustees.

Fortunately, in recent workouts such as the Chase REIT's, where the REIT's interests and the advisor's diverged frequently and acutely, the parties have hired separate counsel. The need to routinize such representation seems so great that a legal or self-regulatory requirement is in order. At the very least, REITs should be required to disclose whether they and their advisors or unaffiliated trustees have separate counsel, and if not why not.

IV • REGULATION

The free market is the ultimate regulator of conflicts of interest. In theory, investors may boycott conflict-laden REITs in favor of those that have fewer conflicts or those whose conflicts are closely regulated by their declarations of trust. Investors who are well informed and sophisticated and making large enough investments to explore in detail such issues as conflicts may indeed favor those REITs that pose the fewest conflicts problems. But few individual investors fit this description.

The experiences of REITs in the past few years have led investors and investment advisors to approach them with caution and have forced promoters and underwriters to try to correct their defects. But the ultimate policy questions are how much the market—made more efficient by full disclosure requirements in the securities statutes—can do to eliminate conflicts, and how much substantive regulation is needed to safeguard the public against conflicts of interest and conflict abuses. The right answers to those questions will enable REITs to enjoy as much public confidence, unfettered by fears of abuses of conflicts of interest, as their economic utility merits. The closest historic analogy, the investment companies that were so scarred by their experience in the 1920s and 1930s, strongly suggests that a system of regulatory safeguards enables investors to enjoy the benefits of the professionally managed, pooled investment concept and thus also redounds greatly to the benefit of the industry.

The current pattern of regulation governing REITs is a mixture of state and federal efforts. Although compliance with these regulations is expensive and time-consuming for the industry, it produces only limited safeguards for investors. In legislating REITs into existence, Congress simply failed to consider what regulatory protection might be needed for investors and the public interest. REIT regulation at the federal level has consisted mainly of disclosure.

Although REITs resemble investment companies more closely than they do any other component of the securities markets, they have not been subjected to regulatory legislation analogous to the Investment Company Act of 1940, which specifically treats almost all types of conflicts discussed in this study, surrounding some with safeguards, prohibiting others, and assuring regulatory oversight and private right to sue. When REITs were first coming into existence, neither the SEC nor any other regulator, let alone the industry or Congress itself, considered analogous protection for them.

Of course, the main body of law governing REITs is the federal tax law, but the purpose of that law has little bearing on problems such as conflicts. The main pertinent federal law is the Securities Act of 1933. This statute calls for the filing of a registration statement with the SEC and preparation of a prospectus to provide detailed, full, and fair disclosure to prospective investors in most public interstate offerings. The act does not regulate the structure of the organization or the offering price; it merely mandates disclosure of all pertinent facts, including investors' rights and obligations under the relevant state's business organization laws governing the entity and its investors. During the boom period, REITs made repeated returns to the public markets for additional equity or debt (because they were barred by tax law from building up retained earnings); disclosure therefore should have been particularly significant to REITs.

Another applicable federal law is the Securities Exchange Act of 1934, which requires most larger publicly owned organizations to file periodic public reports with the SEC; to make full disclosure to investors when soliciting proxies; and to refrain from material misstatements, half-truths, and failures to disclose in connection with the purchase or sale of securities through the use of the mails or involving interstate commerce. Thus, even the "private" or "wholly intrastate" sale of REIT securities falls under some federal rules, although such sales are exempted from the complete registration requirements of the Securities Act of 1933. In addition, under the Exchange Act the SEC regulates the practices of securities broker-dealers, including underwriters and selling group members. As one of its provisions for fair treatment of customers, the SEC prohibits broker-dealers from selling their customers "unsuitable" securities. The SEC has not set forth clear criteria for suitability or enforcement of this provision. Instead, it has left development of such standards to the state regulators and to the National Association of Securities Dealers, Inc. (NASD), an industry self-regulatory group.

Bank-sponsored REITs—which manage about one-third of the industry's assets—are subject to Federal Reserve Board authority under the Bank Holding Company Act. Before the advent of REITs, the Board had imposed safeguards against conflict abuses that might arise when banks engaged in other nonbanking activities (for example, it barred bank affiliates from participating in debt issues on which an affiliate had advised a state or local government) or advised closed-end investment companies (for example, it prohibited the investment companies from using the bank or bank holding company name). But it imposed no such constraints on bank sponsorship of REITs. Even when the massive asset "swaps" occurred around 1975, with the soundness of major banks at stake, only the SEC intervened, tightening the requirements for public disclosure.

State law regarding securities sales within state borders consists of a complex patchwork of requirements involving both disclosure and substantive fairness. State securities statutes antedate the federal acts by several decades. Federal legislation permits the states to regulate securities sales as long as the state does not require something forbidden by federal regulation. A state may, however, refuse to register for sale within its borders an issue cleared by the SEC under the Securities Act. When states refuse to register such issues, they usually cite as their reasons a lack of substantive fairness in the organizational structure, proposed mode of doing business, promoters' or management's compensation, or the price of the issue or the presence of a preclusive conflict of interest—all conditions about which the Federal Securities Act requires only disclosure.

The most controversial issue in federal-state relations regarding securities regulation involves the SEC's refusal to permit the inclusion of projections and "sensitivity analyses" in real estate offerings registered federally. Many market experts agree that numerical projections and sensitivity analyses of key factors, such as occupancy rates, are essential to a determination of the risks and potential profits in a given deal. Several states require such information when the sale is wholly intrastate or otherwise beyond the federal act. But the SEC distrusts projections generally, except in relatively stable or tested situations such as real estate arrangements involving long-term net leases with securely solvent lessees. In less certain situations, the SEC apparently takes the position that projections can seriously mislead investors. To circumvent this prohibition, aggressive salesmen, it is alleged, sometimes relay projections orally to prospective investors.

Another part of the regulatory pattern is state decisional law on the authority and duties of fiduciaries. Such judge-made rules, antedating both the state and the federal securities statutes, apply to the types of conflicts of interest that promoters, managers, and other fiduciaries of a business organization may create and to the duties of fiduciaries in resolving such conflicts as may be tolerated. Most state laws governing REITs are fairly detailed, but they say almost nothing about specific conflicts of interest or their resolution, leaving interpretation of general state law on conflicts to the courts and state administrators.

Federal Securities Regulation

The SEC requires REITs to disclose all material facts, including those relating to conflicts of interest, when registering shares under the Securities Act. The SEC has developed special reporting forms for real estate organizations and has continually updated its requirements. It also has developed special forms for the periodic reports under the Securities Exchange Act.

In 1972 a Real Estate Advisory Committee established by the SEC commented on the adequacy of disclosure:

Although the Committee did not devote a significant amount of time to the specific problems of these entities, it observed that many of the concerns expressed in the Report regarding other real estate securities apply equally to REIT's [sic].

Such problems include, among others, improving disclosure of the complex tax qualification problem faced by REIT's; improving disclosure requirements to provide more investment information on the issuer, including. . . management capability and track record, type of investments and under what criteria they will be made; information as to the capabilities of the investment advisor; specific portfolio performance relating to cash-flow, unit cost, vacancy rates, rent rolls, etc., on properties held by an ongoing trust; and, more meaningful risk factor disclosure.[1]

The Committee "noted considerable room for more effective regulation of these trusts" and recommended further study of them—but otherwise wholly ignored them, focusing instead on tax-shelter offerings sold almost exclusively to investors far wealthier and fewer in number than REIT stockholders.

On the whole the SEC has been less than dynamic in either pursuing breaches of legal requirements or calling for new safeguards. For example, the SEC made grave charges against First Mortgage Investors but dropped them upon receiving assurances that the REIT would behave better in the future, and did not demand reimbursement for stockholders' losses resulting from past misconduct. In May 1975 the SEC undertook a vast investigation of the now-bankrupt Continental Mortgage Investors, which led to the filing of suit nearly three years later.

Apart from those two proceedings, the SEC role in protecting investors and the public interest in this unusually conflict-ridden, huge speculative bubble has consisted of three measures: (1) setting up the 1972 advisory committee that considered REITs as an incidental aspect of the problems in wealthy investors' tax shelters; (2) in February 1975, after the disaster had struck, initiating an economic staff study compiling data (taking inventory, so to speak, of the horses that were gone from the barn) but supplying no conclusions or policy recommendations; and (3) in spring 1976, soon after "asset swaps" began to proliferate, taking the important and valuable step of strengthening disclosure requirements.

Given the SEC's well-deserved reputation for vigor, its record in this sphere has been disappointing, despite the importance of REITs not only to investors themselves (and investors in REITs seem at least as entitled as other investors to active SEC oversight) but also, considering the effects of the REIT bust on the construction industry and real estate markets, to the public interest.

State Regulation

Nearly all states exempt securities listed on major exchanges from securities registration, and even securities not thus exempted are subject to state requirements only when they make a new public offering. For example, the states were responsible for the limits on REIT advisory fees and total expenses; when the 1974 decline occurred and the REITs stopped making new public offerings, many of them also stopped complying with the state regulatory limits. A further limit on the impact of state securities regulation is that when an established public corporation, which for several years has had an active trading market (and accompanying periodic reports to the SEC), makes a new offering, the state agencies simply wave it through the process.

Some states authorize their administrators to require only full and fair disclosure; many authorize the administrator to deny registration unless the offering itself is "fair, just, and equitable"—not merely fully and fairly disclosed; some state statutes fall between these poles. (Nearly all states also allow the administrator to control the selling practices of broker-dealers.) In practice, state regulation is more homogeneous than the statutes suggest; in fact, states with strict substantive fairness statutes do not always require substantive fairness of an offering that is fully and fairly disclosed—as most SEC-registered offerings are. On the other hand, the administrator of a statute that calls only for disclosure or that does not require a strict form of substantive fairness can use his powers to delay, and thus perhaps to kill, what he considers an egregiously unfair offering. (Almost all the adminstrators in the Midwest Securities Commissioners Association administer substantive fairness statutes.[2])

Most REITs made substantial public offerings before they became exchange-listed and therefore exempt from many states' requirements; and REITs have returned to public offerings much more frequently than other kinds of corporations. For those reasons, or perhaps because the statements merely expressed norms the industry wanted or at very least was satisfied to have, REITs generally have followed the statements of policy—as far as they went. State securities administrators—even the "tough" ones—are rarely if ever as independent or vigorous as the SEC. Toughness in state administrators consists not in promulgating general standards but only in dealing with a specific proposed offering or action by a regulated firm. State securities regulation has been weaker than federal securities regulation partly because so many state governments are correspondingly weak but mainly because no single state administrator can be as effective as the SEC in dealing with general problems or large, multistate offerings. Of course, some administrators are more forceful than others. California, for example, has a tradition of special vigor.[3] But it can safely be assumed that state regulation has not required REITs to act or refrain from acting in ways that they found extremely distasteful.

The statements issued by the Midwest Securities Commissioners Association have dealt with the REITs' organization and operating structure, including the relationship with the advisor, and have banned or limited certain kinds of investments.

Although none of the statements has been either thorough or perceptive in the treatment of conflicts, the commissioners have acknowledged the presence of considerable conflicts problems. For example, in 1969 the Midwest Commissioners adopted this resolution on the newly emerging mortgage REITs:

RESOLVED, That the members of this Association view with disfavor the registration of securities . . . of real estate investment trusts with mortgage portfolios whose trust instruments contain no provisions limiting self-dealing transactions between the trust and its trustees, advisers, and affiliated persons.

In 1970 they introduced a requirement that "a majority of the trustees shall not be affiliated with the adviser of the trust or any organization affiliated with the adviser," but they did not define *affiliated*; hence, the REIT's legal counsel and developers relying on the REIT for financing were acceptable as "unaffiliated." They also required self-dealing transactions to be approved by a majority of these unaffiliated trustees; this provision became the principal safeguard against conflict abuses because the other changes in the provisions for self-dealing radically weakened protections that had been provided since 1961.

The first operative section of the original 1961 statement had flatly barred any asset acquisition by a REIT from its advisor, trustees, or other insiders except at the formation of the REIT and with "the profits, if any, thereon disclosed" in the prospectus. But only a few months later, this disclosure requirement was dropped in favor of a requirement that the price be "based on an independent appraisal acceptable to the [state securities administrator]."

In 1970 the Midwest Commissioners modified their provisions regarding self-dealing transactions, making them permissible at any time, not merely upon formation of the REIT. The 1970 statement required that prospectuses include "full" disclosure of self-dealing transactions made upon formation of the REIT, but did *not* call for disclosure of subsequent self-dealing trans-actions or stipulate that "full" disclosure include noting profits. It no longer required that mortgages be independently appraised, like other property, and it dropped the provision that appraisals, where required, be acceptable to the state securities administrator. In place of those safeguards, the 1970 statement required that self-dealing acquisitions of mortgages be "on terms not less favorable to the trust than similar transactions involving unaffiliated parties." (Compliance with this requirement is difficult to verify because of the prob-lems in appraising real estate investments.) The 1970 statement also exempted independent contractors (other than the advisor) from even the relaxed limits on self-dealing. (In addition, it explicitly applied the limits to trustees, the advisor, officers, and anyone affiliated with them and restated the unquestion-ably applicable general law that all self-dealing would have to be "fair and reasonable" to the REIT.)

The 1970 statement, issued just when the number of people and dollars involved in REITs were becoming significant, simply deleted a provision that had been in the statements since 1961.

The declaration of trust, or other instrument forming the trust, shall not contain any provisions relieving any trustee from liability to the trust or its security holders to which it or he might otherwise be subject by reason of acts constituting bad faith, willful misfeasance, gross negligence or reckless disregard of its or his duties.

The typical declaration of trust did relieve the trustees, management, and advisor for liability except for bad faith or gross negligence. The effect of such exculpatory clauses under state common law is unclear. Although both general state law regarding fiduciary duties and any specific securities regulatory provisions are applicable to REITs, such law has not had—and is not likely to have—a broad impact on REITs. Some shareholders' lawsuits may be won in instances of egregious mismanagement or overreaching, but general state law has tended to deny relief to plaintiffs if the subject prompting the complaint was fully disclosed, and especially if it also was in compliance with any requirements of a state securities administrative scheme.

In 1970 the Midwest Commissioners also virtually removed what had been a direct, explicit limit on leverage, in force since 1961, replacing it with a test of "unreasonableness." And they eased the limits on advisory fees and related income, thereby setting the stage for the debacle a few years later.

State regulation treats substantive matters, but the federal law requires only disclosure; the states' substantive requirements—which, moreover, do not apply to the major REITs because they are listed on major exchanges—are neither as thorough and rigorous as those of the Investment Company Act nor applicable at all times instead of only upon offering of securities. The Investment Company Act deals mainly with structure and operation, rather than involving government in decisions about what forms of investments are so risky that they should be wholly barred or what levels of riskiness are tolerable. Many of the state schemes, and certainly the Midwest statements of policy, do not shrink from making such decisions. The relative merits of different regulatory approaches may vary in general. But as a means to the specific end of preventing conflict abuses, where the state schemes were applicable, they were ineffective.

V • CONCLUSIONS

As of early 1978, 9 REITS had gone bankrupt and 14 of the 50 largest had negative net worth. Many others faced the prospect of a long struggle under the burden of problem-laden portfolios. Eighty-seven percent of the industry's assets were selling at share market prices below book value. But a number of REITs had weathered the storm well, and the industry outlook had improved enough by the winter of 1977-78 to prompt even cover stories in financial journals about the revival.[1] Today, the REIT industry is composed of 218 trusts with total capital of $2.78 billion and total assets, through leveraging, of more than $14 billion. But it still functions without proper safeguards; hence, the risk of exploitation of REIT investors remains unnecessarily high. As the stock market regains its vigor, the stage may be set for a new debacle, injuring not only direct investors but a vast number of other people as well, including management and labor involved in construction or real estate.

Neither the REIT industry nor government has attempted to address these problems. The industry's failure to take corrective action is not unreasonable; the REITs have been concentrating on recovery. But it is surprising that so many arms of government—Congress, bank regulators, the SEC, the state securities administrators—have taken no action in response to the near-collapse of over $11 billion in bank debt, the actual collapse of $4 billion in market value of shares held largely by individuals for retirement security, about $1 billion in market value of REIT bonds, and an overblown speculative bubble in real estate that distorted sound land use, ended in bankruptcy for many small firms, and contributed to almost unprecedented unemployment in construction. The total governmental response to these events has been two SEC suits and one day of congressional committee hearings (without preparation before or follow-up after).

Where REITs are concerned, notwithstanding any responsibility owed the investor, Congress has a direct responsibility to the general public to regulate operational problems, such as the trustees' conflicts of interest, more effectively than can be achieved through full disclosure. Congress gave REITs conduit tax treatment to accomplish a number of objectives, including giving the small investor the opportunity to benefit from investments in large diversified real estate portfolios. To justify the resultant loss of revenues and the giving of this discriminatory tax benefit, Congress should insure that the original objectives are in fact accomplished.[2]

Congress should enact a variant of the Investment Company Act, tailored to the special features of REITs. The present Investment Company Act has many features that are inapplicable to REITs and many others that would restrict REITs inappropriately. New legislation also should improve on both those provisions of the present act that experience has shown to be ineffective protections and those that constitute unnecessarily burdensome interference with the regulated firms.

Ideally, Congress'should direct the SEC to study these problems. This study should focus on building safeguards rather than on assigning blame for past misconduct. Since enough is known to make an exhaustive study unnecessary, the researchers should be instructed to report to Congress relatively quickly, say within six months or one year, lest another period of over-optimistic investing begins before the safeguards are put into place.

The SEC has both more expertise than any other federal agency on matters similar and related to REITs and considerable experience in conducting special studies to guide congressional action. Although the SEC's performance with respect to REITs has been unimpressive, its reputation for independence and competence is such that, in calling for the 1963 Special Study of Securities Markets, a subject of which the SEC's past performance was a major aspect, Congress preferred to rely on the Commission's integrity rather than to assume the problems inherent in doing the study itself or assigning it to another agency. A prime topic of such a study must be the overlapping federal and state regulatory schemes and the policies and concerns of the IRS, the bank regulatory agencies, and the insurance regulators; but the SEC is experienced in dealing with precisely these agencies. And, of course, the SEC's recommendations will be subject to full airing and congressional review before any major change can occur.

The result should be a federal Real Estate Investment Trust Act covering at least the following issues:

1. The external management typical of most REITs is less accountable to and less clearly motivated to serve the interests of stockholders than is the internal management typical of most American enterprises. External management may or may not be appropriate for investment companies (a question almost wholly ignored by Congress, the SEC, and the legal literature despite all the recent attention that has been given to investment companies). In REITs the use of external management clearly benefits management but has no obvious advantages for REIT stockholders or the public. The original sponsors of mortgage REITs chose the externalized structure to comply with one of several tax code requirements designed to prevent ordinary real estate companies from claiming the special tax status of REITs. However, other prerequisites for REIT status, such as the requirement of one hundred or more shareholders, seem to serve the same purpose. Many equity REITs use internalized management without calling their tax status into question. If the use of external management confers no benefits on the public or investors that compensate for the conflicts it generates, it should be prohibited.

2. If externalized management is deemed to have compensating advantages, federal legislation should require all or almost all REIT trustees to be unaffiliated and should define *unaffiliated* in terms that assure genuine independence. Probably, the law should require the REIT either to provide or at least to disclose the extent to which it provides unaffiliated trustees with their own counsel and similar resources, independent of the external management. Certainly, the law should require, as the 1970 amendment to the Investment Company Act does, that all trustees be given and be obligated to evaluate full financial information about the external management firm before renewing any advisory contract.

3. The legislation should include measures to eliminate or reduce the incentive that management compensation arrangements now provide for excessive "leveraging" of assets. The Midwest Securities Commissioners Association has prescribed limits on REIT management fees, borrowing, types of investments, and operating expenses. Such substantive financial prescriptions are more common in state than in federal securities regulation. Federal regulation of investment companies does include such prescriptions, although in relatively general terms, but such measures may not be appropriate for real estate investment, which typically involves leveraging. In any event the legislation should assure that management shares the stockholders' interest in avoiding unsound levels of borrowing. It may not be possible to eliminate the link between management fees and leveraging, but, for example, paying management a given percentage of assets that equals stockholders' equity and

additional compensation, on a sharply declining sliding scale, for assets that reflect borrowing, would reduce the incentive for excessive leveraging.

4. Many REITs are managed by firms that also engage in real estate activities for their own accounts. The advantages of expertise, reputation, and financial responsibility that such management confers may outweigh the potential for conflict abuse in the allocation of investment opportunities. (Such conflicts are more acute in REITs than in investment companies because real estate investments lack clearly established fair market values and are not as divisible among accounts as are publicly traded securities.) If so, federal legislation should reconcile the interests of REIT stockholders and stockholders of the sponsoring companies through devices such as giving the REIT effective rights of first refusal or providing for joint participation in investments. And if banks and insurance companies continue to sponsor REITs, safeguards are needed to protect the public interest in the soundness of such institutions.

5. Federal legislation should include provisions regulating self-dealing between a REIT and its affiliated persons or firms. Self-dealing is relatively uncommon and seldom necessary in investment companies. The Investment Company Act requires self-dealing transactions to be approved in advance by the SEC; requests for such approval are rare. The nature of REIT activities is such that a similar requirement might result in a deluge of requests. But legislation should at least require full disclosure and independent appraisals and might well require even more substantial safeguards.

6. Many REIT investors are retired or about to retire. Such individuals tend to seek investments that will yield relatively high and stable income. Legislation should therefore require REITs to emphasize in their prospectuses the riskiness of their investments and the possibility that they will reduce or suspend dividends. Such disclosure should be very specific, including figures and dates regarding dividend experience. In addition, since the nature of real estate investment makes it particularly difficult to evaluate a REIT's riskiness or performance, let alone to compare REITs, those REITs that have externalized management should be required to inform their stockholders (particularly before each year's advisory contract is ratified) of management's income, costs, and other relevant matters.

7. No federal agency now has primary regulatory authority for REITs. Although the economic roller-coaster ride that REITs took in the early 1970s is now over, there is no reason to believe that REIT investment will not embark on another upswing soon. If, when that happens, improved safeguards have not been established, a new generation of investors may suffer from the same old conflict abuses. The SEC is already experienced with investment companies and is the federal body most qualified to assume regulatory authority

over REITs. If that route is found undesirable, then at the very least, a federal coordinator should oversee the regulatory efforts of federal and state agencies regarding REITs and alert them to any jurisdictional gaps.

Many of the problems of REITs do not require new legislation. Even now, the SEC, the bank regulators, and the state insurance regulators have authority and responsibility to protect the public interest, the soundness of financial institutions, and the interests of investors. The time is ripe to reconsider problems such as avoidance of legal loan limits, tie-ins (which may warrant investigation by the antitrust division of the Justice Department), and broker-dealers' compliance with suitability requirements.

Nor is government the only sector that has a duty to focus upon the demonstrated problems of REITs. Groups within the American Bar Association should consider the acute ethical questions raised by what has been the routine practice of having one lawyer or firm represent both a REIT and its sponsor-advisor. Such questions are probably better answered by the Bar's self-regulation than by law.

Fortunately for all efforts to improve this situation, REITs have a well-organized national association, with able staff and significant research competence. The National Association of Real Estate Investment Trusts (NAREIT) might well assist REITs in taking corrective steps.[3]

The Investment Company Act of 1940 was in part a response to the disastrous performance of many closed-end investment companies during the late 1920s and the 1930s. The companies had been riddled with conflicts of interest (for example, the sponsor using the investment company as a dumping ground for securities owned or underwritten by it) and had engaged in over-leveraging. And investors had almost no control over these enterprises.

Congress directed the SEC to examine those problems, and the Commission eventually produced the mammoth five-year-long Investment Trust Study. The investment company industry welcomed remedial legislation to restore investor confidence, and the 1940 act, based on negotiations between the SEC and the industry, provided strong protections for investors.

During the Senate consideration of the 1940 act, Senator Robert A. Taft, Sr., criticized the investment companies for welcoming government regulation. The charge was correct, but the industry was manifesting enlightened self-interest. The act laid the groundwork for the rapid growth of investment companies during the next twenty-five years. And the investment companies have in fact proven remarkably flexible and innovative in providing smaller investors with a chance to obtain a diversified portfolio and professional management and to participate in many kinds of investments.

Similarly, the public interest, including but not limited to the concern for improved real estate financing and the interests of investors, may well be served by the REIT concept. This investment vehicle should be made fully productive and fully fair.

NOTES

I. Introduction

[1]The survey (not published) was conducted in 1972 by the National Association of Real Estate Investment Trusts (NAREIT). It drew a 20 percent response from fifty questionnaires sent to each of twenty-five REITs. The survey report noted that retired persons might be more likely to respond but found that the data received went "beyond 'leisure time' bias."

[2]The minority of REITs whose sponsors opted for internal management did not in fact have tax problems as a result. The internally managed REITs were equity owners of real estate, rather than mortgage lenders, and many in the industry believed that the tax code requirements differentiated between the two types of REITs. The soundness of this belief is questionable. Cf. J. B. Riggs Parker, "REIT Trustees and the 'Independent Contractor,' " *University of Virginia Law Review* 48 (1962), p. 1048.

[3]Since 1974-75 some boards have severed relations with their sponsor-advisors and many have become more independent of the sponsor-advisor as workouts brought divergences of interests into the open, and as numerous suits were brought against trustees as well as advisors for breach of fiduciary obligations. Since there has been no required or voluntary general change in the structure of boards, or in the procedures or criteria for appointment as a trustee, the earlier practice remains the norm and is likely to become nearly universal again as workouts and lawsuits fade.

II. The REIT Industry

[1]It has been argued that REITs received more favorable tax treatment than mutual funds. If a mutual fund had to pay taxes on its earnings, some of those earnings would be taxed three times: first, at the level of the operating corporation in which the mutual fund had invested, second at the fund level, and third at the level of the fund stockholder. The "equal" tax treatment for mutual funds and REITs meant that the mutual fund stockholders' earnings (or at least a portion of them) would not be taxed more than twice, but the REITs' stockholders' earnings would be taxed only once. See Theodore Lynn, "REITs: Problems and Prospects," *Fordham Law Review* 31, no. 73 (1962).

Following the extraordinary economic decline of 1973-74, the tax law requirements were changed; in 1975 changes were made to enable REITs to foreclose on property and sell foreclosed property without losing REIT qualification; the 1976 changes added flexibility to several technical requirements.

[2]National Association of REITs, *REITs Quarterly, 1977* IV, p. 3.

[3]The member states are Arizona, Arkansas, California, Colorado, Idaho, Illinois, Indiana, Iowa, Kansas, Kentucky, Michigan, Minnesota, Missouri, Nebraska, New Mexico, North Dakota, Ohio, Oklahoma, South Dakota, Texas, Utah, Washington, Wisconsin, and Wyoming.

[4]Three member states—Washington, Wisconsin, and Iowa—and three nonmembers—Alaska, Mississippi, and Tennessee. Douglas W. Duval, "Conflict of Interest Problems in the Management of REITs," *Real Estate Law Journal* 3 (1974), p. 34; David G. Epstein, "State Securities Regulation of REITs," *University of Florida Law Review* 23 (1971), pp. 514, 521; and Edmund Polubinski, "The Effect of State Securities or Blue Sky Law Regulation upon the Organizational Structure and Operations of REITs," *The Business Lawyer* 30 (1974), pp. 198-201.

[5]Epstein, op. cit., p. 521.

[6]Hearings on REITs before the Senate Banking Committee, 94th Cong., 2d Sess. (Washington, D.C.: May 1976), p. 275 (hereafter referred to as Hearings on REITs); data from *Realty Trust Review* as of mid-1975.

[7]National Association of Real Estate Investment Trusts (NAREIT), *1977 Fact Book*, p. 11.

[8]At their 1973 peak, REITs did channel $5.84 billion of equity capital into real estate. But more

than half that sum was invested between 1971 and 1973. Operating at that pace, the REITs may have served only to exacerbate volatility in real estate.

[9]As of June 1975. William Zucker, *A Current and Future Assessment of the REIT Industry*, Wharton School Study in Entrepreneurship #2 (1975), p. 3; Hearings on REITs, p. 281.

[10]NAREIT, *1977 Fact Book*, pp. 49, 58.

[11]"How Chase Hopes to Rescue the Chase REIT," *Business Week*, (May 19, 1975), pp. 112, 114.

[12]The second largest source of such lending, the savings and loan associations, had only about 5 percent of their assets in such loans. Data from Zucker, op. cit., pp. 3-4.

[13]Chase Manhattan Mortgage and Realty Trust, *Annual Report 1973*, balance sheet; *Business Week* (May 19, 1975), p. 114.

[14]One of the most notorious instances of lack of depth in management was the Cabot, Cabot & Forbes Land Trust, begun in February 1971 with a $57 million underwriting by Paine, Webber:

Blakely was president of CC&F and chairman of both the Adviser and the Land Trust; Helmuth was senior vice president of CC&F, and president of both the Adviser and the Trust. Neither had any real lending experience, and neither played any major role in day-to-day management and investment decisions. Emerson had had considerable lending experience with John Hancock, but by his own account later, the bulk of his time was taken up with managing the expansion of CC&F's development operations across the country. Only about 20%—perhaps one day a week—was devoted to super-vision of the operations of the Trust, of which he was Managing Trustee. Day-to-day control of business operations, and investments, as it commenced operations in the spring of 1971 was in the hand of Helmuth's bright young protege, 24-year-old Terry Considine, vice president of the Land Trust, former intern under Helmuth at Hale & Dorr, and third-year student at Harvard Law.

In retrospect, the view of several knowledgeable Boston real estate operators is that neither Considine nor most of the front-line staff people working for him had much in the way of actual real estate investment experience. Moreover, virtually no one at the Trust except Emerson had any real lending experience. Considine provided lots of enthusiasm and energy. But as one veteran developer noted, whereas borrowing money successfully for one's own development projects requires an enthusiastic appreciation of what should go right for the project, lending money successfully for other de-velopers' projects requires a somewhat more skeptical understanding of what can go wrong. (Michael Brody, "Law and the Profits," *Barron's* [May 9, 1977], p. 3.)

[15]G. N. Buffington, NAREIT executive vice president and general counsel, address to Asso-ciation of Reserve City Bankers, March 20, 1975.

Interest in growth was so frenetic that one major REIT, Great American Mortgage Investors, reported earnings on a monthly basis.

[16]In the NAREIT survey of stockholders, about 60 percent said they had relied on their brokers' recommendations in buying REIT shares, a proportion substantially larger than that of those who relied on brokers' recommendations in buying other common stocks and more than twice as large as that of those who so relied in buying bonds or mutual funds.

"Income" was by far the most frequent reason cited for buying or holding REIT shares, but a large number of REIT investors also expected growth. NAREIT survey, pp. 115, 126, 135.

[17]The NAREIT survey found that 70 percent of REIT stockholders were over fifty-five years old, and 40 percent were retired. Twenty-five percent had annual incomes of under $15,000; 26 percent more had between $15,000 and $25,000. No data were secured on total assets.

The upper levels of such incomes are happily far from destitute retirement, but even those levels are not high enough—in the case of retirees or near retirees—to suggest capability, let alone willingness, to hold investments that might well suffer reduced or suspended dividends and substantial price declines.

[18]Securities and Exchange Commission Staff Paper 75-1, *REITs: A Background Analysis and Recent Industry Development, 1961-74* (1975), p. 40.

[19]Buffington, op. cit.

[20]NAREIT, *1975 Fact Book*, p. 37.

[21]Before 1970, many states followed, at least as guidelines, the policy statements on REITs issued, starting in 1961, by the Midwest Securities Commissioners Association. The original 1961 statement limited secured borrowing to not more than 10 percent of the assets' values and unsecured borrowing to not more than 2 percent. A statement issued later that year raised the figure to a more realistic 66.66 percent. (Milton I. Baldinger, "Comments Re: Revised Midwest Securities Commissioners Association Statement of Policy Regarding REITs," *Journal of the Bar Association of Washington, D.C.* 29 [1962], pp. 147, 161.)

In 1970, the Midwest Commissioners liberalized their guidelines on leverage:

"The aggregate borrowings of the trust, secured and unsecured, shall not be unreasonable in relation to the net assets. . . and the maximum amount shall be stated [as a percentage] in the prospectus."

Thereafter, many REITs adopt[ed] a 500 percent leverage limitation. (Polubinski, op. cit., pp. 179, 195.)

The 1970 Midwest policy statement added a new provision limiting the issuance of public debt amounts on which the interst would be covered by the "historical cash flow of the trust *or the substantiated future cash flow. . . .* " (Emphasis added.)

Both before and after 1970, one important state, California, maintained a three to one debt-equity requirement for REITs sold in California and not exempted, for example, by listing on an exchange.

[22]Buffington, op. cit.

[23]Quoted in Hearings on REITs, p. 342.

[24]As measured by the NAREIT stock price index, covering all REITs traded on the NYSE, AMEX, and national OTC market; this listing included 165 REITs as of July 1977. See *1977 Fact Book*, p. 21.

[25]*REITs Quarterly, 1977*, p. 2.

[26]Hearings on REITs, p. 343, remarks of Kenneth D. Campbell, president, Audit Investment Research.

[27]Zucker, op. cit., p. 11.

[28]Wyndham Robertson, "How the Bankers Got Trapped in the REIT Disaster," *Fortune* (March 1975), p. 113.

III. Conflicts of Interest

[1]In some corporations, the publicly held shares are nonvoting; such corporations cannot be listed on exchanges. Noncorporate forms of organization, such as limited partnership syndicates and mutual insurance and saving associations, may be structured differently.

[2]Adolph Berle and Gardner Means introduced this notion in their classic *The Modern Corporation and Private Property* (New York: Macmillan, 1933).

[3]As of late 1976, a survey of leading companies showed that two-thirds had outside director majorities on their boards, much more than in previous surveys. However, "outside" merely means nonofficer; outside directors may be, for example, the company bankers or counsel. Heidrick & Struggles, Inc., *The Changing Board* (1976), p. 6.

[4]Almost half of all companies' directors, including outside directors, are essentially selected by the chief executive officer (CEO), not a board. Indeed, as the number of outside directors on

corporate boards has grown, the CEO's role has expanded; thus, management apparently remains fully in charge. The Heidrick & Struggles surveys show that from 1971 to 1976, the proportion of leading companies in which CEOs did most of the selection of directors increased from 14 percent to 46.5 percent. Ibid., p. 8.

[5]The externalized management structure of REITS is a kind of historical accident. The pre-1960 REITs were structured along more normal corporate lines. But what was apparently the first REIT to file with the SEC after the tax enabling legislation happened to be "almost a carbon copy of the typical mutual fund, and included the investment advisory company." By 1962 about half the REITs had followed that lead. Arthur O. Armstrong, Jr., "An Attorney's Viewpoint of State Securities Regulation of REITs," *University of Virginia Law Review* 48 (1962), pp. 1082, 1093. A number of REITs, though, have always had internal management.

For externalized structure's origin in investment companies, see Securities and Exchange Commission, *Public Policy Implications of Investment Company Growth*, House Report No. 2337, 89th Cong., 2d Sess. (Washington, D.C.: (1966), pp. 49-50.

[6]See Peter A. Schulkin, "REITs," *Financial Analysts Journal* 27, no. 3 (May-June 1971), pp. 33, 35, 74.

[7]Kenneth D. Campbell, "Background on the REIT Industry," Practicing Law Institute, *REIT Restructuring* (May-June 1977), pp. 9, 16.

[8]Under the Investment Company Act, in some situations only 40 percent of the board of an investment company are required to be independent of the advisor, whereas REIT boards are required to have a majority of unaffiliated members. But the Investment Company Act also requires investment company advisory contracts to be approved by a majority of the board's independent members; and the difference in number of independent directors required matters much less than the difference in criteria of independence, described below.

[9]Testimony of Abraham L. Pomerantz, Hearings on Mutual Fund Legislation of 1967, Senate Banking Committee, 90th Cong., 1st Sess., Pt. 2 (Washington, D.C.: 1967), p. 691.

[10]Hearings on REITs before the Senate Banking Committtee, 94th Cong., 2d Sess., (Washington, D.C.: May 1976), statement of Kenneth Campbell, p. 121 (hereafter referred to as Hearings on REITs).

[11]Benito M. Lopez, Jr., *The Role of the "Independent" Trustee in a REIT*, NAREIT (1974), p. 2.

[12]In 1965 the Internal Revenue Service (IRS), for which conflicts of interest are hardly a primary concern, issued rulings on matters involving the closeness and complexity of a trustee's relations with a REIT. These rulings, allegedly dictated by the provisions of the 1960 statute, "set the stage for numerous potential conflicts." Michael J. Brill, "REITs: A Current Assessment," *Brooklyn Law Review* 39 (1973), p. 608. The author of this thorough, analytical, and unusually perceptive article was a student. The article appears to be the sole treatment of REIT conflicts by any lawyer or legal academic. The author of another useful article on conflicts is a bank officer; see Douglas W. Duval, "Conflict of Interest Problems in the Management of Reits," *Real Estate Law Journal* 3(1974). Articles on legal requirements for starting or operating REITs are numerous. The scarcity of conflicts articles, given the amount of writing in the securities area, is a sad commentary on the legal profession's concern for fairness.

[13]Lopez, op. cit.

[14]*REITs Quarterly, 1977*, vol. IV, p. 10.

[15]Audit Investment Research, *REIT Advisory Fee Plans—1975: The $100 Million Question* (hereafter referred to as *AIR-1975*), p. 4.

[16]Brill, op. cit., pp. 607-608.

[17]Audit Investment Research, *Realty Trust Compensation Plans—1974* (hereafter referred to as *AIR-1974*), p. 5.

[18]Peter A. Schulkin, "Comparing Advisory Fees: Treacherous Business," *NAREIT Trustee* (October 1973).

[19]Kurt F. Flexner (director, Mortgage Finance Committee, American Bankers Association), "Future of REITs Hinges on Able Management," *Trust & Estates* 100 (1961), p. 542.

[20]*AIR-1975*, p. 40.

[21]Richard D. Marshall (professor of businees administration, Rutgers University Graduate School), "Determining Real Estate Management Fees," *Trust & Estates* 115 (1976), p. 610.

[22]See Audit Investment Research, *Realty Trust Compensation Plans for Advisers—August 15 and October 1, 1973*, p. 11.

[23]In 1972 a REIT known as USF (now Independence Mortgage) stated in proxy materials that state administrators were applying fee and expense limits inconsistently.

[24]"*Fee and Expenses.* The aggregate annual expenses of every character paid or incurred by the trust, excluding interest, taxes, expenses in connection with the issuance of securities, shareholder relations, and acquisitions, operation, maintenance, protection and disposition of trust properties, but including advisory fees and mortgage servicing fees and all other expenses, shall not exceed the greater of:

1. 1½% of the average net assets of the trust, net assets being defined as total invested assets at cost before deducting depreciation reserves, less total liabilities, calculated at least quarterly on a basis consistently applied, or,

2. 25% of the net income of trust, excluding provisions for depreciation and realized capital gains and losses and extraordinary items, and before deducting advisory and servicing fees and expenses, calculated at least quarterly on a basis consistently applied; but in no event shall aggregate annual expenses exceed 1½% of the total invested assets of the trust.

The adviser shall reimburse the trust at least annually for the amount by which aggregate annual expenses paid or incurred by the trust as defined herein exceed the amount herein provided." Midwest Securities Commissioners' Policy, reprinted in *1977 Fact Book*, pp. 85-87.

[25]"A typical fee schedule for instance calls for regular compensation at a monthly fee of 1/12 of 1% of average gross book value of invested assets of a trust, average gross book value of invested assets being defined as average gross book value of the total assets of the trust (excluding goodwill and similar intangible assets, cash, cash items and obligations of municipal, state and federal governments and governmental agencies, other than obligations related to real property or mortgages wherein the liability of the debtor is supported by governmental guarantees or insurance) plus the average of undisbursed commitments of the trust in respect of closed loans and other closed investments!" *AIR-1974*, p. 5.

[26]Ibid., pp. 5-6.

[27]Keefe, Bruyette & Woods, *Bank Loans to REITs: How Serious the Problem?* (May 2, 1975), pp. 3, 6.

[28]Audit Investment Research, *REIT Advisory Fee Plans—1976* (hereafter referred to as *AIR-1976*), p. 1. See also Ibid., p. 37, and *AIR-1975*, pp. 40-41.

[29]Investment Company Act §15 (c). The SEC has promulgated no regulations indicating what minimal information should be secured. As late as 1973, a major investment company's board approved an advisory contract, including revisions favoring the advisor, without sufficient information. See *Galfand* v. *Chestnutt* (S.D.N.Y. 1975), *Securities Law Reporter* (Chicago: Commerce Clearing House), parag. 95, 248, pp. 96, 281.

[30]*AIR-1976*, p. 37.

[31]*AIR-1975*, p. 40. The figures supporting that judgment (set forth in Table 8) do not cover the industry because very few firms published enough data to permit analysis of their profitability. But the data are "selective" only in the sense of excluding firms for which data are not available. There is no reason to believe these figures atypical.

In its 1973 survey, Audit Investment Research published profitability data opening with the statement:

Very little has been documented publicly about the profitability of advisers to a realty trust and for this reason the area remains of unusual interest. The fact that most trust sponsors have chosen to make their major returns in the form of advisers' fees rather than in direct investment in trust shares has fostered the belief that advisers have high profitability. The only generalization possible is that there appears to be a minimum level of expenses involved in advisory operations, and numerous interviews with trusts support the view that advisers of small trusts operate on low profit levels while advisers to larger trusts have higher profit margins. (*AIR-1973*, p. 12.)

In 1974-75 many REITs adopted "expenses only" advisory contracts. Payments under these contracts may be assumed to represent "the irreducible minimum needed to operate REITs."

[32]The surveys covered 112 mortgage REITs in 1973 and 1974, 109 in 1975, 107 in 1976. Data here come mainly from the 1975 survey, p. 44, and 1974, p. 59.

[33]*AIR-1974*, p. 59. Among the 112 major mortgage REITs surveyed, the percentages including unfunded portions were 67.5 in 1971, 64.3 in 1973, and 51.8 percent in 1974.

[34]Ibid., p. 6.

[35]*AIR-1973*, p. 17.

[36]*AIR-1974*, p. 59. The percentage among the 112 mortgage REITs surveyed was much lower in 1971 (26 percent) but rose to 69.6 percent in 1973 and 67.9 percent in 1974. No 1972 data were presented.

[37]Ibid.

[38]Ibid., p. 29.

[39]Ibid., p. 31. Copyright by Audit Investment Research, Inc., and reprinted by permission. All other rights reserved.

[40]*AIR-1975*, p.63.

[41]AIR-1973, p. 9, and *AIR-1974*, p. 32.

Justice changed its name to Metroplex Realty in December 1977 and filed under Chapter XI of the Bankruptcy Act.

By early 1977 Justice had shrunk to $53 million in assets, negative net worth, nonearning investments totaling about 98 percent of its portfolio, and a net operating loss of $12 million for the prior year. For the fiscal year ending September 1976, the advisor received an advisory fee of $595,707. An additional $196,000 was paid to independent managers assisting the trust. The trust, like many others, is the subject of several suits by stockholders.

[42]*AIR-1974*, pp. 30-32.

[43]"Horror Story," *Forbes* (February 1, 1975), pp. 24-35.

[44]*AIR-1975*, p. 1.

[45]*REITs Quarterly, 1977*, vol. IV, p. 10; cf. *NAREIT 1975 Fact Book*, p. 41.

[46]*AIR-1976*, p. 27.

[47]Ibid.

[48]Ibid., p. 23.

[49]Ibid., pp. 23-26.

[50]Ibid., pp. 4-19.

[51]James P. Furniss, "The REIT: Banking's New Profit Partner," *Bankers Magazine* 154 (1971), p. 79.

[52]John Getze, "The REITs—a Good Deal Takes a Dive," *Los Angeles Times*, June 4, 1975, reprinted in Hearings on REITs, pp. 380, 383.

[53]Moreover, some sponsors advised more than one REIT. Merrill Lynch advised five; Continental Illinois advised two; and Sonnenblick-Goldman, a real estate firm, also advised two. Some of these REITs were among the most successful in the industry.

[54]Securities and Exchange Commission Staff Paper 75-1, *REITs: A Background Analysis and Recent Industry Development, 1961-74*, p. 11.

[55]Maynard C. Bartram, "Connecticut General's Approach to the REIT," *Trusts and Estates* 109 (1971), p. 870. The author was a trustee and officer of the REIT who had formerly worked in the insurance company's real estate department.

[56]Of the remainder, one is sponsored jointly by three different banks and called "Tri-South"; and in at least two of the remaining situations, the bank was not the REIT's original sponsor and chose to continue the REIT's original name.

[57]"Banks are Declared Key to Relief for 'Very Sick' First Wisconsin REIT," *American Banker*, (April 22, 1975), p. 1.

[58]Chase Manhattan Corp., *Annual Report, 1973*, pp. 22, 27.

[59]Stephen R. Downes, "Why Chase Manhattan Sponsored a REIT," *Trust & Estates* 109 (1970), pp. 1026, 1027.

[60]A major reason why Connecticut General sponsored a REIT was that:

The capacity of the company's mortgage and real estate organization has in recent times tended to outrun the investment needs of the company even though Connecticut General has been growing faster in sales than most major competitors. (Bartram, op. cit., p. 871.)

[61]"Falling Out: Real Estate Trusts Feud with Advisers over their Obligations," *The Wall Street Journal*, March 13, 1975, pp. 1, 27.

[62]"Too Much Too Soon: How 2 Realty Trusts Gave Backers Big Gains—And then Big Losses," *The Wall Street Journal*, March 14, 1975, p. 1.

[63]Connecticut General's REIT trustee-officer called allocation "one of the major questions," and said the answer was to "give both entities equal access and—if both wanted a particular project—to share it equally." Bartram, op. cit., p. 871.

[64]The Investment Company Act flatly bars transactions between an investment company and its advisor or affiliates, unless specific approval is secured in advance from the SEC, but permits joint participation by an investment company and its affiliated persons under such general rules as the SEC may prescribe. Investment Company Act §17(a), (d).

[65]Testimony of Kenneth Campbell, Hearings on REITs, p. 121.

[66]Citizens and Southern Realty Investors, *Annual Report, 1976*.

[67]Safeguards such as joint participation and rights of first refusal reduce conflict-of-interest problems and the temptation to use the REIT as a dumping ground, but, of course, even without conflicts one can still make unsound investments. For example, see *Realty Trust Review* (December 26, 1975), p. 3.

[68]Nelson, "Regulation of REITs by the Midwest States," Practicing Law Institute, *REITs* (1969), pp. 95, 96.

It might be argued that some self-dealing was made almost inevitable by the tax requirement that the REIT be a "passive investor." The REIT had to secure services other than selection of investments from an "independent contractor"; but for efficiency's sake, the independent contractor selected was often an affiliate of the REIT's advisor.

[69]However, even for investment companies, observers who generally approve of the Investment Company Act and its administration by the SEC have called for relaxation of the flat bar. See Alan Rosenblat and Martin E. Lybecker, "Some Thoughts on the Federal Securities Laws Regulating External Investment Management Arrangements and ALI Federal Securities Code Project," *University of Pennsylvania Law Review*, 124, no. 587 (1976), pp. 640-643.

[70]At least one REIT did flatly prohibit self-dealing. City Investing Corp., a large publicly held real estate and finance company, barred dealings between itself or its affiliates and its REIT, C. I. Mortgage Group.

[71]For an analysis of legal regulation of REITs, see pp. 205-211.

[72]Duval, op. cit., p. 25.

[73]Keefe, Bruyette & Woods, op. cit., p. 69.

[74]Ibid., p. 66.

[75]"Banks and Real Estate Trusts: New and Dangerous Extension of Banking Power," *Congressional Record* (July 15, 1970), pp. 24532, 24533.

[76]Testimony of Roy A. Schotland, *Hearings on REITs*, pp. 96, 102-103.

[77]Keefe, Bruyette & Woods, op. cit., p. 70.

IV. Regulation

[1]Report of the Real Estate Advisory Committee to the SEC (October 12, 1972), p. 93.

[2]John G. Sobieski, "State Securites Regulation of REITs," *University of Virginia Law Review* 48 (1962), pp. 1069, 1072.

[3]For presentations by two of California's securities administrators on their treatment of REITs, see John G. Sobieski, op. cit., p. 1069; and Brian Van Camp, "Securities Regulation of Real Estate Investments: The California Model," *Ohio State Law Journal* 35 (1974), p. 309. For arguments against California's " 'toughest' and most unworkable rules," see Arthur O. Armstrong, Jr., "An Attorney's Viewpoint on State Securities Regulation of REITs," *University of Virginia Law Review* 48 (1962), p. 1082; see also Milton I. Baldinger, "Comments re: Revised Midwest Securities Commissioners Association Statement of Policy Regarding REITs," *Journal of the Bar Association of Washington, D.C.* 29 (1962), p. 147.

V. Conclusions

[1]National Association of REITs, *REITs Quarterly, 1977*, pp. 1, 3. See also articles such as Howard Rudnitsky, "Speculating in White Elephants," *Forbes* (December 1, 1977), pp. 59-68; Henry Scott-Stokes, "Rise in Property Aiding Recovery of REITs," *The New York Times*, January 23, 1978, p. D1; and Dan Dorfman, "REITs are Staging a Comeback in 1978," *Washington Post*, March 1, 1978, p. D9.

[2]Michael J. Brill, "REITs: A Current Assessment," *Brooklyn Law Review* 39 (1973), p. 618.

[3]The NAREIT staff was helpful in the preparation of this study.

Corporate Pension Fund Asset Management
by John Brooks

I • THE PROBLEM OF SERVING TWO MASTERS

Private pension funds, the overwhelming majority of which are sponsored and funded by corporations for the benefit of their employees, now constitute one of the largest pools of private capital in the nation. Covering more than 30 million employees, they currently pay annual benefits exceeding $6 billion to more than 4 million retired persons. According to the Securities and Exchange Commission, as of the end of 1973, the total assets of private noninsured pension funds in the United States were $124.4 billion (book value), of which $79.2 billion were invested in common stocks. Their growth is so rapid that before the end of the current decade their assets will almost certainly exceed $200 billion.[1] (See Table 16.)

Inevitably, this mass of capital in the national economy and stock markets has become a force to contend with. According to one authority, in 1970 private pension fund assets amounted to about one-fourth of the total assets of all nonfinancial corporations in the United States,[2] making private pension fund assets the largest single bloc in the stock market. The existence of this force raises many new economic policy questions and makes it imperative that the reliability of trustees and other investment managers responsible for the investment of pension fund assets be examined. Pension funds have changed the role of bank trusteeship in the United States from a private matter to one of broad public concern. However, concern is slight at present—largely because of unexpected rapid growth and also lack of precedents for regulation.

Conflict of interest is more disturbing in connection with pensions than in most other contexts because it involves the handling (and potential mishandling) of money belonging to employees and earmarked for their welfare in old age. In pension fund investment practices, the potential for conflict has existed in many areas: corporate officers may be tempted to use pension assets

Note: The author expresses his thanks to Nancy Jalet, Barbara A. Patocka of *Institutional Investor* magazine, and Thomas H. Stevenson of the Twentieth Century Fund for counsel and research assistance so valuable and extensive that this chapter should be considered a work of collaboration.

Table 16 Asset Sizes of Some Characteristic Corporate Pension Funds, 1974

EXTERNALLY MANAGED	MILLIONS
General Motors	$3,911[a]
Ford Motor Co.	2,376[a]
IBM Corp.	1,191[a]
Lockheed Aircraft Corp.	964
Boeing Co.	915
Westinghouse Electric Corp.	750
International Paper Co.	325
Xerox	268
Kimberly-Clark Corp.	124
Northwest Airlines	75
Occidental Petroleum Corp.	60
MANAGED WHOLLY IN-HOUSE	
Sears, Roebuck & Co.	2,400
U.S. Steel Corp.	2183[a]
du Pont de Nemours (E.I.) & Co., Inc.	2,000
Bethlehem Steel Corp.	653[a]
Grace (W.R.) & Co.	128
Winn-Dixie Stores, Inc.	75
Wells Fargo & Co.	73
Carter Hawley Hale Stores, Inc.	54
MANAGED PARTIALLY IN-HOUSE	
Exxon Corp.	$1,250
Atlantic Richfield Co.	650
Gulf Oil Corp.	550
American Cyanamid Co.	190
Corning Glass Works	125
National Distillers & Chemical Corp.	110
Norfolk & Western Railway	71
Duke Power Co.	51

[a]Book value; all other figures indicate market value.

Sources: *Institutional Investor*, Pensions Directory, 1975.

in their commercial dealings or to manipulate stock prices or reports of corporate earnings; bank trustees may be tempted to use pension assets invested with them for the benefit of important bank customers; brokerage-connected money managers may be tempted to overtrade the pension fund stock portfolios under their control to generate brokerage commissions for their firms.[3]

Underlying these various temptations, though, has been a single pervading conflict built into the American pension system: corporate pension fund assets are managed either by officers of the sponsoring corporation or by persons or agencies—banks and investment advisors—who are ultimately responsible to the corporation. Therefore the trustees or managers have been necessarily torn

between serving the interests of the corporation and those of the plan participants. Senator Jacob Javits, a leading advocate of pension reform, commented:

As every first-year law student knows, it is a time-honored legal principle that no man
can serve two masters. How pension trusts have escaped application of this principle
eludes me.[4]

Justice Cardozo, in the case of *Meinhard* v. *Salmon*, elaborated on this moral
consideration:

A trustee is held to something stricter than the morals of the market place. Not honesty
alone, but the punctilio of an honor the most sensitive, is then the standard of behavior.
...the level of conduct for fiduciaries [has] been kept at a level higher than that trodden
by the crowd.

Because pension trusts involve so many more people and so much more money
than do conventional trusts, such considerations are particularly important.

The Employee Retirement Income Security Act of 1974 is the first major
federal legislation to take note of many of these problems. In addition to
providing for vesting, disclosure, funding, and termination insurance, the law
also states that any person who exercises control or authority over the pension
fund—which would clearly include bank managers, investment advisors, and
corporate sponsors—is now a ''fiduciary'' and must act ''solely in the interests
of the participants and the beneficiaries'' of the plan. That prescription has
already had important consequences for the conflict-of-interest problems that
have plagued pension funds. But, as will be seen, the law may still fail to
resolve some troublesome questions.

Generally, there have been comparatively few disastrous pension plan
failures to date, and rarely have these been the result of fiduciary misconduct.
There was, for example, the celebrated case of the United Mine Workers'
welfare and retirement fund. Chiefly as a result of the energetic efforts of a
single Washington attorney—Harry Huge of the firm of Arnold & Porter—it
was revealed in 1971 that the union- and company-appointed trustees had, over
a number of years, deposited tens of millions of dollars of fund reserves (for
example, $75 million in 1967, constituting 44 percent of all fund assets) in a
bank controlled by the union—at no interest. The proceeds of this money had
been used principally for the benefit of the union rather than for the beneficiaries. This clear and flagrant case of fiduciary misconduct did not involve a
corporate pension fund—but one jointly administered by employers and a
union.[5]

In the case of the Penn Central Transportation Company employee pension
funds (also 1971), the staff of the Interstate Commerce Commission charged
that two officers of the company, who ''were able to exercise total control over
the investments'' of the funds, had used that power to invest almost $1 million
of pension assets in stock in which the officers were personally interested—

and which subsequently proved to be virtually worthless.[6] The celebrated shortfall of the Studebaker Corporation pension fund in 1964 was probably more significant in terms of social implication than either the Penn Central case or the United Mine Wokers case. (It was this event, incidentally, that first got Senator Javits interested in pension reform.) When Studebaker closed its plant and terminated its pension plan that November, 10,500 workers had pension claims totaling $25 million. The funds were not only insufficient, they were wholly inadequate, creating a desperate situation for 4,000 employees between the ages of forty and sixty, who received only 15 percent of their promised benefits, and for almost 3,000 employees under forty, who received nothing at all.[7]

This was not a fiduciary case but rather a critical inadequacy of funding, a problem that was greatly aggravated by the fact that three years earlier the company had considerably liberalized the benefits it "promised" its workers upon retirement. The liability created by this and earlier plan liberalizations was not yet funded, even though Studebaker was following an "acceptable" funding method. Hence, the necessity for plan termination insurance, as well as for mandatory funding, vesting, and fiduciary standards, became clear to many. To pursue briefly the matter of pension plan terminations, a Senate subcommittee in 1972 reported that the incidence of such terminations, usually resulting in "denial or reductions of promised pensions," rose markedly during the conglomerate era of 1966-69; after a merger, one of the merged companies' pension funds would simply be dropped, presumably as an economy measure.[8]

Such actions vividly illustrated the need for reform in the structure of pension plans, which is probably the major reason that the so-called Pension Reform Act was finally voted in 1974. The new law establishes minimum standards for vesting; it requires that plans be funded according to prescribed formulas; it provides insurance for employees whose plans are terminated without adequate assets to pay vested benefits; and it contains important new provisions for disclosing the plan's benefits and operations to employees.

But a growing number of recognized authorities on pension plans have felt that fiduciary misconduct arises from the fact that it is self-interested corporations or unions, rather than true representatives of the employees, who institute and structure the pension plans that, theoretically, exist for the employees' sole benefit. Such critics see hard-eyed "salesmen" representing actuarial firms, banks, insurance companies, or investment advisory services trying to entice corporations with pension propositions that *appear* to offer maximum benefit to the workers but are in fact structured to keep eligibility, and therefore costs, to a minimum. Thus, a plan is created that provides minimum benefits to participants and maximum opportunity for the corporation to minimize its contributions to the fund, thereby increasing its profits. Mervin C. Bernstein, professor of law at Ohio State University, reflects on part of the problem when he says, "It would be Quixotic of insurance companies, banks, and actuarial consultants to draft plans with [employee] interests paramount so long as employers constitute the bulk of their clients."[9]

As a result of such forces, pension plans are structured so, in the opinion of many authorities, far fewer than half of all corporate employees now covered will ever collect a penny of benefits. Even with the new law, an employee must work for at least five years before he earns a nonforfeitable pension, and, according to the Bureau of Labor Statistics, 58.3 percent of the work force remains with the same employer for less than five years. Bernstein's solution, like Ralph Nader's, is to require immediate vesting and to take the control of pension plans out of the hands of corporations and unions entirely and entrust it to an independent third party. This remedy was too radical for the taste of Congress.

Among the most critical areas of conflict have been the design of the plans themselves, the substantial leeway available for "professional" judgments by actuaries, and the free hand investment managers have had in determining the appropriate investments for the fund and the risks involved in practices such as buying the employing corporation's stock as opposed to other property.

Private pension plans only recently have become a major factor in the economic and social life of the United States. In the nineteenth and early twentieth centuries, when most Americans lived in rural or semirural settings and the elderly generally were provided for by their younger relatives, the need for pensions was limited. The first corporation to set up a pension plan was American Express, in 1875. Railroads and a few closely allied industries had pension plans before 1900; many industrial and craft unions set them up early in the twentieth century. Sears, Roebuck & Company established its famous and highly successful savings and profit-sharing plan in 1916, but as late as 1925, there were only about four hundred private pension plans in operation in the country. It was not until 1926 that Congress took the step, vital to private pension plans' future growth, of granting them tax-exempt status.

The real turning point in the history of pension plan development was the passage of the Social Security Act of 1935, which affirmed national recognition of the needs that had developed now that a historically rural nation had become primarily urban and industrialized, the multigenerational household was fast disappearing, and the aged urgently required protection. A slow but steady growth of private retirement plans, intended to supplement social security, began after 1935 and accelerated in the 1940s, when increased deferred benefits became a happy solution to the problems caused by wartime wage controls. By 1950 almost 10 million employees were covered by private plans (insured and noninsured) with assets of $12.8 billion. A landmark event occurred in 1949, when the Supreme Court affirmed a 1947 lower court ruling in the *Inland Steel* case, holding that pensions were a form of remuneration and therefore an appropriate subject for collective bargaining between labor unions and company managements.

Wage freezes imposed during the Korean conflict stimulated the growth of private pensions as an alternative union demand, as, of course, did the economic boom that lasted through most of the 1950s. By 1960 private pension employee coverage was above 21 million workers and assets were above $50 billion. Then, in the 1960s, a general continuation of good times, combined with a great speculative era in the stock market, contrived for the first time to form the private pension assets into a significant force in the stock market. Those assets, formerly heavily concentrated in bonds and mortgages, were now largely committed to common stocks. By and large this trend toward stock investment constituted a wise and healthy movement toward more liberal and imaginative pension management, enabling beneficiaries to participate in national growth. But in some cases the importance of preserving capital to protect future benefits was forgotten as corporations attempted to cut their costs by increasing investment return. Stock investment also frequently increased the temptation toward conflicts of interest and tended to put pension assets into the hands of men unschooled in the discipline of trusteeship.[10]

Thus, private pensions evolved over the years from a form of gratuity dispensed by a rare benevolent employer to his loyal and long-standing employees into a necessary and powerful aspect of our national life. Meanwhile—without conscious intention—there had grown up perhaps the largest virtually unregulated asset pool in existence. Lack of regulation of pension funds was primarily the result not of negligence but rather of the fact that the very concept of private pensions on a huge scale was so new.[11]

In the past the principal federal agencies with important regulatory jurisdiction over private pensions plans were the Internal Revenue Service and the Department of Labor. Probably the most crucial jurisdiction was that of the IRS, which could take away a private pension or profit-sharing fund's tax-exempt status if the plan did not continue to meet specified criteria. Without tax exemption private plans would not operate on their present scale and many corporations probably would not maintain retirement plans at all. Generally, a plan qualified for exemption under the Internal Revenue Code of 1954 if it benefited exclusively the employees and their beneficiaries, if it benefited 80 percent or more of the eligible employees, and if the contributions or benefits did not favor one class or group of employees over another.[12] Thus, the IRS did not involve itself directly with most real or potential conflict-of-interest situations, and in the matter of self-investment by the plan sponsor, with which it did concern itself to some extent, it tended to be lenient. Moreover, the IRS, as a limited regulator of pension fund activities, lacked real power to prevent abuses; generally, it struck only after the damage had been done and benefits lost. Such recoveries as it did make were payable not to the fund beneficiaries but to the United States Treasury. Hence, if a participant in a plan became aware of practices that were endangering his benefits, he had little motivation to attempt to correct them.

The other important federal regulator has been the Department of Labor. The now superseded and defunct Welfare and Pension Plans Disclosure Act of 1958, amended in 1962, required each plan covering more than twenty-five employees to file with the Department of Labor a statement describing the plan as well as an annual report giving general information on the financial status and investments of the plan. In addition, the plan's administrator was required to deliver to participants or beneficiaries, on their written request, a copy of the description and "an adequate summary" of the latest annual report or to make these documents available for inspection in the plan's principal office. [13]

As a tool for exposing conflicts of interest, however, the act was pathetically weak, principally because it did not require listing the names of specific portfolio holdings. Assets were listed merely by category—such as common stocks, bonds and real estate; loans, notes receivable, and real estate holdings were reported merely by single-line entries indicating the aggregate dollar amounts involved. Even specific party-in-interest transactions—such as investments in the stock of the plan sponsor or of one of his suppliers—did not have to be disclosed if the stocks were traded on any recognized stock exchange. The participant or beneficiary who claimed his right to inspect his company plan's annual report would be unable to determine whether the fund's assets were invested in sound, reputable companies or whether they were invested to benefit others rather than the participating members. In short, having risked the displeasure of his employer by the very act of claiming his disclosure right, he would have learned practically nothing. It is not surprising that few such requests were made by plan participants and that therefore "disclosure" in the past was more theoretical than actual.

Under the new act, regulatory jurisdiction remains with the IRS and the Department of Labor but their power is much increased. The disclosure provisions, for example, are vastly improved over those of the 1958 act. One provision of the new law requires that all participants must be provided a summary description "written in a manner calculated to be understood by the average plan participant." In addition, pension sponsors must report far more detailed information about their funds' investments in an annual report of all holdings required by the Department of Labor, which together with IRS has also taken over the job of policing the vesting and funding provisions of the Pension Reform Act.

Before the enactment of the new law, which preempts state regulation of private pension plans, the principal check on the investment actions of pension asset managers was the state laws governing the responsibilities of trustees. The basic standard of fiduciary law is the famous "prudent man rule," originally expressed by Justice Samuel Putnam of Massachusetts in 1830, which states (with modern and local variations) that a trustee "is to observe how men of prudence, discretion, and intelligence manage their own affairs" and to do likewise in the management of his trust. Durable and equitable as the state-administered prudent man rule had been as a guide to trustees, it fell crucially short as a control on pension fund asset managers because, generally, no body of government enforcers was charged with ensuring compliance. Under the Pension Reform Act, however, the prudent man rule carries more weight because the Department of Labor is responsible for enforcement and the Secretary of Labor is empowered to bring suits for violations of the fiduciary provisions. In effect, the prudent man rule has been nationalized. Under state laws, in contrast, the prudent man rule was essentially enforced only by private suits, and state authorities were plagued with jurisdictional problems when corporate pension funds were interstate. For these reasons the Bankers Trust Company, second largest trustee of pension assets in the country, advocated the adoption of federal fiduciary standards, saying: "Despite the presence of a broad body of trust law at the state level, it has generally proven to be ineffective in protecting the beneficiaries of pension trusts where fiduciary misconduct has occurred."[14]

II • AT LESS THAN ARM'S LENGTH

The most obvious conflict-of-interest temptation facing a corporate officer who is responsible for pension assets is the temptation to encourage the investment of part of those assets in the sponsoring corporation's own stock or other property. This procedure is widely deplored by the banks and other investment managers who handle pension assets—although before the new pension law was enacted, most managers would agree to buy a stock in the sponsoring company if they were so instructed. Now no more than 10 percent of a pension plan's assets may be invested in the sponsoring company's stock, bonds, or real property (although profit-sharing plans may continue to purchase an unlimited amount of company securities). Even with the 10 percent limitation, however, there is still room for conflict of interest, since it would be quite possible for a large fund to fall within the legal limit but still control a large portion of its corporate stock or other property.

As in the past, the Securities and Exchange Commission may intervene if a corporation's self-dealing transactions with its retirement fund appear to violate the securities laws—as in stock manipulating or insider trading. And even before the new pension law was passed, the IRS was empowered to remove a corporate pension fund's all-important tax exemption on a finding that the fund's investments had been made in the interest of persons other than the plan's beneficiaries. But the IRS seldom was inclined to put that interpretation on pension fund self-dealing. Indeed, an IRS ruling, presumably reflecting its attitude before the passage of the pension reform law, revealed a remarkable degree of leniency on the subject. The pension fund of corporation A made an unsecured loan to corporation B when both corporations were substantially under the same ownership; the IRS ruled that the deal was allowable because "the corporation receiving the loan was not the creator of the trust"—which was true in theory but hardly true in practice.[1] Today, however, it is doubtful that such a deal would be permitted.

This is not to say that before the new law, investment of a large amount of pension fund assets in the sponsoring corporation was the general practice. An

SEC survey in the 1950s showed that less than 3 percent of all assets of noninsured funds were self-invested by the sponsoring corporations.[2]

There are cases where self-investment has proved spectacularly beneficial to the plan participants—most notably, the Sears, Roebuck savings and profit-sharing plan, which usually has 80 percent of its assets invested in the company's stock. At the end of 1973, the average value of the account of an employee who was retiring after twenty-five to twenty-nine years was $106,764, and the value of the average retiree's account was $82,304. (It should be noted that the Sears plan—the only plan available to all its employees, incidentally—is a profit-sharing plan, with benefits proportionate to investment performance, rather than a pension plan with level benefits. In contrast, Sears' pension plan is limited to management personnel).[3]

Again, there are cases where self-investment is virtually imposed by market conditions. The American Telephone & Telegraph Company, for example, maintains a rule that none of its pension funds may hold securities of its sponsors; but the pension funds *may* hold securities of other companies within the Bell System—and such securities make up such a high percentage of all blue-chip bonds available that the pension funds can claim to be almost forced to have this type of investment, with the result that some Bell System pension funds invested 8 or 9 percent in Bell System bonds.[4]

Nevertheless, many leading corporate pension fund officials oppose the practice of investment in the sponsor for two reasons: first, because potential for conflict of interest is evident, and second, because the failure of a corporation with a heavily self-invested fund would cost the employees not only their jobs but also part of their pensions. Edward H. Malone, vice president in charge of pension operations for General Electric, says that his company's huge fund ($2.8 billion market value in 1973) has a flat policy against investment in securities of General Electric. International Telephone & Telegraph never holds ITT stock in its pension funds except in a fund acquired through a corporate acquisition; in such a case, the manager of the fund is instructed to sell the stock as soon as practicable. Why then, do corporate pension managers overwhelmingly oppose a flat legal ban on self-dealing? Because, they say, to do so would deprive the pensioners of outstanding corporations of the advantage of profiting from the success of their employers, in effect penalizing them for being on the payroll of, say, IBM. This belief, of course, implies the argument that *no* other investment is as good as the shares of the sponsoring corporation. Tortured as it may seem to be, that argument is the principal one offered by corporate officers who favor wide latitude on pension fund self-investment. Another position is that the corporation understands its own operations and is in a position to know when its shares are a good buy; however, this argument is seldom advanced, since it might imply possible violations of the insider-trading provisons of the securities laws.

The practice of self-investment ranges from outright abuse to a gray area in which the ethics may be questionable but the results harmless or actually beneficial. In abusing his privilege, the trustee may improperly use a pension fund for his personal benefit—and some trustees have done so. George P. Shultz, then Secretary of Labor, reported in April 1970 to a House subcommittee on a case of pension fund trustees, also officers of the sponsoring corporation, who had purchased shares of company stock for the fund while they were selling their personal holdings, with a resulting depreciation of fund assets estimated at over $4.5 million. The five trustees of another corporate plan had borrowed two-thirds of the fund's assets to finance private businesses of their own. Many other such acts—plainly illegal even before enactment of the pension law—undoubtedly go undetected.

A frequently practiced form of self-investment involves real estate. Typically, the trustees of a pension fund use some of the fund's assets to purchase a piece of the sponsor company's property, for example, a warehouse or an office building; the facility is then leased back by the fund to the company, at an appropriate rate of interest. Such a transaction is not necessarily adverse to the interests of fund participants, since sale-leasebacks may be very good deals for the buyer-lessor. The company may be able to say to the fund trustee, "We defy you to find a better investment than this warehouse of ours." If, however, the company wants the leaseback price to be slightly less than the going rental rate or the sale price to be higher than the market rate, the fund trustee may conscientiously refuse to make the transaction—leaving the company, if it wishes to pursue the matter, the option of appointing some other trustee who will be more amenable. Unfortunately, however, in many cases company management and fund trustees are the same people, so they simply deal with themselves, using the fund participants' money.

Among the cases of real estate self-investment that have been publicized in recent years are that of the F. W. Woolworth Company, whose pension trust held 26 percent of its assets in Woolworth property as of 1971 (a top company officer, Robert G. Zimmerman, said of this situation in Senate hearings, "We see nothing wrong with it"[5]) and that of the Whitaker Cable Corporation of Kansas City. In the latter case, the IRS stepped in and temporarily revoked the pension fund's tax exemption, forcing it to correct the alleged fault. In August 1965 the Whitaker pension fund purchased the company's office building for $703,000. A previous appraisal arranged by the company had put the value of the property at $790,000, and so the price apparently was a bargain. But in 1967, through a routine IRS audit of the company, the examining agent appraised the building at only $421,000 as of the date of purchase. After company protests the appraisal was raised to $614,000, which still left the pension fund with an apparent overcharge of $89,000. As a result the plan was disqualified for tax exemption in July 1970, whereupon the company, still under protest, paid the fund the $89,000 balance, and the plan was accordingly requalified as of December 1971. The company's explanation of its pension investment in company real estate—that the fund's investments had been earning only 2 percent over a fifteen-year period while the gross return on the real estate leaseback was 10 percent—seemed reasonable enough. However, if the pension fund had actually been overcharged $89,000 as a result of self-dealing, the additional interest would thereby be canceled out for an extended period.[6] The difference between the low and high appraisal figures—$421,000 and $790,000—clearly shows the potential for abuse in real estate transactions in which the same party is, for practical purposes, on both sides and the discipline of the market or even of independent appraisers is bypassed.

The Whitaker case was exposed because of IRS action, but under the tax and disclosure laws that prevailed before the new pension law took effect, it is impossible to say how many similar cases, or cases more clearly involving abuse, remained undetected. Now, however, any so-called party-in-interest transaction must be reported to the Department of Labor, and there are restrictions on what kinds of employer-related property may be purchased for pension and profit-sharing funds. Nevertheless, because of the inherent difficulty of assigning a market value to real estate, the potential for less than ethical transactions between a retirement fund and its sponsoring corporation remains.

The temptation to invest pension assets in the common stock of the sponsoring company is clearly greatest at times when the company has the greatest interest in maintaining or raising the price of the stock—specifically when the sponsoring company is engaged in an acquisition program based on exchanges of shares and needs a high stock price in order to make favorable deals. (Another obvious temptation to acquisition-minded companies is to invest pension assets in companies targeted for takeovers, but this practice seems to be all but universally condemned, and apparently eschewed, in conglomerate circles.) The most publicized example of pension fund investments in company securities, apparently in connection with an acquisition program, is that of Genesco, Inc., the Tennessee-based conglomerate.

Genesco maintained a pension fund and also an employee stock purchase plan (both internally managed) under which, at their option, employees could regularly purchase Genesco stock through payroll deductions. In the early 1960s, the firm had an aggressive corporate acquisition program. Beginning in 1961 and continuing through 1965, the trustees of the pension fund and the employee stock purchase fund (who were also company officers) bought Genesco stock through regular transactions on the New York Stock Exchange, often in such volume as to influence the price of the stock and sometimes in such volume as to dominate its market. For example, purchases by the two company funds constituted 41.6 percent of all Stock Exchange trading in the stock for the fourth quarter of 1961, 47.4 percent for the first quarter of 1962, and 75.2 and 78.1 percent, respectively, for the second and third quarters of 1962. The percentage fell somewhat over the succeeding three years, but it was still high enough to constitute more than 25 percent of all trading in Genesco in nine quarters during those years; by the end of 1965, the two funds had bought, over the four-year period, about 940,000 of the company's shares. Of these, 41 percent, or about 385,000, had been bought for the pension fund. The result was that as of 1971, almost one-third of the pension fund's portfolio—apart from a large investment in company real estate under a sale-leaseback arrangement—consisted of Genesco stock. (Overall, the fund was invested about 59 percent in Genesco stock or in real estate used by the company or its subsidiaries.)

Meanwhile, the price of Genesco stock, unquestionably helped by all that in-house buying, had been rising; starting at 33 in the first quarter of 1961, it had reached 36 by the end of 1962, 39 by the end of 1964, and 58 by the end of 1965. At the same time, the company was vigorously pursuing its acquisition program; between January 1, 1961, and October 29, 1965, it exchanged over 1 million shares of its common stock for stock or assets of no fewer than 12 other companies in which it thereby acquired controlling or minority interests. Obviously, if the buying program of the two funds had not maintained Genesco's stock price, this cornucopia of acquisitions could not have been accumulated on such favorable terms, if at all.[7]

Had any of this been improper? Not, apparently, by then prevailing laws and the standards of their enforcement. In 1966 the SEC did induce Genesco to enter into an agreement limiting its purchase of Genesco stock to 15 percent of the stock exchange volume for any given week—but it did not make any charge of improper conduct. Indeed, the pension fund participants had not suffered, at least in the short run, since the price of the Genesco stock that was beginning to dominate the fund kept rising steadily. The short-run losers, if any, were those persons and institutions who had sold their Genesco stock to the company's funds at low prices or bought it on the stock exchange or traded their own company shares for it at high prices created in part by the funds' buying. Genesco, after all, was one of the popular, heavily traded, high-flying stocks of that period; it is disconcerting, to say the least, to learn in retrospect that the heavy trading and the high flying were created largely by appendages of the company itself. However, later in the decade, Genesco stock took a dive from its 1965 high of around 60 to a low of 6 early in the 1974. William Wire, Genesco treasurer, at that time, was quite willing to state that the pension and employee stock purchase funds had taken large losses in their Genesco investments and that those losses were instrumental in the company's decision to suspend sales of Genesco stock to employees through the stock purchase fund. More than a decade after the fact, it appears that self-investment measurably damaged the asset value, and therefore the soundness, of the Genesco pension fund. Today, of course, it would be illegal for a pension fund to become so heavily invested in the sponsoring corporation's stock.

Many reform-minded pension authorities maintain that, in spite of particular problems such as AT&T's rule that its pension funds may hold stock of other companies in the Bell Systems, investment of pension funds in the sponsor's securities—whether equity or debt—is wrong and should be banned entirely.

The opportunity for self-dealing is also open to banks that serve as pension fund trustees. In fact, banks currently manage about 80 percent of all noninsured corporate pension fund dollars. Four great New York City banks were trustees for 37 percent of all noninsured pension accounts covered in the SEC's *Institutional Investor Study Report*, published in 1971.[8] As of the end of 1972, the big three of pension fund asset management (Morgan Guaranty, with $16.6 billion; Bankers Trust, with about $15 billion; and First National City, with $9.3 billion) among them held about $40 billion of employee benefit fund money. How these banks invest those assets is obviously a matter of greatest importance to pension beneficiaries as well as to the economy. Overwhelmingly, they invest them in common stocks—at Morgan Guaranty, for example, $13.3 of its $16.6 billion for 1972 was invested in common stocks. All three banks buy and sell fairly actively for their pension fund stock accounts, though less so than most mutual funds; the common stock turnover rate at First National City was 22.5 percent for 1971 and 16.9 percent for 1972. These banks heavily concentrated their investments in thirty to fifty famous growth stocks (thereby creating major and much discussed stock market problems), but in addition, all maintain pooled or commingled pension trust funds structured rather like mutual funds, some of which are invested in smaller, younger companies to provide the bank's clients with more investment opportunity along with concomitant measured risk. At the end of 1972, Morgan Guaranty's largest pooled fund—officially called "Special Situation Investments-Equities" and sometimes informally called "Morgan's crap-shooting fund"—had assets of $971 million, which represented 5.86 percent of the bank's total pension fund assets. This fund constituted a part of about 90 percent of the 653 pension trusts under Morgan management.[9]

The Trust and Investment Division of Morgan Guaranty, the pension fund kingpin, runs its vast asset pool with a total staff of about 800 persons, of whom more than 250 are officers. "The Division functions separately from the rest of the Morgan Guaranty Trust Company," said the bank's first Trust and Investment Division Annual Report, covering the year 1971. (The publication of separate annual reports by the trust divisions of leading banks is a new and obviously healthy development, pioneered by First National City in 1970.) "In our view," the report continued, "the separation is essential to success in the investment division." To achieve equality of performance among the pension accounts it handles, the division distributes all of its purchase of any particular stock on a given day among all of the appropriate client accounts; in addition, the commingled funds provide an automatic way for all participating trusts to share in a desirable new high-risk investment. Until quite recently the bank's performance record has been impressive, considerably more so than that of most of its competitors; from 1961 through 1972, it achieved for its pension clients a median rate of return (counting dividends, interest, and capital appreciation) of over 10 percent per year, with less than 1 percent spread between the best and the worst results for any of its various pension fund clients.[10] But since 1972 Morgan, like most managers, has been badly mauled by the bear market, which fell a staggering 39.4 percent in 1973.

There is considerable variation in the attitude of the biggest trust departments toward self-investment by corporate pension funds under their trusteeship. Morgan, to begin with, no longer (as it once did) accepts categorical direction from a sponsor corporation about investment of its pension assets.

However, suggestions are still acceptable if not welcome, and Morgan is theoretically willing to invest a corporate pension fund in the sponsor's securities to the same extent as it would invest some other fund in those securities—except, of course, if the percentage exceeded the new 10 percent limitation. (Even before the new law, if Morgan were offered trusteeship of a fund in which it considered self-investment excessive and the sponsor refused to change its policy, the bank would have refused to become trustee.)

Bankers Trust took the stand that a pension fund was entitled to be self-invested to the extent that the investment was a sound one; however, a Bankers Trust officer said that even before the new law, self-investment was non-existent or trivial in 99 percent of the funds it managed. First National City, a pioneer among banks in both trust division disclosure and advocacy of structural reform in pensions, had the most categorical attitude toward self-investment. According to Thomas C. Theobald, Citibank's former investment head, the bank has long maintained a rule of limiting to 10 percent the self-investment of pension funds under its management. In practice, he says, the percentage is usually near zero.

This diversity of rules and customs among the major banks that dominate pension fund management might suggest that the new pension law's uniform, legally sanctioned code is a welcome development. However, such codification may encourage abuse because of the difficulty of anticipating every situation. Also it may discourage some worthwhile investments in its effort to prohibit abuses. What is certain is that the law's exposure of trusteeship to open examination was greatly needed. Furthermore, the more defined accountability of the banks and the other investment managers was extremely desirable. As things used to stand, when the sponsor of a pension plan wanted to take investment action of which the bank trustee disapproved, the bank might have been willing to cooperate if it could avoid responsibility by getting a letter from the plan sponsor categorically absolving the bank of any repercussions from that particular transaction. This device, along with the conventional trust instrument that specifically assigned investment responsibility to the bank, enabled each party to shift the burden to the other. For instance, before the new pension law was passed, there was a case in which a good-sized corporate pension fund bought stock from a company that was a major supplier, and thereby a party-in-interest, at a discount of 25 percent from the market price. "We did it quietly without anyone raising questions" the corporate treasurer of the pension sponsor said later in confidence. The stock was subsequently sold at a profit, enabling the corporation to reduce its pension contribution, thereby improving its earnings. In sum, the pension fund had apparently been used in a form of commercial bribery. The bank trustee made no protest; it simply required a letter of absolution from the corporation for that one transaction. Now such practices are illegal, for investment managers and corporate sponsors are both fiduciaries and are liable for a breach of fiduciary duty on the part of another fiduciary when they are aware of the violation but do not make a reasonable effort to remedy it.

Various other possibilities exist for abuse of pension assets by banks. Banks may be tempted to invest assets in the interest of the bank itself or of one of its officers rather than in the self-interest of the sponsor. The bank may, for example, invest pension assets under its management in its own stock, in that of competitor banks, or in the stock of companies on whose boards of directors its own officers sit. It may invest them in the stock of companies that are its important commercial customers. If detected, these practices almost certainly would constitute a breach of fiduciary duty.

On the one hand, the matter of self-investment by banks with pension assets is fairly clear-cut. Morgan Guaranty's trust division has an announced policy of never purchasing J.P. Morgan & Company stock "on its own decision" or recommending such purchase to its clients. Most of its leading competitors follow similar policies. (Nevertheless, in its 1971 trust report, Morgan showed more than $50 million of trust money invested in Morgan stock—most of it presumably stock already in personal trusts at the time they came under the bank's control.)

On the other hand, whatever antitrust or other questions such investments raise, investment of trust assets in the shares of *other* banks is not considered inappropriate even in the most powerful trust circles. Morgan Guaranty in 1973 reported more than $29 million of trust funds invested in First National City (over 5 percent of the outstanding stock), more than $55 million in Bank of America, $47 million in North Carolina National Bank (over 7 percent of NCNB's outstanding stock), and more than $1 million in each of a variety of bank stocks, including Bank of New York, Chase Manhattan, and Harris Bankcorp. Moreover, Citicorp holds $100 million of Morgan stock (under 3 percent of outstanding stock).

As to self-serving investment instigated by banker-directors, leading trust officers scornfully dismiss the subject. Theobald of Citibank does not consider it an area of potential conflict. "If a banker who is a company director should try to press the company's shares on his trust department, nothing could hurt him more at the bank," says Theobald. "No banker can afford to take such a risk." Harrison Smith of Morgan Guaranty says, "The question simply doesn't come up." Nevertheless, interlocks between directorships held by bankers and bank trust investments do exist—at Morgan and elsewhere—and are probably inevitable short of a prohibition of bank officers' sitting on corporation boards. The evidence that such interlocks influence trust investments is flimsy at best, and it appears that they present the bank with more of a dilemma than a conflict.

Finally, there is the thorny matter of reciprocity, in regard to trust investments and commercial loans or deposits, between bank trust and commercial departments. Such reciprocity is widely acknowledged to have been something of a way of life ten or twenty years ago; all leading bankers, however, insist that it has now become a thing of the past. The trust officers of the leading pension-holding banks affirm that commercial operations do not influence their investment decisions and that they are not even allowed to know the size of commercial deposits held by their own banks.[11] Trust officers at Bankers Trust say flatly that none of them knows anything about the bank's commercial operations. Theobald of Citibank says that his investment management group personnel were not permitted to know the amounts of any commercial balances and points out that, in addition, trust and commercial operations at his institution are physically separated—the former being in midtown Manhattan, the latter downtown in the Wall Street area. It is a fact, however, that commercial relationships between banks and corporations are usually publicly known and that it would therefore be almost impossible for an investment department to be unaware of them, no matter how many blocks away it was located.

Morgan Guaranty trust officers also maintain that although their trust and commercial operations took place in the same building until 1974, the separation is emphatic. Smith says, "They hate us in the commercial department because, unbeknownst to them, we may be selling a huge block of stock of one of their best customers." Moreover, he insists that pressure for investment performance in the highly competitive pension field tends to make reciprocity impractical anyhow; that is, the trust division must in every case make the very best investment it can to survive. Until recently, though, there was a strange anomaly in the organization of Morgan Guaranty: the bank had a single investment research department for both the trust and the commercial sides. With the same men working on loans and involved in influencing trust investment decisions, conflicts of interest appeared to be inevitable. Recognizing that fact, in June 1970 the firm changed its structure to separate research activities for the two divisions. All other leading pension-holding banks have separate trust and commercial research divisions.

Bankers like to compare their self-enforced separation of commercial and trust operations to a "Chinese wall." The obvious weakness of this analogy is that the "Chinese wall" could be policed only by constant surveillance and would more than likely be breached constantly by ordinary social relations. Trust officers of all the leading banks agree that people from different departments see each other socially, and when they do they are obviously likely to talk shop. Callaway and Smith, for example, periodically lecture their division's members on the importance of maintaining strict separation from commercial operations; then, as often as not, they go off to lunch with commercial officers of the bank. As a result of such anomalies, critics of pension funds are inclined to take a heavily ironic view of the "Chinese wall," and competitors for pension business—such as investment advisors—go further, to say that such separation is purely imaginary. Duncan Smith, in charge of marketing for the leading investment advisory firm of Lionel D. Edie, said in 1974 that the "wall" is a myth. A small company, he says—one with a single bank upon which it relies for a line of revolving credit—simply cannot afford not to entrust its pension fund to that bank. He says, "I myself have lost a number of pension accounts because of bank commercial relationships. In one case, the president of a pension-sponsoring company said there was no question that Edie could do a better job with its pension fund than had the present bank trustee. But the company was heavily in debt to the bank and had no choice."[12]

In the face of all this skepticism, bankers themselves are defensive. A Bankers Trust officer says, "I know a lot of people think the separation is phony, but it isn't." Some authorities maintain that it is least effective, however, in the many small-town banks where trust departments heavily invest pension assets in local enterprises out of civic booster spirit. At the very least, the "Chinese wall" may be fairly described as a cardboard partition, removable and replaceable on short notice.

The opportunity for self-investment by pension fund sponsors or their designated trustees has been a matter considerable of moral uneasiness among both sponsors and trustees. The new Pension Reform Act limits this opportunity somewhat and appears to represent a stiffer standard of conduct than has existed in the past. But whether self-investment will prove to be limited in practice will depend, in large part, on the vigor of enforcement and the attitudes of the investment managers themselves.

III • JUGGLING THE ASSUMPTIONS

An *actuary* theoretically is the guardian of a corporate pension plan's solvency and as such is a key person in administering the plan. Usually a corporate pension sponsor retains a firm of consulting actuaries to assist in the original structuring of the plan and to recommend, on the basis of various assumptions about future events, how much money the corporation should contribute to the plan each year.

This is the theoretical position of actuaries, but before the enactment of the new pension law their real authority to act as guardians was severely limited. Although actuarial science is as old as modern life insurance, which began to be developed in the eighteenth century, it has never achieved the accreditation and consequent authority granted to accounting and other similar disciplines. Even today, there are four major competing actuarial bodies in the United States rather than a single one with recognized authority. If Congress had not stepped in and required that actuaries must be "enrolled" (that is, approved by a special federal board), it would still be possible for anyone, however ill-trained or untrained, to function as an actuary. As a result of these circumstances, an actuary's recommendations regarding annual contributions to a pension fund have had no force behind them. Regardless of the actuary's qualifications, the ultimate decision invariably rested with the employer, who might decide to ignore the actuary's recommendation or, after the actuary made a recommendation he approved of, might then take credit for the decision, which he referred to as being "based on actuarial factors." Since pension fund contributions are part of a corporation's ordinary costs—sometimes a substantial part—they are an important factor in the corporation's reported earnings. From this situation arises one in which the employer's interest in those earnings is in direct conflict with his interest in the pension plan's solvency.

Before the new pension law, the resolution of that conflict theoretically fell to actuaries, in their quasi-judicial capacity as guardians of the plan's solvency. But according to the president of one of the nation's leading actuarial firms—Robert D. Paul of Martin E. Segal Company—most actuaries tended to be "passive" in dealing with corporations they advised as to pension funds.[1] This situation was hardly surprising, since an actuary who made unpopular recommendations to a pension sponsor and insisted upon them too strongly could simply be fired and replaced. Another actuary—James Curtis, president of Milliman & Robertson—went much further. "Some companies treat an actuary as though he were a legalized bookie," said Curtis two years before the pension reform law was enacted. "They just want us to get figures together that will help their profit picture"[2]—help, that is, at the direct expense of the pension fund.

Before 1966 this ability of a corporation to manipulate earnings by varying the pension contribution from year to year was more or less unrestricted so long as pension funding was at a level that would meet IRS requirements for tax exemption. Some, although by no means all, companies treated pension contributions as a cash item, and therefore every dollar cut from any year's contribution meant a dollar more of pretax earnings that year. Thus in 1958, U.S. Steel, which was having a poor business year, reduced its contribution to $33 million from $140 million the previous year, thereby temporarily making its profit picture look much better. Other companies have resorted to somewhat less visible, but similarly expedient, reductions. In 1966, however, the accounting profession, with its comparatively great authority, stepped in. Opinion #8 of the Accounting Principles Board (APB), then the rule-making body of the accounting profession, issued that year, stated that "pension cost...should be accounted for on the accrual basis" rather than on a cash basis. This opinion formalized a practice that had been previously adhered to by many corporations—that of accounting for its pension cost in any given year on the basis of a variety of actuarial assumptions about future events, such as probable inflation of salaries, probable employee turnover, and expected rate of return on pension investments. A corporation could still improve its cash situation by reducing or eliminating its cash pension contribution in a given year, but for purposes of the balance sheet and its all-important bottom line, it was now required (or virtually required, since an APB opinion lacked the force of law) to deduct from reported income a figure based on the actuarial assumptions.

But the potential for managing earnings through pension contributions, while reduced, had not been eliminated. The potential now lay in simply changing the actuarial assumptions and, in particular, the assumption about investment return. ("Investment return," of course, includes interest, dividends, and the net of capital gains and losses; pension people often speak of it simply as "interest" and the actuarial assumption about such return as the "interest assumption.") A raise in the interest assumption automatically means, on paper, an increase in the amount of funds available to meet pension commitments, hence a reduction in reported pension costs and an increase in reported earnings. In other words a corporation can increase its earnings at will, by the stroke of a pen, by increasing its pension fund interest assumption.[3]

In the 1950s, among companies that accounted for pension costs on the accrual basis, interest assumptions were seldom changed and unrealistically low ones were all but universal. Two and one-half percent was a common figure, even though ordinary bank passbook accounts paid a higher rate of interest.

In the boom periods of the early and middle 1960s, when many companies were reporting increased earnings in every quarter, except for brief temporary setbacks, pension sponsors were under pressure from the Internal Revenue Service to raise their interest assumptions. Such a raise would increase a company's taxable earnings, as we have seen; and the IRS, of course, is in the business of collecting taxes. By and large, though, the companies demurred. "We prefer to be conservative, and keep our assumption at 3 percent or 3½ percent," the companies replied in effect. "After all, who can say when the stock market will drop again and cut our pension assets?" Lacking authority to compel a higher assumption except in flagrant cases, the IRS generally yielded.

After 1965 a whole new set of conditions came into being. Particular groups of stocks were making sensational gains, and a cult of quick performance was gaining ground among institutional investors, particularly mutual funds. Very gradually reacting to this new climate, corporate pension fund sponsors became performance conscious for the first time; they began taking part of their pension funds out of the conservative banks that had previously managed the funds in toto and entrusting it to investment advisors—many of them aggressive mutual fund portfolio managers[4]—who dazzled the pension sponsors with unreasonable promises of annual returns of 12, 15, or even 20 percent. At the same time, pension benefits were being widely liberalized in response to union demands, putting more pressure on the funds for investment performance. Meanwhile, with rising costs of material, labor, and money and a rather sluggish economy, a serious profit squeeze began developing. Under these pressures, the corporate pension fund came to be widely regarded by corporations as a profit center. If the new investment advisor promised more than 10 percent and the pension fund was operating on an actuarial assumption of 3½ or 4 percent, was not the obvious solution to raise the assumption, thereby magically reducing reported pension costs and strengthening the sagging bottom line?

Many companies that took such action did so on bona fide and well justified actuarial advice. After all, interest rates *were* rising to record levels and, until early 1969, stock prices as well were rising. But as Roger F. Murray, professor of banking and finance at Columbia University, has pointed out, among the companies that raised interest assumptions, more faced profit squeezes than did not—providing circumstantial evidence that some of the raises were motivated by the desire to improve reported earnings. At the end of the decade, an ironic situation developed: pension sponsors that had previously held to low interest assumptions against IRS objections were now, in the face of sinking profits—and a suddenly crashing stock market—saying to the IRS, "You finally convinced us—our interest assumption was too low, and we are raising it, just as you asked us to do." In fact, it appears that the sponsoring corporations, which had previously been using low assumptions to minimize taxes in times of rising profits, were now using higher assumptions to minimize costs in times of shrinking profits. The effect was that assumptions, which had been low in a time of high real return on pension assets, were rising as real return was dropping. Obviously actuarial assumptions on corporate pension funds were being widely used as much to manipulate taxes and earnings as to reflect real conditions or to back up pension promises to employees prudently.

In 1965 the average interest assumption was between 3½ and 4 percent. In 1967 the huge General Electric pension trust pioneered in raising it to 6 percent, thereby enabling it to absorb a substantial liberalization of benefits with a comparatively modest increase in corporate contribution. Other large companies that raised their assumptions between 1967 and 1972 were Westinghouse, Firestone, International Minerals & Chemicals, du Pont, Standard Oil of Ohio, and American Telephone & Telegraph. (It should be noted that changed interest assumptions on pension funds have the most dramatic effect on earnings in old companies with many employees and pensioners relative to profits; in newer companies, the effect may be quite small.) This does not imply that the assumptions were raised in each case to improve earnings. While many companies were raising their interest assumption, they were also hiking their wage inflation assumption, an adjustment that lifted the amount that the corporation must contribute for proper funding by increasing the anticipated payouts to beneficiaries. For example, AT&T's across-the-board interest assumption rise from 3½ to 5 percent in 1972 was effectively neutralized by simultaneous drastic revision of an obsolete assumption as to wage inflation. Still, the statistics were striking. In 1972 a study by Chase Manhattan Bank showed that 70 percent of a sample of 465 companies had revised their interest assumptions within the preceding five years and that another 10 percent were currently contemplating doing so. (It may be noted that these five years were a period during which the Dow-Jones industrial average hardly rose at all.) Another 1972 survey, by Standard & Poor's/InterCapital, Inc., now a subsidiary of Oppenheimer & Company, showed the median interest assumption for all kinds of business standing at 4.8 percent—with a range from a low of 2.5 percent to a high of 10 percent. When one company feels, at least for balance sheet purposes, that it can earn on its pension investments four times as much as another company feels it can earn in the same intensely competitive market, these interest assumptions are clearly being used for purposes other than that of faithfully describing real expectations based on past experience.[5]

The passivity, if not outright collaboration, of actuaries in this sudden upthrust of investment expectations was and is matched by a parallel passivity on the part of the bank trustees who manage most corporate pension assets. Banks do not maintain their own actuarial staffs and generally leave the actuarial assumptions of pension funds to the sponsoring corporation and its actuary, except in extreme cases. Theobald of First National City says, "If a pension sponsor told us he wanted to put the assumption at 8 percent or 10 percent, we'd say, 'Hey fellows, we don't think we can make that much for you.' Otherwise, we leave them alone." George Kadel, vice president in charge of pension plans at Bankers Trust, says, "If the rate of return has improved, the corporation is right to look at its assumption." Trust officers at Morgan Guaranty say simply that the bank has no official role in the actuarial assumptions of pension plans for which it is trustee and confines itself to making an informal recommendation if it is asked to do so.[6]

Perhaps the most astonishing interest assumption rise of recent years was that of U.S. Steel in 1971. As the company's chairman, Edwin H. Gott, noted in the Annual Report for that year:

The year 1971 was a difficult year for U.S. Steel—and the steel industry generally— with lower steel shipments, erratic and uneconomical operating levels, labor negotiations, surging imports, government controls over wages and prices, reduced employment and hours of work for employees, and lower dividends for stockholders. . . .Pension costs were lower in 1971 than in 1970. . . .The interest rate assumption for funding pension costs was revised, as it has been from time to time, in light of the actual experience of the pension fund.

Later in the report, the relevant figures, or some of them, were given. The company reported a net income for 1971 of $154.5 million, or $2.85 per share, as against $147.5 million, or $2.72 per share, in 1970. Meanwhile, though, the effect of the interest assumption change (its amount or even nature not announced, but actually from 5 to 6 percent) had been to decrease pension costs from $104.8 million in 1970 to $62.1 million in 1971, thereby giving 1971 pretax earnings a $42.7 million boost. Without the boost, U.S. Steel, instead of showing increased net income for 1971, would have been forced to report a decrease for the third straight year—to the lowest level in many years.[7]

Was this interest assumption change legitimate or manipulative? Under then current disclosure requirements, it is impossible to say. U.S. Steel's reported asset figures for its pension fund were $2.2 billion at the end of 1971 as against $2.149 billion at the end of 1970. This change represents an increase of far less than 6 or even 5 percent, but since the figures include deduction of pension payments and are based on the cost rather than the market value of investments, they are worthless as a measure of actual investment performance. In the absence of full portfolio disclosure, it is impossible for an outsider to know whether the Steel fund was really earning the 6 percent it now claimed for accounting purposes as its future expectation. Again, the change, we are informed by the company's Annual Report, was "based on various actuarial factors. . . determined by an independent actuary"; but we are not allowed to know what the actuarial factors were. Whatever the facts, there is no basis for maintaining that the company's higher assumption and consequent lower contribution endangered the benefits promised to plan participants, since U.S. Steel was one of the major American employers that made a direct contractual promise, as a corporation, to pay the pension benefits specified before the pension law required it. Fulfillment of the contract was thus limited not by the solvency of the pension fund but by that of the corporation itself. Clearly pension payments at Steel were not directly threatened; nevertheless, pension funds sometimes have been used to inflate corporate earnings and confuse investors, since the companies have been required to disclose so little.

Another case, somewhat different but equally instructive, is that of Standard Oil Company (Ohio) in 1972. In that year Sohio, by giving recognition to a greater portion of unrealized appreciation of pension fund assets and by revising actuarial assumptions to reflect increased social security benefits, was able to reduce its pension contribution 65 percent, from $5.7 million in 1971 to $2 million in 1972. This reduction enabled the company to report a solid earnings gain for 1972 over 1971; without the reduction the gain would have been marginal.

At the time of the most recent actuarial valuation before these changes were made, the market value of the assets of Sohio's pension funds exceeded the estimated liability for vested benefits (as is the case with any sound fund), and prior service costs were being amortized "over appropriate periods." No implication is intended that Sohio adjusted its assumptions and drastically reduced its pension contribution merely to manage its current earnings; on the contrary, on the basis of information given, it appears that the change was merely a recognition of past overfunding resulting from ultraconservative policies. But again, as in the case of U.S. Steel, the legitimacy of the change could not really be determined on the basis of available information.[8]

Actuarial assumptions, then, have been a major area of potential abuse in pension fund asset management because they offer a corporation a direct opportunity to improve its reported earnings at the expense of its pension fund. But unfortunately, it has been virtually impossible for anyone outside the sponsoring corporations or their actuarial advisors—including agencies of government—to know when such abuse is occurring and when it is not.

The new law should improve this situation. Actuaries must now "certify" pension plan assumptions and funding methods. Pension plan sponsors must report these assumptions and methods to the Department of Labor and explain any changes in actuaries as well as disclose revisions of actuarial assumptions.

Also, although the issue is by no means settled, it is generally believed that, under the new law, actuaries are fiduciaries.

In the past actuaries have not always adequately fulfilled their duties to be guardians of the solvency of pension plans. In a time when pension benefit levels were rising steadily and rapidly—perhaps too rapidly—widespread reduction of corporate pension contributions through the raising of interest rate assumptions did not, in general, constitute sound practice. It may seem harmless juggling of figures, but the piper will have to be paid someday. Too often the actuaries have seemed to be filling the role of validator of bad or questionable practice—a role rather like that of a medieval king's priest, whose job it often was to confer the mantle of holiness on temporal power, to tell the king and the world that what the king did was right. Before thay can properly fill their designated role—as guardians—actuaries need greater independence and authority. Whether the new Pension Reform Act adequately insures this, and whether the actuaries are ready to assume this greater responsibility and accountability, remain to be seen.

IV • THE SOFT DOLLAR: APPLE IN EDEN

Throughout the institutional investment industry, allocation of brokerage presents a difficult problem. Because of the traditional system of fixed commission rates, the commission on a large stock transaction has been disproportionately high in relation to the service actually performed. The problem has lessened since the New York Stock Exchange by SEC order introduced negotiated commissions on trades above $500,000 in 1971, above $300,000 in 1972, and on all trades in May 1975. But the problem has by no means disappeared. As a result of the anomaly, the customer in a large transaction or series of transactions is enabled to exact from the broker of his choice additional services, apart from execution of the transaction, in exchange for giving his business to that particular broker rather than to another. The institutional investor, knowing that he must pay brokerage commissions in any case, naturally wants to get additional services at no additional cost. Out of this situation arises the entity that Wall Street, with rather astonishing candor, has named the ''soft dollar'': the payment for additional services with commission dollars rather than with cash. In connection with corporate pension funds, the soft dollar is used chiefly as payment for investment research, money management, and consulting services in the selection of money managers.

The soft dollar obviously creates a tempting situation. The SEC formally sanctions assignment of brokerage in exchange for research; beyond that, the matter has largely been governed—if at all—by local custom. Such custom, blinking at an obvious potential conflict of interest, has sanctioned soft dollar payment for pension asset management services when the manager is affiliated with a brokerage firm, for pension performance evaluation services that are offered by a number of brokerage firms, and for assistance to pension sponsors in money manager selection, in cases where the consultant has a brokerage connection.

In the era before 1968-70, the chief conflict-of-interest problem involving brokerage for pension funds was the custom, widespread among bank trust departments that managed corporate pension assets, of allocating pension brokerage in return for demand deposits by the brokers. This practice was exposed and deplored by *Institutional Investor* and other publications and was apparently stopped in 1970 when Washington authorities applied pressure against it and class action suits were filed against several major banks.[1] As of now, brokerage allocation by the great pension-managing bank trust departments seems to be generally based on sound, conflict-free principles. Morgan Guaranty and Bankers Trusts, according to the statements of their trust chieftains, always control the allocation rather than allowing the client or their own commercial departments to control it, and they make the allocation on the basis of the broker's capability to accomplish the best execution of the trade and the quality of the broker's research. First National City says it follows similar guidelines—adopting recommendations of its own research departments about which brokerage firms deserve how much business in exchange for research, and it does a small percentage of its brokerage at the request of the pension sponsor. Since this small percentage is done solely to reward established and objective pension rating services such as those of Becker Securities Company,[2] there is little reason to assume potential conflict.

The small revolution in pension asset management since 1968 has brought new forms of real and potential conflict in brokerage allocation to the fore. As we have seen, at the end of the 1960s, as a result of increased pressures for pension fund investment performance, there arose a practice among corporate sponsors of splitting the pension assets among a varying number of different money managers. To capitalize on this practice, established investment advisory firms changed their areas of specialization from mutual funds and individual accounts to pension accounts, and a number of new pension asset managing firms sprang into existence, most of them made up of men who were already well recognized money managers outside the pension field. Notable among the latter was Jennison Associates Capital Corporation of New York City, numbering among its members the former manager of the billion-dollar United Fund, the former manager of General Electric's Elfun Trust, the former research heads of two large brokerage firms, and former top investment men from Bankers Trust and First National City. By the end of 1972, Jennison managed some $700 million in pension assets belonging to top-drawer clients such as Allis-Chalmers Corporation, Gulf Oil Corporation, Honeywell, International Paper Company, Litton Industries, and Pfizer. Meanwhile, large brokerage firms, seeking to get in on the pension management business and to capture a larger share of the commissions generated by it, began to acquire investment advisory firms as subsidiaries, thereby making it possible for the investment advisory clients to pay their fees partly or wholly in soft dollars. About the same time, with corporate pension sponsors who wanted to split their funds bewildered in having to choose among the thousands of investment management firms, a new breed of broker-affiliated pension consultants sprang up, eager to do the screening for pension sponsors in exchange for soft dollar payments.

Although some pension-specializing investment advisory firms are reticent about their operations,[3] more typical is Bernstein-Macaulay, Inc., which in 1974 managed some $1.14 billion. After merging with a large brokerage and investment banking house, it was accused, with reason, of conflict of interest. Bernstein-Macaulay, originally founded in 1934, was headed during recent years by Peter L. Bernstein, an economist, professor, and author. In 1967 it became a wholly owned subsidiary of Hayden, Stone, Inc., the large old line brokerage and investment banking firm, which wanted to acquire increased research capability.

Bernstein said recently that at the time of the merger, he was concerned about the potential conflicts of interest implicit in a joining of the functions of brokerage and investment banking on the one hand and of money management on the other. A broker friend, Arthur Carter, reassured him by saying, "There's a conflict of one sort or another in whatever you do. It's a question of how you handle yourself."[4]

Bernstein-Macaulay, as a Hayden, Stone subsidiary (as a result of a merger the firm is now Shearson Hayden Stone), immediately began accepting brokerage dollars as an offset against client fees; a 1974 Bernstein-Macaulay promotion booklet showed about one-third of the firm's commission business being executed by Hayden, Stone. This practice, Bernstein found, was strongly encouraged by pension clients who, realizing that they had to pay brokerage commissions anyhow, were glad to be able to discharge part of their investment advisory obligation merely by directing the brokerage to Hayden, Stone. Indeed, one major client complained that not enough of his fund's brokerage was being done in-house. "To us," Bernstein says, "the conflict was in reverse: we wanted to do more brokerage outside, and the client was pressing us to do it inside." In other words the client thought that whatever advantage, such as possibly superior research or technical capability, was being sacrificed by his not being free to choose some other broker was more than balanced by the reduction in his cash investment advisory cost by using Hayden, Stone as broker.

Meanwhile, to avoid conflicts of interest with Hayden, Stone's investment banking arm, Bernstein-Macaulay at first refused to recommend to its advisory clients any securities underwritten by Hayden, Stone. This policy, however, was eventually relaxed under pressure from advisory clients who wanted to have the advantage of Hayden, Stone's specific knowledge about companies for which it served as investment banker. "We did it, in several cases, and it worked out perfectly," Bernstein says. "My hand didn't tremble for a minute." Perhaps, however, it should have trembled.

Today, in fact, the new pension law forbids a money management firm from purchasing securities for a pension fund if the firm has underwritten those securities. Before 1975, however, conflict of interest was seldom alleged unless a deal went sour and someone lost money. The Bernstein-Macaulay deal that went sour involved securities of Topper Corporation, a leading toy manufacturer. In September 1971 Hayden, Stone (at that time known as CBWL-Hayden, Stone) served as investment banker in a private sale of $5,250,000 of Topper debentures, receiving an underwriting fee of $157,500 for its role in the transaction. Hayden, Stone's affiliate, Bernstein-Macaulay, recommended the securities to three pension funds it advised—two of them New York City union funds, the third a union fund in Massachusetts—as a result of which all three funds took positions in Topper. Topper at that time was considered a red-hot go-go security; during 1971 its common stock price had more than doubled, and at one time it had been on the American Stock Exchange's most actively traded list for six consecutive days. Bernstein-Macaulay insists that, in recommending the debentures to its fund clients, it complied with the Investment Advisers Act of 1940 by fully disclosing all pertinent data including the fact that Hayden, Stone represented the seller in the transaction. Indeed, Peter Bernstein, far from acting defensive about recommending the Topper securities, made a virtue of his firm's close association with the company; he wrote at the time to one of his clients, Teamster Local 816, that "our close knowledge of this company gives me confidence that the deal is a sound one" and went on to describe in glowing terms an ingenious new Topper toy intended to teach a child to spell. The funds bought the securities and paid Bernstein's fee with commission dollars.

Unfortunately, though, Topper did not flourish as predicted. In February 1973, hit with heavy returns that forced it to liquidate much of its inventory at discount prices, the firm filed under Chapter 11 of the Bankruptcy Act. It is uncertain whether any of the notes will ever be redeemed, and Teamster Local 816 took legal action to recover its presumably lost investment.[5]

The obvious flaw in the transaction is that Hayden, Stone or its subsidiary represented both the seller and the buyer, and thus the firm was dealing with itself. Although such a transaction is now illegal without an exemption from the Labor Department and the IRS, some people question the wisdom of the ban. Indeed, the professional consensus, as reflected in the investment world's retrospective comments on the Topper transaction, appears to be that such a transaction is all right if it works and is bad to the extent that it "looks bad." *The Wall Street Journal* cited remarks of two investment advisors to the effect that it is entirely possible to act for both sides with complete integrity—but that they would rather not do it. "It isn't good policy to wear two hats," one investment banker was quoted as saying, *"It just looks bad."*[6] [Italics added.] Bernstein himself avers that he realized all along that it would 'look bad" if it went wrong, but he was willing to assume that risk in the interest of giving the pension funds under his management the opportunity to get in on a good thing. "I would do it again," he has said, assuming the conditions of 1971. However, in view of what has happened, he says that he would not recommend another Hayden, Stone issue to his advisory clients.

So the case and the reactions to it put the pre-1975 state of broker-money manager conflicts of interest into sharp focus. When the ethical criterion is success or failure rather than propriety or impropriety and when the ethical sanction is appearance rather than law or even custom, the ethical climate may be said to be unhealthy. More concretely, strict adherence by Bernstein-Macaulay to its original resolve not to recommend Hayden, Stone stock issues would have prevented this setback to the pension clients. Apparently, however, the pension legislation will prevent similar setbacks in the future.

When, in the late 1960s, corporate pension fund sponsors became increasingly performance conscious, a group of broker-related pension consulting services sprang up, most of them directly established by brokerage firms as new departments. Theoretically, the appearance of this new form of competition for the traditional actuarial consultants was a healthy development for pension fund participants. The trouble was that—as with many other brand-new forms of enterprise—this one had no traditions, standards, or entrance requirements, and some of the entrants were not only unqualified but also unethical. As Charles D. Ellis of Greenwich Research Associates, a firm that does marketing studies for investment managers, put the matter, the new business began "attracting a lot of fly-by-nights."[7] Anyone, however inexperienced, could set up as a pension consultant; establishing a soft dollar connection was no great problem, since what a consultant had to offer a brokerage firm was, precisely, a chance for new business.

Even so, the new industry remained fairly small. Of thirty-seven pension consultants polled by *Pensions* magazine in its 1972-73 directory issue, nineteen said they accepted payment in commissions; of those nineteen, eight reported that their services did not include money manager selection, so only eleven were left who selected managers for soft dollars.[8]

Of those few some, by all accounts, operate in a manner beyond reproach. The conflict-of-interest abuse of which some of the others have been accused is that of demanding or accepting soft dollar payments not only from pension sponsors but also from the very money managers they are hired to pass judgment upon. Typically, a broker-affiliated consultant may contract to screen money managers for a pension sponsor in exchange for payment—say, $30,000 or $40,000—in soft dollars. Thus far the arrangement seems in order. But would it be proper for the consultant to go to a money manager and say, in effect, "We like you and will recommend you to corporation X's pension fund—provided that you agree to send a certain amount of the resulting brokerage to us, after you have the job"? Certainly not. As *Institutional*

Investor magazine pointed out early in 1973, this would be similar to a case of a judge demanding payment from those being judged.

Most pension fund money managers and some corporate pension officers say that such things do go on to a limited extent, although, understandably enough, none of these people are willing to blow the whistle publicly on a particular person or firm. For example, Richard B. Lohrer, at the time assistant treasurer and pension officer of Martin Marietta Corporation, has been quoted as saying:

There are very few consultants that I have any faith in . . . . The whole area has expanded so rapidly that it has attracted all kinds of people with [little] expertise. There is also a real problem of integrity among some consultants. Many try to make side deals—"under the table" agreements—with money managers to direct commissions their way in exchange for recommending them to a corporation.[9]

David R. Porter, of the Boston-based investment counsel firm of David L. Babson & Company (not broker-affiliated), says:

It is true that consultants often come to investment counsels such as ourselves with a quid pro quo proposal. More often, at least in our case, the corporation whose pension trust is under discussion introduces the consultant to us and asks us to put some of the brokerage on the particular trust through the consultant. There have been other variations of our meetings and discussions. . . . In general, we are not very happy with our experience with the consultants.[10]

Peter Bernstein said in 1974 of the broker-affiliated consulting business in general, "I have a feeling it's a shocking racket." His impression was that conditions were worst on the West Coast; Bernstein-Macaulay's salesman there, he said, had repeatedly complained of losing pension management appointments apparently because Bernstein-Macaulay was unwilling to enter into a commission arrangement with a consultant representing a pension sponsor. Bernstein also said that he personally was approached several years earlier by a consultant who said to him, on a sound-out basis, "Of course, we expect you to do brokerage through us." Bernstein turned the offer down and has not been similarly approached by a consultant since then.

Duncan Smith, national marketing man for Lionel D. Edie, which manages over $5 billion—and which, of course, had a brokerage affiliation of its own, being a subsidiary of Merrill Lynch, Pierce, Fenner & Smith—is particularly caustic in his comments on pension consultants. Smith divides them into two categories: those offering plan design and actuarial services (some of which have recently added advisor selection services for cash fees), and money manager screening services paid in soft dollars. The first group, he says, is "in the highest professional category," but the second ranges "from highly professional and ethical to outright thieves." The latter group, he says, despite their small numbers, are giving the whole field of pension consulting "a tarnished image." As to a specific occurrence:

We have been approached by a so-called objective consultant, who has a pension-sponsoring corporation as his client, and who asked us directly how much brokerage we would be willing to give his firm in exchange for a recommendation. We threw that son of a bitch out of here so fast he didn't know what had hit him. It only happened once here, in just that way; but I've heard from other investment counselors that it's happened more often with them.

Like Bernstein, Smith feels that pension-consulting abuse is centered on the West Coast, where there is "a plethora of counseling organizations, lots of money, and a promoters' environment dating back to the early days of motion pictures." To deal with the situation, Lionel D. Edie has developed a file on consultants and made a blacklist of those with whom it will not deal under any circumstances. It has not, however, instituted fraud proceedings against any of the firms on its blacklist.[11]

What of the pension participants and beneficiaries? Granting that *quid pro quo* deals between consultants and money managers are morally wrong—and that they may be prosecuted as fraud—do they result in material harm to pension funds? Although actual examples of such damage are unavailable, for obvious reasons, logic and pertinent statistics suggest that the damage occurs. First, a money manager chosen because he was willing to enter into an under-the-table arrangement is certainly less likely to perform well than one chosen because of a record of professional competence. Second, does the allocation of brokerage really matter—that is, can one broker get better prices for a pension fund in its transactions than another broker can? Again, all evidence suggests that the answer is positive. It has been estimated that the quality of execution of institutional buy-and-sell orders can have an impact of 8 to 9 percent[12] on performance in any given transaction.

Some pension advisors maintain that the damage done by dishonest consultants is minimal and transient—that it is "small-time" stuff. Arthur Zeikel, president of Centennial Capital Corporation, a subsidiary of Oppenheimer & Company, believes that consultant abuses involve such a small percentage of the assets of any individual pension fund that no one is likely to get seriously hurt; moreover, he believes that such bad practices cannot perpetutate themselves for long because of the pressure of competition among both consultants and money managers and that, indeed, time and competition are already correcting them. (In the 1972-73 investment climate in which banks were performing better for pension funds than were investment advisory services, Zeikel found the manager selection aspect of the consulting business apparently languishing; as of mid-1973, his firm had not been visited by any consultant, good or bad, for six months.) Zeikel and Peter Bernstein agree that the key factor in eliminating consulting abuses is increased sophistication on the part of the corporate pension officer, who, if he were sufficiently knowing and wary, would evidently not engage a pension consultant who was likely to recommend an investment manager as a result of a bribe. However, the two investment advisors disagree about whether that sophistication is increasing at a rate sufficiently rapid to handle the situation. Zeikel says, "Formerly, the corporate pension man was apt to be an assistant treasurer with many other duties and no knowledge of or interest in pensions. Beginning in 1970 or 1971, with the rise of the profit center concept of the corporate pension fund, he came to be a smart new business school graduate with a good understanding of institutional investing and risk measurement, who can spot a phony consultant." Bernstein—who deals chiefly with union rather than corporate pension funds—is less optimistic. In 1974 he said of fund sponsors, "In general, I'm afraid they're still pretty dumb."

The too-tempting apple of brokerage commissions or underwriting fees, then, is a prime cause for straying from the straight and narrow path on the part of pension professionals. David L. Babson, president of David L. Babson & Company, recently cited "conflicts of interest in the investment community [that] have been multiplying for years" as a prime cause of the "lacklustre results obtained by institutional investors over the past few years."[13] (The specific conflict Babson cited as an example was that of brokerage and underwriting firms managing, through subsidiaries, large amounts of pension assets and sometimes dumping weak securities in pension accounts.)

The greater awareness of the conflict role of the "finder" and the advent of fully negotiated commissions may well correct many of the abuses in this area. In addition, it appears that finder-consultants are fiduciaries under provisions of the Pension Reform Act and that after a two- to three-year transition period, it will no longer be legal to remunerate them with soft dollars unless they can obtain an exemption from the Department of Labor and the IRS.

Another form of conflict could be eliminated by a separation of the function of money management from the functions of brokerage and underwriting. William McChesney Martin, Jr., in his 1971 report to the Board of Governors of the New York Stock Exchange, which served as a blueprint for its reorganization, made the recommendation (not adopted) that brokerage firms be prohibited from crediting commissions received against fees for investment advice.

It appears that, under the provisions of the Pension Reform Act, eventually it will no longer be legal for an investment manager who is affiliated with a brokerage firm to execute transactions through that firm. Thus, unless exemptions are granted, a good deal of the present conflict will be eliminated. Charles W. Shaeffer, chairman of T. Rowe Price Associates, Inc., one of the largest investment counseling firms, goes further and recommends a total separation of brokerage and money management mandated by act of Congress.[14] Those who oppose such separation point out that a pension fund's commission dollars are, after all, one of its assets, of which it should not be deprived; as long as they are used straightforwardly to pay for investment advice, the fund benefits.

These changes, by eliminating soft dollar payments for services, may possibly increase hard dollar costs to pension funds in the form of higher management fees. But presumably, the reduction in soft dollar commission payments, which are charged directly to the pension fund's net asset value, would offset these higher management fees; in the opinion of some it probably would reduce the total true cost of investing.

The new pension law, by forbidding the "fiduciary" to benefit from transactions involving pension assets, appears to reduce greatly the potential for soft dollar abuses. Again, the interpretation of the law by the Labor department, the IRS, and the courts will determine to what extent this is true in practice.[15]

V • THE PROFIT CENTER CONCEPT

Until now we have been dealing with situations in which the trustee or administrator of pension fund assets is tempted, for some reason, because of some conflicting objectives, to take actions that may not be calculated to increase or maintain those assets. Now we turn to a possible conflict of interest that arises paradoxically out of an identity of interest—that is, the case of the administrator who tries to increase the pension assets too much, too fast, or at too great a risk.

The basic identity of interest of the sponsoring corporation and the covered employees is clear. Both parties seek to maximize the size of the pension asset pool per dollar of contribution to the fund. But it should be pointed out that the identity of interest is not complete. The immediate beneficiary of any advantage a pension trustee may gain by successful investment of the fund's assets is the employer, because the level of pension benefits does not automatically rise as a result of such a gain, but the cost to the sponsor corporation does automatically (or nearly automatically) decrease. Bad investment may result in a decrease or cessation of employee benefits, but good investment will not increase them—except to the extent that a larger asset pool will make possible a higher level of benefits should the employer decide or be compelled by collective bargaining to grant them. Regarding the potential decrease in company pension costs, a pension industry rule of thumb is that a 1 percent improvement in fund investment performance means a 10 percent reduction in the corporate contribution—making abundantly clear the corporation's stake in improved performance. Broadly speaking, the upside potential is the corporation's; the downside risk is the pensioner's.

The rise of the "profit center concept" of the corporate pension office, as we have seen, came in the late 1960s with the rapid increase in pension benefit levels and the cult of quick stock market performance that first appeared in the mutual fund industry. The concept quickly became firmly established. The corporate pension officer, formerly treated as a stepchild of management, found his status changed overnight to that of a favored godchild. By 1973 a survey of corporations showed that the majority of managements realized "to a high degree" or "to a very high degree" the importance of pension fund investment to corporate profits.[1] In the opinion of a leading investment authority, Roger F. Murray, this was a generally healthy development. In a paper prepared in 1971 for the Federal Commission on Financial Structure and Regulation, Professor Murray wrote that "intensive competition among investment managers and the growing publicity given to performance evaluation and measurement" led to several salutary developments: "Stodgy and lethargic asset management was exposed. Fresh thinking was applied to the peculiar objectives of a pension fund. Innovation was encouraged.... The size of funds made the engagement of multiple managers feasible, with the introduction of the added factor of direct competition among them for performance." Murray went on to point out the darker side: "Within a wide range of investment alternatives, expected returns increase with the acceptance of greater risk. The less profitable and the less 'safe' [corporate sponsors] tend to accept higher risks. This may be directly contrary to the best interests of employees, who for their retirement years have to prefer a modest but secure level of benefits to a generous but highly uncertain scale."[2]

As a profit center, the corporate pension office, generically, has not achieved impressive results over the years. According to a study by A. S. Hansen, Inc., actuaries and consultants, over the period 1965-71, a representative group of seventy-four commmon stock funds, which contain the commingled assets of many pension and profit-sharing funds, achieved an annual total rate of return of 5.9 percent. Meanwhile, the Standard & Poor's 500 stock average—the average most relied upon by pension measurers—had returned 6.1 percent.[3] Another study, by Becker Securities Company, showed that for ten years before September 30, 1972, 300 major pension funds exactly matched the 10.5 percent total return of the Standard & Poor's 500. Moreover, a Becker officer points out that if the study's cutoff date had been 1971, the results would have shown that six out of ten of the funds measured had failed to match the performance of the average.[4]

Thus, pension asset management, with all its vaunted and high-priced talent and expertise, seemed to be achieving nothing better than could be accomplished by guesswork and a diverse portfolio of New York Stock Exchange-listed stocks. In fact, such a conclusion is too superficial, since pension fund investors labor under special technical difficulties in trying to beat the averages. Pension funds with assets ranging into the billions or hundreds of millions must obviously make most of their investments in very large, successful companies with millions of shares available—precisely the companies that make up the Standard & Poor's 500. Moreover, the auction market system works against very large investors such as pension funds: the very act of buying in huge blocks forces the market up, and selling forces it down. Pension funds' equity holdings amount to nearly 10 percent of the market value of all outstanding New York Stock Exchange shares. It is hard to beat the market and the averages when, to such a marked extent, one *is* the market and the averages. In connection with the problem of liquidity, James J. Needham, then chairman of the New York Stock Exchange, said in 1973, "Institutions can't always sell stocks at their 'paper' prices, because the buyers [for such huge quantities of stock] aren't there these days. This can cause serious questions for the pension funds. . . .Lack of liquidity threatens the whole pension system."[5] AT&T's then pension director John F. Thompson in 1973 went so far as to tell this researcher, "I think it is unrealistic to expect [us] to outperform the averages."

In such an environment, it is easy to see why smaller companies, hard pressed by rising pension costs, and investment advisors, pressured to achieve fast performance with their split-off sections of large funds, are tempted to make higher risk investments that offer greater potential for appreciation. A good measure of the fact that they did so in the late 1960s is to be found in the activity rates of pension fund stock portfolios.[6] Between 1965 and 1969, the activity of bank-managed portfolios rose from 13.7 to 25.7 percent, of internally managed ones from 5.5 to 9.6 percent, and of investment-advisor-managed ones from 27.4 to 55.9 percent.[7] (*Activity* is defined as the average of purchases and sales as a percentage of average total portfolio.) The exceptionally high figure for investment advisors is no accident. As beneficiaries of the then new vogue of splitting big funds among many managers, they were and are under the greatest pressure to perform, often finding themselves entered in performance races with other investment advisors in which sometimes the explicit terms are that only the winners will survive. Of course, such naked competition has a theoretical advantage for fund participants. A few years ago, William A. Dreher and Stephen Rogers, leading fund consultants, wrote: "We feel that the competitive 'horse race' concept still has its place, if coupled with clearly stated investment policies and goals that avoid excess."[8] The danger is that the competitive element may lead the competitors into excess. Peter Bernstein, as an investment advisor who has been entered into such performance derbies, thinks the danger exceeds the advantage. "Pension sponsors don't usually come right out and say that I'm being entered in a horse race, but I get the feeling anyhow," he says. "In 1970, we did have one particular pension client who had said to us right out, 'We want you to swing.' We did—and the client got murdered. His portfolio with us went down 50 percent or so. None of our other clients that year did worse than the Dow Industrial Average" (which incidentally, did better than the more representative Standard & Poor's 500). In assessing Bernstein's comment, it is well to remember that those who enjoy a horse race most are not apt to be the horses.[9]

One of the ways in which advisors have tried to improve pension performance is by going entirely outside of the stock market. Investment in real estate by pension funds is increasing in the form of direct investment in real estate parcels, commingled funds, and through stock purchase in real estate firms. Traditionally pension trustees have been wary of real estate, chiefly on the grounds of its relative illiquidity and difficulty of accurate evaluation. Huge funds such as General Motors's and the Bell System's hold considerably less than 5 percent in real estate. But—to cite a couple of examples—Fred C. Houck, assistant treasurer of Mead Corporation, stated in 1972 that roughly 15 percent of his firm's $125 million fund was then in real estate, and added "I expect real estate investments to represent an increasing percentage of many pension trusts in the next few years"; J. C. Christy, pension fund administrator for the Upjohn Company, said about the same time, "We would like our long-range return to hit 10 percent annually, which might be possible with real estate investments. . . . I see us diverting 25 percent of our new annual contributions—roughly $2 million—into real estate channels." Eventually, Christy said, if the policy proves successful, the real estate share of the entire fund might be raised to as much as 25 percent.[10] More recently a survey of corporate officers revealed that more than 35 percent expected to commit money to real estate in the near future.[11]

Are corporate pension funds, then, in their quest for performance, tending toward taking unreasonable risks, and if so, is their new tendency imprudent under the pension law? Key pension managers seem to be remarkably unworried by the current situation and the legal exposure it implies. With near unanimity they speak of overzealous speculation by pension funds as a phenomenon of the late 1960s, which now is safely in the past. Real estate, according to this argument, is not risky but is a means of diversification, of insuring that not all pension assets are concentrated in the securities market. AT&T says that its turn away from fast performance orientation is indicated by the fact that the pension fund's current asset value is now formally calculated only twice a year, instead of quarterly, as was done a few years ago. Malone of General Electric says that in the late 1960s many funds were evaluated almost daily; General Electric's is now evaluated once a month, and a report to the trustees is made once a quarter. Regarding those trustees—who are also officers of the corporation—Malone says, "In eighteen years in this department, I've never had a call from a corporate officer pressuring us to increase our investment risk. Those guys have a unique ability to take off their corporate hat when they put on their trustee hat."

Attitudes are much the same at the big banks. Theobald of Citibank said in 1973, "At present, client pressure for performance, such as it is, is a constructive force. In the environment of a few years ago there was a very short-term outlook that was dangerous. But now no major customers give us that kind of pressure." Callaway and Smith of Morgan Guaranty say that they see a marked trend in the direction of non-intervention in trustee decisions by corporate pension sponsors. And the pension officers of Bankers Trust, while conceding that some small companies do not properly recognize their responsibilities regarding their pension funds, believe that, in general, pressure for performance from the sponsor is not a problem for trustee organizations.

The trust law that governed pension funds before the Pension Reform Act was enacted was vague about the extent to which a pension trust or similar trust fund might delegate discretionary investing power to an investment manager and about the extent to which the manager might take investment risks. It was to have been tested in a case initiated by a much discussed complaint filed in December 1971, in a United States district court in Indianapolis by Hanover College of Hanover, Indiana, against Donaldson, Lufkin and Jenrette (DLJ), money manager of Hanover's endowment fund from 1967 until early 1971. The complaint charged, among other things, that DLJ had invested the fund in "unseasoned, speculative and volatile securities yielding little or no income but involving a high degree of investment risk." Hanover College went on to comment in the complaint that such securities "might have been acceptable investments for a wealthy, knowledgeable and experienced securities trader willing and able to expose himself to very substantial risks," but they were completely unsuitable and unacceptable investments in view of the character, financial resources, and investment objectives of the plaintiff's account—and the college demanded $2.4 million in damages as compensation for losses on investments such as Colt Industries, Equity Funding Corporation of America, Ling-Temco-Vought, and National Student Marketing Corporation. DLJ replied that, first, Hanover College had categorically pressed DLJ, in writing, to pursue aggressive investment policies and, second, despite the losses cited, the overall results of the firm's management of the Hanover account over the four-year period had been to increase the Hanover fund's value by somewhat more than the Standard & Poor's 500.

Many pension managers viewed the DLJ case with great apprehension. One of them expressed the opinion that a finding for Hanover would result in money managers' being afraid to invest in stocks other than the traditional blue chips. Another went so far as to say that such a finding might mark the end of discretionary management of trust accounts. But the case had no such outcome; indeed, it had no real outcome at all. After almost a year of legal maneuvering, Hanover accepted a settlement from DLJ regarding some relatively minor aspects of its suit; and regarding the crucial matter of excessive risk-taking, Hanover in October 1972 withdrew the charge entirely, thus tacitly conceding that it had been unfounded. [12]

The case ended with no clarification of legally permissible risk-taking by discretionary investment advisors. Risk-taking had not been adequately defined under the new pension reform law either, but most observers believe there will be lawsuits that will ultimately clarify the issue.

A theoretical solution to the problem of the profit center concept of the corporate pension fund is participation in investment decisions by the union as representative of the plan participants. Unfortunately, that solution does not appear to be practicable, since unions almost invariably shy away from such participation, taking the attitude that the responsibility to produce the money to meet pension promises is and should remain solely the company's. A classic exception was the case of the Kaiser-Frazier automobile manufacturing operation, in which the union, shortly before the demise of the company, successfully pressed the demand that the entire pension fund be invested in short-term government obligations. This was probably the only such pension fund agreement ever made. More recently, the United Automobile Workers asked Chrysler Corporation for a voice in pension fund money management, but the point was not pressed and the demand was dropped early in the negotiations. (In view of most unions' alleged lack of investment skill, not to mention the matter of a few unions' disregard for fiduciary standards, the unions' reluctance to participate in the decisions of company-managed funds may be an attitude to be applauded.)

But the problem remains, and it might become more serious. So far as is known, no promised pension payments were defaulted as a direct result of investment losses in the 1970 market crash (although many potential benefits were lost as a result of plan terminations associated with that event through mergers and liquidations). William Hayes, ITT's former pension manager, expresses frank apprehension about what may happen to pension investing in the next speculative market. "The temptations," he said in 1974, "will be great indeed." If the temptations are yielded to, with pension funds now so heavily committed to common stocks and with the percentage of those commitments in frankly risky stocks increasing, it seems inevitable that severe boom-and-bust would shake the whole private pension system to its foundations.

One of the most widely debated features of the new Pension Reform Act is its injunction that all fiduciaries—who now include investment managers—must act "solely in the benefit" of the beneficiaries of the fund. Although many, perhaps the majority, of pension fund experts predicted at the time of the act's passage that this would make little difference in the investment policies, a few believed that the law could force them to adopt ultraconservative investment policies focusing primarily on bonds and cash rather than on equities. Some of the early effects are described in the next chapter.

VI • CONCLUSION

With major new legislation concerning corporate pension funds so recently enacted, it would be the height of folly to make new recommendations at this time about the need for a fresh package of reforms. Although the most important provisions of the Employment Retirement Income Security Act of 1974 may be in the areas of funding requirements, vesting standards, portability, and termination insurance—all topics outside the scope of this chapter—the law is clearly a major step toward correcting many of the more serious fiduciary problems that existed.

The restriction that a corporation may invest no more than 10 percent of its pension fund assets in its own stock, the much more detailed disclosure requirements, the new standards governing actuaries, the federal government supervision and perhaps elimination of soft dollar payments to finder-consultants, the apparent injunction against investment managers executing transactions through brokerage affiliates—all these seem to represent significant progress toward reducing the conflicts of interest that can arise in the management of a corporate pension fund.

At the same time, it is important to recognize what the law did not do. It did not totally restrict corporate pension plans from investing in their own stock. Although the 10 percent limitation is a vast improvement, the opportunity remains for a company to direct that a portion of its pension assets be invested in its own stock when safer or more attractive investments may be available elsewhere.

The law did not specifically prohibit the kind of reciprocity that occurs when a bank trust department is selected to manage a pension fund because it serves as the corporation's commercial banker or a Wall Street firm is chosen because it is the company's investment banker.

Profit-sharing plans, in contrast to pension plans, were not restricted in the amount they could invest in their own company stock. Although there clearly is considerable theoretical justification for this exemption, the fact is that if the profit-sharing program is the only tax-sheltered retirement plan offered a company's employees, as it is in the case of Sears' nonmanagerial employees, savings that many employees probably intend to use to support their retirement may be excessively concentrated in a single security.

Although the 10 percent limitation also applies to corporate real estate, the inherent difficulties in appraising the value of property and structures may continue to invite abuses.

However, these and any other possible failings of the new law will still be subject to what in this context may well be its most important provision: that the bank managers, investment advisors, corporate sponsors, and actuaries—anyone who has control or authority over the pension fund—must make all decisions "solely in the interests of the participants and the beneficiaries" of the plan.

Of course, the application of this principle is open to varying interpretation. However, it appears likely that the bulk of pension fund fiduciaries will probably err more on the side of prudence than risk in exploring its precise meaning. For one thing, enforcement will now be in the hands of the federal government. Perhaps even more important, in the view of some, is that it will now be much easier for beneficiaries to bring lawsuits testing the exact meaning of the fiduciary provisions.

A little more than two years after enactment of the 1974 act, several of its initial effects are clearly discernible. The most disturbing of these is that many smaller employers, unable to afford expensive legal counsel and professional consultants, have found that they simply cannot understand, much less comply with, the new law, and in consequence have decided to terminate their pension plans. Since the law took effect, some thirteen thousand plans have notified the government of their intention to close up—a rate of terminations double the rate before the law was passed. The machinery established the act to deal with terminations consists of the Pension Benefit Guarantee Corporation (PBGC), an independent federal agency on the model of the Federal Deposit Insurance Corporation, which is funded by mandatory premiums from all private pension plans of $1.00 per covered employee per year or $0.50 per employee for multiemployer plans.) These premiums amount to about $29 million per year, and PBGC's fund already totals over $70 million. In theory, PBGC will be able to fulfill all of the pension promises of all terminated plans that are outstanding at the time of termination; however, some six thousand terminated (and inadequately funded) plans have already been turned over to PBGC and with the prospect of thousands more to come, it is easy to imagine that the new agency's fund may prove to be inadequate. There has even been talk about new legislation to exempt small plans from the law, but such congressional action seems unlikely at present. The main corrective action has been a concerted effort by the Labor Department to encourage small employers not to terminate their plans by simplifying the task of complying with the act. Whether bureaucratic reform can save the law from destroying a part of what it seeks to preserve remains to be seen.[1]

The other effect has been a marked change in pension fund investment patterns. The new law's provision making virtually everyone involved in pension fund investing a personally responsible "fiduciary" has, logically, resulted in far more conservative investment policies by managers who fear that they might be held personally liable for imprudent investments. In regard to stock market commitments, pension managers have recently shown a predilection for the "indexing" approach—a systematic effort not to beat the averages but only to match them. Meanwhile, many funds have shown a suddenly revived interest in fixed-income investments. A recent *Institutional Investor* study resulted in the finding that "1976 was the year of the active bond manager." This latest trend obviously represents, to a limited extent, the completion of a cycle: pension portfolios now, although still predominantly in stocks, look somewhat more like they did before 1950 when bonds were the staple and common stocks were regarded as scarlet women. For 1976, when stock performance was erratic, and bond prices rose sharply, the trend seemed sound enough from an investment viewpoint. But any rapid and sustained stock rise in the future will tempt pension managers and bring the fiduciary provisions of the Pension Reform Act into a test of strength with fund managers eager for a piece of the stock market action. Presumably, that test will eventually take place in the courts.[2]

Corporate pension funds are a new industry with awesomely vast and still growing resources and social implications. With the structure resting on a built-in conflict of interest and subject (until 1974) to only state-administered trust law, what is most impressive is how wisely and scrupulously pension managers and trustees as a group have fulfilled their responsibilities over the years.

However, they have not always acted wisely and scrupulously, and with the growing pressures on corporate profits and the mounting aspirations of employees, there would have been no guarantee that the generally favorable record of the past could have been maintained in the future. The new law therefore is welcome. But the need for vigorous enforcement and constant scrutiny remains.

NOTES

I. The Problem of Serving Two Masters

[1]Although corporate plans are by far the largest percentage of these figures, the figures also include the assets of union, multiemployer, and nonprofit organization plans. In addition, the figures include the assets of deferred profit-sharing plans.

[2]Julian Gumperz in *Financial Analysts Journal* (November-December 1970).

[3]Some private pension plans are still "insured," but the total assets underlying such plans are small relative to those of noninsured plans. Under an insured arrangement, the sponsoring company simply pays premiums to an insurance company, which pays the promised pension benefits out of its general assets. The insurance company, not the pension fund, bears the risk of market depreciation and reaps the reward of appreciation. Most of the conflicts of interest discussed in the ensuing pages do not apply to insured funds. Undoubtedly conflicts do occur in insured funds, but they are so much a subject of their own, and so peripheral to the securities industry, that they fall outside the scope of this investigation.

However, it should be noted that when insurance companies establish "separate accounts" for pension funds, their function resembles that of a bank or independent investment advisor, and they may be subject to similar conflicts of interest.

[4]U.S., Congress, Senate, Subcommittee on Labor, *Report on Private Welfare and Pension Plan Study, 1971, Part 2*, 92nd Cong., 1st Sess., p. 880.

[5]*Blankenship* v. *Boyle*, U.S. District Court for the District of Columbia, 1971. The focus of this study is on corporate pension funds. Nevertheless, a few words are in order regarding union-managed funds and those jointly administered by unions and employers, especially since the most publicized, and perhaps the most flagrant, fiduciary scandals of recent years have occurred in connection with funds of the latter kind.

Purely union-run funds, once common, are now rare. Those that exist either have been established for the employees of the union itself or have survived form the era before the Taft-Hartley Act of 1947, which forbids corporations to pay pension money directly to a union and, in the case of jointly administered funds, prescribes an equally balanced union-management board of trustees with one neutral outsider to break tie votes. As a practical matter, the union members tend to dominate these boards, since the labor representatives typically come from the *same* union while the corporate members frequently represent a number of *different* companies. Several technically jointly administered funds (such as those of the Mine Workers and the Teamsters) that were in trouble a few years ago were in fact dominated by unions.

In collective bargaining, with very few exceptions, unions have not asked for a hand in the management of company-run funds. The characteristic union attitude has been the following: We will stick to demanding the benefits and leave you the privilege and responsibility of finding the money to pay them. Most pension critics point out, in fact, that the unions did not press for reform of the structure or the fiduciary standards of company-run funds. A few unions, most notably the United Auto Workers, have pressed for pension plan termination insurance; but too often, it appears, union leadership strives for the semblance rather than the substance of improved benefits (that is, benefits that because of plan structure probably will never be paid) and entirely ignores fiduciary matters. Conversely, in the cases of the fiduciary outrages that have occurred in jointly run funds, the company managements seemed willing to go along with whatever the union leadership wanted to do, in the interest of keeping the union happy.

Why has the most flagrant abuse occurred in those funds dominated by unions? Michael Gordon, minority counsel to the Senate General Subcommittee on Labor Study Group on Pension Plans, sums up their study as follows: union abuse of pension assets is a result partly of inexperience and partly of the fact that some union leaders, having come up the hard way, look on the pension fund as part of their personal reward for success. Gordon, however, is unwilling to say that the conflicts of interest arising out of labor leader misuse of union-run funds are generically worse than those arising out of corporations' attempts to use corporate funds as adjuncts of the corporate treasury. Rather, he says that instances of labor leader misuse tend to be more obvious and dramatic—simple cases of a hand in the till as opposed to equally improper but less easily detected cases of manipulation of pension money for corporate advantage.

In sum, union fund abuses seem to differ from corporate abuses more in style than in substance. Union funds will be managed better when better trained, more financially sophisticated, more ethical union leaders are elected. In the meantime covered employees have at least as much to fear from their unions as from their employers with regard to the management of their pension money.

[6]*The New York Times*, December 21, 1971.

[7]U.S., Congress, Senate, Subcommittee on Labor, *Report on Private Welfare and Pension Plan Study, 1972: Report of Hearings on Pension Plan Terminations*, 92nd Cong., 2d Sess., p. 2.

[8]*The Wall Street Journal*, September 11, 1972.

[9]Address before the 18th Annual Insurance Conference, Ohio State University, March 2, 1967.

[10]U.S., Congress, Senate, Subcommittee on Labor, *Preliminary Report of the Private Welfare and Pension Plan Study, 1971*, 92nd Cong., 1st Sess., pp. 7-10. Also Bankers Trust Company, *The Private Pension Controversy* (New York: Bankers Trust Co., 1973).

[11]Of course, some major corporate interests did resist pension controls vigorously and effectively. Passage of the Welfare and Pension Plans Disclosure Act of 1958 was strongly fought by the leading banks, insurance companies, and pension-sponsoring corporations, particularly in the House of Representatives—a resistance that considerably weakened the disclosure requirements that were eventually enacted.

[12]Ibid., p. 97.

[13]*Institutional Investor Study Report of the Securities and Exchange Commission: Summary Volume, 1971*, p. 69.

[14]*The Private Pension Controversy*, p. 60.

II. At Less Than Arm's Length

[1]*Pension and Profit-Sharing Report* (Englewood Cliffs, N.J.: Prentice-Hall, 1973), vol. XXV, no. 23, p. 3.

[2]Paul P. Harbrecht, S.J., *Pension Funds and Economic Power* (New York: The Twentieth Century Fund, 1959), p. 84.

[3]Because it usually is intended to provide funds for retirement, a deferred profit-sharing plan is often regarded as a type of pension plan. For example, the $124.4 billion that the Securities and Exchange Commission reports as pension fund assets includes profit-sharing funds that are estimated by the Profit Sharing Research Foundation (Evanston, Illinois) at 20 to 25 percent of that total. The significant difference is that a *pension plan* defines the precise benefits an employee will eventually receive, and a *profit-sharing plan* defines the amount the company will contribute each year. In the case of a pension plan, the company benefits or loses depending upon how wisely the assets are invested. In the case of a profit-sharing plan, it is the employee who will do better or worse depending upon the success of the investments.

No criticism is implied here of the Sears fund's self-investment. Such self-investment is probably appropriate, as an employee-incentive feature, to a *profit-sharing* fund as opposed to a pension fund. What Sears may be crticized for is that it maintains no *pension* plan for most employees; therefore, along with the increased opportunity for employees to participate in the company's success goes the increased risk that they may suffer from its failure.

[4]Author's interview with John F. Thompson. Other direct and indirect quotations from corporate managers and bankers in this chapter are based on such interviews unless otherwise noted.

[5]U.S., Congress, Senate, Subcommittee on Labor, *Report on Private Welfare and Pension Plan Study, 1971, Part 2*, 92nd Cong., 1st Sess., p. 730.

[6]Ibid., p. 438.

[7]Ibid., p. 707 ff.

[8]*Institutional Investor Study Report of the Securities and Exchange Commission, 1971*, p. 1007.

[9]Trust division annual reports of Morgan Guaranty Trust Co. and First National City Bank, 1971 and 1972. Bankers Trust Company only began publishing such a report in 1975.

[10]It may be useful here to describe briefly the sort of men who ran the Morgan Guaranty Trust and Investment Division in the early 1970s. Its head was Samuel R. Callaway: born in New York City in 1914; graduate of St. Paul's School and Harvard University, 1936; a Morgan employee since the year of his college graduation; treasurer of the United Hospital Fund, New York; a trustee of the New York Public Library and St. Paul's School; treasurer and trustee of the Juilliard Music Foundation. Its deputy head was Harrison V. Smith: born in New York City in 1919; graduate of Yale, 1941; a Morgan employee since 1946, shortly after he left military service; president of the Visiting Nurse Service of New York; treasurer of Memorial Sloan Kettering Cancer Center, New York. Callaway and Smith speak of their division's operations freely, unguardedly, and even humorously, as well as with evident pride. The very suggestion by an interviewer of potential abuses in their work seems out of place; they appear to resent the idea of legal restrictions forbidding them to do what they would not consider doing anyway. Interior controls based on morality may well be sufficient in some cases but obviously cannot be depended upon in all instances.

[11]In assessing these statements, it should be noted that a contrary position taken by a bank trust officer might constitute an admission of illegal acts.

[12]As Lawrence D. Jones points out in his paper, "Bank Trust Activity and the Public Interest," prepared for the Commission on Financial Sturcture and Regulation (1971), "among the services larger banks are able to offer customers, at a negotiated price reflecting the size of a customer's deposit balances, are the services of the trust department."

III. Juggling the Assumptions

[1]Author's interview.

[2]*Pensions* (Spring 1972), p. 85.

[3]The Financial Accounting Standards Board (successor to the Accounting Principles Board) has the matter of pension accounting, including the interest assumption, under consideration.

[4]Since the rise of investment advisors not affiliated with banks or insurance companies as pension fund managers plays such a large role in this chapter, a word is in order about the fees that lure them into pension fund managing. Large investment advisory firms such as Lionel D. Edie and Scudder, Stevens & Clark charge a rate that is competitive with bank trust departments— generally 0.3 percent of the first $10 million, or $30,000 per year, and higher fees, although on a descending percentage scale, for larger funds. They do not generally solicit funds smaller than $10 million but sometimes take them at a higher fee rate. Smaller investment advisory firms accept smaller funds at rates several times higher—for example, as much as 1 percent per year on $100,000.

[5]Figures obtained from Martin E. Segal Co., Chase Manhattan Bank, and Standard & Poor's/ InterCapital.

[6]Interviews with bankers quoted.

[7]U.S. Steel Corp., *Annual Report* (1971).
[8]Standard Oil Co. (Ohio), *Annual Report* (1972).

IV. The Soft Dollar: Apple in Eden

[1]*Institutional Investor* (February 1973), p. 44.
[2]Becker's is, by a wide margin, the leading pension-measuring service; it has some three hundred employees and three thousand subscribers, including half of the *Fortune* list of the five hundred industrial corporations that have fund assets of nearly $50 billion under their control. Its fees range from $4,200 cash per year upward, depending on the amount of assets. If the fund chooses to pay in brokerage commissions instead of cash, the fee is larger, beginning at $6,000. Becker does not screen or help select money managers.
[3]For example, all of the partners of Jennison Associates (which is not broker-affiliated and thus collects no soft dollar fees), declined to be interviewed by this researcher.
[4]Author's interview.
[5]*The Wall Street Journal*, May 4, 1973.
[6]Ibid.
[7]*Finance* (November 1972), p. 54.
[8]*Pensions* (Winter 1973), p. 69.
[9] Ibid., p. 53.
[10]Author's interview. The same applies to subsequent quotations from money managers in this chapter, except as noted.
[11]As to why not, Smith comments as follows: "Why would we be interested in doing that? Such proposals are made only in private. We'd have to be Watergate North." Moreover, the damage, if any, is to the pension client rather than to the investment advisor.
[12]*Pensions* (July-August 1973), p. 40.
[13]*Commercial and Financial Chronicle* (June 28, 1973).
[14]*New York Law Journal* (June 11, 1973).
[15]In December 1976, *The Wall Street Journal* reported that the Securities Industry Association was urgently pressing for reversal of the provision that would eventually bar securities firms from acting as both broker and investment manager to a pension fund.

V. The Profit Center Concept

[1]*Pensions* (Winter 1973).
[2]Roger F. Murray, "Pension Funds: Newest Among Major Financial Institutions," *Journal of Bank Research* (Winter 1973).
[3]A.S. Hansen, Inc., *Employee Benefit Fund Investment Performance 1965-71, Third Annual Report* (1972).
[4]*The Wall Streeet Journal*, June 7, 1973.
[5]*Business Week* (April 14, 1973).
[6]High turnover is generally taken to imply increased risk-taking; that is, in-and-out fashion conscious trading versus long-term investment in sound, growing companies.
[7]*Institutional Investor Study Report of the Securities and Exchange Commission, 1971*, Chap. 8.
[8]*Pensions* (Winter 1973).
[9]Author's interview.
[10]*Pensions* (Fall 1972).
[11]*Institutional Investor*, (November 1974).
[12]DLJ's investment advisory contract with Hanover, like most such contracts, had stipulated that "DLJ . . .shall not be liable for any loss, unless resulting from its own wilful misconduct or

neglect.'' Moreover, in fairness to DLJ it may be pointed out that among the bad investments specified by Hanover in its complaint was Equity Funding Corporation—which DLJ had sold in 1970 and 1971, at a loss, to be sure, but at far less loss than would have been incurred if the stock had been held until disaster overtook that company in 1973.

VI. Conclusion

[1]*Forbes* (January 15, 1977).
[2]*Institutional Investor* (December 1976).

State and Local Pension Fund Asset Management
by Louis M. Kohlmeier

I • INTRODUCTION

New York City's prolonged and tortuous effort to stave off fiscal insolvency increasingly has involved the use of money from state and local pension funds. Perhaps the city's most dramatic exercise in brinksmanship took place on October 17, 1975, when Albert Shanker, president of the city's teachers union, balked at investing $150 million of the union's pension fund assets in New York securities, an investment on which New York State hinged its own provision of funds to avert formal default. It took a series of negotiations, culminating in a confrontation between Shanker and Governor Hugh Carey, before the former relented. The pressure on him, he later charged, "was intense, amounting to blackmail." But the alternative, he added, was even worse: "The consequences of default would have been an economic, social and political catastrophe."[1]

Since the financial predicament of New York City became widely apparent in early 1975, one of the primary strategies of the politicians and bankers involved in the rescue efforts was to tap the state and municipal public employee pension funds, which together possessed assets of some $15 billion. Shanker was not the only union leader to protest. John DeLury, president of the Uniformed Sanitationmen's Association and a trustee of the City Employee Retirement Association, which earlier in 1975 had bought $95 million of bonds, said that additional purchases would be made only "over my dead body."[2] Al Sgaglione, president of the Police Conference of New York, brought a lawsuit against New York State Comptroller Arthur Levitt, charging him with a conflict of interest in proposing the purchase by New York State retirement funds of $250 million of New York State notes. "As comptroller of the state, he sells state securities," explains Sgaglione. "As trustee of the retirement system, he's supposed to protect our money by making prudent investments. And he also sits on the Emergency Financial Control Board, which is trying to save New York City. We don't see how one man can wear those three hats."[3]

Seldom have the conflicts of interest in the management of public employee pension funds been dramatized as vividly as they have been in New York City's frantic struggle for financial survival. Despite initial protests by unions and notwithstanding a long-term policy of reducing holdings of municipal and state obligations, the New York State pension funds of which Levitt was trustee held $1.3 billion of New York State notes, representing 16 percent of their portfolio, during the state's 1976 borrowing crisis. New York City's five public employee pension funds, which are administered separately from the state pension funds, have invested even more heavily in the frantic attempt to rescue the city. At the end of 1976, the city pension funds held $2.2 billion of city and Municipal Assistance Corporation (MAC) securities among their total assets of approximately $11 billion. At the close of 1976, the city pension funds in addition had commitments that would raise their holdings of city and MAC securities to $3.5 billion by June 30, 1978. Jack Biegel, consultant to the city's pension funds, early in 1977 wrote, "The leaders of the municipal unions, in their capacity as trustees of the city's five retirement systems, have been providing New York City with the only new cash it has been receiving."[4] In Washington the staff of the Pension Task Force in the House of Representatives wrote of the New York City and State pension plans: "While a (New York City) fiscal crisis has been temporarily averted, the solvency of the plans has been impaired and the participants and pensioners are dependent on the uncertain fiscal position of the state and city."[5]

Although no other city has faced fiscal crisis so large and prolonged, the conflicts in New York are by no means unique, nor is their importance limited to New York. Twenty years ago, public employee pension funds in the United States had some $10 billion of assets under management; today, the nation's state and local pension funds control more than $100 billion in assets. These funds are accumulated—and invested—to provide eventual retirement income for hundreds of thousands of government employees. But as the New York experience demonstrates, they are to a considerable degree controlled by city and state employers. The staff of the House Pension Task Force has asserted that the "high level of employer control" of public pension funds and their assets brings along "an attendant potential for abuse unknown in the private sector."[6] In whose interests are public pension funds, in fact, managed?

The first public employee pension funds appeared in the United States roughly a century ago. Like the early private corporate pension plans, which were established about the same time to provide retirement income for a handful of faithful employees, the public pension plans initially had rather modest objectives: to provide a small amount of additional compensation for police and fire department employees in recognition of the hazardous nature of their duties. Pension plan growth, both public and private, remained slow until the 1930s.

It was during that decade that the Great Depression rudely awakened the nation to the desirability of providing greater economic security for all, the old as well as the able-bodied. In 1935 Congress passed the Social Security Act under the apparent assumption that it was carving into statutory stone the centuries-old dream of economic security for the aged. Since then Congress has repeatedly raised Social Security contributions and benefits, and it has amended the act to provide mandatory participation and nearly universal coverage. In the federal government's 1976 fiscal year, Social Security cash outlays will rise to $70 billion, amounting to 20 percent of the federal budget.[7] Yet the Social Security System, operating in an inflationary economy and without resort to general revenues of the U.S. Treasury, has fallen far short of providing Americans with a reasonable measure of economic security in retirement. Even with increased benefits, the average individual Social Security beneficiary received $185 monthly in 1974 and can expect $235 monthly in 1976.[8] The inadequacy of Social Security benefits would seem to be most fundamental, if often overlooked, explanation for the growth of private and public pension funds.

Private and public pension plans were and are essentially voluntary arrangements, initiated by employers or entered into by agreement between employers and employee unions. Pension plans are not mandatory under federal law, and although private and public plans now probably cover (the term *coverage* is subject to various definitions) more than 30 million American workers, pension coverage remains far from universal. A comfortable retirement income still remains elusive for many and impossible for some.

In the early years, when pension obligations were new and small, pensions were commonly paid from the same till as employees' wages—in the case of a corporation, from its current income, and for cities and states, from current tax receipts. A basic attitude, long taken by both private and public employers and acquiesced to by employees and often by their unions, was that pensions were gratuities, awarded with gold watches at age sixty-five for many years of loyal service. The employers' proprietary attitude was also reflected in their long domination of the management of pension fund assets.

These attitudes are slowly changing. Today, usually in theory, frequently in labor-management negotiations, and often in law, pensions are considered deferred wages that the employee has *earned* but can collect only upon retirement. This change in philosophy has caused an important shift from the "pay-as-you-go" financing of the past to a system whereby funds are systematically set aside each year by the employer—and, in some cases, by the employee as well—so when retirement occurs, a good portion, if not all, of the funds necessary to provide a guaranteed monthly income have been accumulated. During the 1950s, and again during the 1960s, the amount of these assets quadrupled. And since 1967, although the assets of public pension funds are still not so large as the $145 billion in private plans, the public funds have been growing at a more rapid pace than private plans. Between 1967 and 1972, the book value of assets of noninsured private pension funds increased by $10.4 billion, or 54 percent. During the same period, the book value of the assets of state and local pension funds increased by $30.6 billion, or 73.7 percent (see Table 17).[9]

Table 17: Assets of All Private and Public Pension Funds (End of Year Book Value, in Billions of Dollars)

	1950	1955	1960	1965	1970	1973	1974	1975
Private	$12.1	$27.5	$52.0	$86.5	$138.2	$182.6	$194.5	$216.9
Insured pension reserves	5.6	11.3	18.8	27.3	41.2	56.0	68.7	84.2
Noninsured pension funds	6.5	16.1	33.1	59.2	97.0	126.5	133.7	145.2
Public	25.8	42.2	56.3	72.8	123.5	161.4	173.1	192.1
State and local	5.3	10.5	19.3	33.1	58.0	81.6	89.0	106.0
Federal								
Federal Old-age and Survivors Insurance	13.7	21.7	20.3	18.2	32.5	36.5	37.8	37.0
Federal Disability Insurance	—	—	2.3	1.6	5.6	7.9	8.1	7.4
Civil Service Retirement and Disability Program	4.2	6.6	10.6	15.9	23.1	31.5	34.6	38.6
Railroad Retirement	2.6	3.5	3.7	3.9	4.4	3.8	3.6	3.1

Note: Figures may not add due to rounding.

Source: Figures are taken from annual surveys by the Securities and Exchange Commission published in the SEC's *Statistical Bulletin.* See *Statistical Bulletin* 34, no. 4 (April 1975).

Although public pension funds were initially begun to compensate police and firemen for the hazardous nature of their work, public funds long ago began to broaden their coverage to all state or local employees, usually on the ground that public service wages generally were lower than wages in private industry. New York City, for example, which established a pension fund for its policemen in 1857, presently has several plans that cover roughly three hundred thousand active and seventy-five thousand retired employees. Today, however, pay scales of all federal, state, and municipal workers appear to equal—and in some cases exceed—pay for comparable jobs in private industry.[10] And yet in general, public employee pension plans continue to offer more liberal benefits than private pension plans. For example, public employees qualify for vested pension benefits sooner than workers in private industry, in some cases as early as five years after employment commences, and an employee may retire after twenty years of service at age fifty. In private pension systems vesting often has not begun until an employee has had fifteen or twenty years of service; and in a few cases, employees are not entitled to any benefits until they reach age sixty-five with twenty-five years of service— although the Pension Reform Act of 1974 mandated a liberalization of such procedures.

The Bureau of the Census' 1972 Census of Governments contains probably the most complete survey of public pension plans and their operations, but the bureau makes its surveys only every five years and the surveys generally are limited to larger plans to which public employees contribute. The 1972 Census of Governments counted 2,304 such retirement systems of state and municipal governments with a total employee membership of 9.1 million. The systems were paying benefits, averaging $223 monthly, to 1.5 million retired public employees. In their fiscal years that ended between July 1, 1971, and June 30, 1972, the systems reported total receipts of $12.6 billion, of which state and municipal governments contributed $5.7 billion, employees $3.4 billion, and earnings from investments $3.5 billion (see Table 18). The House Pension Task Force has attempted to identify all state and local pension funds, including noncontributory plans and small plans with fewer than 100 participants. The Task Force found 6,076 public pension plans in 1975 covering 10.3 million employees.[11] The variation in the findings of the Bureau of the Census and the House Pension Task Force underscores the fact that very little has been known about the operations of public pension funds in the aggregate and the further fact that many individual funds have disclosed to the public very little concerning management of their assets.

It seems likely that the growth of public pension funds will continue at a rapid, if not equally dramatic, pace. In the past fifteen years, nearly one out of every three jobs created in the United States has been in the public sector. From 1960 to 1974, state and local government employment ballooned from 6.1 to 11.6 million. Because the pressure to increase the level and breadth of coverage is likely to continue, and because pressure to raise the level of funding seems certain to intensify, cash flow into public pension funds is also likely to increase. It is the investment of such enormous and growing sums of money that heightens the potential for serious conflicts of interest.

It was in part out of recognition of the temptations of putting self-interest before the interests of participants that Congress established the Employee Retirement Income Security Act of 1974 (ERISA), more commonly called the Pension Reform Act. This law, while not making pension plans mandatory or universal, imposed for the first time some measure of nationwide uniformity and significant regulation on the pension plans of private employers and unions. The purposes of the legislation were also to insure that more and younger employees will actually qualify for pensions when they reach retirement age and to provide increased assurance that private pension funds will be sufficiently funded to pay the benefits they promise. Although the 1974 act did not cover public pension plans, a key congressional committee began to hold hearings in the fall of 1975 on proposals for federal regulation of state and local government pension systems. At least one bill modeled on the Pension Reform Act, the Public Employees Retirement Income Securities Act, was introduced during 1975, and again in 1976 and 1977. But most observers predict that it will take two years before any bill is likely to be passed.

Table 18 Pension Fund Receipts (in Billions of Dollars)

	1962	1966[a]	1971[b]
Private noninsured funds*			
Employer contributions	$4.0	$6.4	$11.3
Employee contributions	0.5	0.7	1.1
Investment income	1.6	2.7	4.1
Public funds**			
Employer contributions	1.9	3.1	5.7
Employee contributions	1.3	2.0	3.4
Investment income	0.8	1.6	3.5

[a]For public funds, fiscal years ending July, 1, 1966, to June 30, 1967.
[b]For public funds, fiscal years ending July 1, 1971, to June 30, 1972.

*Source: Securities and Exchange Commission Statistical Series Release No. 2599, June 28, 1972.
**Source: Bureau of the Census, 1972 Census of Governments, Topical Studies 6, no. 1 (December 1973). The periodic Census of Governments is taken at five-year intervals.

In shaping legislation Congress is certain to run into heavy opposition from city and state politicians who have set their own guidelines on what public pension funds can—and cannot—do. State and municipal laws control the kinds of investments that pension fund administrators and money managers can make.[12] The statutes also create pension fund boards of trustees and sometimes designate who the trustees shall be—frequently including the state treasurer. Trustees not designated are appointed by governors, mayors, or other elected officials. Typically, the trustees are responsible for administering pension benefits as well as pension fund investments. Like trustees generally, pension fund trustees normally devote only part of their time to pension fund affairs. Occasionally, bankers, brokers, insurance executives, or others experienced in investment matters are appointed to pension fund boards. More frequently, the boards are composed largely or exclusively of public officials, employee representatives, and others who are not professionally trained to invest large sums of money.

Public pension fund trustees therefore generally delegate, within the legislatively prescribed guidelines, both the formulation of investment policy and day-to-day investment management. But the extent of delegation varies greatly, and close examination is necessary to determine who in fact exercises what kind of investment authority. Many public pension funds have professional staffs, but they vary widely in size, quality, and investment experience and authority. Some funds have very small staffs, and investment authority in practice is exercised by hired outsiders, most often a bank. At the other extreme are a few large public pension funds with experienced staffs that provide "in-house" investment management.

The dual roles of trustees, pension fund administrators, and investment managers are at the heart of almost all the conflict-of-interest problems of public pension funds. The most fundamental question is: whose interest comes first? Those of employees, for whom adequate pension benefits may well represent the difference between retirement years of grinding poverty or relative comfort? Those of employers, for whom the pension fund is usually just one plethora of competing claims on the tax dollar? Or those of outside investment managers, for whom pension assets under management are a source of income and an entree to other clients?

It is important of course, to distinguish between situations in which a conflict of interest is merely present and situations in which the conflict is actually abused. Whether conflicts of interest develop into serious problems depends upon who carries out the various management functions and how effectively their activities are monitored by the trustees or staffs. But the possibilities for conflict are numerous. For example, some trustees and their staffs decide how the brokerage commissions generated by the fund's portfolio transactions will be allocated; and when they make these decisions, it appears that the commission business is often channeled to favored regional broker-dealers with political influence or friends in the state or city government. But when investment advisors decide where portfolio securities will be bought and sold, other conflict questions arise—for example, when the investment advisor is a bank having commercial relationships with broker-dealers to whom it allocates business. Almost all public pension funds appear to allow their investment advisors to obtain research from broker-dealers through "soft dollar" payments—that is, in exchange for commission business. But few if any pension funds have established controls to insure that the soft dollar benefits obtained by investment advisors accrue to the benefit of the pension funds paying the transaction costs rather than to the benefit of the advisors' other customers.

This study examines these and a number of other conflict-of-interest problems related to the management of public pension fund assets. As these assets continue to grow, if pension fund trustees and staff fail to equip themselves with more sophisticated money management techniques and with more effective surveillance of their hired money managers, conflict-of-interest problems—and abuses—will also continue to proliferate. The problems are compounded by the general failure of public pension funds to make full public disclosure of how investment authority is divided and the methods by which depository banks, investment advisors, and broker-dealers are selected. Some conflicts are unavoidable, and others probably can be avoided only at costs that outweigh likely benefits. But control and surveillance can minimize the effects of the conflicts. And in itself, greater public disclosure should help to prevent the unavoidable conflict from growing into situations that are harmful to both pension fund beneficiaries and the general public, which must ultimately pay the bills.

II • A QUESTION OF CONTROL

The assets of state and local government pension funds had climbed to $106 billion (book value) by the end of 1975.[1] Yet there is still disagreement on the answer to the most basic question concerning those assets: to whom do they belong? To the contributors, to the beneficiaries, or to both?

In a theoretical sense, it may well make little difference as long as the money is available to pay promised benefits to retirees. In a practical sense, important consequences flow from differing attitudes about the ownership of assets. Two examples serve to illustrate the rather extreme differences in pension fund management that can spring from this seemingly small distinction.

The city of Albany, Georgia, has for many years operated a public pension system that, although relatively small, represents the retirement hopes of some one thousand municipal employees and probably is typical of hundreds of other public pension systems in its avoidance of full public disclosure, in the presence on its board of trustees of individuals with political affiliations, and in its low rate of return on investments.

Both the city and its employees contribute to the pension fund, which, as of June 30, 1975, had assets of $3.3 million. A dispute over management of the fund's assets arose in 1972, when it was disclosed that in the prior eleven years, the fund had earned an average annual investment return of only 1.1 percent.[2] The chairman of the city pension board in 1972 was Jim Porter Watkins, a former mayor of Albany. The other four members were the incumbent mayor, the city clerk, a city commissioner, and a representative of the municipal employees. Following the rate-of-return disclosure, Harry Goldstein, the pension fund board member who was also a city commissioner, led a move to replace the Citizens & Southern Bank of Atlanta, the investment advisor that had managed the fund over this eleven-year period. Watkins, who was also a director of the Albany affiliate of Citizens & Southern Bank, opposed replacement of the investment advisor.

When the question was put to a vote, the pension board voted three to two to retain Citizens & Southern. Goldstein thereupon resigned from the pension board, charging Watkins with a "conflict of interest" between his pension board chairmanship and his bank directorship. Watkins in turn charged Goldstein, who was running for reelection to the city commission, with launching "political balloons full of hot air."[3]

A revealing contrast to Albany, Georgia, is the way that the state of Connecticut administers five major trust funds for some eighty-eight thousand state and municipal employees. Connecticut was forced to reform its pension fund operations as a result of a fiscal crisis in the late 1960s, when pension benefits outstripped state contributions by so great a margin that the state had to issue $56 million of long-term bonds to meet its contribution obligations.[4]

In 1971 the Connecticut General Assembly enacted a law providing for a forty-year funding schedule that would cover normal costs plus amortization of unfunded liabilities. The management of the fund's assets, which are pooled and centrally managed under the authority of the state treasurer rather than the funds' trustees, was also dramatically overhauled. Beginning on July 1, 1972, the assets were organized for investment purposes into a fixed-income, a common stock, and a mortgage fund. The state treasurer, Robert I. Berdon, appointed an investment advisory council composed principally of insurance company executives and others with investment experience, but including two employee representatives. The council, chaired by the dean of the University of Connecticut School of Business Administration, helped the treasurer select an in-house investment staff and outside investment advisors. The staff of four, all with investment experience, included a securities trader responsible for executing all stock transaction orders placed by the four outside advisors.

Furthermore, the treasurer created Connecticut Nutmeg Securities, Inc., the first brokerage firm owned and operated by a governmental unit to execute stock transactions. The portfolio holdings of the fixed-income, common stock, and mortgage funds at the end of 1973 amounted to approximately $656 million at market value. The investment yield, calculated on the basis of pooled investments assigned to the State Employee's Retirement Fund, was 6.82 percent in 1972 and 5.61 percent in 1973.[5] The lengthy and reasonably complete semiannual investment reports issued by the Connecticut treasurer's office read more like a detailed mutual fund's report to shareholders than the typical superficial state document.

The contrast between the city of Albany, Georgia, and the state of Connecticut suggests how far many more have to go in changing their attitudes toward the management of public pension fund assets. Many, and perhaps most, public pension funds have been managed as political entities from the city hall or the statehouse. Some funds' assets have been invested heavily in low-yielding state and local bonds, as if the assets were primarily a convenient sinking fund for public debt obligations. Local bankers and brokers have been selected as managers and for transactions, even when outsiders were more qualified. Many plans are underfunded, and few reveal more than a glimpse of their operations. In short, the interests of the employees are not the sole consideration governing the management of public pension funds.

These problems have not gone unrecognized. "There is a general consensus among knowledgeable persons that retirement systems for public employees are much more in need of regulation than the plans of private employers." said Professor Dan M. McGill of the University of Pennsylvania's Wharton School of Finance, testifying in 1972 before the Senate Subcommittee on Labor. "As a group, public employee retirement systems are inadequately funded, poorly designed, and subject to unsound political manipulation."[6] McGill, chairman of the university's Pension Research Council and a recently appointed member of the Advisory Committee to the Pension Benefit Guaranty Corporation, which was set up by the Pension Reform Act of 1974, was urging Congress to apply proposed federal regulations of corporate and union pension plans to state and local government retirement systems.

Most administrators of state and local pension plans, of course, do not agree with McGill. James L. McGoffin, director of the Oregon Public Employees Retirement System, asserts: "Conflict of interest, actual and potential, in our system under public surveillance and reporting procedures such as we have in minutes, monthly reports, quarterly reports and annual reports to our members, to our legislature and to the press, seems less worrisome than under the private system."[7]

Not surprisingly, as Congress considered pension fund regulation in the early 1970s, administrators of state and local retirement systems took the position that their funds did not need to be regulated or, at the least, that Congress should wait until it had studied their funding, vesting, and fiduciary practices.

Although committees of Congress and groups established by the White House had been giving serious consideration to private pension funds since at least 1962, when President John F. Kennedy appointed his Cabinet Committee on Corporate Pension Funds, these investigations of the private system concentrated largely on problems relating to underfunding and to vesting requirements that restricted employee participation in many plans. Although these reports almost invariably also concluded with recommendations concerning the fiduciary responsibility of pension fund trustees, the government's knowledge of fiduciary responsibility and conflict-of-interest problems was neither extensive nor sophisticated. The few nongovernment studies of public retirement systems, usually under university and foundation auspices, also focused more on funding, vesting, and other aspects of the benefits of public pension fund operations rather than on the investment operation and related problems of fiduciary responsibility.

There were a number of reasons why studies concentrated on the private system while relatively little attention was paid to public pension funds. The total assets controlled by private pension funds were considerably larger than those controlled by public funds. Workers in private industry were more vociferous in their complaints that they had been shortchanged in their pension benefits. When private pension plans failed to deliver benefits—as the Studebaker Corporation's plan did in 1964—they received considerable publicity. But Congress and the White House were hesitant to investigate their political allies back home or, indeed, their colleagues in Washington, D.C. (Ironically, at the very time that Congress and the White House were devoting much time and effort to the investigation and reform of private pension funds, the federally operated Railroad Retirement System, in which more than 0.5 million workers were enrolled, was heading toward bankruptcy.[8]) Perhaps the key reason for the relative inattention paid to public pension funds, however, has been the belief that public employees' pensions are considerably more secure than those of private employees. If there is not enough money in a public pension fund to pay benefits as they come due, public employers can fall back on city's or state's power to raise more money by hiking taxes or by issuing bonds, as Connecticut was forced to do in 1969-71, before it switched to its current system of funding.

But the differences between public and private pension funds are smaller than they at first appear. It is unwise to assume that pension promises will always be made good out of current tax or bond revenues. For one thing, future generations of taxpayers may simply refuse to be saddled with liabilities voted by an earlier generation of political officeholders. For another, benefits that are substantially underfunded will become a progressively larger burden on the state of municipal government. The tax resources of American cities—particularly the larger ones with eroding tax bases—are not unlimited. Eventually, the requirement that a city or state meet a large pension fund liability for employee services accrued in the past may well collide head-on with the necessity to allocate more tax resources for education, public health, or other vital needs. Moreover, the failure to fund pension obligations on some reasonable basis conflicts with the increasingly widely held theory that public and private pensions are deferred wages.

The Pension Reform Act of 1974 required private employers to put aside ample funds to cover future benefit obligations, a concept that is also gradually finding its way into public pension fund law. A lawsuit filed by the Illinois Education Association resulted in that state being ordered in 1973 to make payments totaling $1.7 billion over fifty years to the Illinois Teachers' Retirement System. In Detroit a special property tax assessment was levied in 1973 to satisfy an $18 million court judgment requiring additional funding for the pension system covering the city's bus drivers. Other court actions have required large payments to underfunded pension systems in Philadelphia, Los Angeles, and elsewhere.[9] Thus, while Congress was moving toward a uniform requirement for funding of past liabilities of private pension systems, court actions and the threat of court actions have also brought public pension systems close to funding practices that bear some relationship to liabilities.

Although the slow pace at which some public and private pension funds are now funding past liabilities is far from ideal, it is probably defensible on practical grounds. Some of these liabilities are so immense that a more rapid effort to make up for past years of neglect is not realistically possible. Among the more flagrant examples are the Los Angeles' police and firemen's fund in September 1975, which had assets of $400 million and unfunded liabilities of $1.6 billion;[10] the Maine State Retirement System as of June 30, 1974, which had assets of $155 million and unfunded liabilities of $646 million, prompting a state employee representative on the board of trustees to charge that the system is "in jeopardy";[11] and the Nevada Public Employees Retirement System, which had assets of $244 million at the end of 1974 and was told by its actuaries, Martin E. Segal Co., that the fund would soon be facing an unfunded liability of $366 million and that the state should raise its contribution level from 7 to 21 percent of pay or risk insolvency.[12]

The one heartening sign is that at least there is a growing consensus that public pension funds should be properly funded. This is important, because it indicates acceptance of the principle that the public pension fund is, indeed, a form of deferred wage and not a gratuity, employer sinking fund, political promise, or source of business for local bankers and brokers. If that point is accepted, it then follows that a properly managed public pension fund must be run *solely* in the interests of its employees. There should be no conflict between the interest of the employees—which is to receive their full benefits—and the interests of the employers and those who manage or advise the funds.

Unfortunately, many public pension funds still fall far short of accepting this premise. Although some, like Connecticut, have come to understand the importance of completely eliminating all conflicts of interest, too many still have the attitudes of Albany, Georgia.

III • WHO'S IN CHARGE? PUBLIC PENSION FUND TRUSTEES

In creating public pension funds, state and municipal legislative bodies have provided for boards of trustees to oversee the funds' administration. In many cases the governor or mayor appoints trustees to represent state or municipal employers, and occasionally, trustee seats are reserved for public representatives or for appointees with experience in commercial banking, investment, insurance, or other finance-related areas. But the rather surprising—and disturbing—fact is that in few states are *employee* interests well represented on boards of trustees.

Some states—Connecticut, California, and Nebraska, for example—do indeed require the appointment or election of employee representatives. Moreover, employee representatives seem to be found more frequently on public pension boards of trustees than on those of corporate plans. Yet on many public pension fund boards, employee representatives are far outnumbered by those of the employers and, in a few cases, even by so-called public and expert representatives.

Although the boards of trustees of public pension funds, like the boards of directors of some corporations, may exercise relatively little power, their composition is important. If pensions are deferred wages, and pension funds are to be run for the sole benefit of employees, the trustees must be fiduciaries responsible to employees—no less than corporate directors must be fiduciaries responsible to stockholders. Only pension fund trustees who are viewed, and who view themselves, as fiduciaries responsible to employees can resist the political pressures that inevitably are applied to, and that result in conflicts of interest in the operation of, those funds. Only such trustees can hope to expose and eliminate politics and parochialism in the investment practices of public pension funds, whether such practices are legislatively prescribed or are pursued by full-time administrators.

Ideally, a board of trustees should be no more and no less than a board of overseers. Part-time members without investment experience should not involve themselves in day-to-day investment decisions. On the other hand, part-time trustees *with* investment experience certainly should not be selected from among the officers of banks and brokerage concerns that do business with the pension fund. The trustees should oversee the investment policy and performance of their staff and/or outside investment advisors, and the trustees should equip themselves, perhaps by hiring their own investment counselor or consultant, to monitor investment performance. Trustees should also serve the legislature by recommending statutory changes relative to investments, contributions, and benefits.

By those standards very few pension fund boards of trustees are satisfactory. Perhaps the coordinated approach created by California's Public Employees' Retirement Law comes closest. Under the law the Board of Administration of the California Public Employees' Retirement System establishes employer and employee contribution rates, accounts for the contributions, and determines membership and benefit eligibility; it also has exclusive control of the investment of the system's assets. In addition, the law requires detailed public disclosure of investments, a provision that appears to be unique among public pension funds. Although a number of states require periodic disclosure of securities and other investments held by their pension funds, California is the only state that requires disclosure of the names of outside investment advisors and broker-dealers and the amounts paid to them.[1] Further, the law requires that the board, in contracting for investment counseling services, "shall obtain proposals from all interested firms and conduct a public meeting at which a consultant or consultants will be selected by the board."[2]

The board, which has a staff of about 475 to administer a pension system with assets, as of June 30, 1975, of more than $6.9 billion, consists of eleven members. By statute, two members of the board are state officials: the director of finance and a representative of the State Personnel Board. Five members are elected by state and other public employees. The governor appoints four members, one of whom must be a bank officer; another, an official of a life insurance company; a third, an elected municipal government official; and a fourth, a representative of the public.

Although employee and public representatives do not automatically guarantee the best and most efficient management of a pension fund—any more than they insure the presence of independent voices on the boards of corporations, foundations, or other institutions—employees should be represented on pension fund boards because it is their interest that is at stake and their money in the fund, whether it be from direct employee contributions or employer contributions made in lieu of wages.

Teachers seem to have been more successful than general employees in gaining such representation, especially in those states and cities where teachers and general employees each have separate retirement systems. Employees have a majority of seats on pension fund boards in sixteen states, and in some of these, the pension funds cover both teachers and general employees.[3] Through organizations such as the National Education Association, teachers are continuing to press for greater representation with some success. For example, the Ohio legislature in 1973 increased the size of the board of the Ohio State Teachers Retirement System from five to seven, with the two additional seats to be filled by an election among the teachers; the teachers now have a majority, holding four of the seven seats.

However, the progress that teachers have made does not mean that they control, or are near to controlling, their own pension funds. In two-thirds of the states, teachers have not gained a majority of the seats on the boards of pension systems.[4] Moreover, in many of the states where teachers do hold a majority of the seats, they owe their positions to appointment by the governor rather than to election by the pension fund membership. In twenty-four states, there are no elected employee representatives on boards of pension funds covering teachers alone or covering teachers and general employees; these boards are composed entirely of trustees appointed by the governor and/or elected state officials.[5]

The Wisconsin State Teachers Retirement System appears to be the only public pension fund in the nation that is headed by a board consisting entirely of representatives elected by employee members of the system. But the Wisconsin board has no control over investment of the system's assets. Its job is to administer pension benefits. The system's $911 million investment portfolio is controlled by the State of Wisconsin Investment Board, a body commissioned to exercise exclusive control over the investment of money in twenty-three various state funds, including the teachers' retirement system. In Wisconsin, as in Connecticut and several other states—and in New York City as well, investment management has been centralized primarily for the purpose of improving investment efficiency and in the hope of increasing the return on investment. In the process it would appear that some control has been sacrificed—at least, by the employee participants.

Governors, treasurers, comptrollers, and other political officeholders, however, still exert substantial—and in many states and cities—dominant authority over pension fund asset management. Most pension fund boards of trustees necessarily delegate some portion of investment operations to their staffs, to investment committees, or to outside investment advisors, but political officeholders retain substantial or dominant authority, either as *ex officio* members of pension fund boards of trusees or through the power to appoint trustees. In some states political officeholders totally dominate pension fund boards. For instance, in South Carolina the statewide retirement system for teachers and other public employees (with $800 million in assets as of June 30, 1974) is governed by a board consisting wholly of officeholders: the governor, state treasurer, comptroller, chairman of the state Senate Finance Committee, and chairman of the state House Ways and Means Committee. In most states trustees are appointed by governors. The Iowa Public Employees Retirement System, for example, is administered by a commission of three members, each appointed by the governor for a six-year term. Other public pension funds are run by boards consisting of appointees plus *ex officio* members. The Michigan State Employees Retirement System is controlled by a Board of Administration with nine members, four appointed by the governor, and five *ex officio* members who are the state insurance commissioner, attorney general, treasurer, personnel director, and the deputy legislative auditor general.

In few, if any, public pension funds is asset management authority so centralized in political officeholders as in New York. The New York State comptroller, an elected official, is the sole trustee of two pension funds, the State Employees Retirement System, and the State Policemen's and Firemen's Retirement System, which together represent one of the nation's largest public pension fund operations. Under Comptroller Arthur Levitt, assets of the two systems grew from $1.8 billion to $4.6 billion in the decade between 1962 and 1971. In managing the assets, the state comptroller is guided by state statutes that, for example, set maximum limits on mortgage and common stock holdings, and he is assisted by an Investment Advisory Council and a Mortgage Advisory Council, each composed of bankers, insurance company executives, and other outsiders. The New York City comptroller is the custodian of the assets of five municipal employee pension funds, whose combined assets, covering policemen, firemen, teachers, other Board of Education employees, and other municipal workers, grew from $3.2 billion to $6 billion in the decade between 1962 and 1971. The city comptroller, who was Abraham D. Beame during much of the decade, managed the assets with the help of an outside investment advisory committee and outside investment advisor firms. Ultimate responsibility for administration of the five New York City pension funds rests, however, with the board of trustees of each fund. The city comptroller is an *ex officio* trustee of four of the five funds. In general, the other trustees of the five funds are either political officeholders or officers of municipal labor organizations.

The danger of having a close group of political intimates in charge of a pension fund was dramatized early in 1975, when the U.S. Department of Justice accused the former govenor of Oklahoma, David Hall, of approaching John Rogers, the secretary of state and chairman of the state retirement fund's board of trustees, with an investment prospect for the fund. It was alleged that Hall had been paid $50,000 by the Guaranteed Investors Corporation, formed only shortly before for the sole purpose of obtaining pension fund money, to help sway the board to invest $10 million in the company's collateral notes. Hall, in turn, offered $25,000 to Rogers if he would convince the board—the other six members of which were also state officials—to go along with the "investment." The board approved the purchase, but then Rogers exposed the bribe offer, and Hall ended up with a three-year jail sentence. Ironically, Rogers himself was impeached only a few months later for failure to report campaign contributions and other violations of state law, but he resigned before trial.[6]

More typically, *ex officio* members of pension fund boards are limited to state treasurers or finance directors and, in some states, to comptrollers, insurance commissioners, and directors of education. Governors' appointees usually require confirmation by state senates. Statutes generally do not specify qualifications beyond the requirements in some cases that one or several pension fund trustees be public employees or that a given number of trustees be experienced in the banking or insurance industries. Indiana appears to be the only state that requires political bipartisanship; the five trustees of the Indiana Public Employees' Retirement Fund are appointed by the governor, and no more than three may be of the same political party. Moreover, statutes do not attempt to identify and preclude potential conflicts of interest on pension fund boards; it is not uncommon to find trustees who are officers of banks or securities concerns that also do business with the pension fund.

For example, the board of the North Carolina Teachers' and State Employees' Retirement System—which had assets of $1.7 billion as of December 31, 1974—consists of ten trustees.[7] The state treasurer, who also is chairman of the board of trustees, and the state superintendent of public instruction are *ex officio* members. The other eight members, five of whom must be teachers or other state employees, are appointed by the governor. The governor filled the three other positions with the vice presidents of two North Carolina banks— Wachovia Bank and Trust Company and First Union National Bank—and a brokerage house account executive with Reynolds Securities, Inc., a large New York-based concern with offices in North Carolina.

The state treasurer selects the depository for the retirement system's cash-on-hand, which averages about $2 million. Most recently, it was Wachovia. The board of trustees has full power to invest and reinvest the system's monies in government obligations, corporate bonds, common stocks, and insured North Carolina mortgages, all within limitations fixed by statute. But authority to buy and sell stocks is exercised by an investment committee appointed by the board chairman. The members of the investment committee, who need not be trustees, are the vice presidents of Wachovia Bank and First Union National Bank, an officer of a consumer credit company, and a county administrator. An investment officer on the staff of the state treasurer is in charge of selecting the broker-dealers through which the retirement system's portfolio transactions are executed. A retirement system official said that Reynolds Securities participates in such executions. In addition, Wachovia and other banks assist the system in making mortgage investments.

With at least two of the three trustees appointed by the North Carolina governor employed by a bank or broker-dealer that does business with the retirement system, the potential for conflict-of-interest abuses is obvious. In an interview an official of the retirement system acknowledged familiarity with the conflict between a depository bank's interest in maximizing its deposit holdings and a pension fund's interest in minimizing its cash and deposits on hand. Furthermore, North Carolina statutes provide that "No trustee and no employee of the board of trustees shall have any direct interest in the gains or profits of any investment made by the board of trustees, nor as such receive any pay or emolument for his services." But the retirement system official argued that there is no violation of that statute in the present composition of the board.

Many public pension fund trustees seem to lend their banking, investment, and other pertinent business experience to the funds willingly, expecting little or no pay or other emolument. In addition, according to various pension fund administrators, seats on boards of trustees may well be regarded merely as honorary positions, used by governors, state treasurers, and other public officials for garden-variety political patronage purposes. Some trustees are only figureheads, doing little harm or good. A study of the Pennsylvania Public School Employees' Retirement Fund observed: "The existing pro-forma monitoring by the finance committee and the board of individual security acquisitions is at best useless and at worst can weaken the managers' sense of responsibility and their incentive to exert best efforts."[8]

Although many states have laws similar to North Carolina's which appear to bar outright thievery in the form of personal gain through knowledge of or participation in the investment processes of public pension funds, very few states have laws similar to California's, which attempt to spell out or enforce the fiduciary obligations of pension fund trustees. Given the political appointment process and the parochialism of public pension fund administration, it is difficult not to draw the conclusion that very few public pension fund trustees are viewed or view themselves as fiduciaries responsible solely to public employees.

IV • HOME SWEET HOME

One of the most persistent conflict-of-interest situations in the management of public pension funds results from the policy, followed by many funds, of hiring local bankers, brokers, and investment advisors and the practice of investing in local securities, even though better—or lower cost—services and higher yielding investments may well be available outside local boundaries.

Not infrequently, state or municipal law actually requires giving preference to local interests. For example, for many years Pennsylvania restricted state pension fund mortgage investments to Pennsylvania properties, although it seems that the pressures to keep the investment business at home are more frequently exerted informally. Almost all public pension fund executives who were interviewed described such pressures. One official, for example, heads a large state pension fund that is considered to be better operated, more sophisticated, and administered with better defined fiduciary standards than most public pension funds. This executive, who insists on anonymity, says: "I know there is pressure. I feel it all the time. Pressure to work with local brokers who are friends with this politician or that. If I give in, I'm forced to deal with retail firms in this state that have no block transaction capability. I resist. But too often in a lot of states you find local brokers getting pieces of the business, or you find that the investment advisor is the local bank that may or may not have the competence to handle the amount of money involved.'' One of the few public pension fund managers who will speak for the record is Irwin F. Smith, the former chief investment officer in the Office of the Treasurer of the State of Connecticut. Smith, however, is speaking about public pension funds generally, rather than Connecticut specifically, when he says, ''The elimination of politics in the selection of investment advisors and the execution of orders is necessary if the retirement systems are to obtain the maximum rate of return possible within the prudent man rule.''[1]

The desire to keep the pension fund business at home for reasons of political expediency also seems to exert some influence on the selection of investment advisors. In Oregon a local Portland firm was one of the seven outside money managers selected (although it was allotted a smaller amount of equity money to manage than any one of the other six). Idaho's public retirement system, governed by a relatively new and modern statute, initially hired First National City Bank of New York in 1965 as its stock and bond manager. After the fund grew to $100 million, it turned over part of the equity portion's management to Idaho First National Bank of Boise.

Pressure to make local businesses the beneficiaries of fees and other costs is even more apparent in the choice of broker-dealers to execute fund portfolio transactions. In Utah all broker-dealers in the state who are members of the New York Stock Exchange participate in investment transactions of the Utah State Retirement Board, although some out-of-state broker-dealers are used for block transactions.[2] The Bank of North Dakota executes transactions for its state retirement system through the two licensed resident brokers in North Dakota.[3] The Iowa Public Employees Retirement System uses Iowa brokers ''where possible.'' In practice, that means that Iowa's equity investment counselor, Alliance Capital Management, selects the brokers to execute large block trades, and the state treasurer selects the Iowa brokers who will receive the smaller transaction orders.[4]

Even when pension fund administrators attempt to choose investment advisors wholly on the basis of merit, politics often plays a part in the selection of broker-dealers. In an eastern state a few years ago, the legislature revised the pension fund statute by substituting the prudent man rule for detailed investment restrictions, by centralizing the state pension investments under a statewide authority, and by authorizing the fund trustees to hire outside investment counsel. The trustees hired New York and Boston investment advisors, large, experienced advisory firms that manage numerous portfolios for other institutional investors. As the choice was being made, however, concern was voiced about the fate of the twenty-two brokerage houses in the state, many of which had been in business for fifty years and longer. One advisor was told, according to his recollection, that the brokers were ''good guys—we have lunch with them all the time. You're not going to cut them out, are you?'' The advisor explained that he should be allowed to exercise discretion in executing portfolio transactions because the pension fund could save money when, for example, he could execute a block sale by combining the fund's shares of a particular stock with shares held by several other accounts. A thirty-thousand-share block might thus be traded at a favorable negotiated rate or advantageously in the third market, while none of the brokers in the pension fund's state could handle more than one thousand shares.

The trustees apparently agreed, but the state's brokers put pressure on legislators and other politicans, arguing that they deserved preferential treatment because for years they had contributed to the state's economic growth by underwriting state and municipal bonds. If they were now cut out of the pension fund's business, they warned, there would be more empty storefronts on Main Street and more unemployment in the state. The resolution of the problem was a compromise: the pension fund acquired its professional advisors, but the trustees retained the right to direct some of the brokerage commissions to local broker-dealers. Otherwise, the trustees claimed, the state legislature might have enacted a law to keep all the state's brokerage business at home. There was precedent, they said; bills had indeed been introduced in the legislature to require the pension fund to use local banks as custodians of the fund's securities.

Of course, some public benefits, in the form of business activity and employment, may accrue to a state or city that requires a public pension fund to deal with local banks and brokers. But such benefits are difficult to measure against the additional costs to pension funds if they fail either to hire managers who can identify the highest yielding assets or to obtain the best possible executions of portfolio transactions at the lowest charge. The prevailing attitude among pension fund managers who are under pressure to produce the highest possible return on investment is that pension fund assets should not be used for any purposes other than maximum investment return and, ultimately, maximum pension benefits. John E. Menario, chairman of the board of directors of the Maine State Retirement System, has said, "State government should work to further the economic development of Maine and reduce unemployment, but that doesn't mean that the Maine State Retirement System should invest in companies to do business in Maine, nor should the MSRS have any policy that favors Maine brokers, or investment counselors."[5]

Very few public pension funds make any effort to explain publicly the means or standards by which investment advisors, brokers, and banks are selected. Few public pension funds disclose even the names of those institutions that participate in the fund's investment management. Some public pension funds do not routinely report to public employees even the bonds and other securities and mortgages that comprise the fund's investment portfolio. The most complete disclosures appear to be made in the annual reports of the California Public Employees' Retirement System. California not only lists in detail each of the hundreds of securities issues held, bought, and sold, but appears to be the only state pension system that discloses also the amounts of business done annually with each participating investment advisor, broker, and bank. At the other end of the disclosure spectrum are public pension funds such as the Pennsylvania Employees Retirement Board, which issues an annual report on a single sheet of paper and discloses portfolio investments only in nine broad categories. Between the extremes are many public pension funds that disclose somewhat more than Pennsylvania but not as much as California. The annual report of the West Virginia State Board of Investments, consisting of the governor, state auditor, and state treasurer, lists the name and par value of each issue of securities held in a portfolio representing investments of state pension funds and other monies belonging to the state, but the annual report discloses nothing concerning securities traded or the brokers and other financial institutions that participated in the transactions. The annual reports issued by the New York State comptroller, as pension fund trustee, contain relatively complete disclosures concerning stock, mortgage, and other investment holdings, but disclose little or nothing concerning securities traded, the institutions that executed such transactions, or the investment advisors employed in managing the pension assets.

The conflict between the interests that try to keep public pension fund business at home, on the one hand, and the interest of public employees in efficient pension fund operations, on the other, is as well hidden as it is widespread.

V • "SOFT DOLLARS" AND SOFT ADMINISTRATORS

Until the past decade, both public and private pension funds invested most of their assets in government and corporate bonds. In 1950, when the book value of the assets in private, noninsured pension plans totaled $6.5 billion, only $800 million (12 percent) was invested in common stocks.[1] In contrast, by the end of 1972, when total assets at book value of the private funds had grown to $114 billion, about $72 billion (63 percent) was represented by common stocks.[2]

The entry of public pension funds into equities came even later. As recently as 1968, public pension funds' common stock holdings amounted to about $4.1 billion, or only 9 percent of total assets at book value. But by the close of 1972, their stockholdings had swelled to $14.2 billion, or 20 percent of assets.[3] Even the 1973 market decline apparently did not diminish the public funds' appetite for equities. By the end of 1974, the funds' stockholdings at book value had grown to $21.3 billion, 23 percent of total assets.[4] (See Table 19.)

It was probably the scars left by the stock market's crash and the subsequent dismal record during the Depression years that shaped the conservatism of public funds during the 1940s and 1950s. Buying bonds was safer. The few

Table 19: Assets of State and Local Government Retirement Funds (End of Year Book Value, in Billions of Dollars)

	1966	1968	1970	1972	1973	1974	1975
Cash and deposits	$0.4	$0.6	$0.6	$0.5	$0.7	$1.8	$1.7
U.S. government securities	7.9	7.2	6.4	5.1	5.4	5.6	6.8
State and local government securities	2.5	2.4	2.0	1.7	1.4	0.6	2.8
Corporate and other bonds	18.9	24.8	33.8	43.4	48.4	55.9	60.6
Common and preferred stocks	2.1	4.1	8.0	14.2	17.0	17.4	25.8
Mortgages	4.5	5.4	6.8	7.0	7.4	7.7	8.3
Other assets	0.7	1.7	—	—	—	—	—
Total assets	36.9	46.2	57.6	71.9	80.3	89.0	106.0

Source: Surveys published annually by the Securities and Exchange Commission in its *Statistical Bulletin.* See also SEC, Statistical Series Release No. 2599, June 28, 1972.

common stocks in a pension fund portfolio were included primarily for their dividend yield rather than for appreciation potential.

During the 1950s, however, when the stock market staged its broad advance, even conservative investors began to question the wisdom of placing the bulk of their investments in debt securities. Why buy bonds, which yield only 4 or 5 percent, when studies such as those produced by the University of Chicago in 1964 indicated that the annual appreciation of common stocks from 1926 to 1960—assuming reinvestment of both dividends and capital gains— was 9.3 percent?[5] "The salvation of the funds lies in common stocks," said James L. Sublett of the Ohio State Teachers Retirement System, in one of the many optimistic statements of that period.[6]

Before public funds could respond to the lure of stocks, however, impediments had to be removed. For years, a majority of states had restricted common stock purchases by public pension funds to 10 percent or less of the portfolio. If pension funds were to begin buying equities in earnest, those laws had to be rewritten.

Today, the law in Ohio is representative of the new legislatively prescribed investment policy. The Ohio law permits the Ohio State Teachers Retirement System (which had assets as of December 31, 1974, of $2.9 billion) to invest up to 35 percent of its assets in stocks. At the end of 1974, the system reported that $988 million—34.2 percent of its assets—were invested in common and preferred stocks.

Although the Ohio limitations are typical of many states, the range in public pension fund investment policy is still wide. In Pennsylvania, for example, it was not until 1973 that public pension funds were permitted to invest any assets in common stocks. Roughly half the states still limit stock investments to less than 25 percent of the portfolios.

Kansas, on the other hand, has probably gone farther than all but a few states in freeing pension fund managers of detailed statutory investment restrictions. The Kansas statute says simply that the assets ($315 million as of 1974) of the Kansas Public Employees Retirement System ''shall be invested and reinvested . . .to make the moneys as productive as possible, subject to the standard [the prudent man rule] set forth in this act.''[7] However, the Kansas legislation adds that the pension fund managers cannot invest more than 50 percent of the fund's assets in common stocks.

Even among states that now permit sizable investment in common stocks, many still limit the kinds of stocks that may be bought (a long, continuous record of dividends is one favorite criterion) or the percentage of the fund assets that may be invested in any particular industry. In New York, for example, no more than 30 percent of the assets of the state's Common Retirement Fund may be invested in utility bonds.

The movement of public pension funds into common stocks immediately raised some new basic conflict-of-interest problems. Although common stocks have typically generated higher returns, they are a riskier investment than bonds. For example, the rate of return on the Oregon Public Employees Retirement System's common stock portfolio grew from 7.47 percent in 1970 to 9.47 percent in 1971 and 13.87 percent in 1972. Then in 1973 and 1974, the portfolio was off 16.39 and 18.16 percent, respectively.[8] Connecticut provides in many respects a model of progressive pension fund management, but the common stock portion—some 25 percent—of its public employee pension fund assets was off 11.6 percent in the fiscal year ending June 30, 1974. But who should bear the increased risk of stocks, and who should benefit from their potentially higher returns? The taxpayers who pay the cost of pension plans? Or the public employees who collect the benefits?

Those who favor an increased level of common stock investing argue that the higher returns that common stocks have historically produced should ultimately benefit the employee members of the fund. In their view the higher appreciation relieves some of the strain placed on state and municipal tax resources that fund pension plans. Thus, goes their argument, retirement benefits are likely to be higher than if a more conservative method of investment is maintained.

The other view—and the one that seems to have increasing acceptance—is that a pension fund must take only limited risks. Because the assets of the pension fund are, in effect, deferred wages that will ultimately be used to support wokers during the most vulnerable period of their lives, every possible safeguard must be taken to prevent a sharp decline in the value of these assets, which the city or state might have difficulty making up.

Although public pension funds do not appear to have become deeply involved in the speculative excesses of the late 1960s, which David L. Babson, president of a Boston investment counseling firm, once called ''a national crap game,''[9] there were some plungers and losers among public pension funds. Virginia's very modern pension system suffered a $1 million loss on an investment in sixty thousand shares of Equity Funding Corporation, a go-go Los Angeles financial services company that plunged into bankruptcy in 1973 amidst a major scandal stemming from the financial irregularities of its insurance subsidiary.[10] After Arizona's $750 million state retirement fund suffered a $150 million loss in 1974, the State House of Representatives set up a special subcommittee in April 1975 to investigate the fund's operations. The House majority leader, Burton Barr, charged that the lack of supervision of the fund by the state retirement board and investment advisory council was "incredible."[11] The Virginia and Arizona experiences clearly demonstrate the hazards of investing in common stocks. In the pessimistic view of James P. Natale of the Colorado Public Employees' Retirement Association: "Investment in common stocks is too little, too late. There is no way for pension funds to combat inflation. If inflation continues at the rate of 10 percent a year, all pension funds will go bankrupt."[12]

The move of public pension funds into common stocks also entangled their administrators in the full gamut of conflict-of-interest problems that are involved in the allocation of brokerage commissions, the payment of fees for investment management, and the selection of outside managers. Purchasing bonds, after all, had been a relatively simple operation. There was little trading. Most large investors would buy a portion of the original issue of a bond offering and hold the securities until redemption. Only a modest amount of investment analysis was required because the Moody's and Standard & Poor's rating services evaluated the typical major bond issue.

Common stock investing complicated that comparatively serene world. The notion that even a blue chip holding, such as Texaco or DuPont, might sometimes be overpriced made it essential that large investors manage—and trade—their portfolios instead of merely monitoring them. The selection of which common stock to buy and which to sell required an in-depth knowledge of each company's prospects, as well as judgments about market timing. Commission rates for stocks were much higher than for bonds, of course, and portfolio turnover increased the commission dollars even further. How wisely pension funds were spending these commission dollars became a new issue of concern.

Although bond purchases had largely been handled internally, many public pension funds felt they were not equipped to make equity decisions and turned to outside investment managers for that portion of their portfolios. Between 1969 and 1973, for example, the $0.5 billion Oregon Public Employees Retirement System, while continuing to manage bonds internally, hired six outside money managers for equity investments and gave them responsibility for investing a total of $181 million. After several subsequent changes, there are now seven managers: BEA Associates of New York; George D. Bjurman & Associates of Los Angeles; David L. Babson & Co. of Boston; National Investment Services of America of Milwaukee; Columbia Management Company of Portland, Oregon; Fayez Sarofim & Company of Houston; and Rosenberg Capital Management of San Francisco. The Oregon Investment

Council, consisting of the state treasurer and four appointed members, reviews the selections and the performance of the equity managers, assisted by its own outside investment specialist, who is paid on a straight fee basis.

Connecticut also has outside advisors for equity investments: David L. Babson & Co. of Boston, Connecticut Bank & Trust Company, Putnam Advisory Company of Boston, Capital Guardian Trust of Los Angeles, and National Investment Services of America of Milwaukee.

A University of Pennsylvania study of the Pennsylvania Public School Employees' Retirement Fund in 1973 was particularly critical of the conflict-of-interest problems created by outside management of common stocks. The study warned that large investment advisors are often in a position to "derive various side benefits from the management of a large portfolio." For example, said the study, a large account could be used to influence market prices and hence "improve the performance of a small account. . . . In principle, such actions can be carried out only at the expense of the large account and should show up in performance measures. In practice, the effect of such actions may be difficult to detect."[13]

Bank investment advisors may create special problems, said the study, for they "may have an incentive to make loans to [i.e., buy the bonds, notes, or commercial paper] or invest in companies that are customers of the bank. The danger lies in the possibility that the bank trust department will make less secure loans or investments in order to shore-up [the bank's commercial] loans."[14]

A further problem of bank investment advisors is that they may channel commissions to those broker-dealers who maintain the largest deposits with the bank instead of using commissions to obtain the best possible portfolio executions or the highest quality research.

When investment advisors are also broker-dealers, the problem of securing the best executions may become even more critical. Advisors who are affiliated with broker-dealers "may have an incentive to direct trading to their own firms," said the study.[15] Furthermore, because broker-dealer members of the New York Stock Exchange are not allowed to trade exchange-listed securities elsewhere, the pension fund will be denied the advantage of prices that are sometimes more favorable off the exchange floor. An advisor affiliated with a broker-dealer could also engage in excessive pension fund portfolio trading to generate brokerage commissions.

Any investment advisor will certainly channel some of a pension fund's brokerage business to New York Stock Exchange member firms that provide the advisor with investment research and, possibly, other services. The abolishment of the New York Stock Exchange's fixed commission rate structure on May 1, 1975, did not end conflict-of-interest problems. As the University of Pennsylvania study concluded: "These problems do not disappear if commissions are negotiated or if trading is carried out in a dealer market (as with most bond trading). There remains the possibility that the manager may fail to negotiate for the lowest commissions or the best net price in order to obtain services for himself.''[16] Without safeguards and sophistication, the pension fund may not know what it is getting for its money or, indeed, whether the services it is paying for are benefiting the pension fund, the advisor, or the advisor's other clients.

Public pension fund trustees and administrators tend to pooh-pooh such criticisms, arguing that they are buying the best possible investment management and that honorable managers will handle commissions fairly. They allow their advisors to allocate brokerage on the basis of soft dollar services received and have no precise knowledge of whether the fund is getting the services it is paying for or even if the fund is getting good transactions at a reasonable price.

Among larger funds, one of two attitudes prevails concerning the soft dollar services approach. The dominant point of view is that public pension funds should let their commission dollars buy the full bundle of advice, research, execution, and other services, without attempting to break down costs and control expenditures for specific services. A distinct minority of these larger pension funds takes the view that they *should* unbundle the services so they can identify the cost of research, of exemptions, of performance measurement, and of other services.

Oregon illustrates the first attitude. The Oregon Investment Council, according to James L. McGoffin, director of the Oregon Public Employees Retirement System, encourages its investment advisors ''to utilize brokers and dealers who afford them valuable investment research . . . . Only incidentally, if they can find service in the State of Oregon, would they execute here. They go wherever the best price is available and the research is acceptable.''[17] However, although Oregon pays its advisors on a straight fee basis, McGoffin said that ''we are not sure that we recapture any portion of the brokerage commissions in the form of free or reduced-cost investment advice. Yet that service provided to our money managers could and should reduce the cost, at least on a negotiable basis.''[18] In other words McGoffin is saying that the fund is paying the advisor, as an informed professional, to do the fund's investing; and if the advisor has to buy outside help, such as research, he should pay for it by reducing his fee rather than by making the fund foot the bill.

Prudent management of public pension funds obviously requires detailed knowledge of investment costs, and this cannot be obtained when the costs of investment research and transactions are bundled together. Bundling makes it difficult, if not impossible, to judge the value of research and executions relative to cost. The soft dollar game, in which research was supplied ''free'' by broker-dealers wanting commission business, was not ended automatically when the Securities and Exchange Commission (SEC) ended the fixed-commission-rate system in 1975. Even under fully negotiated rates, a pension fund can spend valuable commission dollars on services that do not directly benefit it. But certainly, the end of commission rate fixing, by reducing the costs of trading, diminishes the severity of the conflict.

Some public pension funds *have* attempted to monitor executions and to evaluate costs and quality, but they found it a frustrating undertaking. In Oregon executions were monitored for a year by a San Francisco performance analysis firm. Says James L. McGoffin: "We found that computerized service . . .became in the long run, redundant, not paying for itself in terms of the error factor. It was terminated."[19] In North Dakota, where the pension fund's transactions are executed through the state's two licensed resident brokers, Tor A. Hegland, executive director of the Public Employees Retirement System, says: "The only way we can monitor executions is to compare our net rate of return with that of other state retirement systems."[20]

An investment officer of one of the nation's largest public pension funds, with assets of more than $6 billion, says: "There is no satisfactory way to monitor executions." This fund allows its four outside investment advisors to execute transactions through broker-dealers of their choice, and the fund assumes that the advisors make their decisions on the basis of quality of research and execution. The staff meets frequently with each of the four advisors to examine specific transactions and to try to determine whether any particular broker-dealer is receiving an unusually large amount of commissions. "But none of that is enough by any means to make us certain that we're getting the best executions and the lowest net prices," says the investment officer.

During the past year, as a result of new obligations imposed by the Pension Reform Act as well as the advent of negotiated commissions, an increasing number of private pension funds have renewed their efforts to monitor executions. In addition, a number of commercial monitoring services have sprung up. It remains to be seen, however, whether these efforts will be of sufficient value to justify their continuation.

Guarding against excessive portfolio trading is somewhat more easily accomplished. For example, Melvin Lechner, former administrator of the New York City pension funds as a deputy city comptroller, said he specifically prohibited Alliance Capital Management Corporation from doing business for the fund's accounts with Alliance's parent, Donaldson, Lufkin and Jenrette, a member of the New York Stock Exchange, "to avoid conflict of interest."[21] However, the available evidence suggests that very few pension funds have taken steps to protect against unnecessary turnover—"churning"—to generate added commission dollars.

Because public pension funds do not regularly disclose portfolio turnover rates publicly, it is difficult to tell how much excessive turnover occurs. The general absence of safeguards seems to suggest a lack of sophistication on the part of many pension fund trustees and administrators about the importance of commission dollars. As an example of the amounts of money that can be involved, during the second half of 1971, some seventy New York Stock Exchange member firms participated in New York City pension fund securities transactions. The firms that received the largest share of commissions were

Bear, Stearns & Company, $53,000; Salomon Brothers, $37,000; Becker Securities Corp., $36,000; and Neuberger & Berman, $33,000.[22]

The term *churning* resists precise definition, much as Justice Potter Stewart found it difficult to define hard-core pornography and had to conclude, "I know it when I see it." As would be expected, turnover rates for public pension funds have increased as, in the late 1960s, they moved into common stocks and attempted to boost investment yields. The SEC's *Institutional Investor Study Report* surveyed twenty-five public pension funds and found that common stock turnover increased each year between 1965 and 1969, from 3 to 11.7 percent.[23]

One of the SEC's conclusions was that turnover rates in public and private pension fund stock portfolios are substantially greater when funds are managed by investment advisors, many of whom are affiliated with broker-dealers, than when they are managed internally or by banks.[24] In 1969 the rate for investment advisor managed public pension plans was 49.4 percent; for bank-managed plans, 20.5 percent; and for self-managed private plans, 5.3 percent.[25] Although many public pension funds are managed by multiple investment advisors, apparently few funds compile data systematically and compare each advisor's turnover rate to determine whether advisors affiliated with broker-dealers are generating additional commissions.

On the surface one approach to lessening these problems would appear to be more widespread in-house management of public pension funds. Indeed, perhaps because boards of trustees and investment officers are charged by law with public pension fund investment responsibility, they *appear* to rely more heavily on in-house staffs than do private pension funds. The SEC's *Institutional Investor Study Report* surveyed 105 public pension fund accounts and reported that 72 were self-managed, a much higher proportion than in the corporate world.[26] The SEC study further reported, however, that about half of its sample of so-called self-managed public pension funds had only one or two investment analysts on their staffs and therefore had to rely on investment recommendations purchased from outside advisors. As a result the SEC study concluded that the public funds' purchase of outside investment advice "may mean that these systems are complying with the letter of the state statutes by placing their own orders but in spirit are being managed by outside advisers."[27]

A similar conclusion was reached by the University of Pennsylvania study. At the time the study was completed in 1973, the finance committee of the board of the Public School Employees' Retirement Fund had explicit responsibility for recommending how money was to be allocated among fixed-income, equity, and mortgage investments. The board employed Mellon Bank as its advisor for fixed-income and equity investments and Fidelity Bank for mortgage investment. Although the board was given legal authority for purchase and sale of specific securities, the study found that "in reality such decisions are made by the advisors; inputs into the decision process by the finance committee are minimal and approval by the board is strictly pro forma.'' The major reason was ''that the committee and the board seldom have any basis for questioning the recommendations of the adviser. The committee has neither the time nor the expertise and it does not have ready access to alternative sources of information and judgment.''[28] In addition, the study observed that, although the actual transfers of monies in purchases and sales of securities are carried out through the state treasurer's office, the advisors make the decisions concerning the choice of brokers and dealers who get the commissions.

Pension fund administrators in Oregon and a few other states have been able to build and strengthen their in-house staffs by obtaining authority from state legislatures to pay for pension system investment operations from investment earnings. Most, however, have not been able to obtain such authority, and they must rely for operating money on annual legislative appropriations. The stinginess of appropriations appears to be a principal reason why staffs tend to be small, young, and without depth of investment experience. It is not uncommon for public pension fund executive and staff members to leave to work for a fund's outside investment advisor,[29] if for no other reason than that their salaries tend to be lower than salaries in the outside investment community. The top investment analyst on Oregon's staff, for instance, receives less than $25,000 annually. In sum, the quality and quantity of in-house investment advice is further evidence that even many self-managed public pension funds are heavily dependent on outsiders and, furthermore, that they are ill-equipped for surveillance of the outside managers' performance or indeed for careful selection of those managers.

The conflicts that can arise when untrained, unsophisticated public pension fund trustees and administrators must operate in the world of professional money managers are not easily controlled. The funds require investment advice and research to know what investments to make and when and where to make them. The funds can purchase the assistance of professionals; they can attempt to develop the investment expertise of their internal staffs; or they can follow a middle course of using professional money managers, identifying the conflicts involved, and establishing effective safeguards and surveillance. Most large public pension funds say they follow this middle course. But if the states that have led the way are taken as standards, the great majority of public funds have failed to identify the conflicts and head off potential problems.

The University of Pennsylvania study maps one course toward effective controls. Assuming that the retirement fund will continue to be dependent on outside money managers and that the long-range rate of return from common stocks will be higher than the return from bonds or mortgages, the study recommended that the Public School Employees' Fund retain up to thirteen outside investment advisors or different types of investments. It suggested that the fund's board abandon a mere pro forma review of specific investments. And it proposed methods of monitoring advisors' investment performance by measuring rate of return and risk. While recommending that the legislature lift a number of investment restrictions—incuding the limitation of stock investments to issues listed on the New York Stock Exchange—the study advised keeping some limitations. For example, it suggested that investment in over-the-counter stocks be restricted to 20 percent of each advisor's portfolio, "since lack of historical price data prevents calculation of risk-adjusted return measures as reliable as those available for stocks traded on the exchanges."[30]

Most innovatively, the study recommended that "the compensation of portfolio managers be entirely 'on the table,' that is, limited to the fees paid by the fund."[31] To accomplish this the study said that the retirement fund should hire its own securities trader who would control all of the fund's transactions in common stocks and marketable bonds. The trader would be responsible for choosing the channels through which securities would be bought or sold and for checking the third market and regional exchanges as well as the New York Stock Exchange to obtain "the best execution at lowest net cost."[32] Investment advisors could still obtain investment research services from broker-dealers used by the trader, but they would be required to pay for the services by reducing the cash fees they charge the retirement fund. Thus, advisors who are broker-dealers, or who wish to buy services from broker-dealers by directing brokerage commissions to them, would be asked to submit alternative bids, one in terms of cash compensation and the other in terms of compensation in directed brokerage. "As an example, a manager might submit a bid of $50,000 cash or brokerage of $100,000." The net results, the study stated, "will assure that all benefits from directing trading business will accrue to the fund rather than to the managers. It also will assure that commissions will be fairly negotiated, it will eliminate any temptation by managers to trade excessively for their own benefit, and by combining orders of several managers it will realize trading economies."[33]

No state or municipal pension fund has fully embraced all these ideas. Yet some may be found at the more innovative funds, such as the California Public Employees' Retirement System. With a sizable in-house investment staff and a single outside advisor, California executes its portfolio transactions through a large number of broker-dealers, including third market firms as well as members of the New York and other stock exchanges. In the year ended June 30, 1975, California's stock transaction volume was $264.9 million, of which nearly $44 million represented transactions with third market firms. The fund's annual report noted: "Approximately 16.9 percent of the transaction volume was effected in the 'third market' because of the resultant cost savings to the Public Employees' Retirement System."[34]

Connecticut, too, has attempted with some success to separate investment advisory and brokerage costs by hiring its own trader for executing some stock orders placed by its four outside advisors. In the year ended June 30, 1973, the trader directed 8.7 percent, or $12 million, of the state's equity fund trans-actions to the third market and 0.7 percent, or $2.4 million, to the fourth market, consisting of broker-dealers who are members of the National Asso-ciation of Securities Dealers and who act as agents between institutional investors rather than as principals, which is the case in the third market.

Indeed, Connecticut went one step farther and was the first state to organize and own its own brokerage firm. Connecticut Nutmeg Securities, Inc., as it is called, was organized solely to acquire a seat on the PBW Stock Exchange (formerly Philadelphia-Baltimore-Washington Stock Exchange) and transact orders for the benefit of the state. The firm acquired its seat in December 1972, despite the opposition of some large brokerage houses and of the SEC. In an ensuing court fight, Connecticut's right to a stock exchange seat was supported by only four other states—Oregon, Kansas, Ohio, and Pennsylvania.

Connecticut realized savings almost immediately. Nutmeg's first transaction on the PBW Exchange took place on January 12, 1973. During fiscal 1974 Nutmeg executed approximately 25 percent of all stock purchases and sales for the Connecticut pension funds and reported a net income of $128, 845. "Based on these numbers, it appears that this operation saved the state's equity fund at least 20 percent of the transaction charges which would have otherwise been paid by the state to private securities brokers,"[35] the Office of the Treasurer said.

Lacking Connecticut's knowledge and nerve, the great majority of public pension funds never gained such benefits. For instance, after Connecticut obtained its PBW Exchange seat, the administrators of New York City's much larger pension funds announced that they were studying the formation of a brokerage firm, which, they said, could save the pension funds as much as $1 million annually.[36] The New York City administrators approached the New York Stock Exchange and made polite inquiries about acquiring a seat, and were told that they could not.[37] An affirmative response could hardly have been expected, if for no other reason than that the city's pension fund brokerage business was then spread among seventy New York Stock Exchange member firms and that the funds' $1 million gain presumably would have been the firms' $1 million loss. The city's pension fund administrators appear to have then dropped the matter, neither pursuing New York Stock Exchange membership nor joining Connecticut in its battle with the SEC.

The conclusion that emerges is that most of the nation's public pension funds, despite the very substantial size of their stock portfolios, are not fully aware of the transaction and management costs they are incurring and of the conflicts of interest that exist in the stock market. The reasons for this ignorance may stem in part from pension fund trustees' and administrators' newness to the stock market, but their reluctance may also reflect the old view that holds that interests other than those of employees' should be permitted to influence public pension fund policy.

Some public pension fund administrators express awareness of these potential conflicts of interest. Leonard W. McDonald, executive director of the Utah State Retirement Board, has stated:

It appears to me that brokers, advisers, and counselors should charge for the services that they provide and be paid by the managers for those services. I think the days of lumping all the different services together and including it in a fat commission rate are probably gone. In the future these services become very competitive, and the manager will better know what he's paying, will buy only those services that he feels are necessary, and will go to the organizations which have demonstrated execution capability.[38]

It is unfortunate, however, that even among those administrators who express an awareness of the problems, there are few who have done much about them.

VI • BONDS, CASH, MORTGAGES—AND BANKS

Although the move into common stocks has been the most revolutionary development in public pension funds in the last decade, fixed-income securities remain the major holding of public funds. As of the end of 1975, 74 percent of the $106 billion holdings of the public pension fund system was invested in fixed income securities.

Because fixed income securities involve less risk than stocks, potential conflicts of interest may seem of less consequence to pension fund beneficiaries. But in fact, fixed income securities also create conflict between the interests of beneficiaries and the political, social, or business interests of pension fund officials.

In serving the nonequity needs of public pension funds, banks usually occupy an even more predominant position than they do in the management of stock portfolios. Banks are the principal outsiders involved in managing the funds' investments in corporate bonds, short-term notes, and mortgages; they are the usual depositories for pension funds' cash; and they are frequently the custodians of the funds' bonds (and stock certificates as well). In short, banks play the major role in managing the $75 billion or so of public pension fund assets that are not in common stocks.

One of the most obvious potential conflict-of-interest problems created by this tie between banks and public pension funds involves the funds' cash position. Any assets that are not invested in securities remain in cash. From the point of view of the pension fund, the lower its percentage of cash—presumably the money would earn more if invested—and the higher the interest rate paid on that cash, the better off its beneficiaries will be. But the bank's interest is just the opposite. Its profits grow as the proportion of cash increases and the rate of interest is held low.

In general, public pension funds do not seem to have kept an excessive amount of cash on hand. For one thing it is clear that the cash and deposits of all public funds, as a percentage of total assets, generally have been less than those of private pension funds. Between 1962 and 1974, the figure for public funds ranged between 0.9 and 1.2 percent of total assets.[1] Over the same period, the comparative range for private pension funds was between 1.2 and

1.7 percent.[2] The cash and deposits of local, as opposed to state, public pension funds, however, were proportionately considerably higher than those of private or all public funds, suggesting that at the local level the conflicts may be more severe. Locally administered public funds, during their 1971-72 fiscal years, reported 2.1 percent of total assets as cash and deposits.[3] In the same period, state administered public funds reported cash and deposits amounting to only 0.8 percent of assets (see Table 20).[4]

Table 20: Distribution of Holdings of Public Pension Funds, as a Percentage of Total Assets (Book Value)

	1962[a]	1967[b]	1969[b]	1971[b]	1973[b]	1974[a]	1975
Cash and deposits	1.2%	1.1%	0.9%	1.0%	0.8%	2.0%	1.6%
Federal securities	26.2	16.9	11.9	7.2	6.7	6.3	6.4
State and local securities	17.4	6.2	4.9	3.4	1.7	0.7	2.6
Corporate bonds	40.8	51.6	54.7	56.2	60.0	62.8	57.0
Stocks	3.0	6.0	10.0	15.4	21.1	19.5	24.3
Mortgages and other	11.3	18.0	17.7	16.8	9.5	8.6	7.8

Note: Figures may not add due to rounding.
[a]Calendar years.
[b]For fiscal years ended in the twelve months preceding June 30.

Sources: For years 1962-71, Bureau of the Census, 1972 Census of Governments.
For years 1973-74, SEC, Statistical Bulletin, Annual Survey of Pension Funds.

In the opinion of some public pension fund experts, 2 percent is well above a reasonable level of cash. Naturally, a fund must have some of its assets in cash as money flows in from employees and is paid out to beneficiaries. The abuse occurs when a bank keeps this proportion too high. In this respect a study by the SEC is particularly damning. It found that pension funds managed by banks had substantially larger proportions of fund assets in cash and short-term securities than funds supervised by nonbank investment advisors or in-house managers.[5]

Holding too much cash is bad management. But it is even worse when a bank pays little or no interest on this money. For example, during the early 1960s, the New York State Retirement Systems regularly maintained interest-free deposits of nearly $2 million. At the close of the fiscal year on March 31, 1971, the amount on deposit in interest-free accounts had declined to $480,000[6] and, according to the state comptroller's office, the comptroller in recent years has changed his policy to take advantage of ''the time it takes for checks to clear'' and to improve ''good cash management.''

An interesting case pointing up the growing realization of the importance of managing cash effectively arose early in 1975, when the Kansas Public Employees Retirement System announced it was firing First National City Bank of New York as the manager of $88 million of the $315 million fund because the bank had maintained daily cash balances of $109,000 over the preceding sixteen-month period. Because the balances earned no interest, it was estimated that the fund had lost $8,000 to $12,000 in interest over that period. The bank argued that the daily balance was normal for an $88 million account, but the system withdrew the funds and placed the money with three investment counseling firms.[7]

Some banks that pay no interest defend this practice by arguing that the fees they receive for other investment services are so low that their cost must be covered in some other way. Whether this is true is hard to say. But what is particularly questionable is that in most cases public pension funds do not publicly disclose whether their funds are earning interest. This lack of disclosure provides an invitation for abuse.

Another problem area is in the use of local banks as custodians of pension fund securities, a service that can produce generous fees for the bank. Presumably, this policy was sensible when the funds only invested in fixed income securities that were held until maturity. However, it is not necessarily sound when pension funds frequently buy and sell securities. For example, nominee names are commonly used by many large investors to facilitate trading, but many state laws still forbid the use of nominee names for pension fund holdings, despite their apparent efficiency. The Illinois legislature in 1969 changed its law and permitted the state's pension funds' holdings to be registered in nominee names, but it still required that the custodian be an Illinois bank. An Illinois state investment officer was quoted as saying, "We're lucky we're not in Nevada. At least there are banks in Chicago that can handle our assets."[8]

Other large investors have taken the further step of depositing securities with the Depository Trust Company of New York, formerly known as the New York Stock Exchange Central Certificate Service, and thereby eliminating the need for physical transfer of securities. In 1972 the Virginia retirement system became the first public pension fund to use the Depository Trust Company, but no other public fund was quick to follow, presumably because funds are still required by law to use local banks as custodians.[9] The elimination of this requirement would mean a significant cut in pension fund overhead costs.

Still another concern about fixed income securities is that public pension funds, in turning to local banks for bond management, have taken the attitude that there is little point in actively managing bond portfolios. This is a view that has come increasingly under question, particularly in a period of high interest rates; many investment managers claim that a well-managed bond portfolio can produce an incremental return. Whether or not this view is correct can only be tested by time. But the point is that, by and large, the public pension funds have not even considered the value of active management.

On the other hand, public pension funds have been somewhat more innovative about acquiring direct-placement corporate bonds, which usually carry a higher yield but are less marketable than public issues and, because they frequently include nonstandardized terms, are often riskier. The University of

Pennsylvania study for that state's Public School Employees' Retirement Fund cautioned against a fund's reliance on its own bond investment advisor for evaluating the risk of private placement.[10] Yet most funds that acquire private placements appear to do just that. As far as could be determined, no pension fund with outside bond management takes the precaution of purchasing independent risk ratings of private placements, a service that is readily available.

That precaution seems particularly significant in the light of evidence presented in the study that from 1960 to 1966, the Mellon Bank invested a large proportion of the Pennsylvania teachers fund assets under its management in private placements, yet earned a significantly lower return than that achieved by a group of life insurance companies that invested in similar securities. Although Mellon's performance improved in later years, its relatively poor returns in the early 1960s point up the danger that arises when negotiated private placements are placed in pension fund accounts without independent evaluation or trustee scrutiny.

Perhaps the most severe conflict in the area of bond management, however, has been the practice of investing large portions of assets in state and municipal securities, which, because their interest payments are not taxed, pay a lower interest rate. Public pension funds, however, are exempt from income taxes; therefore, they derive no tax benefits from holding these issues. Thus, a public pension fund that purchased $1 million of state bonds paying a 5 percent interest rate would very probably be passing up a corporate issue of equal safety that might pay 8 percent—$30,000 a year more in yield for the life of the bond. From 1921 to 1961, the New York City retirement funds invested heavily in New York City bonds, with the proportion of these funds in the portfolio reaching a high point in 1961, when the city retirement funds' holdings of the city's obligations totaled nearly $2 billion, some 66 percent of their holdings.[11]

The policy of purchasing tax-exempt securities has a long and somewhat tainted history. The defenders of this practice argued, for the record at least, that public pension funds should be reservoirs of capital available for the borrowing needs of state and municipal governments and for the financing of socially desirable projects—from streets and sewers to low-income housing. Why invest in the projects of distant corporations or other governments when worthy projects were available at home?

In practice, however, the funds' investments in the obligations of their own states and municipalities do not seem to have been made for any high public or social purpose. Although their motivations are buried in unrecorded history, it is likely that the commitments were made by state and municipal treasurers as a matter of convenience—and occasional necessity—to support the market for public obligations or even to fund some pet political project.

Today, the almost universal attitude among public pension fund trustees and administrators is that the funds' assets are, or should be, dedicated to no other objective than the ultimate enhancement of pension benefits. This conviction was strongly stated by James L. Sublett of the Ohio State Teachers Retirement System:

I cannot see why there should be any great interest on the part of tax-exempt organizations in the purchase of tax-exempt securities. The lower yields available on state and municipal debts can only increase the liability of the employer. If we assume that the contributions made by the employer for the benefit programs available to public employees are a matter of deferred compensation, and that alone, then I cannot see why there is any "obligation" in the form of state or municipal purchase. I know of no good reason why public employees, whether they be teachers or other public employees, should utilize their funds in financing public improvements. Public improvements should be the responsibility of all citizens and not of any segment of our population.[12]

A few public pension funds have sold all their state and municipal government bonds and thus eliminated the conflict of interest between public employees and their employers. The Iowa Public Employees Retirement System, for example, holds no such bonds. Many more pension funds still hold small or substantial amounts of state, municipal, county, school district, water district, and other types of tax-exempt bonds. The Ohio State Teachers Retirement System, at the end of 1972, retained $4 million of bonds issued by Ohio counties and universities, a very small portion of its $2.3 billion portfolio.[13] The West Virginia Board of Investments, as of June 30, 1972, still held $2.4 million of county and municipal bonds and $219,000 of State of West Virginia bonds among its total investment holdings of $430 million.[14] The New York State pension funds, administered by the state comptroller, held $39 million of state and municipal government bonds at the end of its 1972 fiscal year.[15] However, locally administered pension funds are the chief perpetuators of this practice. In 1972, when locally administered funds' assets stood at $17.6 billion, their holdings of state and municipal bonds amounted to $1.7 billion, or nearly 10 percent of assets. That compares with only 1.3 percent for state funds.[16]

Some state and local fund administrators have said that they intend to eliminate all such government bondholdings, but others have voiced no such intention. The New York State comptroller's office acknowledges that interest rates on its holdings of public obligations "are much lower than corporate bonds," but says that the public bonds "will not be eliminated."[17] The Arkansas Public Employees Retirement System will eliminate its very small municipal bondholdings "if a buyer can be found without sacrificing too much off par value."[18] In general, public pension funds' unwillingness to eliminate their holdings of state and municipal issues appears to reflect a reluctance to take book losses and a fear of weakening the market for those bonds. Neither, however, is a particularly sound reason from the perspective of the members of the fund.

A somewhat similar conflict-of-interest problem is the practice engaged in by many public pension funds of investing a disproportionate amount of their assets in regional mortgages. Indeed, many public pension funds that hold or have held relatively large amounts of state and municipal government bonds have also invested in mortgages. For example, the New York State pension funds of which the comptroller is trustee have held relatively large investments for many years in both public obligations and private mortgages. On the other hand, the North Dakota Public Employees Retirement System is typical of funds that do not invest in either public obligations or mortgages.

This correlation, plus the fact that many state and municipal governments have required that the investments be confined to real property within the state or city, suggests that the mortgage investments of public pension funds were authorized as much for the benefit of local construction industries, lending institutions, and home buyers as for pension fund beneficiaries. New York State Comptroller Arthur Levitt addressed himself to this potential conflict when he said, "To accept a mortgage investment at below market is to give to a homeowner what a taxpayer must eventually pay." [19]

The growth of mortgage holdings slowed after 1967, presumably because public funds were turning to the stock market for higher investment returns. Although in 1962 public fund holdings of mortgage investments amounted to 11.3 percent of assets, at the end of 1973, the mortgage holdings of public funds amounted to $6.7 billion at book value, a drop to about 7.2 percent of their total assets.

This is not to say that mortgages are not legitimate investments. Mortgage yields historically have been higher than those available from corporate bonds. Furthermore, mortgages that are insured by the Federal Home Administration (FHA), the Veterans Administration (VA), or some other federal agency carry little or no risk. And if yields obtainable within a state or city are comparable with mortgage yields elsewhere, and if an ample supply of mortgages exists within the state or city, there appears to be no reason why a public pension fund should not invest at home. But when local yields are not so high as those obtainable elsewhere, it makes no sense for a legislature to limit mortgage acquisitions to a pension fund's home state or city. The University of Pennsylvania study for that state's pension fund recommended that the Pennsylvania legislature lift the restriction limiting mortgage acquisitions to Pennsylvania properties and also recommended that the fund hire a second mortgage investment advisor, preferably in California. [20]

Such investments do present a difficulty, however: noninsured mortgages and direct real estate investments pose problems of selection, valuation, and surveillance that few public pension funds are equipped to handle. Unlike large insurance companies and banks, public pension funds do not have sizable staffs of mortgage experts and chains of mortgage correspondents. Although local banks and mortgage brokers often put together packages of conventional as well as insured residential mortgages for pension funds, they may derive benefits from their correspondents that, like soft dollar research obtained by stock investment advisors, obscure the true cost of mortgage acquisitions to pension funds. [21]

Because the terms of mortgage investments are frequently reached through negotiation rather than through the action of market forces, the opportunity for abuse is considerable. In one widely publicized scandal, three Ohio residents, acting as finders, presented real estate investment proposals to the investment officer of the Ohio State Teachers Retirement System.[22] The loans were backed by federal mortgage insurance, and the investment officer issued commitment letters covering more than $20 million of the funds requested. But the investment officer, who subsequently resigned, and the three finders, along with other defendants, were cited by the SEC in connection with its investigation of the trading in the stock of Four Seasons Nursing Centers of America, Inc. The federal district court in Columbus in August 1972 entered a temporary restraining order against the investment officer, the three finders, and certain other defendants.[23]

More pervasive political pressures can influence the selection of mortgage investments by public pension funds. In Hawaii two trustees of the Employees' Retirement System resigned in 1969 when a lawsuit seeking their removal was threatened. The trustees allegedly had acquired a financial interest in a $1.2 million loan approved by the retirement system. Hawaii's attorney general was critical of the board of trustees and charged that persons "supposedly privy to vital information" germane to the state's investigation of the system did not come forward with that information. News accounts stated that there had been continuing "subtle pressure placed on the trustees by politicians who apply for loans or represent potential borrowers." It was further alleged that retirement system records at the time "showed that over the past 11 years politicians had been involved in some way in nearly half the loans made by the $300 million system."[24]

Under the best of circumstances, noninsured mortgages and loans cannot be valued in a readily available marketplace. Because risk determinations are imprecise, the University of Pennsylvania study asserted that "It becomes difficult to determine whether managers are acting in the best interests of the fund."[25] Some public pension funds avoid these problems by limiting mortgage investments to FHA- and VA-insured mortgages. In Hawaii, following the resignations of the two trustees, the retirement system placed a one-year moratorium on all commercial loans and thereafter altered loan procedures. At present, the system will purchase only "established" mortgages from banks under an arrangement whereby the bank that processes the loan lends half the amount and the retirement system lends the other half. "We have heard of no other charges of questionable loaning practices,"[26] Fred W. Bennion, director of the Tax Foundation of Hawaii, has subsequently stated.

The continuing conflict between the interests of beneficiaries and the interests of public pension fund administrators relative to fixed income securities most recently and dramatically has been summed up in the course of New York City's financial crisis.

Before that crisis erupted in the summer of 1975, the administrators of both the New York City and New York State public pension funds agreed with most public pension fund administrators that the funds should severely curtail, if not eliminate, their holdings of state and municipal obligations. Arthur Levitt, state comptroller and sole trustee of the state's pension funds (more than $6 billion in 1973), proudly reported that holdings of federal, state, and municipal obligations had been reduced to 31 percent of investments in 1971 from 51 percent in 1962.[27] Melvin Lechner, administrator of the city's pension funds ($6.5 billion in 1973) under then City Comptroller Abraham D. Beame, reported with equal pride that the funds had reduced their holdings of New York City obligations to 7 percent of assets in 1973, down from 57.7 percent in 1962.[28]

But in 1975, when New York City faced the specter of bankruptcy, Comptroller Levitt and Mayor Beame changed their tunes. Under intense political pressure, the decline in the state and city pension funds' holdings of state and municipal obligations was reversed. The New York State pension funds successfully avoided purchasing New York City securities, but the state retirement systems did purchase $25 million of Municipal Assistance Corporation bonds, and by 1976 the state pension funds held $1.3 billion of New York State notes—16 percent of the pension fund portfolio of which the state comptroller is trustee. The New York City pension funds reversed course even more dramatically. In 1975 the city pension funds sold $155 million of corporate bonds at a loss, in order to purchase MAC bonds.[29] By the end of 1975, the city pension funds had brought $1.2 billion of city and MAC securities; the figure had risen to $2.2 billion by the end of 1976 and was scheduled to grow to $3.5 billion in 1978.

This conflict between the interests of pension fund beneficiaries and administrators did not lie in the low interest rate on the bonds, for they had reached a record high for municipal obligations. The problem, of course, was the investor's fear that the city would default on its obligations. The pension funds' purchase of the bonds thus placed city employees in double jeopardy. The city was borrowing to meet its payrolls, and the bonds were purchased for the pension funds despite widespread fears of default.

VII • SUMMARY AND CONCLUSIONS

In theory, the interests of employers and employees in sound public pension fund management are identical. Indeed, the equation seems simple: the more effectively fund assets are managed, the more employer costs may be reduced and employee benefits increased.

In practice, however, many conflicts of interest arise. Trustees, administrators, and their political superiors in statehouses and city halls have not begun to acknowledge, much less erect safeguards against, these conflicts.

The funding problem is one of the most important of the unresolved conflicts. Insufficient funding saves the taxpayers contribution dollars, but it threatens the solvency of the fund. It has been argued that underfunding, which usually arises from liberalizing benefits today while letting another generation of legislators and taxpayers decide how to foot the bill tomorrow, represents no real problem. It is averred that public employees' interests are not really sacrificed, because the fund will always have a legal claim on the tax revenues of the state or city; the problem is merely a fiscal one rather than a conflict of interest. What this argument ignores is that significant underfunding encourages irresponsible benefit liberalization, which in turn is likely to lead to even more pronounced underfunding. Further, underfunding may increase costs if the interest that a state or city is required to pay on underfunded pension liabilities is less than the pension fund could have earned by investing the missing contribution. And even assuming that a future generation of legislators and taxpayers will be willing and able to meet substantial pension liabilities, the past service payments will almost certainly inhibit desirable benefit liberalization.

As Thomas P. Bleakney, a consulting actuary, has said:

The level or kind of benefits to be provided in public employee retirement systems and the financing of those benefits are subject to decisions made under pressure in a political atmosphere. Ideally, orderly procedures should exist to assure that the cost implications of liberalization of eligibility provisions and benefit levels are evaluated before legislators take action. Rarely do such procedures exist, and even when they do, they frequently work imperfectly.[1]

The purchase by public pension funds of securities issued by their own states and municipalities represents another intertwining of pension fund and governmental finances and thus a second major area for possible conflict of interest. If a tax-exempt fund's yield from state and municipal bonds were equivalent to that obtainable from other securities, a case could be made for investing in public obligations. But even under those circumstances, there would be a potential danger in the temptation to use assets as a sinking fund to support the market for local issues, perhaps masking a government's deep-seated fiscal and financing problems. In any event the tax-exempt status of state and municipal bonds does automatically mean that their investment return to pension funds is lower than that of corporate issues of similar quality; so there appears to be no justification for their purchase by public pension funds.

To an important degree, in recent years there have been improvements in the two areas. Increasingly, state and municipal governments have been required by court actions to begin funding past service pension liabilities. Many public pension funds have considerably reduced their state and municipal bond-holdings to obtain higher yields in other securities. Yet important conflicts remain.

There is the political pressure—sometimes written into state and municipal pension fund statutes, but more often covertly applied to pension fund managers—to keep a pension fund's banking, brokerage, mortgage, and other investment business within the state or city. Of course, there is no reason why public pension funds should not channel such business to firms in the pension fund's home state or city, if the firms are capable of providing investment services that are equivalent in quality and price to those available outside. However, the evidence suggests that equivalent services frequently are *not* available at home—particularly for purchases and sales of corporate stocks. At the same time, many have attempted to keep all the business they can at home, regardless of availabilities elsewhere: stock brokerage commissions have been confined to home state or city banks; and mortgage investments have been limited to local real estate and mortgage brokers. When this parochialism dominates investment policy, mortgage investment opportunities are necessarily limited, and the efficiency of security management is often restricted. In addition, states that by law or custom execute stock transactions only through New York Stock Exchange member firms located in the state automatically forfeit the opportunity that may be available to excute transactions at a better price or lower net cost in other locales or markets.

These political considerations may very well produce more subtle, generally unrecognized effects. When inexperienced public pension fund trustees and administrators are tied by law or political custom to particular brokerage and banking institutions, their attitudes and decisions are shaped by existing institutional molds. For example, a pension fund that is tied to New York Stock Exchange member firms has no incentive to hire its own trader, who would allocate portfolio transactions on the basis of best execution and lowest net price. It would be unlikely to have either the will or the way to identify and guard against potential conflicts of interest that arise in the use of soft dollar commissions, in the employment of an investment advisor affiliated with a broker-dealer, or in the allocation of brokerage commissions on any basis other than best execution and lowest net cost.

The inexperience of many public pension fund administrators compounds the problem. To help them cope with these conflicts, public pension funds must be encouraged to acquire, with the help of outside professional investment counsel or in-house staffs, sufficient expertise and knowledge at least to oversee the management of assets. Some public pension fund administrators, such as those in California and Ohio, have built large in-house staffs that have assumed some or most of the functions of professional investment advisors. Connecticut, on the other hand, has built an in-house staff—including a securities trader—to handle a large part of the brokerage and trading functions, but it still relies on outside professionals for investment advice. Oregon has taken a different approach, managing its bonds in-house but relying on outside professionals for both investment advice and trading in the equity area.

But only a handful of states—including California, Ohio, Connecticut, and Oregon—seem to have identified conflict-of-interest problems and taken action to guard against them. It is no coincidence, even though such considerations may not have completely disappeared in those states, that politics appears to play a lesser role in asset management decisions than in many other states.

There also is a correlation in public pension fund administration between political entanglements and secrecy on the one hand and relative political enlightenment and public disclosure on the other. Most public pension funds make financial reports of some kind to the legislature, to the governor or mayor, to employees, and/or to the general public. The great majority of such disclosures are wholly inadequate to allow legislators, employees, or the public to judge the adequacy of fund administration. Quite typical is the Pennsylvania Public School Employees' Retirement Board's annual report to members, consisting of a three-page leaflet listing investments by categories and disclosing receipts and disbursements for the prior years. Some pension fund reports list names and amounts of individual bond, stock, and mortgage holdings as of the end of the year, and other pension funds supply such lists on request. Rarely do reports disclose individual issues or mortgages bought or sold within the year. With very few exceptions, reports that do list individual issues held or traded use par or book values rather than disclosing market values. Names of broker-dealers with whom the pension fund did business are also almost never stated. California appears to be the only state that discloses the names and amounts paid to individual investment advisors, banks, broker-dealers, and mortgage brokers. Moreover, California, in 1974, became the first state to choose its investment advisors after public meetings in which competitive bids are solicited.

Openness and efficiency in the administration of public pension fund investments are not automatically achieved under any particular administrative formula. Politics and secrecy have not necessarily been eliminated by throwing all the politicians and political appointees off pension fund boards, replacing them with employee, union, or public representatives. Employee representatives sit on a number of public pension fund boards that display little enthusiasm for public disclosure. For example, public employee union officers were on the board of Hawaii's retirement system when alleged conflicts of interest arose in connection with mortgage investments.[2] This nation's experience with public representatives on the boards of such institutions as stock exchanges and corporations has been less than impressive. Quite obviously, openness, efficiency, and the other attributes of fiduciary obligation spring from deeper wells.

In those few states where public disclosure is the rule, where conflicts of interest have been identified, and where safeguards have been erected and some efficiencies appear to have been achieved, the guiding philosophy appears to be simply that public pension fund assets are to be managed solely in the interests of employee participants. This attitude does not seem to have sprung from magnanimity but, as in Connecticut, from the fiscal necessity to obtain greater efficiency and the best possible investment return.

Once the interests of the members of the pension plan are recognized as paramount, the use of the plan's funds for political or other public purpose becomes an acknowledged contradiction. For example, Oregon law states that "The Public Employees' Retirement Fund hereby is declared to be a trust fund for the uses and purposes set forth [in the retirement law] and for no other uses or purpose. The state of Oregon and other public employers that make contributions to the fund have no proprietary interest in the fund or in the contributions made to the fund by them."[3] No other state is apparently so explicit in disavowing the use of pension fund assets for political or other nonemployee-related purposes.

The dedication of public pension fund assets to the security and betterment of employee benefits does not dictate employee control of pension fund boards. State and municipal governments and their taxpayers have an equal stake in maximizing investment returns. Employer *and* employee representation is desirable so one group can watch the other, and public representation, too, can be useful if it brings pertinent investment experience to the board. But part-time trustees, whomever they represent, do more harm than good when they pretend to control—or worse, do control— day-to-day investment decisions. The role of trustees, whether assets are managed in-house or by outside professionals, should be to set policy and monitor the managers; and that role should be performed with expert assistance and on the basis of investment results over a reasonable period, rather than by trying to second-guess individual securities transactions.

If California and a few other states are models of openness and efficiency in public pension fund asset management, the great majority of states and cities fall short of that model.Thus, the ultimate goal of providing public employees with income security in retirement remains distant while, at the same time, the fate that has come upon the public pension plans in New York dramatizes for Congress and the nation the conflicts of interest that, to some degree, beset virtually all of the state and local pension funds in the United States.

At least in part because of recession and unemployment, in the past several years, various public pension funds have come under a variety of political pressures to change course by investing large sums in public or political undertakings that may be justified on social or economic grounds but that appear to be unjustified and imprudent if public pension funds are to be managed in the interest of public employees. In Pennsylvania, for example, the public employees and public school employees pension funds, with combined assets of more than $5 billion, came under political pressure in 1976 to supply a part of the $200 million of financing with which Pennsylvania hoped to attract a new Volkswagen assembly plant.[4] The attention of Congress and the nation was focused most dramatically, however, on the conflicts in NewYork.

Comptroller Levitt, as trustee of New York State pension funds, purchased $25 million of Municipal Assistance Corporation bonds, even though an official in the comptroller's office had said, "We do not think it would be prudent for us to buy them. Do we become the lender of last resort for every local government that gets in trouble?"[5] During the state's 1976 borrowing crisis, the state pension funds' holdings of $1.3 billion of New York State notes, representing 16 percent of the funds' portfolio, also was imprudent if the standard of prudence is the 10 percent limitation on such investments written into the 1974 Pension Reform Act that applies to private pension funds. The same 10 percent limitation is contained in the proposed federal statute extending reform to public pension funds. Yet, although the New York State pension funds came to the rescue by purchasing MAC bonds and state notes, Comptroller Levitt stoutly resisted political pressures that would have involved the state pension funds much more deeply in the rescue efforts. He refused to invest more than $25 million in MAC bonds, despite a law enacted by the state legislature directing the state pension funds to buy $125 million of MAC bonds; the state courts held the law to be unconstitutional.

The conflict involving the New York State comptroller is both implicit and explicit. At one point in the fiscal crisis, Levitt addressed himself to the conflict between his roles as state comptroller and as pension fund trustee. Concerning the interest rate to be paid on state notes purchased by the pension funds, Levitt said: "I would like to see, on behalf of the state, as low a rate as possible, and, on behalf of the pension funds, as high a rate as possible."[6] The conflict has been further acknowledged and an attempt to deal with it has been made in an arrangement under which the New York State budget director, rather than the comptroller, approves the rate of interest on any New York State securities sold to the state pension funds.

The New York City pension funds, on the other hand, have been much less successful in resisting the immense political pressures to invest much more heavily in city and MAC securities, and the still larger conflicts have hardly been acknowledged or dealt with.

The House Pension Task Force has asserted that the solvency of the New York City and State pension funds has been impaired, and has said, "Public plans in general do not appear to be operated within the general financial and accounting parameters established by custom and practice in the private retirement plan field. The absence of any external independent review has perpetuated a level of employer control and attendant potential for abuse unknown in the private sector. Numerous instances of the use of plan assets to finance the operations of governmental units sponsoring the plan were entered into the hearing record."[7]

If public pension plans cannot or will not themselves move toward the goal of prudent asset management, it seems reasonably certain that, sooner or later, the responsibility for fullfillment of the retirement expectations of state and municipal employees will be assumed by the federal government.

VIII • A NOTE ON THE SOCIAL SECURITY SYSTEM

In the United States, responsibility for employee retirement income security is divided between private and public pension funds and the federal government, which operates the Social Security System as well as pension systems for railroad workers and federal government employees. If in the future the private and public sectors are unable to provide a satisfactory level of supplementary retirement benefits to a sufficiently wide range of workers, the federal govenment could assume total responsibility through enlargement of the benefit structure of the Social Security System—a possibility that is frequently mentioned by critics of the private and public pension systems. Although federal assumption is not an imminent likelihood, the possibility clearly exists in the federal government's power to withdraw the tax deduction it accords to corporate pension fund contributions and to the capital appreciation of funds, diverting those additional tax revenues into the Social Security System. Although the same federal stick would not reach state and municipal pension funds, those funds presumably also could be absorbed into the Social Secuity System because most state and municipal employees are now enrolled in that system. Therefore, a brief examination of Uncle Sam's performance as money manager is pertinent as a postscript to a study of the investment shortcomings of public funds.

The Department of the Treasury is designated by law to hold and manage the assets of a number of federal trust funds containing monies that are accounted for separately from general revenues and expenditures. Among such funds the Railroad Retirement System is the only federally administered pension plan for the employees of a single industry. The Department of the Treasury also holds and manages the assets of the Civil Service Retirement and Disability Fund, covering federal civilian employees. It is, in addition, the custodian of the four Social Security funds: the Federal Old-Age and Survivors Insurance Trust Fund, the Federal Disability Insurance Trust Fund, the Federal Hospital Insurance Trust Fund, and the Federal Supplementary Medical Insurance Trust Fund. The Social Security cash benefit and Medicare programs are financed through the four trust funds. Each of the four federally administered trust funds is nominally headed by a board of trustees consisting of the Secretaries of the Treasury; Labor; and Health, Education and Welfare. The railroad pension system is nominally administered by the members of the Railroad Retirement Board. The Secretary of the Treasury is designated by law as the fiscal agent of the board and is assigned the duty of investing the Railroad Retirement System's assets in interest-bearing obligations of, or guaranteed by, the United States.

The uniqueness of the federal government notwithstanding, interest earned on the federal funds' investments can help to meet rising benefit costs no less than they can help to meet the rising costs of other public and private pension plans; the federal trust funds, like other public and private plans, must meet their costs from contributions and investment earnings. If or when general public revenues are used to subsidize the federal funds, Social Security will no longer be a trust function but will become unmistakably and completely a general welfare scheme. Therefore, the Secretary of the Treasury, like many other money managers, has been under considerable pressure, in this case from Congress, to improve the trust funds' investment returns. There has been no suggestion that the Secretary plunge into the stock market with the funds' billions, but there are opportunities for higher returns that the Secretary has not seized because of the inherent conflict between his duty to manage the total public debt at the lowest possible cost to taxpayers and his obligation to obtain the best possible investment return for the beneficiaries of the federal trust funds.

The plight of the Railroad Retirement Fund reflects, in part, the effects of the Secretary of the Treasury's conflict. This is not to say that the Secretary will be at fault if the fund should become bankrupt; the Railroad Retirement Fund, like almost all other private and public pension funds, has been grossly underfunded, and to that extent, the Secretary's ability to produce investment earnings has been limited. In 1974 Congress voted to restructure, and in effect bail out, the Railroad Retirement Fund. But the long-range problems of the fund, and of a Congress trying to cope with them, are not an overdrawn example of what could happen to private pension funds in other mature industries, and to public funds in some states and cities, as benefit costs rise in the face of grossly inadequate past funding and investment earnings.

The failure to fund future pension obligations as they are incurred has reflected the belief that benefit costs will be met on a pay-as-you-go basis, that is, by contributions from present and future generations of employers and employees. The implications of that assumption, as it applies to the Social Security System, are staggering. That system covers almost the entire U.S. working population and rests on the premise of an ever-expanding American economy. The unfunded liabilities of the Social Security System are vastly larger than those of any other public or private pension fund. Social Security fund reserves held by the Department of the Treasury are now less than one year's benefit costs.[1] Yet the system has been stated to be "actuarially sound."

Theoretically, the general revenues and taxing powers of the federal government are behind the Social Security System in the event of an emergency, but Congress has not yet seen fit to dip into general revenues (with the exception of certain limited, specific categories of welfare-oriented Social Security benefits). Whatever the validity of the system's actuarial assumptions, there is one particular reason for being very wary about funding the Social Security programs more fully. Members of Congress have time and again proved themselves just as politically motivated as state legislators when they vote to increase benefits without simultaneously increasing contributions. If Social Security programs were more fully funded, Congress would be still more tempted to liberalize benefits with even less regard for future costs.

The assumption about the ability and willingness of future generations to pay the bill for incurred liabilities has come upon hard times when applied to a single, mature industry: the railroads. The Railroad Retirement Act was passed in 1935, but as it turned out, railroad employment had reached its peak during World War I and had declined steadily thereafter (except for a temporary increase during World War II). Declining employment increased the ratio of retired beneficiaries to active workers and benefit payments relative to contributions. By 1971 railroad employment was down to approximately 600,000, but the number of retirement system beneficiaries was up to 980,000. What is more, during the years of declining employment, benefit provisions were liberalized numerous times, generally at the same time that Congress was increasing Social Security benefits. Railroads and their employees contributed almost twice as much to their fund as employers and employees covered by Social Security, but retired railroad workers also collect benefits about twice as large as Social Security benefits. Although the assets of the Railroad Retirement Fund grew to more than $5 billion, contributions and investment earnings were never large enough to fund the system on an actuarially sound basis; and in 1972 the system's unfunded liability was estimated to be $14 billion.[2] In 1971 for the first time disbursements exceeded receipts, and the following year the Commission on Railroad Retirement predicted that, on the basis of its projections of railroad employment and retirement rolls, the fund would experience annual deficits growing to $330 million in 1980 and $578 million in 1985, and that it would be bankrupt three years after that.[3]

On June 30, 1974, the public debt stood at $486.2 billion (not including obligations of government or government-sponsored agencies); and of that amount $140.2 billion, or 28.8 percent, was represented by government securities held in federal government investment accounts (not including holdings of Federal Reserve banks).[4] In 1962, when the public debt stood at $298.2 billion, the percentage had been markedly lower, 18 percent. Most of the holdings, of course, are in the trusts of the Social Security, Civil Service Retirement, Railroad Retirement, and other large accounts managed by the Department of the Treasury.

In 1935, when the Social Security and Railroad Retirement Acts were first passed, the Secretary of the Treasury had only $29 billion of public debt to manage. But it appears that Congress was concerned even then that the Secretary of the Treasury would be tempted to finance the public debt in part by selling low-interest federal debt obligations to the trust accounts. Congress, in enacting the 1935 law that designated the Secretary of the Treasury as the fiscal agent of the Railroad Retirement Board, authorized the Secretary to issue to the Railroad Retirement Funds special obligations, redeemable at the Retirement Board's request at par and bearing interest equivalent to the average market yield on all marketable, interest-bearing U.S. obligations, but not less than 3 percent annually. In 1935 the 3 percent rate represented the approximate current average yield on U.S. long-term obligations. Congress made similar provisions for certain of the other retirement funds for which the Secretary of the Treasury was the designated managing trustee. For two decades the 3 percent rate turned out to be quite advantageous for the trust funds because, until the mid-1950's, the average yield on U.S. bonds in the open market was considerably below 3 percent. The special Treasury issues also had two advantages over other marketable government issues: immediate placement and the assurance of liquidity stemming from prompt repurchase at par by the Treasury. The special issues, of course, provide complete safety, disregarding the effects of inflation.

Inasmuch as interest rates on government obligations began to rise above the 3 percent level in the mid-1950's, in more recent years the statutory formula covering special issues has worked to the disadvantage of the trust funds. Nonetheless, the trust funds managed by the Secretary of the Treasury continue to be invested heavily in the special, nonmarketable, nonpublic Treasury issues, although each trust fund holds some marketable Treasury notes as well as bonds. Interest rates on newer special issues sold to the trust funds have naturally risen as average market yields on marketable U.S obligations have risen. On the other hand, however, yields on the special issues have not gone up so much as the highest yielding marketable Treasury bonds.

Moreover, the Department of the Treasury appears to have pursued certain policies that have had the effect of depressing trust fund investment returns. For instance, the Advisory Council on Social Security has stated: "The practice of investing in relatively long-term obligations when interest rates are low, and in shorter-term obligations when rates are high, will obviously be disadvantageous to the trust funds in the long run."[5] The Commission on Railroad Retirement asserted that the Secretary of the Treasury's policy has been to purchase marketable issues for the Railroad Retirement Fund only when it has been necessary or desirable for the Secretary to sustain the price of marketable U.S. securities during a "disorderly market."[6] This practice is not only unrelated to the railroad retirement system's purpose of maximizing investment return but also tends to reduce the yield on marketable federal issues, the commission noted, concluding, "this is a reasonable practice by the Secretary insofar as he is protecting his own capacity to enter into the market on behalf of the U.S Treasury,"[7] but it has not served the purpose of the trust funds.

The Secretary of the Treasury has also refused to invest more than token amounts of trust fund assets in government and government-sponsored agency securities, which carry higher interest rates than U.S. obligations. The Secretary's reluctance continues despite an opinion written by the Attorney General in 1966, which advised the Secretary that such securities are lawful investments for the trust funds. In 1972 there were outstanding nearly $11 billion of federal agency securities, such as those of the Export-Import Bank and Tennessee Valley Authority, and nearly $42 billion of government-sponsored agency securities, including those of the Federal Home Loan banks, the Federal National Mortgage Association, and banks for cooperatives. Both the Commission on Railroad Retirement and the Advisory Council on Social Security were critical of the Secretary of the Treasury's failure to make regular fund investments in such securities.

The incentive to buy federal agency securities was further vitiated several years ago by the adoption of the "unified budget." After the Attorney General's ruling in 1966, the Treasury had indeed purchased certain small amounts of federal agency securities for the Social Security, Railroad Retirement, and other trust funds. But no further agency securities appear to have been bought for the funds since the President, in coordination with the Treasury and other departments, decided in 1968 to adopt the unified budget concept for 1969 and subsequent fiscal years. The unified federal budget combines the operations of the trust funds with the general operations of the federal government, and thus presumably presents in a single budget a truer picture of the size of the federal government and the impact of its activities on the nation's economy. But federally sponsored agencies are outside the unified budget, and therefore, any purchases of agency securities for the trust funds would have to be treated as budgetary outlays, increasing total federal expenditures and deficits. It is apparently for this reason that the Secretary of the Treasury has purchased no agency securities for trust funds since the adoption of the unified budget. The Commission on Railroad Retirement has commented:

Because the budget managers are normally eager to hold down the apparent size of the budget outlays and of the budget deficit, the budgetary treatment of "agency" securities issues limits their availability as an investment medium [for the Railroad Retirement Fund]....This is an extraneous criterion which is bound to be contrary to the interests of the trust fund and its beneficiaries.[8]

The Advisory Council on Social Security has taken a similarly dim view of the effects of the unified budget on Social Security trust fund income.

The Commission on Railroad Retirement accepts "the evident fact" that the Department of the Treasury

is open to the criticism that it sits in a dual role as both trustor and trustee. The department is first and foremost concerned with managing the total public debt to achieve for the general taxpayers the lowest possible interest rates over the long run. Simultaneously, however, the Treasury is also the fiduciary for the trust funds, and in this capacity it should be seeking to maximize the yields to these funds on behalf of their beneficiaries. It is clear that these two objectives may be in conflict with one another.[9]

Uncle Sam, as a manager of other people's money, is not quite so different from other managers as is perhaps generally thought. Not surprisingly, reform proposals covering the federal system sound similar to suggestions for alleviating the conflicts of interest of other public pension funds. The Commission on Railroad Retirement has suggested the "simple and minimal" requirement that the Secretary of the Treasury report annually to the beneficiaries and the public that he has met his fiduciary obligations to the trust funds. The Railroad Commission and the Social Security Advisory Council have further suggested that the boards of trustees of the federal funds be expanded to include non-governmental representatives.

When Congress in 1974 undertook the reform of the private pension systems, Professor Mervin C. Bernstein, a leading critic of private funds and of congressional attempts to reform them, commented, "If that's private pension reform, make mine Social Security."[10] An examination of the federal government's performance as a money manager should give pause to those who propose federal assumption of total responsibility for retirement income security through the Social Security System. If it does happen, however, it might well be only the first step, followed someday by the ultimate solution to the retirement income security problem. And that solution will consist of subsidizing the Social Security System with large infusions of general tax revenues, thereby converting Social Security into a general welfare system. Whether that solution is good or bad might be debated, but the possibility certainly should not become a probability simply through the default of the present private and public pension systems.

NOTES

I. Introduction

[1]*The New York Times*, October 18, 1975, pp. 1, 16.

[2]*The New York Times*, October 19, 1975, section 1, p. 7.

[3]*Pensions and Investments* (October 13, 1975), p. 11.

[4]*The New York Times*, February 2, 1977, p. A23.

[5]*Interim Report of Activities of the Pension Task Force of the Subcommittee on Labor Standards*, Committee on Education and Labor, House of Representatives, 94th Cong., 2d Sess. (Washington, D.C.: March 31, 1976), p. vi.

[6]Ibid., p. vii.

[7]*The Wall Street Journal*, October 9, 1975, p. 5.

[8]The Budget of the U.S. Government, Executive Office of the President (February 3, 1975), Part 5, p. 135.

[9]Most public pension funds report their assets in terms of book value—purchase price—rather than market value—the price at which the securities are currently trading. Financial reporting based on book value can be misleading; in recent years, with many bonds selling at prices well below their book value, this practice has resulted in overstatement of the assets of many public pension funds.

[10]See "Public Worker Pay Emerges as Growing Issues," in *The National Journal* 7, no. 34 (August 23, 1975), p. 1198.

[11]Ibid., p. 1.

[12]For a recent survey regarding these laws, see *Public Pension Funds: A Financing Survey*, prepared by The Chase Manhattan Bank, N. A., Trust Department, 1211 Avenue of the Americas, New York, New York 10036.

II. A Question of Control

[1]SEC, *Statistical Bulletin* 35, no. 11 (November 1976), p. 554.

[2]Statistics concerning the Albany, Georgia, pension fund taken from the Bureau of the Census, 1972 Census of Governments, U.S. Department of Commerce (1973), pp. 34-35.

[3]Details of events in Albany are from the *Albany Herald*, June 30, 1972, p. 1. See also the *Albany Journal*, July 7, 1972, p. 1.

[4]Annual Report of the Treasurer, State of Connecticut, Hartford (June 30, 1972), p. 8.

[5]Letter from Henry J. Rigney, chief of the Retirement Division, State Retirement Commission, Hartford, Connecticut, September 18, 1973.

[6]Retirement Income Security for Employees Act, 1972, Hearings, June 20-21, 1972, Labor Subcommittee, Labor and Public Welfare Committee, U.S. Senate, 92nd Cong., 2d Sess., Pt. I, p. 208.

[7]Letter from James L. McGoffin, August 17, 1973.

[8]*The Railroad Retirement System: Its Coming Crisis*, Report of the Commission on Railroad Retirement, House Doc. 92-350, 92nd Cong., 2d Sess. (Washington, D.C.: June 30, 1972).

[9]See *The Wall Street Journal*, June 25, 1973, p. 1.

[10]*Business Week* (September 15, 1975), p. 80.

[11]*Pensions and Investments* (July 21, 1975), p. 22.

[12]Ibid., November 4, 1974, p. 1.

III. Who's in Charge? Public Pension Fund Trustees

[1]California Public Employees' Retirement Law, Part 3, Chap. 2, Sec. 20206.5.

[2]Ibid., Sec. 20206.

[3]See *Survey of State Retirement Systems*, June 30, 1972, published by the National Association of State Retirement Administrators, Montgomery, Alabama. See also *Teachers Retirement Systems, 1971*, a publication of the National Education Association, Washington, D.C.

[4]Ibid.

[5]Ibid.

[5]*Pensions and Investments* (February 3, 1975), pp. 1, 2; (March 31, 1975), p. 1.; (May 12, 1965), p. 1; (June 23, 1975), p. 27; (July 7, 1975), p. 22.

[7]Letter from Richard T. Allen, research and planning officer, Department of the Treasurer, State of North Carolina, Raleigh, August 30, 1973.

[8]Jack M. Guttentag and Hans R. Stoll, *Performance, Policy and Management of Pennsylvania Public School Employees' Retirement Fund*, University of Pennsylvania, Fels Center of Government (February 1973), Chap. 1, p. 7.

IV. Home Sweet Home

[1]Letter from Irwin F. Smith, August 20, 1973.

[2]Letter from Leonard W. McDonald, executive director, Utah State Retirement Board, Salt Lake City, August 22, 1973.

[3]Letter from Tor A. Hegland, executive director, North Dakota Public Employees Retirement System, Bismark, August 28, 1973.

[4]Letter for Iowa Public Employees Retirement System, Des Moines, August 29, 1973.

[5]*Pensions* 2, no. 2 (May-June 1973), pp. 45-46.

V. "Soft Dollars" and Soft Administrators

[1]Securities and Exchange Commission (SEC) *Statistical Bulletin* 32, no. 8 (April 4, 1973), pp. 286-287.

[2]Ibid.

[3]Ibid.

[4]Ibid., vol. 33, no. 16 (April 17, 1974), p. 456.

[5]Lawrence Fisher and James H. Lorie, "Rates of Return on Investments in Common Stock: The Year-by-Year Record, 1926-65," *Journal of Business of the University of Chicago*, 1 (July 1968), pp. 291-316.

[6]The statement was made at a pension conference sponsored by the National Legislative Conference of the Council of State Governments held at Nashville, Tennessee, June 27-30, 1973.

[7]The "prudent man rule," as stated in Kansas law, is that "In acquiring, retaining, managing and disposing of investments of the fund there shall be exercised the judgment and care under the circumstances then prevailing, which men of prudence, discretion and intelligence exercise in the management of their own affairs, not in regard to speculation but in regard to the permanent disposition of their funds, considering the probable income as well as the probable safety of their capital." Kansas Public Employees Retirement Act, K.S.A. 74-4901, 4921, revised through July 1, 1972.

[8]Figures on return of the Oregon Public Employees Retirement System.

[9]See *Investment Policies of Pension Funds*, Hearings before the Fiscal Policy Subcommittee, Joint Economic Committee, 91st Cong., 2d Sess. (Washington, D.C.: April 27-30, 1970), p. 219.

[10]*The Wall Street Journal*, June 25, 1973, pp. 1, 16.

[11]*Pensions and Investments* (April 4, 1975), p. 11.

[12]The statement was made at a pension conference sponsored by the National Legislative Conference of the Council of State Governments held at Nashville, Tennessee, June 27-30, 1973.

[13]Guttentag and Stoll, op. cit., Chap. 5, p. 19.

[14]Ibid.

[15]Ibid., p. 20.

[16]Ibid., p. 22.

[17]Letter from James L. McGoffin, August 17, 1973.

[18]Ibid.

[19]Ibid.

[20]Letter from Tor A. Hegland, August 28, 1973.

[21]Interview, New York City, August 4, 1973.

[22]*The Wall Street Journal*, January 23, 1973, p. 4.

[23]SEC, *Institutional Investor Study Report*, published as House of Representatives Doc. 92-64, 92nd Cong., 1st Sess. (Washington, D.C.: March 10, 1971), vol. 3, pp. 1166, 1196.

[24]Ibid., pp. 1106, 1196.

[25]Ibid., p. 1151.

[26]Ibid., p. 1106.

[27]Ibid., p. 1163.

[28]Guttentag and Stoll, op. cit., Chap. 5, p. 1.

[29]*Pensions* 2, no. 2 (May-June 1973), p. 41.

[30]Guttentag and Stoll, op. cit., Chap. 1, p. 10.

[31]Ibid., p. 11.

[32]Ibid., Chap. 5, p. 22.

[33]Ibid., Chap. 1, p. 11.

[34]Forty-Second Annual Report, for fiscal year ended June 30, 1973, Board of Administration, California Public Employees' Retirement System, Sacramento, pp. 74-76.

[35]Semi-Annual Report of the Treasurer, State of Connecticut, Hartford, for the period ending December 31, 1973, p. 7.

[36]*The Wall Street Journal*, January 23, 1973, p. 4.

[37]Ibid., December 14, 1972, p. 3.

[38]Letter from Leonard W. McDonald, August 22, 1973.

VI. Bonds, Cash, Mortgages—and Banks

[1]Bureau of the Census, 1972 Census of Govrnments, op. cit., p. 10, and SEC, *Statistical Bulletin* (April 17, 1974), p. 458.

[2]SEC, *Statistical Bulletin*, op. cit.

[3]Bureau of the Census, 1972 Census of Goverments, op. cit., p. 10.

[4]Ibid.

[5]SEC, *Institutional Investor Study Report*, p. 1168.

[6]See 51st Annual Retirement Systems Report, New York State Comptroller, Albany (March 31, 1971), p. 23.

[7]*Pensions and Investments* (February 3, 1975), pp. 1, 23.

[8]*Pensions* 2, no. 2 (May-June 1973), p. 40.

[9]*Pensions* 1, no. 3. (Fall 1972), p. 10.

[10]Guttentag and Stoll, op. cit., Chap. 4, p. 50.

[11]*Trusts and Estates* (January 1972), pp. 30, 32.

[12]Letter from James L. Sublett, August 16, 1973.

[13]Ibid.

[14]West Virginia State Board of Investments, Annual Investment Report (June 30, 1972).

[15]Bureau of the Census, 1972 Census of Governments, op. cit., pp. 46-47.

[16]Ibid., p. 10.

[17]Letter from Bruce W. Boyea of the staff of Arthur Levitt, New York State Comptroller, Albany, September 5, 1973.

[18]Letter from Fred E. Henne, executive director, Arkansas Public Employees Retirement System, Little Rock, October 23, 1973.

[19]*Investment Policies of Pension Funds*, Hearings before the Fiscal Policy Subcommittee, Joint Economic Committee, 91st Cong., 2d Sess. (Washington, D.C.: April 27-30, 1970), p. 143.

[20]Guttentag and Stoll, op. cit., Chap 5, p. 16.

[21]Ibid., Chap. 4, pp. 16-17; Chap. 5, p. 17.

[22]These details were supplied by John Cooper, investment officer of the Ohio State Teachers Retirement System, Columbus, in a telephone interview, July 31, 1973. Cooper was not the investment officer at the time the commitment letters were issued.

[23]SEC, Litigation Release No. 5508 (August 21, 1972).

[24]Information relative to the Hawaii Employees Retirement System was provided by letter from Fred W. Bennion, secretary of the Tax Foundation of Hawaii, Honolulu, August 3, 1973. See also *State and Local Employee Pension Systems*, (New York: Tax Foundation Inc., 1969), p. 46.

[25]Guttentag and Stoll, op. cit., Chap. 4, p. 4.

[26]Letter from Fred W. Bennion, August 3, 1973.

[27]51st Annual Retirement Systems Report, New York State Comptroller, Albany (March 31, 1976).

[28]See an address delivered by Melvin Lechner before the Society of Security Analysts, New York, August 3, 1973.

[29]*The New York Times*, December 5, 1975, p. 13.

VII. Summary and Conclusions

[1]Thomas P. Bleakney, *Retirement Systems for Public Employees*, published for the Pension Research Council, Wharton School of Finance of the University of Pennsylvania (Homewood, Ill.: Richard D. Irwin, Inc., 1972), p. 13.

[2]See *State and Local Employee Pension Systems* (New York: Tax Foundation, Inc., 1969), p. 46.

[3]Oregon Revised Statutes 1971, Chap. 237, Sec. 237.271.
[4]*The Wall Street Journal*, July 8, 1976, p. 4.
[5]*The New York Times*, July 25, 1975, p. 30.
[6]*The New York Times*, October 3, 1975, pp. 1, 14.
[7]*Interim Report of Activities of the Pension Task Force*, p. v.

VIII. A Note on the Social Security System

[1]*U.S. News & World Report* (July 15, 1975), p. 27.
[2]*The Railroad Retirement System: Its Coming Crisis*, p. 27.
[3]Ibid., p. 18.
[4]See *Statistical Appendix to the Annual Report of the Secretary of the Treasury* (June 30, 1972), pp. 62-63, 234-235.
[5]Reports of the 1971 Advisory Council on Social Security, House Document 92-80, 92nd Cong., 1st Sess. (Washington, D.C.: April 5, 1971), p. 61.
[6]*The Railroad Retirement System: Its Coming Crisis*, p. 424.
[7]Ibid.
[8]Ibid., p. 423.
[9]Ibid., p. 421.
[10]Merton C. Bernstein, professor of law, Ohio State University, in a letter to the editor of *The New York Times*, April 2, 1974, p. 33.

Union Pension Fund Asset Management
by Richard Blodgett

I • INTRODUCTION

In September and October 1976, twelve of the sixteen trustees of the Central States Teamsters pension fund resigned under heavy federal pressure,[1] and the fund itself announced "a major reorganization" of its board, replacing the old sixteen-member joint union-industry board with a streamlined ten-member joint board.[2]

Then on November 26, the Internal Revenue Service announced that the new board of trustees had agreed to enter negotiations with federal investigators for procedures to safeguard the fund's assets, including possible systems for monitoring the fund and the creation of independent checks on its activities.[3]

After nearly two decades of articles in the press charging conflicts and abuse within the Central States fund, the first tangible actions were being taken toward reforming the $1.4 billion institution and providing better protection for the interests of fund beneficiaries; these actions were taken only under extreme federal pressure, including an Internal Revenue Service threat to revoke the fund's tax-exempt status.[4]

But although these actions were a refreshing move in the right direction, they were essentially cosmetic in nature; they did nothing to cure the basic structural ills of the Central States fund and indeed of almost all union pension funds.

Jointly trusteed union pension funds, established under the provisions of the Labor Management Relations Act of 1947, more familiarly known as Taft-Hartley Act,[5] actually provide very little of the structural protection for pensioners' interests that was sought by the drafters of that law. And the widely reported allegations against the Central States fund—of lending money to mobster-controlled enterprises, lending money to friends of the Teamsters union leadership, and failing to provide adequate controls over the disbursement of funds[6]—are a sign of deeper problems that, in all the clamor over specific abuses, have remained totally unaddressed by the Congress, federal regulators, and the press.

Of course, relatively few union pension funds besides Central States have been accused of flagrant abuses. The great majority of union pension funds appear to be managed by boards of trustees genuinely concerned about the interests of beneficiaries and in no way dishonest in their practices. Structural conflicts do not automatically lead to abuse.

Yet the structural deficiencies of union funds are significant enough to raise questions about whether an alternative type of structure, more directed toward the needs of pensioners, should be legislated by Congress.

One basic type of structural conflict that has made union pension funds vulnerable to abuse results from the shortcomings of jointly trusteed boards as mandated by Taft-Hartley. The drafters of Taft-Hartley saw joint trusteeship, with equal representation on the board by labor and management, as the best way to achieve built-in checks and balances to protect fund beneficiaries against misdoings by either side.[7] They were particularly concerned that, without management trustees on a union fund board, the fund would end up merely becoming an appendage of the union, with fund assets being managed in ways designed to help the union's cause (or personally benefit the union leadership), rather than in ways aimed at providing workers and their families with the best possible pensions. There was a specific fear that some union pension funds would be turned into union "war chests."[8]

However, in the thirty years since enactment of Taft-Hartley, the very circumstance that the act was supposed to prevent—unrestrained union control of members' pension monies—has occurred regularly despite the provisions of that law. Management trustees have no real incentive to take an active role, and many are actually quite willing to let the union trustees dominate, in clear opposition to the objective of Taft-Hartley.

Often, despite the presence of management trustees, it is very difficult to distinguish between the pension fund and the union. It is standard practice for the top officers of the union to appoint themselves for indefinite terms as union trustees of the fund.[9] In the majority of cases, the fund and union share the same office space. Often, the general counsel to the union serves as attorney for the fund. The union sometimes acts as unofficial collection agent for the fund when employers are delinquent in their payments. It can be argued that a close relationship between union and fund is an efficient arrangement, avoiding duplication of space and personnel and putting management of the pension monies in the hands of union officers who are more concerned than anyone about protecting the rights of the fund beneficiaries (who are, after all, essentially the same group as the union members).

But the arrangement also puts the union representatives on the fund board in a position of conflict, pledged as union officers to act in the best interests of the union and pledged as fund trustees to act in the best interests of the fund and its beneficiaries.

A similar conflict exists in most corporate pension funds and in most state and local government pension funds, where representatives of the sponsoring organization typically dominate the board of trustees of the fund. In other words this is a common arrangement throughout the pension field, not a problem unique to union funds. And although there may be variations from one class of pension funds to the next in the specific types of potential abuses arising out of this conflict, there appears to be little difference in terms of frequency of abuse short of criminal conduct.

Earlier studies in this series on conflicts of interests in various sectors of the securities markets discussed, for instance, how corporations have sometimes used their pension funds to manipulate the market in their own stock[10] or even in honest ways to buy stock or finance mergers [11] and how municipalities have used their pension funds to buy their own debt securities.[12]

In the case of union pension funds, examples of potential conflicts include instances where the union may use the investment power of the fund as a bargaining or organizing tool and where, as happened with the United Mine Workers pension fund in the late 1950s and 1960s,[13] the fund deposited large sums of money interest-free in a bank controlled by the union. Also, there is a heightened risk that the union trustees, with the acquiescence of the management trustees or without their knowledge, will abuse the fund for their personal gain—for instance, through loan kickbacks, loans to close friends, or excessive pension payments to themselves.

In a somewhat different vein, union pension funds, because of their relationship to the labor movement and the goal of that movement to better the lot of mankind, also may find themselves under special pressures to invest in ways that do social good or to avoid investments in anti-union companies or to use a portion of their investment funds to help create jobs for union members. (Construction loans by pension funds in the building trades are an example.) There would seem to be no pat answers in any of these specific areas, except that the fund trustees must obviously maintain a high degree of concern for protecting the fund assets and maximizing investment returns for the benefit of pensioners. Often, though, investing in socially acceptable ways or to create jobs for union members can be accomplished without undue risk or loss of investment income, and so, in those instances, the conflict is more theoretical than real.

Some conflicts of interest are unavoidable. Even when they can be eliminated, the costs may be higher than the envisioned benefits. The best answer in such cases is reasonable, workable controls.

However, in the instance of the union funds, the controls being relied on through the provisions of Taft-Hartley have not really worked. In fact, they may have made matters worse because they appear to provide adequate controls but, in reality, do not.

The dangers of union domination are intensified by the funding and pension payout structure of the typical union pension fund. Unlike most corporate pension funds, in which pensions are set at a fixed level and annual employer contributions vary as needed to finance those levels, the arrangement is reversed in most union pension funds.[14] Contributions are the fixed item, negotiated through collective bargaining between union and employers, and pension rates are the variable. Pension rates are determined periodically by the trustees, based on monies available from employer contributions and investment income.

The result is that employers lack the same kind of intense financial interest in maintaining an active hand in the management of the fund and assuring that investment income is maximized since they generally suffer no direct financial consequences if investments are managed poorly or monies are siphoned off. Indeed, employers may be tempted to "attack" the union pension fund as a key pressure point in labor-management relations, by purposely delaying their fund contributions or by directing the management-appointed trustees to obstruct the orderly administration of the fund in retaliation for union activities that offend the employers. Employers are relatively free to do this because they hold no direct financial stake in efficient fund performance.

However, employers may eventually lose this freedom from financial responsibility as an indirect result of the Employee Retirement Income Security Act of 1974 (ERISA). Sometimes referred to as the Pension Reform Act, that law established tough new standards for all private pension plans, corporate and union, in the areas of funding; fiduciary responsibilities of trustees and advisors; financial dealings with trustees, officials of sponsoring organizations, and sponsoring organizations themselves; and public disclosure of fund assets and investments. But ERISA is relatively new, and neither its applicability to the problems of union pension funds nor its enforceability has been adequately demonstrated.

Title IV of ERISA created the first federal insurance program to protect fund beneficiaries in the event of default by a private pension plan. Insurance coverage is financed through premiums paid by the funds. The Pension Benefit Guarantee Corporation (PBGC) was created by the act to administer this insurance program.[15] Insurance is mandatory for most "defined benefit" plans, and the PBGC has interpreted this term to include all union pension funds—even those plans described in their trust indentures as being "defined contribution" plans. Soon after the PBGC began operations, the trustees of the Operating Engineers Pension Trust for Southern California and Southern Nevada brought suit in federal district court in Los Angeles to be exempted from pension coverage, contending that despite the position taken by the PBGC, the Operating Engineers fund was not a defined benefit plan covered by Title IV of ERISA. In March 1976 the court ruled in favor of the fund,[16] but the PBGC has appealed that ruling to the U.S. Court of Appeals for the Ninth Circuit. The issues of insurance coverage and of whether union pension funds are defined benefit plans or as they have long been considered defined contribution plans have caused a split in the ranks of the union funds. The National Coordinating Committee for Multiemployer Plans, representing a number of funds in the construction trades, favors insurance coverage and has filed an *amicus curiae* brief siding with the PBGC. On the other hand, an attorney for the Operating Engineers Pension Trust has claimed that if the PBGC wins on appeal and is able to establish that all union funds are actually defined benefit funds, the future of these funds will be threatened.[17] He contends that: (1) employer liability for specific pension contributions, but not for the ultimate pension benefits, is essential to the collective bargaining process; (2) many existing union funds would not be able to survive a midstream change from a fixed contribution to a fixed benefit arrangement since the guaranteeing of specific pension rates might require greater resources than these funds have at their disposal. However, another labor expert has suggested that, regardless of the final outcome of the Operating Engineers court case, many union pension funds may be forced to adopt the defined benefit approach.[18] He says that these plans may turn out to be underfunded according to future interpretations of ERISA, and that, to avoid potential legal liability from funding deficiencies, labor and management may have to start bargaining directly over the size of workers' pensions.

Union pension funds have remained a significant blind spot in our understanding of how institutional capital is managed in the United States. Although they have been the subject of numerous newspaper and magazine exposés (particularly those concerning the Central States Teamsters fund), they have largely escaped the more serious and systematic analysis that has been directed at other major capital pools by the federal government.

Despite their many structural and legal differences, union pension funds are typically considered with their big cousins, the corporate funds, when pension fund asset management practices are studied and, for that reason, are seldom really analyzed at all. The most notable exception is the Securities and Exchange Commission's (SEC) 1971 *Institutional Investor Study Report*, one of the few serious research projects to undertake a separate analysis of union funds. But even that study was limited to nineteen union plans and did not deal with potential conflicts of interest.

Political considerations also have helped protect the union funds. With labor unions wielding immense political power, federal regulation of their pension activities has remained weak. Union pension funds are something of a hot potato in the legislative and executive branches of government; the current Department of Labor investigation of the Central States fund illustrates this very point. Although allegations of abuses have persisted since the late 1950s, it was not until the fall of 1975 that the executive branch finally undertook a thorough and far-ranging investigation. Even with such an obvious need to get to the root of these allegations, Teamster president Frank E. Fitzsimmons complained bitterly about the Department of Labor probe,[19] and Secretary of Labor W. J. Usery compromised his department's position by publicly praising Teamsters leaders at the very time that his subordinates were looking into their alleged misdoings.

In sum, even though they have considerable investment power and serve as a key link in our nation retirement income program, union pension funds represent uncharted waters. Five questions, in particular, can help focus attention on those areas needing a more thorough study:

1. Just how widespread is self-dealing by union pension fund sponsors? Do only a few sponsors engage in such practies or is self-dealing commonplace? In addition, are union funds any worse than corporate-managed pension funds?

2. Aside from self-dealing what are some of the more subtle and basic areas for potential conflicts of interest, especially conflicts that are unique to pension funds?

3. How do union pension funds routinely deal with these potential problem areas?

4. How are union pension funds structured, and in what ways, if any, does the typical structure fail to protect the interests of the funds' beneficiaries?

5. Are current federal laws adequate to the task of preventing abuses, and if not, how should these laws be changed?

This last question may be the most timely because union pressure is mounting in the other direction—for a rollback of the strict ERISA prohibition against dealings by pension funds with "parties-in-interest," such as employers who contribute money to a plan and unions whose members are covered by the plan. In 1974, with ERISA, Congress established the first blanket prohibition against loans by pension funds to parties-in-interest, purchases of property from them, and similar types of financial dealings with individuals and organizations related to the fund. This prohibition is aimed directly at anyone who, having a special relationship with the fund, might be tempted to take advantage of that relationship. In ERISA Congress flatly banned some types of practices that actually had been fairly common. These practices include loans to and financial transactions with participating employers and union officials. To provide flexibility the law specifies that exemptions may be granted jointly by the Department of Labor and Internal Revenue Service (IRS) for specific types of transactions that, in the view of these agencies, are administratively feasible to exempt, are in the best interests of the funds, and do not harm the rights of beneficiaries. However, Labor and the IRS have been extremely slow in responding to requests for grants of exemption. In some cases requests have been pending nearly two years without response. As of late 1976, the two agencies had acted on only sixty of approximately 480 requests for exemption, from both corporate and union funds, submitted since passage of ERISA in September 1974.[20] A major fight appears to be brewing over what many fund managers consider to be the government's unresponsiveness to their geniune needs. A number of labor leaders, contending that the item-by-item exemption process is much too impractical and restrictive, are calling for the complete elimination of ERISA's ban on transactions with parties-in-interest. These labor leaders are seeking a reversal of the process; all transactions with parties-in-interest would be permitted except those banned through administrative action by Labor and

IRS. In support of this position, Representatives John H. Dent (D.-Pa.) and John N. Erlenborn (R.-Ill.) have introduced legislation that would reverse the process for both union and corporate pension plans.[21]

Strong crosscurrents are at work: some unions are calling for much less restrictive laws; some reformers, such as Merton C. Bernstein, professor of law at Washington University, St. Louis, Missouri, and Karen Ferguson of the Pension Rights Center in Washington, D.C.,[22] are calling for tougher laws or even a federal takeover of all corporate and union pension funds; and the Department of Labor and Internal Revenue Service, just beginning to exercise their vastly expanded powers under ERISA, represent the great unknown.

Even the seasoned observer, in trying to sort out these complex issues, will find few clear guidelines. The problem of analyzing union pension funds is so basic that there are no official figures on the number and combined assets of such funds. The Department of Labor estimates that there are seventeen thousand union and "multiemployer" benefit funds of all kinds—pension funds, health and welfare funds, insurance funds, and so on.[23] But the department says it does not know how these funds break down by specific category or the total assets involved, either for the seventeen thousand plans or for any of the individual categories. However, in line with its expanded responsibilites under ERISA, the department does hope to begin compiling such data by mid-1977.

Similarly, the SEC, which currently issues the most definitive statistics on financial institutions, publishes a combined figure for both corporate and union funds. On June 30, 1976, that combined figure was $152.8 billion at book value.[24]

The 1976 edition of the *Money Market Directory*, which contains probably the most comprehensive, organization-by-organization listing of U.S. financial institutions and their assets, presents further evidence that union pension fund assets are undisclosed.[25] This book singles out union pension funds as an area that has defied definitive analysis because of both a lack of overall statistics and incomplete and inadequate reporting by many individual funds.

The best unofficial estimate appears to be that the union funds control about $35 billion of assets, or about 23 percent of the combined corporate-union total. The $35 billion figure has been reported by *Pensions & Investments*,[26] probably the foremost publication in the pension management field, and supported by Noel Arnold Levin,[27] a leading labor attorney who has written extensively about union pension funds. The ten largest union pension funds have by themselves a total of about $5 billion in assets, which would further indicate that an industry-wide figure of $35 billion is at least within reason. It also has been unofficially estimated that 9 million U.S. workers are covered by union pension funds[28]—nearly 15 percent of the work force in the private sector. (See Table 21.)

Like corporate pension funds, the union funds have enjoyed enormous growth over the past twenty years. Most of the larger funds were established in the 1950s and grew rapidly during the 1960s, when labor unions pressed for

Table 21: Assets of Ten Large Taft-Hartley Pension Funds, 1976

FUND	(MILLIONS)
Western Conference of Teamsters Pension Fund, Seattle, Washington	$1,479
Central States, Southeast and Southwest Areas Pension Fund, International Brotherhood of Teamsters, Chicago	1,363
The Bakery and Confectionery Union & Industry International Pension Fund, Washington, D.C.	387
Joint Industry Board of the Electrical Industry Pension Funds, Flushing, New York	300
International Ladies Garment Workers Union National Retirement Fund, New York	298
National Maritime Union of America Pension Fund, New York	206
International Union of Operating Engineers Central Pension Fund, Washington, D.C.	200
Carpenters Pension Trust Fund for Northern California, San Francisco	185
International Longshoremen's Association & New York Shipping Association Pension Fund, New York	150
Southern California Pipe Trade Trust Fund & Retirement Fund Trust of the Plumbing, Heating and Piping Industry, Los Angles	150

Source: *Pensions & Investments*, pension fund annual reports filed with the Department of Labor

increased pension contributions from employers to offset inflation. The growth pattern of the Teamsters' Central States fund is fairly typical. That fund was created in 1955, and ten years later it held assets of $326 million.[29] By 1970 the figure was $718 million, and by 1975 it was $1.4 billion, a ten-year compound annual growth rate of more than 15 percent.

Union pension funds are set up as independent legal entities; each fund is managed by its own board of trustees and, in theory, is neither company-nor union-controlled. The purpose of these funds is to collect the dollars negotiated in collective bargaining, invest these monies, and disburse benefits to union members and their families.

Such pension plans are often referred to as "multiemployer" pension funds, "Taft-Hartley pension trusts," or "jointly administered" pension funds. Strictly speaking, the term *union pension fund*, although widely used, is inaccurate because very few pension funds are actually administered directly by labor unions. Under federal law only three types of pension funds qualify for unrestricted union control: (1) those plans funded by a union to provide pensions for its own officers and employees, such as the Employees Pension Plan and Trust of the International Union of Electrical, Radio, and Machine Workers; (2) those corporate plans funded solely through worker contributions; and (3) those union-managed plans for corporate employees, including those for which the corporation puts up the cash, created before January 1, 1946, a cutoff date established by the Taft-Hartley Act.

In reality, few plans qualify for these exemptions because the overwhelming majority of pension plans for corporate employees were created after the 1946 cutoff date and are financed through payments by employers.

For these corporate-funded plans, two main types of structures are possible under the law: (1) a joint board of trustees with equal representation from labor and management (''union'' plans) and (2) exclusive appointment of trustees by the funding corporation (''corporate'' plans). Jointly administered funds generally take their name from the supporting union and usually are housed in union headquarters—thus, the use of the term *union pension fund*.

The choice between having a corporate-appointed board or joint appointment of trustees is essentially a matter of the dynamics between company and union. Where the union is small and weak and the company is big and powerful, it is understandable that corporate-run plans dominate. The automobile industry is a case in point: Even though the unions are strong and pension benefits are subject to collective bargaining, individual pension funds have been established on a company-to-company basis, and administrative control of these funds has remained in the hands of corporate managements.

Jointly administered (or ''union'') plans, by contrast, are most prevalent in industries characterized by a combination of aggressive, industry-wide unions and employer fragmentation (i.e., hundreds of smaller companies rather than a few large ones). Examples include construction, trucking, the garment industry, coal mining, and the maritime industry. In such industries it was generally the union that first established a pension fund and then signed up employers. Often, the union is the natural party to assume primary sponsorship of the plan because the corporate mortality rate in these and other highly fragmented industries tends to be high, and the union may be the most stable organization in sight.

A jointly administered pension fund is typically organized along union jurisdictional lines and will cover union members working at anywhere from half a dozen to twenty thousand different companies. For instance, the Bakery and Confectionary Workers Union, one of the larger funds, provides coverage for approximately one hundred thousand members at twenty-one hundred companies.[30] In contrast, a major corporate fund, such as the General Motors pension plan for hourly employees, involves corporate negotiations with eighteen different unions and covers four hundred thousand workers at a single company.[31]

II • JOINT BOARDS AND UNION CONTROL

Both the Taft-Hartley Act of 1947 and the Employee Retirement Income Security Act of 1974, two of the major federal laws governing union pension funds, specify that these funds must be managed for the exclusive benefit of plan participants—that is, workers, retirees, and their families.

Taft-Hartley speaks in terms of plans having to be managed "for the sole and exclusive benefit of the employees and their families and dependents,"[1] and ERISA specifies that a plan fiduciary "shall discharge his duties with respect to a plan solely in the interest of the participants and beneficiaries" and for the "exclusive purpose" of providing benefits to participants and of "defraying reasonable expenses of administering the plan."[2]

Nowhere does either law allow the use of pension monies to further the cause of the union or its leaders. Indeed, by assigning full and exclusive rights to fund beneficiaries, federal law clearly forbids the use of pension monies on behalf of the union or its leaders.

The purpose of joint boards of trustees is to insure compliance with the law. But it is one thing for the law to require management to be represented on the boards of union pension funds and quite another to force these representatives to be active and interested participants.

The issue is a critical one because it is the trustees who are in control. They are invariably vested with broad powers over all aspects of fund operations, including collecting contributions, managing investments, determining how large pension benefits should be, and disbursing these benefits. Although specific duties often are delegated to an administrative staff or outside consultants, the ultimate responsibility nonetheless rests with the board.

The Taft-Hartley Act, which created the concept of jointly appointed boards for union pension funds, specifies that, in addition to being represented equally on the board of trustees, labor and management may, if they see fit, appoint one or more neutral trustees to the board, although in practice such appointments are rare. If neutral trustees are not appointed, the two sides are supposed to agree on an impartial mediator to settle disputes in the event of a deadlock. If they cannot even agree on a mediator, one may be appointed by a federal district court on petition from either side.[3]

The natural implication is that such an arrangement will insure that neither labor nor management dominates the fund and that the interests of beneficiaries are given absolute priority, as the law says they must be. The arrangement might work—if management trustees took their responsibilities seriously. But as we shall see, they seldom do—and the door to abuse is left ajar.

The consequences of this problem have surfaced in a number of ways: from the occasional looting of pension funds by union leaders to a wide variety of other, more subtle practices that clearly do more to benefit the union or its leadership than the fund participants. This latter category includes an instance cited by Bernard F. Curry, senior vice president of Morgan Guaranty Trust Co.[4] Morgan's trust department was serving as investment manager to a union pension fund whose parent union happened to go on strike against a company of which a Morgan officer—not in the trust department—was a director. "The union got after us to tell our guy to settle," Curry recalls. Morgan refused; eventually, it lost the pension account.

This interesting case illustrates how a union-controlled pension fund can easily stray from its supposedly exclusive task of providing pensions for union members. It could be argued that pensioners benefit when the fund is used to pressure for a strike settlement, to force companies to buy union-made products, to discourage the "exporting" of jobs to overseas manufacturing facilities, or similar ends that may seem to be for the economic good of the union membership as a whole. But such activities actually create great potential risks, by eroding any distinction between fund and union and by diverting attention from the job of providing maximum benefits for the fund participants. One specific danger in these pressure tactics is that, contrary to sound business practice and the intent of the law, pension managers will end up being hired for their willingness to cooperate with the union instead of their ability to manage money.

Because so many conflicting pressures may exist within a union pension fund—between union and management trustees, between the goals of the fund and the goals of the union, between the desire of retirees to receive the maximum possible pension benefits and the institutional self-interest of the union, which may lead it to hold down pensions and build up assets so the fund can be used to wield more investment power—some attorneys and governmental regulators claim that jointly trusteed pension funds are a structural monster and that (perhaps an overstatement) it is a wonder that the workers' interests ever come first.

The joint board arrangement originally came about because of congressional concern over the United Mine Workers pension and welfare fund, which Senator Robert Taft described as administered without restriction to the point where "practically the fund became a war chest for the union."[5] Fears about the power of the United Mine Workers fund were heightened by the fact that, at the time, the union was seeking to establish a formula under which the union-run plan would collect, from the industry, a fixed amount per ton of coal mined.

Specifically, Taft-Hartley bars companies from making direct payments to unions but allows them to make pension money payments into independent trusts that have joint labor-industry boards. The clear intent of Taft-Hartley was to drive a wedge between unions and their members' pension plans so union leaders could not use these growing pools of money for their personal advantage or for the purpose of the union. Corporate managements, by their presence on the fund boards, were supposed to serve as watchdogs against abuses by their natural adversaries, the unions.

Today, however, it is almost universally acknowledged by experts that the unions have continued to dominate their members' pension plans, in spite of the law. The only dispute is over whether union domination is necessarily bad.

Gerald M. Feder, voicing a view held by many other individuals in the labor movement, argues that it is natural and appropriate for unions to dominate because they are more likely to do a good job of protecting their members' interests.[6] Feder, an attorney for the National Coordinating Committee for Multiemployer Plans, an offshoot of the construction trades division of the AFL-CIO, doubts that it was ever the intent of Congress to build an insurmountable wall between labor unions and union pension plans. He thinks the joint-board arrangement recognized the fact that pension funds are subject to collective bargaining and that some sort of continuing management involvement is needed beyond the mere making of contributions to the fund.

But even the most minimal standards of management involvement seem to be lacking in many funds. Noel Arnold Levin, a New York labor attorney who serves as a management trustee on a number of jointly administered pension plans, says that the general passivity of management trustees shows up in several ways: (1) their chronic absenteeism at board meetings; (2) their lack of involvement when they do show up; and (3) their tendency to rubber-stamp the decisions of the union trustees.[7] Basic to the problem, Levin says, is the general feeling among management trustees that pension funds are the "workers' money" and so are of proper concern only to the workers and their unions, not to employers.

Labor lawyer Theodore W. Kheel, who has served as a neutral trustee on one fund and is familiar with the operations of many others, says that "managements tend to follow the lead of the unions rather than abdicating totally."[8] Kheel finds some reason for hope in ERISA. By making clear the legal responsibilities of *all* trustees, he says, this law is causing many management trustees to reevaluate the risks of remaining aloof. Under ERISA the Department of Labor has been given the authority to go to federal court to seek either civil or criminal relief against pension funds that have allegedly violated federal law, and it has been vested with the authority to seek the removal of trustees who have failed to act in the best interests of fund beneficiaries.[9] Kheel tells of one jointly trusteed pension fund whose management representatives are pressing for full investment responsibility, pushing the union representatives totally aside, because they feel that under ERISA they are liable. The union, however, has refused to comply.

In general, the full implications of ERISA are just beginning to be realized, but whether or not the Department of Labor vigorously enforces the law remains an open question. Kheel finds that many managements are content, for the time being at least, to leave the pension fund to the union: "The fund gives the union something to do. Employers like this [arrangement] because otherwise the union may find something else to do and cause trouble." He notes that in disputes between labor and management, the pension fund can serve as a harmless (to management, at least) focal point, reducing the possibility that such disputes will extend into areas of greater concern.

The implications here are extremely troublesome. Amplifying on Kheel's point, an official of a large New York-based labor union contends that when management trustees do assert themselves, it is often in reprisal for previous union actions.[10] For instance, the union may become obstreperous during contract negotiations, or its members may engage in a wildcat walkout. Management, in turn, may tie up the administration of the pension fund by instructing its trustees to vote against all proposals coming before the board. Such antagonism does not arise every day; management trustees, unlike their union counterparts, generally come from different organizations with varying viewpoints, and it usually takes great adversity or impassioned anger to make them act in unison against the union. Jointly administered pension funds are nonetheless one of the most sensitive pressure points in labor-management relations. And management, in particular, is sometimes willing to exert pressure through the fund because it is the union and its members who suffer most when fund administration breaks down.

This vulnerability stems not only from the joint-board arrangement but also from the basic financial structure of most union pension funds. It is important to understand that the financial structures of most corporate pension funds and most union funds differ significantly.

Corporate pension funds. Nearly all of these funds are of the "defined benefit" type. This means that disbursements are fixed at a specified level, while employer contributions vary. High investment returns typically enable the corporation to reduce its contributions, and low returns force the corporation to contribute more. Essentially, the corporation is underwriting all pension benefits and, if the fund is managed poorly, must make up the difference to keep retirement benefits at the specified level. Understandably, corporate managements are anxious to do whatever they can to achieve maximum investment returns and avoid any actions that might undermine the smooth administration of the fund.

Union pension funds. In the great majority of union pension funds, the formula is reversed,[11] making these funds vulnerable to pressure from management. In these funds contributions are fixed, and benefits are variable. Typically, management negotiates for a fixed contribution per worker; then, on the basis of these contributions and the flow of investment incomes, the trustees determine the size of the pensions. Thus, the workers, not the employers, suffer when investments do poorly. Corporations simply do not have the direct financial stake in most union funds that they have in most corporate plans.

Collective bargaining is the final element that deters management from taking an interest in union pension funds. In most cases management's primary concern in collective bargaining is with the overall dollar cost of the settlement, not with the allocation of individual elements. Because both wages and fringe benefits are deductible from federal income taxes, the separate elements in the settlement make no difference to management in terms of after-tax cost. Once an overall dollar figure is agreed upon, labor generally structures the individual elements as it sees fit. Management and labor might agree on a total package of $9.50 an hour; then the union might decide, for example, that the breakdown should be $8 for wages, 90¢ for contributions to the pension fund, and 60¢ for other fringe benefits. Management views all elements in the package as matters between the union and its members—but the law says that management must get involved in supervising the funds set aside for pension benefits.

Taft-Hartley, although establishing the requirement for joint boards, allows union and management to decide freely on the number of trustees and their specific identities. In practice, fund boards tend to range in size from two to sixty members, the latter figure being the number of trustees on the board of the International Ladies Garment Workers Union National Retirement Fund.[12] Almost without exception, the union trustees also are key officers of the union. In fact, the union presidency is usually concomitant with a position on the fund board. Management trustees, on the other hand, come from a more diverse group and often include individuals such as trade association lawyers, corporate presidents, and labor relations executives.

The Teamsters' Central States pension fund is a case in point. The five union trustees are all officers of various Teamsters organizations and include Frank Fitzsimmons, president of the International Brotherhood of Teamsters; Roy L. Williams, president of the Central Conference of Teamsters; Loran Robbins, president of the Indiana Conference of Teamsters and of Joint Council 69; Hubert L. Payne, secretary-treasurer of Teamsters Local 519 in Knoxville; and Robert E. Schlieve, president of Local 563 in Appleton, Wisconsin. In 1975 longtime Central States trustee William Presser, vice president of the International Union and president of Joint Council 41 of the Teamsters in Cleveland, was temporarily forced off the Central States board after the passage of ERISA, which bars anyone from serving as a trustee for five years after a criminal conviction. Presser had pleaded guilty in 1971 to misusing $590,000 in union funds. While he was off the board, his position was filled by his son Jackie, also a Cleveland-area Teamsters official. However, several months after returning to the board in 1976, William Presser resigned again, reportedly at the urging of other trustees, after he invoked his Fifth Amendment rights and declined to testify in connection with the Department of Labor's investigation of the Central States fund.[13]

Of the other nine largest Taft-Hartley pension trusts—from the $1.5 billion Teamsters' Western Conference fund through the $150 million Southern California Pipe Trade trust fund—the top union officers are, in almost every case, also the union trustees on the fund. These are individuals who, on the surface at least, would not have an easy time separating their deep and long-standing commitment to their union from their responsibilities to the fund.

The five management trustees on the board of the Central States fund come from regional trucking associations in the Midwest, Southeast, and Southwest. They are by no means strangers to the Teamsters leadership and include individuals who regularly meet with Teamsters officials on labor relations matters, who play golf with them, and who otherwise enjoy a friendly relationship and frequent contact. It is hard to imagine them as independent watchdogs.[14]

As with most other union pension funds, the current Central States trustees —union and management—do not have any previous experience in pension management or administration, although they have hired, again in line with common practice, a full-time administrator responsible for the day-to-day management of the fund.

The Central States fund has another basic similarity to almost all other jointly administered pension funds. The trustees serve indefinite terms at the pleasure of the party that appointed them. In fact, the trustees of nearly all private pension funds, both union and corporate, serve on this basis, and the result is structural conflict. The trustees are supposed to act solely in the interest of fund beneficiaries, but they are dependent on union or management for their very jobs. Rare is the pension fund that provides some sense of independence for the trustees by creating terms of specific length. (The author was able to find only one example among union pension funds: The United Mine Workers fund, whose trustees serve three-year terms under an arrangement mandated by court decree.[15]) Among jointly administered funds, at least, the by-laws typically state that any trustee can be removed from office at any time and for any reason by the appointing party. Through this mechanism alone, the union leadership maintains complete and unchallenged control over the affairs of the fund, particularly when management does not play an active role. The trustees become an extension of the appointing party—indeed, the appointing party and the trustees often are one and the same—rather than separating the union or managment from the pension fund.

This incestuous arrangement is reinforced by the fact that in the great majority of cases, the attorney for the union serves as legal counsel to the fund. There is some uneasiness in the legal profession about such dual representation, and the National Coordinating Committee for Multiemployer Plans asked the Department of Labor in late 1974 for a ruling that dual representation of a union and its pension fund by the same attorney is not a violation of ERISA. The department has yet to respond and may never formally do so. As a result there is growing disquiet over whether the arrangement is legal.

Moreover, if a conflict of interest were to develop between a union and its pension fund, the attorney would be serving two masters. Such a conflict might arise, for instance, if that attorney were to discover in his official capacity as counsel to the union the the union had in some way misused the assets of the fund. The information would presumably be protected by client-attorney privilege. Yet the attorney might have an even more overriding responsibility as fund counsel to bring the matter to the attention of the fund trustees or, if they did not act to curb the abuse, perhaps even seek to correct the situation himself. One lawyer who serves both a union and its fund confesses that he has "serious ethical problems" with the arrangement, but he argues that legal restrictions against dual representation might actually do more harm than good by robbing many pension funds of the services of attorneys who are in a position, by reason of their union affiliation, to serve the funds inexpensively, knowledgeably, and well. This is an instance of the familiar fact that reducing or eliminating conflicts involves taking on new costs and, possibly, worse problems than the conflicts raised.

The broad issue of union control of members' pension funds came to a head in 1971, in the landmark case entitled *Blankenship* v. *Boyle*.[16] Ironically, this case involved the very same union—the United Mine Workers—that Congress had sought, through passage of Taft-Hartley, to curb from misusing the power of its pension fund. That law, it turned out, had not done its job.

Blankenship is a union member who decided that the United Mine Workers was misapplying the power of its members' welfare and retirement fund in ways that benefited the union rather than the fund participants, and he sued in federal district court. His suit brought to light two specific ways in which the United Mine Workers was using the fund to its own ends:

1. The fund had over a period of years deposited up to 44 perent of its assets interest-free in the National Bank of Washington, of which the union was 74 percent owner. When the Blankenship suit was filed, the fund had $28 million in checking accounts and $50 million in time deposits in the bank. Judge Gerhard A. Gessel of the U.S. District Court for the District of Columbia found this practice to be a breach of fiduciary obligation by the trustees of the fund.

2. The union had developed a broad plan for using fund investments to pressure electric utilites to buy union-mined coal. Two utilites were singled out: Cleveland Electric Illuminating Co. and Kansas City Power & Light Co. Between February and April 1955, the United Mine Workers' fund bought thirty thousand shares of Cleveland Electric stock; in March of that year, the fund loaned money to Cleveland industrialist Cyrus S. Eaton, who was sympathetic to the union's goals, to buy another twenty thousand shares in his own name. Eaton, who was given a general proxy for the fund shares as well as holding full voting rights to his own shares, then got himself elected to the Cleveland Electric board. Similarly, between January and March 1955, the fund bought fifty-five thousand shares of Kansas City Power & Light stock and in June loaned Eaton the money to buy an additional twenty-seven thousand shares. During 1962 and 1963, when the campaign for union coal focused on Cleveland Electric, the fund bought another ninety thousand shares of that company's stock. At the time of the 1962-63 purchases, Gesell noted in his decision, one of the fund trustees was president of the principal coal company that stood to benefit from Cleveland Electric purchases of union coal. Gesell found the transaction to be "a clear case of self-dealing" that, like the bank deposits, represented a breach of trust.

Gesell forced a major restructuring of the United Mine Workers' fund by throwing out two of the three trustees, by requiring that the fund obtain "independent professional advice" to help in formulating an investment policy, by forcing the fund to stop doing business with the union-controlled National Bank of Washington, and by specifying that the fund could no longer maintain noninterest-bearing accounts at any bank in excess of current cash needs.

Since then, the fund has emerged as what some people in the pension field consider to be a model of independence from its sponsoring union. The fund is managed by a three-man board of trustees.[17] Harry Huge, a Washinton, D.C. attorney who represented Blankenship and almost single-handedly waged that case, is now the union trustee, appointed in 1974 by the United Mine Workers' president and the chairman of the board. Huge's appointment broke the long-standing tradition that the position of union trustee be filled by the United Mine Workers' president himself. Another basic change has been the appointment of an active and strong-willed neutral trustee: Paul R. Dean, former dean of Georgetown University Law School. All three trustees—Huge, Dean, and C.W. Davis, the management trustee, who is very active in fund operations—are serving fixed three-year terms that are specified in the United Mine Workers' contract with the coal operator.

Huge says the fund board has tried to make the fund independent from the union and the industry. Investment management has been placed in the hands of six outside counselors, who have been given broad investment guidelines by the fund trustees but who are free to make individual investment decisions on their own. By giving the managers discretionary authority, the trustees hope to assure that investments are not chosen on the basis of whether they might benefit the union. The fund also has established a written, detailed conflict-of-interest policy that bars all fund officials and employees from taking any personal advantage of their relationship with the fund. And unlike most other union pension funds, the United Mine Workers' fund is currently in the process of creating its own independent field staff to serve the needs of pensioners. Huge believes this field staff will remove the fund from disputes between labor and management and that it will eliminate the internal power that union field representatives have traditionally acquired by solving pensioners' problems.

But the United Mine Workers' fund, in its court-mandated efforts to achieve independence, is unique. It is naive to assume that the interests of fund beneficiaries are similarly protected in other funds. In the absence of effective institutional controls, protection of the beneficiaries' interests depends on one of three things: (1) the assertion of rights by the beneficiaries themselves; (2) strong governmental oversight and enforcement efforts; or (3) the good faith of the union leadership to do what is right for the beneficiaries.

The beneficiaries, however, seldom have the power or the interest to intervene in an area about which they know very little. They tend to follow the union on these matters and do not complain as long as steady pension increases—or at least the appearance of steady increases—are achieved through collective bargaining.

Government efforts at regulation have in the past been clearly inadequate—the Teamsters' Central States case is a prime example—although ERISA may eventually change this situation.

For the moment, therefore, the primary power for faithful and honest administration of union pension funds is in the hands of the unions themselves.

Certainly, there are many unions that have, year in and year out, managed their workers' pension monies well. But until the basic structural conflicts of these funds are remedied by Congress, the possibilities for abuse by less dedicated union leaders, accommodated by passive, even neglectful, management trustees, will probably remain.

III • INVESTMENT CONFLICTS

A few years ago, the trustees of the United Mine Workers' retirement fund discovered that one of the outside investment managers had purchased shares of J.P. Stevens & Co. stock on behalf of the fund. Because J.P. Stevens is widely regarded in labor circles as anti-union, the trustees immediately directed the advisor to sell the shares; in addition, they instituted a specific policy—which was passed on to all fund managers—against investing in companies that were strongly anti-union. [1]

On another occasion the United Mine Workers' fund found itself in the strange position of holding shares in the Southern Co., an Atlanta-based electric utility, at the same time the union was picketing against importation of South African coal by that very corporation. [2]

In the opposite direction, the Teamsters' Central States fund has sometimes been used by the union *against* nonunion companies. In several instances, the Central States fund has loaned money to a corporation or purchased its shares on the open market, and from that position of strength, the union has been able to pressure management into supporting organization of the company's workers by the Teamsters. [3] (The presence of management trustees on the board of a union pension fund, even when these trustees are active, provides little protection against this tactic because it is actually in the best interests of unionized employers to eliminate the use of less expensive, nonunion labor by their competitors.)

Still other funds, particularly in the construction trades, often invest in ways designed to create jobs for union members.

Because they invest at all, union pension funds are, like any other investor, bound to encounter problems. In the case of the union funds, these problems often are heightened by the fact that essentially the unions stand in opposition, both philosophically and economically, to the corporate world in which their pension funds are invested. Union funds are unique in this regard. Among major types of financial institutions, none holds such a position of ambiguity in terms of its relationship with corporate America. Unions bargain for higher wages and benefits, seek cost-of-living wage escalation clauses, and strike to protect their members; such actions tend to hold down corporate profits. But as investors, the union trustees on a Taft-Hartley fund are expected to hope for rising profits that will increase stock prices.

Understandably, it may sometimes be difficult for labor unions to separate their strong commitment to the economic well-being of their workers from the investment needs of their pension funds. They confront a number of hard questions; for example.

1. Should a union pension fund take into account any pro- or anti-union bias of a company in deciding whether to invest in its stock?

2. Should it avoid investments in foreign securities—on the theory that foreign companies, when they prosper and sell goods to the U.S. market, take jobs from American workers?

3. Should a union pension fund choose investments that might create job opportunities for union members, even when such investments are economically inferior to alternative choices?

4. Should fund investments ever be used as a bargaining tool or organizing lever?

5. Should union pension funds, because of the labor movement's historic commitment to improving the quality of life, emphasize "social responsibility" in their investment policies—that is, invest in ways that will in general terms benefit society as a whole and avoid investments of questionable social merit?

Union funds are under especially strong pressures on the "social responsibility" issue. On the one hand, politicians and labor leaders have repeatedly called for union funds to do a better job of managing their investments in socially responsible and economically productive ways. On the other, if maximum investment returns are sacrificed in the process, there is the danger that fund beneficiaries will suffer financially. According to one widely accepted estimate, a fund can typically increase its pension payouts by 10 to 20 percent for every percentage-point gain in the overall rate of return on its portfolio.

Union pension funds also face potential conflicts in the area of investments in the securities of employers that contribute to that fund. Congress, through enactment of ERISA, has sought to reduce the danger of abuse in this area by prohibiting both union and corporate pension funds from investing more than 10 percent of their assets in the marketable securities of contributing employers and by establishing a total ban against direct loans to these employers.[4] But in any case the temptation to invest in the securities of contributing employers has always been much milder for union funds than for corporate pension funds, and the by-laws of a number of major union plans—including those of the National Maritime Union[5] and the Textile Workers Union[6]— actually contain total bans against investments in the securities of participating employers.

Union pension funds have good reason to avoid investing in contributing employers. If a union pension fund were to invest in such securities the question would immediately arise regarding which ones to buy and which ones to shun, and very few broadly based union funds want to risk opening that Pandora's box. In addition, as a trustee of one large union fund says, "I can just see us getting into a very bad position if we were to invest in companies in our own industry. What happens if you want to strike? To me, it conjures up all sorts of problems." This trustee adds, however, that, even with a flat ban against such investments, problems can still arise. He cites the theoretical case of a fund investing in a conglomerate that subsequently acquires a company whose workers are represented by the union. He says his own fund's by-laws, while outlawing industry investments, give no guidelines about what the trustees should do in a more complex case such as this.

Besides facing their own special areas of potential conflict, union pension funds differ from corporate funds in a number of other ways: They tend to invest more heavily in bonds and less actively in stocks, primarily because investment losses by a union fund generally are not made up by the contributing employers. A recent study by Becker Securities found the median equity commitment of Taft-Hartley pension trusts to be 59 percent at year-end 1974, versus 70 percent for corporate funds.[7]

Union funds also have a reputation for being less sophisticated in their investment practices than their corporate counterparts. A bank trust officer says, for instance, that union funds hate to take realized losses on their holdings. "So sometimes you're forced to stay with securities longer than otherwise in hopes you'll get back to cost," he adds. "It doesn't make any sense, but this happens to be part of the animal." One explanation for the lack of sophistication among union funds, if this criticism is indeed true, is that the trustees typically come from the ranks of corporate labor relations officials and union officers, and the trustees of corporate pension funds are likely to be corporate financial officers with day-to-day business experience in investment matters.

In line with this alleged lack of sophistication, some investment managers say there is a tendency, particularly among the smaller funds, for union plans to make a certain number of low-grade, questionable investments. One bank trust officer complains that several of his bank's Taft-Hartley clients have made such investments even against the bank's specific advice. These investments, the bank official says, include New York City bonds by a number of New York-area crafts union pension funds, low-grade bonds of corporations that employ union members, and Israeli bonds acquired in fund-raising drives with which union leadership was involved. In the past the bank official says the bank has gone along with these investments as long as the fund trustees have submitted a letter absolving the bank of all legal liability. However, under ERISA exculpation of outside managers is no longer possible; they share full responsibility regardless of any special arrangement with fund trustees. So, the bank official says, his bank is beginning to fight all attempts by unions to make investments with which the bank disagrees.

Although ERISA seems to be solving the problem of lower grade investments, more deep-seated conflicts involving broad social and economic issues remain. And unfortunately, when a union does encounter such issues, the answers are seldom clear. A corporate pension plan might easily buy J.P. Stevens stock without considering that company's anti-union stand. But by its nature a union pension fund cannot be expected to ignore such considerations totally. If a union fund refuses to invest in J.P. Stevens, it may find itself accused of molding its investment policy to suit its sponsoring union rather than the fund beneficiaries; it it does invest, however, it may come under fire from other unions and even, perhaps, from some fund beneficiaries themselves. Trustees of union funds must therefore think through the issues carefully and decide on the basis of what works best for their individual fund; rigid guidelines cannot be established in this area.

A few union pension funds, such as the $299 million Internation Ladies Garment Workers Union plan, simply avoid investing in common stocks at all, both on ideological grounds and in line with a conservative investment policy that seeks to protect assets rather than to achieve capital growth. This fund holds approximately 30 percent of its assets in triple-A and double-A rated corporate bonds and the remainder in U.S. guaranteed securities and mortgages.[8] (But does this policy really benefit fund participants, particularly because the fund has sacrificed capital growth?) Even within that limited investment realm, this fund gives some consideration to the union policies of companies in deciding which bonds to buy.

In general, however, bank trust officers and independent money managers say that suprisingly few union pension funds give much thought to such issues. An official of one major New York bank, which is among the leaders in the number of Taft-Hartley pension trusts under its management, says that perhaps 10 percent of the bank's client funds have asked the bank to avoid anti-union or foreign investments. Even less concern is reported by Morgan Guaranty Trust Co., which, although number one in overall trust assets under its management, is down the list in the specific area of Taft-Hartley funds. "We have not had any instance in which a Taft-Hartley board of trustees has told us not to buy any type of stock or buy a specific type of stock," says Bernard F. Curry, senior vice president of Morgan. "As a practical matter, this just doesn't happen."[9] (Of course, Morgan is well known for assuming full investment authority for client portfolios and for refusing to allow clients to interfere even if they want to.) Curry adds that Morgan would not be averse to a general prohibition by a union pension fund against buying stocks in the fund's own industry but probably would object to any prohibition against specific stocks.

There apparently is no concern at all over broader social and humanistic issues related to the general thrust of unionism. Lawrence Smedley, associate director of the AFL-CIO department of social security, recently argued that pension fund assets "should be invested in more socially useful objectives than is now the case."[10] His statement echoes a call to action that comes from leaders of the labor movement every two or three years. But a lawyer who has served on the boards of a number of funds says that there is seldom any follow-through at the level where it counts: fund boards of trustees. He says, for instance, that he has never heard any discussion of avoiding investments in South Africa. "You'd be laughed out of the room if you raised such issues," he says, adding that rank-and-file union members tend to be very conservative. A specific example recently surfaced in the press, although not involving a union pension fund per se. In this case a Hartford, Connecticut, firemen's union sued to block the city-run firemen's pension fund from investing $500,000 with a black-owned savings and loan association. The union charged that the savings association offered 6.75 percent interest, while some insurance companies offered 9 percent.[11]

The United Mine Workers' fund has been seeking to lend $100,000 at bargain rates to a union-affiliated hospital in Illinois to equip a clinic for the treatment of black lung disease.[12] Obviously, this loan would benefit all union members, although not fund participants as a specific class. But the transaction has been delayed for twenty months pending a requested Department of Labor exemption from the prohibited transaction rules of ERISA. People in the union pension fund field generally agree that, without special Department of Labor dispensation, "socially conscious" investments are legal for union funds under ERISA only if the potential investment returns are equal to those available elsewhere.

Calls for more social awareness in pension fund investment practices have repeatedly and specifically enjoined organized labor to build housing and to create jobs. AFL-CIO president George Meany has taken this stand on many occasions, as have prominent members of Congress. In 1969, for instance, Senator Jacob Javits (R.-N.Y.) called on organized labor "to put its pension trust funds to work toward eradicating slums and creating jobs in poverty areas."[13] In 1970 Congressman Wright Patman (D.-Tex.) introduced legislation to require certain nonprofit funds to invest a percentage of their assets in home mortgages. Although the Patman bill did not pass, it reflects a fairly widespread view in Congress that nonprofit financial institutions have an obligation to invest in socially productive ways.

But as a matter of fact, ERISA has terminated much of this activity, and some people in the labor movement are very upset. In particular, ERISA has slowed the very common practice of lending money in ways that create jobs for union members in the construction trades. A number of funds have traditionally invested heavily in short-term construction loans and home mortgages as a means of spurring activity in their industry. An outstanding example is the International Brotherhood of Electrical Workers pension fund. About 50 percent of that fund's $750 million in assets (including monies it invests for the Electrical Contractors Associations) is in Federal Housing Administration and

Veterans Administration guaranteed mortgages on one family homes. To qualify for Electrical Worker financing, homes must be built completely with union labor.

The issues here tend to be very complex and, at times, even contradictory; for despite the obvious merits, there are dangers. Christopher J. McClellan, a portfolio manager specializing in real estate for Kennedy/Boston Associates, Inc., in Seattle, has pointed out that union-built homes can be more expensive to build than nonunion built homes.[14] These higher costs, in his view, subject such housing to potentially higher mortgage default rates, even though investment returns are generally not higher and do not compensate for the added risk. Other problems cited by McClellan include: increased risk when a union fund invests only in real estate within the union's own jurisdictional boundaries, the possibility of conflict-of-interest abuses when the union invests in housing being erected by employers contributing to the fund, and the difficulty of distinguishing between union-built structures and those built wholly or in part by nonunion labor.

Specifically, ERISA banned all loans by pension funds to contributing employers—superficially, a reasonable and well-intentioned action. Because of the absence of arm's-length negotiating, loans to participating employers present special difficulties, and the fund may not receive a fair market return for its money. In addition, there have been a number of cases in which funds have failed to obtain adequate security from participating employers and in which union officials have allegedly received kickbacks.

The Department of Labor, under pressure from the unions, issued a partial exemption in March 1976, fifteen months after ERISA took effect. Under this exemption, short-term construction loans to participating employers are allowed through a bank, insurance company, or federally chartered savings and loan association. However, that intermediary must have full discretionary authority to approve the loans and negotiate the terms; hence, obviously, there is no guarantee that the loans will go to the intended employers and create jobs for the union members. In addition, short-term loans to one employer cannot exceed 10 percent of the fund's assets, and those to all employers cannot exceed 35 percent. These rules apply only to short-term loans. Because the department declined to exempt permanent mortgages to contributing employers, such long-term mortgages are still prohibited by ERISA.[15]

Union pension funds remain free to invest in nonunion construction, but that, of course, is not what unionism is all about. These conflicts—the desire to invest in housing, thereby benefiting the public and creating jobs, versus the potential abuses when union pension funds lend money to contributing employers—defy clear solution. The current thrust is very strongly in the direction of preventing abuse with little concern for the union member who is out of work. A balanced approach, more freely allowing construction loans with reasonable controls, would seem to be a better solution for both pension beneficiaries (who, after all, are not likely to be concerned about potential

investment conflicts if they cannot even find jobs) and the funds themselves
(which prosper most when contributing employers prosper).

IV • SELF-DEALING: HOW WIDESPREAD IS IT?

The specter of Teamster pension abuses hangs over the entire pension field.
Union fund trustees, complaining that outsiders tend to assume that all union
funds engage in self-dealing, find themselves in a terrible bind: if the federal
government, through the departments of Labor and Justice and the Internal
Revenue Service, aggressively investigates alleged Teamster abuses, the resulting bad publicity will hurt all pension funds. If, on the other hand, the
government does not pursue the matter aggressively, abuses may continue and
eventually prove even more damaging. Some pension managers worry that
either course could create congressional support for a takeover of union
funds—and perhaps of corporate pension funds as well. In fact, Ira M.
Shepard, minority counsel to the Senate Labor Committee, suggests that union
pension abuses decisively influenced the passage of ERISA in 1974.[1] Others
may dispute this view, but it reflects widespread concern that the union funds,
because of their alleged misdeeds, may be bringing the weight of the federal
government down on all pension funds.

A third possibility for resolution of the current Teamsters controversy, of
course, is that the Central States fund could reform itself. This possibility may
actually be the most logical of the three, particularly in light of the greatly
increased legal responsibility of fund trustees under ERISA.[2] A number of
newspaper reports already have suggested that the Central States trustees are
sweating out their increased legal exposure and are curtailing the fund's heavy
investment activities in real estate, the area that seems most susceptible to
fraud.[3]

Just how widespread are self-dealing and other forms of abuse in the union
pension field? Are the union funds actually any worse on this count than
corporate pension funds? These questions remain largely unanswered.

Despite public opinion to the contrary, thousands of union funds remain
untainted by self-dealing and fraud. Even among the various Teamsters funds,
although some seem to be constantly in trouble, others are not. There are about
forty separate Teamster pension funds in the United States, including the two
largest union pension funds of all—the $1.5 billion Teamsters' Western Con-
ference fund and the $1.4 billion Teamsters' Central States fund. Although the
Central States fund has been repeatedly accused in the press of abuse, the
Western Conference fund has conducted its affairs quietly, honestly, and
efficiently. The Central States fund manages most of its investments internally
—a procedure that perhaps allows greater latitude for fraud if trustees are
indeed so inclined. The Western Conference fund has turned all its assets over

to the Prudential Insurance Co. of America for management[4] and in that way may have helped shield its trustees and staff from even the temptation to abuse.

There are actually two broad areas of possible abuse: criminal fraud, including embezzlement, and self-dealing, which may or may not violate criminal law.

The term *self-dealing* refers, not surprisingly, to dealing with oneself. Examples of self-dealing include investments by a fund in enterprises controlled by a fund trustee, the arranging of loans to friends or relatives, and the hiring of organizations that are controlled by the trustees or their relatives. The major identifying points are an absence of arm's-length negotiation and the likelihood that the person (or persons) arranging the transaction stands in some way to benefit from it.

Clearly criminal activities such as embezzlement and kickbacks do not involve "self-dealing" so much as blatant fraud. The union or corporate treasurer who steals $50,000 from the pension fund is engaged in ordinary thievery, not "self-dealing."

Criminal activities would seem—on the surface, at least—to represent a very special problem for the union sector of the pension industry. Charles Ruff, former chief of the management and labor section of the criminal division of the Justice Department, has asserted that there are opportunities for fraud in three general areas of union pension fund operations: collection of contributions, payment of benefits, and investments.

In the first area the plan's staff is charged with receiving the weekly or monthly payments made by the plan's members which, depending on the size of the plan, could total as much as several hundred thousand dollars a month. Whenever this kind of money flow is present, particularly in small, less organized health and welfare plans, there is room for larceny. The second area presents somewhat more sophisticated problems, for the danger here is that the plan's assets (whether welfare or pension) may be misused by having benefits paid to persons not entitled to them. This may involve anything from mere technical violations of the plan's regulations concerning eligibility to clear cases of payments to persons who have failed to keep up the required contributions, or who are total strangers to the plan. The third area is the most troublesome since misuse of funds can be easily concealed, violations are more complex, and it is frequently difficult to distinguish between criminal misuse and unwise judgments that may call only for civil redress.[5]

There is a widespread feeling that outright graft is more of a problem with union pension funds than with corporate funds. One factor that may explain the higher incidence of fraud in union funds, if it is indeed higher, is that some union leaders, having literally fought their way to the top, are perhaps inclined to consider pension abuse as the spoils of office.

The charge that union funds are more susceptible to embezzlement and other types of blatant graft would seem to be borne out by the fact that during 1975-76 at least seven indictments for criminal fraud were delivered in cases involving union funds,[6] but the author of this report was unable to find a single criminal indictment during that same period involving alleged abuse of a corporate pension fund. However, more definitive proof is lacking, and it certainly is possible that the major difference between fraudulent activities in union pension funds and those in corporate funds is a matter of style rather than degree. Union funds may simply be looted in more spectacular and heavy-handed ways that, when discovered, make headlines and are easier for prosecutors to understand.

What are we to make of criminal fraud, then, as it relates to "conflicts" and "self-dealing"? The prevalence of thievery indicates that better structural controls are needed, perhaps including mandatory appointment of strong neutral trustees. Moreover, the current "defined contribution" financial structure of most union pension funds, although a natural outgrowth of collective bargaining, has created a situation in which neither management nor union is financially liable for a set level of pension rates, and so neither side has much incentive to institute strict financial controls. But it is unlikely that mandatory appointment of strong, neutral trustees would, for instance, put a stop to all random embezzlement by bookkeepers, investment managers, and union presidents. The ultimate answer—not a very revolutionary one—is that structural changes must be combined with continued strict enforcement of the criminal laws.

Thornier issues arise in transactions that are more purely "self-dealing" in nature. A number of practices have come to light, especially involving cases where:

- Certain borrowers have consistently been given highly favored treatment by the pension fund, for reasons that are not always clear.
- Investments have been made in companies in which one or more fund trustees have a personal investment stake.
- There have been direct financial dealings between the fund and the union, sometimes to the apparent detriment of the interests of the fund.
- Fund trustees have been paid what appear to be excessive fees by the fund, while also drawing salaries as full-time officers of the union.
- Outside "consultants" have been given favored status or paid seemingly excessive fees.

Since the beginning of 1975, when ERISA took effect, both union and corporate pension funds have been prohibited from engaging in any type of financial transaction with an "interested party"—that is, a fund trustee, union officer, employer officer, employer organization or the union itself.[7] But whether such an across-the-board ban is workable, and is indeed putting an end to self-dealing, remains to be seen.

Evidence of self-dealing is difficult to sort out completely from evidence of criminal fraud since all existing studies have lumped the two together.

The most damaging evidence about the degree if self-dealing/fraud goes back more than twenty years, to two reports by a special Senate subcommittee.

That Committee, originally chaired by Senator Irving M. Ives (R.-N.Y.), studied the general characteristics of union pension funds. The Ives Report analyzed twenty-seven Taft-Hartley funds and concluded that thirteen could be characterized as having questionable management practices and seven as having been grossly mismanaged.[8] Then in 1955 the committee, under the chairmanship of Senator Paul H. Douglas (D.-Ill.), investigated alleged mismanagement in the welfare plans of the Laundry Workers International Union and Local 52 of the Painters, Cleaners, and Caulkers Union. The Douglas Report went into more detail and expressed especially great concern about highly inflated commissions and fees being paid to insurance agents.[9] The report described how Louis B. Saperstein, an insurance agent, arranged with Security Mutual Life Insurance Company to receive a flat 10 percent annual commission for Laundry Workers Union's group insurance plan. Normally, a 10 percent commission would be paid only in the first year, with the rate declining sharply thereafter. During the period from April 1950 through September 1953, Saperstein collected $262,500 in commissions, versus the $18,125 he would have received under standard commission rates. When Security Mutual informed Saperstein in 1953 that it would have to reduce his commissions, he simply switched the policy to another company and collected an additional $91,000 until the new insurer in turn canceled. The committee found the practice of switching carriers to boost commissions to be widespread; more generally, it found a clear pattern of abdication of responsibility for fund operations by the participating employers, inadequate controls over disbursement of benefits, and excessive administrative costs.

Despite the warning implicit in the Douglas Report against the siphoning of monies by means of excessive insurance commissions, such practices have continued in at least a limited number of cases.

One example came to light in June 1976, when a Senate subcommittee released a report charging that in the late 1960s and early 1970s, the severance trust fund of Teamsters Local 195, New York, was depleted by $1.1 million through irregular administrative practices and that only $200,000 of this sum was ever recovered. The report cites an instance in which the fund paid $800,000 in life insurance commissions to an individual who, previously convicted of theft, did not even have a license to sell life insurance in New York. An accompanying General Accounting Office report says that the commissions would have totaled a mere $10,000 if the fund had contracted for more conventional group coverage rather than individual whole life benefits.[10]

This kind of favored treatment of certain outsiders is the most troublesome aspect of union fund self-dealing. Relatives, friends, insurance agents, or "advisors," rather than the trustees personally, are usually on the receiving end of good deals; thus, many transactions have been beyond the reach of the law.

For instance, in the 1960s the Teamsters' Central States fund loaned $12.3 million to Valley Steel Products Co. of St. Louis, Missouri.[11] Valley's president was the father of Robert Crancer, who was James Hoffa's son-in-law as well as a Valley executive himself. The loans were made while Hoffa, serving as international president of the Teamsters, was the dominant trustee on the Central States board. To complicate matters further, the Teamsters Union represented Valley's employees.

Another Central States example involves a series of loans by that fund to Morris Shenker, a St. Louis attorney who for years represented Hoffa. In one transaction the fund invested $116.7 million in the Penasquitos land development project in California. Shenker was co-owner of Penasquitos. But the Penasquitos project was slow in getting off the ground and the Central States fund was forced to take control with only $5.8 million of its loans repaid. However, under the unusual terms of the 1973 takeover agreement, the fund will owe a 20 percent equity interest to Shenker if Penasquitos ever becomes profitable. Furthermore, the 1973 agreement, while giving Shenker an equity stake, absolved him of all personal liability for Penasquitos' debts to the fund.[12]

Despite the setback suffered by the fund in the huge Penasquitos deal, the trustees went ahead and agreed in 1974 to lend Shenker $40 million to finance an expansion of the Dunes Hotel in Las Vegas, of which he is controlling stockholder. But the Dunes loan was held up pending approval by the Nevada Gaming Commission, and when that approval was finally given in May 1976, the Department of Labor stepped in and suggested that the transaction would violate ERISA. The fund trustees, who were under extreme federal pressure at the time to institute stricter administrative and investment practices, thereupon canceled their commitment, and Shenker sued the trustees for restoration of the loan.[13] The matter is now in the federal courts.

Another more successful borrower is Allen R. Glick, a thirty-four year-old real estate operator who seems to owe almost his entire business career to easy access to Central States loans. In one 1972 transaction, the fund foreclosed on $13 million of loans to Beverly Ridge Estates in California and then sold the property to Glick for $7 million, financing the entire purchase price by issuing Glick a twenty-five-year mortgage at a mere 4 percent annual interest.[14]

In the past federal pension laws have been limited in their scope and very rigid in the penalties that could be applied and therefore not especially effective in dealing with anything less than clear-cut cases of criminal abuse.

Before ERISA federal legislation relied heavily on the questionable concept that financial disclosure was the most effective means of preventing pension abuse. The key piece of pre-ERISA legislation was the Welfare and Pension Plans Disclosure Act of 1958—a direct outgrowth of the Ives and Douglas reports. Senator Douglas, expounding on the 1958 law, expressed his hope that "sunlight" would prove to be "a great disinfectant."[15] The 1958 act required for the first time the filing of annual financial reports with the Secretary of Labor but did not give the Secretary any power to enforce this requirement. Because of that glaring weakness, the law was controversial from its enactment. Amendments passed in 1962 provided for more detailed financial reports and gave the Secretary of Labor the authority to investigate filing violations and to refer suspected criminal violations to the Department of Justice. The 1962 amendments also tightened existing criminal liability by creating three special provisions prohibiting: (1) direct theft of plan assets; [16] (2) the filing of false reports or the making of false entries in the books of a plan;[17] (3) receiving kickbacks that influence performance of administrative duties.[18] Such activities were presumably prohibited under existing law, but the 1962 amendments strengthened the prosecutor's tools by specifically barring these activities in relation to a union or corporate pension fund.

Until ERISA, then, responsibility for preventing criminal abuse by union pension funds rested primarily with the Department of Justice and the individual states. In addition, the IRS held (and still holds) an all-or-nothing enforcement weapon—the revocation of the tax-exempt status of any pension fund that it considered to be in violation of the tax law—but it was unable to respond in more measured ways when it believed that less drastic action was appropriate. The Department of Labor, meanwhile, was responsible for maintaining and monitoring the financial reports of funds and for referring possible violations to the Department of Justice.

The enactment of ERISA radically changed the thrust of federal enforcement efforts by: (1) creating a variety of new civil penalties for violations of the law, supplementing the previous rigid system under which only criminal statutes were available to federal prosecutors; (2) giving the Department of Labor greatly expanded authority to pursue alleged violations, both criminal and civil; (3) placing greatly expanded responsibility on all those involved with a pension fund, either as trustees or advisors, to act in the exclusive interests of the fund beneficiaries; and (4) establishing the first blanket ban against all financial dealings between a fund and its contributing employers, sponsoring union, trustees, and/or advisors, although this ban will not necessarily remain absolute. The law provides flexibility by giving the Department of Labor the power to exempt specific categories of self-dealing as long as such transactions are, in the department's view, administratively feasible to exempt, are in the best interests of the funds, and do not harm the rights of plan beneficiaries.

However, one increasingly apparent problem is that ERISA assigns overlapping responsibilities to the Department of Labor and the IRS. The printed law includes a four-page section explaining which agency is responsible for enforcement of which specific provisions of ERISA and emphasizing the need for coordination between Labor and the IRS. But there has been a great deal of in-fighting between the two over which agency will assume primary responsibility for bringing charges against violators of the law and for issuing administrative exemptions. James D. Hutchinson, who resigned in August as the Labor Department's chief administrator of ERISA, has been quoted as saying he did so because of frustration over bickering between Labor and the IRS and the resulting inefficiency of either side in granting exemptions to the prohibited transactions rules and enforcing the rules themselves.[19]

Nowhere has the dispute between Labor and the IRS shown up more clearly than in the current federal investigation of the Central States fund. Relying on ERISA the Department of Labor announced in October 1975 that it was undertaking a major investigation of that fund.[20] Then eight months later, the IRS, without advance warning to the Labor Department, launched its own action against Central States by revoking the fund's tax-exempt status.[21] Department of Labor officials reportedly were furious. Since then the IRS has backed off somewhat by granting a series of temporary extensions of the fund's tax-exempt status. As this report went to press, the latest of these extensions was scheduled to expire on February 28, 1977.

Meanwhile, the Department of Labor is continuing its investigation and should complete it by late 1977 or early 1978. The Central States case looms as the first key test of whether ERISA really works.

So far, two civil lawsuits involving union funs have been brought under ERISA by the Department of Labor:

1. In November 1976 the department sued in federal district court in Knoxville, Tennessee, for the removal of five trustees of the Southern Labor union pension and welfare funds.[22] The suit charges that the trustees engaged in prohibited transactions by, among other things, leasing an airplane for the fund from a company partly owned by two of the trustees. One of the two trustees— Ted Q. Wilson, the union's general counsel—has denied any violation of the law, saying that after passage of ERISA, the two trustees gave their stock in the aircraft company to the pension fund to avoid any conflict.[23] The case is pending in court.

2. In January 1977 the department filed suit in federal district court in Brooklyn, charging that George Snyder, secretary-treasurer of Teamsters Local 806, received $1 million from the local's three pension and welfare funds, apparently in return for services as a trustee of the funds. The suit alleges that, in the case of the pension fund, the payments to Snyder equalled 80 percent of the employer contributions to the fund during the most recent fiscal year and that such payments were excessive. The suit further alleges a series of transactions in which thirteen past and present trustees of the funds, including Snyder, improperly spent $380,000 to redecorate offices at Local 806 headquarters. In addition, the suit alleges that the pension fund made an unsecured loan of $180,000 to the union local in 1971. When state investigators discovered the loan and ordered it repaid, the local allegedly repaid the loan by borrowing $300,000 from a bank using pension assets as collateral. The Department of Labor, in its suit, originally sought the removal of all fund trustees and appointment of an interim receiver. Three weeks later the department backed off and agreed to allow four of the defendants—three of them officers of the union local—to stay in charge of administration of the funds at weeky salaries of $825, $750, $600, and $300 each, in addition to their union

salaries. The four are being paid as employees of a service corporation the department wants dissolved on the ground that it is a dummy operation set up to milk the funds. The department also has agreed to let Snyder remain as the sole union trustee on one of the funds. Under the terms of a consent decree, all thirteen defendants, except the four administrators, have agreed not to take any direct or indirect payments from the funds. Although Department of Labor officials have defended this agreement as providing the best possible protection for fund beneficiaries pending ultimate court resolution of the department's lawsuit, Rep. John F. Pickle (D.-Tex.), member of a House subcommittee that is investigating welfare fund abuses, has objected vehemently, contending that "on the surface it looks like worse than a conflict of interest to have four defendants operating as quasi-receivers."[24]

But the big test of ERISA still lies ahead, in the outcome of the Central States investigation. This investigation may provide the first clear indication about whether self-dealing has continued to occur in the face of that law and whether the Department of Labor has the skills and willpower to be vigorous in challenging self-dealing and other abuses. Although ERISA has been in effect for more than two years, the record on both those issues remains very much open to question.

V • HOW EMPLOYERS SOMETIMES SHORTCHANGE UNION FUNDS

Abuses by union officials are not the only source of problems for union pension funds. Contributing employers can at times be equally difficult. One fund lawyer says that delinquent employer contributions—and what to do about them—probably represent the largest single day-to-day problem for the great majority of union pension plans.

Few funds escape this problem. Of 459 Taft-Hartley funds surveyed in 1974 by the International Foundation of Employee Benefit Plans, less than twelve reported that all employer payments to the fund were up to date.[1] The typical delinquency rate of total payments due is 2 to 3 percent annually, and in the construction industry, where many employers are only marginally profitable and bankruptcies are commonplace, delinquencies are often 5 percent or more. The International Foundation study found that, despite the obvious problem, about 20 percent of the 459 funds had not instituted adequate collection procedures and that 44 percent wanted federal legislation to (1) make failure to pay required contributions a criminal offense; (2) give fund contributions the same priority as wages in bankruptcy proceedings; (3) require bonding of employers or make it a mandatory topic in collective bargaining; (4) hold delinquent employers personally liable.

The issue of delinquencies is obviously an important one, for contributions are the lifeblood of any fund and generally far outpace investment income as a source of new cash. Most union funds are supported by contributions from hundreds or thousands of different employers, and these small to moderate sums can add up to a substantial annual cash flow. The largest union fund, that of the Central States, collects about $336 million annually from twenty thousand employers and disburses about $240 million in benefits, for a net annual cash flow, excluding investment income, of approximately $96 million.[2] Even a relatively small fund like the $7.1 million Albany, Schenectady, Troy and Vicinity District Council of Carpenters Pension Fund collects $1.3 million a year from three hundred fifty employers.[3]

On the positive side, the tremendous diversity of the sources of this income shields union funds from the financial risk in relying on one employer—a risk that is inherent in corporate pension plans. This diversity, however, also creates control problems and may lead to three specific types of abuse:

1. A union may privately arrange for certain employers to pay reduced rates or even suspend payments for a certain period. Union funds are especially vulnerable to this tactic when management trustees, who should obviously want *all* employers to pay their fair share, allow the union to control the fund. The union might offer reduced payments as a bargaining or organizing tool. For instance, it might secretly arrange for a company to be granted reduced pension payments for the first year if the company agrees to allow the union to organize the company's workers. This tactic, although difficult to document, is said to have been employed by a number of major union funds. All sorts of variations on the theme of reduced payments also are possible—in each case to the benefit of the union and certain employers and to the detriment of the fund and its beneficiaries. The union officers might grant reduced payments in return for kickbacks, or they might temporarily forego contributions from certain companies whose officers serve on the fund board if these officers agree to ignore fund loans to friends of the union. Regardless of the specific arrangement, the key point is that legal controls are often inadequate to prevent such abuses.

2. Some employers more commonly delay payments on their own, perhaps in response to a dispute with the union over a matter unrelated to the fund or perhaps simply to use the cash. Again, it is the fund and its beneficiaries who suffer.

3. Finally, there is the practical problem of how to collect overdue contributions, particularly from employers who are only marginally profitable or who appear close to financial collapse. The key question is: what is in the best interests of the workers? If the fund presses for immediate payment, it may force the employer out of business and cost union members their jobs. If, on the other hand, the fund lets the matter ride, it may eventually have to write off the

contribution as uncollectible, ultimately creating an atmosphere of laxity in which all employers can feel free to delay payments at will. The International Foundation of Employee Benefit Plans study found that delinquencies often involve the same employers—an indication that there may be a tendency for some employers to take advantage of the absence of legal penalties for failure to pay on time. As many as 5 percent of the contributing employers to a major fund may be consistently late in their payments.[4]

The Department of Labor recently tried to address these problems and in June 1975 issued tough new rules governing such delinquencies,[5] but it was forced to relent considerably because of both the complexity of the issues and the opposition from union funds and some employers.

Under the original Department of Labor proposals, funds were required to take court action against any employer that failed to pay its scheduled contributions within sixty days of the original due date or within twenty-four months if the employer provided the fund with a secured note in lieu of payment. Such a note would have carried interest and been payable in installments. Exemption from these requirements would have been allowed by the Department of Labor only on a case-by-case basis and on specific application. The stated purpose was to stop such abuses and bring a measure of conformity to union pension collection practices.

The Department of Labor received 162 written comments on its proposals, almost all negative. Critics—primarily from the union funds—noted that the proposals overlooked the practical problem that delinquencies often are not discovered for months or even years after they occur; to require court action within sixty days of the delinquency would be unworkable. They also contended that, in those cases where it was possible to discover delinquencies quickly, the proposals would trigger a wave of bankruptcies among employers who were legitimately unable to pay their fund contributions on schedule. In general, the union funds asked that they be allowed to continue responding to delinquencies on an individual basis.

In March 1976 the Department of Labor withdrew its original proposals and issued final regulations that are much more general in nature.[6] In the proposals delinquent payments were a violation of ERISA, and legal action could be avoided by a union fund only if it acted within the proposed Department of Labor guidelines. In the final regulations, delinquent contributions are not a violation of ERISA. "However," the regulations state, "if the plan is not making systematic, reasonable and diligent efforts to collect delinquent contributions, or the failure to collect is the result of an arrangement, agreement or understanding, express or implied, between the plan and the delinquent employer, such failure to collect a delinquent employer contribution may be deemed to be a prohibited transaction." In addition, the regulations permit a plan to allow an employer to delay contributions only if (1) the plan has previously made "reasonable, diligent and systematic" efforts to collect the money; (2) the terms of the agreement are established in writing and are "reasonable"; and (3) the agreement is entered into for "the exclusive purpose of facilitating the collection of such contribution." Finally, it is legal for a plan to settle for less than the full amount of a delinquent contribution or to write off the contribution completely, but only if it already has complied with steps one and two.

Thus, the Department of Labor has given union pension funds the legal responsibility to make a reasonable and systematic effort to collect all employer contributions without establishing specific guidelines about how to go about this process. Moreover, the Department of Labor, for all its good intentions, appears to have left the door open to abuse because the regulations, directed exclusively at the pension funds, ignore the reality that the way to correct delinquencies is to put pressure on the employers and unions. Employers remain free to delay payments without restriction—unless the fund can force them to pay by threatening a court action or the union by threatening a work stoppage. Department of Labor officials must have been aware of this reality. But some fund lawyers suggest that, although the department holds the legal authority to force union funds to tighten their collection procedures, its authority to force contributing employers to pay on time is much less clear-cut. (Department officials themselves declined to discuss this matter with the author.) Any authority that the department does have over employers is contained in one of two sections of ERISA: Part 3, which deals with the funding of pension plans but does not discuss delinquent employer contributions, or Part 4, which establishes the duties of fund fiduciaries, outlaws all self-dealing, and establishes the funds' collection regulations. Part 4 prohibits pension funds from lending money to "parties in interest," including contributing employers, without approval. The Department of Labor views delinquent contributions as loans to employers and, despite protests from many union funds, on that basis established collection regulations. However, Part 4 apparently fails to give the department any real power over the employers. It says very specifically that "a fiduciary" shall not cause a plan to engage in a prohibited transaction; it does not, however, include contributing employers within its definition of fiduciary. Delinquent employer contributions, therefore, are a form of abuse that has apparently escaped ERISA's jurisdiction, except for whatever indirect pressure the Department of Labor has applied to the funds to force them to deal with the problem.

The chain of events in the contribution process begins in collective bargaining, where labor and management agree to a specific sum per worker to be paid into the pension plan. However, this agreement does not guarantee that all employers will contribute regularly or fully. The system tends to be loose, and the fund can suffer greatly when employers are lax. Typically, it is the union, rather than the fund, that tries to police the employers. The theory is that, because labor and management are adversaries and the union has a direct interest in enforcing the terms of its collective bargaining agreement, the union will serve as the most aggressive collection agency for the pension fund. But not all unions are equipped to fulfill their responsibility, and in a few cases, the union may actually work in collusion with certain employers to the detriment of the workers' interests. Certainly a better system, and one less susceptible to potential conflicts, would be for the pension fund to establish its own independent collection program and for federal legislation to support the funds by requiring employers to meet their obligations to the fund.

The problem of delinquent contributions is heightened by the long delays that often occur between an employer's failure to pay the full amount and the fund's discovery of that failure. Employers, like taxpayers filing tax returns, file forms stating the amount due and enclose a check. Because the system relies almost totally on the good faith of the employer, delinquencies may not come to light for months—and then only because a payroll audit was made or a worker filed for benefits and it was discovered that no contributions were made on his behalf. Spot checks of employer records could ameliorate this situation but generally are made only every two or three years. Furthermore, only about 39 percent of all union funds have full-time payroll audit programs.[7]

Union funds have wrestled for years with the problem of collecting overdue contributions. At times, because of inadequate legal remedies, the fund may be reduced almost to beggar's status. There is very little the union can do against a chronically delinquent employer except threaten a work slowdown or strike, a rather drastic step. The fund itself might ask for a secured or unsecured note for the overdue payments, but the employer is under no obligation to comply. Ultimately, the fund can sue for payment in court. But that can be a long and difficult process, and even when the fund is successful, all it receives is the payment itself with, perhaps, interest—a point that hardly encourages employers to pay their delinquent contributions.

The welfare and pension funds of Bakery Drivers Local 194, Union, New Jersey, describe their collection process this way:

Upon occasion we have taken notes, accompanied by a bond and warrant for confession of judgment, to enforce payment of delinquent accounts. It is our practice to seek personal endorsement or some other security, plus interest, to guarantee payment. However, this is not always successful and we have exercised our best judgment, with the advice of counsel, whether to forgo the endorsement, security or interest in order to recover contributions due. Among the factors we consider is the employer's past record, the contributions due, the effect of institution of suit and entry of judgment upon the employer's ability to continue in business and thereby continue current contributions while paying the delinquency, whether entry of an immediate judgment will result in other creditors filing a bankruptcy petition against the employer, etc.[8]

New legal remedies are clearly needed to deal with chronically delinquent employers. This abuse is widespread and will not be eradicated until the law imposes greater penalties on company officials who sanction delayed or reduced payments to their workers' pension plans.

VI • CONCLUSIONS

Union pension funds have grown rapidly over the past twenty years and now control an estimated $35 billion of invested assets. Traditionally, the investment activities of union pension funds have been subject to only weak federal controls, and fund beneficiaries have suffered because their interests often are considered after the interests of the union and the union officers.

In addition to inadequate federal controls, a number of other factors have heightened the vulnerability of union funds to abuse: (1) the lack of accountability when fund assets are depleted; (2) the general passivity of management trustees; (3) the resulting dominance of the union, through its own handpicked trustees; and (4) the tendency of some union leaders to view the fund as the spoils of office, rather than monies being managed for the exclusive benefit of fund participants.

Problems of abuse are intensified by a number of unique structural conflicts that, although not in themselves sinister, make the job of managing union pension fund assets for the exclusive benefit of fund participants a difficult one. One of these basic conflicts revolves around the fact that the unions stand in opposition, both philosophically and economically, to the corporate world in which their pension funds are invested. No other major financial institution maintains such an ambiguous relationship with corporate America. Understandably, it can be difficult for unions to reconcile their strong commitment to the labor movement with the investment needs of their pension funds. Specific issues that can arise out of this dilemma include: Should a union pension fund consider a company's pro- or anti-union bias in deciding whether to invest in its stock? Should fund investments ever be used as a bargaining tool or organizing lever? Should a union pension fund select investments that will create jobs for union members or select such investments when they are economically inferior to alternatives?

Although the majority of union pension funds are administered honestly and with the interests of fund beneficiaries foremost in mind, there is nonetheless great leeway for abuse. The honest management of union pension funds depends largely on the goodwill and integrity of union leaders rather than on any built-in system of controls.

The Employee Retirement Income Security Act of 1974 represents a major step forward in curbing the blatant wrongdoings that so often make the headlines: loans to organizations controlled by fund trustees or their friends, the looting of union funds by organized crime, investments made for the direct benefit of the union rather than in the interests of the beneficiaries.

Although ERISA is potentially strong, its enforcement by the Department of Labor remains a great unknown. The department holds primary responsibility for enforcing the fiduciary, vesting, and reporting requirements, and it is still too early to determine if the department will do its job well. The department's investigation of the Central States pension fund may, as Senator Jacob Javits has suggested,[1] prove to be a key test of whether (1) ERISA is actually effective in preventing abuses by both union and corporate funds and (2) the Department of Labor has the willpower and resources to investigate charges of corruption. One question is whether the unions will use their political power to try to block government action against abuses by union funds, particularly alleged abuses by the Central States fund. The Teamsters union has been very active politically during the past decade; its leaders have been honored guests at the White House, and the union has made substantial contributions to the election campaigns of many senators and congressmen. Only time will tell if the relationship between the federal regulators and the organizations they regulate is too strong to allow a truly thorough and independent investigation to be conducted.

In addition to ferreting out corruption, under ERISA, the Department of Labor is jointly responsible with the IRS for responding quickly and reasonably to requests for exemptions from the more technical aspects of the law. In this area these two agencies have so far failed to give much reason for optimism—although, of course, it is still fairly early and they may be suffering from some temporary growing pains. When ERISA was first introduced in Congress, there were two conflicting versions: One would have permitted private pension funds to continue dealing with "parties-in-interest"—contributing employers, unions, union officers, close relatives of union officers, and so on—except those transactions specifically prohibited through administrative action by enforcing agencies. This approach was to provide maximum operating flexibility for private pension funds, giving Labor and IRS responsibility for outlawing clear types of abuse. The other version, the one that prevailed, took the opposite route and banned all dealings with "parties-in-interest" except those transactions exempted by Labor and the IRS.[2] This approach was to ban all transactions that even hinted at abuse and to provide flexibility through an administrative exemption process. Because the second version was enacted by Congress, it is important that the Department of Labor and the IRS establish an efficient and evenhanded procedure for responding to exemption requests. If they do not, private pension plans, union and corporate, may become so entangled in red tape that they will not be able to function. So far Labor and the IRS have responded to very few of the many requests for exemptions; in those cases when they have responded, they have taken up to two years to do so. This timidity is unfortunate and may ultimately harm the interests of fund beneficiaries—despite the fact that ERISA is aimed at helping them. Loans *by* the union *to* the fund are an example of the type of transaction upon which the Department of Labor and the IRS refuse to reach a decision. In late 1974 the National Coordinating Committee for Multiemployer Plans requested a ruling that such transactions not be a violation of ERISA. Short-term loans from a union to its members' pension plan when the plan faces a temporary shortage or cash may, with proper controls, be in the best interests of fund beneficiaries. The enforcing agencies, however, have yet to address this issue either positively or negatively, and so the legality of union loans to union pension funds remains unresolved.

Although ERISA gives the Department of Labor the power to challenge flagrant abuses in union pension funds, it does little or nothing to resolve the most overriding conflict of all: the continued domination of these funds by their sponsoring unions. In spite of the jointly trusteed boards mandated by Taft-Hartley to correct this situation, an effective system of internal controls does not exist, and until new federal legislation resolves this conflict, a considerable measure of abuse, both petty and gross, is likely to continue in union pension funds.

Delinquent employer contributions also have escaped ERISA's jurisdiction, and new legislation may be needed to correct abuses by contributing employers who consistently fail to pay on time. Pension contributions are part of the workers' total wage package and deserve the same kind of preferential treatment in the law as cash wages and Social Security contributions. One underlying problem is that the interests of the three major groups involved in any union pension fund often conflict with one another: (1) the employers' interest lies in saving money by minimizing contributions to the fund; (2) the unions' major objective may be to maximize fund assets, thereby creating a power base for union organizing and bargaining activities; and (3) the pension fund's goals are to avoid all disputes between the employers and the union, to disburse benefits fairly, and to make sure that assets are not eroded—through excessive current pensions, questionable investment practices, or delinquent employer contributions—to the point where future benefits are imperiled. The current collection approach—under which the union, rather than the fund itself, generally holds the only meaningful power to police employer contributions— offers too many opportunities for secret deals between union and employer and should be replaced by an arrangement whereby the fund, backed by tough federal laws, serves as its own collection agency.

Also unresolved is the problem of conflicting values in the area of "socially responsible" investments by union pension funds. Over the years politicians and union leaders have repeatedly called for all private pension funds, particularly union funds, to make investments that facilitate the construction of new housing, clean up slums, create job opportunities, and in general provide direct benefits to the public. Because the roots of trade unionism are deeply intertwined with the efforts of social reformers to improve humanity's lot, it is often argued that union pension funds have an underlying responsibility to develop economically positive investment practices. The most tangible result of this theory is that a number of union funds have traditionally invested heavily in home construction—providing much-needed support for this lagging sector of our national economy and, even more specifically, creating jobs for union members in the construction trades.

But ERISA has stopped much of this activity. Congress apparently gave little thought to such side effects or how these side effects conflict with the oft-stated request that pension funds be sensitive to the social and economic implications of the investments they make. The key question is this: Is it more important for union pension funds to manage their assets in ways that finance new construction and create jobs for union members, with the potential for some abuse, or for abuse to be brought under strict control? These issues remain unresolved, and Congress and the Department of Labor should consider the pros and cons more objectively, instead of blindly seeking to crack down on abuse.

Specifice Proposals

1. Taft-Hartley should be revised so it can finally accomplish one of its major objectives: to remove pension funds from the uncontested control of their sponsoring unions. Two broad approaches are possible: a federal takeover of the management of union pension funds or a reorganization of fund boards to include independent, third-party trustees or to force management trustees to assume the active role envisioned by the framers of Taft-Hartley.

A government takeover, although occasionally suggested by critics of union funds and by some reformers as a step needed for all funds, would probably create as many problems as it would solve. Government officials are, after all, subject to as many human shortcomings as are union officers and management trustees. Furthermore, to have the government take over when the Department of Labor and the IRS are having trouble digesting their expanded regulatory authority under ERISA does not make any sense at all.

Even with government management of union pension assets, certain types of conflicts would simply be replaced by others. Currently, conflicts can arise when a union fund invests in employer securities. In the event of federal management, a similar conflict would exist when investments were made in government bonds or Treasury bills.

A government takeover of union pension funds would have a profoundly negative effect on the U.S. capital markets. The present system is rich in diversity and flexibility; the monolithic concentration of capital in the hands of a few government bureaucrats would, in the absence of competition, probably result in a rather heavy-handed, conservative, risk-free investment approach.

On the positive side, a government takeover of union funds would sound the death knell for most types of abuses that exist today. It also would automatically eradicate the central conflict of the union funds: union domination of monies that are supposed, by law, to be managed for the exclusive benefit of fund participants. But conflicts are an ever-present part of life and, in themselves, are not necessarily evil or dangerous. It is, rather, the abuses that flow from these conflicts that must be brought under control. And in the case of union pension funds, it is possible to control these abuses short of a government takeover.

The second, more logical, approach is to strengthen the independence of fund boards so unions no longer dominate. Along these lines, ERISA has provided a degree of help by holding trustees—union and management—responsible for fund misdoings. In some cases management trustees, fearing legal repercussions, already have become more active.

Three additional steps are possible: further legal changes that reinforce the seriousness of management trustees' responsibilites; the mandatory appointment of strong neutral trustees, in line with the United Mine Workers example; and specific terms of office for all union and management trustees, thereby creating some independence from the appointing party.

These steps recognize the basic advantages of having a union involved in, not controlling, the management of its members' pension fund. Union involvement is a logical outgrowth of the collective bargaining process; it is natural that labor and management, having agreed to pension terms in collective bargaining, should then jointly supervise the implementation of those terms. In addition, most unions are likely to be the most persistent and concerned spokesmen for their members' rights.

Mandatory one-third representation on the fund board by neutral trustees, coupled with one-third representation each by labor and management, provide a beginning to offset absolute union control. Like any approach, this one has problems—most notably, that of making sure that third-party trustees are qualified and active. Perhaps the most practical system would be to leave the selection of third-party trustees to labor and management, with court appointments where the two sides are unable to agree. Minimum professional standards might be established by law for third-party trustees: an accounting or law degree, for instance, or a minimum ten years' business experience in investment management.

To create an additional sense of independence for all trustees, minimum terms of office—perhaps three years—should be established by law. Under current practice trustees can be replaced at any time and for any reason by the appointing party. As a result trustees are forced to vote as the appointing party directs or risk immediate removal.

Beyond that it also is worth considering whether Congress should establish minimum standards of participation by all union pension fund trustees: mandatory high quorums, which will cause active management trustees to pressure chronic absentees to attend; regulations requiring that any trustee who misses two or three meetings without a valid reason be deemed to have resigned; and smaller boards—perhaps with a maximum of twelve members—so membership means something.[3] Regarding this last point, the sixty-member board of the International Ladies Garment Workers Union National Retirement Fund, although hardly typical, is an example of how a fund board can expand until a trusteeship becomes little more than an honorary position, bestowed on many and of significance only to those few trustees who dominate.

The above steps are all practical and workable. The United Mine Workers retirement fund, which has instituted similar practices under court mandate, has clearly shown how a union pension fund can establish an arm's-length relationship with its sponsoring union. Until other union funds are forced to do the same, it would be naïve to believe that the interests of fund beneficiaries will automatically come first.

2. New laws are needed to resolve the long-standing problem of delinquent employer contributions. Currently, delinquencies are subject to the same remedy used for almost all other types of contract defaults—civil suit in the courts. On the surface, at least, this arrangement may seem reasonable. But it actually reinforces union dominance of pension plans because only the unions have effective economic weapons—the threat of a strike or a work slowdown—to force delinquent employers to pay up. It is important, if funds are to be independent of their sponsoring unions, that the trustees be a separate group and have a stronger legal position to pursue delinquent employers. At the minimum management trustees should be held as personally liable for delinquencies as they are for delinquent Social Security contributions. A strong argument also can be made for the mandatory bonding of employers against contribution defaults; the one drawback is cost. There also are good reasons for changing the law to give unpaid employer contributions the same priority in bankruptcy proceedings as wages and Social Security contributions —which are, after all, part of the same overall worker payments package as pension contributions.

3. Congress should reconsider whether it really wants, through ERISA, to block union pension funds from investing in ways that create jobs for union members. As a preliminary step, Congress or the Department of Labor should undertake a detailed study of the construction industry to find out just how dependent the industry is on loans from union funds, just how widespread the abuses are when union pension funds make such loans, and whether there is any effective legal system under which such loans can once again be made.

It is still too early to suggest other changes in ERISA. The broad thrust of ERISA is certainly a positive one, although some specific sections of that extremely complex law may eventually prove to be inadequate and others excessive.

The major issue now facing Congress is whether to eliminate the across-the-board ban on transactions by private pension funds with "parties-in-interest." The Department of Labor and the IRS have been slow to assume their responsibility to provide flexibility by granting exemptions from this ban when circumstances warrant. This hesitation has opened the way for the unions to lobby for a reversal of the process. A number of unions and labor trade organizations are currently seeking to have ERISA amended to permit all transactions except those that the enforcing agencies specifically forbid, and legislation has been introduced that provides for just such a rollback, for both union and corporate pension plans.[4]

This move represents a major retreat from the broad intent of ERISA and should not even get to the floor of the House. But the Department of Labor and the IRS must recognize that pension funds cannot operate in a straitjacket.

Until these agencies institute reasonable administrative procedures for dealing with exemption requests, strong pressure for an ERISA rollback will continue.

Ultimately, of course, Congress has the responsibility for making sure that the enforcing agencies are both aggressive in stamping out abuse and open-minded in responding to requests for exemptions. Only if the agencies fulfill these goals will ERISA be the landmark legislation that it was intended to be.

NOTES

I. Introduction

[1] Lee Dembart, "Teamsters Pension Fund Board Revamped as 11 Resign," *The New York Times*, October 27, 1976, p. 18.

[2] Ibid. See also Lee Dembart, "Teamsters Tell IRS of Changes in Pension Fund, Arguing That It Again Deserves Tax-Exempt Status," *The New York Times*, September 21, 1976, p. 18.

[3] Lee Dembart, "Teamsters Consent To Discuss Pensions," *The New York Times*, November 27, 1976, p. 1.

[4] "Favorable Tax Status for Teamsters Fund Is Extended by IRS," *The Wall Street Journal*, November 29, 1976, p. 12.

[5] Labor Management Relations Act (Taft Hartley Act), § 302, 29 U.S.C. § 185 (1964).

[6] One of the better articles summarizing the changes made over the years is A.H. Raskin, "Can Anybody Clean Up the Teamsters?" *The New York Times Magazine* (November 7, 1976), p. 31.

[7] See Senate, *Congressional Record*, 80th Cong., 1st Sess. (Washington, D.C.: 1947), pp. 4892-94.

[8] This fear was voiced specifically about the United Mine Workers Pension fund by Senator Robert Taft, ibid.

[9] See Department of Labor, *Major Collective Bargaining Agreements*, Bulletin 1425-12 (May 1970), pp. 34-35.

[10] *Corporate Pension Fund Asset Management*, pp. 224-266, this volume.

[11] Ibid.

[12] See *State and Local Pension Fund Asset Management*, pp. 267-319, this volume.

[13] See *Blankenship* v. *Boyle*, 329 F. Supp. 1089 (1971).

[14] See *Major Collective Bargaining Agreements*, p. 40.

[15] Employee Retirement Income Security Act of 1974, § 4002, 29 U.S.C. 1001.

[16] *Connolly* v. *PBGC*, F. Supp.———(U.S.D.C. 1976); See *Prentice-Hall Pension and Profit Sharing Guide*, parag. 135, 201.

[17] The attorney is Wayne Jett, who represents many union pension funds in the Los Angeles area. See "Lawyer Thinks ERISA Threatens Unions' Vitality," *Pensions & Investments* (January 3, 1977), P. 43.

[18] Arthur Smith, Jr., of the Cornell School of Industrial and Labor Relations, cited in "ERISA, NLRA Gang up on Taft-Hartley Plans," *Pensions & Investments* (December 6, 1976), p. 19.

[19] "The Teamsters Fear Rough Treatment at the Hands of Federal Investigators," *The Wall Street Journal*, November 18, 1975, p. 1.

[20] These figures were cited by Senator Jacob Javits in a speech before the Seventh Annual Conference of Human Resources System Users, Chicago, Illinois, November 8, 1976. In that speech Javits termed the backlog of unresolved requests for exemption "inexcusable" and called on the Department of Labor and the Internal Revenue Service to give "their first priority" to improving their administration of the prohibited transactions section of ERISA "under a rule of reason" that "does not abort legitimate transactions."

[21]H. R. 7597, 94th Cong., 2d Sess. (1976).

[22]Bernstein is a leading advocate of merging all private pension funds into the Social Security System. See his letter, "Pensions: Reform Has Not Been Achieved," *The New York Times*, March 16, 1976, p. 34. Ferguson, who favors a government takeover through either Social Securitiy or a separate mechanism, expressed her views in an interview with the author.

[23]Author's interview with H. Ned Shreve of the Department of Labor.

[24]Securities and Exchange Commission, *Statistical Bulletin* 35, no. 10 (October 1976), p. 501.

[25]*Money Market Directory* (New York: Money Market Directories, Inc., 6th ed., 1976), Introduction (pages not numbered).

[26]"Economy, ERISA Head the List of the Taft-Hartley Funds' Concerns," *Pensions & Investments* (November 10, 1975), p. 1.

[27]Author's interview.

[28]"Economy, ERISA Head the List of Taft-Hartley Funds' Concerns," p. 1.

[29]The asset figures for the Central States pension fund are taken from that fund's D-2 financial reports, on file with the Department of Labor.

[30]"Bakery and Confectionary Union and Industry International Pension Trust," *Pensions & Investments* (November 10, 1975), p. 9.

[31]Author's interview with Harry Turton of General Motors.

II. Joint Boards and Union Control

[1]Labor Management Relations Act, § 302 (c) (5).

[2]Employee Retirement Income Security Act of 1974, § 404 (a) (1), 29 U.S.C. 1001 note.

[3]Labor Management Relations Act, § 302 (c) (5) (B).

[4]Author's interview.

[5]See Senate, *Congressional Record*, 80th Cong., 1st Sess. (Washington, D.C.: 1947), pp. 4892-94; S. Rep. No. 105, 80th Cong., 1st Sess. (Washington, D.C.: 1947), p. 52.

[6]Author's interview.

[7]Author's interview. See also Noel Arnold Levin, *Successful Labor Relations: An Employer's Guide* (New York: Fairchild Publications, 1967), pp. 313-15.

[8]Author's interview.

[9]Employees Retirement Income Security Act, § 502 (a).

[10]In the text, when no source is given for a quotation or paraphrase, it may be assumed that the statement was made in the course of a confidential interview.

[11]See *Major Collective Bargaining Agreements*, p. 33.

[12]Intenational Ladies Garment Workers Union National Retirement Fund, form D-1 for 1975, on file with the Department of Labor.

[13]A. H. Raskin, "2 in Teamsters Fund Are Forced To Quit," *The New York Times*, September 18, 1976, p. 1.

[14]"Teamsters Make Shifts in Pension Fund Board Due to U.S. Pressure," *The Wall Street Journal*, November 1, 1976, p. 17. The close relationship between union and management trustees on the Central States board is discussed in *Teamster Democracy and Financial Responsibility* (Washington, D.C.: PROD, 1976), pp. 86-88.

[15]*Major Collective Bargaining Agreements*, p. 34.

[16]*Blankenship* v. *Boyle*, 329 F. Supp. 1089 (1971).

[17]Information on the United Mine Workers fund comes from an author's interview with Harry Huge, chairman of the board of trustees, and from the fund's 1975 annual report.

III. Investment Conflicts

[1]Author's interview with Harry Huge.

[2]Ibid.

[3]See Noel Arnold Levin, *Labor-Management Benefit Funds* (New York: Practicing Law Institute, 1971), p. 212.

[4]Employee Retirement Income Security Act, § 407 (c).

[5]Richard Frye, "Electrical Workers Fund is a Model on the Socially Responsible Course," *Pensions & Investments* (November 10, 1975), p. 15.

[6]Author's interview with Theodore H. Kheel, who is a trustee of the Textile Workers Union fund.

[7]Taft-Hartley Portfolios Examined," *Pensions & Investments* (November 10, 1975), p. 9.

[8]Ibid.

[9]Author's interview.

[10]"No Social Investing," *Pensions & Investments* (January 19, 1976), p. 7.

[11]"Around the Nation," *Pensions & Investments* (May 10, 1976), p. 19.

[12]Letter dated June 27, 1975, from the United Mine Workers health and retirement funds to John Bowen, chairman, UMWA Union Hospital, West Frankford, Illinois. A copy of this letter was filed with the Department of Labor by the National Coordinating Committee for Multiemployer Plans.

[13]*Labor Relations Reporter* 72 (1969), p. 153.

[14]Christopher J. McClellan, "Special Real Estate Skills Essential for Taft-Hartley Funds," *Pensions & Investments* (June 21, 1976), p. 18.

[15]*Federal Register* 41, no. 60 (March 26, 1976), p. 12940.

IV. Self-Dealing: How Widespread Is It?

[1]Author's interview.

[2]Employee Retirement Income Security Act of 1974, §§ 404, 405

[3]"Teamster Tamer?" *Newsweek* (August 16, 1976), p. 63. See also Lee Dembart, "U.S. Aide Hints Teamster Pension Bid," *The New York Times*, August 9, 1977, p. 24; and James C. Hyatt, "Study of the Teamsters Pension Fund Grinds On, Makes Some Progress; but Skeptics Still Abound," *The Wall Street Journal*, February 3, 1977, p. 34.

[4]"14 of the largest Taft-Hartley funds profiled,"*Pensions & Investors* (October 25, 1976), p. 19.

[5]Charles Ruff, "Welfare and Pension Plans: The Role of the Federal Prosecutor," *Santa Clara Lawyer*, 12 (1972), p. 501.

[6]In August 1975, a New York produce dealer named Loretta Lustig was indicted on charges of conspiring with the late administrator of the United Paper Workers International Union pension fund, James Fabio, to embezzle $812,000 from that fund. In December 1975, New Jersey Teamsters official Anthony Provenzano and two other men were indicted on charges of conspiring to arrange a kickback for a Teamsters pension loan to be secured by a New York City hotel. In March 1976, a Long Island businessman named Andrew De Lillo was indicted on charges of embezzling $1,497,629 from the pension and welfare fund of Local 138, International Union of Operating Engineers, Farmingdale, New York, through a complex series of transactions in which he purchased a motel/golf course/restaurant from the union fund. In April 1976, seventeen individuals—ten union officials, five contractors, an attorney, and a contractor association employee—were indicted on charges of arranging that unearned pensions be paid to themselves from the pension find of Local 89, San Diego, of the International Laborers Union. In July 1976, Howard N. Garfinkle, a Miami real estate operator, and Bernard Tolkow, secretary-treasurer of Amalgamated Local Union 355, Queens, New York, were indicted on charges that Garfinkle paid $165,000 in kickbacks to Tolkow for loans from the union pension and welfare fund. In July 1976, Saul Durst, president of Local 150, New York, of the Bakery and Confectionery Sales Clerks Union, was indicted on charges that he stole more than $50,000 from the union pension and welfare funds. In November 1976, Alvin Baron, former asset manager of the Teamsters' Central States Pension fund, Chicago, was indicted on charges of accepting a

$200,000 kickback for a $1.3 million fund loan to a California cemetery owner. Lustig and Durst both pleaded guilty; all other individuals in these cases have pleaded innocent.

[7]Employee Retirement Income Security Act, § 406.

[8]Senate, Committee on Labor and Public Welfare, *First Interim Report*, 84 Cong., 1st Sess. (Washington, D.C.: 1955).

[9]S. Rep. No. 1734, 84th Cong., 2d Sess. (Washington, D.C.: 1956).

[10]Senate, Permanent Subcommittee on Investigations of the Committee on Government Operations, *Staff Study of the Severance Pay—Life Insurance Plan of Teamsters Local 295*, 94th Cong., 2d Sess. (Washington, D.C.: 1976), p. 103.

[11]Paul R. Merrion, "Teamsters' Troubles," *Pensions & Investments* (July 5, 1976) p. 23.

[12]Jonathan Kwitny, "Union Financiers: Insiders and Mobsters Benefit from Loans by Teamsters Fund," *The Wall Street Journal*, July 23, 1975, p. 1.

[13]"Teamsters' Fund Sued in Loan Deal," *The New York Times*, June 26, 1976, p. 26.

[14]Jonathan Kwitny, op cit.

[15]Senate, *Congressional Record*, 85th Cong., 2d Sess. (Washington, D.C.: 1958), p. 7053.

[16]18 U.S.C. 664.

[17]18 U.S.C. 1067.

[18]18 U.S.C. 1954.

[19]Paul R. Merrion, "Hutchinson Quits Over Staffing Tiff, Prohibited Transactions Breakdown," *Pensions & Investments* (September 13, 1976), p. 18.

[20]"Teamsters' Central States Pension Fund Is Being Investigated Anew, Dunlop Says," *The Wall Street Journal*, October 17, 1975, p. 2.

[21]Lee Dembart, "Teamsters Lose Tax Exemption for Pension Fund," *The New York Times*, June 29, 1976, p. 1. See also James C. Hyatt, "Teamsters Fund Contributions Clarified by IRS," *The Wall Street Journal*, July 7, 1976, p. 3.

[22]Michael Clowes, "Labor Department Files 1st ERISA Lawsuit Against Five Trustees of Southern Union," *Pensions & Investments* (December 8, 1976), p. 1.

[23]Ibid.

[24]A. H. Raskin, "4 Defendants Keep Teamsters-fund Jobs," *The New York Times*, February 15, 1977, p. 1. See also "Teamsters Unit Sued Under Pension Law by Labor Agency; Board Remedies Asked." *The Wall Street Journal*, January 24, 1977, p. 13.

V. How Employers Sometimes Shortchange Union Funds

[1]"Collection Practices and Procedures," Survey Report No. 1. International Foundation of Employee Benefit Plans (June 1974).

[2]Terry Robards, "Teamsters Fund Kept No Files on Pensioners," *The New York Times*, July 11, 1976, p. 20.

[3]Form D-2.

[4]"Collection Practices and Procedures," on file with the Department of Labor.

[5]*Federal Register*, 40 (June 2, 1975), p. 23798.

[6]Ibid., 41 (March 26, 1976), p. 12740.

[7]"Collection Practices and Procedures."

[8]Letter dated June 24, 1975, from Bakery Drivers Local 194 welfare and pension funds to the Department of Labor and Internal Revenue Service, on file with Department of Labor.

VI. Conclusions

[1]"Success of Pension Law Tied to Teamster Inquiry," *The Wall Street Journal*, September 19, 1975, p. 24.

[2]Employee Retirement Income Security Act, § 406.

[3]These suggestions are based in broad terms on similar suggestions made by Noel Arnold Levin in *Successful Labor Relations: An Employer's Guide* (New York: Fairchild Publications, 1967).

[4]H. R. 7597, 94th Cong., 2d Sess. (1976).

Investment Banking
by Nicholas Wolfson

I • INTRODUCTION

> *The underwriter, realistically regarded, is a salesman.*
> —Securities and Exchange Commission, March 18, 1940

In the years ahead, the capital needs of U.S. business are projected to grow enormously, with the actual billions needed representing astronomically high sums. In the past such projections have been regarded as expressions of growth and burgeoning wealth. Today, though, raising the hundreds of billions of dollars seems an extremely difficult job to many leaders of the financial community and, indeed, of the administration, which has been proposing such incentives for investors as tax-free treatment of dividends.

A critical element in the capital-raising process is the role of the investment banker—or underwriter[1]—a role that as currently practiced creates conflict both for the investment banker and for the capital-raising mechanism itself. Unless the conflict is lessened, potential investors, large and small, will have greatly diminished trust in the securities markets and will continue to be driven away. It has to be determined whether there are ways to mitigate the conflict that *must* arise when the investment banker finds himself, as he does, obligated both to a corporation issuing securities and to an investor purchasing those securities. The need is *not* to destroy the investment banking business; on the contrary, because its work is of critical importance, it must be preserved.[2]

The investment banker's position is permeated with conflict. On the one hand, he has to make a profit and act in the best interests of corporate issuers. On the other hand, he has a responsibility under the securities law to act in the interest of the purchasers.[3] How does he, or indeed can he, resolve this conflict, born as it is of this dilemma?

Corporations want to present themselves in the best possible light. Publicizing adverse information can only depress the price of their stock or credit rating.

New investors are entitled under federal law to negative as well as positive information about a company's financial outlook to make a reasoned appraisal of its securities.

The seller, of course, wants to receive the highest possible price for its stock, but a buyer looks for the lowest. What is fair?

The investment banker, himself, wants as big a profit as he can get. But every dollar he receives is a dollar less for the issuing company. What is a reasonable markup?

Securities are sold, not bought, and this fundamental fact is at the heart of the investment banker's conflict. Indeed, a group of investment bankers put it precisely that way in a 1974 statement to the Securities and Exchange Commission about the shares of public utilities. "It is clear that public utilities are not *bought* by individual investors on their own initiative," said the underwriters. "[T]hose stocks must be *sold* to them by security salesmen who have sufficient conviction and are given sufficient financial incentive to induce individuals to buy . . ." (emphasis in original).[4] In short, more than any other skill, investment banking requires salesmanship.

The importance of the salesmanship element has been supported by economic research. Economics Professors I. Friend and J. R. Longstreet determined that over the " . . . post-World War II period, the average price performance of new issues in the five years after sale to the public was below that of the market as a whole, with virtually all of this difference taking place in the first two years after issue."[5] The researchers stated that the findings might be explained by the " . . . greater [initial] selling effort attached to new than to outstanding issues."[6] In other words it is possible that new issues are initially oversold.

Actually, these conclusions should evoke little surprise. Salesmen's underwriting commissions are generally two, three, or four times the rates negotiated on trading outstanding issues of stock. A risky venture may even boost underwriters' compensation to six or seven times the secondary market rate. Obviously, there must be a selling effort to launch a new issue. The more generous commissions provide the marketing incentive. But the confessions of the investment bankers and the findings of the Friend-Longstreet study raise the most serious questions of whether investment bankers have, indeed, priced their securities fairly and whether under a commission structure that rewards the sale of new issue securities more than others, investment bankers can be counted on to act only in the best interests of the buying public.

Another category of conflict is structural and results when underwriting is only one source of certain firms' revenues. In recent years the archetype of these firms has been Merrill Lynch, Pierce, Fenner & Smith, because its underwriting capital and retail brokerage distribution capabilities [7] combine to guarantee the success of its underwritings.

But the combination brings with it the danger of conflict. A firm with a large retail brokerage business will be reluctant to take its retail clients out of a corporate client's stock and jeopardize its investment banking relationship with the latter. But this threatens the fiduciary relationship between the investment banking firm and its small individual clients. If the firm acquires confidential information from its investment banking client, it may violate the confidence and alert retail clients who own the stock or want to buy it, or it may remain silent and protect its investment banking client at the expense of retail investors. This is the nub of the conflict.

This study proceeds chronologically from the beginning of an underwriting (pp. 367-389) to after-market trading (pp. 390-405). The remaining sections consider several special problems, such as private placement and the link between investment banking and broker-dealers.

Underwriting is a major element of the securities industry. Underwriting revenues of investment banking firms in 1972 and 1973 totaled some $900 and $500 million, respectively, constituting 12.1 and 9.2 percent, respectively, of total broker-dealer revenues.[8] In the years ahead, if the economy recovers, the volume of new offerings and underwriting compensation as a percentage of Wall Street's total business seems likely to increase markedly.

Unfortunately, almost every step of the underwriting process is permeated with serious conflict problems. This study shows why this is so and suggests what may be done about it.

II • THE SELECTION OF INVESTMENT BANKERS

*Very seldom do you really have arms-length nego-
tiations between an underwriter and issuer....*
—The First Annual Institute of Securities
Regulation, 1970

Need to Improve the Standards of the Law

Potential conflict of interest begins when an issuer selects its investment banker. In theory, corporate management chooses its underwriters on the basis of integrity, cost, and expertise. In practice issuers and investment bankers are linked by past business relationships, interlocking directorships, equity ownership by the investment banker, and personal and social associations.

Such close relationships, however, are not necessarily bad. They can lead to mutual trust and to the application of the investment banker's expertise to the business of the issuer. Nor is the competition left out; it is not unusual for one investment banker to displace another. Moreover, close relationships do not violate federal antitrust laws. Twenty years ago the Justice Department took the position that a number of prominent investment bankers had conspired in the 1930s and 1940s to violate the antitrust laws by dominating issuers and preserving traditional positions with corporations. But the government lost its case in the federal district court.[1]

Close relationships, however, do tempt underwriters and corporate officers to select one another for mutual benefit instead of in the interests of public investors.[2] Without competitive bidding the issuer and the investment banker also lack a free market evaluation of their negotiations; and this, too, tempts the investment bankers to look for overly generous compensation and the corporate insider to downplay shareholder and investor interests.

But partly because of tradition and partly because an investment banker's evaluation of a corporation takes time and money, the habit of negotiating with one prospective underwriter, rather than with several, is ingrained. At a recent session of the Practicing Law Institute, a speaker advised his fellow corporation attorneys to "avoid shopping the issue," that is, stop soliciting bids from among several underwriters.[3]

Ideally, of course, the management and directors of a corporation will be able to balance the less tangible advantages of a lengthy investment banking relationship against the more direct benefits claimed by a rival firm and reach a decision that is in the best interests of the company. The problem is: what happens if they fail to exercise this duty diligently?

Until recently, not very much. In 1945 a stockholder brought suit against the officers and directors of the Pennsylvania Railroad, charging that $1 million had been lost in the sale of $28 million in bonds, because corporate officers and directors had refused to provide an investment banking firm, Halsey, Stuart & Co., with information that would enable it to bid.[4]

Instead, the railroad had negotiated the bond offering with its traditional investment banker, Kuhn, Loeb & Co. It did no good for the stockholder to point out that a better price might have been received for the bonds or, in a glaring conflict, that a director of a parent corporation of the railroad owned 50 percent of the stock of one of the members of the Kuhn underwriting syndicate. The court sided with the management and the directors.

At the time the judge followed the principle that the law did not hold directors to high standards in the performance of their duties. Today, however, the courts in the area of securities law are saying that the directors are fiduciaries in every sense of the term. The list of grounds on which stockholders can start a suit, incidentally, has grown steadily, and the number of suits resulting in awards is so threatening to executives and directors that the purchase of malpractice insurance is common.

There is no need to go so far as to require that a corporation solicit formal competitive bidding. But modern courts, at least whenever there are conflicts of interest, should require solicitation and genuine consideration of informal bids from competing investment bankers. The failure to shop around, obviously, can cause a loss of significant sums of money to the corporate issuer. Moreover, intelligent shopping around leads to an offering price that is set by competition. Permitting corporate managements almost total discretion, as in the railroad case, invites abuses.

Competition in Investment Banking

Although a stronger legal doctrine is one important step that could be taken to reduce the potential conflicts in the selection of underwriters, it would be less important if there was genuine rivalry among underwriters.

In this regard in recent years there have been some encouraging signs. In the past the investment banking industry was dominated by firms such as Morgan Stanley & Co. and First Boston Corporation. These giants, and others like them, lacked individual retail brokerage departments but had important institutional clients and long-lasting relationships with many of the leading U.S. corporations.[5]

But the entry of Merrill Lynch, Pierce, Fenner & Smith, a retail-oriented firm, has changed things. Howard Sprow, general counsel of Merrill Lynch, says his firm does not wait for investment banking clients to approach it but woos clients of other investment bankers.[6] With Merrill Lynch the leading investment banker today, other firms have engaged in the same aggressive competition.

Some industry representatives have expressed the fear that the institution of competitive commission rates in May 1975, for transacting business on the New York Stock Exchange, will lead to the demise of the smaller regional broker-dealer firms and with it their underwriting functions. The basis for this fear was effectively demolished by Professors Irwin Friend and Marshall Blume in their study, *The Consequences of Competitive Commissions on the New York Stock Exchange,*[7] which satisfactorily demonstrated to Congress that small firms would not be the ones mainly affected by competitive commission rates. Indeed, the study indicated that under the new regime of competitivie commission rates the more efficient small firms might experience an increase in profits.

Unfortunately, however, hundreds of broker-dealer firms have dropped or are dropping out because of failure or merger as a result of the operational back office disasters of 1968-70 and the bearish state of the U.S. economy today. As concentration grows there is a danger that the number of investment banking firms will shrink to a handful of giants.

Moreover, the increasing size of utility and industrial debt issues and the uncertain state of the market have placed a strain on the capability of all but the largest and best-capitalized firms to handle major issues. Mr. Sprow of Merrill Lynch points out that spreads in the big competitive bid deals have already dropped sharply.[8] The pressures grew so great that in March 1974 Lehman Bros., a major underwriting firm, sharply curtailed its competitive bidding for new clients.[9]

The industry's prospects, however, are by no means as bleak as they are sometimes painted. The claim of many underwriters and brokers that negotiated commissions will lead to a large number of failures of brokerage firms and thus weaken the underwriting process is simply not supported by the evidence. Rather, the major reason for the underwriting industry's current difficulties is the depressed state of the stock market, which has led to a sharp reduction in the number of common stock offerings, traditionally an extremely important source of profits for underwriting firms. The future of the underwriting business, like that of most other industries, is tied closely to the economy. If the economy falters and common stock prices decline, still more firms undoubtedly will drop out of the underwriting industry. But if, as is widely predicted, the economy continues to recover and common stock prices rise, the underwriting business, even though somewhat smaller than in past years, probably will prosper.

Competitive Bidding

For many the solution to the problem of improper relationships between issuers and underwriters is a system of formal competitive bidding for securities. Inviting bids has been the accepted method of financing in the sale of municipal, state, and other securities since the turn of the century.[10] On the federal level, in 1944 the Interstate Commerce Commission required that all future debt securities, with limited exceptions, be sold by competitive bidding.[11] The Federal Power Commission amended its rules in 1939 to require competitive bidding in many circumstances.[12]

The greatest spur to competitive bidding came from the SEC in 1951 with the promulgation of Rule 50 under the Public Utility Holding Corporation Act.[13] That rule requires competitive bidding for equity as well as debt in most circumstances for public utility holding corporations. In 1973, out of fifty-five registered utility holding company issues sold, valued at $2.71 billion, all but three were competitively bid.[14]

The basic economic argument for competitive bidding is that it is a proven method by which an issuer "can most effectively canvass the broadest range of market opinion and obtain binding bids, in accordance with its own specifications, for the marketing of its securities on terms most advantageous to it."[15] Related to this, of course, is the belief that underwriting profits are lower in competitive deals than in negotiated deals. Moreover, competitive bidding eliminates the potential for improper relationships between issuers and their investment bankers.

There are, of course, arguments against competitive bidding. According to Sidney M. Robbins, professor at the School of Business of Columbia University:

competitive bidding...does not necessarily reduce domination of the investment banking field by a comparatively small number of companies. . . .[In addition], some of the benefit of expert advice gained in arranging the details with a competent underwriter may be lost. Even more important, the process is inflexible. It is not readily adaptable to special situations. . . . Difficulty may also be experienced in attempting to market very large or extremely small issues by means of competitive bids. . . .[16]

Many of Professor Robbins's points are valid. Competitive bidding has not been used for relatively small and untried issuers, because the bidders cannot afford the time and money to make so exhaustive an investigation as they can in a negotiated transaction. The underwriting groups, only one of which will get the deal, have relatively little incentive or opportunity to do an independent investigation of the issuer's operations. They tend to rely on the issuer's bidding prospectus and registration statement, which have been prepared in advance by the issuer and its lawyers. In the case of small issues, and particularly for relatively new corporations, the cost of competitive bidding makes it an impractical procedure.

In very large offerings, there can also be other problems with competitive bidding. Rapid distribution, especially in times of uncertain bond markets and falling investor demand, is essential. But in competitive bidding the sales effort is delayed until the day the successful bidders are announced. Before that it is not worth a bidder's effort to try to sell an issue it may ultimately not be selling. Moreover, selling a large issue may require the efforts of almost all of the major investment banking houses, an alliance that is possible in a negotiated deal but not in competitive bidding. That alliance also lends itself to timing an offering for the most propitious moment, something quite necessary during unsettled market conditions.[17] For example, if the market breaks on the day of bidding, the bids will naturally drop. In negotiated deals it is easier to defer the offering and then to sell the securities quickly when the market firms up.

It was these considerations—plus the negative impact on investors of Consolidated Edison's apparent financial crises in 1974—that led major investment bankers in that year to request that the requirement for competitive bidding on common stocks of regulated utilities be suspended. The SEC held public hearings on the issue in January 1975.[18]

The Securities and Exchange Commission equivocated on the proposal, first temporarily suspending competitive bidding on November 7, 1974, then ending the suspension on March 31, 1975.[19] Unfortunately, as of this writing, the SEC has not taken the opportunity to solve the conflict-of-interest problems inherent in the peculiar process in competitive bidding by which the actual "due diligence" investigation (of the financial condition of a corporation) is conducted.

Ironically, the due diligence investigation is one of the reasons that competitive bidding is not necessarily the best solution to the conflict-of-interest problem. The standard practice under SEC Public Utility Rule 50 is for the corporate issuer of the securities to choose an "independent" legal firm that will eventually work for the successful bidding underwriter. As soon as counsel is designated by the issuer, he begins working with the issuer's counsel to prepare the SEC registration statement, bidding papers, prospectus, and related documents. During this period, because bidding has not yet taken place, the underwriters' counsel has *no specific client*.[20]

Because the issuer selects the counsel, it seems likely that counsel will view the issuer, not the underwriter, as his true client, and this can create difficulties. For example, if counsel conducts an active and adversary scrutiny of the issuer's registration documents, will the issuer be eager to designate him in the future? Will the managements of other corporations who learn of the counsel's zeal tend to avoid him in their deals?

Some of the difficulties with the use of issuers' counsel were described in 1975 by a partner in Salomon Brothers. Criticizing the inadequate disclosure obtained in utility issue competitive bidding, he asserted: "The competitive bidding process, in which 'due diligence' is performed to a large extent by counsel for the bidders appointed by the issuer, has, in many cases, unfortunately led to a certain 'hardening of the prospectuses.' " [21] In other words the prospectus contains insufficient disclosure about utility issuers. The actual pluses and minuses of the investment are hidden in dense verbiage or are actually omitted.

What makes this problem even more significant is the trend in securities law toward changing the role of corporate lawyers from partisans of management to representatives of public stockholders. Although it remains to be seen how far this trend will progress, it adds to the difficulty of squaring the responsibility of the independent counsel to the investment banker—and ultimately the public—with the way the system is actually working. As such it is one of the major defects in the competitive bidding process.

It is clear that formal competitive bidding is no panacea for the selection problem. In the case of small firms, it is simply impractical. In larger issues there are serious obstacles to competitive bidding, because the investment banker lacks the time to undertake a thorough investigation of the issuer and the law firm is tempted to owe its allegiance to the issuer rather than to the public.

The SEC and the industry should explore the possibility of bringing underwriters into the due diligence process much earlier than is the practice. The SEC already has warned attorneys about their role as "errand" runners for managements. Perhaps underwriting groups could also be required to appoint due diligence "teams," including counsel, that would replace the old process of issuer-designated counsel. Such teams would go to work a considerable time before awarding the winning bid.

With respect to negotiated underwritings, the standards of the law on the selection process should be improved. The law should impose a strong presumption that directors are at fault unless they actually solicit multiple offers from investment bankers.

There is no easy answer to the selection problem. What is clear, however, is that it is presently too easy for the system to work imperfectly. Changes in the law, added competition, and increased awareness by underwriters' lawyers of their responsibility to the public would improve that state of affairs.

III • DUE DILIGENCE

In view of the good reputation and demonstrated record of success, at least in the stock market, of the. . .promoters, we were indeed flattered to be selected as the underwriter. It would have been regarded as poor taste if we had made any further investigations of the company. . . .

In any event, we made no further investigation of the company, the industry or the management except that both my partner and I visited the company's restaurant where we each ate a humburger with no ill effects.
—SEC *Hot Issue Hearings*, 1972

Introduction

The fox is not put in the chicken coop to guard the chickens. Rather, that trusty old friend of man, the dog, is used for that chore. In the world of finance, the question is whether the investment banker is the fox or the dog. The law solemnly says that due diligence means he is to protect and inform investors. The economic facts of life, however, place him in a three-way conflict: his duty to the buying public, his obligations to corporate issuers, and his own self-interest.

Moreover, securities laws require the investment banker to probe into the financial and operational details of a company and to indentify its weaknesses publicly. In a sense he is the people's tribune, with the reponsibility to protect them from the tendency of company management to exaggerate prospects.

Securities laws also expose the investment banker to civil liability for misstatements in a prospectus unless he had, "after *reasonable investigation,* reasonable ground to believe and did believe"[1] that the material in the prospectus was true. The standard of reasonableness is "that required of a prudent man in the management of his own property."[2]

The difficulty with these legal principles is that the investment banker also has a number of strong economic incentives to sell an issue to anyone who can be convinced to buy it.

Consider the pressures:

- In firm commitment underwriting, the investment banker is selling a product that he has taken a significant risk to purchase and that he must sell or suffer a severe financial setback.

- If he criticizes the securities, the corporation may be angered and never retain his services again.

- The cheaper the price he pays to the corporation and the higher the price the public pays, the greater his profit.

Even when the investment banker acts as agent, rather than as principal for his own account, the temptation to puff the securities is enormous, because the investment banker receives three or four times or more the commissions normally applicable to ordinary transactions. If, out of excessive solicitude for the anonymous masses of the public, the investment banker turns down deals too often, he will soon be looking for a new line of work. In addition, there may be other conflicts. A partner of the investment banker may be a director of the issuer. And the investment banker is a member of a syndicate he wants to be invited to rejoin in future deals.

The investment banker's principal legal shield against these pressures is the doctrine of due diligence contained in the Securities Act of 1933. To the extent that the doctrine is strict, precise, and adequately enforced, the public has considerable assurance that its interests will be protected by the investment banker. The question is how well the due diligence doctrine measures up to its objectives.[3]

In this respect the record is mixed. Before the mid-sixties, it is fair to say that standards were lax or unclear. However, in 1968 a decision in the *BarChris* case sent shock waves through the financial community. An investment banking house, one of whose partners was a director of the issuer, was held to have failed to detect a number of clues that foretold the collapse of the company, which occurred eighteen months after its stock was sold to the public. The danger signals were visible, the court decided, but the investment banker overlooked or ignored them.[4]

The court decision struck terror in lawyers, investment bankers, and accountants, because many investigating practices that had been followed for decades were found inadequate by the federal district court judge.

The lead underwriter was Drexel and Co., a fairly well-known investment banking firm. Seven other investment bankers also took part in the underwriting, and the court observed that they made absolutely no investigation of the accuracy of the prospectus: "They all relied upon Drexel as the 'lead' underwriter."[5] This, of course, is standard operating procedure in the investment banking industry,[6] because it would be impractical to permit each investment banker to conduct an independent investigation of one company.

The 1972 SEC public hearings on investment banking procedures[7] correctly determined, however, that participating investment bankers never even take any steps to establish whether the lead investment banker is doing a responsible job. However, the court's most important criticism of the underwriting procedures focused on the quality of the due diligence investigation conducted by Drexel and Co. and their law firm. As in many underwritings, the bulk of the investigation had been conducted by the underwriter's law firm. However, the lawyers' job was a disaster: they failed to call for key minutes of the executive committee; they did not read the major contracts; they neglected to check out management's claim as to backlog; and they failed to detect emergency officer loans to the hard-pressed, cash-tight corporation. The key failure was that no "effectual attempt at verification [of management claims] was made."[8] Questions were asked, and presumably satisfactory answers were received, but no effort was made to *verify* the accuracy of the answers.

The court held that due diligence inherently required that the investment banker verify the assertions of management,[9] and it is disturbing that this rather elementary proposition brought horror and consternation to numerous investment bankers and their law firms. Hundreds of nervous lawyers attended special extension programs on the *BarChris* case. Dozens of law review articles were devoted to the topic.[10]

The court was unyielding in its description of the underwriters' obligations:

The purpose of [the Securities Act] is to protect investors. To that end the underwriters are made responsible for the truth of the prospectus....[11]

Unfortunately, in 1971 another federal district court, in *Feit* v. *Leasco Data Processing Equipment Corporation,*[12] gave lip service to the principle that underwriters will be held to a very high standard of diligence, but then found that the underwriters had "barely" established that they had been duly diligent. The court, in essence, permitted the investment banker to rely on the company and its counsel in regard to certain key facts and did not demand that the underwriter verify the accuracy of the information.[13]

Leaving the establishment of standards of diligence to the courts, in a case-by-case process, would be a long procedure indeed. Perhaps the most expedient way to seek practical understanding of the due diligence process would be to go directly to a well-respected underwriting firm. One such firm is Merrill Lynch, which has indicated that (1) the most important ingredients in forecasting the future earning power of a corporation are highly subjective and (2) they never appear in a prospectus.

In the SEC Hot Issue Hearings, Merrill Lynch spokesman Thomas L. Chrystie, then vice president and director of the Investment Banking Division, said: "I think the most *subjective,* and yet the most important aspect of our investigation centers around who is really managing the company, how strong is the management."[14]

In evaluating management Merrill Lynch inevitably raises questions such as: ''How do you manage the company?. . .How do you measure the progress of the divisions of your company? Is it against past performance? Is it against budget?. . .Do you make five-year forecasts and update each year?''[15] Few of these questions and their answers appear in any prospectus, nor are they available to prospective investors. Chrystie emphasized that the key indicators are frequently subjective and are not conducive to an acceptable analysis in a lengthy written report,[16] which, of course, is exactly what a prospectus is.

Because Merrill Lynch, as the largest underwriter of all, decides whether to underwrite a company largely on a *subjective* evaluation of management and an analysis of earnings projections that are not available to the public, some perplexing questions must be raised about the lengthy prospectus that the SEC requires, which, even after recent reforms, is woefully inadequate in disclosing such evaluations of management's ability and the company's earning prospects. If Merrill Lynch's approach is correct, the wisdom of the SEC's forty-year-old disclosure philosophy is open to serious doubt.

SEC Recommendations for Reform

Given these defects, how can due diligence be improved? In its 1972 Hot Issue Hearing, the SEC concluded that ''one of the major problems in a hot issue market is the distribution to the public of securities of new ventures which have little or no actual economic viability.''[17] In addition, although the Commission exonerated the majority of investment bankers, it concluded that the apparent inadequacy of investment bankers' due diligence techniques required pervasive new regulations in all offerings—whether of new or established corporations.[18]

The SEC, however, decided not to regulate directly. Instead, it called upon the National Association of Security Dealers (NASD) to handle the problem.[19] On March 14, 1973, the NASD proposed three reforms, which were eventually withdrawn in 1975. The first recommendation was that every managing underwriter establish and maintain written due diligence procedures. The procedures included a list of sixteen areas of investigation, such as inspection of the issuer's plant, review of pertinent management techniques, and investigation of the issuer's relationships with banks and suppliers.[20]

Although the NASD procedures were an improvement, they were inadequate in many areas; for example, they omitted for investigation the company's customers, advertising, and SEC filings. Certain items were totally impractical, such as the review of *all* marketing and scientific reports concerning the corporation and its products for the previous ten-year period. In addition, other items, such as ''budgets,'' were described far too vaguely to be useful.

The NASD also made several other proposals. One would require the managing underwriter to certify in the agreement among underwriters that it had followed adequate inquiry procedures in accordance with the sixteen-item checklist. In theory, this certification might permit the general public to sue the underwriters if the agreement is violated.[21]

Another proposal would have tightened suitability requirements for companies in the promotional or developmental stage. Unlike the past NASD suitability rule, which places no obligation on the broker-dealer to gather facts about the investor, the new proposal would have required the investment banker to make its purchase recommendation only after an investigation of all the important facts concerning the customer's investment objectives and financial situation. The new proposal also would have required broker-dealers to maintain written documentation detailing the basis and the reasoning upon which such determination of suitability was estalished.[22]

The NASD proposals were in general too sketchy and summary to be of any practical use. The due diligence checklist had the usual disadvantages of such lists. It left out some important items and covered the rest in bare outline form. The suitability proposal, to begin with, was limited in its applicability to very new or speculative corporations. Moreover, it would be difficult to implement since it was not drafted with sufficient exactitude.[23]

On April 25, 1975, the NASD publicly announced the withdrawal of these three proposals regarding due diligence and suitability.[24] As bad as they were, the replacements are worse. In lieu of the due diligence checklist and certification prodecures, the NASD proposed a general statement of policy on due diligence. Although it mentions a few of the items omitted from the checklist, it amounts to no more than a warmed over rehash of legal clichés. It will be of no help to the public. The new suitability proposals merely add to the NASD manual a few hortatory words of guidance to broker-dealers. The old defective rule is retained. The SEC should now address itself vigorously to articulate, detailed, and tough new due diligence and suitability rules.

Recently, the SEC moved in a related area to make the disclosure results of due diligence more meaningful. It proposed to permit prospectuses to disclose projections of future economic performance, subjective data of the kind used by Merrill Lynch in its due diligence investigations. The SEC recognized that ''persons invest with the future in mind'' and that projections are sought by all investors. The SEC further recognized that ''management's assessment of a company's future performance . . .is . . .of significant importance to the investor. . . .''[25] The standards, when eventually finalized, would be designed to insure that the projections have as reasonable a basis as possible. Moreover, in the last two years, the SEC under the leadership of John Burton, its new chief accountant, has embarked on an ambitious new program to make accounting and finance disclosure more meaningful to experts and general investors.[26]

Due Diligence in Competitive Bidding

While the SEC and NASD were in the process of recommending certain reforms, the due diligence procedures of large utility company offerings came under fire in private litigation.[27] On May 1, 1974, a stockholder sued Consolidated Edison Company of New York, Merrill Lynch, First Boston Corporation, Halsey Stuart & Co., Inc. (an affiliate of Bache & Co., Incorporated), Blyth, Eastman Dillon & Co., Inc., Lehman Brothers, Inc., and Salomon Brothers, the successful bidders on Con Edison's March 7, 1974, offering of $150 million of bonds. The stockholder alleged that the underwriters and Con Edison knew, or should have known, that a cash bind was imminent and would probably result in omitting a dividend and lowering the rating on Con Edison's bonds. Because all this contributed to a large decline in the value of the $150 million bond offering after it was sold, the stockholder sued, claiming the information should have been in the prospectus.[28]

The investment banking fraternity is understandably distressed by the suit. If successfully pursued it might force changes in the established routines of competitive bidding. It potentially challenges the efficacy of the old system of designated counsel and due diligence procedures.[29] At the least the lawsuit may spark an exhaustive examination and critique of due diligence and the related techniques used in competitive bidding.

In the past the utility industry had appeared "relatively impregnable"[30] to lawsuits of this kind. Indeed, the due diligence and issuer-designated counsel procedures were predicated upon the safety of such investments.[31] Those assumptions no longer hold. The need for searching due diligence is now clear.[32]

The Prospectus and the Individual Investor

Until now the views of investment bankers, SEC officials, and judges have been expressed. The ordinary individual investor has not spoken. What actually influences his decision to buy new issues? Does he read the prospectus? Does he understand it? Does it influence his decision? Is he aware of the underwriters' conflicts of interest? Does he blindly rely on the investment banker or broker-dealer? Does he or can he intelligently evaluate the current methods of due diligence or its product? Does he make his own decisions? Does he view stock investment as a wager or a gamble?

Suggestive answers to these questions, at least in the context of hot new issues, were given in the third phase of the SEC Hot Issue Hearings in December 1973.[33] That phase was concerned with eliciting information from investors who purchased at premium prices in the aftermarket three first-time offerings that experienced dramatic price increases. The answers are revealing. One witness was a Wall Street lawyer with eight years' experience in corporate law. He said:

. . .when the broker says he has got a stock I'm very interested in what the stock is, if I know the broker and I like the broker, if he feels it is a good buy I will go ahead and buy it. . . .

Q. Do you recall reading the prospectus?
A. I'm sure I did not read it.[34]

A stock margin clerk was asked:

Did you read the prospectus?
A. Not thoroughly. The only thing I wanted to bid into something like that, and at the time had mobile homes which did good by me and I thought that might be another one because they were very similar. . . .[35]

Another investor with an eleventh-grade education was asked:

Q. . . . Do you recall looking at the prospectus?
A. I might have, I didn't understand it, but I looked at it.[36]

An experienced criminal and negligence attorney had this to say:

My frank opinion when it comes to a prospectus [on a new issue] is that it's difficult to understand it and to determine whether that is a good investment from that prospectus. . . .

* * *

Q. You feel that the prospectuses have limited usefulness in making a decision as to whether to buy a new issue.
A. Yes. . . .
Q. Do you recall whether the broker encouraged or discouraged the sale?
A. . . . He said it is a gamble probably.[37]

Another investor with two years of college was asked:

Q. How would you characterize your investment goals?
A. I was strictly a gambler. . . . A gambler looking for a quick dollar and . . . I don't look a stock over and I don't analyze it and I am not that well versed. I look at it like horses.
Q. How did you first learn of the offering of stock in International Furniture Galleries?
A. On the job I guess where I work, let's put it that way. I went to the broker. The broker didn't come to me. . . . I just asked him [the broker] what he thought about the stock and he said, you know, said it looks all right. . . . As I said I went to him with it. . . .[38]

Another witness was a real expert. He was a stockbroker.

> Q. How did you first learn of the public offering of International Furniture?
> A. Off the record.
> Staff: Stay on the record.
> A. We do a business with———who is a secretary . . . and she came into our office and wanted to buy 50 shares of International Furniture, and that is how we became acquainted with International Furniture. . . . We . . . executed [her] transaction, and as a lark bought some ourselves.[39]

Another witness was a secretary.

> Q. Did you make the decision to buy the stock?
> A. No he [the broker] does. . . .
> Q. Did he tell you anything about the security and the company?
> A. No, I think he sent me a prospectus . . . after I bought it . . . I usually leave it [buying] to his discretion.[40]

Another witness was a graduate student in psychology.

> Q. Did you purchase shares of Cabana Coach Corporation?
> A. I didn't purchase them. They were purchased for me by an investment counselor. . . .
> Q. Did you give this investment counselor discretion to buy and sell for you?
> A. Yes.
> Q. Without your prior approval?
> A. Yes.[41]

Another witness:

> A. I would like to make it clear that we are generally very satisfied with the integrity of Mr. ———. . . . It also was represented to me as speculative since it was a new company and I agreed with Mr. ——— that these investments should be made.[42]
> Q. How did you first learn of the public offering of Cabana Coach Stock?
> A. Through my broker who called me, told me, gave me a brief summary about it, thought it would be a good investment. . . .
> Q. Did he send you a prospectus?
> A. I don't recall. . . .
> Q. What information did you consider the most significant in your decision to purchase the security?
> A. That he was recommending it and had researched it.[43]

The testimony suggests that many individual customers, including brokers, do not read prospectuses (at least of speculative new issues), and those who do often do not understand them. Some investors rely on tips from friends, and many rely heavily on their broker's judgment, the assumptions of which may or may not be explained. Very few do any independent financial analysis of their own. Large institutional buyers read prospectuses, of course, but they can take care of themselves with or without a prospectus. The individual, on the other hand, needs protection. This conclusion should not surprise anyone who is familiar with the investment banking process. As a distinguished federal district court judge has observed:

In at least some instances what has developed in lieu of the open disclosure envisioned by the Congress is a literary art form calculated to communicate as little of the essential information as possible while exuding an air of total candor. Masters of this medium utilize turgid prose to enshroud the occasional critical revelation in a morass of dull—and to all but the sophisticates—useless financial and historical data. In the face of such obfuscatory tactics the common or even the moderately well informed investor is almost as much at the mercy of the issuer as was his pre-SEC parent.[44]

As we have noted, in recent years renewed efforts have been made by the SEC to improve due diligence and its product, the prospectus. Indeed, new accounting disclosures, projections, and additional subjective data are in the process of being permitted in the prospectus.[45] The hope is that they will be sufficient in their magnitude and scope.

One reform that I suggest would require the prospectus to contain a new section in which the underwriter first fully discloses his conflicts of interest, such as a comparison between his compensation in underwriting deals and in ordinary brokerage transactions.[46] The new section should also contain both the underwriters' subjective evaluation of the future prospects of the corporation and the prospective plans of corporate management. The danger of unscrupulous underwriters who might write puff portraits would be eliminated by SEC rules requiring full disclosure of the factual bases for the prediction and evaluation. The purpose of this section would be to highlight the conflict issue and at the same time present in the prospectus those subjective judgments that Merrill Lynch and other underwriters honestly make in determining whether to bring the issue to the public.

The point is that the subjective evaluation of management and the corporation are the name of the game in the stock market. Reams of historical facts do not necessarily enable the ordinary investor to predict future values of his investment. The expert, honest judgment of corporate management and underwriters about corporate prospects are of great value to the general investor. The pages of the prospectus should illuminate the investment decision, not obfuscate it.

IV • PRICING THE ISSUE

> *God Almighty does not know the proper price-*
> *earnings multiple for a common stock.*
> —Burton G. Malkiel, *A Random Walk Down*
> *Wall Street*, 1973

When a company makes its initial stock offering, underwriters play a key role in pricing the securities. In fact, this is the chief decision the underwriter makes during the entire underwriting process, because the initial price determines the cost of the investment to the public and its value to the issuer and thus will determine the ultimate success or failure of the offering. If the issue is priced too high, the price may plummet in later trading, and the public will lose money on its investment. If the price is too low, the corporation will lose money. Moreover, a low price can artificially inflate public demand, ballooning an issue that eventually deflates, harming investors.

In competitive bidding many of these difficulties are minimized, because the issuer enjoys a range of prices from which to select. Although a characteristic tendency may be to overprice in rising markets and underprice in declining markets, the bidders' submissions not only reflect their personal perceptions of the marketplace but also try to take into account their competitors' bids.

In a negotiated underwriting, pricing a new issue does not result from the interaction of impersonal competitive forces of supply and demand. Because a corporation that is not yet public issues stock that is comparatively new and untested, the price must be determined by the underwriters and the company. Investment bankers derive a sense of the likely demand for the issue by talking with potential buyers; at best the price to initial buyers approximates a rough estimate, the accuracy of which is tested in the marketplace *after* the initial buyers put their money up, not before.

If judgment alone were involved, the test would be difficult enough, but the investment banker is also entangled in a conflict of interest. As Paul Risher of Newberger, Loeb, a medium-sized underwriter, has said: "We are in a middleman position. I do not want to overly represent the company, nor can I ever disregard, in any way, the public interest."[1]

The pricing decision might be thought of as the modern version of ancient soothsaying and entrail reading. An extreme, and illuminating, example was the 1968 underwriting of Metropolitan Quarterback, a new corporation that was selling its first issue of stock. J. V. Grimm, of Grimm and Davis, Inc., has described his calculation in a letter to the SEC:

Metropolitan Quarterback was introduced to us by three people who were instrumental in organizing the Company; . . .In view of the good reputation and demonstrated record of success, at least in the stock market, of the . . .promoters we were indeed flattered to be selected as the underwriter. It would have been regarded as poor taste if we had made any further investigation of the Company, so we did not. We spent about 30 minutes negotiating the terms of the deal. We have no written record of the negotiations, but as I remember it, the promoters wanted $5 per share; we suggested $3 and we compromised on $4. The negotiations were concluded in June of 1968, and the proposed offering represented a step forward for us in the realm of corporate finance since prior to that time we had not underwritten a stock at a price in excess of $4 per share.[2]

At a later public hearing on the case, Mr. Grimm elaborated, saying that the major factor of concern was the price paid by the last investor in a corporation. In Metropolitan insiders had paid $1 per share before the company went public. J. V. Grimm thought "the relationship between their [$1] price and the public offering price was a reasonably good one, certainly in relation to many of the deals which were coming out at that time, in which you know that your markup could be 10, 15, or 40 times what the last guy had paid."[3]

Grimm was asked whether he had access to any sales or earning projections. He had not, he answered, the promoters being people of stature who "must certainly have done some of the homework that would be required in order to make an investment of that type."[4] His honesty about the arbitrariness of his pricing decision is at least refreshing.

Grimm and Davis specialized in underwriting new issues of untested companies with highly unpredictable earnings prospects. However, judgment is also a necessity for underwriters who manage the offerings of companies with established earnings histories. For example, A. Robert Towbin, a partner in C. E. Unterberg & Towbin Co., says that the investment banker should first consider the type of business the company conducts. Does the business have growth potential? Does it excite the imagination of the investment banker? Next, the investment banker evaluates the personalities of the company's managers and reviews its financial history. Then the banker examines the price earnings multiples of similar companies that have gone public and focuses on the company's view of what the price should be.[5]

Towbin may include supply and demand factors in determining his offering price, but in an apparent contrast, First Boston Corporation, one of Wall Street's largest and most prestigious investment bankers, says that it tries to establish an "intrinsic value" and largely ignores short-run supply-demand pressures. "What we are trying to do," says Gregory Doescher, a senior officer of First Boston, "is to place a fair value on the security almost irrespective of what the investor is willing to pay for it."[6] Even if First Boston detected a significant demand that seemed likely to propel the stock price to an immediate premium, the firm would "try to stay with the intrinsic value."[7]

The mystery, of course, is how a "fair" or "intrinsic" value is determined. Doescher says that the main criteria is to set the price-earnings ratio of the company's shares approximately equal to those of similar companies that are already publicly owned. He draws a significant distinction. Namely, when a company is selling shares, he finds it reasonably easy to persuade management not to adjust the opening price upward in response to great demand. "Usually we are able to convince an issuer...that we should stay with the intrinsic value.''

But when insiders sell their personally owned shares, his negotiations become more complex. The insiders, he says, are ''looking for top dollar''[8]— thus, the underwriter is presumably under greater pressure to charge the public more when insiders' shares are sold than in sales by the corporation.

With so many voices declaring their interest, the investment banker—the middleman—faces two serious questions: Whom does he represent? To whom does he owe a duty?

First-tier investors. The investment banker must insure that the price is low enough to constitute a reasonable buy for his customers. Too low an offering price, however, starves the corporation of needed working capital and harms members of the buying public attracted by long-term investment prospects.

Second-, third-, and fourth-tier buyers. An artificially low offering price may inflate demand and release a runaway hot issue in which the price of the stock climbs rapidly in aftermarket trading. Soon the stock price may descend rapidly, burning the unlucky members of the public who bought the stock at a premium from its initial purchasers. These unfortunates were not smart enough or well connected enough to buy the new issue at the lower offering price. Should the investment banker come out with a higher initial offering price to protect the second-, third-, and fourth-tier buyers? (See pp. 390-405 for a detailed discussion of hot issues.)

Corporate issuer. The price must be fair to the company going public. In other words the price must provide adequate proceeds so the corporation can do those things that caused it to go public in the first place. How should the corporation and the underwriter measure the price?

Minority shareholders before the public offering. Investors who already hold shares in the corporation and who want to continue to hold them will benefit from the highest possible initial offering price. The more others pay in, the greater the worth of their initial investment. Investors who want to sell will profit from a lower offering price, ballooning a hot issue and allowing them to sell at the inflated hot issue aftermarket prices (See pp. 390-405).

Corporate insiders. The investors who control the corporation profit from a high offering price, because the value of their equity holdings increases as the price rises. But too high a price may chill the issue. On the other hand, a low price may create a wild hot issue after-market in which they can unload at great profit.

The investment banker makes his pricing decision amid this welter of conflicting pressures, and we cannot conclude this discussion without a description of his personal stake. The investment banker does business for profit, not charity. His underwriting spread must produce a profit, or, more bluntly, his self-interest is to buy cheap and sell dear. In best efforts deals, his commission hinges on his success in selling the issue to as many investors as possible. If the issue sours, his prestige will suffer in direct proportion to the seriousness of his mistake. Too high or too low an initial price can damage the investment banker, occasionally beyond repair. His interest in satisfying management and the relative ignorance of the buying public may combine and tempt him to set a higher price than he would have recommended had the public been his only client. Unlike Caesar's wife, his final pricing decision is not above suspicion. In recent years the SEC has attempted to require more public disclosure to the pricing decision and the reasons behind it. Until 1973 the prospectus of a new corporation did not reveal the estimated price of its new security; this was made public the day before the prospectus was declared effective by the SEC. Buying securities was like venturing into an auto showroom for a new car and having the dealer refuse to tell you the price until the moment you decided to buy and reached for your checkbook. In August 1973 this practice was amended. The Commission ordered that the prospectuses of newly public companies should disclose a bona fide estimate of the maximum offering price.[9] Moreover, the old boiler plate discussions of the initial offering price were rejected. These statements often mouthed trivia such as "such price has been established by negotiations between the underwriter and the registrant."[10]

Unfortunately, conveniently vague language has a habit of never fading away. Below is a sample of the new boiler plate.

Cover: "Prior to this offering there has been no public market for the Company's Common Stock. It is currently estimated that the proposed initial public offering price per share may range from $23 to $25. Based on that price range, the market value of the presently outstanding Common Stock of the Company would range from approximately $230 million to $250 million. See 'Underwriting' as to the method of determining the initial public offering price."

Underwriting: "There has been no previous market for the Common Stock of the Company. The major factors considered by the Company, the Selling Shareholders and the Representatives in determining the public offering price of the Common Stock, in addition to prevailing market conditions, are the price earning multiples of publicly traded common stocks of similar companies, the growth rates and the earning of the Company and similar companies in recent periods and factors relating to the Company's earnings potential."[11]

The shares of the above offering were sold at $27. In the final prospectus, dated September 13, 1973, the statement about the market value of all the outstanding shares was transferred to the Underwriting heading and the following caution inserted:

However, due to the varying nature of the above factors and the securities markets in general, there can be no assurance that the market value of the presently outstanding Common Stock of the Company will remain at this level.[12]

More stringent SEC requirements are needed on proper disclosure. (Perhaps an excerpt from an eighteen-minute tape, with no gaps and with expletives included, of the hectic pricing discussion between a company president and the managing underwriters should be in the prospectus.) Adequate disclosure should include all the reasons behind the pricing decision; then the investor or his advisor has a fair opportunity to assess the offering. The prospectus should describe the exact processes that led the investment banker to his pricing recommendation. To the extent that price-earnings ratios of other corporations in similar businesses were used for comparison, they should be identified and the comparative computations spelled out. The reason why the issue was valued at a higher or lower price-earnings ratio than similar corporations should be disclosed. Psychological factors, such as evaluation of investor demand and taste, should be discussed.

The SEC should continue its efforts to punish and deter underwriters who manipulate the price of new issues in violation of the SEC's antifraud and manipulation statutes. In addition, adoption of the recommendations given on pages 390-405, on solving the hot issue problems, will significantly lessen conflicts in this area.

V • UNDERWRITERS' COMPENSATION

There is a danger of overreaching.
—SEC Director of Enforcement at
a conference of lawyers, 1970

Although many of the conflicts in underwriting involve the competing interests of the issuer and the purchaser, one of the most direct conflicts concerns the compensation of the underwriters, whose commissions are typically much greater than for regular brokerage transactions. In common stock offerings, a company may pay the underwriters from 3 to 13 percent of the total anticipated revenue from the offering. In 1971-72 the average rate was 7.68 percent for firm commitment deals and 12.77 percent for best efforts underwritings. Add other expenses, such as legal and accounting fees, and in 1971-72 the average rate of total costs as a percentage of proceeds was 11.13 percent for firm commitment deals and 20.02 percent for best efforts underwritings.[1]

The underwriters' compensation is frequently determined by competitive forces. The managements of some investment banking firms and corporations, however, form close-knit relationships that preclude tough arm's-length nego-tiations on compensation. Irving Pollack, now a commissioner of the SEC, claimed when he was director of its Division of Enforcement that ''in some instances corporate officials are not concerned with how much they pay for the underwriting services, because they feel that the public actually is doing the paying.'' Pollack warned that there is often a risk that ''distribution isn't really a legitimate raising of capital but instead is a plan to enrich the underwriter....''[2]

Both the SEC (indirectly) and a number of state governments (directly) have moved to limit the underwriters' fee. At the federal level, this has been left primarily to the National Association of Securities Dealers.[3] At the state level, it is usually the province of a bureau of securities law. But at both levels, the premise is basically the same: bureaucratically limiting the amount of money an underwriter can charge for his services will somehow protect the investor. This premise may not work out well in practice and may be wrong in theory.

What are NASD's standards? Publicly the NASD has said that the under-writers' compensation may not be ''unfair or unreasonable.''[4] Compensation consists of the gross amount of the investment banker's discount, total ex-penses payable by the company to or in behalf of the underwriters, the underwriters' counseling fees, and any other item of value paid to the under-writer.[5]

Stock and stock options received by the investment banker are also included in the NASD's definition. Stock is valued by computing the difference be-tween the cost of the stock and the proposed public offering price. (However, if the underwriter agrees not to sell the stock for a substantial time, the NASD will value it somewhat lower.[6])

No formula is mandated for options or warrants received in connection with the underwriting. The NASD states that it will consider the number and term of the warrants, their cost, their lowest exercise price, the date at which they become exercisable, and ''other relevant factors.'' The NASD prohibits options or warrants for terms in excess of five years, or exercisable below the intial public offering price, as being unfair and unreasonable underwriting compensation.[7]

Surprisingly, the NASD has never published any percentage of dollar figures specifiying unreasonable aggregate underwriters' compensation. Commis-sioner Pollack has said that the reason for not publishing specific guidelines is to keep the investment banker honest. If precise fees were published, the invest-ment banker, he contends, would probably always charge the limit.[8] One observer, a lawyer, has remarked:

It has not been easy for underwriters to find out from the NASD just what permissible maximum underwriters' compensation is. There was a kind of cat-and-mouse game. You made your filing with NASD. . . . Then the NASD staff might come back and say, ''That's too much.''

You say, ''How much can I get?''

''Well that's your problem. You work it out again, and we will let you know whether we think it's reasonable.''

This could go on and on with the underwriter gradually reducing his contemplated compensation until it reaches a level acceptable to the NASD.[9]

This commentator also concluded from his research that investment banker compensation for a medium-sized firm commitment underwriting ($3 to $10 million) will not be permitted to exceed 18 percent of the public offering price. In the case of smaller offerings, the NASD may permit compensation in excess of 18 percent. In offerings over $10 million, compensation may be considerably less than 18 percent.[10]

Although the NASD's decisions often seem to vary from case to case, a possible case is as follows:

Assume an investment banker manages an offering of two hundred thousand shares to be priced at $10 per share. He receives an underwriting spread of 10 percent ($1 per share) and warrants for four thousand shares. Four months before the offering, he purchased sixteen thousand shares at $5 per share. The 10 percent spread is $200,000. The sixteen thousand shares, calculated at the difference between $5 and $10, amount to $80,000. An unpublished NASD deduction of 20 percent is then applied, due to the one-year holding period of the cheap stock, for a net sum of $64,000. For the warrants the NASD uses an "undisclosed" formula. The securities bar has made the informed guess that the NASD uses a figure of 2 to 4 percent of the stock offering or 20 percent of the offering price of the shares underlying the warrants. (These figures vary with the terms of the warrants. At 20 percent, the sum is $8,000.) Finally, $40,000 of the investment banker's expenses are paid by the issuer. Therefore, the total compensation to the underwriter is $312,000, or 15.6 percent of the $2 million offering, somewhat below the guessed-at 18 percent limit.[11]

In effect, by dictating the price of investment banker services, the NASD is price-fixing. A failing of its approach is the use of secret guidelines, which makes it practically impossible to judge the extent to which the NASD formulas coincide with economic reality.

Government price-fixing normally at least attempts to follow efficiency criteria. When a governmental authority regulates the price that a public utility may charge, some means are used to regulate price, profits, and consumer services. Permissible rates of return on equity, or profits as a percentage of gross sales, are fixed with a view to providing low-cost, efficient consumer services. The rates are also commensurate with the utility's need to pay for equipment, meet operating costs, and provide incentives to keep and attract talented management. It is impossible to judge the extent to which the NASD secret guidelines conform with such standards.

Although few economists believe in the ability of government to fix prices successfully and allocate resources in any industry, it is difficult, if not impossible, to imagine any economist championing a secret formula based on undisclosed criteria. Moreover, as a matter of political theory, it is hard to justify any secret formula. The public, whom government is supposedly formed to protect, can contribute no rational input, because the formula can be developed without considering public opinion.

It is possible that the NASD does not employ secret formulas but merely adopts a series of in-camera hunches and visceral reactions. If true, this would be even worse than secret formulas: it would mean that the investment banker's price is determined by NASD fiat, which does not necessarily have a logical relationship to investment banker efficiency, public protection, or any accepted economic standard of reasonable profit.

Even if the guidelines were made public, problems with government or NASD regulation of underwriters' compensation would continue to arise. Indeed, perhaps the crucial question involving guidelines, public or secret, is whether they make it more difficult for companies to raise capital. James S. Mofsky, professor of law at the University of Miami, has analyzed state regulations governing underwriter compensation; he concluded that they may well inhibit the capital-formation process of small issuers.[12] He points out that many of the published regulations of the several states are aimed primarily or exclusively at the smaller stock flotations of newly promoted ventures. The impact on the larger offerings of established businesses is minimal.

Securities statutes in many states limit underwriters' compensation and issuers' expenses to amounts ranging from 15 to 20 percent of the aggregate value of securities offered.[13] Professor Mofsky has compared the limitations on underwriters' compensation to the actual cost of underwriting a new issue, and he concludes that as the size of the issue diminishes the actual costs "more closely approach," equal, or are greater than many state limitations. A very recent SEC cost study supports those conclusions.[14]

The NASD regulations may have a similar impact on small companies, argues Mofsky:

It should be noted that there is an informal NASD standard, nowhere appearing in writing, limiting underwriters' compensation to a range of 15 to 18%. Based on the statistics cited in this article, underwriters' compensation for some small offerings exceeded the NASD limitations during certain periods. Accordingly, that NASD regulation may be having effects similar to those of the blue sky rules discussed above.[15]

It is pertinent to note here that private financing may be unavailable. Indeed, banks and other financial institutions are traditionally loath to lend funds to fledgling corporations.

In conclusion, there is no evidence that the benefits of NASD or state regulation, if any, exceed the chilling effect upon the promotion of new businesses. As suggested in an earlier chapter, the prospectus should highlight the comparison between the underwriter's compensation in the public offering and his remuneration in ordinary brokerage transactions. The fraudulent cases of secret compensation will never be disclosed to the NASD and state authorities and will be stopped only by vigorous SEC and NASD enforcement activities.

VI • TRADING IN THE AFTER-MARKET

> *"A fisherman is selling a barrel of sardines for
> $1. Along comes a farmer who says: 'Just $1
> for a barrelful of sardines? I'll take 'em.' Then
> the farmer walks around the corner and sells
> them to a shopkeeper for $2, who in turn sells
> them to a customer for $3. But when the
> customer lifts the lid, the stench nearly knocks
> him over. The sardines are rotten. The cus-
> tomer and shopkeeper catch up to the farmer,
> and all three confront the fisherman. 'How
> dare you!' they say. 'Nobody can eat those
> rotten sardines.' The fisherman looks puzzled.
> 'Why are you angry? I didn't say they were
> sardines for eating. They're sardines for sell-
> ing.' "*
>
> —The fisherman's version of a hot issue
> adapted from *Forbes*, June 15, 1974

Another major area of investment banker conflict of interest is after-market
trading of public offerings when investment bankers, new issue market
makers, and other broker-dealers sometimes create "hot issues" to benefit
themselves, corporate insiders, and favored customers. The results are damaging both to other investors and to the capital markets.

The obligation of investment bankers is to help create an orderly after-
market. If investment bankers have done their job well, the after-market price
will be only moderately higher than the offering price. The right premium will
satisfy investors, please the issuer, and demonstrate that a reasonable offering
price has been selected. In contrast, a drastic drop or jump in price, at best,
suggests that the investment banker has made a costly error in judgment or, at
worst, has manipulated the market.

A hot new issue is one in which the price of the stock rises sharply soon after
the public offering.[1] Examples of stocks rising from 50 to 100 percent are not
uncommon. The New York Attorney General's Office studied forty companies
that went public in 1968 and found that by January 1969 the price of thirty-
three of them had increased more than 50 percent:[2]

NUMBER OF COMPANIES	PERCENT INCREASE
7	Up to 50%
5	Between 51 and 100%
10	Between 101 and 200%
11	Between 201 and 300%
3	Between 301 and 700%
4	Over 1,000%
40	

The New York State study, as well as the SEC Special Study in the early 1960s, established that some investment bankers and corporate insiders help create hot issues to unload their personal holdings at the highest possible prices. The buyers too often are innocent members of the public whose high priced shares turn to worthless junk when the price plummets.

Not all hot issues, of course, are tainted offspring of investment bankers' manipulations. Many are the result of the seemingly insatiable demand of the investing public for speculative new issues, a trend that peaked most recently in the late 1960s. Since then the new issue market has been dead, but the trend is likely to emerge again in the future as it has so often in the past.

Profile of a Hot Issue

SEC public hearings in the spring of 1972 detailed how, even in the hands of honest people, a typical hot issue develops. The key *dramatis personae* are the issuer, the underwriters, and the market makers who specialize in new issues.

The first act of the drama unfolds at a meeting of an underwriter's representative and a corporation's president. After several weeks of investigation, the underwriter may decide to proceed with an offering.

As the issuing date draws nearer, the managing underwriter and members of the syndicate receive indications of the interest from prospective individual and institutional customers as well as reactions from potential market makers. In a matter of days or sometimes weeks before the sale of the securities, the underwriters will be able to sense whether they have a hot offering.

That unique species of market maker, the specialist in new issues, gears up for the new offering. (Another group of new issue market makers devotes a primary portion of its business to making markets in seasoned issues.) These new issue dealers gauge the demand, too, for the proposed new issue through discussions with retail brokerage houses, members of the underwriting syndicate, and institutional customers. The SEC Hot Issue Hearings indicated that these market makers often learn more than the underwriting syndicate manager about demand, or lack of it, for the issue.[3]

The SEC effective date arrives, and the bell rings for the opening round. At, say, 10 a.m. on a Thursday, the market maker delivers his opening quote, based on knowledge, "feel" for the market, and guesswork. If he has received what he regards as a significant number of indications of interest at certain prices on the buy and/or sell side, he will "wrap" his opening bid and ask quotes around those prices, just as the exchange specialist calculates his opening quote for the day. If the opening quotation is considerably above the public offering price, and stays above it for the first day or two, the market has a hot new issue.

Immediately following the first quotation, the market maker adjusts his bid in response to the flow of purchase and sale orders. This process parallels that followed by any over-the-counter market maker in a seasoned issue or by an exchange specialist on the floor. In the SEC Hot Issue Hearings, it was described by an over-the-counter market maker:

Q: All right, now let's take the various possibilities.
   Are there situations where you will open a market without having received any order or indication of interest?
A: Well, if we check around and . . . the stock is not all sold, we know the stock will have to sell at the issue price and the underwriter usually puts in a syndicate bid, no penalty, a syndicate bid with a penalty or a syndicate bid with a penalty and with a legend. So we are then able to trade around that bid.
Q: That is where there has been a relatively weak demand?
A: That is correct.
Q: Now, let's take the case of a very hot issue high demand, what happens then generally?
A: In a case like that we once again flash all our wires hoping—
Q: Excuse me. . . . You flashed your wires after you received word from the underwriter that trading commenced; is that correct?
A: That is correct.
Q: All right, go ahead.
A: We flash all our wires hoping to get an order one way or the other, a buy or sell order . . . trying to form a market around that order.
Q: These are actually orders, am I correct that you are trying to get not indications?
A: Oh, it has to be an order. Then if you get an order one way, in other words, say the stock comes out at ten, somebody's research department feels that they should put their clientele in this stock at 18, it has merits of, say, a $25 stock, they are willing to pay 18. We then open our market around that bid and we can open the market at 17 to 20 hoping to buy some at 17 where we have an out at 18. . . .
Q: You commenced absolutely flat?
A: That is correct.
   Usually when a new issue is released and you do get an order one way or the other the markets are fairly wide. In other words, it's sort of a protection for the trader to have a wide market just to form the picture when he is trying to feel what is going on the way or in his shop. So, in other words when this deal comes out at 14 or ten dollars, the market opens up 17 to 20, the trader has some sort of protection until a real market forms as well as volume is concerned.[4]

In a hot new issue, the volume of trading within the first few days is very large. Many fortunate first-tier buyers, namely, those who bought at the public offering price, sell off via retail brokers to the new issue market maker. Thus, a new tier of buyers emerges at a higher price. The purchases at this point are also through retail brokers, who obtain the shares from new issue market makers. Purchase and resale continue during the first few weeks of the new issue. In extreme cases of feverish demand, most of the original offering may be redistributed to a new group of investors within a few days. Ultimately, the stock is sold at progressively higher and higher prices to gullible investors. Then, all too often, the price plunges abruptly, and the investors stuck with the stock suffer accordingly.

During the early stages of a hot issue's evolution, the underwriters are prohibited by SEC Rule 10b-6[5] from making a market in the new issue until their distribution has ended.

Soon an interesting phenomenon occurs: the market makers who specialize in new issues terminate their activities because volume is dropping and underwriters are now competing. Market making is no longer profitable to them, and they move on to other new issues.

Hot Issue Horrors

Wild hot issue markets have become an apparently incurable disease in the securities market. As long ago as April 1946, the SEC proposed a rule prohibiting a broker-dealer who was taking part in a distribution from offering any portion of the issue at a premium above the initial prospectus price, unless a bona fide public offer at the prospectus price was continued for a reasonable period. Bona fide offers would exclude distribution to partners, officers, directors, or employees of the broker-dealer firm.[6] The September 1946 market decline eliminated the immediacy of the problem, and the proposal died. In 1950 the NASD adopted its withholding and free-riding rule, which forbade, under specific circumstances, selling a portion of a public offering to persons connected with the broker-dealer.[7] In both 1946 and 1950, the target was investment bankers who in effect remove a substantial number of securities from the public market, restricting supply and driving up the price.

At the beginning of the swinging sixties, the NASD rule proved too weak to control the excesses surrounding the hot issues. In his 1973 book on Wall Street, Burton G. Malkiel, professor of economics at Princeton University, includes a table that records the boom-and-bust history of some stocks during the era.[8] Malkiel observes that ten years after the new issues described in the table below, the shares of equity of the bulk of the corporations were almost worthless.

The New York attorney general's 1969 study analyzed 103 companies that went public in the hot issue craze of 1968-69. The study concluded that many corporations were not bona fide investments but were creatures of investment bankers who designed them for quick stock market profits. David Clurman, the director of the investigation, stated that "faith in a company's long-term prospects was not a significant factor in inducing purchases of its securities."[9] Rather, the investors gambled on winning quick short-term profits.

David Clurman put the conflict-of-interest problem this way:

Company insiders and investment bankers took full advantage of the opportunities presented to them by the generally heated situation, *a situation that was partially of their own creation*. At times, underwriters . . . withheld part of the issue for their own accounts and then sold when they thought the market had reached its peak.[10]

Table 22 Representative New Issues

SECURITY	OFFERING DATE	OFFERING PRICE	BID PRICE FIRST DAY OF TRADING	HIGH BID PRICE 1961	LOW BID PRICE 1962
Boonton Electronics Corp.	March 6, 1961	5½[a]	12¼[a]	24½[a]	1⅝[a]
Bristol Dynamics	March 20, 1961	7	16	23	3⅛
Geophysics Corp. of America	December 8, 1960	14	27	58	9
Hydro-Space Technology	July 19, 1960	3	7	7	1
Mother's Cookie Corp.	March 8, 1961	15	23	25	7
Seaboard Electronic	July 5, 1961	5½	8¾	15½	2¼
Universal Electronic Labs	November 25, 1961	4	4½	18	1⅜

[a]Per unit of 1 share and 1 warrant.

Source: Burton G. Malkiel, *A Random Walk Down Wall Street*, p. 52 Copyright © 1973 by W. W. Norton & Company, Inc.

In such situtations the underwriter is under extraordinary temptation to induce the public to purchase new issue stock that it is anxious to sell. The unusual profit motive inherent in hot issue deals is sufficient to slant investment advice given to customers.

Clurman went on to detail the tie-in between investment bankers and corporate insiders:

Resales by insiders occurred in approximately twenty-three percent of all cases analyzed. This figure, which is based on our questionnaires, is undoubtedly low since further insider resales must have occurred after we received the completed questionnaires.[11]

In addition to investment bankers and corporate insiders, the business associates, friends, and favorite customers of investment bankers are a third group that may benefit from a hot issue. The members of this group receive good hot issue allocations either as a reward for past favors and business transactions or in return for expected future business dealings with the investment bankers. Because stocks in hot issues are hard to obtain, the power of investment bankers to allocate is really the power to spread largesse to a fortunate few.

The New York State study concluded as follows:

The big winners were underwriters, insiders of the issuing companies and those with contacts in these groups. The losers were those investors who purchased at inflated prices and the economy itself.[12]

Restricting supply and increasing demand remain the basic method used by investment bankers to overheat a new issue. The most common way to decrease supply is called *free riding and withholding*, a technique by which investment bankers withhold shares from the general public in favor of themselves, friends, employees, relatives, and affiliates. Frequently, the withheld shares are later sold to the public at premium prices. NASD rules prohibit free riding and withholding, but the enforcement in the past left much to be desired.

Investment bankers deploy a battery of other stratagems to artificially restrict supply and stimulate demand. Among the more common are:

1. Requiring customers to purchase shares in the after-market in order to obtain shares in the public offering. This artificially heats up activity in the after-market.

2. Allotting shares to discretionary accounts over which the investment bankers exercise continuing control in the after-market. Investment bankers can use their discretionary power to control purchases and sales in the new issue market.

3. Calculated delay in notifying customers that they have received allotments of new issues. As a result customers who do not know how many securities they have bought will not sell them.

4. Failure to deliver stock certificates for weeks, thus effectively preventing customers from selling.

5. Distribution of enthusiastic market letters, news releases, and other calculated bullish publicity.

6. Deliberate fixing of a low initial offering price to stimulate after-market activity.

7. Requiring customers to buy the new issue as a condition to being allotted future attractive hot issues. This artificially both creates demand and may affect the offering price. This practice also unjustifiably precludes other public investors from acquiring such hot issue shares.

8. Discouraging public investors from selling their hot issue shares by threatening them with loss of future hot issue deals. This dries up supply.

9. Allotment of offered securities to over-the-counter trading firms. These firms are then expected, in return, to make a market in the new issue. As a reward, they sell their allotment at premium prices in excess of the prospectus price. The premium is created in part by their overactive market making.

Three Proposals for Reform

I. MERIT REGULATION

One theoretical solution to the hot issue problem is federal regulation of the fairness and viability of the offering. Approval of the offering price value of the issuer and the investment banker's compensation might be required. Many states have attempted this kind of merit regulation, with highly questionable results. Professor Mofsky of the University of Miami Law School portrayed in 1971 a realistic horror scenario of the blue sky (i.e., state) merit regulation. The model was based upon a Florida blue sky law, but it typifies state merit regulation. [13]

E., a promoter, wishes to raise about $500,000 for a promotional venture. The Florida rule on best effort deals requires that promoters or insiders contribute 15 percent of the initial capital. This means that E. and his friends must post a minimum of $65,000 (the public offering will be $435,000). If E. has only $10,000, he must raise the balance in a private offering.

Consequently, it will be very hard for E. to retain control. Assume that the issuer's capital structure will be one-hundred thousand shares of common outstanding after the public offering. E. may very well be forced to relinquish, say, twenty-two thousand shares, or 22 percent, of the voting stock to the private offerees in return for their $55,000 investment. Assume further that E. seeks to retain fifty-one thousand shares for himself and that ten thousand shares are reserved for the issuer's lawyers and other insider professionals. Thus, only seventeen thousand shares will be available for public sales to raise the $435,000. The public offering price would be about $26 per share.

However, Florida limits the per share public offering price to an amount ranging from two to eight times the per share price paid by insiders. In arriving at a public offering price that is "fair, just and equitable," as the law puts it, the state may also consider net asset value, management ability, and other factors. [14] But the primary factor is the ratio of the proposed public offering price to the amount paid by promoters or insiders for their stock. The ratio permitted is ordinarily less than eight to one. In E.'s case the average consideration per share is $0.90 ($65,000 divided by seventy-three thousand shares), and thus the maximum public price per share is $7.20.

At $7.20 per share, a public offering would bring in only $122,000, less than one-third of the needed amount. To combat this problem, E. could take fewer shares for himself. For example, on the basis of an eight times multiple, he could take twenty-seven thousand shares, and the public investment would then be sold about forty-one thousand shares for $435,000, which works out to a price of $10.64 per share, about eight times the average price of $1.33 that the founders and other insiders paid. This arrangement would create a serious control problem for E. and might sway him toward abandoning the new venture. As Mofsky states, "There may always be someone at the margin like Mr. E. who, if costs (in the form of restrictive regulatory provisions) were a little less, would clearly go ahead with the venture, whereas in the posture described, there may literally be no feasible arrangement satisfactory to all individuals involved."[15]

Apparently, no data exist that prove that new investments in Florida are deterred by these regulations, but it is hard to believe that such is not the case. The supporters of this type of regulation have never demonstrated that the regulation does not deter new investments, and they should bear the burden of proving its worth.

New issue excesses may occur because of speculative frenzy and problems in after-market trading rather than because of the low level of economic viability of the new issuer. Thus, even if merit regulation were established and only a few certified issuers filtered through the regulatory screeen, this would not guarantee an end to hot new issue excesses. Speculative frenzy and after-market trading excesses could be just as serious a problem for government-approved issues. Indeed, the U.S. seal of approval could exacerbate speculative frenzy, in which case investors would still end up with overpriced stock and large investment losses.

Investment bankers are hard pressed to predict successfully the future viability of issuers. To put federal government bureaucrats in the business of evaluating new issues—deciding which issue is a future Xerox, which a future Equity Funding—is foolhardy. Were a large percentage of speculative hot new issues eliminated, the new issues market in general might also disappear, a case of tossing baby out with the bathwater.

State securities administrators have never demonstrated the dollar savings, if any, derived from the regulations. They have not explored the possible losses to the capital market and to the economy from the denial of entry to new issuers. Moreover, the larger investment bankers do not generally underwrite the type of offerings that are affected by state regulation and thus have no incentive to urge that it be reformed. Indeed, they gain a competitive advantage, because smaller investment brokers, who tend to underwrite the more speculative deals, are hit hard by state legislation. Federal merit regulation would probably increase the competitive advantage of large investment brokers even more.[16]

2. REFORM OF THE PHANTOM INVESTMENT BANKER

One of the most intriguing aspects of the new issues market is the existence of the phantom investment banker, that is, the new issue market maker. Should his methods of operation be reformed? Does he serve a useful function?

Conventional myth maintains that the investment banker underwrites a new issue, and the over-the-counter market makers establish the initial trading market. But in reality, for very active new issues the over-the-counter new issues market makers act as the true underwriters. They take the stock out of the hands of the first-tier buyers and place it in the hands of new buyers.

In very active new issues, the redistribution assumes mammoth proportions. A spokesman for Kenneth Bove & Co., an over-the-counter market maker and underwriter (since defunct), described one new issue the firm had underwritten and in which it had also made a market:

> SEC Staff: Taking the two-week period [immediately after the effective
> date], how many shares were sold back to you? [And resold?]
> Answer: Maybe, 70% of the issue.
> SEC Staff: Is that characteristic of other hot issues?
> Answer: Yes.[17]

In another issue:

> SEC Staff: I asked what your opening offer was.
> Answer: $10.
> SEC Staff: And, your offering price to the public was $4?
> Answer: Yes.

* * *

> SEC Staff: The initial offering was an aggregate of $500,000?
> Answer: Yes.
> SEC Staff: . . . The first day you opened, you sold approximately 25,000
> shares or a quarter of a million dollars of the stock . . .?
> Answer: Yes.[18]

Mr. Rosenthal of L. M. Rosenthal & Co., Inc., another market maker, spoke in these terms:

> [Y]ou have two different types of customers. You have one customer [i.e., the second- and third-tier buyer] who is buying it basically because he would like a large position to hold as an investment medium.
>
> And then you have another customer [i.e., first-tier buyer] who basically wants it because he wants a *present*.[19]

The over-the-counter dealer continued his description of active new issues: "During the first few days is where you have the exchange between those two customers."[20]

The description is honest and revealing: The over-the-counter market maker referred to the first-tier buyer as the recipient of a "present." The reason for the gift is that the favored first-tier buyer stands to make a huge gain off the premium. Explained Mr. Rosenthal: "By definition [the buyer] is not a speculator. . . .he is getting a gift."[21]

The gift, as we have already learned, is bestowed by the investment banker in return for past and future business.

The key question was then put to Mr. Rosenthal:

Q: Are you performing more of an underwriting function than a market-making function?

A: Redistribution . . . is typically done through the marketplace and we are definitely providing a conduit mechanism for that redistribution.

But I believe that is a function of the market and not a function of underwriting.[22]

There is no doubt that in many cases the new issues market makers act as a conduit for stock redistribution to a new group of investors. Thus, it is clear that they are performing investment banking functions in active new issues.

New issue market makers perform this function without being subject to the formal due diligence obligation of the traditional investment banker. Moreover, they generally act without regard to SEC Rule 10b-6, which prevents the investment banker from commencing his own new issue market making functions until the completion of his distribution, to make it impossible for him to bid the price of the stock artificially.

The new issue market makers are clearly involved in a conflict situation. As the actual, although not official, underwriters of many issues, they are classified with the typical over-the-counter marketplace dealers, who are not required to protect affirmatively the interests of purchasers of new issues. Instead, they appear to have the responsibility to comply with the due diligence responsibilities of underwriters as well as to examine the suitability of each specific issue for their customers. In short, like the "official" underwriters, they have a duty to the public buyer of the corporations' securities.

Unfortunately, their self-interest and that of the issuer insiders and investment bankers dictate that they raise the price as high and as fast as possible. Their self-interest encourages them to permit, or create, a bubbling hot issue market harmful to the buying public. Because the volume will grow if the price rises rapidly, and because the greater the trading volume, the greater their chance for profit, their desire for a hot market conflicts with their duty to, and the interest of, most shareholders for a rational, orderly market.

The new issues over-the-counter dealers' object is profit, an honorable goal as long as it leads to efficient capital formation and protection of investors. Because over-the-counter market makers maintain a new issues market for only a few days and then depart for yet another new issue, the question is: do they perform a useful economic function? Far too often, in fact, they skim the profit off the temporarily high volume and then leave quickly when the market making gets rough.

To this criticism the over-the-counter dealer replies that he adds important depth and liquidity to the market during the crucial first days of the new issue. Many argue that enough market makers do continue to stick with the stock, providing sufficient liquidity as trading volume diminishes.

Unlike exchange specialists and over-the-counter market makers in seasoned issues, who stand to gain in the long run if they make orderly markets—

because this will attract continuous investor interest and build confidence in the security—new issues market makers have no economic inducement to maintain sound markets. Their markets are temporary; their interest is in big volume and quick profit, not in the long-run success of the security. Their profit depends largely upon investment banker miscalculation of the offering price. The higher the price rises in the after-market, the better off they will be. Frederick B. Whittemore, of Morgan Stanley & Co., Inc., described how his firm curbed the excesses of one new issues market maker:

> To give you a specific example on————when we [the investment bankers] were making an immediate market . . . we found that there was one of the notorious market makers. . . . He knew we were there . . . and every time he started to run it one way or the other . . . we shorted it or sold it to affect that orderliness.[23]

In other words, Morgan had commenced making a market as soon as it completed its investment banker distribution. When the over-the-counter dealers allowed the new issue price to soar, Morgan sold; and when the price began to drop too sharply, Morgan bought. This kept the over-the-counter new issues market makers in line.

Imposing market making responsibilities, similar to the obligations of a specialist on the New York or American Stock Exchanges, might solve the problems caused by new issues market makers.

Three steps could be taken:

1. Establish formal standards for new issues market makers, including a requirement that they help maintain a fair and orderly market in the new issue for, let us say, six months.

2. Increase capital requirements for new issues market makers to insure their ability to make orderly markets.

3. Establish comprehensive reporting requirements for the new issues market makers, exposing their operations in a timely fashion to the SEC and the public.

Admittedly, the first two suggestions have defects. The problem with them is that market making regulations on exchanges have not been an unqualified success. But in view of the grave problems present here, it is advisable to try them. The special nature of the after-market trading and the temptation of new issues market makers to trade to excess create a special need for stringent market making regulations. The special duty of new issues market makers to help create a fair and orderly market should be part of the SEC regulations.

In effect, over-the-counter dealers and the public engage in auction market bidding for the new issue. Unfortunately for the issuer, the auction process does not result in increased proceeds. It results, instead, in increased profits to the over-the-counter dealers, first-tier public buyers, and those investment bankers who also make a market in the new issue that they have underwritten.

Another possible albeit Draconian remedy for this abuse, in addition to the reforms mentioned above, would require investment bankers and over-the-counter market makers to return to the issuer a specified sum formulated on the amount of the immediate after-market premium. This could be done in the form of a levy on profits. This would reduce the conflict between the self-interest of dealers and the interest of the investing public.[24]

3. SEC AND NASD PROPOSALS FOR REFORM

Some of the most drastic reform proposals were included in the famous 1962 SEC Special Study of the securities markets. Rules prohibiting broker-dealers from initiating a trading market for a limited period of, say seventy-two hours after the effective date were made but never adopted.[25]

The New York State study recommended similar steps. It proposed state legislation granting the attorney general the power to issue an order suspending the trading in a particular stock for up to a ten-day period, when he discovers a lack of business information to support price variations of new issues. He could issue an order imposing a standard one- to three-day trading gap between the issue date and the start of the after-market trading for *all* new issues whenever he finds a dangerous hot issue syndrome developing.[26]

A temporary ban would help solve the hot issue problem. Initial trades in the after-market are often prearranged or induced by the underwriters and the over-the-counter market makers. In the immediate after-market, few read the prospectus in its final form. The immediate rise in the after-market price convinces many to buy their full allotment of the new issue, lures new buyers into the after-market, and induces buyers to unload immediately. This engenders the speculative frenzy that reaps profits for the crooks. A trading ban would permit time to evaluate the issue. The theory of the trading gap is that original purchasers and potential new investors will turn cautious during the holiday.

The rebuttal to this recommendation is that delay may place a temporary lid on demand. But lift the ban and demand could erupt. Indeed, some assert that a temporary ban may only whet the appetite of traders, creating a delayed speculative frenzy. Moreover, a ban will eliminate the investor's right to sell his stock. If the overall market were to drop suddenly, the investors would be temporarily stuck with their purchases until the government released them.

But considering the grave and recurrent nature of hot issues, the trading ban proposal should be adopted by the SEC, adding to the reserve arsenal of weapons available to curb hot issue excesses.

Anticipating a new wave of hot issues, the SEC staff began its most recent study of them with a series of public hearings on February 28, 1972. The study resulted in the so-called July 26, 1972, proposals, many of which were implemented in the amendments to SEC reporting and registration requirements announced on June 1, 1973.[27] Ironically, the July 26, 1972, proposals concentrated on changes in prospectus-disclosure requirements, although the Commission pointed out in its release that the major difficulties with hot issues were the methods and patterns of distribution and after-market trading, rather than disclosure inadequacies. One proposal recommended that the NASD consider establishing guidelines defining a bona fide public offering. This proposal would require wide distribution of new issues to new investors and prohibit undue concentration of sales to a few. Factors that restrict supply in the after-market would hopefully be eliminated. For example, the new proposal would require that new issues be spread in relatively small amounts among a large number of investors, thus creating a more effective market for orderly public trading.[28] In April 1975 the NASD rejected the proposal, stating that it would "infringe on the management prerogative of the issuer."[29]

The NASD did, however, propose at that time a number of helpful alternate plans.[30] First, it recommended a change in the NASD rules to prohibit underwriters from accepting from an issuer any instruction to reserve or direct securities to any specified person. This amendment would prevent corporate insiders and their friends from artificially stimulating the price of new issues. More shares of a new offering would be available for purchase by the public.

The second proposal would prohibit underwriters from allocating new issues to customer accounts over which they hold discretionary power. Situations in which an underwriter has discretion (i.e., has total power to buy and sell for a customer) represent an acute, distressing conflict of interest. The underwriter is sorely tempted (and often succumbs) to place an issue with such accounts. Underwriters have manipulated discretionary accounts to control artificially the after-market in new issues and to create false demand.

The NASD also proposed a crackdown on the underwriters' practice in best efforts deals of maintaining strict control on the supply of shares in the market by refusing to deliver stock certificates of new issues to their customers.

In December 1973[31] the NASD somewhat extended the scope of its "free riding and withholding" interpretations. Under the old rules, an investment banker could sell relatively small amounts of a hot issue to partners or employees of his firm, accountants and attorneys for the investment banker, and senior officers of institutional-type accounts. The restrictions were that the amount sold must be "insubstantial" and "not disproportionate" in size to public sales and that the securities be acquired in conformity with "normal investment practices."

The new interpretation imposes a number of revisions: First, no portion of a hot issue may be sold to the partners or employees of the underwriters or to members of their immediate families. Second, no hot issues may be sold to hedge funds if an investment banker or his partners have an interest in the funds. Third, the rules on sales to senior officers of banks or other institutional-type accounts are tighter.[32]

These changes and proposals are very important steps in the right direction, assuming that the NASD adopts the proposals and vigorously enforces the free riding rule. They do not, however, eliminate the problems associated with new issue market making. Also they do not prevent the allocation of sizable blocks of hot issue stocks to a coterie of favored customers and business associates of the investment banker in return for favors, past and future.

As of January 1977, the proposals, the general details of which were suggested by the SEC in 1972, had not yet been adopted. Indeed, the issuer directed proposal has recently been liberalized by the NASD to permit up to 5 percent of the offering to be directed by the issuer to its officers and directors. Moreover, a NASD spokesman informs the author that the due diligence proposal (see page 377) may be withdrawn.

In its proposed Rule 10b-20 (which would prohibit certain tie-in arrangements), the SEC recently inched partway toward the controversial concept of requiring a nondiscriminatory first-come, first-serve concept for distribution of hot issue allotments to customers.[33] The SEC specifically refused to go the full distance. Although such a procedure has the disadvantage of possibly preventing a broker-dealer from innocently favoring substantial old customers over new and relatively inactive customers, a first-come, first-serve approach might help end the hot issues problem by reducing the chances of the underwriters and their friends to profit. The requirement could perhaps be improved by limiting its applicability to customers with some minimum level of annual volume. Although admittedly a Draconian reform, it should be explored because of its attack on the allocation problem and the excesses of hot issues.

The Sticky Issue

The saga of the investment banker and conflict in after-market trading cannot end without referring to the curious concept termed *stabilization*. This is a legal manipulation used by investment bankers to facilitate the distribution of a slow or sticky issue. It is an SEC-approved exception to the prohibitions of Rule 10b-6.

Stabilization has been defined as "the buying of a security for the limited purpose of preventing or retarding a decline in its open-market price in order to facilitate its distribution to the public."[34] Rule 10b-7[35] permits such purchases by underwriters as long as the purchase prices do not exceed the initial public offering price or the highest current independent bid price in noninitial offerings where a market exists. Generally, these provisions permit the underwriter to bid for or buy portions of the slow issue (i.e., peg the price), provided he does not raise the price or follow a rise with increasingly high stabilizing bids to further accelerate the rise. Otherwise, the underwriter falls within the prohibitions of Rule 10b-6.

In 1940 the SEC stated that it was "unanimous in recognizing that stabilizing is a form of manipulation."[36] The SEC, however, balanced the evils of stabilization against its supposedly beneficial results (i.e., easing the work of the underwriting fraternity) and opted for a program of regulated stabilization.

The Commission pointed out that American underwriters do not have sufficient capital to risk buying new securities for any length of time. "They can afford to [enter into underwriting agreements] only on the supposition that they will, with great speed, be able to sell the securities to the multitude of direct individual investors. . . .[The] underwriter's ability to resell the issue [swiftly], in certain conditions of the market, in turn, depends on his ability to stabilize."[37]

Not everyone viewed stabilization as helpful. In 1940 SEC Commissioner Healey dissented from the SEC statement of policy on underwriter stabilization of security prices. Commissioner Healey observed: "What is a proper price if it is not one established by the market based on supply and demand unaffected by unnatural restraints and stimulation? The stabilizing rule puts a premium on improper pricing in that the burden thereof may be passed to the public."[38] Although Healey particularly objected to an SEC rule, since repealed, that permitted stabilizing in connection with an offering "at the market," that is, not a fixed price, his remarks were also directed to stabilizing in general.

Stabilizing in fixed-price offerings has been accepted for over thirty years. It constitutes a built-in SEC-permitted conflict of interest. Whenever an issue is sticky, the investment banker, despite his duty to deal fairly with the public, can artificially peg the price and induce public demand in his self-interest—which may be opposed to the public interest.

A conflict problem also arises in slow or declining markets when the underwriter—for whatever reason—has an equity position in the issue subsequent to the offering. This could perhaps occur when the offering was slow and the investment banker was stuck with part of the issue. Typically, the underwriters and corporate insiders terminate their bidding or buying—in market jargon, "the plug is pulled"—just after they sell out their investment. The buyers are stuck with stock that abruptly collapses.

A classic case in the middle 1960s involved Shearson Hammill & Co. (now called Shearson, Hayden, Stone, Inc.), a large broker-dealer firm.[39] Several partners and employees of Shearson, in cooperation with issuer insiders, underwrote an issue of United States Automatic Mechandising Company (USAMCO) stock. Employees of the underwriter held a substantial equity position in the issue after the offering. They had an obvious interest in maintaining the price of the stock until they could unload their holdings. Their conflict of interest vis-à-vis customers was clear.

After the distribution was ostensibly terminated, Shearson emerged as the dominant market maker in the stock and was both the primary wholesale and retail dealer in USAMCO stock. Several months later the Shearson employees and partners who held USAMCO stock discovered to their consternation that demand was insufficient to cover their public sales. A "workout" market was immediately established, involving the following scenario:

No sell orders from customers were accepted unless offsetting buy orders were in hand.

Although Shearson continued to publish bid and ask quotations, these bids were phony, because Shearson had no intention of purchasing USAMCO from other broker-dealers.

Shearson employees solicited customers' buy orders. While they did this, they continued to quote Shearson's phony bid and ask quotes.

Partners and employees of Shearson sold their holdings of USAMCO to retail customers, even though prior sell orders of retail customers remained unexecuted.

Several of these unexecuted sell orders had been entered at floor prices *lower* than those the Shearson employees received in their sell orders.

Shearson employees advised retail cutomers not to sell their USAMCO holdings.

After the Shearson insiders unloaded their holdings, the manipulative work-out market ended, and the price of the stock plunged. The Shearson customers who still owned the stock were badly stung.

The firm was held to have violated Rule 10b-6 and other antimanipulation and antifraud rules of the SEC.

VII • INVESTMENT BANKING AND BROKER-DEALERS

> *But segregation as a specific remedy for all the multifarious possibilities for conflicts in the complex securities business could not be a simple segregation in any traditional sense but would have to involve fragmentation of the business to a point where (as facetiously pointed out in a recent magazine article) each investor would have his own broker who would not be permitted to act for any other customer or for himself.*
> —Report of Special Study of the Securities Markets, 1963

The Problem

In 1936 the SEC published a report dealing with the segregation of the functions of dealer and broker.[1] Although much of the report focused on the problems of exchange members, underwriting was not ignored. In language that evokes sympathy today, the SEC asserted that

the over-the-counter house which conducts a brokerage business and which also takes underwriting positions. . . . is under temptation to induce its brokerage customers to purchase securities which it is anxious to sell. . . .Whenever the broker and dealer functions are thus combined the profit motive inherent in the latter may be sufficient to color investment advice or otherwise affect the brokerage service rendered to customers.[2]

The SEC concluded that it lacked sufficient data to justify recommending segregation of brokerage and dealer functions. Thus, the matter rested for forty years.

In 1972 a lawsuit revived the issue in a modern setting. A stockholder named Renee Slade charged that Shearson Hammill & Co., Inc., an investment banker to Tidal Marine International Corp., learned that a large percentage of Tidal's fleet was damaged; yet Shearson permitted several registered representatives to promote Tidal stock to Shearson brokerage customers.[3] The registered representatives allegedly were never apprised of this adverse news.

Shearson, like many Wall Street firms, had set up a so-called Chinese wall[4] between its investment banking department and its retail-brokerage arm. (One prominent investment banking firm calls its wall the "Iron Curtain.") No inside information was permitted to flow from the investment banking unit to the account executives in the brokerage end of the firm. Moreover, Shearson had a policy, again quite common, that forbade formal "buy" recommendations being issued for the securities of investment banking clients. This policy was no doubt designed to prevent the firm from officially recommending a security about which Shearson's investment banking department had received adverse news before it had become publicly known. Apparently, individual account executives, however, were permitted to undertake their own independent research and to advise their clients to buy or sell securities of investment banking clients. The wall prevented such individual ad hoc advice from being based on inside information. It was in this setting that several registered representatives had innocently recommended that their retail customers buy Tidal stock at the same time that Shearson's investment banking department had allegedly learned of the adverse news. Shearson's investment banking department tried to convince Tidal to disclose the news publicly. When it failed Shearson finally threatened to go to the regulatory authorities. After Tidal finally did disclose the information to the SEC, Shearson terminated its investment banking relationship.

The federal district court held that Shearson's registered representatives were prohibited from soliciting customers without disclosing the adverse information.[5] Since disclosure might violate Shearson's duty to its investment banking client, its only alternative, the judge stated, was to refrain entirely from recommending the stock. This policy placed it at a competitive disadvantage with those retail brokerage firms with no investment banking clients.

Shearson, on appeal, argued that the district court had for the first time imposed on a broker the duty to use material nonpublic information, sometimes called "inside information," for the sole benefit of its own brokerage customers. Shearson argued that recommendations should not be based on material nonpublic information.[6] The U.S. Court of Appeals for the Second Circuit did not disturb the district court ruling, but returned the case to it for further fact-finding, stating: " . . . this is precisely the kind of case in which the implications are so considerable and the issues so complex that in the proper exercise of judicial restraint, an abstract answer to an abstract question is the least desirable of *judicial* solutions."[7]

If the district court's rationale is ultimately approved in the Second Circuit, or in other appellate courts, investment banking firms that also do a retail brokerage business may have to choose between these two. Otherwise, they will run the risk of violating the law whenever they deal simultaneously with retail clients and investment banking clients. No matter how it is decided, the case forcefully illuminates the dilemmas created by the combination of underwriting and brokerage functions within the same firm.

A lengthy series of SEC and judicial cases on SEC antifraud Rule 10b-5 have made it clear that brokers cannot use nonpublic material information in connection with either the sale or purchase of securities or recommendations to customers to buy or sell securities. Indeed, the doctrine has been expanded to bar more or less inadvertent recipients of inside information, so-called tippees, from so acting.[8]

A famous illustration of this line of judicial and SEC authority is the 1968 *Douglas* case, which involved Merrill Lynch, Pierce, Fenner & Smith.[9] Members of Merrill Lynch's investment banking department had been informed of adverse news about the earnings of Douglas Aircraft. Merrill Lynch's investment banking employees gave that news to members of the firm's sales department, who in turn leaked the news to several institutional clients. The clients quickly sold out their Douglas stock to investors who, obviously, did not have the information. To prevent reoccurrences the SEC required the firm to set up a barrier between the investment banking department and all other branches of the firm and to establish procedures that clearly prevent such inside information from being used for any other purposes.[10] Other large underwriter brokerage firms have set up similar barriers.

The policy seems sound, but there are complications, as in the Shearson incident. In that case, the firm *failed to use* material inside information, unlike Merrill Lynch, which was charged with *improper use*.

The Shearson argument would allow unknowing customers of any broker-dealer to buy into an investment that the firm knows to be overpriced. The conflict is mind-boggling. On the one hand, as an SEC amicus curiae brief stated, a security dealer under the antifraud rules of the Securities Act "cannot recommend a security unless there is an adequate and reasonable basis for such recommendation. . . . By his recommendation he implies that a reasonable investigation has been made and that his recommendation rests on the conclusions based on such investigation."[11] On the other hand, the investment banker owes a duty to its corporate clients not to release confidential information prematurely.

The *Slade* case puts the investment banking community in a difficult position. If the district court's decision is upheld, the effective use of the Chinese wall may be thwarted. But if the Chinese wall is dropped, even worse dilemmas could arise. At the moment three principal directions, all unsatisfactory, seem possible.

1. The multiservice securities firm maintains a Chinese wall. Whenever the firm receives adverse or favorable nonpublic news concerning the security of an investment banking client, the security will be placed on a restricted list and registered representatives will be forbidden to recommend purchases or sales of the security. This is called the *reinforced Chinese wall policy*. But as soon as their license to advise is pulled, the danger grows that the decision to pull the license will trigger a flood of rumors on Wall Street as well as alert retail customers to the existence of inside information. In certain cases this might constitute an indirect tip of inside news in violation of Rule 10b-5. The argument in favor of the no-recommendation rule is that there will not be tips or rumors because the market will not know whether the inside news is bullish or bearish. This argument fails for the following reasons: (a) The stock market bubbles with gossip. The no-recommendation decision is likely to give rise to rumors and speculation that will have a disturbing impact on the market. Customers will make guesses about the nature of the inside news and will buy or sell based upon their hunches. Cautious investors will infer that the inside news is bad. Optimists will speculate that it is good. Trading will result from hunches not rational evaluation of economic values. (b) The imposition of a "no-recommendation" rule will be regarded by many investors as confirmation of an old rumor. As Leonard Chazen pointed out, "Imagine, for example, the market impact of a notice that a public company, rumored to be a prospective tender offer target, had been placed on the restricted list of an investment banking firm known to have counseled the rumored tender offeror."[12] (c) In many cases the brokerage firm will pull its recommendations after the firm has made a public recommendation to buy. This will operate as an almost unmistakable (or irresistable) clue that negative inside information has been received, in possible violation of Rule 10b-5.

2. A variation of the reinforced Chinese wall policy is to prohibit registered representatives from giving advice at any time on any security issued by an investment banking client, whether or not the investment banking department is in possession of inside news. This prohibition, however, places the integrated investment banker-broker-dealer firms at a severe competitive disadvantage. Their range of advice will be narrowed compared with that of nonintegrated investment banking firms. (This bad effect will result from the first direction also.) Indeed, the larger the underwriting department grows and

the more issuer clients it has, the less competitive its other departments can be. Beyond the competitive problem is the impact of a no-recommendation rule (whether of the first or second variety) on the professional worth of investment advice given by broker-dealer firms. The customer expects to receive and indeed deserves first-rate investment advice. But the larger the firm's restricted list, the more limited is the range of investment alternatives the firm can offer. Ultimately, all of these factors might force firms to separate their investment banking and retail functions.

3. There is yet a third direction. In the *Slade* case, there was no explicit discussion of the extent to which the Shearson registered representatives may have cautioned investors that their recommendations were not based upon official Shearson research, or whether they warned that, because Tidal was an investment banking client, it was possible that inside information was not being disclosed. It is, therefore, conceivable that future judicial decisions would be different, if registered representatives were to advise customers that, because the firm has an investment banking relationship with a company, the research department is prohibited from advising on the stock, and that the customer, in addition to being insulated from inside information, is only receiving the individual judgment of the registered representative, not the official opinion of the firm. This direction might be termed the *naked Chinese wall plus notice* position, or in other words a position that the Chinese wall standing tall without the reinforcement of a restricted list/no recommendations policy is sufficient to protect customers and at the same time insulate the broker-dealer from Rule 10b-5 liability.[13]

There are three major arguments for this choice of direction. First, it would preserve the economic viability of integrated investment banking firms. Second, it would fulfill the broker-dealer duty to preserve confidential data of investment banking clients. Third, it would make the retail client fully aware of the limited nature of the advice being offered.

But there are also a number of very convincing arguments against this direction. First, this policy would permit a broker-dealer to place a customer in a bad investment, even though the firm possesses inside information that the security was grossly overpriced. This is an indefensible policy on grounds of commonsense justice and equity. Second, it violates the firm's legal duty to its customers based upon the well-accepted SEC-judicial shingle theory, which requires the investment banker-broker-dealer to be honest about its recommendation and to treat its customers fairly. It entails that a firm must reveal to its customers (see page 407) any material knowledge in its possession that contradicts its recommendations to buy or sell. Third, the public will lose confidence in the integrated investment banker-broker-dealer once it understands that one employee may be recommending a stock on the basis of information that other employees in the investment banking department know to be untrue. Fourth, the policy is bad economics since it permits the firm to help misallocate economic resources by making recommendations that the firm knows are based upon incomplete or inaccurate public information.

However, assume for a moment that the Chinese wall is abandoned. Then the integrated firm is in even greater trouble. Consider this scenario:

Shearson's investment banking department has just learned of nonpublic adverse news and tells the registered representatives in the brokerage department. A valued customer who holds Tidal stock telephones his Shearson registered representative, and asks, "Shall I hold, sell, or buy more Tidal stock?"

The Shearson employee, using the inside information derived from the investment banking department, advises the customer to sell. The customer's sale, based upon *use* of nonpublic news, would clearly violate federal antifraud rule 10b-5. This was made clear in both the *Merrill Lynch* case and *SEC* v. *Texas Gulf Sulphur Co.*,[14] which determined that individuals who obtain nonpublic inside material information must abstain from trading in, or recommending purchase or sale of, the stock. The doctrine is fair. Why should Shearson customers be permitted to use inside information and sell Tidal stock to an unsuspecting public?

In short, tearing down the wall would quickly lead to totally unacceptable consequences.

In an *amicus curiae* brief in the Shearson case, Salomon Brothers, one of Wall Street's largest institutional broker-dealers, argued that the district court opinion should be affirmed, distinguishing between what it termed, "solicitation" and "affirmative recommendation." Salomon maintained that when Shearson *affirmatively recommended* the purchase of a security, which some members of the firm with access to inside information knew to be overpriced, the firm was, indeed, acting unlawfully. However, argued Salomon Brothers, when a firm *solicits* a customer order, instead of actively recommending, then, in spite of the fact that the firm possessed adverse inside information, the *solicitation* should be legal.

But the emphasis Salomon places on the distinction between solicitation and affirmative recommendation is largely explained by the character of Salomon. Most Wall Street firms do a considerable amount of retail business, and this almost always requires an affirmative recommendation of a security. Salomon Brothers, in contrast, does little retail business and is a dominant block trader. Unlike the retail house, according to Salomon Brothers, the block trader does not make "affirmative recommendations." Rather, he "solicits" business, that is, "merely contacts a customer to determine if a customer is interested in buying a particular security . . . no recommendation of purchase is made."[15] With a large inventory of securities constantly on hand, Salomon Brothers, which is also an underwriting firm, would probably be severely restricted by the application of the Shearson ruling to its business—thus, the attempt to differentiate its activities from those of most other Wall Street firms.

Paine, Webber, Jackson & Curtis, a prominent retail firm, criticized this distinction in an *amicus curiae* brief. It argued in part as follows:

In its brief Salomon takes issue with the District Court's use of the word "soliciting," rather than "recommending," in the certified question. (Salomon Br., footnote,
at 1.) By drawing the distinction in a footnote, rather than textually, and by characteriz-
ing the District Court's use of the word "soliciting" as only "unintended" (id.),
Salomon might have this Court believe that it is engaging in little more than a semantic
quibble.

The fact of the matter is that the distinction between "soliciting" and "recommending" is critical to Salomon's way of doing business and, therefore, critical to Salomon's
entire position. If this Court should answer the certified question in the affirmative but
limit the scope of its decision to "recommendations," and not "solicitations,"
Salomon will have succeeded in gaining a distinct and entirely unjustified competitive
advantage over most other major securities firms. These firms, like Paine, Webber and
unlike Salomon, market securities primarily based upon research through recommendations to customers. . . .

Salomon's brief is quick to point out, however, that such policy should not extend to
"soliciting" customers. This is readily explained by the fact that Salomon's business
consists, in part, of "soliciting" institutional customers to purchase large blocks of
securities from Salomon's inventory of securities. In such transactions, of course,
Salomon is acting as a principal for its own account and not simply as a broker for
others. Its customers buy securities from Salomon as the owner and seller of such
securities and not merely as an intermediary. . . .

In its brief, Salomon suggests that "solicitation" is far removed from the affirmative
act of "recommending" a security for purchase. (Salomon Br., footnote, at 1.) That is
decidedly not the case. As defendant-appellant correctly points out in its reply brief (at
14) Salomon's trades "are scarcely as mechanical as Salomon represents them to be."
In selling securities from its inventory, Salomon does not simply sit back and wait
dispassionately for customers to place unsolicited orders, or mechanically execute
orders for customers who dial its telephone number. It affirmatively and aggressively
seeks out its customers, hoping to induce them to buy a particular security at a particular
time and at a quoted price.[16]

These dilemmas are not limited to the retailing of securities or to the large
institutional block business. Market making is another vulnerable activity. A
market maker maintains a market by being prepared both to buy and to sell
specific securities at quoted prices on a continuous basis. If the investment
banking unit of a dealer receives adverse nonpublic material news, can the
firm's over-the-counter department continue making a market in that stock
without public disclosure? The market maker's usual argument is that it trades
passively and simply reacts to the forces of supply and demand, never setting a
price based upon its own research. Moreover, market makers argue that market
making transactions do not involve any opinion on the value of the securities.

There is another point of view that holds quite the opposite. The Supreme
Court *Affiliated Ute* case held that market makers could not "stand mute"
while making sales in a market that they "had developed and encouraged and
with which they were fully familiar."[17] The SEC has been moving toward
requiring market makers to make public the financial status of the issuers of the
securities they trade. Specifically, SEC Rule 15c 2-11 makes it illegal for any

market maker to trade a security unless he obtains financial information about the issuer and makes it available to his customers. [18]

As a practical matter, firms realize that if their trading pattern even *appears* to be based on inside information, a court is likely to conclude that the firm's Chinese wall was breached and that trades were, indeed, a result of inside tips. Of course, everyone agrees that if the Chinese wall is, in fact, penetrated, the dealer is liable.

Particular concern is frequently expressed about national wire house firms like Merrill Lynch that use their vast individual retail departments to boost the distribution of their underwritings. How can such large wire houses reconcile the conflict between their duty to issuers and their duty to retail clients?

Some observers, noting this conflict, have argued for a divorce of these two functions. However, this solution misses the fundamental point about securities: They are sold, not bought; therefore, all underwriters, whether or not retail wire houses, have to supply distribution prowess to sell the issue.

Large commissions have proven necessary to induce registered representatives to convince customers to buy. This is true even in secondary trading. Underwriting historically involves commission payments three or four times the average trading commission, because the selling effort is so much larger and more difficult than in small, casual trading in the secondary market. In recent years the sales commission component in underwriting spreads involving equity issues has been an increasing source of profit, because distribution efforts have proven so crucial. [19]

Therefore, if Merrill Lynch or other integrated firms were eliminated, they would need to be invented anew for the underwriting business to continue. Investment bankers, if limited to underwriting alone, would be forced to set up syndicates with other firms that did have distribution capacity. Those firms, in turn, would receive large commissions to induce them and their salesmen to make the necessary selling effort.

This is precisely what firms such as Morgan Stanley presently do to compete with firms such as Merrill Lynch for investment banking business. Syndicate groups of regional broker-dealers with retail clients are established. These syndicates involve precisely the same conflict problems as the Merrill Lynch system. They have, on the one hand, a duty to the public buyer to protect his interests, and on the other, an obligation to the issuer to push its stock.

Solutions

What is the best solution? One approach is to cut the Gordian knot of conflicting duties by divorcing investment banking from brokerage, block trading, and market making. The difficulty here is that a loss of capital would result that would irreparably harm the underwriting functions. Moreover, recent developments demonstrate that successful underwritings require a retail brokerage operation. The growth of Merrill Lynch into a leading investment banking firm is testimony to that fact. Further, divorcing the functions and thus splitting up capital resources would seriously impair the market making function, because a very large percentage of all over-the-counter market making is conducted by firms, again such as Merrill Lynch, that also have investment banking departments. To remove all these firms from market making would impair the liquidity of the over-the-counter markets. Such a divorce would also impair the block trading function of firms by depriving them of needed capital. Also, dividing up firms into separate brokerage and investment banking units would result in costly replication of research resources now employed in one entity. Indeed, a split in function would so destroy the usual operations of the equity and debt markets, that as the SEC has stated, "The capital-raising capability of the industry and its ability to serve the public would be considerably weakened."[20]

The best solution to the Slade dilemma is an SEC or legislative mandate requiring the *immediate* public disclosure of all material inside corporate news by the issuer or, if the issuer defaults, by its investment banker (whether in the retail, block business, or market making area). In the *Slade* case, for example, that rule would have required Shearson's *immediate* public disclosure of the adverse news. Such an approach is consistent with the recent trend of disclosure doctrine of the New York and American Stock Exchanges and the SEC. Although there are good reasons for temporary corporate secrecy, on balance such reasons must give way when corporations enter into investment banking relationships with dealers. When the value of immediate full disclosure to the public is balanced against the risk to corporations, the former weighs more heavily. Otherwise, the lack of public confidence in the markets is likely to accelerate, and even more investors will desert forever.

The presence of public shareholders and the decision to go public create a need to share corporate news immediately with stockholders and the general public. The lessons learned from Watergate about the dangers of secrecy in the political arena should be applied to the corporate arena as well.

Immediate disclosure is the only realistic solution for the ordinary public investor. Swift, total, and immediate public disclosure of all material news must be the rule. This policy will not create de facto segregation, because all issuers, whether they deal with nonintegrated or integrated houses, will be required to comply. Also, they will have no choice among investment banking firms on this issue, because all underwriters will be subject to the same mandate. The principle of prompt disclosure is consistent with the SEC's present trend to require disclosure by issuers during the SEC-registration waiting period.[21]

The proposal is practical because issuers and investment bankers will know the requirements in advance. Planning will be based upon a ground rule applicable to everyone.

On balance, the fiduciary obligation of the broker-dealer to its buying and selling clients requires it to tell the full truth. If this disclosure rule is implemented, future Slade-type dilemmas will be avoided.

VIII • PRIVATE PLACEMENTS

. . . reliance on the private offering in any transaction
[is] a calculated business risk at best.
—Southwestern Law Journal 503, 512 (1966)

In public offerings the basic conflict of interest arises between the investment banker's duties to the issuer on the one hand, and to the buying public on the other hand. The SEC's new private-offering Rule 146 exacerbates this basic conflict in the realm of the private placement.

A private placement is a sale of securities to a limited number of purchasers. Enormous amounts of securities are sold in this manner. In many private placement deals, particularly the larger ones, a professional investment banker plays a pivotal role in setting the terms and placing the securities. A study of investment banking completed in the middle 1960s pointed out the basis for this practice:

During a firm's first recourse to such financing the firm is likely to have only limited knowledge regarding potential buyers, acceptable procedures, and what might constitute reasonably competitive terms.[1]

Even after the first private placement, however, the study concluded that a majority of issuers continue to rely on investment bankers for future private placements.[2]

Unfortunately, conflict of interest abounds in many private placements. Consider the following all-too-typical scenario: An investment banker and a corporation consider the advisability of a private placement. After the decision to proceed is made, the investment banker begins lining up the prospective purchasers. The investment banker, naturally, will receive a handsome fee for his successful services. At the same time, under SEC Rule 146,[3] he is acting as offeree representative, presumably protecting the interests of potential purchasers. Yet, if the investment banker recommends against the purchase to any offeree, the deal may founder, and the investment banking fee will be forfeited.

Qualified private offerings are exempt from the registration requirements of the Securities Act of 1933, including the necessity to prepare a prospectus. Basically, the exemption assumes that prospective purchasers are sophisticated and that, therefore, the registration provision is unneeded. A thicket of judicial decisions, however, had grown up around private placements. The new SEC Rule 146, effective June 10, 1974, marked an effort by the SEC to clarify and simplify an increasingly complex area.

One of the innovations introduced by Rule 146 involved the creation of the "offeree representative,"[4] who was to represent the interests of unsophisticated investors. The rule provides that individual offerees need not themselves satisfy the financial sophistication requirements when they are represented by experts. It was at this point, however, that the conflict problem arose. Initially, the SEC defined the offeree representative as any person who "*is independent of the issuer* and is not acting on behalf of the issuers in connection with the transaction. . . ."[5] This language would have prevented the investment banker who placed the deal from serving as the offeree representative.

The revised rule dropped the offending language. The offeree representative no longer needed to be "independent of the issuer." The new requirement stipulated only that he not be "an affiliate, director, officer or other employee of the issuer, beneficial owner of 10 percent or more of any class of the equity securities or 10 percent or more of the equity interest in the issuer . . . ."[6] Thus, the investment banker (who is usually an independent contractor and not an employee of the issuer) and offeree representative could be the same. This means that the underwriter-offeree representative can wear two hats in the same deal, that is, have conflicting interests and yet qualify the deal by the Rule 146 exemption from SEC registration.

The focus is shifted from regulation to disclosure, requiring that the offeree representative *disclose* to potential investors any present or likely material relationships between it and the issuer. However, the rule cautions that such disclosure "does not relieve the offeree representative of its obligation to act in the interest of the offeree."[7]

Another subtle change in language emphasizes the new approach. The original rule required that the representative be "duly authorized by the person for whose account securities are to be purchased *to act as agent* for such person. . . ."[8] The new language merely requires the representative to be "acknowledged by the offeree, in writing, during the course of the transaction, to *be his offeree representative*. . . ."[9] The deletion of the word *agent*, a legal term denoting fiduciary responsibility, highlights the lessening of concern with the problems of conflict of interest.[10]

Rule 146, then, was the SEC's effort to simplify the elusive legal booby trap known as the private offering exemption. It is fair to conclude that many corporate lawyers view the rule as a technical failure and a legal nightmare. From the conflicts standpoint—our concern—it is also a failure and indeed makes matters worse than before the rule was enacted.[11]

IX • CONCLUSION

The SEC made headlines in 1974 when it charged Hayden-Stone, Inc., a prominent investment banker, and Seaboard Corp., a mutual fund advisor, with civil fraud in connection with the underwriting of the fund manager's securities.[1] The SEC allegations involved many of the conflicts discussed in this book. In a settlement with the SEC, in which it neither denied nor admitted the allegations in the SEC complaint,[2] Hayden-Stone consented to various disciplinary actions and to a permanent court injunction.

The SEC complaint asserted that the investment banker, as managing under-writer for a public offering of securities issued by Seaboard, sold 543,100 units of securities for $13.50 per unit. Each unit consisted of two shares of Seaboard common and one warrant to purchase an additional share. In addition, Arnold Bernhard & Co. sold 60,000 shares of Seaboard common at $5.75 a share. However, the prospectus failed to disclose the following highly questionable activities.

In 1969 Hayden-Stone had made a private placement of sixty thousand shares of Seaboard's stock to Bernhard. To induce Bernhard to buy, the investment banker gave the firm an option to sell the stock back to the investment banker at $5.25 per share if the shares could not be sold in a registered public offering within six months. When the time came to under-write the public offering, Hayden-Stone found the deal a difficult one to syndicate because of the desperate financial condition of Seaboard. Its demise, in fact, was a possibility. At the same time, Hayden-Stone could not find a buyer for the sixty thousand shares it had agreed to take back from Bernhard, and it informed Seaboard's insiders of this, saying that Hayden-Stone itself would have to buy sixty thousand less shares from Seaboard than those originally agreed on. The reduction, of course, would substantially decrease the proceeds to Seaboard.

Seaboard insiders reacted, according to the SEC, by persuading a private investor to buy the sixty thousand shares. The purchase would aid the offering by creating an illusion of demand, and it would prevent the adverse publicity that would arise if the investment banker was forced to cut back on the size of the offering. The sweetener was the insiders' secret agreement to give the buyer the right to sell the shares back to the insiders at a guaranteed profit six month after the public offering.

In addition, the Seaboard officers entered into secret deals with professional dealers to create a fictitious market in Seaboard stock before the public offering became effective. The purpose was to support the price of its securi-ties to facilitate the distribution.

During the underwriting negotiations, Seaboard secretly promised that a subsidiary of Hayden-Stone would become the investment advisor to Competi-tive Capital Corporation, a mutual fund operated by Seaboard. Indeed, the proceeds of the offering were to be used to complete the purchase of Competi-tive Capital Corporation. This secret commitment, which was not disclosed in the prospectus, meant additional compensation to the investment banker.

The prospectus also failed to disclose that the investment banker had sold 42 percent of the offering to the discretionary and advisory accounts managed by the investment banker subsidiary.

In addition, the SEC complaint stated that the sale to discretionary accounts was made despite the fact that Hayden Stone's corporate finance department had prepared a report that said Seaboard had financial and operational de-ficiencies and questioned whether the market price of Seaboard was justified.

Finally, the SEC staff asserted that the investment banker violated Rule 10b-6, because it encouraged customers to buy Seaboard common stock before distribution.

The Seaboard allegations[3] knit together many of the investment banker conflicts discussed in this book:

1. *Discretionary Accounts.* The investment banker sold 42 percent of the Seaboard issue stock to discretionary accounts. The profitable sale by an agent of property he owns to his principal, where the agent controls the principal, is fraught with obvious peril. The fruit of such conflict is overreaching, as was the case in Seaboard.

2. *Due Diligence.* The investment banker did not disclose the secret arrangements made by Seaboard management and the related manipulative activity designed to facilitate the success of the underwriting.

3. *Pricing.* The investment banker overpriced the issue and knew, or should have known, that an offering price based on current market price was not justified.

4. *Compensation.* The investment banker received secret underwriting compensation.

5. *Issuer Choice of Investment Banker.* The investment banker and issuer had a series of close relationships, including the private placement to Bernhard and the arrangement for using the investment banker subsidiary.

6. *Integration of Underwriter and Retail or Advisory Functions.* The investment banker's subsidiary was a money manager. The investment banker's investment judgment was subject to a conflict, because it had a secret commitment from the issuer to employ its subsidiary's services.

The *Seaboard-Hayden-Stone* case is a dramatic illustration of the problems that exist in investment banking. Conflict of interest is built into the very essence of the profession.

There is a temptation to suggest the Draconian surgery of segregation of broker-dealer functions to cure these problems. But drastic surgery, for the reasons already discussed, would be unwise.

There is no simple one-shot solution to the conflicts problem. Furthermore, many conflicts are unavoidable; they are inextricably part of the system and cannot all be totally extinguished except at a cost that exceeds the benefits derived from the system. The combination of intelligent disclosure policies, certain regulatory changes, and vigorous SEC enforcement policies are the only effective curbs. This report on investment banking has made many specific suggestions. For example, in the new issues area, the SEC and the NASD should promulgate a comprehensive code of due diligence and suitability requirements to govern investment banking procedures and responsibilities.

Further, the SEC should help develop and clarify the legal standards that govern a corporate director's responsibilities in regard to the competitive selection and supervision of the issuers' investment bankers. Moreover, the SEC should set forth standards for the public distribution of new issues, such as minimum percentages to be distributed to the general public and strict limits on or prohibition of directed sales to insiders. Such standards will lessen the issuers and underwriters' ability or motive to manipulate new issue prices.

The SEC could also improve the 1933 act's prospectuses by encouraging greater use of projections and other "soft," that is, subjective data, and by requiring disclosure of underwriters' conflicts and a clear description of the process by which the underwriter and issuer arrived at their offering price. In addition, there is the recommendation to require immediate disclosure of material inside information by investment bankers and their corporate clients. This policy would lessen the conflict danger that results from the combined function of investment banking and retail brokerage.

Finally, it is necessary to maintain and to increase SEC enforcement resources and activities. At present, the SEC professional enforcement staff numbers only about four hundred—a ridiculously small number to cover the U.S. securities markets. These changes and the others discussed here will improve the system of investment banking, while preserving its great strengths, enabling underwriting to play an important role in raising the large sum of capital that the American economy will require in the late seventies and beyond.[4]

NOTES

I. Introduction

[1]There are two basic kinds of underwriting—*best efforts* and *firm commitment*. In the former, the investment banker usually acts purely as a broker and takes no risks. He sells the corporate securities for the issuer and receives a commission for his services. In firm commitment underwriting, which comprises most of the larger and more important deals, the underwriter purchases the securities from the corporation and resells them at a higher price to the public.

Firm commitment underwritings are either competitively bid or negotiated. In *competitive bidding*, two or more investment banking groups submit sealed bids to the issuer, and the highest bidder becomes the underwriter.

In the typical *negotiated* deal, a corporation informally contacts one or perhaps several investment bankers, then selects a lead underwriter—the one who, it hopes, will charge the least and whose standards of dollar size and financing are met by the issuer. In practice established companies usually contact an underwriter with whom they have worked before, and the neophyte corporate issuer can choose a member of that segment of the investment banking industry that caters to new or recently established corporations. There are times, of course, when investment bankers, especially the more aggressive ones, seek out prospective clients.

Firm commitment underwritings involve two separate tasks. The first is the underwriter's commitment to buy the issuer's securities, thereby accepting the risk that the public may not buy the issuer's stock.

The second step is the sale of the securities to the public. In the past many underwriters relied on retail firms for distribution, but during the past ten years, the trend has been for underwriters to sell directly to investors.

It is the lead underwriter who manages a firm commitment underwriting. It investigates the financial strength of the issuer and assembles an underwriting syndicate ranging from a handful to over one hundred firms who will share the risk and buy a percentage of the shares being offered to the public. The syndicate is formed on the basis of a pecking order, called "bracketing," in which the biggest firms get the largest share of the underwriting.

In the case of a firm commitment deal, the underwriters are compensated by a discount from the public offering price and cheap stock or warrants. The discount, or spread, is shared among the firms in the underwriting syndicate.

The lead investment banker may get a cut of 20 percent of the discount. Another 50 to 60 percent is typically paid to the firms that actually sell the issue to the public. The balance of 20 to 30 percent is prorated among the investment bankers according to the number of shares they bought from the issuer. In recent years the share given for a successful selling effort has been increasing in equity deals. Investment bankers who are able to sell more than they buy (i.e., underwrite) get a selling commission on all those shares as well.

In both competitive and negotiated underwriting, the law requires the underwriter to investigate the financial resources and prospects of the issuer. In a negotiated deal, the underwriter typically begins this investigation well before the offering of the security.

In competititve bidding, however, the underwriters have little opportunity to conduct a lengthy investigation.

Bids are based upon a prospectus prepared by the corporation, and the winning investment bankers immediately take the issue to the public for sale.

The practice may undercut the underwriter's "due diligence" responsibility, set forth in the Securities Act of 1933, to protect the public from misrepresentation of the corporation's financial and business status.

The drafting of a prospectus for filing with the Securities and Exchange Commission and distribution to the public is a cooperative project carried out by the lead underwriter and the issuer. After an SEC review of the prospectus (but not approval), the issuer's stock can be offered to the public.

If the stock is not listed and traded on an exchange, over-the-counter dealers usually make a market in the stock, with the managing underwriter committed to supporting the security. To do this the underwriter may act as an over-the-counter market maker or may recommend the stock to public investors, including its own customers.

In summary, American investment bankers perform four functions: 1. they purchase securities from the issuer; 2. they distribute those securities to the public; 3. they sponsor trading in those issues; 4. they act as financial counsel to the issuer.

What is significant about these functions is that they are linked to the merchandising ability of the underwriter. Securities are sold, not bought.

[2]For a general discussion of investment banking, see Carosso, *Investment Banking in America: A History* (1970); Friend, Longstreet et al., *Investment Banking and the New Issues Market* (1967) [hereafter cited as Friend et al.]; 1. L. Loss, *Securities Regulation* (1961, 2d ed.) [Hereafter cited as 1. Loss]; Securities and Exchange Commission, *Report of Special Study of Securities Markets*, Pt. 1 (1963) [hereafter cited as *Special Study*]; *Hearing on Hot Issues Securities Market Before the Securities and Exchange Commission* (1972-1973) [hereafter cited as *Hot Issue Hearings*]; *U.S. v. Morgan*, 118 F. Supp. 621 (S.D.N.Y. 1953).

The main focus of this study is corporate issues. Mutual fund shares are sold and redeemed continuously, use unique distribution methods that are very different from those employed in corporate issues generally, and are not included in the study.

[3]See, for example, *Escott v. BarChris Const. Corp.*, 283 F. Supp. 643 (S..N.Y. 1968).

[4]Submission of Morgan Stanley et al. to the SEC staff, File No. S7-529 (June 1974), p. 3.

[5]See Friend et al., p. 41.

[6]Ibid.

[7]Ibid., p. 503. The researchers stated that another possible explanation, *inter alia*, was that corporate issuers tap the capital markets when their common stock is selling at unusually high multiples " . . . or, in other words, when their common stock was being evaluated on the basis of exceptionally optimistic forecasts." Ibid., p. 502. It should be noted that the researchers found that the difference between new issue and market as a whole performance was greater in the pre-SEC years. Friend, "The SEC and the Economic Performance of Securities Markets," in H.

Manne et al., eds., *Economic Policy and the Regulation of Corporate Securities* (Washington, D.C.: 1969), p. 197.

[8]SEC, *39th Annual Report* (1974), p. 140; SEC, *40th Annual Report* (1975), p. 145.

II. The Selection of Investment Bankers

[1]*U.S.* v. *Morgan*, 118 F. Supp. 621 (S.D.N.Y. 1953).

[2]See, for example, Blackstone, *Developments in the Broker Dealer Area: Underwriters' Compensation and Related Problems*, First Annual Institute on Securities Regulation (Practicing Law Institute; Fleischer, Mundheim, and Glazer, eds., 1970). p. 293.

[3]Eppler, "Preparing for a Public Offering." 1. *How to Go Public: An Introduction to the Securities Laws* (Practicing Law Institute, S. Friedman, Chm., 1974), p. 229.

[4]*Otis & Co.* v. *Pennsylvania R. Co.*, 61 F. Supp. 905 (E.D. Pa. 1945), aff'd 155 F. 2d 522 (3rd Cir. 1946); accord *Casey* v. *Woodruff*, 49 N.Y.S. 2d 625 (Sp. T. 1944).

[5]Robertson, "The Underwriters Have to Offer Even More," *Fortune* (January 1973), p. 117.

[6]Interview with Howard Sprow, General Counsel for Merrill Lynch in New York City, May 8, 1974.

[7]I. Friend and M. Blume, *The Consequences of Competitive Commissions on the New York Stock Exchange*, reprinted in Hearings on S. 1369 before the Subcommittee on Securities of the Senate Committee on Banking, Housing, and Urban Affairs, 92 Cong., 2d Sess., (Washington, D.C.: 1972), pp. 395-397.

[8]See note 6 above.

[9]See "Bloodbath in the Bond Market," *Institutional Investor* (June 1974), p. 35.

[10]1. Loss. p. 388; see also Henkel, "The Auction Block for Securities"*Virginia Law Review* 36 (1950), p. 701 [hereafter cited as Henkel].

[11]Henkel, p. 702. The current regulation is 49. C. F. R. pt. 1010 (1974).

[12]Henkel, p. 702-703.

[13]17 C. F. R. § 250.50 (1974).

[14]See SEC, *39th Annual Report* (1974), p. 111.

[15]Peterson, "Negotiated vs. Competitive Debt Financing," *Vanderbilt Law Review* 1 (1948), pp. 531, 551.

[16]Robbins, "Competitive Bidding in Sale of Securities" *Harvard Business Review* 27 (1949), pp. 646, 663.

[17]See Ricotta, "Southern Bell Deal Highlights Otherwise Dull Week," *Investment Dealers' Digest* (February 19, 1974), p. 6.

[18]Hearing on Temporary Suspension of the Competitive Bidding Requirements of Rule 50 with Respect to Common Stock of Holding Companies Registered Under the Public Utility Holding Company Act 1935, S 7-529 (January 6-9, 1975), p. 3 [hereafter cited as Public Utility Hearings]. See also Public Utility Holding Company Act Release No. 18646 (1974).

[19]See SEC, Public Utility Holding Company Act Release No. 18898 (1975).

[20]Henkel, pp. 714-715. See also Holding Company Release No. 3118 [1941 Transfer Binder] *CCH Fed. Sec. L. Rep.* §75,219 (1941).

[21]Public Utility Hearings, p. 108.

III. Due Diligence

[1]Securities Act of 1933 §11(b)(3), 15 U.S.C. §77k(b)(3) (1970).

[2]Securities Act of 1933 §11(c), 15 U.S.C. §77k(c) (1970).

[3]Another source of his responsibility lies in the SEC's antifraud and suitability doctrines, which require broker-dealers in general to have a *reasonable* basis for their recommendations and their belief that their investment recommendations are suitable in light of an investor's finances, personal condition, investment objectives, and net worth. NYSE, AMEX, and NASD have each adopted suitability rules for the selling activities of their members. The SEC has adopted a rule to apply to those brokers or dealers who are not members of NASD. See Article III, §2, *CCH NASD Manual. parag. 2151 (1974);* Rule *405, 2 CCH NYSE Guide,* parag. 2405 (1974); Rule 411, 2 *CCH AMEX Guide,* Parag. 9431 (1974); Rule 15b10-3, 17 C.F.R. §240, 15b10-3 (1974).

[4]*Escott* v. *BarChris Const. Corp.*, 283 F. Supp. 643 (S.D.N.Y. 1968).

[5]283 F. Supp. p. 692.

[6]See SEC Securities Act Release No. 5274 (1972).

[7]The Commission ordered a public investigation of hot issues securities on October 20, 1971. The first stage of the hearings began February 28, 1972, and continued through June 8, 1972. The second stage concentrated on broker-dealer, underwriting trading, and selling practices and began on October 25, 1972. A third phase was held in December 1973.

The author of this paper was an SEC staff member and participant in the first phase of the SEC hearings.

[8]283 F. Supp., p. 696.

[9]283 F. Supp., pp. 696-697.

[10]See, for example, *Symposium on Escott* v. *BarChris Const, Co., The Business Lawyer* 24 (1969), p. 523; Comment, "BarChris: Easing the Burden of 'Due Diligence' under Section 11," *University of Pennsylvania Law Review* 117 (1969), p. 735; Comment, "BarChris: Due Diligence Refined," *Columbia Law Review* 68 (1968), p. 1411.

[11]283 F. Supp. pp. 696-697.

[12]332 F. Supp. 544 (E.D.N.Y. 1971).

[13]Two noted commentators have analyzed this case as follows:

...The Feit case gives lip service to this same principle, but then holds that the underwriters have "barely" established that they exercised due diligence. The court says that the company "should have known" after the August 1 agreement by which Roberts withdrew his opposition to the exchange offer that he would have cooperated in a calculation of "surplus surplus"; but it never asked him. But the underwriters also knew of this agreement, and they also never asked him; if the company "should have known," why shouldn't the underwriters? The court tries to buttress its distinction in this regard between the company and the underwriters by referring to the actual fact of cooperation by Roberts after mid-September, which may have been unknown to the underwriters, and suggests that perhaps the company is liable because it did not thereafter supplement the registration statement. However, this is clearly wrong: Section 11 only imposes liability for a misstatement or omission in the registration statement when it *"became effective."* Any liability for failure to correct a statement which becomes false or misleading thereafter can only arise under Section 12(2) or Rule 10b-5—possible bases of liability which the court refuses to consider in the Feit case.

The court also states that the company and the insiders were liable because Mr. Hodes didn't have one of his associates try to calculate "surplus surplus," and therefore they had made no investigation at all (which presumably isn't a "reasonable" investigation). But the underwriters and the same information which was available to the company prior to the effective date; shouldn't they have had one of their security analysts who specialized in insurance securities try to calculate "surplus surplus"? It would seem that he would have had a better chance of succeeding than a junior associate in a Wall Street law firm. [R.W. Jennings and H. Marsh, Jr., *Securities Regulation: Cases and Materials*, (1972), 3rd ed., pp. 1023-1024.]

[14]*Hot Issue Hearings, Testimony of Thomas L. Chrystie, director of the Investment Banking Division, Merrill Lynch, Pierce, Fenner & Smith, Inc.*, File 4-148 (1972), p. 1995 (emphasis added).

[15]Ibid., pp. 1995-1996.

[16]Ibid., 2002.

[17]SEC Securities Act Release No. 5275, (1972), p. 2.

[18]Ibid., p. 3. The SEC Study was directed at negotiated underwritings. Competitive bidding was not considered as such. The emphasis of the SEC on the need for a high level of investment banker's due diligence, however, appears to apply to both kinds of underwriting.

[19]It is interesting to note that in 1974 the SEC introduced a kind of due diligence requirement in the commercial paper area. It required Goldman, Sachs & Co. to follow appropriate investigatory procedures in connection with its participation in the sale of commercial paper as part of a judgment of permanent injunction by consent. *SEC v. Goldman, Sachs & Co.*, Civ. No. 1916 (HRT)(S.D.N.Y., filed May 2, 1974).

[20]The proposed list reads as follows:

PROPOSED ARTICLE III, SECTION 35 OF RULES
OF FAIR PRACTICE CONCERNING UNDERWRITER
INQUIRY AND INVESTIGATION STANDARDS
RESPECTING DISTRIBUTIONS OF ISSUES
OF SECURITIES TO THE PUBLIC

Obligation to Establish and Maintain Written Procedures

(a) Every member engaged in investment banking activity as a managing underwriter shall establish and maintain written procedures which shall be followed by it in its inquiry and investigation of any issuer for whom it is acting in connection with the distribution of an issue of securities to the public. Such procedures shall include, but not necessarily be limited, to the following:

(1) Review by underwriters' counsel of the issuer's corporate charter, by-laws, and corporate minutes;

(2) Examination of the audited and unaudited financial statements of the issuer, including footnotes, for the preceeding ten year period or for the entire period of the issuer's existence if less than ten years;

(3) Review of all changes in auditors by the issuer within the preceeding ten year period if applicable and the reasons therefor;

(4) Review, with the issuer's auditors, of the financial statements which will appear in the prospectus or offering circular;

(5) Review of the issuer's budgets, budgeting procedures, and order/backlog figures;

(6) Review of internal projects of the issuer, including the intended use of the proceedings of the offering;

(7) Review of all pertinent marketing, scientific and/or engineering studies or reports concerning the issuer or its products during the previous ten year period or for the term of the issuer's existence if less than ten years;

(8) Consideration as to the necessity of third party review of appropriate portions of the inquiry if the issuer is a promotional organization or engaged in marketing high technology or previously unmarketed products;

(9) Investigation of the issuer's current and past relationships with banks, creditors, suppliers, competitors and trade associations;

(10) Communication with key company officials and appropriate marketing and operating personnel regarding the nature of the issuer's business and the role of each of the above individuals in the business operation;

(11) Inspection of the issuer's property, plant and equipment;

(12) Examination of business protection devices and related data such as trademarks, patents, copyrights and production obsolescence, among others;

(13) Review of available information with respect to the issuer's position within its industry;

(14) Review of pertinent management techniques, organization of managment and the background of the management personnel of the issuer;

(15) Preparation and maintenance of memoranda pertaining to all meetings and/or conversations regarding the issuer held during the member's performance by it of its obligations of adequate inquiry;

(16) *Tax-Sheltered Program*—In addition to the above, when considered appropriate, written procedures relating to inquiry and investigation of tax-sheltered programs shall include, but not necessarily be limited to, the following:

(i) Investigation to determine that the management of a tax-sheltered investment program has experience and a working knowledge of tax-sheltered investments sufficient for the proper handling of investment monies and the maintenance of the tax-sheltered program.

(ii) Physical inspection of all properties described in the prospectus as being acquired by the tax-sheltered program, a review of all documents pertaining to such acquistions and an examination of the facilities of any servicing function performed by the tax-sheltered management, if any.

(iii) Examination of applicable partnership agreements.

(iv) Review of available information with respect to the issuer's position within its industry including:

(i) Examination for proper disclosure of all conflicts of interest of the sponsor of the tax-sheltered program; and

(ii) Examination of all records submitted by appraisers, engineers, financial consultants and other independent consultants with emphasis respecting the procedures utilized in the formulation of their analysis of the tax-sheltered investment, and study of all tax aspects of the tax-sheltered program to insure that the described or anticipated tax benefits will, in fact, accrue to the investor. [See 194 *BNA Sec. Reg. & L. Rep.*, (1973), pp. 13-14.]

[21]Proposed Article III, §35c, ibid., p. 14.

[22]See Proposed Amendment to Article III, §2 of the NASD Rules of Fair Practice, ibid., p. 15. The proposed new suitability rule (since withdrawn) would apply to corporations organized within one year before the filing of a prospectus that have not had a net income from operations. It would also apply to corporations organized more than one year before the filing of the prospectus that had not had net income from operations for at least one of the two fiscal years immediately preceeding the filing of the registration statement.

[23]See Phillips, "Suitability and Bona Fide Public Offerings" *N.Y. Law Journal Symposium on Hot Issues—First Time Filings* (1972), p. 299.

[24]NASD Notice to Members 75-33 (April 25, 1975). The NASD is also finalizing proposals to require experienced and knowledgeable personnel to conduct due diligence. They will be called "qualified underwriter principals" and will have to pass an exam in certain cases. Ibid., p. 3.

[25]SEC Securities Act Release No. 5362 (1973), *CCH Fed. Sec. L. Rep.* [1972-73 Transfer Binder], parag. 79, 211, p. 82,667. SEC Securities Act Release No. 5581 (1975); *CCH Fed. Sec. L. Rep.*, parag. 80, 167, p. 85,299.

[26]*BNA Sec. Reg. & L. Rep.* No. 284, A-10 (1975).

[27]The procedures were described in 1950 as follows. They are essentially the same today.

Where securities are offered for competitive bidding under Rule U-50, it is customary practice for the issuer to select independent counsel to act for the successful bidders. The fees of such counsel are paid by the underwriters who, before they submit their bid, are informed of the estimated amount of such fees. The fees are subject to the approval of the Commission and the bidding papers must provide that in the event the actual fee is less than the estimated fee the difference is paid to the company rather than returned to the underwriters. As soon as underwriters' counsel are selected, they begin work in collaboration with the company and its counsel on the registration statement, bidding papers and other documents relating to the transaction, although generally speaking the primary responsibility for drafting most of the documents is assumed by company counsel. Underwriters' counsel, having no specific client at the time, must be guided primarily by their experience in past transactions, whether as independent counsel for the underwriters or as company counsel . . . .

The respective underwiters have very little opportunity to question officials of the company about operations or prospects and accordingly meetings of prospective underwriters are arranged by the company, the time and place of such a meeting or meetings is set forth in the bidding papers furnished to the interested groups. These meetings have taken many different forms. In some instances only one meeting is held, in other, meetings are held in different sections of the country. . . . At these meetings, the company executives, company counsel and accountants and underwriters' counsel are present and the meeting is thrown open for questioning by all those present. In some instances the issuers have arranged at their own expense inspection trips, but in view of the larger number of underwriters evidencing interest in many of the issues, this has been obviously impractical both from the standpoint of time and expense. The companies do, however, welcome any questions and if the underwriters desire, will usually make arrangements for inspection of the properties at the expense of the underwriters. [Henkel, ''The Auction Block for Securities'' *Virginia Law Review* 36 (1950), pp. 701, 714-715, 718-719 (footnotes omitted).]

In the absence of previous independent investigation of data and verification of issuer's claims, the due diligence meetings are not very helpful. Moreover, in the negotiated deal, there is a general consensus that such meetings are pure form with no substance. They are designed to help bolster the legal position of members of the syndicate (who do no independent investigation) in case of lawsuit.

The underwriters depend upon the investigation of designated counsel for the bidders. As we have seen in the *BarChris* case, this is a dangerously risky maneuver. Lawyers are generally not equipped or trained for financial and business analysis.

In 1941 the SEC worried about the problem. It sent out a questionnaire to investment bankers and insurance corporations on the practice. The overwhelming consensus of investment bankers was that ''no practicable substitute for the present method of selection was forthcoming.'' Holding Company Act Release No. 3118 [1941 Transfer Binder] *CCH Fed. Sec. L. Rep.* (1941), parag. 75,219, p. 75, 485. The majority of the life indurance corporations who responded to the questionnaire (and who bid on underwritings along with investment bankers) objected to the practice. The SEC decided to continue the practice.

[T]he Commission has concluded that the existing practice of designation by the issuer of independent counsel to represent the bidders will be permitted to continue, but that adequate disclosure of such matters as the identity of the independent counsel and the proposed fees of such counsel to be paid by the successful bidders will be required and close scrutiny will be given to the reasonableness of such fees and to the relationship of the independent counsel to the issuer. (Ibid., p. 75,486.)

Merrill Lynch, in materials filed in the Public Utility Hearings on competitive bidding before the SEC, January 1975, described the problems with issuers' counsel in due diligence as follows:

It is the opinion of our firm that the participation of the managing underwriter in the prospectus drafting sessions will more adequately ensure the investor that a full due diligence investigation has been carried out on his behalf thus promoting full disclosure of all material events. In a negotiated offering, the managing underwriter will closely coordinate with underwriters' counsel throughout the preparation period. In a competitive offering, however, the underwriters' counsel has to function without the benefit of his prospective client's guidance and assistance. [Merrill Lynch, Pierce, Fenner & Smith Exhibit #1 (SEC file S7-529).]

[28]Complaint of Plaintiff, *Shapiro* v. *Consolidated Edison Co. of N. Y. et al.*, Civ. No. 1906 (S.D.N.Y., filed May 1, 1974), pp. 5-6.

11. (a) Edison and the underwriters knew or should have known at the time of the Bond offering that Edison was in a desperate cash position and was experiencing a

severe cash shortage which would not be alleviated by the expected upturn in the results for March, 1974.

(b) Therefore, Edison and the underwriters knew or should have known at the time of the Bond offering that all of the above would necessarily occur (i.e., that the dividend would be omitted, that Edison's bond rating would be reduced, that the value and price of Edison's bonds [including the Bond] would decline substantially, and that Edison would no longer be able to raise debt or equity capital except on extremely unfavorable terms).

(c) Despite the knowledge of Edison and the underwriters, these facts and their necessary consequences were omitted from the registration statement.

12. The registration statement violated § 11 of the Securities Act in that it omitted to state the aforesaid material facts.

[29]See Submission of Morgan Stanley et al. to the SEC staff, File No. S7-529 (June 1974). This concern is also suggested by informal talks with several prominent investment bankers. See also Public Utility Hearings, pp. 138, 139.

[30]Ibid., p. 7.

[31]Salomon Brothers, at the Public Utility Hearings before the SEC, pointed out that " . . . because of the current state of utility industry, and particularly the Con Edison situation, issuers had become much more sensitive to the situation and more requests for information are made and those requests granted." Salomon Brothers also pointed out that as a result of the Con Edison situation " . . . underwriters in competitive bidding began to do more . . . work themselves. . . ." (Ibid., pp. 138, 139.)

[32]The problems with due diligence in competitive bidding transactions were described by Salomon Brothers in the Public Utility Hearings on Rule 50 in January 1975 as follows:

. . . the traditional process for due diligence in compeititve bidding of utility securities was that the issuer would appoint a counsel for the bidding groups who would perform some analysis and some investigations. The bidder group traditionally would not do very much themselves. This was a historical development based on the high quality of utility issues. . . .

Basically, because of the fact that underwriters have felt that because they did not have the assurance of winning the issue that there was not sufficient economic justification to participate in the competitive bidding as fully as they would in the negotiated underwriting and therefore that they would rely upon the counsel for the bidders to do that for them, which had been the traditional accepted practice.

The other aspect of this is there had been occasions in the past when members of the bidding groups would attempt to get additional information from either the issuer or the counsel for the bidding groups and these people felt that because of the competitive nature of the situation, that it might seem collusive for information to be furnished to one group that was not furnished to all of the groups and therefore these requests were turned down. (Ibid.)

[33]See note 7 above.

[34]*Hot Issue Hearings* (December 10, 1973), pp. 60-61.

[35]Ibid. (December 10, 1973), pp. 85-86.

[36]Ibid. (December 11, 1973), p. 7.

[37]Ibid.

[38]Ibid. (December 12, 1973), pp. 5, 6, 8, 20.

[39]Ibid. (December 12, 1973), pp. 5-6.

[40]Ibid. (December 10, 1973), pp. 18-19, 21, 25.

[41]Ibid. (December 10, 1973), pp. 30-31.

[42]Ibid. (December 10, 1973), p. 49.

[43]Ibid. (December 10, 1973), pp. 7-9.

[44]J. Weinstein, *Feit* v. *Leasco Data Processing Equipment Corp.*, 332 F. Supp. 544, 565 (E.D. N.Y. 1971). For an excellent critique of SEC disclosure policies, see Kripke, "The SEC, the Accountants, Some Myths and Some Realities," *New York University Law Review* 45 (1970), p. 1151.

[45]See Schneider, "Nits, Grits and Soft Information in SEC Filings," *University of Pennsylvania Law Review* 121 (1972), p. 254.

[46]See the report of the *Center for Applied Ethics, New York Society for Ethical Culture: Conflicts of Interest and Professional Inadequacies in the Securities Industry* (1974).

IV. Pricing the Issue

[1]*Hot Issue Hearings, Testimony of Paul Risher, Newberger, Loeb & Co.*, File 4-148, (1972), p. 2104. The pricing dilemma is most acute in the case of issues that have no public market and no public price for their securities.

[2]Letter from J. V. Grimm to SEC, July 19, 1972, pp. 2-3, Exhibit 1, to *Testimony of J. V. Grimm, Grimm & Davis, Inc.*, File 4-148 (1972).

[3]*Hot Issue Hearings, Testimony of J. V. Grimm, Grimm & Davis, Inc.*, File 4-148, (1972), p. 4265.

[4]Ibid., p. 4266.

[5]Address of A. Robert Towbin, Partner, C. E. Unterberg, Towbin Co., New York, "Considerations of an Underwriter in Determining Whether of Not to Underwrite; Pricing the New Issue." *New York Law Journal Symposium on Hot New Issues, First Time Filings* (November 16, 1972), pp. 331, 335-336.

[6]*Hot Issue Hearings, Testimony of N. Gregory Doescher, First Boston Corporation*, File 4-148, p. 2448.

[7]Ibid., p. 2447

[8]Ibid., p. 2448

[9]SEC Securities Act Release No. 5396 [1973 Transfer Binder] *CCH Fed. Sec. L. Rep.* (1973), parag. 79, 384, pp. 83, 125.

[10]Ibid., pp. 83, 125-126.

[11]Preliminary Prospectus of Pioneer Hi-Bred International, August 8, 1973, quoted in Johnson, *Recent and Proposed SEC and NASD Regulations Governing Distributions of Securities*, in Fifth Annual Institute on Securities Regulation (Practicing Law Institute, A. Fleischer and R. Mundheim, eds. 1973), pp. 153, 161-162.

[12]Ibid., p. 162

V. Underwriters' Compensation

[1]*SEC Study of Cost of Flotation of Registered Issues*, 1971-1972 (December 1974), p. 15. For additional general data, see Mendelson, "Underwriting Compensation" in I. Friend, J. Longstret et al., *Investment Banking and the New Issues Market* (1967), p. 394.

[2]Blackstone, *Developments in the Broker-Dealer Area: Underwriters' Compensation and Relation Problems*, First Annual Institute on Securities Regulation (Practicing Law Institute, Fleischer, Mundheim, and Glazer, eds. 1970), pp. 293, 301 [Hereafter cited as Blackstone].

[3]See Article III, §1, Rules of Fair Practice Interpretation of the Board of Governors, *CCH NASD Manual*, parag. 2151.02, p. 2020.

[4]Ibid., p. 2021.

[5]Ibid., p. 2031.

[6]Ibid., pp. 2031-2032. The NASD has a fixed rule that stock or shares underlying warrants acquired by the investment banker in connection with the underwriting must by held for a minimum period of one year from the effective date of the registration statement.

NASD regulations, in addition to including the value of stock or warrants in determining the permissible *amount* of underwriting compensation, also set a fixed limit on the *number* of shares.

The number of shares of stock and shares underlying warrants acquired by the investment banker as part of its compensation may not exceed more than 10 percent of the total number of shares in the proposed offering. The persons covered by this aggregate 10 percent rule include the managing underwriter; the other underwriters; counsel to the underwriters; financial consultants; any member of the selling group; and any officers, directors, or employers of such persons. Ibid., pp. 2029-2030.

[7]Ibid., p. 2032.

[8]Blackstone, p. 301.

[9]Ibid., note 2 above, p. 295. Materials must be filed with the NASD director, Corporate Financing Department at the Executive Office of the Association, 1735 K St., N.W., Washington, D.C. See note 3 above, *CCH NASD Manual*, parag. 2151, p. 2024.

[10]Ibid.

[11]Figures based upon Matteson, *NASD Review of Underwriters: Compensation and Related Problems*, 2d Annual Institute on Securities Regulation, pp. 183, 195.

[12]Mofsky, "Adverse Consequences of Blue Sky Regulation of Public Offering Expenses," *Wisconsin Law Review* (1972), p. 1010 [hereafter cited as Mofsky]; and Mofsky, "Reform of the Florida Securities Law," *Florida Southern University Law Review* 2 (1974), p. 1.

[13]Mofsky, pp. 1011-1017.

[14]See note 1, above, p. 15. This study shows that total costs were 24.46 percent of proceeds in firm commitment deals under $500,000 and 23.44 percent for like size best efforts deals. The figures were 20.59 percent and 21.42 percent, respectively, for offerings of $500,000 to just under $1 million.

[15]Mofsky, p. 1024, n. 69.

VI. Trading in the Aftermarket

[1]On Hot Issues, see SEC, *Report of Special Study of Securities Markets*, Part 1 (1963) [hereafter cited as *Special Study*]; "Hot New Issues—First Time Filings," *New York Law Journal Symposium* (A. Levenson and A. Sommer, Co-Chm., 1972); Sowards and Mofsky, "The 'Hot Issue'; Possible Hidden Causes," *St Johns Law Review* 45 (1971), p. 802; Prifti, "The Hot Issue," *The Business Lawyer* 24 (1963), p. 311; Rotberg, "The Hot Issue" *The Business Lawyer* 17 (1962), p.360. A recent source of extensive data is the *Hot Issue Hearings*.

[2]Clurman, "Controlling a Hot Issue Market," *Cornell Law Review* 56 (1970), p. 78 [hereafter cited as Clurman].

[3]This results from the fact that certain underwriters will be more honest with the market makers about their distribution efforts than they are with the syndicate manager due to their fear that the manager may bump them from future offerings and from their hope that the new issue market maker will steer institutional customers to them.

[4]*Hot Issue Hearings, Testimony of R. Friedman of A. P. Montgomery, Inc.*, File 4-148, pp. 3965-3967.

[5]17 C.F.R. §240. 10b-6 (1974). For a discussion, see Wolfson, "Rule 10b-6: The Illusory Search for Certainty," *Stanford Law Review* 25 (1973), p. 809.

[6]See SEC Securities Exchange Act Release No. 3807 (1946).

[7]See Article III, Sec. 1, Interpretation of the Board of Governors, *CCH NASD Manual*, parag. 2151.06

[8]B. Malkiel, *A Random Walk Down Wall Street* (New York: 1973), p. 52.

[9]Clurman, note 2 above, p. 75.

[10]Ibid., p. 78 (emphasis added).

[11]Ibid.

[12]Ibid., p. 82.

[13]See J. Mofsky, *Blue Sky Restrictions on New Business Promotions* (1971). The hypothetical example set forth in the text is taken substantially as is from Professor Mofsky's book. Ibid., pp. 48-54.

[14]See Fla. SEC, Comm'n Rule 330-1.15 (1969), quoted ibid., p. 55, n. 26.

[15]Mofsky, *Blue Sky Restrictions on New Business Promotions*, pp. 53-54.

[16]Another suggestion to regulate new issues is a net worth rule, for example, no new issues for persons with less than $XX,000 per year plus $XX,000 net assets, plus perhaps a requirement that the investment banker in new issues have a prior established track record. The theory is to limit the risk to those who can bear it. The writer must confess to a strong aversion to telling individuals below a certain dollar standard that they cannot decide where to put their money. Moreover, in the absence of careful empirical investigation, which proved the contrary, I would be concerned that the dollar cutoffs might impede the ability of worthy new businesses to raise capital. On the other hand, I would want empirical investigation to determine whether such a cutoff approach is meaningful, that is, in the past perhaps only an insignificant number of individuals below the wealth cutoff bought new issues. With respect to restricting the investment bankers who can underwrite new issues, for example, requiring a record of experience or size, this might limit the pool of investment bankers who underwrite new issues. The validity of that approach is not self-evident. Perhaps only the smaller or newer investment bankers will be willing to underwrite new ventures. The general objections set forth in the text to merit regulation, I believe, apply to these areas.

Subsequent to the publication of this study in January 1976, a study of merit regulation in Wisconsin, which endeavored to prove the value of merit regulation appeared. See Goodkind, "Blue Sky Law: Is There Merit in the Merit Requirements?" *Wisconsin Law Review* 79 1976. This study is effectively criticized by Professors James S. Mofsky and Robert D. Tollison in "Demerit in Merit Regulation," *Marquette Law Review* 60 (1977), p. 369. The Wisconsin study, *inter alia*, measured relative price performance of issuers denied registration and issuers granted registration. Professors Mofsky and Tollison in their article stated as follows:

The study's data were derived from three year periods, 1968-71, 1969-72, 1970-73. In the category of price, issues denied registration outperformed those registered after one year. However, in that same category, registered issues performed better than those denied registration after three years. The author somehow decided, without supporting rationale, that the particular three year periods were a better standard than the one year time frame, and thus concluded that investors on balance were benefited by Wisconsin's merit regulation.

The study failed to recognize, however, that different investors have different time horizons. Some investors trade securities on a six month basis. Others after twelve months. And still others only after longer holding periods such as three years. Some market participants do not trade on the basis of price or time at all, and hold securities until some external events, such as wedding expenses or medical bills, dictate their sale. While Wisconsin's merit rules may have benefited investors who held for the particular three years, those rules were harmful for someone whose time horizon was one year and for those who withdrew from the market for other reasons after only one year. Why is it better to protect three year holders rather than one year purchasers? We can find no rational answer to that question.

[17]*Hot Issue Hearings, Testimony of Albert Holtje and Timothy Murray, Kenneth Bove & Co., Inc.*, File 4-148 (1972), p. 2629.

[18]Ibid., pp. 2637-38.

[19]*Hot Issue Hearings, Testimony of L. M. Rosenthal, L. M. Rosenthal & Co., Inc.*, File 4-148 (1972), pp. 3365-3366 (emphasis added).

[20]Ibid.

[21]Ibid., p. 3368.

[22]Ibid., pp. 3381-3382.

[23]Ibid., *Testimony of Frederick B. Whittemore, Morgan, Stanley & Co.*, File 4-148 (1972), pp. 3518-3519.

[24]The new issue market makers do not limit themselves to corporations going public for the first time. They also will make short sales of the securities of companies that are already public

but now plan to sell additional shares. The short sales beat down the market price and, of course, the offering price as well. The over-the-counter dealers may sometimes then cover the short sales with shares purchased in such offerings, although this activity is illegal manipulation. In addition to the manipulation, it probably also transforms the over-the-counter dealers into underwriters of the securities sold short in violation of the Securities Act of 1933 on the theory that because the shares are fungible, when they sell short and later on cover with registered shares, they are in effect selling registered shares without adequate disclosure in the prospectus.

The Commission has proposed new Rule 10b-21 to prevent these practices and ordered public administrative proceedings against A. P. Montgomery & Co., Inc., and Richard S. Friedman, its president, based upon allegations that they had made such short sales. Also named were two other New York broker-dealers and a number of investment funds. The SEC staff asserted that the investment funds allegedly made their sales through A. P. Montgomery, which knew of the scheme.

Ironically, the short selling, when and if it occurs, is manipulation that drives the offering price of a secondary *down*. Hot issue manipulation drives the price of a new issue *up*. Either way, the public is gouged, and the broker-dealer is rewarded. See SEC Securities Exchange Act Releases Nos. 10,636, 10,637, and 11,328 (1974).

[25] See *Special Study*, pp. 557-559.

[26] Clurman, pp. 80-81.

[27] A second area the Commission considered in July 1972 related to suitability requirements on hot issues. In response to this, the NASD proposed to establish suitability regulations with regard to the distribution of certain unseasoned securities. These new proposals were discussed in the section on Due Diligence above.

Three other proposals were announced in June 1973 and became effective August 1, 1973:

1. When a corporation is not subject to the public reporting requirements of the 1934 act, it will be required to identify any principal underwriters who intend to confirm sales to discretionary accounts and to include an estimate of the amount of securities to be so confirmed. Apparently, this new disclosure had a real bite, because Alan Levenson, director of the SEC Division of Corporate Finance, stated to this writer that his office had received a great deal of "flack" as a result of the new requirements. SEC Securities Act Release No. 5395 [1973 Transfer Binder], *CCH Fed. Sec. L. Rep.*, parag. 79,383 (1973).

2. The Commission will require complete disclosure to the discretionary account customer of the potential conflict of interest in the situation. The SEC pointed out that, because an underwriter has a selfish interest in the success of the offering, the placement of a portion of an offering in a discretionary account raises a serious potential conflict of interest. SEC Securities Act Release No. 5393 [1973 Transfer Binder], *CCH Fed. Sec. L. Rep.*, parag. 79,386 (1973).

3. In certain cases there must be an undertaking by the issuer to provide to underwriters, at the closing, stock certificates in such denominations and names as to permit prompt delivery to each purchaser. Moreover, any request for SEC acceleration of the transaction must be accompanied by a representation from the underwriter that the issuer has been requested to provide stock certificates in such denominations as to permit prompt delivery. These requirements apply to registration statements where equity securities are to be offered and the registrant has not previously sold securities registered under the Act. SEC Securities Act Release No. 5395, above.

* * * *

On February 11, 1974, the Commission proposed new rule 10b-20, which would prohibit investment bankers and other broker-dealers from explicitly or implicitly demanding from their customers any payment in addition to the announced offering price. This rule was proposed to eliminate the practice in some new issues, when public demand is inadequate, that purchase of the slow offering is tied to certain sweeteners, such as the chance in the future to obtain really attractive hot issue shares. The inducement may have a self-fulfilling nature in that many people will be encouraged to buy certain future new offerings, thus artificially heating them up. The rule proposal was modified on April 2, 1975. SEC Securities Exchange Act Release No. 10,636 [1973-74 Transfer Binder] *CCH Fed. Sec. L. Rep.*, parag. 79,645 (1974) and SEC Securities Exchange Act Release No. 11,328, Securities Regulation & Law Report E-1 (1975).

[28]See Securities Act Release No. 5275 (1972), pp. 4-5.

[29]NASD Notice to Members, 75-33 (April 25, 1975).

[30]Ibid.

[31]See Fleischer, "Less Free 'Free-Riding' Rules," *Institutional Investor* (January, 1974), p. 33.

[32]Ibid.; see also Interpretation of the Board of Governors, "Free-Riding and Withholding," *CCH NASD Manual* (1974), parag. 2151, pp. 2039-2045.

[33]See note 27, above.

[34]SEC Securities Exchange Act Release No. 2446, 2 *CCH Fed. Sec. L. Rep.* parag. 22,512 (1940), p. 16,555-5.

[35]17 C.F.R. Section 240. 10b-7 (1974).

[36]Securities Exchange Act Release No. 2446, 2 *CCH Fed. Sec. L. Rep.* (1940), parag. 22,512, p. 16,555-52.

[37]Ibid., pp. 16,555-5-16,556.

[38]See separate statement of Commissioner Healey, Securities Exchange Act Release No. 2446, reprinted in R. Jennings & H. Marsh, *Securities Regulation* (1972), pp. 883-884.

[39]In the matter of Shearson, Hammill & Co., SEC Securities Exchange Act Release No. 7743 [1964-66 Transfer Binding] *CCH Fed. Sec. L. Rep.*, parag. 77,306 (1965).

VII. Investment Banking and Broker Dealers

[1]SEC, *Report on the Feasibility and Advisability of the Complete Segregation of the Functions of Dealer and Broker* (1936).

[2]Ibid., pp. 75-76.

[3]*Slade* v. *Shearson, Hammill & Co., Inc.* [1973-74 Transfer Binder] *CCH Fed. Sec. L. Rep.* (1974), p. 94,329.

[4]On the "Chinese wall" and related matters, see SEC, 5 *Institutional Investors Study* (1971), pp. 1539-1540; in re Merrill Lynch, Pierce, Fenner & Smith, Inc., Securities Exchange Act Release No. 8459, *CCH Fed. Sec. L. Rep.* parag. 77,629 (Exhibit A) (1963); Cook, "The SEC and Banks," *Banking Law Journal* 89 (1972), pp. 499, 508; Comptroller of the Currency, Proposed Amend., 12 C.F.R. 9, 39 Fed. Reg. 14510 (1974); Yellon, "Trust Investments; Problems Regarding Exchange of Information, between the Trust Department and other Departments within the Bank," *Chicago Bar Record* 54 (1973), p. 405; SEC, *The Financial Collapse of the Penn Central Company* (1972), pp. 205-206; Gillis, "Inside Information: Are Guidelines Possible?" *Financial Analysts Journal* (May-June 1974) p. 12; and Fleischer, "Inside Information: How Solid Are 'Walls'?" *Institutional Investor* (May 1974) p. 31. For a particularly good succinct analysis of the Slade case, see Bernstein, "Securities Class Actions," *New York Law Journal* (January 28, 1974), pp. 1, 4.

Some of the basic facts, such as the actual integrity of the Chinese wall and when Shearson learned of the inside information, are at issue in the trial, and if decided in certain ways, will permit the Second Circuit to avoid the issues discussed in this section.

For a recently published provocative debate on the Chinese wall, which discusses, in great detail, the pros and cons of the three principal directions referred to on pp. 406-412, see Lipton and Mazur, "The Chinese Wall Solution to the Conflict Problems of Securities Firms, *New York University Law Review* 51 (1975), 459; Chazen, "Reinforcing the Chinese Wall: A Response," *New York University Law Review* 51 (1976), p. 552; and Lipton and Mazur, "The Chinese Wall: A Reply to Chazen, " *New York University Law Review* 51 (1976), p. 579.

[5]*Slade* v. *Shearson, Hammill & Co. Inc.*, note 3, above.

[6]Memorandum in support of Defendant and Third-party Plaintiffs Petition for Leave to Appeal Pursuant to 28 U.S.C. Section No. 8 1292(b) in *Slade* v. *Shearson, Hammill & Co., Inc.*, Civil No. 72-1779 (S.D.N.Y., filed January 12, 1974), p.1.

[7]*Slade* v. *Shearson, Hammill & Co., Inc.*, [Current] *CCH Fed. Sec. L. Rep.*, parag. 94, 914 (1974), p. 97,172.

[8]See, for example, in the matter of Investors Management Co., Inc. Securities Exchange Act Release No. 9267 [1970-71 Transfer Binder] *CCH Fed. Sec. L. Rep.*, parag. 78,163 (1971).

[9]See SEC Securities Exchange Act Release No. 8459 [1967-69 Transfer Binder] *CCH Fed. Sec. L. Rep.*, parag. 77,629 (1968).

[10]Material information obtained from a corporation by the Underwriting Division in connection with the consideration or negotiation of a public or private offering of its securities and which has not been disclosed by the corporation to the investing public, and conclusions based thereon, shall not be disclosed by any member of the Underwriting Division to anyone outside that Division except to

(a) senior executives of the firm and its Legal Department;

(b) lawyers, accountants and other persons directly involved with the underwriters in connection with the proposed offering;

(c) appropriate personnel of the Research Division whose views in connection with the proposed offering are to be sought by the Underwriting Division; and

(d) members of the buying department of other firms who are prospective members of the underwriting group for the purpose of enabling such other firms to decide whether, the extent to which or the price at which, they will participate in the proposed offering.

Any employee of the firm who receives such information pursuant to the foregoing shall not disclose such information or any conclusions based thereon except as provided above for members of the Underwriting Division. (Ibid., pp. 83,351.)

[11]Brief for SEC as Amiscus Curiae, p. 7 [quoting *Hanley* v. *SEC*, 415 F.2d 589, 597 (2d Cir. 1969) (footnote omitted)], *Slade* v. *Shearson, Hammill & Co. Inc.*, above, note 3.

[12]See Chazen, "Reinforcing the Chinese Wall," note 4 above, p. 575.

[13]Of course, this approach could be further modified by relying on the wall and eliminating even the notice requirement. We will assume for the sake of argument that notice is given. If the notice plus wall aproach fails *a fortiori*, it will fail without a notice requirement since the notice operates to make the customer aware of his risks.

[14]401 F.2d 833 (2d Cir. 1968), cert. denied, 394 U.S. 976 (1969).

[15]Brief for Salomon Brothers as Amicus Curiae, footnote, p. 1, *Slade* v. *Shearson, Hammill & Co., Inc.*, note 3, above.

[16]Brief for Paine, Webber, Jackson & Curtis, Inc. as Amicus Curiae, pp. 5-6, 7, 8, and 9, *Slade* v. *Shearson, Hammill & Co., Inc.*, note 3, above (footnotes omitted).

[17]*Affiliated Ute Citizens* v. *United States*, 406 U.S. 128, 153 (1972).

[18]17 C.F.R. Sec. 240. 15c2-11 (1973).

[19]Robertson, "The Underwriters Have to Offer Even More," *Fortune* (January 1973), p. 116.

[20]SEC, "Statement on the Future Structure of the Securities Market," in [*Special Studies*] *CCH Fed. Sec. L. Rep.*, (1972), parag. 74811, pp. 65, 623.

[21]See SEC Securities Act Release No. 5180 (1971).

VIII. Private Placements

[1]Longstreet and Hess, "Characteristics of Corporate New Issues in the Post-SEC Period," in I. Friend and J. Longstreet et al., *Investment Banking and the New Issues Market* (1967), pp. 332, 346.

[2]Ibid.

[3]17 C.F.R. § 230.146 (1974) [hereafter cited as Rule 146].

[4]Rule 146(a) (1).

[5]See SEC Securities Act Release No. 5336 [1972-73 Transfer Binder] *CCH Fed. Sec. L. Rep.*, (1972), parag. 79, 108, p. 82401 (emphasis added).

[6]Rule 146(a) (1).

[7]Ibid., note 3, above.

[8]SEC Securities Act Release No. 5336, [1972-73 Transfer Binder] *CCH Fed. Sec. L. Rep.*, (1972), parag. 79, 108, p. 82,401 (emphasis added).

[9]Rule 146(a) (1) (iii) (emphasis added).

[10]Another potential conflict arises when discretionary accounts are involved. Would an investment banker who puts securities from a private placement in a customer's discretionary account be an appropriate "offeree representative"? Fortunately, the new rule provides safeguards against the result. Although securities may be technically placed with discretionary accounts, advance consent must first be obtained. The rule accomplishes this by requiring that the offeree representative be "acknowledged . . . during the course of the transaction" by the offeree to be his representative (Ibid.). As a result, the discretion in the discretionary account is effectively taken out of the transaction by the rule.

[11]In March 6, 1978, the SEC in Securities Act Release No. 5913 issued a proposal to amend Rule 146 so a person receiving compensation directly or indirectly from the issuer would not qualify as an offeree representative. If adopted, this would eliminate the Rule 146 conflict position of the investment bankers as described in this chapter. The proposal was subsequently withdrawn.

IX. Conclusion

[1]See Complaints of Plaintiff, *SEC* v. *The Seaboard Corp. et al.*, and *SEC* v. *Hayden Stone, Inc. and Marshall S. Cogan*. Civ. No. CV 74-567 and 74-1014 MML (C.D. Cal. filed March 5, 1974). See also *The Wall Street Journal*, March 6, 1974, p. 4.

[2]See SEC litigation Release No. 6269 (March 5, 1974). Final judgment by Consent 74 Civ. 1014 (March 5, 1974).

[3]The allegations in the complaint were neither denied nor admitted by the investment banker.

[4]Subsequent to the preparation of this study in pamphlet form at the end of 1975, Exxon Corporation used the so-called Dutch auction offering in two cases: The first was a $54.9 million issue of pollution control bonds in November 1976 and the second was a $250 million revenue bond issue in May 1977. The Exxon sales avoided the traditional fixed-price underwriting syndicate. Although most of the purchasers were dealers (and indeed in the second offering only NASD members were permitted to make the initial purchases), the usual fixed price syndicate arrangements were missing. Dealers were permitted to resell the securities at any price or prices they could obtain. As Chris Welles stated in a recent article, "Fortunately for Wall Street, no other corporation has seen fit to emulate Exxon." See Chris Welles, "Wall Street's Last Gold Mine," *Institutional Investor* 12, no. 2 (February 1978), p. 134.

Also occurring subsequent to the research and preparation of this study in pamphlet form was the appearance of the *Papilsky* case and its ramifications. Papilsky, a holder of shares in the Affiliated Fund claimed that Lord, Abbett & Co., the fund's manager, had failed to recapture the selling discounts on underwritings by becoming a member of the underwriting syndicate arranging the distribution of securities that the fund purchased. A New York District Court determined that recapture of underwriting commissions were permissible. The court decision would permit an investment advisor to a registered investment company to participate in the underwriting as a syndicate member and credit against the advisory fee underwriting commissions received by it. If fund managers or other entities can effectively recapture underwriting commissions, this might eliminate the fixed price offering. That is to say, if an underwriter purchases a security at $3 and resells it at $4 to the general public, but remits all or a portion of the $1 underwriting commission to certain institutional buyers (such as funds or their designees), those institutions are in effect purchasing the stock at a discount off the public offering price. The NASD felt that such a practice would discriminate against certain customers, particularly small investors. The NASD at the end of 1977 was proposing to solve what it deemed to be a problem by strengthening its rules barring discounting. See Welles, " Wall Street's Last Gold Mine."

Broker-Dealer Firms
by Martin Mayer

I • INTRODUCTION

In spirit, if not always in fact, broker-dealers are central to American public finance. Investors large and small, informed and uninformed, rely on their brokers—and on dealers as if they were brokers—to advise them on the purchase and sale of securities. Advertising by broker-dealers, to the public and within the trade, stresses the great trust that can be placed in the firm's recommendations, often comparing the obligations of the broker-dealer to those of the doctor or lawyer. These claims would impart a fiduciary quality to the relations of broker-dealers with their customers even if the fiduciary responsibilities of broker-dealers were not, at least in part, codified in law. As the first Securities and Exchange Commission (SEC) study of the broker-dealer put it in 1936: "The relationship between broker and customer is fiduciary in nature . . . . In the performance of his duties, the broker is held to the same high standard of conduct as the law imposes upon attorneys, administrators, executors, guardians, bankers, public officials, and other persons vested with fiduciary powers."[1] Since then, a number of courts have held that essentially the same standards are applicable whether the broker-dealer is acting as a broker or as a dealer.

Still, the scope of the broker-dealer's fiduciary obligations remains a source of speculation, controversy, and, when the stakes are large enough, litigation. Some of the difficulty of definition arises from the fact that, more than any other fiduciary active in the securities business, the broker-dealer operates in a conventional market where merchandise is purchased and sold. Thus, all broker-dealer transactions involve the conventional marketplace conflict where the interests of the seller are pitted against those of the buyer. Other troublesome conflict-of-interest questions are inherent in the peculiar multiplicity of broker-dealer operations, for the broker must act as agent and principal, lender and borrower, advisor and salesman, investment manager and underwriter, insider and fiduciary—for a variety of clients and with a diversity of fee schedules during the course of a single day's operations.

For example, the broker-dealer may function as a broker for an investor who wishes to buy one hundred shares of General Motors. The seller of these shares will be another investor, remote and unknown. In this transaction the broker's responsibility is to search out the best values in the securities market, acting on behalf of the customer.

The broker-dealer may function as a dealer for the same investor, now seeking to buy one hundred shares of American Express. In this transaction the seller is the dealer himself; the investor is actually purchasing shares from an inventory in the dealer's vault, much as he might buy a refrigerator or a toaster from a store. The broker has no stake in the merchandise; the dealer does. As the SEC warned: "Where the broker and dealer functions are combined in a single person his own interest may conflict with the interests of those to whom he owes a fiduciary duty."[2]

In the old SEC report, the danger is spelled out in greater detail: "The over-the-counter house which conducts a brokerage business and which also takes underwriting positions, or participates in distributory syndicates or sells securities at retail is under temptation to induce its customers to purchase securities which it is anxious to sell."[3] Since that report, written in 1936, striking advances in commercial morality and legal liability have been made in many areas of the financial industry; but the broker-dealer conflict remains unchanged.

Conflicts in the financial markets are a special case of the general problem of policing selling activities in a partly free, partly regulated society. That problem, unfortunately, is inherently very hard to manage, as witnessed by the sad history of the Federal Trade Commission, which for nearly sixty years has served both the government and the business community as a vermiform appendix that has no function but to become inflamed.

The conflict problems of the broker-dealer are far from unique. The life insurance agent who collects commissions from the insurance company will represent himself to his customers as "your" insurance agent; the real-estate broker who will be paid by the seller and can offer only the houses that sellers have made available to him will put up a fine show of working in the interests of the purchaser. All selling, as the attentive viewer of television commercials may observe, rests on the pretense—which both parties may actually believe— that the salesman is really serving the customer.

When the purchaser is unable to evaluate the quality of what is sold, we use the word *professional* to describe a standard of competence and diligence that applies to the seller. When money or property is involved, making it especially easy and tempting for the seller to take advantage of the purchaser's ignorance, helplessness, or absence, we use the word *fiduciary* to describe his obligation to protect and serve the purchaser's interest rather than his own.

Almost no one feels free to follow unbridled self-interest in his business conduct. Grocers, undertakers, and used car salesmen believe, along with lawyers, doctors, and brokers, that they are subject to a code that both limits their permissible expressions of self-interest and works for the benefit of their customers or clients. Nor is there a sharp line between fraud in the marketplace and conflict-of-interest abuses in what are considered professions. A dealer who pushes a "concept" stock when he knows the concept is imaginary will probably be articulate and fast on his feet; a butcher who gives short weight will probably be slow of speech and hard put to justify himself; but the difference between them is nowhere near so great as the dealer or the student of finance likes to think.

Customer skepticism remains the best protection against abuse of conflict of interest in any trade or profession. Neither court nor bureaucracy can protect a fool from his folly or a hog from his greed. Many conflicts are unavoidable: like thermal pollution from a power plant, they are externalities of productive behavior. The question is whether institutional arrangements enlarge or diminish the uninvited harm done by such conflicts, and whether the costs of changing the arrangements exceed the benefits to be derived.

Variables in Broker-Dealer Conflicts

It is useful to assign broker-dealer conflicts to one of three separate though overlapping categories:

1. *Zero-sum conflicts between broker-dealer and customer, when each dollar the house gains is a dollar the customer would have gained had the house acted in the customer's interest rather than its own.* Such conflicts arise most obviously in the dealer relationship, when the house is selling merchandise from its inventory. This problem is very common in Europe, where banks underwrite securities and manage customer monies on a discretionary basis. The bank brings out an issue and finds that some fraction of it cannot be sold in the market at the issue price. Rather than cut the price and take the loss (or reduced profit) on its underwriter's inventory, the bank sells the leftover to the customer accounts it controls.

In the United States, banks and their trust departments are barred from underwriting corporate securities, and investment bankers who also manage money are forbidden to sell new issues to managed accounts without the informed consent of the account owners. But less stringent rules apply when the underwriter—or any broker-dealer—is handling or participating in a secondary offering[4] of existing securities exempt from the registration provisions of the Securities Act of 1933. To the extent that specialists on the exchange and broker-dealers who position blocks in the institutional trading market are presumed to be operating as agents for others, decisions they take in their own interest may produce direct zero-sum conflicts of this nature.

Another direct conflict resides in the employment by the broker-dealer of customer funds (and to a lesser extent, securities) left with the firm. Historically, this money has been considered an interest-free loan from customer to broker-dealer. Broker-dealers gain from maximizing the amount of interest-free money ("free-credit balances") at their disposal; customers gain from minimizing the proportion of their assets not at work for them. Obviously, such interests conflict.

2. *Variable-sum conflicts of interest, when broker-dealers, acting to maximize their own profits, may harm their customers, although the customers may also win.* These conflicts arise from the compensation system of the brokerage business, by which the broker's income derives from commissions on his customer's trades. The more often the customer buys and sells, the greater the revenues of the brokerage house (and of the "registered representative"— colloquially, "customer's man"—who handles the account and is in effect paid a percentage of the commission). Customers may or may not benefit from active trading; brokers definitely do benefit. Further complications arise on the interface between the traditional securities market and the new "options" market because a customer's options trading may yield his broker greater commission revenues than can be garnered from trading in conventional securities.

Related conflicts may exist on the dealer side of the broker-dealer operation, when registered representatives are paid commissions for their customers' purchases but not for their customers' sales, creating a bias on the buy side that may or may not meet the needs of the customers. When securities are to be sold from a portfolio to provide funds for purchases, the customer's man (who receives full commissions for an auction market sale) may be tempted to recommend the sale of exchange-listed stocks rather than over-the-counter stocks—a process that could switch an account from more seasoned to more speculative issues.

Any situation in which a broker advises a continuing customer whose activities generate the broker's income involves a potential conflict of interest. After June 1977, subject to exceptions that may be granted by the Secretary of the Treasury or of Labor, the Pension Reform Act of 1974 will prohibit broker-dealers from taking both advisory fees and commissions from pension funds in their care; after May 1978, unless current efforts at revisions are unexpectedly successful, brokers will be forbidden to take both advisory fees and commissions in *any* institutional account. How this rule is to operate in an age of negotiated commissions has not yet been explained.

3. *Conflicts between two customers, when the broker-dealer has undertaken to serve as agent for both.* The clearest of the many examples of such conflicts is the wire house that solicits common stock underwritings. As investment banker to the issuing company, the firm acquires one set of fiduciary obligations, including that of establishing the highest possible price for the issuer client; as broker for its customers, the firm has a separate conflicting set of fiduciary obligations, including that of obtaining the lowest possible price for the investor clients. These conflicts are compounded when a broker-dealer who retains an investment-banking relationship with a corporation also makes

a market in its securities. A special case of such conflicts arises in the smaller stock exchanges, where a specialist may be a member of a firm that is active in underwriting securities traded under the specialist's aegis.

Cases described in the newspapers (and in the SEC reports) as abuses of inside information also belong in this category.

Conflict Resolution

Conflicts, as William J. Casey argued when he was chairman of the Securities and Exchange Commission, can be taken care of "by disclosure, the professional's sense of fiduciary obligation, and regulation—a combination of the three."[5] This approach, carried through, takes care of some categories of conflict better than others.

For zero-sum conflicts of interest, regulation is necessary and probably sufficient; it can be very simple regulation of the kind municipal authorities impose to assure that scales give true weight and the taxi-meter does not charge for more miles than the taxi travels. But in other kinds of conflicts, regulation might find itself in a maze—for example, in the complex of relationships between institutional investors and block positioners. In that instance disclosure can be significant.

For variable-sum conflicts, when the broker-dealer's actions result in an assured gain for himself but may involve risk for the customer, disclosure suffices. But the disclosure should probably be considerably more extensive than anything now demanded—that is, a broker-dealer firm informing a customer that it holds a position in a recommended security should probably also be required to disclose the average price at which the firm's position was acquired. (Such information is, of course, on the front page of the prospectus for any new issue for which the broker-dealer is acting as underwriter.) Ideally, the customer should know whether the broker-dealer is still accumulating a position or is now running it down. The greater the disclosure, the less the chance that variable-sum conflict will turn into zero-sum conflict.

In 1976 the Securities and Exchange Commission proposed a new Rule 10b-10, which would require broker-dealers to disclose to a customer the price at which they purchased a security they are selling to him, if that purchase was made specifically to fill this customer's order, leaving the broker-dealer a "riskless principal" in the transaction. The explanation of the rule specifically exempts from disclosure requirements, however, "the price at which a dealer purchases or sells securities from or to others or the inventory profit on a particular transaction" if the broker-dealer is a market maker in the security and acts in the market independently of specific customer orders.[6]

When conflicts have been institutionalized in the workings of the market, it can be argued that the institutions should be changed. If accident insurance protection had developed in such a way that the lawyer for the insurance company was also expected to represent the victim, we can be sure that our consumerist age would reorganize the insurance industry to make certain that each side of a dispute had its own representative. In the broker-dealer situation, altering the compensation structure may be the kind of institutional change necessary to eliminate or reduce abuse of conflicts.

Is Responsible Resolution Possible?

Conflict-of-interest discussions deal primarily with what the systems experts call worst-case analysis. It is assumed that institutionalized conflict will lead to individual misbehavior. But good men may make any institution work right, and "responsibility for the man who feels it," as Arthur Dewing once wrote, "is not made clearer by legal subtleties."[7] For responsible people consciousness of conflict produces a personal and extraordinarily scrupulous code of business conduct.

Such ethical codes are not made public, but they are not uncommon. The following example was observed firsthand by this writer:

In 1972, when the new issues market was enjoying a temporary revival following the debacle of 1969-70, a privately held manufacturing company in the Midwest went public at $30 a share. It had earnings of $2.75 in 1971, up from $2.35 the previous year and $1.98 in 1969. The debt ratio was under 15 percent; it was a growth company and salable.

But not long after the stock appeared on the market, investor opinion changed, and by spring of 1973—with earnings at $3.25—the price was down to $16. A handful of dealers was making a market in the stock, but the only one of any size was the investment banker who had managed the original underwriting. The house was embarrassed, as was the board of the company; but the price reflected the realities of the market, and nothing much could be done. A good portion of the money that had been raised by the issue was still in the till, invested in bank Certificates of Deposit (CDs) and tax-anticipation notes. The board began to discuss the possibility of buying in some of its own stock, partly (though this would not have been admitted) to keep the price from sagging any further, partly because, at less than five times earnings, the stock seemed an extraordinarily good buy. It was tentatively decided at a meeting—subject to telephone check if the possibility actually arose—to buy for the company itself any stock that might be offered below $15 a share.

Among the purchasers of the original issue had been several bank trust departments that were now disheartened by the performance of the stock and wanted out. Two such banks in the same city, with about sixty thousand shares between them, began feeling around the market to see what they could get. The investment banking house that was making the largest of the markets became aware of their interest in selling, although the bank trust departments in the early stages of their exploration went only to the other market makers. Nothing approaching the size the banks wished to sell was available at the lesser market makers, and finally, the trader for one of the two banks took the initiative and called the original underwriter, telling him that he had about thirty-five thousand shares. The underwriter commented that a colleague in the same city had twenty-five thousand more. The trader replied that he knew about the other block, and that both were willing to put all sixty thousand shares into one deal. They understood that a sale of that size would have to be made well below the price prevailing in the fairly thin over-the-counter market, and in fact, they were willing to take $12 a share to get this particular dog out of their portfolios.

The officer of the underwriting house who was approached with this proposal said he thought he could find a customer for the stock at $13 and would take an eighth-of-a-point commission on the transaction. The trust department trader said that he was not authorized to make brokerage arrangements in the over-the-counter market: it would have to be a straight deal at a net price. "Do you mean," the underwriter said incredulously, "that you'd rather take twelve dollars net than thirteen dollars less an eighth?"

"Those," said the trader, "are my orders."

"I won't do business that way," said the underwriter. "We have obligations to this company, and I will not be in the position of a riskless principal in any transaction in this stock. If you won't do the deal on a brokerage basis, we don't do it at all."

The trust department trader said he would have to check upstairs and would call back. Meanwhile, the underwriter had his secretary set up a conference call with the board of directors of the company. He told them that two blocks were coming onto the market from bank trust departments, and that he thought he could buy the stock at $14 a share, with an eighth-of-a-point commission to his firm to be paid by the seller. The board of directors authorized the purchase.

When the trust-department trader called back with approval from both holders to proceed on the basis of $13 less an eighth, the underwriter told him that his customers were willing to pay $13.50, and the deal was in fact made—sixty thousand shares at $13.50, less an eighth for the brokerage. A separate call was made to confirm the participation of the second bank. The underwriter then told the board of the company that they had bought back sixty thousand shares of their stock at a net price of $13.50 a share.

In this situation the underwriter's opportunity for self-dealing was enormous. He could have purchased the sixty thousand shares for $12 a share and quickly resold them for $14.50 a share, reaping a $150,000 profit on the deal. Or he could have netted $40,500 within the mark-up rules of the National Association of Securities Dealers. But he did not seriously consider such conduct. He was happy to make $7,500 for his firm while performing a service that he considered important both to his customers in the trust departments and to his corporate client.

Nevertheless, both of his clients might have questioned his actions. He never revealed to his corporate customer that the bank trust departments were willing to sell for as little as $12 a share, at which price the corporation might have saved $90,000. On the other hand, his bank trust department clients might have justifiably felt aggrieved if they had known that the buyer was willing to pay $90,000 more than they received. What was the underwriter's responsibility? "My business is learning to live with conflicts," he later explained. "To be fair to both sides."

II • ZERO-SUM CONFLICT SITUATIONS

Broker-dealers, like other businessmen, have a continuing need for cash. They must pay regular salaries, rentals on office space and computers, telephone bills, postage, paper and pencils, taxes. Underwriters and dealers must pay for maintaining the inventory they are selling to their customers; block positioners, who help institutions dispose of large blocks of stock by taking some of it into their own portfolios while seeking out institutional buyers, must put up cash for the blocks they hold. Operationally, brokers buy and sell from and to each other, and transactions between them must be consummated whether or not the customer's payment has come through. Mistakes, fractional delays, and forgetfulness may create situations in which the brokerage house must supply money to the market that its customers have not supplied to the house.

Again like other businesses, the broker-dealer firm relies in large part on bank credit to carry the inventory and bridge the time gap between costs incurred and revenues received. In addition, the securities laws and regulations established by the exchanges and the National Association of Securities Dealers require broker-dealers to place their own capital in the business.

The capital requirements are not onerous. Even under the new and relatively strict requirements established by the Securities and Exchange Commission in early 1973, a broker-dealer can hang out his shingle and do a "general securities business" on an investment of only $25,000, which is less than the amount required to open a Kentucky Fried Chicken franchise. The capital required to continue in business is only one-fifteenth of the aggregate indebtedness of the firm: that is, a firm with $25,000 capital can legally have $375,000 in bank loans if it can find banks willing to make the loans, which it usually can. (On the New York Stock Exchange, the failure of established firms in 1969 and 1970 resulted in further tightening of the capital rules; now a member firm with a ratio worse than ten to one may be forbidden to advertise, hire additional representatives, or open new offices. New SEC regulations require any broker-dealer with a capital ratio worse than twelve to one to file reports so detailed and expensive to prepare that the effective legal ratio for small houses is now near what the NYSE demands from its members.) Although part of the purpose of the capital rule is to insure the safety of investors who have left cash or securities in the custody of the broker-dealer firm, this capital requirement in no way constitutes a "reserve." It is an earning asset of the firm and, until recently, could even be invested in common stocks. In the past brokerage firm capital has been invested in the market, earning its keep independently; until the decline that began in the late 1960s, one of the attractions of being a limited partner in a Wall Street house was the opportunity to participate in the firm's own investments. Not the least of the reasons for the appalling back-office tangles of the period 1968-71 was the failure of most broker-dealer firms to invest their capital in modernizing and improving their own operations.

Such investment simply did not occur to many broker-dealer firms; they had always run the business on their customers' money. This money comes to the firms in four ways:

- As proceeds from interest and dividend payments made to the brokerage house for the customer's account (rather than directly to the customer) because the securities are held in "street name"
- As payments made by customers for securities not yet delivered by the broker or dealer on the other side of the transaction
- As payments made by customers in the form of deposits before opening an account or in anticipation of purchases to be made subsequently
- As proceeds of sales for customers' accounts, which the customers have left with the house either because they expect to use the money to buy something else soon or because the proceeds are from a short sale, which by law cannot be paid out[1]

In his book *Wall Street: Security Risk*, Hurd Baruch, then special counsel to the Division of Trading and Markets of the SEC, gave the total of customer cash balances and equities as at least $5.8 billion as of June 30, 1969.[2] Less detailed analysis shows about $5 billion at the end of 1971.[3] The figures have dropped since then with the troubles in the stock market, and as of mid-1974, the broker-dealers may have had less than $4 billion of customer cash. But this figure approaches the total equity capital behind the broker-dealer business in the United States.[4]

In 1970, according to Baruch's figures, the total amount of customer cash at the disposal of Merrill Lynch, Pierce, Fenner & Smith on the day such figures had to be reported to the SEC totaled $566,605,361.[5] At 7 percent interest the imputed income from this sum would be $39,662,361 over the course of a year. Actual Merrill Lynch income before taxes in 1970 was $76,390,000. Interest rates in fact were over 7 percent for much of 1970; the value of customer monies to Merrill Lynch was considerably more than half its profits before taxes for the year. Percentages for the smaller wire houses would probaby be roughly comparable. There are cases when the income from the use of customer cash at the prime rate exceeds the total profits on the enterprise. In 1970 "interest income on customer account" (amounting to $379,568,000) was 84 percent of operating income ($449,589,000) for the nation's broker-dealers as a whole.[6] In 1973-74, when total profits to the broker-dealer firms were very low, the income that can be imputed from customer cash more than accounted for the total profitability of the industry.

An analysis by the Internal Services Group at Merrill Lynch, covering activities in five hundred-twenty thousand accounts from December 1970 through May 1971, indicates that customer free-credit balances (which account for about 60 percent of the total customer cash and float available to the brokerage house) are very high-velocity monies. Only half of this money remains loose in the accounts for as long as five days; 90 percent of it is removed within thirty days.

Until the end of 1972, broker-dealers had unrestricted access to these funds for their own purposes. Customer money was routinely commingled with the firm's own money either to finance the inventory positions of the dealer operation or as a source of loans to the partners' own trading accounts. If the executives of a broker-dealer house thought they could use another branch office or wanted to experiment with television advertising, they did not have to reach into their own pockets to pay the costs or convince a skeptical bank that they had a good proposition: they could simply tap their customer's funds.

But the inability to make good on this indebtedness to customers was the major reason for the collapse of a number of brokerage houses in 1969-70. In 1972 the SEC published amendments to Rule 15c3-3, prohibiting many of these uses—and abuses—of client cash. Under the new rules, customer money may be used only to finance customer debits; that is, to lend to margin customers, to borrow securities for customers who have made short sales,[7] and to borrow securities for customers who have sold shares but temporarily failed to deliver the certificates.[8] Customer money remaining must be placed in escrow in a special bank account.

To the outsider it may seem odd that the SEC should regard the speculative activities of a firm's more adventurous customers—margin purchases and short sales—as a "safe" employment of the money the more conservative customers have left in their accounts, forbidding the use of this money in the broker-dealer's constructive and vital activities of underwriting and trading. Pragmatically, however, the SEC's judgment is doubtless correct: the margin account is thoroughly secured in nearly every case by the stock itself, which is unlikely to become valueless before the brokerage house can sell the margined customer's stock to repay the loan; and it is next to impossible for a stock that has been sold short to rise so rapidly that the brokerage house cannot protect itself by purchasing the stock for delivery before the customer's margin has been breached. One of the reasons for the previous abuse of customer balances had been that bank loans to support margin accounts were acquired more easily than loans to support other broker-dealer activities.

The new Rule 15c3-3, however, does not treat all of the conflicts inherent in *any* free use of a customer's money by a broker-dealer. Cash accumulations that yield nothing to the customer benefit the broker-dealer, who can usually find enough margin and short-sale business to absorb the balances. Money advanced to these accounts returns interest to the brokerage houses at a rate conventionally set at 0.5 percent or 0.75 percent (depending on the house and the customer) above the current broker-dealer rate, which is closely tied to the prime rate of the banks and automatically adjusted whenever the prime rate moves.[9] Why should the broker-dealer, and not his customer, receive this income earned on the customer's money?

Brokerage houses provide a two-part defense of their practices. First—to quote the Merrill Lynch analysis published by the former Association of Stock Exchange Firms (since merged into the Securities Industry Association)—they argue that customer credit balances are "maintained for the convenience of customers. The use of such funds by brokers represents the most economic employment of these dollars. It results in lower commission rates, permits brokerage firms to provide a broader range of services to individual investors, and obviates the necessity of brokers using bank credit to support their normal operations." Second, brokerage houses claim that no conflict between broker-dealer and customer will arise because the broker's commission income when the customer buys is much greater than his interest income on an idle balance; thus, the broker's interest, like the customer's, lies in rapidly finding new employment for the customer's funds.

The first part of the defense seems a little disingenuous. Something more than the convenience of customers is involved in the free use of billions of dollars of other people's money, and it is impossible to see why either a firm's customers or the public at large should want to spare brokers the normal business need to finance their activities with bank loans. Commissions should cover the costs of performing brokerage services; there is no reason why customers who leave money at a brokerge house should subsidize lower commission rates for those who do not.

More can be said for the second part of the defense, although perhaps not as it is usually argued. With the interest rates of recent years, the return to the brokerage house on the free use of customer money compares rather favorably with the return from customer activity in the market. In 1974 interest income for approximately six weeks equaled commission income from a stock purchase. The interest income was earned virtually without cost to the house, but the commission income was acquired through the normal expenditures the house incurs whenever it does business. The customer does not deal, however, with the brokerage house but rather with his customer's man, who does not participate in the income from interest on credit balances but does participate in commission income. Operationally, even in situations when the house might rationally prefer to see the customer leave his money in the account, the customer's man will press him to put it to work.

At bottom, however, after due obeisance to the shibboleths of the fiduciary relationship, the customer's man works for the broker-dealer, not for the customer. Tightening the ties that bind the customer's man to his employer is a commonplace suggestion when experts are drawing up proposals for the reform of the securities industry. (Indeed, SEC rules once appeared to require that registered representatives be compensated by salary rather than by commission, but the rules were interpreted to classify commissions as salary.) When securities are held in street name, dividend and interest payments to the customer are commonly, although not invariably, retained in the house unless the customer gives contrary instructions; and there is little pressure to reinvest these sums, unimportant in the individual account but impressive in the aggregate. Finally, although one can expect relatively quick reinvestment of the proceeds of most sales of securities, the same assurances cannot be given for the proceeds of maturing debt instruments.

Although hard evidence is not available, it seems reasonable to assume that pressure on customer's men to keep their accounts fully invested varies with changing conditions. The only way to eliminate the conflict growing out of uncompensated use of customer balances is to require the payment of compensation. The point is especially clear today, because the Securities Investor Protection Corporation (and supplementary commercial excess-line coverage) now helps assure the safety of customer balances: brokers who once built such balances simply by letting nature take its course can now tell customers that cash left in the house is protected up to the stated amount. [10]

Some brokers argue—and some even believe—that the Glass-Steagall Act, which forbids them to accept "deposits," also forbids the payment of interest on customer balances. But these balances can be treated as loans to the house rather than as "deposits," and some houses do pay interest on balances to their more sophisticated customers. Baruch reports $23,500,000 of interest payments to customers by the New York Stock Exchange firms in 1969, which he estimates at less than one-tenth of their revenues from lending customers' money. [11]

Often, of course, individual customer balances are far too small to be considered interest-bearing accounts. At Merrill Lynch the average customer cash balance is $70, and the median time it remains on the books is five days. Interest to the average customer would be about ten cents, a tiny fraction of bookkeeping costs. In these accounts all customer cash balances could be considered part of a fund to be invested in Treasury bills. Periodically—perhaps quarterly—this fund could declare a dividend, probably at a rate close to 150 basis points below the broker-dealer's actual average earnings on the fund during the quarter (to compensate the house for the nuisance). Each customer would participate in the dividend *pro rata* to the share of his average daily cash balances in the total customer cash held by the house. Minor adjustments to the computer program that handles customer accounts would make this operation manageable. At a fee of 150 basis points, it would even be profitable—although far less so than the current system of paying nothing at all for the use of the money. In fairness to the industry, it should be said that in 1973-74, when very high short-term interest rates produced customer pressure to put that money to work, a number of firms did propose pools of customer balances to be invested for customer benefits in bank CDs and Treasuries—and were blocked from proceeding by SEC opinions that such pools would constitute securities subject to registration under the 1973 act.

Another possibility under a system of negotiated fees is to allocate credit toward commission charges from the earning on money left with the brokerage firm. In effect this procedure is being followed by Merrill Lynch in its new "sharebuilder" program, to reduce commission charges on small transactions. Most public attention has been directed to the provision in the program that delays the customer's actual purchase until the opening transaction of the next day, but the plan also provides for immediate rather than five-day payment, giving Merrill Lynch the use of the money in the interval before settlement at the clearing house, and giving the customer some of the benefits of the return on it.

The new capital rules mandated by Act of Congress in spring 1975 include a gimmick that may influence some broker-dealers' attitudes toward customer balances. As an alternative to the fifteen-to-one ratio of capital to total indebtedness, broker-dealers after December 1975 will be permitted to measure their capital adequacy by comparison to their net customer balances. A firm that opts for this alternative will be considered adequately financed if its net capital (after formula deductions) equals at least 4 percent of its net customer credits (after deducting 96 percent of customer debits). The impact of this law is impossible to estimate in advance; but it should be noted that the new rules could act as a stimulus to the promotion of short sales, which by increasing customer debits reduce the broker-dealer's capital requirement.

Conflict and Fraud

Conflicts relating to customer balances are direct but at least arguably subtle, and in the case of the ordinary customer, they may fall by the rule of *de minimis*, in ethics as well as in law. But the dealer function gives rise to conflicts that are obvious variants of the standard marketplace "conflict" between the seller who wants top price and the buyer who wants a bargain.

Problems arise whenever a dealer maintains an inventory in a security his salesmen are recommending to his customers. Some houses that do an over-the-counter business acquire a sizable position in such a stock before issuing this recommendation. (This practice used to be called "scalping.") One explanation of such behavior is that if the house does not acquire a position in advance, demand from its customers may push up the price, to the customer's detriment. The danger here is not cured by insisting that the customer be told before his order that the sale comes from the firm's inventory—an insistence that has had the force of law since the opinion of the Second Circuit Court of Appeals in *Chasins* v. *Smith, Barney & Co.* in 1970. In fact one of the most effective sales pitches the customer's man has in dealing with a naïve customer is a statement that the firm thinks so highly of this stock is has acquired a substantial position in its own account.

In a wire house, where customers normally expect the broker at the other end of the phone to be acting as their agent, a research report recommending purchase of a stock in which the house makes a market is advertising material for a seller. Such material is policed by the SEC when it involves an under-writing, but far looser standards (including those for disclosure) are applied to research reports for securities already being traded over-the-counter. Proposed rules to tighten these standards are still in an early discussion stage. The customer's man typically receives a higher commission payment from his employer when his customer purchases an over-the-counter security in which the house makes a market. This compensation system clearly increases his capacity to suspend disbelief in a research recommendation. Even in situations when the recommendation is right on target and the stock is a good buy for the customer, its promotion by the research department of the house may increase the price the customer must pay and the returns to the house on its inventory.[12]

In the "hot stock" situations of the 1967-68 boom, the conflict between customer and house was more often one of time sequence: whose order got priority? But the continuing and most serious conflict occurs in situations when the stock is rapidly losing strength. The customer has a position in the stock; the dealer has a trading inventory. Who gets out, and who gets stuck?

SEC Commissioner Irving Pollack recalls from his youth a veteran at Burnham & Co. who told him, "The brokerage business was built on the idea that the captain of the ship got off last." Pollack adds, "In those days, if a man violated fiduciary obligations he was *destroyed*—people wouldn't talk to him. Now you get people like those at I.O.S., who'll say, 'Those simpletons—why should I knock myself out for them?' "

The promotion of worthless stock to credulous customers is normally re-stricted to the bottom level of the broker-dealer community, where men who do not really expect to stay in business, or with the same firm, are intent on extracting illegal gains. But it can happen in large houses as well, if manage-ment grows careless. The senior executives of Shearson, Hammill & Co., for example, earned punitive suspensions from doing business a few years ago, after a West Coast office put a number of customers into the stock of USAMCO, a vending machine company that had not been able to make the placements in schools and factories that the stock salesmen were saying had been made. False bids were placed in the quotation sheets; customers were encouraged to buy and discouraged from selling; and several customers' men and traders profited by their customers' losses.

Because some people in the firm knew that the information given the customers was false, the USAMCO case appears to fit under the heading of "fraud" rather than "conflict." But from the customer's point of view, the result would have been the same if everyone at Shearson, Hammill had innocently accepted the information USAMCO offered. The firm would still have shown profits on its trading inventories, and the customer would ulti-mately have borne the losses. The sheets would not have been impeded—but as long as the customers' men, the traders, and the firm had positions in the stock, enthusiasm would do almost as much danger as conspiracy.

The danger inherent in dealer-customer conflicts are disturbingly detailed in the matter of Penn Central commercial paper and Goldman Sachs & Co., the sole dealer in a money market instrument believed to be and recommended as completely safe, which became worthless overnight.

Commercial paper is a way to borrow money for a short term outside the banking system. It became a significant element in American finance in 1966, when the Federal Reserve System failed to raise the maximum interest rates that banks could pay on their certificates of deposit. Corporate treasurers with some surplus cash to manage for brief periods became willing to pay some visible but small premium over the rates on Treasury bills and CDs.

The credit is completely unsecured and junior to virtually all other indebtedness of the borrowing corporation. In theory, the paper is marketable; in fact, the term is so short—normally ninety days—that transaction costs make trading uneconomic, especially in competition with the well-oiled Treasuries market.

Issuers may place their paper directly or through dealers who operate by purchase and resale rather than by commission, choosing to keep their own surplus funds (in days past their customers' free balances) in these instruments rather than in Treasuries. Commercial paper running less that nine months is essentially unregulated; the issuer obtains from the SEC a "no-action" letter freeing the issue from registration, and the Federal Reserve System lacks supervisory authority. Because the dealer's mark-up is necessarily very small, his motivation is the access afforded him to other business from the issuer and purchaser. Because the trading market for commercial paper is so limited, both issuer and dealer have been known to repurchase the paper before maturity to accommodate a customer who finds himself with an unexpected need for cash.

Goldman, Sachs was the leading dealer nationally in this sort of instrument, and the leading expert on the theory of why investment bankers were less expensive and more useful intermediaries than commercial bankers. The company was also experienced in the use of commercial paper to promote other business from the issuer; the SEC report on the Penn Central collapse lists half a dozen auxiliary relationships between Goldman and Penn Central that were created or discussed in the two years that Goldman was selling the company's paper.[13]

As late as March 1970, despite a string of unfavorable reports from the company, Goldman, Sachs still awarded Penn Central its "prime" rating and was active in persuading the National Credit Office (NCO, a Dun & Bradstreet subsidiary)[14] to give Penn Central an apparently dependent "prime rating" that carried more credibility. An internal memo from Robert Wilson of Goldman, Sachs informed the senior partners of the firm that the director of NCO had said "that as long as Goldman, Sachs was going to continue to handle the company's c/p (commercial paper) he would keep the prime rating."[15]

Goldman, Sachs salesmen, however, continued to stress the NCO rating as an outside appraisal in their discussions with customers.

Until late April 1970, Goldman, Sachs salesmen kept recommending Penn Central paper to the firm's customers, scoffing at stories that the company's cash flow would not sustain its debt structure. But the firm's own inventory, which had been as high as $15 million in February, went down to zero. Ten million dollars of that total was bought back ahead of schedule by the struggling railroad itself at Goldman, Sachs' insistence; the remaining five million was taken back when the paper expired. When the ship went down, Goldman, Sachs as captain was safely aboard another ship; its customers were dunked to the extent of $82 million.

Some of the customers to whom Goldman, Sachs sold Penn Central paper were highly sophisticated investors: the last large sale, on May 1, 1970, was $5 million to American Express. The interest rate required to move Penn Central paper after February 1970 was significantly higher than that being paid by other "prime" borrowers in this market—partly because Penn Central was trying to sell longer term paper—and this difference should have alerted even less experienced customers to the possibility of risk. But the customers were not told that Goldman, Sachs was no longer carrying an inventory of Penn Central paper—or that the firm was using its management of Penn Central's commercial paper offering as an entrée to what appeared to be very profitable business ("could amount to as much as a billion-dollar underwriting"[16]) from the railroad.

The SEC report on this situation concluded that "most of the institutions and corporations" that purchased the paper "were not sophisticated in terms of their ability to gather and analyze the necessary information. . . . And . . . almost all of the customers were relying on Goldman, Sachs' recommendation."[17] Two examples were cited in the report. One was a textile manufacturer in Clinton, South Carolina, for whom Goldman, Sachs had arranged mergers in 1964 and 1968, who had $1 million to invest pending the closing of another merger; the textile man instructed his treasurer to put the money in commercial paper, "relying on the recommendation of Goldman, Sachs and no one else."[18] The other was Muhlenberg College in Pennsylvania, which added $300,000 to an existing inventory of $400,000 of Penn Central paper on March 30, 1970, relying on a representation by a Goldman, Sachs saleman that "there was no need for concern since total assets exceeded 6½ billion."[19]

In defense Goldman, Sachs argued that the Dun & Bradstreet credit raters were not so dependent on its advice as the SEC staff contended; that its reduction of its Penn Central inventory was consonant with its action as dealer in the commercial paper of other, wholly solvent companies during the tight-money period of early 1970; that the saleman did not specifically push Penn Central paper but marketed a full range of commercial paper; and that the SEC staff went into print with comments from Goldman, Sachs' customers without seeking Goldman, Sachs' side of the story. But the firm has entered into one of those SEC consent decrees that permit it to say that it did nothing wrong but would not do it again. Virtually all the holders of defaulted Penn Central paper sued Goldman, Sachs. The firm settled cases involving more than half of the money its customers lost, paying off at a rate varying from twelve to twenty-six cents. More patient customers may collect more; in the first cases to come to trial, in September 1974, a jury awarded the holders of the commercial paper the full face value, to be paid by Goldman, Sachs.

Options Brokerage

Options to buy securities (''calls'') have been purchased and sold (or ''written'') since the dawn of securities trading. Until the 1970s each such transaction was a unique event, producing a contract between the buyer and the seller that could not be transferred without consent of both and thus could not conveniently be traded. Moreover, options were not significantly standardized: different options on the same stock would carry different prices at which the option could be exercised, different dates of expiration, and different ''premiums'' (that is, purchase prices for the options themselves). In 1972 the Chicago Board of Trade organized a new system of options writing and a Chicago Board Options Exchange to operate a continuous auction market for options produced under that system. Three innovations characterized the Chicago system:

1. Although all transactions still represent a deal between an options buyer and an options writer, in the Chicago system, the contract between these two lapses at the moment of consummation. It is replaced by two other contracts that involve each party separately with a Clearing Corporation associated with the options exchange. The purchaser of the option now has a claim upon the Clearing Corporation entitling him to purchase a given stock at a stated price while the option runs. The writer of the option now has undertaken an obligation to the Clearing Corporation to supply this stock at that price at any time up to the stated day. Now the holder of a claim can sell his option as he might sell any other asset, to any purchaser; and the writer of the option can buy his way out of his obligation as he might gain surcease from any fixed liability.

2. Options are written only for one hundred-share lots of the underlying security, to be exercised at established uniform prices. These prices are set at ten-point (sometimes five-point or twenty-point) intervals. For each stock, several ''striking prices'' are available, at least one of them normally below the current market price of the underlying stock. The price of the option will therefore reflect a time value (itself a function of the anticipated price volatility of the underlying security) plus a possible intrinsic value if the market for the stock is above the striking price on the option. The price of the option fluctuates as a function of the market price of the stock and the time remaining before the option expires.

3. Options are written to expire on uniform dates. There are four "series" a year, each series expiring on the same day for all the underlying securities. Each series is offered with a life of roughly nine months. Because options are continuously created and extinguished by traders, of course, the life of each option is determined by the time remaining between the date of the transaction creating it and the expiration of the series. Pre-Chicago, options were "ninety-day" or "one hundred and eighty-day" options; in the Chicago plan, they are "July" or "October" options. This system has since been adopted for options trading on the American Pacific, Philadelphia, and Midwest Stock Exchanges.

Normally, there will be at least six option contracts available on an exchange for each of the underlying securities accepted for options trading: two striking prices for each of three expiration dates. (Usually, there are more than six, because options are offered at more than two different striking prices.) Thus, the market provides arbitraging possibilities both among different option contracts and between the option and the underlying security. Most options are quite cheap—those involving a striking price considerably above the current price of the stock will sell for pennies.

"Buying call options offers many investors exactly what they're looking for," proclaims the Chicago Board Options Exchange in its introductory pamphlet: "A potentially large profit from a relatively small investment with a known and predetermined risk . . . Selling—or 'writing'—call options offers other investors exactly what they're looking for: An opportunity to increase— often substantially—the income derived from their securities investments."[20] You bet.

It's a nice business for broker-dealers, too. Total commission revenues to the brokerage community from options trading are unknown and essentially unknowable in an age of negotiated commissions. Because options are traded on an exchange, publicly held brokerage firms reporting on their activites can subsume their options commission revenue under the general heading of "listed securities" in the 10-K form, and they do. Merrill Lynch, however, does break out options commissions on its 10-K. In 1975 the revenue from that source ran almost to $40 million, nearly 10 percent of all commissions revenue. For the industry as a whole, then, something slightly short of half a billion dollars in commissions would seem indicated for calendar 1976.

Most of the conflicts questions raised by the emergence of the options exchange fit into the next chapter, but one element of the arbitrage situation seems to pit the brokerage community in its entirety against the customer community as a whole in a game that is at least superficially zero-sum. For the existence of separate options and stock exchanges enables a broker in effect to generate commission revenues for himself without orders from customers.

The most obvious example of this opportunity comes when an option is "in the money"—that is, when its striking price is below the market price of the underlying stock, so the stock purchased by exercising the option can be sold simultaneously at a profit on the exchange. A customer, however, does not profit if the striking price plus option price lies narrowly below the market price: his trade must cover the costs of commissions on the exercise of the option (which is commissionable) and on the sale of the stock. Thus, to give an example in numbers, an option with a striking price of 50 and a premium of 3 will not be profitable to the customer when the stock sells at 53½, because the two commissions together will more than absorb the $50 gross on one hundred shares. This combination of prices will be profitable, however, to a broker-member dealing for his own account, for whom the marginal cost of a trade is very low. He can purchase and exercise the call, simultaneously selling the stock short (short sales matched with purchases of calls are not subject to the "up-tick" rule). In effect, especially as the calls near their expiration date, the existence of the two markets creates for member-brokers a sure, small profit that lies somewhere within—probably not far within—the commissions that would be paid by a nonmember performing the same trades.

Other, more complicated exploitations of membership privileges are also possible. One such exploitation, slightly risky, involves purchasing a stock and writing a call shortly before an ex-dividend date. After collecting the dividend, the broker-member sells the stock and in effect buys back the call; the price of the call is unlikely to rise much more rapidly (or decline much more slowly) than the price of the stock, leaving most of the dividend received as a trading profit. This profit, although too small to cover a customer's commission costs, can be rewarding to the broker: 1 percent isn't much, but when it is 1 percent in two weeks it is 26 percent a year, which is not bad for a safe game, even on Wall Street.

The revenues of the broker-members on such transactions must come out of the pockets of the nonmember participants in the market: there is no other place they could come from. But the economics of the system are not simple because there are values to all participants in the tight articulation of the markets that results from this arbitrage, and there is at least a possibility that commission rates are lower than they would otherwise be because the member firms have a relatively assured supplementary income from their work in these markets. Still, no one knows: data should be gathered and the analysis performed one of these days, preferably soon.

The Stock Marketplace

Stock exchanges in the United States, in theory, are auction markets, and the literature that describes them speaks lyrically of the flow of bids and offers that meet on the floor to create the changing prices of securities. But the market is not composed of flows; bids and offers even for the most active stocks reach the floor discontinuously. The exchanges guarantee to process firm orders "at the market" expeditiously; someone must stand ready to sell to the bid or buy from the offer if the appearance of a flow is to be maintained.

On all exchanges this market maker is called a specialist, and he is a broker-dealer with special rights, responsibilities, and obligations. His work is limited to a relatively few stocks, rarely more than a dozen actively traded securities (plus a varying number of inactive securities). The exchange assigns these stocks to him, and he agrees to maintain an orderly market for them. In the absence of bids, therefore, he must stand ready to buy stocks offered on the market; in the absence of offers, he must stand ready to sell. He deals with brokers, and on most exchanges he is forbidden by the rules to deal directly with the large institutional investors (although not, oddly enough, with the noninstitutional public).

The prices at which the specialist buys and sells are supposed to bear a reasonable relationship to the recent trading pattern of the stock. If the stock has been going up, he can indeed sell at a higher price than the previous sale; if it has been going down, he can buy at a lower price. But even though he may think the price will continue to rise, he may not join the crowd to build an appreciating inventory and bid the price still higher; nor may he sell out on the way down, lowering the price. He is supposed to see to it that prices move smoothly, and even if he believes a stock that started the day at, say, $50 will end it at $54, he is expected to sell continuously at only gradually increasing prices into a market that swarms with buyers.

An exchange evaluates a specialist's performance primarily on the basis of the percentage of his trades made against the market—that is, selling into a rising market or buying from a falling market. Such transactions do not necessarily lose money for the specialist. Assume a stock selling at 51. The next sale is at 50⅞, down a tick; the specialist buys. The sale after that is 51 again, up a tick; the specialist sells. In both cases he has traded "against the market." He has made a "jobber's turn" of $12.50, and earned two brownie points. Nevertheless, the specialist's is a risky enterprise; if the market in his stocks moves all one way, up or down, he can suffer very substantial losses in a brief period.

What he gets in return is unparalleled quantities and qualities of information, plus a commission on the trades he executes for brokers who leave orders in his "book." These orders come in three general categories: *limit orders*, for customers who want to buy a stock if it declines to a certain price (or sell if it rises to a certain price); *stop orders*, for customers who want to cut their losses and sell on a decline to a certain price (or buy, closing out a short position, on a rise to a certain price); and sometimes *market orders of essentially undefined size* to be executed at the specialist's discretion as part of a program of accumulation or distribution by some customer of the broker who has left the order. Every time the specialist executes an order left in his book, he gets a piece of the commission the customer pays to the broker who left the order. [21]

The orders in the book establish fiduciary obligations for the specialist, and, like other fiduciary obligations, they create conflicts of interest. From 1910 to 1922, the rules of the New York Stock Exchange forbade specialists to buy from or sell to their own book: orders in the book were to be triggered only by public bids and offers, and the specialist could never act as a dealer with his book taking the other side of the transaction. But this rule destroyed the possibility of effective stop orders, because the market could easily skip over the stop price before satisfying the size of the stop order. Since 1922 the specialist has been permitted to deal directly with his book, provided the broker who placed the order agrees (which he can scarcely refuse to do). The problem then became one of policing situations where a specialist believing that a selling wave has crested, deliberately triggers a stop order for his own profit, acquiring stock for sale into what he expects will be a rising market or, believing that a buying flurry is coming to an end, fills an existing order on his book, expecting to repurchase shares in a declining market. Opportunities for specialists to profit from conflicts arise most often today in connection with block trades when a sale has been negotiated at a price below a stop order on the specialist's book. Specialists typically execute these orders at the block price, not infrequently taking them into their own inventories for later resale into what is usually (not always) a rising market. Such situations are impossible to police, although brokers who have watched specialists behave this way often refuse subsequently to leave stop orders in their books.

What troubled the Special Study in 1963 was the specialist's "ability to outbid and underoffer his customer."[22] A limit order in the book, if it had some size, made a floor under the stock, and only the specialist, whose book is confidential, would know about it. If he agreed with the customer that a stock down that low was a good buy, he could stand guard at an eighth of a point above that price, acquiring an inexpensive inventory with the certain knowledge that, if his judgment was wrong, he could dispose of the stock only an eighth of a point down—which would still yield him a profit, because he would get a commission on the purchase by the book. (A mirror image of the same no-risk arrangement is found, of course, in the limit order; in this case the specialist could safely sell at a price just under the price in the book, knowing that if there continued to be buying pressure in the stock he could bail himself out at an apparent cost of an eighth of a point, and a real profit after commission.)

The coupling of the specialist's market making function and his proprietorship of the book came about accidentally in the history of the New York Stock Exchange. At the turn of the century, there were competing specialists in most significantly traded stocks; each kept a book but did not take positions or make a market. Not until the late 1930s did the New York Stock Exchange begin to require specialists to make a market and take the associated risks, and not until after World War II did the Exchange act to assign stocks to specialists as monopoly franchises—thereby eliminating competition among market makers in a single stock on the Exchange floor. The rationale was that this was the only effective way to develop the adequately staffed and capitalized specialist units needed to keep pace with the increase in the volume of trading and the number of securities listed.

In recent years this system has come under increasingly strong attack. The American Society of Corporate Secretaries has demanded that the New York Stock Exchange permit a listed company to secure a change of specialists whenever the company believes the specialist is not doing an adequate job in its stock. "Many companies are unhappy," according to Harold L. Glasser, secretary of Kayser, Roth and president of the Society. "Whether it's subjective or objective, they want a change. I'm not making the claim that the specialists are feathering their own nests; but if he knew he could lose a stock, a specialist would be bound to perform better."

From within the community of specialists, Irwin Schloss has argued for a return to the prewar system under which stocks were assigned to more than one specialist: "With competitive books, you will get a broader market in both depth and continuity, and you'll have less need for rules and regulations to govern the market." Schloss would like to see the Exchange establish for each of the heavily traded stocks a list from which a competitive specialist would be chosen; any evidence that the two were operating collusively would force a new choice from the list. In 1976 the Exchange did open an opportunity for competing specialists at a post. The first serious attempt to establish a competing specialist unit, however, is generally regarded as an effort to gain revenge on a specialist who has expanded his public brokerage business through well-advertised rate-cutting; and in general, the rules change was seen as an opening for personality conflict rather than for profitable enterprise. As the stock markets move to the national quota system, with market makers on different exchanges and over-the-counter submitting their bids and offers for simultaneous display on computer terminals all over the country, the issue of competing specialists on any one exchange must become moot.

On the new Chicago Board Options Exchange (CBOE), the functions of bookholder and market maker are separated. A "board broker" keeps the book; a specialist makes the market without knowing what is in the book. Several commentators have suggested that the CBOE has been able to fight off the competition of options trading on the American Stock Exchange, because brokers prefer to do business in a market where a book is neutral. On the German stock exchanges, the book is kept by employees of the exchange itself, and any broker can see what is in it. Nothing would be easier than the establishment of a computerized book that would feed into the current quotations system, which gives brokers bid-and-asked figures for all listed stocks displayed on a cathode ray tube (CRT) at the touch of a key. Riskless principal transactions should be discouraged whether the actor call himself a dealer or a specialist; the reconstructed American stock exchanges of the future should separate the market making and the broker's broker functions.

Although conflicts of interest are frequent in his day-to-day work, the specialist has relatively few problems in which his conscience must be his guide. His opportunity to abuse confidential information for his own gain is recognized by all, and before he can be approved as a specialist, he must take solemn oaths—some of them more or less enforceable by the exchange through its own "self-regulatory" procedures—that he will not do certain things that could make him money and will do a number of things that may cost him money.

Rules that require people to act against their self-interest are notoriously likely to be breached, and specialists are consequently the most closely monitored of all the participants in the securities markets.

The New York Stock Exchange, for example, constantly measures the ''price continuity'' of trades in each stock (''defined as the percent change in price from trade to trade''), the spread between bid and offer as a percent of price for every stock at every specialist's post, and the ''depth'' of the market for the stock (as measured by the net price change in the stock for every thousand shares traded, and also by ''the frequency of participation by the specialist in various sizes of trades'').[23] A good deal of this monitoring, moreover, is the market equivalent of wiretapping: the specialists themselves are not told the details of the parameters in the computer program, the rating they receive from others, or many of the third-party observations of the market in the stocks for which they are responsible. This surveillance has apparantly been effective. In panic situations, like the market that followed the assassination of President John F. Kennedy, most specialists tend to forget their professional obligations, but on routine days specialists are apparently quite responsible in conducting their activites. The Special Study of 1963, the largest single investigation of specialist activites, rated specialists as a group surprisingly high in obeying rules.

Problems remain, however, and some recent changes have had unfortunate side effects. Traditionally, for example, newspaper stock tables have reported the opening price of every stock. Perhaps the specialist's most important single task on the floor is weighing the bids and offers that have come in overnight; he determines the price at which they should be matched to start the day's trading. And there is a temptation here: because the specialist is usually involved as purchaser or supplier in the opening transaction, he can acquire stock easily by setting the opening price a little higher or dispose of stock by setting it a little lower. Today, the relationship between the opening price and the subsequent market is hidden from view, omitted from the tables to make room to print the *price earnings* ratio, which expresses the relationship between the closing price of the stock and its post-tax per-share profits over the most recent reported twelve months. Although officials of the exchanges know the opening price and can punish any abuse of this specialist's power, the trading community—even the brokerage community—cannot routinely monitor his performance of this sensitive task.

On the lesser exchanges, where specialists are often members of firms that do an ordinary brokerage business with the public, conflict situations may arise without any possibility of publicity—and without any clear rules for the specialist's guidance. Theodore Bilharz of Robert W. Baird & Co. in Milwaukee and Norman Froehling of Froehling & Co. in Chicago stand across the floor from each other at the Midwest Stock Exchange, both specialists, both partners in brokerage houses. Baird has a rule that any order for a stock in which Bilharz is the specialist must be given up to a floor broker for execution;

Bilharz never knows when a customer of his own firm is buying or selling. The Froehling firm, on the other hand, informs a customer that the company may well be on the opposite side of any trade in a security in which its partner makes the Midwest Stock Exchange market, and the confirmation slip is rubber-stamped to state that the firm has acted in this sale as both principal and agent. Froehling & Co. never issues a research report on any stock for which its partner is specialist; Bilharz assumes ''that our Milwaukee office does not put out recommendations on my stocks. I have nothing to do with it. Usually I'm the last to find out.'' Both these positions are acceptable to the Midwest Stock Exchange.

At the American Stock Exchange, the specialist-brokerage situation is complicated by a rule that permits a brokerage house to be a limited partner in a specialist's book, supplying capitalization but not participating actively in the specialist's operation. Here there are some fixed prohibitions: houses affiliated with a specialist may not handle institutional orders in that specialist's stocks, issue literature or advice regarding those stocks, or solicit orders in them. They may, however, accept unsolicited orders from individuals and execute them in a routine manner, without informing the customer that this transaction may have been formally different from others. The purpose of the rule is simple and, Exchange vice president Norman S. Poser believes, accomplished: ''You're trying to prevent the guy who's making the market from influencing that market.''

Block Positioners and Specialists

Concern about conflicts at the specialists' posts has recently given way to anxiety about their ability to perform their function at all. As Harold L. Glasser put it in his speech to the Corporate Secretaries, ''Institutional investors are trading in 250,000-share lots in a system designed to handle 100-share round lots, and specialists 'with insufficient capital and insufficient guts' are losing command.'' The total capitalization of the seventy-two specialist units on the New York Stock Exchange at the end of September 1973 was $305 million; the total market value of the stocks in which they are supposed to maintain an orderly market was then $780 billion, and the daily trading of those stocks was running at a rate of $600+ million. Specialists operating on so small a base cannot resist even minor shocks to the market. In 1973-74, when major shocks became commonplace, the specialists seemed to stop trying; daily price movements of 3 percent for medium-priced issues were not unusual.

In this context concern about the specialist's abuse of his book acquires a rather old-fashioned flavor. Even without considering institutional trading, the specialist's book today is thin. In a climate of negotiated rates, brokers are reluctant to split their commissions, and greater price volatility has increased their reluctance to leave orders with a specialist, lest they be executed at the inflection point of a fluctuating market.

When compared to the enormous orders mutual funds, bank-managed pension funds, charitable endowments, and insurance companies may place for immediate execution, the orders in the specialist's book are trivial. These institutional blocks are traded via large and well-financed broker-dealer firms through the exchanges, by over-the-counter dealers, or directly between the institutions themselves in the so-called 'fourth market.' At the exchanges much of the business in very large orders is done on a straight brokerage basis with negotiated fees. The most successful firms in this field also stand ready to act as dealers, purchasing for their own accounts whatever the market will not absorb at the agreed-upon price and taking the risk of subsequent distribution.

Twenty years ago the idea that block business could or would be done through the facilities of a stock exchange was nothing less than visionary, and whatever else is to be said for or against the block positioners, they have made possible the maintenance of open trading of the shares of the great corporations. One of the two groups in the SEC Advisory Committee on a Central Market System has recommended recognition of block positioners as "upstairs market makers," with responsibilities for limiting excessive price swings and giving priority to public orders not unlike those of the specialist. [24] Not all observers, however, are enthusiastic about the services rendered today: "Intellectually there's a complete split," says specialist Irwin Schloss, "a block trader services a customer, a market-maker services a market."

Block positioning is a glamorous business, where a firm may show a profit in millions in one month and a loss in millions the next. Inescapably, it exemplifies the basic marketplace conflict, in which buyer is pitted against seller. The selling institution wants to receive the highest possible price for its stock; the block positioner wants to buy at a price low enough to insure that it can fairly quickly dispose of the stock at profit or at least without loss. And the price to the block positioner is not necessarily what it seems. When he arranges the transaction—makes a "cross" between seller and buyers—the block broker receives both buying and selling commissions on everything his customers dispose of and acquire. He also receives the sell side commission on the part of the trade he takes into his own position. By the most restrictive definition, then, the price of the stock to him is not what appears on the tape but that figure less a commission on what he has purchased. By the more practical definition, the price to him should be seen as what prints on the tape, less both the commission on the stock he has acquired and his profits on the commission for the rest of the trade. Unless he puts discretionary accounts into the deal, however, the "cross" does not leave the block trader wearing two or more hats; he clearly represents only the "active" side of the trade, the initiating institution, although he collects from both sides.

Until the early 1970s, block trading was conducted on exchange floors largely to get under the umbrella of minimum commission rates, which were fixed on the basis of one hundred-share lots and permitted no volume discount for larger trades, because the execution of a forty thousand-share trade does not cost brokers anything like four hundred times as much as the execution of a one hundred-share trade (twenty times as much would be a generous estimate), fixed commission rates generated quite a lot of surplus revenue for brokers.

But not all this revenue stayed with the house that put the trade together. Until late in 1968, customers could direct their brokers to split their fee—to ''give up'' to other brokers some part of the commission earned by the trade. Some of these give-ups went to pay for services performed on behalf of the institution. Mutual funds sweetened the pot for firms that sold the fund's shares to the public; bank trust departments rewarded brokers who kept large deposits at the bank; and every institution used give-ups to pay for research reports and recommendations. When blocks were positioned by the broker at his own risk, the fixed commission provided a cushion against losses on the disposal of the stock.

The management companies of a few funds even found a way to funnel much of the excess commission payment back to the management company itself, usually through the acquisition of a brokerage firm on one of the regional exchanges and instructions to the New York Stock Exchange firm to give up some of the business to the captive firm on the other exchange. (NYSE rules forbid control of member firms by any outside organization; the SEC under its new Rule 19b-2, adopted in January 1973, has ordered all exchanges to permit the ownership of member brokers by other financial institutions, provided the member does at least 80 percent of his business with customers other than the controlling institutions. The 1975 amendment to Section 11-A of the Securities and Exchange Act, apparently written to override 19b-2, will force exchanges not to deny membership to any firm qualified to do a securities business.) Some fund managers even arranged to have excess commission revenues routed around to their own personal benefit, usually through instructions that part of a transaction must be given up through a specified customer's man in a specified firm, who then presumably invested the proceeds in the manager's personal account.

Although the give-up system was essentially pernicious, and often worked in a manner contrary to the interest of the funds, endowments, and other institutions, it did provide a convenient mechanism for rewarding expertise. Muriel Siebert, for example, the first female member of the New York Stock Exchange, was able to establish herself as an authority on aviation and air freight, and institutions interested in those stocks could give her very large orders, with the understanding that a substantial piece of her commission income from the transaction would be given up to other brokers who had a closer relationship to the fund. With the end of the give-up mechanism, the expertise offered by Miss Siebert came into competition with the more tangible services performed by larger houses, and, reportedly, she lost a considerable piece of her business, as did others similarly situated. In 1976 Miss Siebert became one of the small group of New York Stock Exchange members offering public customers deep discounts for no-frill execution services.

But the end of give-ups in late 1968 did not bring about anything like the changes its advocates had anticipated; the market found other ways to accomplish the same results. In the spring of 1971, the SEC went after the root problem: the overcompensation of brokers by their customers for the work involved in putting together a block trade. Starting in April 1971, the SEC eliminated fixed minimum commissions on that portion of every trade beyond the first $500,000; in April 1972 the limit was lowered to $300,000; and in May 1975 fixed commissions were eliminated entirely. Stockbrokers, like other businessmen (but unlike real estate or insurance brokers), now must operate in a context of price competition.

With the end of fixed commissions on block trades, excess commission income went out of the stock market; in the first half of 1973 and most of 1974, in part because of negotiated commissions on large blocks, the brokerage business as a whole lost some money. (In early 1975, with volume at record levels, the business got some of it back.) Institutional customers now account for 70 percent of all New York Stock Exchange business (and NYSE business is nine-tenths of all brokerage business). Institutions carry so much weight that, when fixed commissions went off on larger trades, they displayed surprising force in stipulating the commission fees they would pay. Because they were under constant threat of lawsuit if they paid anything more than a minimum price, they tended to set the fees quite low. Typically, on all but the largest blocks (where the broker retains leverage, especially if he will have to position any part of the block), the procedure now is that the institution calls in the order, the broker executes it, and the institution then informs the broker, a day or two later, how much the commission will be. Figures are hard to come by, but Ben Ames Williams, Jr., of Boston's Old Colony Trust has estimated the saving in commissions on large blocks at $3 million a year for his bank alone.

A troublesome conflict in block trading arises from the situation of the broker-dealer who also performs investment-management functions.

As the Institutional Investor Study put it, mildly:

A potential conflict of interest exists when a block trade assembler places its discretionary accounts on the passive side of the block trades. Insofar as the participation of such accounts eliminates or reduces the need for block positioning, it allows the block trade assembler to avoid a very risky and often unprofitable activity, while at the same time increasing its commissions earned to the extent of that participation. The block trade assembler may well be tempted to put its account into such transactions at unfavorable prices to earn the brokerage commissions on both those shares and the other shares in the block trade.[25]

The study then gave two cases of "more real conflicts of interest." In one the block trade assembler had made a bid for its own account, which the seller had rejected. Thereupon the broker bought the bundle for a discretionary account at a slightly higher price, earning $29,000 in brokerage commissions

—a maneuver not unlike that of a Swiss bank that sells securities it has underwritten directly to its managed accounts; the activity would be illegal for underwriters in the United States without elaborate disclosure precautions, but is not illegal for block positioners.

In the other case, the block trader bought a position for its own account from an account under its management at a price 4 percent below the previous sale and 6 percent below the opening price for that day; the purchase price was so attractive—and early rebound so likely—that "the specialist unit also bought almost 50,000 shares even though slightly long at the time, the odd lot dealers bought the unusually large amount of 2,000 shares and the specialist's book took more than 14,000 shares." The author of the study added drily: "The price of the stock that day rose immediately."[26]

The elimination of fixed commissions on larger blocks also expanded the opportunities for institutions and the block trader to establish a community of interest at the expense of other investors. Before 1971 the price of the block as printed on the tape had a known meaning. If fifty thousand shares changed hands at $50 and the commission at that price worked out to 1 percent, the world knew that the buyer had paid $50.50, the seller had recieved $49.50, and the block broker had taken $1; and if he positioned ten thousand shares, he had done so at an effective price to him of $49.50 (and if he sold out at $48.50, he was still going to make money on the total deal, because he had $40,000 of gross commission income on the cross to set against his $10,000 loss on positioning).

Today, when a *cross* (a transaction where the same broker represents both buyer and seller) prints at $50, no one can tell if that was really the price. With commissions negotiable the broker and his customers can allocate differing proportions of the money to commission and to price. It may make a considerable difference to the positioner's profitability on his acquired inventory whether the price of a fifty thousand-share deal prints at $49.75 or at $50.25; under the new rate structure, he and his customers can decide which of these numbers they would like to see on the tape.

"Even the printed price doesn't mean anything," a senior partner at one of the oldest Wall Street investment banking houses insists, "because you never know what the side deal is." Institutions and the block brokers are constantly doing busines with each other; the institution that sells to the broker today will be buying from him tomorrow. Thus, a party that gains an advantage on one deal can make amends on the next. Such back-scratching has infinite possibilities. Penn Central in its headlong rush to bankruptcy still experienced months when it had a good deal of loose cash, some of which went into the purchase of commercial paper from other Goldman, Sachs clients. Salomon Brothers, while handling blocks of Equity Funding common stock, was dealing with Equity Funding as a customer for the debt instruments of others.

An institution can and does do favors for a block house that bails it out of an unwanted position; the *quid pro quo* can be a somewhat high print requested by the broker to help prop a stock. A block trader can and does eventually see to it that a generous allocation of a hot issue is made to an institution that once cleaned up the end of a sale or offered its facilities for parking part of a block that was being accumulated for others. The SEC has begun to look into at least two possible arrangements of this kind, says Stanley Sporkin of the SEC Division of Enforcement. "We hear rumors, but so far it's just statements [that are being taken]," he adds. A specialist, contrasting his work to that of a block trader, says insinuatingly: "Of course, I'm not influenced by what happened yesterday in the corporate bond department, or by the chance for a trade in the municipal bond department . . . ."

When a wire house does a block business and distributes securities to its retail customers, the legal, ethical and practical elements of decision are difficult to assess. The customer does benefit from the broker-dealer's whole-sale purchase price and from elimination of the commission charge. On the other hand, securities are made available at retail in connection with a block transaction only when wholesale customers cannot be found, and presumably the wholesale customers know what they are doing. Merrill Lynch has an absolute rule that such distributions will be made only when the research department independently recommends the stock, and several others say they are "comfortable" with such operations only when they have a research recommendation. But decisions to do a block must be made quickly and are usually based on the feel of the market rather than on more fundamental judgments; only a firm with a large research department can follow all the stocks that may be offered in blocks. (Obliging research departments at smaller firms can of course supply "instant analysis" of stocks they are not following. Moreover, lawyers for some of the block houses doubt the legal propriety of issuing research recommendations on stocks the firm is distributing—or of undertaking distributions in stocks very recently promoted to the public by research.)

Using the firm's discretionary accounts as purchasers or as parking places for a block that has not found other customers is clearly improper in the absence of specific informed consent by the owner of the account. Although probably not illegal per se, it subjects the broker-dealer to the risk of damage suits when a deal works out badly. Such suits are relatively rare; legislation should be written to assure that the occasion for them cannot arise.

The struggle between block positioners and specialists centers on two situations. The first is the disruption by the specialist of a *clean cross*, an arrangement whereby a large buyer and a large seller have come together upstairs in the block trader's office (or rather, via his telephone) and have agreed on a size and price for a trade. The broker, as a New York Stock Exchange member, is required by Exchange rules to bring his trade to the floor, to be officially executed at the post and printed on the tape. The specialist now may and should require that any public orders on his book that would be triggered by this trade be incorporated in the deal. He may also demand that he be permitted to acquire a position on the floor, especially if the sale is made perceptibly below the market and he can expect it to stimulate public buy orders that he would otherwise have to fill from inventory acquired at a higher price.

The specialist sometimes operates out of pure greed, demanding that he be permitted to ''write up'' some of the block, as though he were performing a brokerage function on it, and collect his usual broker's commission. (''Like a tip to a doorman for not getting you a cab,'' says Arthur Lipper, formerly a New York Stock Exchange member.) Unless he wishes to create a row within the Exchange, about the only recourse the block trader has at this point is to transfer the deal to a regional stock exchange—cutting out the orders ahead of the block on the New York specialist's book.

A second cause of bad blood between traders and specialists is the situation in which the broker is attempting to dispose of, or acquire, a large block for an institution through normal auction-market means, buying or selling a little at a time—without informing the specialist that this is what he is about. In theory, the specialist should be pleased to see the business coming to his post as part of the normal flow; it confirms his feeling that he is providing a useful service and, in the long run, brings him profits. But he is at the mercy of the broker who comes to him with, say, a three thousand-share selling order on Monday, another on Wednesday, and another three thousand order on the Tuesday following, each time saying that as far as he knows that is all there is. A broker who routinely works in this way may eventually find, for example, that the ''spreads''quoted him by the specialist are wider than they used to be.

In most situations, of course, a broker assembling a block deal will want the specialist's help and will keep him informed, paying through split commissions for the help he gets. Such disputes as arise tend to be about the size of the specialist's cut. In past years such fights were of intramural interest only, because the cost to the customer was the same; however, the insiders divided their fees. Today, as an unexpected by-product of negotiated commission rates, broker-dealers may be afraid to appear to be ''in collusion'' with the specialist, and may doubt the propriety—or even the legality—of giving him part of their commission, especially in situations where a lawyer could argue that the net result was an increase in the commission paid by the customer. The result has been an increase in friction between block traders and specialists.

These disputes occur along a fault line between two quite separate stock markets that by historical accident have wound up on the same floor. One is the traditional auction market, where bids and offers meet, with the specialist smoothing the path; the other is the lumpy institutional market, where insurance companies, trust departments, and pension funds pretend their enormous holdings in common stock are really liquid investments, qualitatively different from, say, the ownership of an office building. Here prices are strongly influenced, although not entirely controlled, by prices in the auction market, and thus the specialist's ordinary work has some significance for the block brokers. On some deals, moreover, the block traders may want the specialist to take a residual piece of a sale for his own inventory, using the auction market to clear the lumpy market.

Block positioners are in a sense specialists of the lumpy market, except that they are under no obligation to maintain orderly conditions; they seek to return quickly to a zero balance if any stock circumstance has led them to position. A position taken by a specialist does in effect clear the market, because he may be prepared to hold it for a while; Federal Reserve regulations make it possible for him, moreover, to borrow from the banks to carry such an inventory without the constraints of Regulation T, by which the Federal Reserve Board limits the extension of credit to broker-dealers for the purpose of holding securities. A position taken by a block broker, on the other hand, leaves a block still overhanging the market, because the broker will be seeking to dispose of it as soon as possible. (Since 1973, however, the block broker has been able to claim for relatively short periods some of the specialist's exemption from Federal Reserve regulations.) Genuine bear raids by hedge funds or by a disgruntled specialist are possible at the expense of a block positioner, and from time to time they happen. Fights between specialists and block brokers have a distinctive characteristic: both sides are well equipped to take care of themselves. The public observing them might as well take the attitude of the West Virginia housewife who looked out the kitchen door to find her husband battling a bear: ''Go it, husband! Go it, bear!''

III • VARIABLE-SUM CONFLICTS

In a perfect world, stockbrokers would be recompensed like the legendary Chinese doctors who are paid only when their patients stay well, for the big winner in finance is the man who buys Haloid in 1947 and sells Xerox a generation later. In our imperfect world, brokers are paid only when their customers trade. Most brokers advising their customers to sell one stock and buy another unquestionably believe they are serving the customer's interests and may be doing so. But the fact remains that brokers make money every time there is a trade.

When a broker deliberately leads a customer to trade constantly, without regard for the customer's interest, his activity is called *churning* and it is a crime. ''Churning,'' says a young enforcement officer of the New York Stock Exchange, ''is really theft.'' There are truly amazing cases on record. One customer's man at Reynolds & Co. in the 1950s turned over one account twenty-nine times in forty-six months, and another one thirty-four times in fifty-six monthes. The customers started with $57,300 and $66,000, respectively. One bought $1.665 million in securities and sold $1.652 million; the other bought $2.276 million and sold $2.235 million. The first lost $36,000;

the second, $19,000—while commissions to the brokerage house ran $27,000 and $38,000, repsectively.[1] Today, the brokerage would be even higher, because commissions are higher; and the losses presumably would be greater; the SEC, of course, would still get there after the horse was stolen. In only one case—J. Arthur Warner Co. (a.k.a. ''The Doubling Company'') in 1955—has the SEC compelled a brokerage house guilty of churning to make good the losses of its customers.[2] In late 1973 Bache & Co., denying any wrongdoing, settled for a $250,000 damage suit for churning in its Miami office.[3]

Conflicts between the fiduciary role of the broker and the compensation structure in the market are necessarily most severe in a ''discretionary account,'' an arrangement by which an investor permits a broker-dealer to buy and sell securities in his name without consulting him. For years the SEC moved on ''churning'' only when there was evidence that the customer had not given specific consent for each transaction. The New York Stock Exchange manual *Supervision and Management of Registered Representatives and Customers Accounts* expresses disapproval on the subject and observes that ''many firms refuse such accounts under any circumstances. If a firm permits discretionary accounts, it should scrutinize the reasons why the customer wishes to open such an account. It is extremely dangerous to permit a discretionary account to be opened for trading purposes.''[4]

Rule 408 of the Exchange requires that the customer provide and periodically renew written authorization for the exercise of discretion. If a customer gives the firm discretion over his account while he is away on a trip (an entirely reasonable thing for him to do), the house is expected to have a system that automatically revokes the discretionary authority on his return (also reasonable, but often forgotten). At well-run houses, discretionary accounts are given a separate code number, to flag the attention of the office manager or the computer; and the Exchange recommends that the order room require every ticket a customer's man writes for such an account to carry a legend stating whether discretion was exercised. When discretion has been exercised, moreover, the ticket is supposed to carry the manager's initials before the order room will process it. Even at less well-run houses, NYSE rules require that a manager keep himself informed *post facto* of all trades in discretionary accounts.

Unfortunately, because the brokerage business runs on the telephone, it is almost impossible for a branch manager to know whether a customer's man he is supervising has called the customer before putting in the ticket. The New York Stock Exchange kindly permitted this observer to accompany one of its inspectors on a visit to a branch office of a large wire house. The inspector required the manager to answer a long questionnaire, one section of which included no fewer than twenty-seven separate items on the handling of discretionary accounts. His answers seemed satisfactory; discretionary accounts could be opened only with prior approval by both the branch manager and the head office, and they expired automatically on June 30 of each year, unless specifically renewed in writing; all tickets for trades made at the discretion of the customer's man had to be marked "PTA" (Partner's Approval required) and shown to the branch manager before the order could be processed. But in fact the policing was minimal; the customer's men made very little use of the PTA legend, because it was a nuisance; and the branch manager was clearly guessing at the number of trades made on the basis of his employees' discretion.

"Many branch offices," the Exchange manual reports, "appear to be in need of up-to-date information regarding discretionary accounts. In a disturbing number of instances, branch managers have been found to be completely unaware of the existence of discretionary accounts in their office."[5] The worst situations of all are in firms that in theory do not permit discretionary accounts, because their branch managers probably never know when a customer's man is churning. A customer who has been making money (or has had his eye fixed on the pot of gold at the end of the rainbow) may be reluctant to complain to a firm that he did not know what the customer's man was doing with his account—especially since such complaints are virtually impossible to prove. (The written confirmation of an order goes from the firm to the customer, not vice versa.) On a certain proportion of losing trades, a branch manager may expect the customer to complain that he never authorized the purchase or sale, even though in fact he did.[6] Such complaints, therefore, do not necessarily trigger a significant investigation by the firm.

Most of the larger broker-dealer firms have hired "compliance officers," usually lawyers with substantial experience on the other side of the table at the SEC. Their authority, title, and salary vary a good deal from firm to firm, but their status has been rising steadily since 1965, when the SEC for the first time punished the senior partners of Shearson, Hammill & Co. personally for their failure to supervise a branch office. "The compliance function is widely supported because management guys are too wealthy, and they have worked too hard, to want to let some salesman ruin their reputation," says the compliance officer of a major firm. Nipping problem situations in the bud, he adds, is especially welcome, because "you have to remember that the SEC tries its cases in the newspapers."

The most important aspect of compliance work is establishing a computer program and monitoring its output. Every morning the compliance officer finds on his desk a sheaf of printouts detailing all trades by all members and employees of the firm for their own account, trades that bring a customer's account above certain rule-of-thumb prescriptions of maximum activity, and trades associated with unusual activity or unusual price changes in any stock, especially in any stock in which the house is a market maker. Secondary distributions are troublesome: "You don't know whose interest is being served—the issuer, the customer, or the salesman who needs the business. Unless you have a research recommendation on the stock—that sanitizes it."

Keeping an eye on the research recommendations is another central element in the compliance officer's job—"watching the language, seeing that it doesn't get inflammatory." Most houses have a rule forbidding registered representatives to buy for their own account any stock recommended by the research department until at least forty-eight hours (in some houses seventy-two hours) after issuance of the research report. There is supposed to be a wall between the analysts and the customer's men: "If I find a research guy is leaking to the salesmen the fact that he's writing up a company, he is out," a compliance man says.

At the exchanges themselves, staffs of enforcement officers keep an eye on the flow of the market and look into customer complaints. The New York Stock Exchange requires all members to report all severances of employment of registered representatives, voluntary or involuntary, with statements of the reasons for parting. Several firms have been disciplined (although not publicly) for failing to tell the Exchange the reason why certain customer's men had "resigned."

At the exchanges, too, the basic tool is the computer program, which automatically flags any price movements that are out of the ordinary. At the American Stock Exchange (ASE), an hourly statement reports the thirty-five most active stocks during the previous hour. If a stock is unexpectedly active, an exchange officer calls the specialist, finds out which houses are doing the trading, and then checks out with the broker-dealer: "Who are the customers?" Frank Savarese of ASE says, running down his catechism. "Is it all one salesman? All one area of the country? Did you put out a research report? Are the orders solicited or unsolicited? . . ." Such queries are made about a hundred times a week at the New York Stock Exchange, fifty to eighty times a week at the American Stock Exchange. Usually, the answers are sufficient, but not always.

A general source of frustration in the industry is the difficulty of getting new customer's men to take compliance rules seriously. A training director for a large wire house, agonizing over the problem, asks, "What about the branch manager? Isn't it his first responsibility to comply, and see that his people comply?"—then answers the rhetorical question: "No. His first responsibility is his sales." At the office visited by this writer, the branch manager estimated that he put half of his time into taking care of his own customers and half into supervision. He knew a great deal more about each man's "production" month by month than he knew about the handling of discretionary accounts.

In the real life situation in an office, the great majority of sales by customer's men fall somewhere between actual discretion and mere order-taking. Many customers merely assent to a recommendation, assuming that the customer's man knows what he is doing. For the last dozen years, the SEC has been considering such situations as indicative of churning; today, any account may be considered a victim of churning if it turns over more than once every two months, unless the customer's man can demonstrate that the client initiated the trades himself. The SEC also has gradually developed a "suitability" rule, to draw the line between defensible and indefensible advice to a customer. Switching customers from one mutual fund to another, for example—with a loss of an 8½ percent sales charge to the customer, and a gain of perhaps 5 percent for the broker-dealer—would be *prima facie* indefensible, although perhaps justifiable in special circumstances. Things such as short selling in custodian accounts actually happen, and the branch manager must be held to blame if they happen more than once.

The NYSE manual offers a list of ten "potential sources of problems" that a branch manager should be alert to spot:

1. Evidence of excessive activity in an account
2. Substantial purchases of any one security
3. Extremely large orders
4. Purchases of low priced or highly speculative securities
5. Day trades
6. Short sales
7. Mutual fund purchases just under the breakpoint in the sales charge
8. Mutual fund switches
9. Transactions of employees and their families and any possible relation between these and customers' transactions
10. Sale of possible control stock[7]

Further problems arise with the growth of options trading. Although options can be put to entirely legitimate—even conservative—use as hedges and as a limited-risk timing tactic, most participants in the market use them as a form of off-track betting. As the literature issued by the options exchanges correctly stresses, an option is a wasting asset: a mistake on a stock will cost an investor some fraction of his money, but a mistake on an option probably means a dead loss. The number of people who should be invited to play the options market is much smaller than the number who are attracted to it.

The options exchanges have required every member firm to designate a registered Options Principal responsible for policing his firm's conduct in this area, and among his duties is the administration of special questionnaires by which customers are qualified to buy or write options. Each customer must be separately certified as an option customer and must be assigned a trading limit by the firm. Here as elsewhere the rule of "know your customer" really protects the firm: the Clearing Corporation as the option creator holds brokers responsible for their customers' trading, so the firm itself will pay the piper if an overly adventurous customer writes a naked option (that is, sells a call on a stock he does not own, the functional equivalent of a short sale with potentially unlimited losses). Still, from the customers' man's point of view it is attractive business—lots of action—and because the sales pitch for buying options or writing covered options is the limit on the customer's risk, he may think that all the special restrictions are just formalities.

The temptation is especially great to sell "spread" options, whereby the customer acquires a call on one hundred shares at one striking price—say, 50—while writing a call at another striking price—say, 60. Assume the stock is now selling at 49, and the prices of the two options are $350 and $125, respectively. If the price of the stock fails to rise, so neither option is exercised, the customer's maximum loss is $225 (the purchase price of the 50 less the sales price of the 60); if the price goes to 60 or above, his profit is $775. Reversing the transaction during the lives of the options cannot yield a profit greater than $775 (because 10 points is the absolute ceiling on the difference in value between a 50 option and a 60 option) and will probably yield less because the bigger they are, the harder they fall: the larger time value of the option at the lower striking price goes *pari passu* with the smaller time value of the option at the higher striking price.

Customers tend to be attracted to this sort of low-risk little flyer, and the numbers presented without commission costs may be appealing. But four commissions may be involved here—two for each option—and taken together they will cut profits substantially. Within the trade the spread option is known as "the alligator" because, as one broker explained, "the commissions will eat you up alive." Someone should be policing the volume of spread options on the exchanges.

The Use of Margin

One of the more subtle conflicts between the broker-dealer and his customer arises in the use of *margin*—that is, funds loaned by the broker-dealer to the customer to cover some fraction of his purchase price. The use of margin increases the profitability of correctly calculated short-term trades but also increases losses on mistakes and usually reduces the profitability of investments held for any period (especially when interest rates are higher than dividend ratios). Therefore, it is generally agreed that relatively few stock purchases should involve margin. But SEC rule 15c3-3, which prohibits the use of customer balances except for the financing of margin accounts, has heightened the already considerable incentive for brokers to push credit on their customers—and the option of measuring net captial adequacy as a fraction of the difference between customer credits and customer debits may make margin accounts look even more attractive.

The numbers are striking. Assume a $5,000 purchase in April that is sold in October. On a straight cash basis, the brokerage house receives a pair of commissions amounting perhaps to $150. If the customer buys with 60 percent margin, the broker receives the same pair of commissions as well as six months' interest on a $2,000 loan that cost him nothing (additional revenue of $100, assuming a 10 percent interest rate).

Then the broker has the right to use for his own purposes the securities the margin customer has purchased on credit. Another customer of the house, for example, goes short on a stock that is in the margin customer's account. By the terms of the standard margin agreement, the broker is authorized to lend a margin customer's stock to consummate a short sale. The borrower pays interest on the value of the borrowed stock. Assuming the stock is still worth $5,000, a 10 percent rate would generate another $250 over a six-month period, bringing the total revenue on the transactions to $500—more than three times the revenue a straight nonmargined transaction would have generated for the brokerage house. The broker may do even better if he uses a margined securities held ''in the box'' to cover what would otherwise be naked calls in the options market. The *naked call* being simply a short sale at a somewhat higher price (the purchaser of the call paying a premium for the limit on *his* risk), the proceeds to the coverer will be greater than the interest yield on the loan for a short sale. (It should be noted in passing that short sellers with behavior patterns of bad judgment are best off selling naked options, because they can cover by purchasing the unexpectedly rising stock as it crosses the striking price and actually show a profit on their mistake.)

Even if the opportunity to cover an option or to lend the stock does not present itself, the brokerage house may benefit by its right to pledge the margin customer's stock as security for bank loans the broker may make for his own use. The SEC rules also permit brokerage houses to make another rather charming use of margined securities. If the firm's back office is disorganized, it can lend margin customers' securities to cash customers' accounts to make up deficiences that otherwise have to be borrowed outside or bought.

Although there is no evidence that brokerage houses pay customer's men higher percentages of the firm's commission on margin purchases than on cash purchases, salesmen are anxious to open margin accounts, because they enable investors to purchase more securities than they could otherwise buy and because margin accounts tend to trade more actively than fully paid accounts. At various times is has been suggested that buying stocks with borrowed money should be prohibited, but any such prohibition would be artificial and fruitless. Anyone with a house can get a mortgage, and as long as timely payments of interest and principal are made by the borrower, the bank will not inquire whether the proceeds of the mortgage were invested in the stock market. In fact Section 221.3(s) of Regulation U, the Federal Reserve System rule on activity by banks in financing stock purchases, permits the lending of money for such purposes without restriction when the loan is secured by collateral other than stocks.[8] The Federal Reserve does impose a limit on the valuation that can be made of securities as collateral for ''purpose credit''—

loans to carry stock purchases—but for other credit, banks may give securities whatever collateral value they choose in "good faith." A loan to a going business may be put in the market with no one the wiser; the lending officer has better things to do, and the bank examiner has no reason to look behind the file.

An interesting example of the violation of Regulation U emerged from the investigation of the Penn Central collapse. A group of officers of Penn Central and their friends had been borrowing from the Chemical Bank, on no security but the stock itself and their signatures, the full purchase price of securities they bought for a private investment fund. In explaining to his subordinates his approval of these loans, William S. Renchard, then chairman of the board of the bank and its chief executive officer, noted that "the rate on the proposed loan is too low, but, in view of the size of the deal and the fact that it has such good friends connected with it, [Renchard] felt it was preferable not to quibble."[9] The Penn Central officers urged Renchard to join their investment club himself, but he explained to them that he could not possibly do that, because the Federal Reserve prohibits loans by banks to their own executives. In other words, although Renchard thought he had to take Regulation O seriously, he considered Regulation U a matter of taste. Even after the publication of the Penphil story, the Federal Reserve administered neither a penalty nor a rebuke to Chemical Bank.

The SEC enforces Regulation U violations for the Federal Reserve, bringing suit on the cases referred to its division of enforcement. Such referrals are apparently infrequent. Division Chief Sporkin reports that "the Fed [which examines member banks with state charters] is much better than the Comptroller [which examines nationally chartered banks]." In general, he adds, "the bank regulators' attitude is much more paternalistic than ours."

In matters relating to Regulation U and Regulation T (the control over loans by brokers, which is also legally the responsibility of the Federal Reserve), the SEC can be paternalistic, too. Regulation T requires that the brokerage houses automatically charge customers interest on money still owed for a cash purchase concluded more than five days before. The brokers do not comply with this regulation, but no one ever gets in trouble. In fact, when a federal district court held that six broker-dealers victimized by a defrauding colleague could not put the fellow into bankruptcy, because they were at fault when they extended credit to him in violation of Regulation T, the SEC entered a brief *amicus curiae* on appeal. It urged, among other things, that "if a special cash account customer has a credible explanation for a brief delay in delivery, a broker-dealer may in good faith rely on this explanation."[10]

Historically, the problem with margin accounts has been their role in the pyramiding of purchases. In the 1920s, when stock could be bought on 10 percent margin, a rise of 10 percent in the market value of the stock purchase would enable the customer to double his holdings without any additional investment. Conversely, a very small drop in the price would first trigger "margin calls" for additional equity, then force sales of the stock if the margin calls were not met. Today, the Federal Reserve requires that the major fraction of any purchase be paid immediately or covered by the pledge of wholly owned securities worth much more than the loan; hence, the pyramid at worst has a gentle upward slope and a peak not too far from its base. But there is still some danger that lower prices will produce sell-offs; the severity of the decline of so many prices in the summer and fall of 1974 was attributed to forced sales by margin customers.

Brokerage houses claim to control tightly the opening of margin accounts. They require extra credit references and permit only customers who can afford to supply the equity for substantial initial purchases—$3,000 to $5,000 is a common range—to play on other people's money. If brokerage houses were forbidden to have margin accounts, the brokers argue, customers would borrow the money elsewhere, and the authorities would have even less control than they have now over the use of credit in the market. Moreover, no particular public policy would be served by shifting from brokerage houses to banks the interest income from borrowing to support stock purchases.

Nevertheless, a case can be made that the market, the country, and the customer would be better off if banks or third-party lending institutions were made the source of credit in the stock market, provided that the bank supervisors would give some priority to examining such loans. Presumably, such a restriction would reduce both the dangers of pyramiding speculators' access to funds, result in the application of more independent judgment on the desirability of the loan, and imbue the borrower with a somewhat greater sense of the responsibility he has undertaken. At least according to this theory, banks (the regulation of which is enforced by agencies with public policy functions) should be more likely than brokers (whose regulation is enforced by a policeman) to know whether loans are made for desirable (capital formation) or undesirable (commodity-inflation) purposes. This is theory; in practice the bank examiners do not investigate the purpose of loans, and the Federal Reserve and other supervisors do not control undesirable lending. But perhaps they could be required to do so.

The Institutional Customer

The victims of churning and the abuse of margin accounts are, most often, unsophisticated individual customers. Quite different problems arise in the relationship of the broker-dealer and the institutional customer, especially when the institutional customer is affiliated with a brokerage house—as, for example, the Oppenheimer Fund is with Oppenheimer & Co. Here a committee of "disinterested directors" of the fund meets monthly and reviews all business relations between the fund and the brokerage house, which gets about one-third of the fund's brokerage business. Oppenheimer as dealer cannot sell to the fund at all without prior SEC approval, which Oppenheimer would never seek, not because the SEC would say no, but because approval would take a month and yield ghastly publicity. Under the terms of the Investment Company Act of 1940, the fund also is barred from any action whatever in connection with blocks that Oppenheimer positions or underwritings in which Oppenheimer participates.

After 1978, by the terms of the 1975 amendment, a brokerage house managing money will have to give up the brokerage business to others; the industry is unhappy about the amendment, but an outsider cannot avoid suspecting that the pain from the new rule is the sort of thing that can be assuaged by a little judicious back-scratching. Probably because of doubts about the likely effectiveness of the prospective rule, the SEC staff in early 1977 floated a trial balloon emblazoned with the legend that the 1975 amendments merely permitted and did not mandate the separation of money management and brokerage functions: the SEC has a choice. The staffs of the congressional committees involved promptly shot down the balloon, but the principals have not yet been heard.

The rules are not quite so strict when the money a broker-dealer manages comes from a pension fund or some other source than a publicly offered mutual fund. To make sure they need never work through the right way of handling the conflicts that would arise from such a situation, Salomon Brothers refuses to manage money; so does First Boston Corporation. But even when the broker and the fund are institutionally at arm's length, the fund may rely on the broker for research and advice, paid for by brokerage commissions—and for sales of the fund itself, which have historically been paid for by brokerage commissions in addition to the broker-dealer's share of the sales load.

This "reciprocity" and the related reciprocity of brokerage orders given by a bank trust department as a reward for the maintenance of deposits in the bank have now been formally prohibited. Of course, it is still possible for a fund to acknowledge the excellence of the research services supplied by a big wire house that sells a lot of the fund's shares. And a senior executive of a large broker-dealer reports that the bank trust departments still "come around and say, 'We think your research reports warrant the business—and we expect you'll maintain your balances.' It's as blatant as that."

Statistics gathered for the Institutional Investor Study demonstrate that the rate of turnover of pension fund and other institutional portfolios increased rapidly through the later 1960s and that funds managed by investment advisors (rather than by banks or insurance companies) had the highest turnover rates. The text of the study is Delphic on this subject, advising, among other things, that "accounts having higher turnover rates, older accounts, and accounts holding larger numbers of stock issues have higher turnover rates."[11] But the figures are clear and revealing:

- For corporate benefit plans, bank trustees showed activity rates rising from 14 percent in 1965 to 26 percent in 1969; investment advisors managing similar accounts showed a rise in activity rates from 20 percent at the beginning of the period to 56 percent at the end.[12]

- For multiemployer plans, bank management showed activity rising from 10 percent in 1965 to 22 percent in 1969; investment advisors managing similar accounts showed a rise in activity from 14 percent at the beginning to 34 percent at the end.[13]
- For state and local government plans, bank management showed activity rising from 14 percent in 1965 to 38 percent in 1969; investment advisors managing similar accounts showed a rise in activity from 15 percent at the beginning to 48 percent at the end.[14]
- For endowments, bank management showed activity rising from 12 percent in 1965 to 23 percent in 1969; investment advisors managing similar accounts showed a rise in activity from 10 percent at the beginning to 29 percent at the end.[15]

Between 1965 and 1968, most of these investment advisors outperformed the rising market, refuting the general misconception that accounts that turn over rapidly must be losers and demonstrating that variable-sum conflicts of interest can produce profits for both parties. During what John Brooks has called the go-go years, employers were able to reduce their contributions to pension funds, and universities were able to increase faculty salaries, partly because increasing turnover of their investment portfolios yielded a greater rate of return to the institution. (The effective rate of return, moreover, was much greater than an individual investor could have hoped to achieve, for most of these institutions pay neither income tax nor capital gains tax on their profits.) But when the market turned down in 1969-70, the common sense ratio reasserted itself. Higher turnover was associated with greater losses; the volatile "special situations" section of investment management houses evaporated; and in the case of offshore funds and hedge funds, when investment advisors and brokers were relatively unrestricted in what they could do with customers' money, the conflicts of interest inherent in the compensation structure pushed down the value of customer investments at an accelerating pace.

These conflicts were succinctly stated by the Special Study a decade ago: "While it is the mutual funds themselves whose portfolio transactions provide the brokerage which constitutes the currency of reciprocity, its principal beneficiaries are not the funds but their investment advisors and principal underwriters."[16] The dimensions of the conflict have been reduced in recent years by the end of fixed commissions and by pressure for both the bar and regulatory agencies to push mutual funds, banks, and nonprofit institutions toward maximum recapture of commissions for the beneficiaries of the funds.

At the same time, however, the SEC has become increasingly concerned about the unprofitability of the broker-dealer firms and has moved to restrict the use of captive brokerage houses that rebate upstream to the controlling institutions—a practice forbidden on the New York Stock Exchange but encouraged on the Philadelphia- Baltimore- Washington Stock Exchange, which tripled its share of the exchange brokerage business between 1965 and 1972. Rule 19b-2, adopted by the SEC in early 1973 and challenged by the PBW Exchange, forbids firms to be members of any exchange unless at least 80 percent of their brokerage transactions are executed for customers other than their own internally managed accounts. Few institutions can meet this provision and thereby recapture commissions.

Rule 19b-2 requires 195 pages of a single-spaced mimeographed book to state, explain, and defend. Its basic purpose is to increase the potential capital resources of brokerage houses and specialist firms without placing at too great a disadvantage those exchange members who do not choose to accept institutional control. The rationale for the 80-20 percent provision is particularly interesting in the context of these present pages, because it asserts that, in a stock market context, other values may sometimes take priority over the total dedication to the client's interests usually demanded by a fiduciary relationship.

The Commission argues:

If a broker is dependent upon business from public customers he will have an incentive to perform these public services efficiently and in a manner that will not adversely impact on the markets, since his economic self-interest will be dependent on a consistent public order flow, maintainable only by public confidence that an account will be serviced efficiently and an order treated fairly. To upset the market with any particular order would be self-defeating since he must not discourage other public participation. On the other hand, if a member is engaged in transactions solely on behalf of an affiliated account his responsibility to and dependence upon that account may conflict with the trading restrictions and regulations of the exchange and with the interests of public investors at large. The mere potential for large investors to ignore the spirit if not the letter of such restrictions may undermine the confidence of other investors in the fairness of the nation's securities markets.[17]

That this principle reads better than it applies is suggested by the situation of J. Walter Sherman, proprietor of the small brokerage firm of Sherman, Dean & Co., and manager of a small mutual fund that participates in the firm's commissions.

Sherman reminisces:

The SEC was very happy with us. We had no load, no advertising, no salesmen, no giveups, no expenses—two and a half people altogether. We had an arrangement with the New York Stock Exchange by which the management fee on the fund was reduced by one-third of our commissions in handling business for the fund. We were the only firm doing that, and the Exchange didn't talk about it.[18] Then Abe Pomerantz had somebody from the Exchange on the stand in the Dreyfus case, and asked if it was possible for a brokerage house to make a fund the beneficiary of its commissions, and the man on the stand said very reluctantly, Yes, there was a way, and Sherman, Dean was doing it. . . . Now the SEC comes up with this eighty-twenty rule; and my firm, which the SEC was using as an example, turns out to be the only one that will have to lose its membership on an exchange . . . .

Under the 1975 amendments, as noted in the Oppenheimer discussion, the 80-20 rule will be junked, and brokers managing mutual funds will be compelled to do their funds' trading through other brokers. Sherman will be out of business under the amendments, too.

In fact, the situation is even more complicated than it seems. Much competent opinion calls for the "unbundling" of brokerage services, so brokers would charge separately for executions, research, portfolio planning, custodial care, and so forth. But mutual funds operate under state blue sky laws that establish ground rules for their accounting procedures, and banks must invest trusts by the terms of trust agreements. In the majority of the states, the law requires that operators of mutual funds treat direct payment for research or advice as their own expense, although they may make payments for brokerage out of the assets of the fund. Similarly, under most trust agreements, any research or advice purchased for the account must be taken out of the bank's fee, and brokerage commissions come out of the trust assets. Unbundling, therefore, would raise the cost of brokerage house research and might even make it unavailable to mutual funds and trust managers (or their shareholders and beneficiaries). The expenditure of "soft" commission dollars for the purchase of auxiliary services from broker-dealers is not necessarily a losing proposition for shareholders and beneficiaries. Congress, in the 1975 amendments, specifically revoked the state laws that now require bank and fund managements to pay for research from their own fees rather than from the income of the fund or trust. But consumer advocates are sure to object, and the congressional mandate is by no means sure to stand up in court.

In any event legal challenges to the mutual funds and the bank trust departments have cut deeper than that. If the fund or the bank is liable to the shareholders or beneficiaries for any unnecessary expenditure of brokerage commissions, the only really safe course of action for the managers is to buy and sell at net prices. Charged with paying more than a bare-bones minimum commission, the manager of an institutional fund could claim that the house that got the business delivers a better execution—but any junior lawyer could easily argue the case that such claims are self-serving, as well they may be.[19]

Judges are not likely to be very sophisticated in this area and might tend to interpret "best execution" as the fastest processing of the transaction. Although the SEC regards it as proper for a fund or a bank to give brokerage business as a reward for research, judges may well find such rewards improper in any case where the advice turns out to be wrong—something that can happen even in the best of families. But not even a senior lawyer can prove that a net purchase or sale of a large block of securities could have been made at a better price with some other dealer, because in the lumpy market of big blocks each transaction is unique.

It is fashionable to say that the institutional market is already a dealer market, and no doubt the trading of big blocks of stocks is made possible by the willingness of some houses to take positions. But most block trades go through an intermediary whose function is less that of a stockbroker than that of a real estate broker (or marriage broker). If we are indeed to change from a stock market formed as an auction market to a stock market openly operated on the jobber principle, the decision should be based on considerations of effectiveness and efficiency; it should not be a by-product of rulings by courts that have neither the resources to explore nor the competence to evaluate the consequences of judgments based necessarily upon retrospective evidence. Insistence on net prices rather than brokerage in today's market would lead to a proliferation of riskless principal trading—the worst of both worlds.

The Broker-Dealer Split

Differences in the compensation system of auction market and dealer market are the heart of the case for segregation of the broker and dealer functions. There is no question that broker-dealer firms change their emphasis according to the relative profitability of different market activities at different times. When auction market volume is heavy, wire houses hire squads of new customer's men, circularize mailing lists, and broadcast research recommendations. As has often been observed, selling razor blades is better than selling razors: very high volume with very small unit profits per transaction is the surest way to get rich. When auction market volume is light, Wall Street begins looking for a higher profit per item; and because the mark-up on dealer transactions is almost always higher than brokerage commissions, attention shifts to the dealer side of the firm.

"Interestingly," an article in *Barron's* proclaimed in late 1972, "new-issue volume [has risen] despite the lack of widespread public enthusiasm. Part of the gain stemmed from the relatively sparse brokerage business, particularly for the small houses, which turned to new issues to bolster revenues."[20] That this activity is not necessarily in the interest of customers is suggested by the next sentence in the article: "In addition, a number of institutions often found it necessary to buy stock in offerings they didn't want, to get a piece of the action in those they did." In other industries such behavior would be a clear violation of the Robinson-Patman Act.

Shifting of emphasis between broker and dealer activities are by no means indefensible, and in fact have defenders. William Freund, chief economist for the New York Stock Exchange, has observed that:

If you were to separate the agency markets and dealer markets in the United States, the results would be disastrous. The costs of agency [broker] trading would rise enormously. There are economies from the fact that agency and dealership are joint businesses. This is a labor-intensive business and a cyclical business. As you mitigate the cycle, you reduce risks. In 1968 the firms stressed brokerage; in 1969-70 they stressed bond trading and the commodities business. Without the alternatives, earnings would have been even more volatile than they were. The greater the risk, the higher the return has to be. If we had an agency business only, the volatility would be greater, you would have to have greater earnings in good years, there would have to be greater charges to customers.

A study conducted by Jacob Nussbaum of the New York Stock Exchange research department buttresses Freund's argument. From 1969 to 1970, securities commission income of NYSE member firms dropped from $3.035 billion to $2.157 billion. "Diversified" firms doing a predominantly retail business nevertheless increased their pretax return on capital from 8.5 percent to 9.5 percent; "nondiversified" firms doing a predominantly retail business saw their pretax return on capital drop from 5.7 percent to 1.4 percent.[21]

Many knowledgeable insiders see little or no problem in the combination of broker and dealer. "It was a big issue once, " says a senior partner of an important house, a man now in his sixties. "But you don't hear people talking about it any more." William J. Casey, while chairman of the SEC, observed, "The inside information thing is a lot more important than conflicts. Conflicts is mostly nickels and dimes; information is ten, twenty, thirty percent."

In a discussion of conflicts of interest at a section meeting of the American Bar Association convention in 1972, the late Thomas O'Boyle, then a senior partner of Shearman & Sterling, contrasted the real estate transaction, where "the decision to buy or sell is normally reached by the principal for his own reasons" with the securities transaction, "where the broker through his advice provides all or most of the motivation for the customer's decision to buy or sell." Under these circumstances, O'Boyle argued, the broker's temptation to earn himself some extra commissions is not really different in kind from the dealer's temptation to make himself some extra profit on a direct sale. The present law, he claimed:

> ... recognizes the facts of life in the securities business: (1) that the form of a particular transaction, whether agency [broker] or principal [dealer], is in large measure accidental and under the control of the broker-dealer; and (2) that, to the extent the public requires protection against the possibility that the broker-dealer, for reasons of financial self-interest, may induce transactions improperly, such protection is required regardless of the form of the transaction. In the aggregate this system imposes a duty on the broker-dealer to act fairly in all transactions . . ..[22]

SEC Commissioner Philip A. Loomis, participating in the same panel, was not quite so sure everything worked out that well. Historically, he pointed out:

> ... there is a tendency or there has been . . . to represent to customers of all kinds that the firm is sort of in the estate planning and advisory business and you can rely on them as your family counselors in the financial field. And when that impression is given, then you have a problem if you have a position or an upcoming underwriting . . . . When a customer has been accustomed to doing an agency business with a firm, a statement on

the back of the confirmation of a particular transaction that the firm acted in the legal capacity of principal is not going to be very informative or enlightening to him. Thus firms when they shift from one position to another have a duty to make a better disclosure than that . . . . I have noted a tendency in papers and financial magazines for firms to suggest that they are capable of moving a block because they have a distribution system. One wonders what disclosure they make to their customers, if that is what they are doing?[23]

The problems raised by the underwriting activities of broker-dealer firms, Loomis added, were minor next to the problems that could come up when a wire house handled a secondary distribution of a block of already issued stock that a large holder was selling off to the public. In an underwriting, he said, "the customer may review the prospectus which says who the managing underwriter is and who the people in the underwriting syndicate are and in that way disclosure may be accomplished." An exempt secondary provides no such information. "I remember," Loomis said, "when I was in private life and had not become accustomed to the securities business, I was very pleased when my broker called me to say he had a good stock for sale on which he wouldn't charge me a commission. I thought I was getting a bargain. That kind of thing is, I think, questionable."[24]

In at least some cases, "questionable" is an understatement. In one recent situation, a large wire house disposed of four hundred thousand shares of a major oil stock in a secondary after four weeks in which its customers had bought virtually none of this security on the established auction market. The firm's customer's men had received four weeks' notice of the upcoming secondary and knew their commissions would be two and one-half times the normal figure for each share sold in the secondary distribution.

A financial analyst who used to be a customer's man in the Washington area, for a different house, reports that he stopped working for brokers because of the pressure applied to him to sell secondaries:

You're told,"———himself [a New York principal of the House] is interested in this." They tell you, "You've got some good customers who will take some of it." If you object, they say, "Look, there's at least a fifty-fifty chance the customer'll make money on it." The sales pitch you're ordered to use is the "no-commission, no-odd-lot-differential" line. And when you make the sales, it's not just a bigger commission for you; the manager comes around with a tax-free hundred dollars in small bills . . . .

Slightly less anecdotal evidence for the existence of such procedures at the highest levels of the broker-dealer business comes from the SEC complaint against Merrill Lynch in the Stirling Homex case, settled by consent decree in summer 1975. The Commission in passing mentioned an unspecified issue sponsored by an unspecified affiliate of Merrill Lynch, peddled to the public through "the assignment of local sales quotas, mandatory evening and week-end solicitation sessions, and extra inducements to salesmen."[25] A pending class action against Merrill Lynch alleges that its customers have been in effect defrauded by the firm's open and aboveboard custom of awarding extra "sales credits" to registered representatives who successfully put out paper the firm has underwritten.

Recent years have seen a growth in what the trade calls "riskless principal" business, in which broker-dealers enlarge what are really commissions by taking a mark-up on purchases they make from others in reponse to a customer order to them. "People in the securities business don't want to take the risks of being dealers," says Donald Feuerstein, Salomon's chief compliance officer, "but they want the prices the dealer gets." It is widely understood in the business—although not much advertised—that the institution of a computerized "central market system" is likely to make this problem a great deal worse. In each wire house, the order room will have a computer-serviced CRT that displays the current bid-and-offer around the country. If a customer's bid exceeds the best offer by more than the amount of the commission, the broker-dealer will have an incentive to execute orders in-house on a net basis. When the dealer mark-up exceeds what would have been the brokerage commission on a sale to a managed account, the SEC has ruled in a case involving Kidder Peabody that riskless principal activity violates the Investment Advisors Act. On customer orders, however, the house may let its conscience be its guide.

Rule 394 of the New York Stock Exchange, which prohibited members from trading listed securities off-board, was lifted by government pressure at the start of 1977, presumably to permit Exchange members to seek the best markets for their customers. All Exchange rules still forbid in-house crosses not taken to the floor, but the wire houses are mounting a campaign for full freedom. Dean Witter has already announced plans to begin handling customer orders for fifty popular stocks without recourse to the marketplace.

SEC Rule 10b-10 as proposed will ventilate such activity and, at the least, discourage the creation of a system in which the firm takes both a trading profit and a commission on the in-house cross of orders for a listed security. It might be wise, however, to tighten the time-stamp rules on dealer trading so the customer can discover precisely rather than only approximately when his trade occurred.

Some institutional customers have already pressured brokerage houses to do business on a net basis, for reasons that are, to say the least, undesirable. This is an old story: the original SEC 1936 study on segregation of functions noted that "securities are largely bought and sold in the over-the-counter market for the account of institutional investors such as banks, trust companies, insurance companies, investment trusts, and educational and charitable foundations."[26] In 1971 the Institutional Investor Study reported that, in custodian accounts:

... some banks ... trade directly with the market-makers at net prices and add a charge equal to the commission which would have been charged had the bank given the order to a non-market-making broker-dealer. This charge is retained by the bank. At least six of the 50 banks studied charged a full NYSE commission on net trades; at least two others charged half of a NYSE commission. [27]

Under these circumstances the broker-dealer who does business net has yet another advantage to offer an important group of customers.

Such concerns were in the minds of the congressmen who sought to legislate separation of the broker and dealer functions in 1934 and only reluctantly consented to leave the matter for study by the new Securities and Exchange Commission. The report that recommended this approach spoke of the "inherent inconsistency in a man's acting as both a broker and a dealer. It is difficult to serve two masters." But, the report continued:

The combination of the functions of dealer and broker has persisted over a long period of time in American investment banking and it was found difficult to break up this relationship at a time when the dealer business was in the doldrums and when it was feared that the bulk of the dealer-brokers would, if compelled to choose, give up their dealer business and leave, temporarily at least, an impaired mechanism for the distribution of new securities. [28]

This was the argument of the industry. When the SEC report was finally written, its authors saw a quite opposite danger, especially with relation to the regional exchanges, where members were permitted to deal in listed stocks over-the-counter as well as on the floor:

One of the serious problems confronting the smaller exchange is a preference on the part of its members to fill orders as dealers over-the-counter rather than as broker on the exchange. This preference is based upon the fact that the opportunity for profit is greater in the former type of transaction than in the latter. [29]

It is generally believed today on Wall Street (and at the SEC) that the 1936 staff study of the "feasibility and advisability" of segregating the broker and dealer functions came up with a recommendation against segregation. In fact, the staff report was positive and brushed aside all worries about the impairment of liquidity that might result if firms could not be both brokers and dealers. [30] One of the few arguments against segregation to which the 1936 staff gave full credence was that it would destroy the regional exchanges, because the members, forced to choose, would opt to retain their dealer rather than their brokerage business. The current wave of reforms does in fact threaten to drown the regional exchanges, which may be just as well: they have stayed afloat, after all, mostly by offering opportunities to members to avoid certain New York Stock Exchange rules.

Confusions have long been common in this area. Old-timers recall that in the 1920s, before securities advertising was regulated, houses would advertise blocks for sale at a net price "plus commission," although they owned what they were advertising. Before the middle 1920s, the investment banking and brokerage functions were in practice quite separate; brokers did not make markets or take positions, and market makers did not deal directly with the public. Underwriters were wholesalers to the trade only; selling syndicates were paid for selling efforts and took no risks. Different functions, in short, were performed by different firms.

The creation of the Securities Investor Protection Corporation and the imposition of Rule 15c3-3 have reduced the danger to brokerage customers from the dealer activities of their brokers. (It is interesting to note in this connection that, as long ago as 1934, John M. Hancock of Lehman Brothers suggested to Congress a need to "prohibit loans from the brokerage portion to the issuing portion of the business."[31] Rule 15c3-3 was merely thirty-nine years late.) Former Chairman Casey is probably right in his belief that the inherent conflict of the mingling of broker and dealer functions is now a matter of nickels and dimes. Yet there remains something fundamentally distasteful about a situation in which a firm may choose in any given transaction to act as its customer's agent or as a retailer selling to him, without any real sense of the part of either the customer or his contact at the firm that these relationships are drastically different in both law and ethics.

Some authorities say there is no way out. Clearly, the London market, with its rigidly separated brokers and dealers, is an inadequate model for the United States. Among the opponents of segregating the broker and dealer functions, SEC Commissioner Irving Pollack, until recently head of the SEC Division of Enforcement, observes:

When you break things apart, you create all sorts of hand-washings and back-scratchings, like the eye glasses and eye doctor. The individual is better off when he knows there may be a conflict. The public is better off when everyone knows a conflict exists, and then says, "How do we regulate it?"

Unfortunately, not everyone does know that the conflict exists. Relatively few individual investors realize that their broker-dealer's commission on a secondary offering may be as much as five times his commission on a conventional brokerage transaction. At the very least, it would seem that a broker-dealer should be required to state prominently and clearly how he profits from any transaction.

IV • CONFLICTS OF ETHICS

Anyone at all acquainted with Wall Street knows professionals who are highly sensitive to their fiduciary obligations, who would never do anything that would give rise to even a suspicion that these obligations have been violated. But others work on Wall Street for whom such sensitivity is the mark of the fuddy-duddy.

According to the director of one of the larger training programs on Wall Street:

If you go before a bunch of registered reps who haven't established a business yet, forget about honesty. They're going to say *anything* to make a sale. For most of them, the classes we give in compliance are like a criminal learning what the law is—he wants to know how far he can go without its being a felony. These guys are twenty-six to twenty-eight. They're married and they have a family. They may have had their own small business, or they've been field officers in the military. They've traded, so they think they're big-deal brokers; in an academic sense, they know nothing. You give them six months' training, then put them in a situation where all the pressure is to make sales. When the market goes bad, they get panicky, even those whose personalities would incline them to comply. I don't blame them.

On Wall Street as in so many other areas of human endeavor, the way to get better performance is to recruit and hold better people. Most observers would say that in the 1960s the industry made real progress in that direction, but that since then, simply because Wall Street was attractive in the 1960s and is not attractive today, it has suffered some backsliding.

Unfortunately, the current organization of the financial markets also produces situations where the best of its intentions cannot avoid conflict-of-interest situations. When a partner in a broker-dealer firm sits on the board of an issuing corporation, the firm underwrites the corporation's new securities and sells its commercial paper; the firm's research department puts out reports on the desirability of purchasing, holding, or selling the corporation's securities; the customer's men recommend trading activity in the stock; and the money management department operates the corporation's pension fund investments—well, the conflicts are simply unmanageable.

Norman S. Poser, now executive vice president of the American Stock Exchange in charge of its Legal and Regulatory Division, insists on drawing a distinction between those conflicts of interest that a broker can handle through professional self-control and those created by the broker's undertaking to serve different parties whose interests are in conflict. The most obvious (but inescapable) conflict is the clash between the interests of two customers, both of whom have been led to believe that the broker-dealer is acting exclusively in their interests. Allocations of ''hot stocks'' (when there are such), priority in the receipt of important information, timing of purchases and sales in one fund or discretionary account rather than another—all these decisions have created anguish in the offices of responsible broker-dealers and bad blood between the industry and some of its most important customers. Only a few firms have taken the simple but highly desirable step of disclosing the priority of their accounts—announcing that they may rank institutional accounts ahead of individual accounts or large ones before small.

In most instances a customer is in a house because he has a personal relationship with the man who handles his account, and the conflict is resolved by political warfare on the inside; no individual normally feels an equal sense of responsibility to all his customers. But large broker-dealers sell their services as impersonal agencies to discretionary accounts and endowment or pension funds. They must then make important but essentially buried decisions regarding the allocation of personnel to one account rather than another, and the customer who gets the most perceptive, aggressive, or politically potent partner will receive the best service.

Such conflicts between the interests of different customers are found in bank trust departments, in advertising agencies, and (although they might not admit it) in large law firms. But the financial house also must solve the problem of a conflict between different kinds of clients. The matter comes to a head when a representative of a financial institution sits on the board of directors of a publicly held corporation.

This issue goes back at least sixty years, to the report of the Pujo Committee of the House of Representatives, followed less than a year later by the resignations of J. P. Morgan, Jr., and his partners from the boards of twenty-seven corporations. ''An apparent change in public sentiment in regard to directorships seems now to warrant us in seeking to resign from some of these connections,'' Morgan said. ''Indeed, it may be, in view of the change of sentiment upon this subject, that we shall be in a better position to serve such properties and their security holders if we are not directors.''[1]

In 1968, citing conflicts of duty, the Philadelphia brokerage house of Butcher & Sherrerd announced that its partners had resigned all thirty-six directorships they had previously held; members of some other brokerage houses privately backed off other boards. The problem is not easy to resolve. Companies that are young and moving into the big time especially benefit from the presence of an investment banker on the board. Such companies need help in handling what are for their executives new financial concerns, and no one will give such help more willingly than an underwriter who has at least to a degree put his reputation on the line by publicly promoting the company's stock. But directors are privy every day to information that is not and cannot be available to others, and the obligation to keep that information secret conflicts with a broker's obligation to customers who have bought or are thinking about buying or selling the company's stock.

And a broker-dealer who manages the underwriting of new issues does not avoid conflict of duties merely by not being on a board. A potential underwriter is at least as privy as any director to the internal operations of a corporation; an underwriter who will sell such securities directly to his own brokerage customers subjects himself to a totally irreconcilable conflict.

The price of a new issue is established by the lead underwriter with the advice and consent of the larger houses in his group. In his relations with the issuing corporation, the underwriter accepts an obligation to obtain the highest reasonable price the market can be expected to pay for the newly issued stock or bond. But in recommending purchase to its retail customers, the house accepts an obligation to promote only securities that are a good buy at the price. In setting a price, the managing underwriter who expects to sell mainly to his public customers is caught between the principals.

Wire house interests push in both directions at once: the house needs both issuing corporations to get itself new business and happy customers to keep the business going. Most people automatically believe that the house resolves these conflicts for the benefit of the corporation, which is part of its own crowd. In fact, such conflicts tend to be resolved in favor of the customer, because the mechanics of underwriting require the house to buy the new securities from the issuer before resale to its customers. If prices are set too high, and customers prove recalcitrant, the house rather than the issuer will take the loss. Unless the corporation has other business to give out—brokerage on its pension fund investments, for example—the pressure to make the selling job a little easier by keeping the price down may be greater than the pressure to get the corporate client top dollar.

Full disclosure will not eliminate this fundamental conflict of duties. The customer told that he is buying at a net price does not really understand that this means his broker, whom he considers his financial advisor, is, for this transaction, in the pay of the corporation selling the stock. Indeed, the spread is calculated to reflect the presumed difficulty of making final sales. Like the magazine or the television network, the wire house is selling its circulation—and its seal of approval. A large brokerage house with many customers gives a corporation sponsorship for a stock issue the house underwrites. But one of the clearest statements in equity is that a man cannot sell his agency. The broker-dealer that becomes an underwriter does in fact sell out the agency of its customers.

This criticism applies most obviously to Merrill Lynch, Pierce, Fenner & Smith, where underwriting revenues rose from just over $11 million in 1963 to just under $72 million in 1972, a compounded growth rate of 24.6 percent.[2] Merrill Lynch's president Donald T. Regan gives a long, eloquent justification:

There is an inherent good in the distribution of new issues, and for that distribution there has to be someone in the middle. The SEC holds us to a suitability rule—issues can't go direct to the public without an undertaking that the purchase is suitable for the customer. Under the suitability rule the distributor who is not an underwriter has the same liabilities as the underwriter: he has to stand behind the merchandise. Why shouldn't he underwrite?

We feel we know good merchandise when we see it. We try to hire good people whose outlook is not that of the seller or of the buyer, but of Merrill Lynch, Pierce, Fenner & Smith. Banks came to us to underwrite closed-end bond income funds [in 1973], and we turned them down, because we didn't think it was good merchandise. Turning them down cost us not only the underwriting business but also business from bank trust departments. We do have standards. We won't underwrite things we don't believe in, and we won't break faith with our customers.

The cardinal principle laid down by Charles Merrill is that our people should show our merchandise to their customers. If the customer says, "What do you think?", our account executive can say, "I think there's a better deal coming."

We give our people added recompense for selling the merchandise we underwrite. It will not move unless it's sold. Very few people are self-motivated to go out and buy a book that hasn't been brought to their attention, either.

Admitting all that, however, it still seems unfortunate that the nation's largest brokerage house, with 1.5 million individual customers, is also the nation's largest manager of corporate underwritings sold to the public. It may or may not be more efficient to do business this way: one man's economy of scale is another man's muscle. What is unquestionable is that an investment banker undertakes fiduciary obligations to his corporate client, and a broker undertakes fiduciary obligations to his customer, and, under the current system, it is impossible to avoid situations where these obligations conflict.

The problem shows up in bold relief whenever the government or the press—or customers—become upset about the use of inside information. Merrill Lynch has been the subject of several such flaps. Back in the go-go days of 1966, when fixed commission rates made brokerage for institutions almost unbelievably profitable, Merrill Lynch was managing underwriter for a proposed debt issue by Douglas Aircraft. During the course of readying this issue for market, the underwriting division of the firm discovered that the company's outlook was bleak. According to the SEC, this news was passed on to the institutional salesmen, who promptly got on the telephone and told some of their best customers to clear out their Douglas Aircraft. Ultimately, Lazard Freres was brought into the situation, scurried about soliciting merger bids from other airframe companies, and got the Douglas stockholders away from the brink via a takeover by McDonnell. But, says the SEC, a number of the funds the Merrill Lynch salesmen had called were long gone out of the stock, at a good deal better price, thanks to the information they received from Douglas's prospective investment banker.

This very clearly will not do, and after proceedings before the SEC, the funds involved were censured. Few inside or outside the business had a good word to say for the behavior of the Merrill Lynch salesmen. But meanwhile, in another part of the forest, the California courts were establishing an entirely contrary rule in a case growing out of the misbehavior of officers of Shearson, Hammill & Co. in connection wih the over-the-counter stock of USAMCO, described in a previous chapter. Here the undisputed facts were that a partner in the brokerage house, who was a director of the company, knew that claims for the stock being made by the firm's salesmen were in fact false. The bad news had not yet been made public, and the partner pleaded in his own defense that to release such information unilaterally would violate his duties as a director. The court disagreed: "We have been given no sufficient reason for permitting a person to avoid one fiduciary obligation by accepting another which conflicts with it.''[3] This case, *Black* v. *Shearson, Hammill*, was generally regarded as an aberration until spring 1973, when the SEC adopted its logic in starting an action for fraud, with Merrill Lynch again as the target.

The transactions that formed the basis for the latter complaint had occurred four years earlier in the stock of Scientific Control Corp., one of a number of companies which mistakenly decided in the later 1960s that its success in competing with IBM in the market for computer peripherals implied a real prospect of successful competition in the market for larger machines. On recommendations from the Merrill Lynch research department, a number of the firm's customers had bought the stock. Because Merrill Lynch customers held the stock, banks with loans endangered by the company's deepening financial troubles came to Merrill Lynch to propose a public issue that might carry the company through what the banks argued was a temporary period of losses. When the underwriting department looked into the company's condition, it discovered evidence of significant management miscalculations. The *Douglas* case was then recent history, and as part of its settlement with the SEC, Merrill Lynch had agreed to insulate the rest of the firm completely from the work of the underwriting department. Nothing was said to the researchers or the customer's men about what had been uncovered at Scientific Control; research reports and telephone calls from customer's men continued to recommend purchase of stock in a company that the underwriting department knew was only a few small jumps ahead of the sheriff.

In its public statement of reply to the SEC charges against it, Merrill Lynch pointed out that two of its customers with losses in Scientific Control had already brought and lost civil suits and that the federal judge in Dallas had found ''no evidence that Merrill Lynch's opinions in 1969 were in any way fraudulent or negligent or inaccurate in stating facts known by it about Scientific . . . . The evidence does not establish that Merrill Lynch was negligent in ascertaining facts about Scientific.'' But as a matter of common sense, a customer cannot help feeling that a financial analyst is negligent if he fails to pick up information about a stock that is available in the files of the underwriting department down the corridor.

Moreover, it appears increasingly likely that this commonsense view is in fact the law, that it was not *Black* v. *Shearson Hammill* but *Douglas Aircraft* that was the aberration, created by a need to find law to punish clear misbehavior. The SEC has persisted along the lines of *Douglas Aircraft* in the *Bausch & Lomb* case of spring 1973, when it moved against Faulkner, Dawkins & Sullivan for withdrawing the company's stock from its ''buy list'' without explanation, on the basis of bad earnings news prematurely revealed to a securities analyst by the chairman of the board of the company. (This action was widely noted by the trade, because the house was regarded as especially expert on this industry—as, obviously, it was.) But the *Scientific Controls* case, especially as presented to the press in the initial announcement (refinements have been attempted subsequently), does take a directly opposite tack, and it is that tack which the federal courts have been following in *Slade* v. *Shearson, Hammill*,

In this case a broker-dealer appears to have incurred liability to its customers by following the *Douglas Aircraft* decision to the letter, insulating its broker-age department entirely from bad news that was being developed by its underwriting department in an attempt to set up a new issue for a company called Tidal Marine. The brokerage department issued recommendations for the stock in all innocence, using only public information. A purchaser who bought pursuant to the recommendation and lost money thereupon sued, and the trial court ruled that the broker-dealer company as an entirety was liable for statements that any part of the company knew were false. On appeal the SEC intervened as *amicus curiae* and offered the following argument:

A BROKER-DEALER MAY NOT MAKE A RECOMMENDATION TO ITS CUS-TOMERS ON THE BASIS OF INFORMATION WHICH IT KNOWS TO BE SUB-STANTIALLY INACCURATE, EVEN THOUGH ITS KNOWLEDGE RESULTS FROM MATERIAL INSIDE INFORMATION WHICH IT IS NOT ALLOWED TO USE IN EFFECTING SECURITIES TRANSACTIONS.[4]

The situation at this writing, then, is that a broker-dealer assisting a cor-porate client in the preparation of a public issue undertakes an obligation to the client to help work out rather than publicize any difficulties their joint explora-tion may uncover. If the broker-dealer reveals this information to its cus-tomers, it is legally liable to other purchasers (following *Texas Gulf Sulphur* and *Douglas Aircraft*). If it fails to reveal this information to its customers, it is liable to those customers (following *Scientific Control* and *Tidal Marine*) for their losses. If it merely removes the stock from its buy list (following *Bausch & Lomb*) it is liable to administrative penalties. The SEC stoutly denies that it is forbidding broker-dealers to act as underwriters, but the conclusion of these lines of argument is exactly that. One may believe that the law *should* forbid any firm to exercise both these functions without admiring the way the SEC has gone about establishing this prohibition.

In the Stirling Homex matter, settled by consent decree in summer 1975, the SEC dropped the other shoe. Now Merrill Lynch was accused of: (1) failing to pass on information acquired as underwriter to this fraudulent operation; (2) mishandling the information developed by the research department; and (3) pushing the securities at its customers "in such a manner as to induce the customers to make hasty and ill-considered decisions." In accepting the con-sent decree, the court noted that the customers were suing—and that if by some chance the customers lost their suit the court retained the power to make Merrill Lynch disgorge its profits on its Stirling Homex business by means of a fine.

In the seminar on conflicts at the 1972 American Bar Association conven-tion, Richard H. Paul, a specialist in securities law at Paul, Weiss, Rifkind,

Wharton & Garrison, said that in looking at conflict situations "my own and only touchstone is this: in assessing them, I ask myself, 'How would it look in *The New York Times*?' "[5] Given that touchstone, debates about the price of new issues and secondaries should occur in the marketplace rather than behind closed doors at a firm representing both seller and buyer; what happens in the marketplace is more likely to be publicized. Prohibiting financial houses from performing conflicting functions might increase marginally the cost of marketing new issues, but putting daylight between people whose roles are in conflict is clearly preferable to putting walls between them.

Advance Information

Continuing underwriting relationships create conflicts whenever they mix with other financial functions. Nationwide investment houses like A.G. Becker and (until recently) Paine Webber, Jackson & Curtis, Inc., among others, have operated as specialists on the Midwest Stock Exchange; whenever the head office takes a participation in an underwriting in one of the stocks such firms service as specialists, they disclaim the exchange floor function until the underwriting is over and then recapture it. Another conflict, between the underwriting function and the money management function, is universally visible. Less visible, but nearly as obvious, is the unavoidable conflict in a house that has an underwriting department and also issues research reports and recommendations for the guidance of customers and potential customers.

As has often been noted, such reports lean overwhelmingly toward buy recommendations, because the solicitation of buy orders is something a customer's man can do with his entire list of old, new, and possible customers. The promotional value of sell recommendations is greatly limited, because the customer's man can use them seriously only on the restricted group that owns the stock. The business value of hold recommendations is nil, of course, because the broker makes money only when the customer trades rather than holds. Add to this natural bias toward buy orders the looming presence of a corporate client of the underwriting department—who certainly does not expect to see his own investment banker drive down the price of his stock with negative evaluations—and the financial analyst in the research department may well be distracted from focusing on the firm's duty to its customers.

When a firm has an investment advisory business among its subsidiaries, it may find itself legally liable for advice to a client that it should buy an issue sponsored by the firm. Teamster Local 816 in New York is now in the courts to recover from Hayden, Stone, Inc. (now Shearson Hayden Stone), and its Bernstein-Macaulay subsidiary $250,000 that the local's welfare fund invested in September 1971 in debentures of Topper Corp., which had been underwritten by the parent house. Two partners of Hayden, Stone were on the board of Topper, which filed under Chapter 11 of the Bankruptcy Act seventeen months after the debentures were recommended by Bernstein-Macaulay and bought routinely by the welfare fund. In the light of the previous pages, it should be noted that Merrill Lynch will not permit its investment advisory subsidiary, Lionel Edie & Co., to recommend to clients securities the parent is underwriting. The investment advisor is not a salesman. Even the absence of investment banking relations with corporations that must be rated, the broker who publishes research recommendations is soon enmeshed in conflicts. There is simply no way to avoid getting this information to some customers before others receive it: telephone calls must be made in some sequence, mail gets to people near the main office faster than it gets to people in the boondocks, telegrams are delivered with varying degrees of efficiency in different places. If it has discretionary accounts, the house will be wrong if it either puts research recommendations to work immediately for the benefit of these accounts (buying stocks on their behalf before other accounts even know there is a recommendation; this is forbidden by SEC rules) or arbitrarily withholds action in discretionary accounts until after independent customers have had a chance to move (depriving the discretionary accounts of possible gains to which the beneficiaries may well consider themselves entitled). During the late 1960s, when every week saw a new issue of "hot stock," priority questions became a source of constant irritation within brokerage houses that accept discretionary accounts and of suspicion among their customers. Most of the time, it seems, such questions were not answered in ways that helped the rich get richer; in fact, "hot stocks" were often allocated to accounts that had been doing poorly, as a courtesy to an unlucky customer and a favor to an endangered customer's man.

The conflict between duty to discretionary accounts and duty to other customers is magnified whenever the brokerage house manages investments for a fund or endowment. The conflict escalates when the management fee is calculated on a "performance" basis. One of the uglier stories of recent years concerned a fund associated with a published investment advisory service. Shortly before the end of the fund's fiscal year, the service put out a strong buy recommendation on a depressed stock held in some quantity by the fund. As the result of the increase in the price of that stock during the last two weeks of the year, the management of the fund (identical with the management of the published service) received not only the normal fee but an additional one based on the sudden success of the fund.

V • CONCLUSIONS

In the hearings on the abortive Banking Reform Act of 1971, Congressman Tom S. Gettys (Democrat-South Carolina) declared:

I am worried about our attempt here maybe to legislate morals. I do not think you can do it. I think we have got still to rely on industry responsibility, on individual responsibility, on individual character, and that if a man breaks the law, if he is crooked, if he is dishonest, then he should be punished according to the criminal laws of the country. But to start with the presumption that everybody is crooked and base our laws on that type of presumption, I think, is the wrong approach.

What is a conflict of interest? And on the interpretation of some of the people I talked with today, there is nobody that is competent to serve in the Congress, or to become a member of a board of directors of a bank, or a financial institution. You have got to have a history of having accomplished nothing at all, and being absolutely no good, in order to avoid a conflict of interest. To be able to serve on, say, the Banking and Currency Committee you cannot be a banker or if you are a lawyer you cannot serve on the Judiciary Committee. If you are a farmer you cannot serve on the Agriculture Committee. What is a conflict of interest, when does it start, when does it end?[1]

Gettys' frustration over the conflict-of-interest issue is easy to understand. Defined sweepingly enough, conflict of interest becomes a dominant feature of our society: the medical profession gives much better treatment to wealthy patients than to poor ones; journalists are expected to report the full story, yet need to cultivate their sources; an employee is torn between his responsibilities to his job and to his family.

Yet it is also clear that conflict of interest, covered up or ignored, can create enormous problems. Even when the abuses are only imagined, the resulting loss in confidence can corrode the institutions that make light of the dangers.

"Most conflicts questions," says Ralph S. Saul, formerly of First Boston Corporation, "subsume a healthy securities industry that performs an economic function. We are faced with an industry that is not healthy, and there are sounds of thunder that seem to portend a change in function."

History judges those it notices by their performance in emergencies, and Wall Street has a bad name because it handles emergencies badly. The recent economic crisis was not an exception. Blame can be laid on many hands: on the SEC and the Congress for simple-minded treatment of symptoms of underlying disorders, on the very many greedy men of finance who abused the opportunities for unconscionable profit that the market structure of the later 1960s presented, on the customers who formed an unrestrained cheering section for such activities, and on a financial press that found some of the shadiest characters the most interesting stories.

In fact, Wall Street has not been the villain of our present disorders, although there has been some jiggery-pokery around the market. Especially in the late 1960s, when the exchanges (and the SEC) allowed broker-dealers to include in their capitalization loans subject to repayment on demand, there was a great deal of early flight from sinking ships by those on the bridge, and there has clearly been some fiddling with capital requirements by major houses. Compliance officers at both the New York and American stock exchanges report that it is common to see houses whose officers are on the board of client corporations out on the floor buying stock just before the publication of good news or selling it just before the publication of bad news. In preparation for a block trade or an underwriting, sales are occasionally printed on the tape that was collusively arranged off the floor for just such purposes. But the computer-based routine check of all transactions on the floor almost certainly prevents the large-scale abuse of market mechanisms that was common fifty years ago.

An old-timer says that if enough people had cared, most inside information and collusive trading situations could have been policed long ago, without computer printout or organized staff surveillance: "The minute anything like that starts up the post gets noisy, with all sorts of brokers running over to find out what the hell is going on." Even today, the most important evidence on compliance comes from the telephone calls made after the computer has spoken. "There's a suspicious amount of activity in a stock," says an exchange compliance officer, "and you call the brokers involved. 'Who was your customer?' The buyer says it was a Swiss bank. The seller says it was the same Swiss bank. Well... we can cancel any trade." To some extent the concern over conflicts of interest reveals a step forward in the morality of the marketplace, for it means that open fraud has become far less common.

Still, the present is prologue no less than the past: what counts at any given moment is the trend line, and the trend line is troubling. The strength of the American financial markets has been their ability to command resources from a wide spread of the population. Increasingly, this breadth is being sliced away, and knowledgeable observers fear a time not far off when American financial markets, like those of Europe, will simply be places where large borrowers find access to an inner group that controls large pools of money. Meanwhile, broker-dealer firms that do maintain a public business are becoming what they like to call "financial department stores." The phrase is not new; it was used by the National City Corporation in the later 1920s, and what the phrase ultimately meant in that company, in terms of unloading mistakes onto the public, can be found in horrifying detail in the record of the Pecora investigations of 1933. Nothing that raw is likely to happen now, but it seems unlikely that the managers of a full-grown financial department store, enmeshed as they would be in recurring conflicts of interest and duty, could retain any great sensitivity to the nature of their commitments to the customers.

Quite a number of Wall Street houses are likely to disappear within this decade, and it is hard to see why they should not be allowed to go in peace. Between 1950 and 1970, the number of jobbers on the London Stock Exchange fell from 187 to 27, the number of brokers from 364 to 177, benefiting the institution and its customers alike. No comparable consolidation occurred here, largely because the embattled firms pulled their wagons into a tight circle and stayed in place, fighting off the Indians. The sin against the spirit of enterprise is not the conspiracy to raise profits (which is unlikely to hold up, because one greedy conspirator can connive for more than his share, breaking up the combination), but the conspiracy to protect against losses: fear makes all men brothers. Even after the trauma of 1969-70, many firms found it impossible to improve their efficiency in any substantial way, because most of the costs of the broker-dealer operation are personnel costs, and the stock market as it now operates is a terrible consumer of people time. From the little old men carrying manila envelopes to the brokers along the back streets in the Wall Street canyons, too many people are doing just what they did a quarter of a century ago, for wages or fees very much higher than they were.

Modern technology, especially computer-based information services and transfers of securities and money, can change the stock market into something very different from what exists today. What is needed is not a way to make that technology serve the old structure but a way to create the right new structure.

Almost every service sold to a large public involves a tax on some customers for the subsidy of others, and a competitor permitted to pick off the most profitable parts of the service—an insurance company that handles only selected risks, a discount-house book department that stocks only bestsellers, a microwave telecommunications system that works only between Chicago and St. Louis—can reduce costs to those it serves and present an appearance of greatly increased efficiency. But the social costs may be considerable, and the savings from eliminating redundancies and inefficiencies may prove illusory —as witness the 1974 struggles for scarce commodities or components by companies that had previously rewarded their comptrollers for cutting out the expenditures associated with "excess" inventories. (Then, of course, the pendulum swung to panicky hoarding.) If fair-trade laws had permitted the mom-and-pop store to survive on the city streets, the subsidy paid by the consumer in the form of higher prices might well have been less than the costs of urban decay. In this context the continuation of institutionalized conflicts can be justified in the new central market system.

But the stock market of the 1980s must abandon the fiction that institutional holdings valued in tens of millions of dollars are liquid assets. And disparate services must not be bundled together as a single commissionable item without a compelling reason for public benefit. The financial department store looks attractive to the industry, essentially because it offers opportunities to over-charge for some merchandise while using other merchandise as a loss leader. This is all wrong. Instead, the industry should be geared toward unbundling whenever a combination of services creates a conflict of interest. Certainly, no one should dream of tampering with the basic caveat contained in the Glass-Steagall Act: even the professionally unflappable should be terrified of the prospect of banks again becoming brokers on anything more than the most minimal service basis.

For anyone who watched the advertising business learn to live without a fixed 15 percent commission, the agony of modern Wall Street has elements of déjà-vu. If finance wishes to consider itself a profession, it must not flinch from the prospect of fee-for-service payment. The execution of customer orders for listed securities is not an inherently expensive activity; it is made to seem so only by the inefficiency of an archaic processing system and by a number of extraneous services provided under the commission umbrella. One can measure the costs of offering separate advisory and execution services, but one cannot measure the costs arising from the conflict of interest when the broker-advisor is paid in commissions. No doubt it would be more expensive on a short-term basis to make underwriters form a management group that would set the terms of the issue and have no relations with ultimate customers —but the long-run costs of coupling agency for buyer and seller in one house may be greater still. Organizing stock transfer and depository functions as trust companies (which can, under the Glass-Steagall Act, accept deposits) would eliminate the bar to an all-cash market with instantaneous transfer of cash and securities debits and credits—and put an end to the situation where a broker benefits from his customers' free balances.

In the rush to establish a central market system, most of these problems are now being neglected. The system proposed in March 1975 by the SEC Committee on the Implementation of a Central Market System is a computer network ganglion with tentacles reaching everywhere, each ending in a CRT. Every stock listed on the new National Securities Exchange would be traded on any of the nation's stock exchange floors or by over-the-counter dealers. Each floor would have at least one specialist in each stock accepted for trading. A broker punching his computer terminal would be presented with all the bids and offers from all the market makers in that security all over the country; he would then put his customer's order through to whatever floor (or office) was making the best market.

The proposal is vaguely troubling—mostly, perhaps, because the United States used to have a national securities exchange, called the New York Stock Exchange, which did the overwhelming bulk of all business in these markets. It was quite elaborately connected to brokerage offices all over the country, with tickers to report trades virtually as they occurred, and telephone lines by the hundreds to permit, among other things, rapid transmission of the bid-and-asked prices at the trading post for all the listed stocks. Part of the information system—the activity and feel around the post—was available only to insiders, but they were the ones who needed it most and could interpret it best. Although a number of securities traded on the New York Stock Exchange also were traded on the Midwest and Pacific exchanges, New York was dominant. During the hours when the New York Exchange was open, specialists on the floors of the other exchanges were likely to adjust their inventories by buying or selling on the New York Exchange, if the stock in question was an NYSE listed stock. Only the New York market was deep enough to handle large orders. Exactly *how* deep the New York market was could never be determined with any certainty, because the specialist revealed neither the content of his book nor the dimensions of his own inventory. But an experienced man approaching a post could pick up impressions of size and confidence on his antennae.

For various reasons, some of which have been presented here, this system is no longer adequate even to its own task in trading the most widely held securities. But the new system will have its costs as well as its benefits. The locus of decision will move from the man on the floor, who is in direct touch with the trading situation, to a man in an office, who is necessarily isolated in some degree from the day's activity. Moving trades to secondary markets will become much easier. To get out from under the New York City stock transfer tax, to find markets where costs are a little lower, or simply to keep others in the dark, the members of the new national market are likely to shift business out of New York. In the meantime they will be subject to all the old conflicts pressures and some new ones. There are always reasons, after the fact, for having gone to one market maker rather than another, and not even the most assiduous supervisors of the National Securities Exchange will be able to police the costly back-scratching that arises from conflicts of interest.

The recent legislation on the organization of the securities markets addressed itself to improving the efficiency of the system much more than to conflict problems. Lawyers hunting out villainous behavior to attack and social critics seeking shoddy practice in capitalist institutions can look forward to finding the objects of all their respective quests in the years ahead.

NOTES

I. Introduction

[1] Securities and Exchange Commission (SEC), *Report on the Feasibility and Advisability of the Complete Segregation of the Functions of Dealer and Broker* (Washington, D.C.: June 20, 1936), p. xiv.

[2] Ibid., p. xv.

[3] Ibid., p. 75.

[4] Redistribution of a block of stock already in the hands of a previous purchaser. The sale is handled off the exchange by a securities firm or a group of firms. Shares are usually offered at a fixed price related to the current market price of the stock.

[5] In the text, when no source is given for a quotation, it may be assumed that the statement was made in the course of an interview.

[6] SEC Release 34-12806, September 16, 1976, p. 2.

[7] Arthur Dewing, *Financial Policy of Corporations* (New York: Ronald, 1953), vol. 1, p. 8.

II. Zero-Sum Conflict Situations

[1] In theory, receipts from short sales are deposited with another broker as security for stock borrowed to enable the customer to make delivery. For the lender of the stock, these receipts are an additional source of money. In the large firms, such borrowings are done in-house. The broker in any event has the use of the payment the customer must make (from 50 to 100 percent of the market price, depending on Federal Reserve and Exchange regulations) to initiate a short sale.

[2] Hurd Baruch, *Wall Street: Security Risk* (Washington, D.C.: Acropolis Books, 1971), pp. 30-31.

[3] *Thirty-eighth Annual Report of the Securities and Exchange Commission* (Washington, D.C.: 1972), pp. 144-145.

[4] Ibid. Wholly accurate figures are impossible to get, because more than half the assets and nearly half the liabilities of registered broker-dealers as reported by the SEC are in areas "not related to the securities business," that is, insurance. At least half the $10 billion or so of equity in the firms should also be credited to the insurance business.

[5]Baruch, op. cit., p. 41; additional calculations by the author; Baruch includes in his totals customers' fully paid securities not segregated in the firm's vaults, which are not quite the same as cash on hand.

[6]SEC, op cit., p. 143.

[7]When a security is borrowed for delivery to the purchaser as the result of a short sale, the selling broker must deposit with the lender an amount equal to the entire market price on the day of the transaction. This money is supplied by the proceeds of the sale, but there may be a friction loss, because the stock must be borrowed before it can be delivered and thus there is a brief need for credit to complete the transaction.

[8]This stopgap use of customer balances is permitted, however, only for the thirty calendar days after the date of the sale; if the customer has not delivered by then, the broker must either make the customer produce the stock he owes or take the risks on his own rather than on his customer's money.

[9]The base rate is officially the ''call loan rate,'' but there are no call loans in American finance these days, and so the rate is really the prime rate for short-term money.

[10]SIPC, a government corporation with reserves provided by assessments on securities firms, protects customers against any losses of cash or securities up to $50,000 (not to exceed $20,000 in cash) in the event of insolvency of broker-dealers.

[11]Baruch, op. cit., p. 25.

[12]The same ''conflict'' occurs when a broker recommends a stock in which he holds a position; the increased value of his inventory is no less real than the dealer's quick trading profit. Indeed, the dangers here are even greater, because the *Chasins* rule does not apply. But the conflict is not of the direct zero-sum nature that is our concern in this chapter, because the house does not benefit at its customer's expense from the higher price of the security. If the advice is good, both gain; if the advice is bad, both lose—assuming, of course, that both get out together.

[13]SEC, *The Financial Collapse of the Penn Central Company: Staff Report of the Securities and Exchange Commission to the Special Subcommittee on Investigations, House of Representatives* (Washington, D. C.: U.S. Government Printing Office, 1972).

[14]Dun & Bradstreet's commercial paper rating activities were transferred two years ago from the National Credit Office to its Moody's Diversified Services subsidiary.

[15]*The Financial Collapse of the Penn Central Company*, p. 283.

[16]Ibid., p. 287.

[17]Ibid., p. 290.

[18]Ibid., p. 289.

[19]Ibid.

[20]Chicago Board Options Exchange, *Understanding Options* (Chicago: 1974), p. 1.

[21]Although specialists are permitted to do business with individuals, the rules prohibit them from taking into their book small market orders ''not held'' to a price; doing so could cut out the broker and create direct conflicts between the specialist's market-making functions and his service to exchange customers. But they are permitted to help when the broker is assembling a large trade.

[22]SEC, *Report of the Special Study of Securities Markets* (Washington, D.C.: 1963), vol. 2, p. 143.

[23]New York Stock Exchange, ''Description of New Measures of Specialist Performance,'' mimeo (February 1972), p. 1.

[24]''Report to the Securities and Exchange Commission by the Advisory Committee on a Central Market System,'' mimeo (March 6, 1973), p. 27.

[25]SEC, *Institutional Investor Study Report*, House Doc. 92-64, 92nd Cong., 1st Sess. (Washington, D.C.: March 10, 1971), vol. 4, p. 1596.

[26]Ibid., p. 1597. It should be noted in fairness that the trader sold another thirty-six thousand shares at higher prices later that day from other discretionary accounts but did not entirely dispose of its own position for three weeks; the final reckoning showed the trader with a loss of $1,000 on the position and commissions of $25,000 on the transaction.

III. Variable-Sum Conflicts

[1]Reynolds & Co., 39 SEC 902.

[2]J. Arthur Warner Co., SEC Litigation Releases 910, 920.

[3]*The Wall Street Journal*, December 17, 1973.

[4]New York Stock Exchange, *Supervision and Management of Registered Representatives and Customer Accounts* (New York: 1967), p. 16.

[5]Ibid., p. 23.

[6]Not the least of the problems in regulating (or writing about) the stock market is the blindness of the law to the greed and cupidity of customers. Legislators assume that broker-dealers can protect themselves against antisocial customers but that customers are defenseless against chiseling brokers. This assumption by no means covers all the possible relationships of broker-dealers and customers.

[7]New York Stock Exchange, *Supervision and Management of Registered Representatives and Customer Accounts*, p. 25.

[8]Board of Governors (Federal Reserve System), *Securities Credit Transactions* (Washington, D.C.: November 1971), p. 43.

[9]*The Financial Collapse of the Penn Central Company*, p. 307.

[10]*Naftalin & Co., Inc. v. Merrill Lynch, Pierce, Fenner & Smith, Inc.*, CA 8 71-1634, 71-1672, cited in SEC 1972 Report, p. 83.

[11]*Institutional Investor Study Report*, vol. 3, p. 1048.

[12]Ibid., p. 1105

[13]Ibid., p. 1149.

[14]Ibid., p. 1198.

[15]Ibid., p. 1244.

[16]*Report of the Special Study*, vol. 1, p. 171.

[17]SEC, *Adoption of Rule 19b-2 Under the Securities Exchange Act of 1934* (Washington, D.C.: 1973), pp. 127-128.

[18]In fairness to the large houses that manage mutual funds, it should be noted that the Institutional Investor Study found that "the broker-dealer affiliation factor is associated with approximately a 12 percent reduction in fee rate. The result of the brokerage offset is particularly striking for registered investment company [i.e., mutual fund] accounts. The reduction in fee ratio for these accounts is approximately 40 percent, other things being the same," Vol. 2, p. 213.

[19]In fairness, again: the SEC has found that in the early years of negotiated commissions "some brokerage firms with affiliated investment companies" have charged those affiliates "the equivalent of the lowest rate the broker has negotiated at arm's length with any unaffiliated institutional customer on similar transactions." *Adoption of Rule 19b-2*, p. 142n.

[20]Charles Biderman, "Hot and Cold: New Issues, Secondaries Will Set a Record This Year," *Barron's* (November 20, 1972), p. 3.

[21]Jacob Nussbaum "The Impact of Diversification Upon the Brokerage Industry," New York Stock Exchange Research Department, mimeo (September 8, 1971).

[22]"Conflicts of Interest and the Regulation of Securities: A Panel Discussion," *The Business Lawyer* (January 1973), p. 569.

[23]Ibid., pp. 578-579.

[24]Ibid., p. 579.

[25]*The Wall Street Journal*, July 3, 1975, p. 10.

[26]SEC, *Feasibility and Advisability of Segregation*, p. 67.

[27]*Institutional Investor Study Report*, vol. 4, p. 2257.

[28]H. R. Report No. 1383, 73rd Cong., 2d Sess., p. 15 (1934), cited in *Rule 19b-2*, p. 61.

[29]SEC, *Feasibility and Advisability of Segregation*, p. 52.

[30]"The prominence of the quality of liquidity increases the inclination, already too prevalent, of buyers of securities to think in terms of the appreciation of the value of the security rather than the promise of continued and substantial earnings. This inclination impairs the value of the

market as an accurate barometer of investment opportunities and thus tends to vitiate the judgments of even those buyers who do think in terms of underlying worth." Commentators on market conditions, the report urged, should not "regard existing liquidity as a fetish." Ibid., p.100. Wow!

[31] Vincent P. Carosso, *Investment Banking in America* (Cambridge, Mass.: Harvard University Press, 1970), p. 378.

IV. Conflicts of Ethics

[1] Carosso, op. cit., p. 180.

[2] Merrill Lynch, Pierce, Fenner & Smith, Inc., *Annual Report 1972*, pp. 12-13.

[3] 72 Cal. Rep. 157 @161; cited in Norman S. Poser and Raymond L. Aronson, "Conflicts of Duty," *The Review of Securities Regulation* (New York: Standard & Poor's, November 4, 1969), vol. 2, no. 10, p. 825.

[4] U.S. Court of Appeals for the Second Circuit, *Slade* v. *Shearson, Hammill*, brief of the Securities and Exchange Commission *amicus curiae*, mimeo, p. 4.

[5] "Conflicts of Interest and the Regulation of Securities," *The Business Lawyer* (January 1973), p. 568.

V. Conclusions

[1] *The Banking Reform Act of 1971*, Hearings before the House Banking and Currency Committee, 92nd Cong., 1st Sess. (Washington, D.C.: 1971), p. 302.

[2] British Financial Institutions, HMSO (London: 1971), p. 45.

Nonprofit Institutions
by Chris Welles

AUTHOR'S PREFACE

As a journalist I approach the task of reporting on conflicts of interest in nonprofit institutions somewhat differently from an academic researcher. Although I read and studied reports from over two hundred endowment funds and foundations, as well as much other material, the findings of fact and conclusions of this report are not based on rigorous statistical analyses or formal surveys and questionnaires. My research consisted primarily of wide-ranging interviews with various individuals who I thought might be knowledgeable about what conflicts of interest exist, how serious they are, and what ought to be done about them. Having weighed and judged the diverse viewpoints I encountered and having examined as much information as I could obtain from endowment funds and foundations, I gradually developed my own conclusions.

This report focuses principally on foundations and educational endowments. Although such institutions as hospitals, symphony orchestras, ballet companies, and museums also operate on a nonprofit basis, foundations and educational endowments hold the bulk of the assets in this category.[1] (Churches also hold immense assets, but because they are subject to few disclosure requirements, little information is available to the public about their holdings or financial operations.) According to figures compiled by the New York Stock Exchange (NYSE), as of 1975, foundations owned $22.1 billion in NYSE-listed stocks, educational endowments owned $7.2 billion, and all other nonprofit organizations owned $8.7 billion.[2] In 1975 the Securities and Exchange Commission, which does not compile data on nonprofit institutions other than foundations and endowments, put the total assets of foundations at $34.2 billion and those of educational endowments at $13.8 billion.[3] If the other nonprofit institutions invested a similar portion of their assets in NYSE stocks, the total assets of nonprofit institutions would amount to about $62 billion (slightly less than the $66 billion held by mutual funds[4]), of which foundations and endowments would account for about 77 percent.

The investment-related conflicts of interest to which foundations and educational endowments are prone seem quite similar to those of other nonprofit institutions. The basic problem is that all nonprofit institutions, particularly those that receive contributions from affluent donors or investment income from endowments, depend on benefactors from the business world. Thousands of nonprofit institutions are unable to obtain sufficient support from government programs, operating income, or donations from the general public. Businessmen and those associated with business wealth enable these institutions to survive. Businessmen and their heirs are virtually the only creators of private foundations, which themselves are important sources of funding for other nonprofit intitutions. Although these individuals are generally well intentioned, they sometimes have difficulty separating their philanthropic and fiduciary activities from their personal business interests. When they permit the latter to take precedence over the former, the conflict of interest inherent in the situation degenerates into abuse, and the affected nonprofit institution, as well as its beneficiaries, inevitably suffers.

My research suggests that although conflicts of interest and conflict abuses in foundations and educational endowments may be less serious now than in the past, they still remain widespread. Surprisingly little action is being taken to combat them. In response to some particularly lurid revelations in the 1960s, the Tax Reform Act of 1969 imposed some important controls on private foundations. Yet several major problem areas were relatively unaffected by the act and continue to breed abuses. No federal laws and only a few, generally very mild or unenforced, state laws deal with conflicts of interest in other nonprofit institutions. But recent events indicate that unless trustees of nonprofit institutions take the initiative in purging their organizations of conflict-of-interest problems, they may eventually face a new wave of public criticism, legal challenges, and perhaps even new federal legislation.

EDUCATIONAL ENDOWMENTS

I • INTRODUCTION

In 1966 Ford Foundation president McGeorge Bundy made his now famous observation that "over the long run caution has cost our colleges and universities much more than imprudence or risk-taking."[1] This criticism, reinforced in later pronouncements by the Ford Foundation,[2] spurred a massive overhaul of investment policies at many colleges and universities. A large number of schools, which had invested heavily in fixed-income securities and steadfastly eschewed all but minor commitments in equities, hastily built up their stock portfolios. They made their purchases at what proved to be the peak of the 1960s bull market.[3] During the inflationary-recessionary 1970s, of course, many endowment managers wished they had held onto their pre-Bundy portfolios.

But Bundy's statement also led to beneficial change in the way many colleges and universities managed their endowment funds. Previously, according to Roger F. Murray, professor of banking and finance at Columbia University and a man with wide experience in nonprofit institutions, many if not most funds used "management by crony."[4] The funds were often little more than the private preserves of the schools' boards of trustees; often, they were incestuous hotbeds of interest conflicts and abuses. In many cases the funds investment advisors, banks, and brokers were so tightly involved with the schools' trustees, donors, and alumni that the interests of the fund and the school were lost in a tangle of cozy self-dealing and mutual back-scratching. Not only the public but even concerned beneficiaries of the funds such as students and faculty members were usually ignorant of these relationships because most funds released little if any substantive information about investment policies, portfolio composition, or the identities of their managers or advisors. In a 1970 article in the Philadelphia *Evening Bulletin*, business writer J. A. Livingston provided the following illuminating example of the sort of conflict situation common during this period.[5]

For many years before the bankruptcy of Penn Central in 1970, Howard Butcher III, a senior partner of Butcher & Sherrerd, one of Philadelphia's largest brokerage houses, had been a trustee and chairman of the investment committee at the University of Pennsylvania. Butcher was not only a Penn alumnus but also one of Penn's most important donors. At the time, his firm was the paid investment advisor to and one of the principal brokers for the university's $100 million endowment fund. Butcher also was on the board of the Penn Central Railroad Company. At one time he had been the largest individual holder of Penn Central stock, and he had been instrumental in bringing about the merger between the Pennsylvania Railroad and the New York Central. Butcher was an enthusiastic booster of Penn Central's stock; at his urging, his family, several friends, and a number of his firm's customers had become major stockholders. His firm also was a holder and an underwriter of Penn Central securities issues. At Butcher's recommendation the University of Pennsylvania's endowment fund had paid more than $8 million for 113,214 shares. This block was the largest in the university's portfolio, except for American Telephone & Telegraph Co. The university's president, Gaylord P. Harnwell, was on the railroad's board as well.

During 1969 and 1970, Penn Central's fortunes began faltering badly. Butcher, convinced the troubles were only temporary, steadfastly refused to lighten the university's holdings. For a time he even disregarded the instructions of the rest of the investment committee to unload. Only when Penn Central's difficulties become so extreme that even Butcher could no longer overlook them did he commence a wholesale dumping of the stock. Yet according to Livingston, Butcher was more diligent in disposing of his, his family's, and his friend's Penn Central holdings than of the university's. The price of the railroad's stock was falling steadily, and because, on average, the university's shares were sold later than those of the other holders whom

Butcher advised, Penn realized a lower average price per share than the other holders. According to Livingston, this delay may have cost the university as much as $279,639; the university's total loss on its Penn Central investment was $3,029,807.

Butcher himself does not dispute Livingston's figures, but he denies any deliberate wrongdoing. In putting Penn into the stock, he maintains, "I thought I was doing the best thing for the university. It was just bad judgment on my part." But if Howard Butcher and his firm had not been so tightly involved with Penn Central, the university might have acquired fewer Penn Central shares, sold them sooner, and lost less money.

Bundy's recommendations have helped endowments in a number of cases to free themselves from incestuous relationships of this nature. In recent years trustees at many schools have retained independent investment managers, whose selection has been based solely on competence and cost, to improve investment performance and reduce the potential for conflict-of-interest abuses. Although retaining the right to establish broad guidelines, the boards of many endowments have given the managers complete discretion in making specific portfolio selections. A few schools with large endowments, such as Harvard and the University of California, have established professional in-house management teams who enjoy considerable discretion to assemble portfolios under broad guidelines laid down by the trustees. Increasingly, trustees designate custodian banks and brokers solely on the basis of competence, performance, and cost.[6] Many schools now publish detailed financial reports containing descriptions of investment policy, breakdowns of portfolio holdings, and reports on investment performance.

As a result of these developments, when I began my research for this report, I assumed that the traditional management by crony form of conflict of interest had all but disappeared and that the principal problem area now lay in the rapidly expanding partnerships among educational institutions, corporations, and the government.[7] Colleges and universities today are major recipients of corporate and government grants and are frequent partners with corporations in research ventures. For example, in North Carolina, Duke University, the University of North Carolina, and North Carolina State University have joined forces to build and maintain a fifty-two-hundred-acre enterprise known as Research Triangle Park. The park houses government and industrial tenants including the U.S. Army, the Environmental Protection Agency, IBM, Monsanto, Becton Dickinson, and Richardson-Merrell. Among other things the three schools share the surpluses of the nonprofit foundation that operates the park and maintain a joint research institute that provides services to industrial and government tenants. According to a Research Triangle Park brochure:

The facilities and technically skilled staffs of the three schools work closely with triangle industrial and government personnel in a wide variety of fields involving planning and execution of cooperative research. Such association has resulted in close personal relationships and the free exchange of information of mutual interest.

Other colleges are going into business themselves, establising subsidiary corporations to purchase revenue-producing property. Jerome P. Keuper, president of the Florida Institute of Technology, which operates several for-profit subsidiaries, has been quoted as saying, "We're going to get into anything that looks profitable, is honest, and doesn't compete unfairly with business in our community."[8]

These trends may, over time, lead universities to orient their curricula, or the thrust and philosophy of their educational services, toward furthering their outside relatonships rather than toward meeting the needs of their students. This shift may already be taking place. One observer sees

. . . a coalescence of higher education and business that is a radical departure from the older notion of the university as an independent seeker of truth, beholden to no one.

In the past the university was relied upon to serve as a social critic, insulated from the kinds of pressures that inevitably dictate accommodation in business and government. Today that independence is rapidly being lost as the universities join with industry and government in mutually appealing endeavors.[9]

Universities, of course, have never been as independent or as insulated as this quotation suggests. Yet whatever the broader implications and problems presented by this coalescence, no informed observer questioned for this report considered its impact on the investment of educational endowment funds to be significant. Of course, the alliance of universities, industry, and government may yet generate conflicts of interest and actual abuses at educational endowment funds, but at present, the main conflict-of-interest problem of endowments is still management by crony.

Although many institutions have made significant progress in this area, the improvement over the pre-Bundy days amounts to less than is generally believed. Conflicts as blatant as those in the Penn Central episode at the University of Pennsylvania are unusual, and instances of deliberate self-enrichment by fiduciaries appear to be very rare. But boards of trustees that rigorously maintain arm's-length relationships and pursue the best interests of the endowment fund above all still tend to be more the exception than the rule. And in far too many cases, colleges and universities still consider management of their endowment funds to be a private matter between the school and its trustees and refuse to release anything more than the most rudimentary data about their funds.[10]

The available information suggests that the following conflict-of-interest situations are not uncommon:

• A businessman who is a trustee of a university gives the school a large block of his company's stock. Although the endowment fund's managers are technically free to dispose of the block if they judge it to be unsuitable for their portfolio, they hold it for fear of antagonizing or upsetting the donor, who clearly believes that his company's stock is a good investment. As a result the school's portfolio is insufficiently diversified and thus exceedingly risky. If gifts to the fund are pooled and the fund, because of the large block it is holding, performs badly or has a very low yield, the contributions of other donors also diminish in value. Moreover, in such situations as tender offers, management compensation plans, and shareholder resolutions, the trustees and managers invariably vote the block in favor of management, even though doing so may not be in the best interests of the institution as a stockholder.

- Some endowment funds deal with investment advisors whose officers serve on the boards of trustees or who are associated with major donors and fund-raisers, rather than seek out the best and least expensive advisory services regardless of such associations. Other funds are internally managed, and the trustees' investment committees are heavily involved in stock selection. When the portfolio does not perform well, the other trustees are reluctant to be as critical of their peers, friends, and business associates or as eager to alter investment procedures as they would be if the portfolio were being managed by an outsider.
- When trustees are involved in the stock selection process or the advisor is linked to the trustees, the fund tends to invest in companies with ties to the trustees. This favoritism is not based on some nefarious scheme to manipulate stock prices but is a natural by-product of mutual friendship, nourishment, and support. But the portfolio that results is seldom what a disinterested manager would have chosen and may not be in the best interests of the fund.
- Instead of making use of firms that offer the best executions at the lowest price, a fund directs brokerage commissions to firms associated with the school's important donors, fund-raisers, and trustees. Similarly, the fund maintains banking and custodial relationships with institutions selected not for the high quality and low cost of their services but for their ties to trustees, donors, and fund-raisers.

To the extent that considerations other than the interests of the endowment fund influence the selection of its managers, advisors, and banks, they inhibit efforts to obtain services at the lowest cost and to achieve the best performance. Hence, they may impose on colleges and universities costs that are unnecessary and unjustifiable, given the financial plights of many schools. But such costs are difficult to measure, and they may not be large. According to one estimate, a typical endowment fund's custodial, administrative, professional, and brokerage costs per year are about 0.5 percent of average assets.[11] Fees to an outside manager may run between 0.1 percent and 1 percent. Paying at a rate of 1 percent of assets for all these expenses, a $50 million fund would incur total costs of $500,000 annually. Of course, a portfolio containing a large block of donor stock may not necessarily perform worse than a more disinterestedly assembled portfolio, and a trustee-linked investment manager may not necessarily achieve less satisfactory results than a disinterestedly selected manager. Moreover, the contribution of endowment fund income to college and university budgets is low and continues to decline. A survey of 214 colleges and universities indicates that, as of 1971, endowment income accounted for only 6.9 percent of the schools' total income.[12] Although endowment income is more important to independent institutions, whose financial health is sometimes precarious, than to state-supported institutions, the direct financial cost of endowment fund conflict-of-interest abuses is probably small relative to the other expenses of the average college or university.

Other costs, although less quantifiable, may be more significant. Since Watergate, public concern has focused on the ethical conduct of the nation's institutions. In the past, the trustees of nonprofit institutions tended to regard themselves as free of the outside scrutiny and accountability to which corporate board members were properly subject. Even today, very few colleges or universities have adopted a formal conflict-of-interest policy for their endowment funds. According to one observer:

Since there are no "owners" in the ordinary sense of the term, no specific beneficiaries, no general or uniform rules for the disclosure of financial or other types of information, nonprofit trustees in effect are not answerable to anyone. Within very broad limits, they are their own masters. The words "irresponsible power" are harsh words, but they are relevant . . . . The trustee's problem is compounded—or simplified, depending on the point of view—by the absence of any systematic, generally accepted criteria that define satisfactory performance on their part.[13]

As a result of some recent events, though, trustees are now in danger of losing some of this freedom. In compliance with recently adopted accounting standards, colleges and universities, as well as other nonprofit institutions, may soon be including in their financial statements lists of "related party transactions," many of which may carry conflict-of-interest potential. Such disclosure should focus public attention on once secret relationships, such as links between trustees and investment managers. Moreover, a recent court finding[14] that the trustees of a nonprofit hospital had breached their fiduciary duty through self-dealing and other abuses may have set a precedent, according to some attorneys, for similar court actions against college and university trustees.

Lawsuits are not the only potential problem. To a much greater degree, perhaps, than any other single group of institutions (with the possible exception of churches), colleges and universities are viewed by the public as upholders of the best standards of ethical conduct. Schools that permit questionable practices in the management of their endowments may increasingly find themselves subjected to embarrassing and damaging criticism.

To be sure, trustees and university officials have made substantial progress in bringing impartial, professional management to endowment funds. Yet the evidence indicates that there is still a long way to go before the regrettable traditions of management by crony are completely expunged.

II • THE TRUSTEES

The root of most endowment fund conflicts of interest is the trustee. Formally, the board of trustees of a nonprofit institution, like the board of directors of a for-profit corporation, is the principal policy-making body. In addition, non-profit institutions, much more than corporations, use board membership as an honorific mechanism; at colleges and universities, board membership serves to fortify the school's ties with its major benefactors and fund-raisers, whose philanthropic contributions are often critical to the school's financial health. Since most wealth derives from business success, many trustees, as well as other important donors and fund-raisers, are businessmen, usually chairmen and presidents of corporations located in the same geographical area as the school. Richard Aldrich of the Association of Governing Boards, which collects data on the subject, estimates that five thousand corporate executives may be serving as college and university trustees. The concern that business-men feel for the success of a local college or university is not always purely altruistic. The presence of a nearby, highly regarded school lends prestige to their own business. The school also may be useful as a source of research and development assistance and new recruits, a purchaser of corporate products and services, or simply a general boon to the regional economy.

Many colleges and universities are inextricable components of their respective communities' industrial and financial power structures. A researcher seeking to identify the business establishment of a city might find the listing of trustees of a local college or university a good place to start. For example, the seventy-member board of trustees of Case Western Reserve University in Cleveland includes present or former executives of five of the seven largest industrial corporations headquartered in Cleveland—TRW, Inc., Republic Steel Corp., the B. F. Goodrich Co., Standard Oil Company (Ohio), and Eaton Corp.—as well as executives from the city's two largest banks, Cleveland Trust Co. and National City Bank of Cleveland. About three-quarters of the trustees have business affiliations. Among the numerous close links between Case Western Reserve and local business interests is University Circle Research Center, a $100 million industrial research project established by the university and local businesses.

Similarly, Northeastern University in Boston includes among its 175 corporation officers senior executives from Boston-area concerns such as Raytheon Co., New England Telephone & Telegraph Co., Foxboro Co., USM Corp., Foster Grant Co., Boston Edison Co., Arthur D. Little, Inc., the Gillette Co., Sprague Electric Co., and Polaroid Corp. It also includes representatives of Boston's financial community: The Boston Co., State Street Bank and Trust Co., First National Bank of Boston, New England Merchants National Bank, National Shawmut Bank of Boston, New England Mutual Life Insurance Co., John Hancock Mutual Life Insurance Co., Liberty Mutual Insurance Co., Massachusetts Financial Services, Inc., and Putnam Management Co. Over three-quarters of the officers of the Northeastern Corp. are businessmen.

Despite the formal extent of their authority over the institutions on whose boards they sit, college and university trustees, like the trustees of other nonprofit institutions, usually lack the time or the inclination to become very deeply involved in the school's affairs. Perhaps as a result, as one observer has put it:

[M]ost trustees simply do not understand the "nitty gritty," "day-to-day," "real world" work of the hospital, museum, dance company, university, or foundation that has invited them to serve. (And they would be the first to say so. The invitation to serve is a civic honor that is hard to turn down.) Trustees, well intentioned as they usually are, often are quite unfamiliar with the operations, budgeting, and spending of the institution. So these "operating finances" or expenditures are usually left entirely to the administration. On the other hand, the responsibility for income is divided into three parts. The administration is responsible for setting fees for admission, membership, tuition, and so forth. The administration divides with trustees the responsibility for fund raising. And the trustees, usually without a clear knowledge of the current financial future of the institutions they are striving to serve, are given full responsibility for the endowment. (After all, they're financial people. And besides, what else can they do?)[1]

The legal obligations of trustees in managing college and university endowment funds have never been clearly spelled out: "There is virtually no statutory law regarding trustees or governing boards of eleemosynary institutions, and case law is sparse."[2] A recent judicial decision regarding trust funds states that trustees have a duty to "maximize the trust income by prudent investment."[3] Directors and trustees of nonprofit institutions also are considered "obligated to act in the utmost good faith and to exercise ordinary business care and prudence in all matters affecting the management" of the organization.[4] Good faith, prudence, and care would seem to require that trustees maintain a "Chinese wall" between the investment of the endowment fund's assets and their own personal financial interests.

Many trustees strive diligently and successfully to maintain that Chinese wall. D.F. Finn, executive vice president of the National Association of College and University Business Officers, contends that "trustees often rise above themselves when they take on the responsibility [of being trustees] and become much more statesmanlike and ethical than before." Hazel Sanger of Thorndike, Doran, Paine & Lewis in Atlanta, which acts as investment manager for several endowment funds, says, "We see a very general shift in the direction of avoiding any appearance of conflicts of interest.[5] Trustees are becoming increasingly scrupulous."

Yet at fund after fund, portfolio investments and the suppliers of financial services to the fund are linked to the outside business and financial affiliations of the trustees and of important donors and fund-raisers. The management of the trust fund is not isolated from the tight interrelationships among the school, its trustees, and local businesses, but is a part of those interrelationships.

It is important to understand the atmosphere and context in which the overwhelming majority of these conflicts and abuses occur. The trustees involved are not dishonest individuals furtively conspiring to channel business to friends or to enrich themselves at the fund's expense. Rather, they are essentially well-meaning, basically honorable individuals engaging in practices with which they sincerely see nothing wrong. In many cases trustees believe that a little business from the fund for their corporation is a justifiable *quid pro quo* for the time they contribute to the institution by serving on the board.

Despite their nonprofit status, colleges and universities experience many of the same financial problems as profit-making corporations. But perhaps because they need not show a profit, trustees still tend to regard them as institutions to which some accepted practices of good business are not applicable. "The things that govern your behavior in your own business do not seem to apply when you become a trustee," says Hans H. Jenny, vice president for finance and business at the College of Wooster in Ohio. "You're making the same kinds of decisions. But your behavior changes, and you tolerate things you wouldn't sit still for in your own business." For example, in overseeing the management of a corporation's pension fund, the performance of which directly affects the corporation's earnings, a corporate executive typically conducts an elaborate competition to secure the best managers and does not hesitate to fire a manager who performs poorly. He will assiduously demand that whoever manages the fund shop diligently for brokerage and custodial services. He will make sure that the portfolio includes nothing but those securities most likely to produce the greatest return at the designated risk level. Yet in his capacity as a college or university trustee, the same individual often sees nothing wrong in allocating fund commission business to firms associated with a well-known alumnus, selecting as investment manager a firm run by an important donor, and permitting the portfolio to hold securities chosen not for their investment merits but because they are associated with other trustees.

It is from this still prevalent double standard that the worst conflict-of-interest abuses at endowment funds flow.

III • THE PORTFOLIO

The most visible evidence of the breach in the Chinese wall between the interests of endowment funds and the private interests of trustees, as well as donors and fund-raisers, is the presence in endowment fund portfolios of securities linked to the business affiliations of the trustees.[1] Most often, positions in these securities are the result of gifts from trustees that the managers of the fund have chosen to hold. Gifts of appreciated securities are popular, of course, because the donor can deduct the full market value of the gift when he makes it and need not pay a capital gains tax on long-term holdings. In some cases the trustees themselves have supervised purchases by the fund of stock in their own companies. Some examples of apparent trustee influence on portfolios:

- As of August 31,1976, Emory University's endowments and trust funds had a market value of $169,708,000. Some 46.5 percent of that, or $78,737,000, was invested in a single company: the Coca-Cola Co. Emory has long been closely linked to large individual holders of Coca-Cola stock, particularly members of the Woodruff and Candler families, whose gifts of stock account for most of Emory's holdings. Charles W. Duncan, Jr., former president of Coca-Cola, was a member of the boards of both Coca-Cola and Emory until his appointment as Deputy Secretary of Defense. Emory's vice-president for health affairs is on Coca-Cola's board. George Woodruff and C. Howard Candler, from whose family the Woodruffs purchased Coca-Cola in 1919, are listed as trustees emeriti. Emory has a total of thirty-three trustees on its board.
- Close to 40 percent of the University of Rochester's $342,523,655 worth of endowment assets, as of December 31, 1975, consisted of two holdings: 825,000 shares of Eastman Kodak Co., worth $87,553,000, and 735,000 shares of Xerox Corp., worth $37,393,000. Executives of the two companies have been major benefactors of the university. Three executives of Kodak, including the chairman and the president, and two executives of Xerox, including the chairman, sit on the university's thirty-four-member board of trustees. The endowment fund also holds positions in Sybron Corp., Lincoln First Banks, Inc., and Security New York State Corp. All these concerns have their headquarters in Rochester, and their chief executives (or, in the case of Lincoln First Banks, that of the local bank of which Lincoln First Banks is the holding company) are trustees of the university. W. Allen Wallis, chancellor of the university, is a director of Eastman Kodak and Lincoln First Banks. Emanuel Goldberg, a board member of Sybron, is head of the university trustees' investment committee. The endowment fund's positions in Kodak, Xerox, Lincoln First Banks, Security New York, and Sybron were acquired in part through purchases on the open market.
- The largest single equity position in the $63,063,078 portfolio of endowment and similar funds held by Swarthmore College, as of June 30, 1976, was 68,976 shares of Standard Pressed Steel Co., worth $1,043,662. Most or all of this stock was a gift from H. Thomas Hallowell, Jr., chairman of Standard Pressed Steel. Hallowell is a member of Swarthmore's thirty-four-member board of trustees and its investment committee. Swarthmore also

owns 56,344 shares of Scott Paper Co. worth $855,090, largely acquired through gifts from Thomas B. McCabe, a former chairman of Scott Paper who, for many years, was chairman of Swarthmore's investment committee. The current finance committee chairman at Swarthmore is J. Lawrence Shane, Scott Paper's chief financial officer.

- As of June 30, 1976, Washington University in St. Louis held $158,173,000 in endowment and similar funds. Included in its portfolio, as of November 30, 1976, were positions in Interco, Inc., The May Department Stores Co., McDonnell Douglas Corp., Mercantile Bancorporation, Inc., Mallinckrodt, Inc., Monsanto Co., and Olin Corp. Included on its forty-nine-member board of trustees were executives or directors of those concerns, all of which are located in St. Louis. Families linked to several of the companies, such as Olin, Mallinckrodt, and McDonnell Douglas, have made sizable gifts to the university. The co-chairmen of Washington University's investment committee are the chairmen of Interco and the honorary chairman of Olin. The fund acquired several of its trustee-linked investments, including Monsanto and Interco, largely on the open market.

- Northwestern University's $225,667,868 portfolio of endowment and similar funds, as of July 31, 1976, held positions in American Hospital Supply Corp., Combined Communications Corp., Continental Illinois Corp., Illinois Tool Works, Inc., Johnson Products Co., First Chicago Corp., G. D. Searle & Co., Sears Roebuck & Co., and Standard Oil Co. of Indiana. Executives of these companies, which have their headquarters in the Chicago area, are on Northwestern's thirty-eight-member board of trustees. The university acquired its two largest blocks of stock, $17,378,932 worth of American Hospital Supply and $8,952,510 worth of Searle, as gifts. Daniel C. Searle, chief executive of G. D. Searle, and Karl D. Bays, chief executive of American Hospital Supply, are trustees of the university. The head of Northwestern's investment committee is John J. Louis, Jr., chairman of Combined Communications; Northwestern holds 50,550 shares of his company's stock, acquired on the open market and valued at $524,456. The university acquired at least part of its holdings of other trustee-linked securities—including Illinois Tool Works, Johnson Products, Standard Oil of Indiana, and Continental Illinois—on the open market. Harold B. Smith, president of Illinois Tool; Blaine J. Yarrington, executive vice president of Standard Oil of Indiana; and Tilden Cummings, formerly president and still a director of Continental Illinois, are on the investment committee with John Louis.

These colleges and universities publish lists of their portfolio investments. Many others do not. One such institution is the California Institute of Technology, which, as of June 30, 1976, had $145,241,000 in endowment and similar funds. Henry J. Tanner, Caltech's assistant treasurer, reports that it is a policy of the trustees not to release investment data. ''I don't know if it is really something we want the public to know," he states. "Why should we?" Tanner goes on to explain:

We have quite a broad board of trustees, and some of the stock in their companies is held out of proportion to what might be held in the average portfolio. We have some holdings of a substantial size in certain companies that are not normally held. This may be one sensitive reason. Mr. X may have given us some shares in his company and he might not like the outside world to realize he had done this.

Caltech's forty-member board includes the presidents or chairmen of such major West Coast corporations as Atlantic Richfield Co., Rockwell International Corp., Union Oil Co. of California, TRW, Inc., Twentieth Century-Fox Film Corp., MCA, Inc., Security Pacific Corp., BankAmerica Corp., Wells Fargo & Co., and Pacific Mutual Life Insurance Co. Most of these executives or their companies are important donors to Caltech and sponsors of various university programs. Twenty-two corporation executives who are trustees are members of "visiting committees" who "play a vital role in directing the future development of education and research at the California Institute of Technology."[2]

Of course, not all trustee-linked investments are harmful to the interests of the universities involved. The University of Rochester has unquestionably benefited from its Kodak and Xerox holdings. But most such acquisitions are less successful. In 1969, at the urging of a trustee, Worcester Polytechnic Institute, which has an endowment of $27.3 million, put $6 million in a private placement mutual fund that had just been organized by the Paul Revere Life Insurance Co. The trustee was an officer of the mutual fund. "It went nowhere but downhill and didn't even pay us a dividend," recalls WPI treasurer David E. Lloyd. Finally, after the school had suffered a loss of about $1.5 million, the trustee recommended that the stock be sold and WPI unloaded its position. "It really killed us," says Lloyd. "We don't even like to think about it."

This investment involved a conspicuous risk. But even some relatively more conservative trustee-linked investments seem inappropriate for a university endowment. Coca-Cola stock, a very lackluster market performer for many years, is selling at half its price of three years ago, and it has recently been yielding about 4 percent.

Publicly, most treasurers assert that their endowments maintain positions in trustee-linked securities strictly for their investment merits. "They represent our best investment judgment," says John B. Borsch, Jr., director of the investment department at Northwestern, which manages its fund internally. "I have never really felt any inhibition in regard to our securities holdings simply because there was a trustee involved."

A few university officials publicly admit to the presence of other considerations. "If the stock is considered investment grade," says Merl M. Huntsinger, treasurer of Washington University, "we have a policy, if we get a big gift of stock and we know there is more stock out there, of hanging on to it.'' But most university officials, as well as outside investment managers and trustees, will only discuss such considerations anonymously.

"There are plenty of cases where universities feel a reluctance to dump the stock,'' says the head of an investment advisory firm with a number of endowment clients. "They feel that if they don't antagonize the donor, he'll give them more stock.''

"There are circumstances under which this college continues to hold a certain stock because of the personal relationship involved,'' says the treasurer of one southern college. "We will not offend a significant donor to the college or an important trustee by apparently expressing some doubts about his company. Take our big holding of ——— [a company in which his fund held a large block]. It may not be a very good investment. But on the other hand, it didn't cost us anything.'' Asked why an eastern university continues to hold a large block of stock donated by one of its trustees, the trustee in question responds, "Nothing has ever been said about that, either by them [the college's investment officers] or by me. But there is a kind of understanding about . . . well . . . why disturb it?'' A trustee who leads the investment committee at another school says, "I guess we'd have a consultation with the interested trustee before there was any sale just in case some upset would happen.'' He adds that he is not sure just what the policy would be because "I don't think we've ever tried to sell any of the sensitive stocks that have been given to the university.''

In addition to accepting gifts, endowment funds often purchase trustee-linked stocks on the open market. At Washington and Northwestern universities, the endowment funds have acquired positions in companies with which members of the trustee investment committees were affiliated. Noting that the trustee involved always abstained from voting on the decision to buy or hold his own stock, the treasurer of one large college conceded, "You can't really blame them if sometimes they recommend each other's stock. After all, these people know each other very well.''

Few trustees whose companies are represented in the endowment portfolios they supervise appear to have derived any significant financial benefit from the institution's holding. Open market buying on the scale of Washington's or Northwestern's purchases almost certainly had no readily discernible effect on the stocks' prices. The price effects of sales may be more significant. But even if Washington abruptly unloaded its 30,785 shares of Monsanto or 71,739 shares of McDonnell Douglas, the prices of the stocks would be affected at most very temporarily. And Northwestern could easily dispose of its 576,984 shares of American Hospital Supply (1.5 percent of the total outstanding) or Emory of its Coca-Cola holdings (also 1.5 percent) without permanently affecting stock prices by reducing its positions gradually or, in the case of securities unregistered with the SEC, selling them through a well-managed registered secondary offering. Endowment funds hold these positions not because the trustees are seeking to enrich themselves or to shore up their own portfolios but to make the trustee or donor feel good, to reinforce his ties with the school, to avoid embarrassing him. If a trustee-linked position were liquidated, the damage, if any, would be not to the trustee's portfolio but to his pride, and to his loyalty to the school.

Shareholder votes, especially those involving hostile tender offers or proxy fights, are more dangerous to the personal financial interests of trustees than simple buy or sell decisions. For the management of the company involved, a successful takeover can be tragic. Often many of the existing top managers are fired. For shareholders, though, the same situation can be a windfall. Outsiders making tender offers usually are willing to pay an attractive premium over the current market price; hence, if the offer is a success, shareholders enjoy a substantial capital gain. Shareholders also can benefit if a badly managed company is absorbed by a well-managed concern that installs a fresh group of executives.

The voting of large endowment fund blocks, such as Northwestern's 1.5 percent of American Hospital Supply or Swarthmore's 1.7 percent of Standard Pressed Steel, might be decisive in a closely contested takeover struggle. But endowment funds are unlikely to vote important trustee-linked blocks against management. Asked how he would feel if the university considered voting a large block of stock he had donated in favor of an unfriendly takeover aspirant, one trustee expresses astonishment at the proposition: "I would think that if they're interested in getting more contributions over the years," he says. "They would say to themselves, 'Let's not aggravate this guy by voting the stock the wrong way. Otherwise, he may not give us any more.' That's just common sense. Goddamn it, they don't get big chunks of stock from everybody."

Some corporate executives have used the technique of donating major blocks to colleges and universities both to keep the shares from being liquidated to pay estate taxes after their deaths and to assure that their families or chosen successors will continue to control their respective companies. Galen J. Roush, co-founder of Roadway Express, Inc., and, until his death last year, a trustee of Hiram College in Ohio, donated a large block of Roadway Express to Hiram and made it the beneficiary of a nonvoting trust explicitly for that purpose. Members of Roush's family own 41.9 percent of the company's other shares. The trust and the shares the college owns make up 40 percent of its endowment.

Washington University has one-third interest in a trust consisting of 1,534,344 share of Mallinckrodt, Inc., a large drug and chemicals concern that was established by the late Edward Mallinckrodt, Jr. Before his death, Mallinckrodt appointed as trustees of this trust a number of the directors of his company; he further arranged for their trusteeship to end in 1982 and for the university to assume voting control at that time. According to Washington University treasurer Merl M. Huntsinger, "His whole idea was to avoid the possibility of a takeover'' of the company he had founded. The trust in which Washington has an interest and another family trust constitute 24 percent of the company's stock. At the moment, Harold E. Thayer, Mallinckrodt's chief executive and a trustee for the trusts, is a trustee of Washington University. William H. Danforth, chancellor of the university, is a director of Mallinckrodt.

Gifts and bequests of major blocks for such purposes may be on the rise. At one time the standard practice of corporate executives seeking to keep control stock in friendly hands was to establish private foundations.[3] But the Tax Reform Act of 1969 sharply reduced the usefulness of foundations as control mechanisms by imposing limits on the portion of a company's stock a foundation could hold. Now a foundation that receives a large block of stock generally must reduce it to no more than 20 percent of the company's outstanding shares within five years. This rule may divert the donation of control stock from foundations to other nonprofit institutions. According to John G. Simon, a professor at Yale Law School and the president of the Taconic Foundation: "[T]here are hundreds of thousands of financially hard-pressed colleges and churches which would be delighted to receive control stock with all kinds of informal voting understandings . . . . [T]here is evidence that such diversions are being actively solicited . . . ."[4]

Among its many drawbacks, the presence of large, trustee-linked blocks in a portfolio can increase investment risk by reducing diversification. The financial future of Emory University, for example, is closely linked to the continuing prosperity of Coca-Cola. "Coca-Cola has done very well over the years," says D. F. Finn of the National Association of College and University Business Officers, "but if the university had had all that money in Penn Central, it would have been tragic." The University of Rochester's endowment income, which supplied 17 percent of the school's revenue during 1975-76, could be materially affected by a major change in the fortunes of Kodak and Xerox. And in the past two years, these two stocks have lost much of the glamour they had during the 1950s and 1960s. Although few universities hold such large blocks, many are heavily and probably excessively concentrated in companies within a small geographic region whose prosperity is vulnerable to shifts in, for example, government spending and demographic patterns. Still other schools are excessively concentrated in a single industry. Some 36 percent of the common stock portfolio of Rockefeller University, which is effectively controlled by the Rockefeller family, is invested in energy issues, principally Exxon Corp. The Rockefeller family, of course, has many ties to the energy industry.

Failure to diversify portfolio assets is regarded by nearly all investment experts and some courts as inherently imprudent. The trustee's duty to diversify, long an integral part of trust law, is codified in *Restatement of Trusts (Second)* as follows: "Except as otherwise provided by the terms of the trust, the trustee is under a duty to the beneficiary to distribute the risk of loss by a reasonable diversification of investments, unless under the circumstances it is prudent not to do so.''[5] The Employee Retirement Income Security Act of 1974 imposed the duty to diversify investments on all pension trusts and other employee benefit plans covered by the act.[6] According to attorney Marion Fremont-Smith:

One aspect of the application of the prudent man rule to trust departments is the question of diversification of risk. Common sense dictates that it is not prudent to keep too many eggs in one basket. The question of diversification is particularly important to trustees of the many charitable foundations to which donors have contributed large amounts of stock of a closely held corporation. Unfortunately, the cases do not make clear how far a trustee is subject to liability for failure to diversify investments. The requirement for diversification has been specifically recognized in the courts in some juridictions and has been imposed by statute in others.[7]

It seems at least possible that failure to diversify could subject a school's trustees to legal challenge, especially if it could be shown that such failure jeopardized the endowment fund's assets.

Imprudent investments can affect the contributions of all a school's bene-factors because most schools pool their endowment fund assets. When a new gift is received, it is added to the pool and credited with units or shares in the pool. The value of the gift then becomes the value of its shares, and like a mutual fund shareholder, the gift benefits on a pro rata basis from the return of the endowment fund as a whole. If a large, trustee-linked block performs badly, has a very low yield, or subjects the portfolio to excessive risk and volatility, all gifts, and their designated uses, from scholarships and pro-fessorships to student loans and libraries, will suffer accordingly.

Investment manager John W. Bristol, whose firm has several endowment clients, approaches the problem from a different perspective: ''I think a little potential conflict of interest is not too much of a price to pay, considering the alternative of cutting off the golden goose.'' A badly performing, undiver-sified block of stock is after all better than no stock at all.

This counter-argument has merit. But it does not provide a blanket justifi-cation for golden-goose coddling and cozy trustee-portfolio relationships. College and university investment officers should confront the issue directly, weighing the dangers of a possibly risky, undiversified portfolio, the appear-ance of conflict-of-interest abuse, and the possibility of embarrassing criticism or even legal action against the hope of future donations and the chances that the golden goose would actually stop producing if his previous gifts were unloaded.

Some trustees make it very clear that they consider the donated block a ''good investment'' for the endowment and that it should be left alone. But as John W. Bristol notes: ''Often the reluctance to sell is exaggerated because sometimes the donor couldn't care less.'' Both the University of Pittsburgh and Carnegie-Mellon University have disposed of substantial portions of Gulf Oil stock donated to them by members of the Mellon family without causing noticeable concern to their benefactors. Unfortunately, the subject of abuses and problems resulting from trustee-linked stock positions comes up at all too few trustee meetings, either because no one thinks anything is wrong with the practice or because no one is willing to risk giving offense. Leigh A. Jones, vice president for finance at Berea College in Kentucky, which has worked hard to minimize interest conflicts, recalls the reluctance of some new investment firms he had hired as endowment fund managers to accept his assurances that a large holding of Ralston Purina Co. stock, part of which had been donated by the Danforth family, which had founded the company, and one of whose members, Donald Danforth, was a Berea trustee, could be sold whenever the managers deemed it appropriate:

We told the managers they had complete discretion, but it took them a while to get used to it. Once, one of the managers called me and said: "Leigh, what about the Ralston stock?" I said: "What about it? We told you you could do whatever you wanted with it." He said: "Do you really mean that? What happens if I sell it? Aren't I going to get in dutch?" Even though I said he wouldn't, I know that for a while at least the manager thought twice about coming before the investment committee with Danforth sitting across from him and explaining why he felt some of the stock should be sold.

Not all investment managers are timid. Hazel Sanger of Thorndike, Doran, Paine & Lewis reports that when her firm is confronted with a sensitive block: "We think it is our fiduciary obligation to point out to the trustees the risks of nondiversification or any specific risk in the company. Then if the trustees feel that despite the risks they want to hold the stock, then at least they have made an informed decision." If they decide to hold the stock, Thorndike segregates it in a special account away from the rest of the portfolio.

"You have to push trustees' noses into the [conflict-of-interest] question," says Columbia University professor Roger Murray. "They hope it'll go away or that you won't nag them about it." But if more investment managers confronted the trustees with the issue and more trustees and university officials took the trouble to analyze the advantages and disadvantages of holding such blocks, they might eliminate many of the existing abuses.

IV • INVESTMENT MANAGERS, BROKERS, AND BANKERS

At one point during the early 1960s, the board of trustees at a large New England university was looking for a full-time investment advisor. The trustees had run the endowment fund's portfolio themselves for many years, and although the treasurer and one or two of the more enlightened trustees had convinced the others that the time had come to secure the services of a well-qualified outside professional, the trustees refused to pay an advisor more than $6,000 per year. One of the trustees was assigned the difficult task of finding the right man for the job. After much searching, the trustee discovered a brilliant young analyst who hated New York, where he was then employed, loved the idea of working on a tree-shaded campus, and did not mind the low salary because his wife came from a very wealthy family. The trustees rejected the man because he had graduated from the university's traditional football rival.

In the last decade, universities have made substantial progress in eliminating intramural sports rivalries and other extraneous considerations from the selection of those who provide advisory, managerial, brokerage, and banking services to endowment funds. Today, for numerous colleges and universities, competence and cost are the only relevant criteria. Yet in too many instances, competence and cost receive lower priority than affiliation with trustees and prominent donors.

Investment Managers and Advisors

Perhaps the most visible change since the old days of management by crony has been the now common practice of hiring independent professional managers. In the past the head of the investment committee often employed his own firm to manage the endowment. Today, numerous educational institutions give outside investment managers discretion to make portfolio investments subject only to broad policy guidelines. Despite its close ties to Nashville, for instance, Vanderbilt University divides up management of its $124 million endowment fund among four outside managers: Capital Guardian Trust Co. in Los Angeles; First National Bank of Chicago; Thorndike, Doran, Paine & Lewis in Atlanta; and United States Trust Co. in New York.

Ohio State University in Columbus, Ohio, which also is closely associated with its community, uses Thorndike in Atlanta and Alliance Capital Management Corp. in Minneapolis for its $49.3 million endowment. Several schools, including Harvard, the University of Chicago, the University of California, the University of Pennsylvania (which has completely reorganized and professionalized its investment staff since the Penn Central episode), and Syracuse, maintain a staff of in-house professionals who generally have discretion to make individual portfolio selections and are often advised by outside firms. The portfolios of these schools tend to be well-diversified assemblages of institutional grade securities largely free of trustee-linked aberrations and discernible conflicts of interest.

The internal management system of schools such as Harvard operates with relatively little trustee involvement and, according to some treasurers, is cheaper, more efficient, and more responsive to the school's needs than outside management would be. But internal management can increase the risk of conflicts of interest. Both Northwestern University and the University of Rochester, where links between portfolio holdings and trustees are especially evident, are internally managed.

One of the advantages of paid professional management is that it can always be replaced if the portfolio's performance is unsatisfactory. Colleges and universities at which the members of the investment committee or merely of the board are closely involved in the portfolio's management have no such recourse. "What happens if the trustees flunk the test?" asks Hans H. Jenny of Wooster College. "Who's going to say you really goofed? I've seen this happen with many institutions I've consulted with. Nobody spanks Mama because she might leave you a million bucks. So you have to put up with a lot of bad or hands-off management just so you won't ruffle trustee feathers." The interests of the fund thus are subverted to avoid upsetting or embarrassing the involved trustees.

At a large number of schools, the job of managing the endowment is an apparent captive of one or more local institutions, usually banks, that are closely linked to the school and its board of trustees. At the University of Pittsburgh, the Mellon Bank manages most of the $88,913,454 in endowment assets (as of June 30, 1976); the Pittsburgh National Bank manages the rest. The Mellon family, which controls the bank, has been the university's most important donor. Of the university's twelve charter trustees, one is James H. Higgins, chairman of the board of Mellon National Corporation, the bank's holding company, and four more are directors of Mellon National Corporation. The board also includes Merle E. Gilliard, chairman of Pittsburgh National Bank, and two members of the board of his bank's holding company. Of the university's $43.9 million in current and loan funds and plant funds, $16.3 million is invested in Mellon National and Pittsburgh National securities. The endowment portfolios run by the two banks are relatively free of large holdings of securities linked to the university's trustees or Mellon interests. Nevertheless, as trustees and fiduciaries, the chairmen of Mellon Bank and Pittsburgh National Bank have apparently voted to award, or at least acquiesced in the award of, the management of the university's endowment fund to themselves. If the bank's most recently published fee schedule is applicable, during the fiscal year ending June 30, 1976, Mellon received approximately $65,000 for managing its portion of the university's portfolio.

Management of Case Western Reserve University's $82,990,247 in endowment and similar funds (as of June 30, 1976) is divided up among the Cleveland Trust Co., the National City Bank of Cleveland, and Central National Bank, the city's three major banks. The vice-chairman of Cleveland Trust and the chairman of National City Bank are on Case Western's boards of trustees and overseers. Eight corporations whose present or former officers are trustees of the university are also represented on the board of National City Bank. Case Western Reserve president Louis A. Toepfer and a Case Western professor are board members of CleveTrust Corp., the holding company for Cleveland Trust, as are three corporate executives who are also Case Western trustees. Several partners from Jones, Day, Reavis & Pogue, a powerful law firm closely associated with Cleveland industry, are trustees of the university and are on the boards of all three banks. A listing of stocks in Case Western's endowment portfolio (as of November 30, 1976) shows positions in National City Corp., CleveTrust Corp., and CleveTrust Realty Investors SBI, as well as in ten other companies whose executives are on the university's board of trustees. Most of these companies are located in Cleveland and have commercial and trust relationships with the three major local banks.

Emory University's endowment has one outside manager, Trust Company Bank of Atlanta, which also is a lender to the school. Emory's board includes no fewer than four present or former executives of the bank: Robert Strickland, chairman of the bank; William R. Bowdoin, head of the bank's executive committee; George S. Craft, former chairman of the bank; and James B. Williams, head of Trust Company of Georgia Associates, an affiliate of the bank. Three other directors of the bank are also trustees. The Trust Company Bank also has been very close to Coca-Cola ever since Ernest Woodruff, who formed the syndicate that bought control of the company in 1919, headed the bank. A former chairman of the bank, the current honorary chairman, and a director of Trust Company of Georgia, the bank's holding company, are on Coca-Cola's board of directors. J. Paul Austin, chairman of Coca-Cola, is on the bank's board. The bank is also manager of much of the Woodruff family money, including the $205 million Emily and Ernest Woodruff Foundation.

The University of Rochester is not the only school in that city with conflicting relationships. Rochester Institute of Technology's (RIT) $63,246,399 in endowment and similar funds (as of June 30, 1976) is managed by Lincoln First Bank of Rochester. Alexander D. Hargrave, chief executive of Lincoln First Banks, Inc., the holding company, is a trustee of RIT. Three other trustees or officers of RIT are directors of Lincoln First Banks, Inc. If Lincoln First Bank of Rochester's latest published fee schedule is applicable, the bank received about $55,000 for its services as manager during the past fiscal year.

At times factors other than trustee affiliation can affect the direction of management business. The University of Minnesota, with an endowment of $83,085,349 (as of June 30, 1976) is a case in point. In the late 1960s, after many years of internal management, a system of outside managers was organized. The university's regents, who are appointed by the state legislature and are not usually important members of the local business establishment, had no objection. But D. P. Benda, manager of investment and cash management for the university, recalls being under "an awful lot of political pressure, particularly by the state legislators, to avoid managers from outside the state of Minnesota." The firms selected included: Rowe Price Associates from Baltimore; Thorndike, Doran, Paine & Lewis from Atlanta; Brokaw, Schaenen, Clancy & Co. from New York; Alliance Capital Management, headquartered in New York but with an office in Minneapolis; and—the sole local manager—Northwestern National Bank in Minneapolis.

The state legislators were irate. In 1971 Brokaw, whose performance had been below that of the other out-of-state firms, was fired and replaced by First Trust Company of St. Paul and Investment Advisors, Inc., of Minneapolis. As a result the endowment now has three local and three out-of-state managers (if

Alliance is counted as a New York firm), and the legislators are somewhat appeased. But the outsiders currently manage over 80 percent of the endowment fund.

Many treasurers of endowment funds, although unhappy that the management of the fund is an apparent captive of local institutions, assume that the relationship is too strong to be broken. Yet the possibility of change may be greater than they realize. For example, for many years Carnegie-Mellon University in Pittsburgh used the Mellon Bank and Pittsburgh National Bank to run an endowment that amounted to $110,488,584 (as of June 30, 1976). On the surface the management of this fund appeared to be as locked up as that of the University of Pittsburgh. The Mellons, of course, are heavy donors to Carnegie-Mellon. In addition, Donald C. Burnham, former chief executive of Westinghouse Electric Corp. and chairman of Carnegie-Mellon's board of trustees, and John D. Harper, former president of the Aluminum Co. of America and vice-chairman of the board of trustees, are both directors of Mellon National Corp.

In 1975, however, treasurer George O. Luster and other university officials succeeded in switching a major portion of their endowment assets to four new managers: Capital Guardian Trust in Los Angeles; Delaware Investment Advisors in Philadelphia; and F. Eberstadt & Co. and Fischer, Francis, Trees & Watts in New York. "The only way you can overcome reluctance to change," Luster says, "is to put forth your argument in a logical fashion supported by documentation that change is necessary." The argument Luster used in presenting the plan to the trustees was "risk diversification," the usefulness of dividing up the portfolio among different managers with different philosophies. According to Luster's latest report:

The diversification of management philosophy and risk proved to be of substantial benefit in the first year of operation. The investment performance of the equity manager group exceeded the return achieved by the Standard & Poor's 500 Index without any loss in quality and with a decrease in the volatility of the portfolio.

Quite likely at other institutions as well, the apparently very close links between universities and their endowment fund managers are more the product of tradition and inertia than of active, self-interested efforts by trustees affiliated with the managers to perpetuate a profitable captive relationship. Perhaps if presented with persuasive reasons why a change would be beneficial, trustees would be willing to go along.

Trustees may be less willing to go along with the idea of putting some or all of their endowment assets in "index funds," which have been widely discussed in the investment business in recent years.[1] The idea derives from the notion, elaborately documented in statistical studies, that the stock market is "efficient"—that the price of each stock accurately reflects all publicly available information about the stock's future as well as investors' feelings and opinions about it. If the stock market is indeed efficient, in this sense, it is virtually impossible, except through luck, to assemble a portfolio of securities that will consistently outperform the market as a whole. Academicians have long advanced this theory,[2] but it did not begin to gain acceptance in the investment world until a large number of studies of the performance of actual institutional portfolios revealed that, over time, few outperformed broadly based market indices such as the Standard & Poor's 500.

Index funds do not try to beat the market. They merely seek to match it or, more accurately, to match the S&P 500 or one of the other widely followed indices, by assembling portfolios of all or most of the stocks in the index they are trying to evaluate. Such index funds outperform most conventionally managed portfolios, whose performance is weighted down by the heavy costs, in brokerage commissions and research, of trying to beat the market. The cost advantage of index funds over conventionally managed portfolios is compelling. Batterymarch Financial Corp., a Boston investment manager that offers index services, publishes an annual estimated relative cost comparison for management of a $25 million fund. Index funds have negligible turnover—just 2 or 3 percent to compensate for changes in the index. Hence, the brokerage commissions on $25 million would be $2,500 if the money were in an index fund or $53,000 if it were in a portfolio whose managers were continually buying and selling securities in their efforts to achieve high performance. The administrative costs of index funds are very low because they require no investment research; Batterymarch's management fee for running the $25 million portfolio would be $25,000, as against $154,000 for a conventional manager, who would need to pay a large staff of analysts and buy outside research and statistical services. Batterymarch also claims to save additional money in trading costs because, unlike active managers, it does not tend to chase the same groups of stocks up and down at the same time. Batterymarch calculates the total annual cost of managing $25 million as $61,500 under indexing and $438,000 under conventional management.

Impressed by these cost comparisons, pension fund trustees, including those for major corporations such as AT&T, Exxon, and Ford, have invested some $2 billion in index funds to date. According to some Wall Street estimates, the figure could be $10 billion in a couple of years.[3]

Although no college or university is known to have invested its endowment money in index funds, many school treasurers, unhappy with the cost and performance of conventional managers, are attracted by the idea.[4] According to a survey conducted by the National Association of College and University Business Officers (NACUBO), for the ten years ending June 30, 1976, the seventy-seven participating pooled endowments achieved an average annual return of 3.71 percent; the S&P 500 received an average return of 4.70 percent.[5] "I'm kind of enamored with [index funds] at this point," says Leigh Jones of Berea College. "If you're a long-term investor like a college, where you're looking ahead 25 or 50 years, maybe it's the best route to go." But Jones admits, "I'd have a hard time selling my board or my finance committee." The chairman of Berea's finance committee is Kroger Pettengill, former president of the First National Bank of Cincinnati and now head of an investment counseling firm. Nearly all conventional money managers are opposed, often heatedly, to index funds. "Maybe if you're a money manager," says Jones, "you keep thinking, I can do it, I can win."

Numerous experts with less of a vested interest than conventional money managers still argue that superior performance can be achieved. "Let's agree that only one out of ten managers consistently outperforms the averages after transaction costs," says Roger Murray of Columbia:

If you're lazy or incompetent and you don't know how to find the manager who can deliver superior performance, then use an index fund. But if you're not and if you think your responsibility is to maximize the productivity of the endowment fund, don't accept a second-best solution. Go to work and find the one out of ten. There is no question in my mind it can be done. I've done it myself enough times.

Given the apparent cost savings, though, college and university trustees may have to consider index funds seriously, especially if they have an affiliation with the existing manager of the endowment fund. J. Peter Williamson, professor at the Amos Tuck School of Business Administration at Dartmouth and an expert on endowment funds, says:

It may not be too long before college and university trustees will be in trouble if they have not explicitly considered index funds and made a decision for or against them with evidence to support that decision. That doesn't mean that it is imprudent not to go into an index fund. But prudence demands that you have to have at least looked into it. And if your own performance has been below the level of an index fund, you had better be prepared to explain why you prefer your own managers to an index fund.

Rejecting index funds out of hand may come to be regarded as a conflict-of-interest abuse, a case of the trustee pursuing his own vested interest in perpetuating the fund's relationship with a manager with which he is affiliated or simply protecting his own uninformed prejudices and preconceptions rather than the interests of the endowment fund and, as a result, costing the endowment fund money it otherwise might not have had to spend.

Brokers

It has long been a common practice in the investment business to use brokerage commissions to pay for numerous other services besides execution of stock and bond transactions. Some of the services, such as research, are relatively legitimate. Others, such as a *quid pro quo* paid by trust departments for deposits by brokers,[6] raise serious questions.

Colleges and universities commonly use commissions to reward trustees and donors for their services—most often, apparently, because the trustees and donors demand them. "The pressure is very, very heavy, and I don't see it ever relenting." says Roger Murray of Columbia. "There are a lot of alumni who will be absolutely open about it. For every dollar of commission business they receive, they say they will make a contribution of fifty cents.''

Investment manager John W. Bristol adds: ''There have been more abuses in this area than any other. Alumni at brokerage houses are always crying to the treasurer, talking about how generous they are during annual giving. Trustees feel it is important to support alumni at brokerage houses who are or could be potential givers.'' For many years at one southern university, the head of the trustees' investment committee insisted that all the commission business be sent to his own brokerage firm. Although some of the other trustees complained, he maintained he could do the business as well as anyone else.

Many treasurers strive to resist such pressures from alumni and donors. ''The problem comes up, but we duck it,'' says Leigh Jones of Berea. ''We tell people we've given the authority to the managers and that they handle the brokerage.'' Other treasurers admit to going along. Merl M. Huntsinger, treasurer of Washington University, reports that he and the trustees give the three local banks and two investment firms who manage the endowment fund ''guidelines'' on how the commission business should be allocated:

We tell them, all things being equal, these are the brokers we want you to use. We tell them to spread it around in accordance with the weighting we give them. The list is put together from people who work with us in various ways. For instance, there is one small local firm who gave an endowed professorship a few years ago, and needless to say he is close to our hearts. So we remember him when we have some brokerage business that his firm can do. It's this type of thing: people who work with us, who are members of the investment committee, or people who help the university raise funds or who are substantial contributors.

(The member of the investment committee to whom Huntsinger was apparently referring is Elliot H. Stein, president of Scherck, Stein & Franc, Inc., a small St. Louis-based brokerage house.) Northwestern has sent commission business to brokerage houses represented on its board, including Smith Barney, Harris Upham & Co., Dean Witter & Co., and First of Michigan Corp.

This practice can lead to some rather blatant abuses. One investment manager tells of a southwestern college that was considering switching management of it endowment fund from a local bank, which had performed poorly, to a New York investment counselor. The move was vetoed by partners at three local brokerage houses who are members of the board of trustees. They were enjoying most of the fund's commission business and thought they might not receive the same consideration from the New York house, which had a policy of not accepting brokerage direction from clients.

A respected endowment executive claims firsthand knowledge of an instance involving a college trustee whose bank handled a major part of the college's $30 million endowment. The bank churned the account vigorously and in one year generated for itself $200,000 in commissions, much of it for unnecessary transactions. The accountant for the fund brought the unnecessary transactions to the attention of the school's president. But he declined to take action because the trustee was one of the school's largest donors.

Few trustees would condone such churning. Yet, according to John W. Bristol, many trustees have the "misguided belief" that merely spreading commissions around to the firms of donors and similarly deserving parties is harmless. This belief stems in part from the fact that, before May 1, 1975, the brokerage commissions charged by members of the New York Stock Exchange and other exchanges were fixed. Cheaper executions often could be obtained in the "third market," the over-the-counter market in issues listed on the Big Board. But the third market, in part thanks to NYSE propaganda, was regarded as somewhat illicit. Investors who wanted to deal with a "reputable" NYSE firm had to pay the fixed rate. Since all NYSE members charged the same rate, the reasoning went, why not send the orders to the university's friends?

Investment houses vary considerably in execution ability, however. Few small regional firms of the sort most likely to be receiving commissions from an endowment fund due to trustee or donor ties can match the ability of the major New York firms, particularly in handling large blocks. If using a local firm costs an endowment fund only a quarter of a point in unloading a five thousand share position, the school loses $1,250.

In any case, on May 1, 1975, fixed rates were abolished and brokerage commissions became competitive. By the end of 1976, price competition had become fierce, and some firms were offering discounts as high as 70 to 80 percent off the old rate.[7] Discounts vary widely from firm to firm and from customer to customer. To a large extent, the cutomers who bargain the most vigorously pay the lowest commissions. Endowment funds do not release breakdowns of the commissions they pay by amounts and recipients. But it seems reasonable to assume that endowment funds generally receive smaller discounts from local firms headed by a trustee or loyal alumnus than they would from the 70 percent-off "deep discounters," as the firms are called. If the trustee's firm gives only a 20 percent discount, a major portion of the commission the endowment fund pays is not an unavoidable payment that might otherwise go to a firm unconnected with the school but simply a reward for the trustee's loyalty or generosity. The available evidence indicates that very few people who oversee endowment funds have ever actually weighed the contributions or services received against the added commission costs. If a university receives $2,500 in donations from a loyal almunus and pays his firm $5,000 in unnecessary commission business, the relationship costs the university $2,500 and subjects it to the potential embarrassment of engaging in a practice that, if not exactly illegal, is certainly questionable as well as unfair to donors or trustees who do not happen to be in the brokerage business. Hazel Sanger of Thorndike, Doran, Paine & Lewis says that her firm requires trustees to supply in writing all brokerage instructions not predicated on best price or best execution. In such cases, she reports, "we make sure the trustees know what kinds of discounts are available elsewhere so that they can assess the competitiveness of the brokers they want us use. If they choose to direct brokerage on a noncompetitive basis for what they may consider the broader interests of their institution, at least they will have made an informed decision.''

Bankers

Custodianship of investment securities and other banking services can be a major cost to endowment funds and thus a major area for cost savings. According to J. Peter Williamson, professor at Dartmouth's Amos Tuck School of Business Administration:

Selecting a custodian calls for a careful comparison of costs, services, and quality of service among candidates. The best assurance that the present custodian fees and services are appropriate, of course, will come from ''shopping around.'' The bank and custodial arrangements and the level of efficiency in an institution's handling of cash call for regular evaluation. The sums of money at stake can be quite substantial compared with the income on the endowment.[8]

Instead of permitting large noninterest-bearing cash balances to build up at its bank, the managers of an endowment fund should keep these balances as low as possible and keep the fund's cash constantly at work in the most productive way. Instead of permitting the custodian to accumulate dividends and interest for days or weeks before crediting them to the endowment fund, managers should make sure that this money is credited on settlement day. Many colleges and universities work assiduously to obtain the best banking and custodian services at the lowest price. Many manage their cash as efficiently as large corporations. Harvard, which has put a great deal of study into obtaining the most efficient banking services, maintains no balances at commercial banks. But a number of other schools have long-standing arrangements with trustee-linked banks for the usual reasons and with predictable results. According to Williamson, bank relationships are the most important single area of conflict-of-interest problems at endowment funds:

The way it works—and this is on the basis of talking to quite a few people who have explored it—is that you have the president or chairman of the local bank on your board of trustees. It is not the trustee deliberately having the college maintain excessive balances. It is the financial officer of the college thinking he could get a better deal for the college, but being very reluctant to go to the bank and say either you give us a better deal or we'll switch banks. Instead, he decides not to make a fuss because it would upset the college's relationship with the trustee, who may be a big donor. Colleges and universities have been very slow in getting the best banking services and the reason is that it is often not very comfortable for them to do so. It's not comfortable to get tough with someone who is on your board of trustees.

Colleges and universities do not disclose the terms of their banking relationships. But in case after case, the custodian for an endowment fund, and thus quite possibly the school's commercial bank as well, also manages the endowment fund and has a representative on the board of trustees. Case Western Reserve's custodians are the same three Cleveland banks that manage the fund and are linked to the board of trustees. Washington University's custodians are the four St. Louis banks that manage its fund and are represented on its board. The custodian banks for the University of Rochester's endowment fund are Central Trust Company, Lincoln First Bank, and Security Trust Company. The chief executives of all three banks are trustees of the university. In such circumstances trustees are apparently voting or acquiescing in the allocation of business from the trust for which they are fiduciaries to institutions with which they are affiliated.

These universities may be receiving excellent, low-cost service from their banks. Perhaps the banker on the board even directs his bank to give the school a cut-rate price. But in most cases the university is a captive customer. Logic suggests that a tough customer, inclined to shop around, may receive better service than a docile, captive customer.

The extent to which schools are the captives of local or trustee-linked banks has become apparent through the experiences of the Common Fund, a nonprofit operative endeavor that offers several pooled investment vehicles specifically designed for educational institutions. The Common Fund, which began operations in 1971 with the aid of a Ford Foundation grant, has not been so successful in attracting assets as its organizers had expected.

The failure of many schools to invest in the Common Fund's equity vehicle may be due in apart to its disappointing performance. But nearly everyone agrees that the performance and structure of the Common Fund's pooled cash management vehicle, the Common Fund for Short Term Investments, has been extremely good. It provides participants with an elaborate wire transfer mechanism that allows them to make immediate additions and withdrawals. Shortly after the fund was established in 1974, George F. Keane, executive director for the Common Fund, estimated that colleges and universities had close to $5 billion in liquid assets, which potentially could be invested in the fund.[9] Yet by the end of 1976, the fund had attracted only slightly more than $50 million.

"The whole concept [of the short-term fund] is working out beautifully, just as well as we had hoped," says Roger Murray of Columbia, who is a Common Fund trustee:

It is a very effective device for managing cash and keeping balances to a minimum level. But we're not getting the volume and the activity. If you ask a treasurer why he doesn't participate, he'll say, well, we already have a pretty good system, or we already watch our balances. But you can't help but think that it is partly due to his unwillingness to create problems with his local banker who is a trustee. There is a certain tightness about these local relationships. The treasurer doesn't want to let go of the money. He doesn't want those relationships reduced. In the development of the Common Fund, this is a problem we've run into repeatedly.

The treasurer of a West Coast college reports that his recent proposal for participation in the Common Fund's short-term fund was vetoed by two local bankers who were trustees of the school and handled the school's banking business.

For many years a local bank had been investment advisor and custodian of the endowment fund of The College of Wooster in Ohio. When Hans H. Jenny, Wooster's vice president for finance, expressed dissatisfaction with the quality of service and proposed to switch, he ran into intense opposition from three trustees. One was an accountant whose firm handled the local bank and who was on the local bank's board. Another was an officer of a large bank of which the small bank was a correspondent. The third, as Jenny put it, "was just miffed because we were violating a long historical relationship." The bank officer and the traditionalist had been important donors; in protest, they stopped giving. But Jenny's biggest problem was with the accountant. "We had a terrible hassle with him," Jenny recalls. "When the administration came up with proposals for switching banks, he said, 'We can always find new administrators.'" When the college finally chose a new bank, the accountant resigned from the board of trustees. The other two trustees remained and eventually began making donations again. But making the switch and "establishing peace on the board," says Jenny, "took three and a half years."

V • CONCLUSIONS

Incestuous relationships, apparent self-dealing, and other conflicts of interest remain widespread at educational institutions mainly because many trustees see nothing wrong in them. Yet over the years to come, these practices may become grounds for legal action and, as a result, the focus of growing public criticism. Much attention, in this regard, is being focused on an important 1974 court case involving the Sibley Memorial Hospital, a nonprofit institution in Washington, D.C., with about $5 million in assets.[1] According to one commentator, the case

presents for the first time an exhaustive review of the legal standards of care to be exercised by trustees of nonprofit organizations. It is a landmark decision and one which is being studied carefully by trustees and legal counsels of nonprofit organizations.[2]

The five defendants in the *Sibley* case were trustees and members of the hospital's investment committee as well as officers or directors of local financial institutions. The charges, brought by the hospital's patients in a class action, involved conspiracy, mismanagement, nonmanagement, and self-dealing. The self-dealing charges entailed a clear conflict of interest: the hospital did considerable business with the institutions with which the trustees were affiliated. The relationships included noninterest-bearing demand deposits, a mortgage loan, and an investment advisory contract. Two of the defendants were officers and directors of two local banks. The hospital's checking account had alternated between those two banks. In the year before suit was brought, the account held about $1 million, more than one-third of the hospital's investable funds, an amount that District Judge Gerhard A. Gesell found not justified by the defendants, although he also found that the plaintiffs had not established that the practice was "the result of a conscious direction on the part of" the interlocked directors who were the defendants.

In addition, Judge Gesell found that each of the defendants had "breached his fiduciary duty to supervise the management of Sibley's investments."[3] Although noting that District of Columbia law, like that of most jurisdictions, does not bar trustees from placing funds under their control in banks with which they are affiliated, the judge said the defendants had failed to disclose adequately to other persons involved in approving the transactions their outside interests or their knowledge of better terms available elsewhere. In some cases, including the awarding of an investment advisory contract to Ferris & Co., whose chairman and principal stockholder, George Ferris, was a trustee, the defendants had participated in or voted in favor of decisions to transact business with their own firms.

Because the hospital did not thereby suffer any measurable injury and because the defendants had neither engaged in actually fraudulent practices nor profited personally from their actions, Judge Gesell did not rule that they were financially liable. Nor did he approve the plaintiffs' requests for injunctive relief such as removal of the defendants as trustees and an absolute ban on dealings between the hospital and firms with which any of its trustees had an affiliation. He noted that the hospital had recently adopted a new by-law based on new conflict-of-interest guidelines issued by the American Hospital Association.[4] However, he did decree, among other measures, strict rules for disclosure by trustees of outside affiliations.

Altough the remedies he chose were modest, Gesell also included in his decision a strongly worded and subsequently widely read passage on the hiring of new trustees by the hospital:

The tendency of representatives of [financial institutions joining the board] is often to seek business in return for advice and assistance rendered as trustees. It must be made absolutely clear that Board membership carries no right to preferential treatment in the placement or handling of the Hospital's investments or business accounts. The Hospital would be well advised to restrict membership on its Board to the representatives of financial institutions which have no substantial business relationship with the Hospital. The best way to avoid potential conflicts of interest and to be assured of objective advice is to avoid the possibility of such conflicts at the time new trustees are selected.[5]

According to Charles T. Stewart, general counsel for J. C. Penney Co. and a trustee of Cornell University, the precedent set by the *Sibley Hospital* case should dispel the "sense of euphoria" that trustees of educational institutions have "probably had . . . as a result of the absence of specific beneficiaries to whom the trustees were accountable."[6] In an earlier decision in the same case,[7] Judge Gesell found that the patients of Sibley Hospital had standing to bring a class action against the trustees on the grounds of a breach of trust; that decision, Stewart said, "indicates that colleges and university trustees should be concerned about being held accountable under certain circumstances to students, faculty, employees, or even alumni."[8]

In a recent interview, Stewart elaborated on this point:

These are a lot of people who don't think this is a serious problem. But I'm convinced it is. If you have a situation where the endowment fund has a terrible experience in the stock market, while at the same time enrollment is down and the school has to raise tuition 25 percent, and on the board of trustees you have some serious conflicts of interest, it's not impossible that a student or a group of students would sue, and I think they would have standing to sue.

A group of benefactors also might bring a class action, charging that, by imprudently holding on to a large block of trustee-donated stock whose performance or yield had been inadequate, the managers and trustees of the endowment fund, due to pooling, had caused the value of the donors' bequests to decline. "There are potentially dozens of cases [like the *Sibley Hospital* case] lurking around [among endowment funds]," says Daniel Robinson, a partner with the accounting firm of Peat, Marwick, Mitchell, Inc., who oversees his firm's nonprofit clients. He adds:

This is a litigious society, and I don't think educational institutions will remain exempt from that kind of activity. As soon as you have a suit against trustees where the plaintiff collects some money, a good piece of change, you'll see five hundred of those cases in the next three years.

Several possible courses of action are open to trustees and educational administrators seeking to protect themselves from lawsuits and public criticism and to reduce the still wide prevalence of conflicts of interest:

1. **A total ban on conflicting relationships.** Judge Gesell's opinion implies that such a ban may be advisable. And some institutions have chosen this course. As a result of local publicity several years ago about business dealings between the University of Minnesota and firms in which regents held stock, the University of Minnesota is not permitted to invest its endowment assets in any company in which a regent owns an interest, even though the university gives complete discretion to outside managers in the selection of portfolio securities.

The Common Fund has a formal conflict-of-interest policy that, among other things, prohibits any trustee or fund officer from having an affiliation with or interest in any investment manager, custodian bank, or securities firm with which the Common Fund does business. The fund had issued a policy statement specifying that "each affected person should avoid interests of any kind which, in the performance of any services for the Corporation or the Fund, might in fact or in appearance divert him from continued loyalty to the Corporation and the Fund." Because the Common Fund gives its investment managers discretion, in most cases, this policy does not prohibit trustees and officers of the fund from owning the same securities owned by the fund.

A total ban has certain disadvantages, according to Charles T. Stewart of J. C. Penney and Cornell:

[I]t is questionable whether a college or university board should restrict its membership to representatives of financial institutions which have no substantial business relationships with the institution.

The effect of such a requirement would be to eliminate from potential board membership a number of persons whose business experience, ability, and financial capacity would enable them to make important contributions of expertise and money to the institution or, conversely, to require the institution to do business only with second-rate investment and financial organizations.[9]

This view is perhaps overstated, except perhaps for very small colleges in very small communities. Most endowment funds may obtain satisfactory service from any of dozens of investment advisors, banks, and brokers that would not present conflicts with existing trustees. And yet the close network of relationships between universities, their communities, local businesses and financial institutions, and major donors may also provide very valuable nourishment to a university. Moreover, a contract between an endowment fund and an institution whose chief executive is on the board of trustees is not necessarily unfair or inequitable, although it is more likely than a contract with a nonaffiliated manager to be so. Finally, the evidence suggests that many apparent conflict-of-interest abuses are the result of timidity or eagerness to please on the part of officers of the educational institution rather than the venality of the trustees. Of course, in some cases trustees have approved of actions benefiting institutions with which they were affiliates. But the most serious self-dealing activities in the *Sibley Hospital* case were initiated by the hospital's treasurer, who apparently felt a personal obligation to favor institutions represented on the board.

Not all institutions are likely to find it necessary or possible to adopt a total ban on conflicts without undue inconvenience and disturbance of valuable relationships. But complete avoidance of conflicting relationships is a goal toward which all educational institutions should strive.

2. **A prohibition on voting on questions involving an outside institution with which one has an affilation or interest.** Judge Gesell stated flatly: "The trustee of a charitable hospital should always avoid active participation in a transaction in which he or a corporation with which he is associated has a significant interest."[10]

But is this prohibition by itself sufficient protection? William C. Porth, general counsel for New York University, has stated:

Over the years we have had officers or directors of major New York banks and trust companies on the University's board of trustees including some from institutions which handled major portions of our financial transactions. We can perceive no objection to this relationship provided always that any such trustee would not participate in any board decision which might present a possible conflict. Neither should there be any inhibition concerning ordinary business transactions between the institution and a firm with which a trustee is connected provided the trustee does not improperly influence such activities.[11]

Northwestern University also has an informal policy to the same effect. Yet as that school's portfolio holdings suggest, the members of some boards have close personal and business relationships and are unlikely to vote to fire a firm associated with a friend. A voting ban in itself is not necessarily a panacea against conflict-of-interest problems, although it is obviously better than nothing at all.

3. **Formal affirmation of a strict policy of avoiding conflict-of-interest improprieties.** After noting the problem of interest conflicts at nonprofit institutions and considering a complete prohibition on self-dealing situations, the Commission on Private Philanthropy and Public Needs recommended:

that all tax-exempt organizations be required by law to maintain ''arm's length'' business relationships with profit-making organizations or activities in which any member of the organization's staff, any board member, or any major contributor has a substantial financial interest, either directly or through his or her family.[12]

Educational endowments should seriously consider putting themselves formally on record against any but arm's-length relationships. They should adopt strict procedures requiring disclosure by trustees to other trustees of relevant outside affiliations. If the trustees choose to do business with an organization with which a trustee has an affiliation, the record should clearly show that alternatives were carefully considered, that the selection was in the best interests of the fund, and that the interested trustee did not participate in the decision.

4. **Public disclosure.** Trustees and endowment fund officers could go a long way toward establishing their concern for avoiding improprieties and toward curbing temptation to engage in questionable practices if they broadened their standards of public disclosure. The investments and investment policies of an educational endowment fund are not a private matter. Given the numerous groups of people which are affected by the activities of a typical college or university, anything short of complete financial disclosure is un-

justifiable. A comprehensive financial report should include the following items:

The affiliations of trustees. Most major corporations disclose the business and professional affiliations of their directors in annual reports. Many even list directors' outside board memberships. Most colleges and universities do not routinely disclose this information, and several even refused requests by the author for it. In addition, members of the trustees' finance or investment committees should be identified.

Portfolio investment. Some schools release detailed breakdowns of their portfolios, but most do not. Publication of this information and the list of trustee affiliations would make relationships between the two easy to spot and might inhibit trustee-linked investments.

The identity of investment managers and bank custodians. A few schools disclose this information. The University of Minnesota, the University of Pittsburgh, and Lawrence University, among others, even publish portfolio lists for each of the managers of their portfolio. But most do not. Schools also should disclose their broad investment objectives and philosophies and the degree of discretion given outside managers.

Fund performance. Most major colleges and universities now follow the reporting standards of the *Industry Audit Guide: Audits of Colleges and Universities*, which was prepared in 1973 by the Committee of the American Institute of Certified Public Accountants on College and University Accounting and Auditing. According to the *Audit Guide*, "The financial statements or notes should set forth the total performance (i.e., yield and gains or losses) of the investment portfolio based on cost and market value."[13] Yet too many schools still do not provide enough information to indicate to the reader how well the school's endowment fund has performed.[14] All should.

Conflict-of-interest relationships. Schools should disclose all trustee affiliations with or substantial stock interests in investment managers, brokerage houses, custodians, of banks that receive endowment fund business. Such disclosure is basically what Judge Gesell required of the hospital in the *Sibley Hospital* case. Charles T. Stewart, in his capacity as a Cornell University trustee, is working on a conflict-of-interest policy that would require trustees to make public disclosure of substantial stock holdings and outside directorships. In 1975 the American Institute of Certified Public Accountants published a policy statement on the disclosure of "related party transactions," requiring the reporting entity to release information on relationships whose effect is to prevent one of the parties "from fully pursuing its own separate interests."[15] According to Daniel Robinson of Peat, Marwick, Mitchell, this requirement may be applicable to relationships of the trustees of educational institutions with investment advisors, brokers, and banks with which the institution does business and to portfolio holdings in companies in which a trustee has a very large personal stock interest.

Accounting firms, however, have apparently been very slow to apply this policy to their audits of colleges and universities. Although the AICPA statement became effective for reports on periods ending on or after December 26, 1975, very few school financial reports for periods after this date disclose this information.

Disclosure, of course, is no panacea. But it could still go a long way toward reducing the still prevalent conflicts of interest and associated abuses at college and university endowment funds.

FOUNDATIONS

VI • INTRODUCTION

In 1961 Wright Patman (D.-Tex.) stood up on the floor of the House of Representatives and declared:

I am . . . concerned with, first, foundation-controlled businessess competing with small businesses; second, the economic effect of great amounts of wealth accumulating in privately-controlled, tax-exempt foundations; third, the problem of control of that capital for an undetermined period—in some instances perpetuity—by a few individuals or their self-appointed successors; and fourth, the foundation's power to interlock and knot together through investments, a network of commercial alliances, which assures harmonious action whenever they have a common interest . . . .[1]

With this speech, Patman and his Select House Committee on Small Business began a historic eight-year fight against private foundations. Foundations have always been the richest of the nation's nonprofit institutions, subsisting not on donations from the general public but on the income from sometimes mammoth endowments created by bequests from wealthy donors. According to the latest edition of the authoritative *Foundation Directory*, published by the Foundation Center, 2,504 foundations in the United States each have assets of over $1 million. The assets of these foundations, as of reporting periods during 1972-73, totaled $31,497,000,000. The 22,421 foundations with assets of under $1 million apiece had total assets of $2,599,410,000.[2]

When Patman began his investigation, foundations were remarkably free to do whatever they liked with this wealth. To maintain their tax-exempt status, foundations had only to adhere to the very vague and broad general requirement, set forth in Section 501 (c) (3) of the Internal Revenue Code, that they be "organized and operated exclusively for religious, charitable, scientific, testing for public safety, literary, or educational purposes, or for the prevention of cruelty to children or animals . . . ." Foundation trustees were even more autonomous than the trustees of educational endowments and other nonprofit institutions. Depending on the donor's expressed wishes, foundation boards could set criteria for the recipients of foundation funds and alter the criteria at will. They could spend as much or as little as they wanted. And unlike colleges and universities, which are inevitably the focus of public attention, foundations were able to operate, if they wished, in almost total secrecy. Even the Internal Revenue Service (IRS) accorded them only cursory attention. To a large extent, the tax exemption that foundations and other nonprofit institutions enjoy is subsidized by taxpayers, who must bear an additional financial burden to compensate for the taxes that foundations and their donors avoid. Yet foundations conducted themselves as if they were wholly private organizations to which no outsider need be given access.

In the absence of constraints, it was, perhaps, almost inevitable that abuses should develop. Section 501 (c) (3) provides, among other things, that "no part of the net earnings" of a foundation can inure "to the benefit of any private shareholder or individual." In six voluminous reports, packed with data and prefaced by often vituperative (but not always accurate) recitations of specific examples, Patman and his staff asserted that this provision had been violated regularly and on a very broad scale.[3]

The most dramatic of the instances cited by Patman were conflict-of-interest abuses deriving from extensive and incestuous linkages between foundations, donors, and companies with which donors were associated. In many cases the linkages were so intimate and complex that is was impossible to tell where one facet of the relationship left off and another began. Whatever the arrangement, the common theme was near-exclusive dedication of the foundation to the financial interests of the donor and his company, with the interest of charity running at best a poor second. Self-dealing was widespread. Foundations made loans to the donor or his company at low or no interest rates, purchased assets or interested parties at excessively high prices, sold assets for excessively low prices, and made grants to the donor's friends and family. They participated in elaborate kickback schemes with the donors and his associates, paid high salaries to the donor's friends and relatives for services as foundation trustees, and subsidized the donor's personal living expenses.

More broadly, the Patman material illustrated the widespread use of the foundation mechanism as a combination tax-free private bank and holding company for donors. Having given a foundation a large block of his company's stock, a donor could deduct the stock's market value from his taxable income as a charitable contribution and avoid capital gains taxes on the stock's appreciation. Then he would install himself, his family, and his friends as trustees. Thus, he could retain control of the block and his company while using the foundation's assets to promote his own and his company's fortunes. Foundations were not required to pay taxes on the dividends and interest they received or on the appreciation of their portfolios. Apart from channeling an occasional token grant to charity, foundations were an ideal device for storing enormous accumulations of resources to be employed in accordance with the donor's wishes. When the donors died, control of foundations and their assets passed smoothly to their heirs and chosen successors without the inconvenience of estate taxes; thus, foundations provided a means of perpetuating family dynasties and corporate power.

During the late 1960s, public outrage at the activities of foundations reached a crescendo. The publication of Patman's reports coincided with growing concern, on the part of liberals, over the inequities of the tax laws in general and, on the part of conservatives, over revelations of leftist tendencies in the grant programs of several foundations, especially the giant Ford Foundation. And everyone was upset by disclosures that foundation funds were being used to corrupt public officials. The discovery that Justice Abe Fortas, for instance, had accepted an annual fee from a foundation controlled by Louis E. Wolfson, a stock manipulator under federal indictment, led to Fortas's resignation from the Supreme Court.

Aggressive foundation lobbying defeated some of the most stringent of Patman's proposed measures, including a Senate Finance Committee amendment that would have forced foundations to dispose of all their assets after forty years or pay a regular corporate income tax. But the Tax Reform Act of 1969 was far from toothless. It subjected private foundations to stiff controls, many of them specifically designed to curb conflicts of interest. The act defines private foundations as organizations other than churches, schools, and hospitals that are covered by Section 501 (c) (3) and receive more than a third of their support from investment income. The Internal Revenue Service enforces the provisions of the act, penalizing violators, in most instances, by means of excise taxes—an initial tax upon discovery of the violation and a much higher tax if the violation is not remedied within a prescribed period. The provisions of the act deal with conflict-related issues such as:

1. *Self-dealing (Section 4941).* The self-dealing rules essentially prohibit all transactions between a foundation and "disqualified persons" and their families. The act defines disqualified persons as substantial contributors to the foundation, the foundation's managers and trustees, and persons holding more than a 20 percent interest in a business or enterprise that has been a substantial contributor to the foundation. (The act also provides for exceptions. For example, a foundation may pay a disqualified person reasonable compensation for personal services to the foundation necessary to accomplish exempt purposes and, if certain requirements are met, may enter into certain limited dealings with disqualified persons.)

2. *Required distributions (Section 4942).* Since failure to expend funds had been cited as frequently associated with abuses, this provision is designed to prevent an unreasonable accumulation of foundation assets. The act requires

a foundation to pay out in ''qualifying distributions'' the larger of its ''adjusted net income'' or the ''minimum investment return'' on fair market value of the foundation's assets. The Tax Reform Act of 1976 permanently put the minimum investment return and thus the minimum required payout at 5 percent of a foundation's assets.

3. *Excess business holdings (Section 4943)*. This series of rules is designed to reduce foundation holdings in and control of outside businesses. The Patman evidence showed conclusively that foundation control of businesses was the leading source of abuse. To avoid imposing excessive burdens on foundations with large holdings, the act distinguishes between holdings received by a foundation before and after May 26, 1969. For post-May 26, 1969, holdings, a foundation and related disqualified persons together may not own more than 20 percent (35 percent if a third person has effective control of the company) of the voting stock of a corporation. A foundation has five years after receipt of a holding to reduce it to the required level. For pre-May 26, 1969, holdings, the act provides for two phases of divestiture to bring a holding down to the 20 (or 35) percent level. In the first phase, which lasts ten to twenty years, depending on the original percentage, with longer periods for higher percentages, aggregate holdings of the foundation and disqualified persons must be reduced to 50 percent. In the second phase, which lasts fifteen years, the holdings must be reduced to 25 percent if disqualified persons own more than 2 percent, or 35 percent if they own less than 2 percent.

4. *Jeopardy investments (Section 4944)*. A foundation may not make investments that would financially ''jeopardize'' the foundation's ability to carry out its exempt purposes. (This provision does not apply to stock received from donors or investments made before 1970.)

5. *Disclosure (Section 6056)*. All foundations with more than $5,000 in assets must file with the IRS information such as the names and addresses of foundation managers and substantial contributors; income, expenses, and disbursements; a balance sheet including detailed information about securities holdings; and the names of foundation managers with a 10 percent or greater interest in an outside business in which the foundation owns a 10 percent or greater interest. This information is available to the public.

Discussions with foundation executives, investment managers, state attorneys general, and others suggest that the prevalence of abuses, particularly at the major foundations, has been significantly reduced by the 1969 act. Law enforcement authorities, who, before the act, had taken an almost laissez-faire stance toward foundations, have since 1969 sharply increased the intensity of their oversight. Using the proceeds of a 4 percent tax on foundation investment income imposed by the 1969 act, the IRS has substantially added to the resources devoted to foundation audits. State attorneys general, who have broad powers over foundations because most foundations are organized under state law, have stepped up their surveillance. The effect of this swelling enforcement effort has been to drive out of business many small foundations established mainly to serve the donor's interest and to force larger foundations to abandon questionable practices for fear of penalties.

Many large foundations with large holdings of donor stock, such as the Robert Wood Johnson Foundation (Johnson & Johnson), the Edna McConnell Clark Foundation (Avon Products), and the Kresge Foundation (S. S. Kresge), have been selling off large portions of these holdings. The Mellon foundations have been reducing their massive positions in Mellon-affiliated concerns such as Gulf Oil Corp. and Aluminum Co. of America. Perhaps the most spectacular divestiture, though, was conducted by the James Irvine Foundation, whose allegedly unscrupulous dealings with the Irvine Co., a large California landholder and developer of which the foundation owned 54.5 percent, were the subject of a report by Wright Patman. Because the 1969 act required the foundation to reduce its holdings to 2 percent by 1979,[4] the company decided to put itself up for sale. In July 1977 a consortium called Taubman-Allan-Irvine, Inc., acquired the company for $337.4 million.

In many cases the ties between donors, their companies, and their foundations are becoming unraveled. Symbolic of this trend was the resignation of Henry Ford II as trustee of the Ford Foundation in early 1977. In his resignation letter to the foundation, Henry Ford was quite critical of the foundation's policies and staff and suggested the foundation was insufficiently appreciative of the capitalistic system that had made the foundation possible. Over the past twenty years, the Ford Foundation has followed a policy of continually divesting its giant position in Ford stock, which once comprised 88 percent of the total outstanding. The foundation now owns no Ford stock and has no members of the Ford family or executives of the Ford Motor Co. on its board of trustees. Its only tie to the family that founded it is its name.

The John A. Hartford Foundation also has changed, for more obviously compelling reasons. John A. Hartford's father was George Huntington Hartford, who, in the nineteenth century, had founded the Great Atlantic & Pacific Tea Co.(A&P). John A. Hartford established the foundation in 1929, explicitly intending thereby to insure continuity of control of the company "as we know it today."[5] For years the trustees of the foundation loyally adhered to Hartford's intent. The foundation remained dominated by the company; Ralph W. Burger headed both the company and the foundation for twelve years. The foundation, which owned 34 percent of A&P's stock, steadfastly refused to cooperate with outsiders who considered taking over the company. Under foundation protection the company's management became increasingly ingrown and the company stagnated.

By 1972 A&P's troubles had become acute. A desperation price-cutting campaign to revive sagging sales had produced staggering losses; in 1972, A&P lost $107 million.[6] The Hartford Foundation, which had about three-quarters of its assets in A&P, felt the full force of the company's traumas. As the price of A&P stock dropped from 70 in 1961 to 16 in 1972, the value of the foundation's A&P holdings shrank from $585 million to $135 million. The foundation became an object lesson, as one senior executive with another foundation puts it, on "what failure to diversify can cost charity." Meanwhile, A&P, which had been steadily reducing its dividend, eliminated it entirely, wiping out most of the foundation's income.

"It was very hard for them [the foundation trustees] to believe that A&P could really be in trouble," says Michael McIntosh, president of the Josephine H. McIntosh Foundation. (The McIntosh Foundation had most of its assets in A&P shares, which McIntosh, whose mother was an A&P heir, had been unable to unload.) "Gradually," McIntosh recalls, "there was an awareness on the part of a sufficient number of the trustees of the foundation, probably helped out by the example of Penn Central, that even the finest companies if poorly enough managed for a long enough time can go down the tubes." In 1974, spurred by numerous disenchanted shareholders and the company's own board of directors, which had begun to worry mightly about shareholder suits, the Hartford Foundation took the lead in displacing the old management and bringing in a new chief executive from the outside. The foundation, meanwhile, embarked on a diversification program. In June 1976 it sold through a public offering a fifth, or $21 million worth, of its once inviolate A&P holdings, reducing its percentage of the company's stock to 25.5 percent. In early 1979, with the foundation's active support, the Tengelmann Group of Germany bought control of A&P. Tengelmann has acquired or has an option to acquire all of the Hartford Foundation's and McIntosh Foundation's A&P shares.

Today, few of the nation's large foundations show evidence of the egregious abuses and self-dealing of the sort highlighted in the 1960s by Wright Patman. But the conflicts of interest that remain, although often extremely subtle and perfectly legal, still permit foundations to serve as mechanisms for the perpetuation of corporate power and impair their ability to fulfill their responsibilities to help meet the nation's charitable needs. Few foundations conform to the standards set by the Ford Foundation—with its broad group of trustees, its diversified, professionally managed portfolio, its generous grant program (critics even argue that this generosity is severely depleting the foundation's assets), and its exclusive dedication to the public's well-being.

Two chief problem areas remain only marginally affected by the 1969 act:

1. Numerous foundations continue to possess extremely close links with donors, the donors' families, and the donors' companies. Although they have in some cases sold blocks of the donors' stocks, they have done so solely to comply with the 1969 act, and they clearly intend to continue holding as much stock as the law allows. The 1969 act limits the percentage of a company's stock a foundation can own, but it places no limits on the percentage of a foundation's portfolio that can be invested in a single stock; hence, many

foundations continue to keep almost all their assets in shares of their respective donors' companies.

In many cases substantial overlaps remain between a foundation's trustees, the donor and his family, and the associated company's management and board of directors. Trustees of such foundations typically continue to view the foundation as a mechanism for corporate control. In conflicts between the charitable obligations of the foundation and the private concerns of the company, charity is likely to come off second best. Citing some of these relationships, Waldemar Nielsen, a prominent foundation critic, concluded that "the boards of the big American foundations are currently ridden with conflicts of interest incompatible with their objective and exclusive devotion to philanthropic purposes and the public interest."[7]

2. Despite the self-dealing rules, many foundations maintain very close ties with local banks and other organizations that provide them with services. In numerous cases executives and directors of the bank serve as trustees, the bank serves as investment manager and custodian, and the foundation has invested heavily in the bank's securities and those of other companies represented on the board of trustees. As in the case of endowment funds, the relationships lessen the foundation's ability to secure disinterested, low-cost services and to employ its assets in the most productive way.

Because a large portion of their assets consist of tax money foregone by federal, state, and local governments, private foundations are really quasi-public institutions. Arguably (it is not the function of this report to make a judgment on the point), foundations serve an important social role and are entitled to their indirect public subsidy. But they are not justified in sacrificing their ostensibly charitable goals to serve the private interests of those who control them.

VII • THE DONORS AND THEIR COMPANIES

In 1945 Otto Haas, a German immigrant and founder of the Philadelphia-based Rohm and Haas Co., established a foundation and named it after his wife, Phoebe Waterman. In 1970, a year after her death and a decade after his, the foundation was renamed the Haas Community Fund. In 1975 its name was changed again to the William Penn Foundation. Yet despite the increasingly cosmopolitan orientation implied by its name changes, and without violating the Tax Reform Act of 1969, the foundation remains as much a creature of the Haas family and of their company as it was in 1945.[1]

John C. Haas, Otto Haas's younger son, is chairman and president of the foundation and chairman of the company. F. Otto Haas, Otto Haas's elder son, is vice-chairman of the foundation and vice-chairman of the company. Also on the foundation's board of directors are the two Haases's wives and one of their sons. As of the end of 1975, all but $7,537 of the $124,048,622 in assets in the foundation's principal account was in 2,376,266 shares—18.5 percent of the total outstanding—of Rohm and Haas stock. These shares, combined with other shares controlled by the Haas family, make up 47.7 percent of the total.

The William Penn Foundation's holdings of Rohm and Haas do not violate the excess business holdings provision of the Tax Reform Act of 1969. But Rohm and Haas is not a big income producer for its shareholders. Recently, the stock was yielding about 2.8 percent in dividends. The foundation also receives income from several Haas family trusts. But to meet the minimum payout requirement, the foundation has had to sell small portions of its Rohm and Haas holdings.

Rohm and Haas has not been much of a capital gains producer for shareholders either. The stock was recently selling at its lowest price in seven years, down two-thirds from its 1973 high. The foundation's treasurer is unwilling to talk publicly about investment policy or any other aspect of his work, but the foundation has shown no sign of an intent to diversify its portfolio or to sell any more Rohm and Haas than necessary to meet the minimum payout requirement.

The nature of charitable grants made by the William Penn Foundation has given it a reputation as one of the more innovative foundations. The Haas brothers take an active interest in philanthropy. But it appears that the foundation serves a dual purpose. During hearings on the 1969 act, a spokesman for the foundation told the Senate Finance Committee that it had been created ''to establish a major philanthropy and to enable the family to satisfy their desire for such philanthropy without jeopardizing their control of the family business. . . .The company is a prime target for raiders and is protected only by the fact that as much as 49 percent of the stock can be considered in friendly hands.''[2]

Whatever its charitable purposes, the William Penn Foundation is clearly an instrument for the retention of corporate control. An asset-rich chemical concern with sales of over $1 billion and a net worth of over $550 million, Rohm and Haas has often been regarded covetously by acquisition-minded conglomerateurs. The foundation's policy of keeping its entire portfolio invested in a single company whose stock pays a low dividend and has had a lackluster growth record is not the product of disinterested investment analysis and an effort to make the maximum amount available for charity in accordance with a prudent level of risk. It is, rather, the method by which the Haas-controlled board of directors of the foundation seeks to perpetuate the entrenched corporate position of the Haas family.

The 1969 Tax Reform Act penalizes investments that jeopardize a foundation's tax-exempt purposes. An instruction booklet issued by the IRS to assist foundations in complying with the act defines jeopardizing investments as "those which show a lack of reasonable business care and prudence in providing for the long- and short-term financial needs of the foundation."[3] The booklet further states: "to avoid the application of the tax on jeopardizing investments, a careful analysis of potential investments must be made and good business judgment must be exercised." (The booklet also note that the IRS will not use hindsight in evaluating foundation portfolios for this purpose.) Because it was acquired before 1970, the William Penn Foundation's Rohm and Haas holding is exempt from these provisions. But it is hard to avoid the conclusion that the foundation's steadfast retention of Rohm and Haas stock has little to do with the exercise of reasonable business care and prudence or with the furtherance of the foundation's charitable purposes.

As the American economic system matures, the prevalence of large, family-run and -controlled corporations is declining, and although relatively common in the past, absolute family control of a company and its associated foundation is also becoming rare. Yet many large foundations still invest most of their assets in a single stock. Of the ten largest foundations, accounting for close to a third of all foundation assets, six, with assets of over $4 billion, have more than half their money invested in one company. Despite the limitations and intent of the 1969 act, all six of these foundations are the companies' largest single stockholders, and their blocks are essential for control of the company. Most one-stock foundations are dominated by a combination of relatives or descendants of the original donor and current or former executives of the donor's company. Over time the descendants of donors have become dispersed and have tended to lose interest in the company or the foundation. Under these conditions, one-stock foundations increasingly are becoming simply adjuncts of the corporations—nonprofit, management-controlled holding companies. For the corporation executives in charge, the foundations are a valuable mechanism for resisting challenges and preserving their tenure in office.

Some examples of current foundations structure and control:

The Duke Endowment. Established by James B. Duke, founder of the Duke Power Co. (an electric utility serving North and South Carolina), this foundation, as of the end of 1975, had 75.3 percent of its $379,137,219 portfolio invested in Duke Power securities. Its common stock holdings represented 24 percent of the company's total shares outstanding. Of the fourteen trustees, two are family members (including James Duke's daughter), two are former executives or directors of Duke Power, one is a current director of the company, and three are executives with the foundation.

James Duke's trust indenture specified that the foundation's holdings were not to be changed "except in response to the most urgent and extraordinary necessity" and that if some securities were sold, the proceeds could be invested only in Duke Power securities or U.S. Treasury issues. In 1963 the foundation's trustees sought a South Carolina court judgment that would permit the foundation to diversify. But the request was turned down. Three years ago they tried again and this time succeeded. But their purpose in seeking the court judgment apparently was not to sell Duke Power. Since the favorable decision, the foundation has disposed of most of the large blocks of Alcoa and Alcan Aluminum that also were among the original securities donated to the foundation by James Duke. John F. Day, secretary of the foundation, explains: "We think we lost the first case because we couldn't convince the court we weren't talking about selling the Duke Power but some of the other things that we held." The foundation apparently made the point more clearly to the state court the second time. Beyond what may be necessary to comply with the 1969 act, the foundation does not contemplate reducing its Duke Power holdings.

In 1968 an official with the smaller, family-controlled Mary Duke Biddle Foundation, which also holds most of its assets in Duke Power stock and whose chairman is a trustee of the Duke Endowment, stated that its Duke Power holdings were "sacred." That attitude apparently continues to prevail among the family and corporate trustees of the Duke Endowment today.

The Lilly Endowment. As of the end of 1975, the Lilly Endowment had $687,730,590, or 90.3 percent of its assets, invested in Eli Lilly and Co. Its holding of 13,289,480 shares constitutes 19.25 percent of the company's outstanding shares. The foundation's eight-member board of directors includes: a member of the Lilly family, which started the foundation and the company; the present chairman of the company, the head of its finance committee, and two of its former presidents. (Eli Lilly, an early organizer of the company and honorary chairman of the board of trustees of the foundation, died in early 1977.) Another trustee is the chancellor of Indiana University, a major recipient of the foundation's grants. Five of the trustees are members of the board of Eli Lilly and Co. and are themselves major holders of Lilly stock. The foundation and the Lilly family together control 40.5 percent of the company. The foundation has sold off some of its Lilly shares to comply with the 1969 act but does not appear to be planning any further sales.

W. K. Kellogg Foundation. In conjunction the Kellogg Family Trust, which it controls, this foundation held 36,176,480 shares of Kellogg Co., worth $917,978,180, as of August 31, 1976. This block, 95.1 percent of the foundation's assets, represented 49.1 percent of the company's outstanding shares. Of the foundation's nine directors, five are executives and/or board members of the Kellogg Co. (four of them own Kellogg stock), and they comprise the foundation's finance committee. Through sales of Kellogg stock, the foundation has complied with the 1969 act stipulation that it own under 50 percent of the company by 1979. The act also stipulates that the foundation should hold no more than 35 percent of the company by 1994. But according to foundation president Russell G. Mawby, the Kellogg Foundation has no immediate plans for further sales. As he puts it, "1994 is a long time away."

Many other one-stock foundations control important blocks of a company's securities and have links with the company.[4] For example, the Henry Luce Foundation (assets: $55 million) is dominated by current and former Time Inc. executives, their relatives, and members of the Luce family. The foundation has some 91 percent of its assets in Time Inc. stock. That block, plus blocks owned by two other foundations of which Time Inc. board members are trustees, makes up 9 percent of Time Inc.'s shares.

The Danforth Foundation ($106 million) had 84 percent of its money in Ralston Purina Co., a 5 percent ownership. William H. Danforth, chairman of the foundation's board of trustees, is a board member of the company, and Donald Danforth, Jr., another trustee, heads a Ralston Purina subsidiary.

Over half the assets of the Pew Memorial Trust ($485 million) and 95 percent of the assets of the J. Howard Pew Freedom Trust ($58 million) are invested in the Sun Co., accounting for close to 20 percent of total outstanding Sun Co. stock. The sole trustee for the foundations is the Glenmede Trust Co., which is controlled by the Pew family, which founded Sun Co. Among Glenmede's directors are the corporate secretary and a retired chairman of the Sun Co.

Virtually all of the assets of the Frank E. Gannett Newspaper Foundation ($150 million) are invested in shares of the Gannett Co. Those shares, as a result of the 1969 act, have been reduced through sales and donations from 27 percent to just under 20 percent of the total outstanding. Gannett Co. chairman Paul Miller is president and trustee of the foundation. Gannett Co. president Allen H. Neuharth and four other present or former Gannett officers and directors are trustees and officers of the foundation. All are Gannett stockholders; together, they own $10 million worth of the company's stock.

Similarly close foundation-corporation linkages are evident at the $34 million Rowland Foundation (Polaroid Corp.), the $45 million Boettcher Foundation (Ideal Basic Industries, Inc.), and the $94 million Henry J. Kaiser Foundation (Kaiser Industries Corp.), and the $110 million Moody Foundation (American National Financial Corp.).

Other large nonprofit institutions closely allied with corporations escape the restrictions of the 1969 Tax Reform Act through a loophole that excludes ''medical research organization[s] directly engaged in the continuous active conduct of medical research in conjunction with a hospital.'' The best-known organization that has attempted to take advantage of this loophole is the Howard Hughes Medical Institute (HHMI), a research facility in Miami, Florida, that was one of Wright Patman's prime targets. The HHMI was organized in 1963, when Howard Hughes transferred to it the shares of what was later called Hughes Aircraft Co., a major defense contractor. Hughes, who derived considerable tax benefits from the transfer,[5] installed himself as sole trustee, with complete contol over HHMI's affairs. Hughes requested tax exemption for HHMI, but the IRS turned him down, maintaining that the institute was simply a tax dodge. In 1967 the IRS reversed itself, allegedly as a result of the efforts of Richard Nixon in return for a $205,000 Hughes Aircraft loan for his brother. In 1970 the HHMI applied to the IRS for a ruling that it is a medical research facility not covered by the 1969 act.

If the IRS were to rule that the HHMI was a private foundation covered by the 1969 act, the institute would then have to divest controlling shares of Summa and Hughes Aircraft and substantially step up its contributions to charity. Hughes Aircraft has paid no dividends to the HHMI, which subsists instead on "distributions" from the company. Until 1976, these distributions amounted to only $3.5 million, 0.35 percent of Hughes Aircraft's value. (In 1976 Hughes Aircraft earned about $60 million on sales of $116 billion.)[8] If the IRS were to rule that the HHMI was not covered by the 1969 act, the institute would become, in effect, a $3 billion, tax-exempt industrial complex controlled by Gay and Davis and not required to demonstrate more than minimal concern for charity. In 1978, a memorandum issued by the IRS indicated that it would reverse an earlier ruling by the local IRS office and would consider the HHMI exempt from the 1969 act.

As of this writing, the disposition of the Howard Hughes estate remains unsettled, and controversy continues to rage over which, if any, of several candidates was Hughes's legal will. During his lifetime Hughes occasionaly expressed the desire to make the institute his sole beneficiary, a move that would avoid taxes on the estate. The institute thus stands at least a good chance of eventually acquiring his estate, principally Summa Corp., a holding company for most of Hughes's other business properties. Shortly before he died, Hughes is said to have appointed as members of the executive committee of HHMI Frank W. Gay, until recently president of Summa, and Chester C. Davis, until recently Summa's chief counsel. Under the by-laws of the HHMI, the executive committee was empowered to succeed Hughes as the institute's trustee.[6] If the HHMI obtains Summa, Gay and Davis would then possess direct control, through a nonprofit institution, of corporate properties worth perhaps as much as $3 billion: $1 billion for Hughes Aircraft and $2 billion for Summa.[7]

A large foundation that has succeeded in taking advantage of the loophole is the Nemours Foundation. This institution is the beneficiary of and receives most of its income from the estate of Alfred I. Du Pont, one of the organizers of E. I. Du Pont De Nemours & Co. After he died in 1935, his estate was taken over by the Florida National Bank of Jacksonville and three individual trustees, the senior being Edward Ball, Alfred's brother-in-law. Ball built Du Pont's legacy into an immensely remunerative empire worth over $1 billion.[9] The estate holds large blocks of Du Pont and General Motors stock. But its principal asset is a 74 percent interest in the Jacksonville, Florida, based St. Joe Paper Co., which Ball built from a tiny paper mill into a sprawling conglomerate that, besides its extensive paper operations, controls two railroads, a sugar refinery, and "what is believed to be the largest and richest collection of real estate in Florida,"[10] including dozens of acres of downtown Miami.

Until 1970 most of the proceeds of this empire, usually between $10 million and $15 million a year and mostly from dividends from the Du Pont and General Motors stock, went to Alfred Du Pont's third wife, who was Ball's sister. In 1971 she died, and the money began flowing into the Nemours Foundation. The chief function of this foundation has been operation of the Alfred I. Du Pont Institute, a small hospital and research center for crippled children in Wilmington, Delaware. When it began its operations, the foundation sagely obtained a ruling from the IRS designating it as a medical research organization exempt from the 1969 act. With no payout rules to govern its operation, the money was soon piling up faster than the foundation seemed able or willing to spend it.[11] Recently, the foundation decided to appropriate some of its surplus, now over $50 million, for an addition to the hospital, but it has actually spent little of the money as yet.

Last year, Alfred Du Pont Dent, Alfred Du Pont's grandson and the only blood descendant of Du Pont on the Nemours Foundation board, commenced a series of moves to, among other things, broaden the foundation's activities and increase its return from the estate. His grandfather, Dent pointed out, had expressed the belief that "it is the duty of everyone in the world to do what is within his power to alleviate human suffering . . . ." His grandfather's will specified that the foundation should serve not only cripped children but also the elderly and "other worthy charitable institutions." Yet over the forty years in which he has managed Alfred Du Pont's estate, Ball appears to have been "dedicated more to the accumulation of economic power than the care of the needy."[12]

Dent's chief aim is to get the foundation to sell its interest in the St. Joe Paper Co., which in 1975 earned $187 a share but paid a dividend of only $4. The foundation has been reaping a return of just $280,000 on a 74 percent interest in an asset worth perhaps $500 million or more. If the foundation sold its St. Joe shares and invested the proceeds in more productive investments, Dent has claimed, it could increase its income and thus its distributions to charity by as much as $50 million annually.

Edward Ball and his associates vehemently oppose Dent's proposal. Along with three executives and directors of St. Joe and its subsidiaries, whom Ball, now eighty-nine and in failing health, wants to succeed him as stewards of the estate, Ball controls the foundation's five-man board of trustees.

Dent is not surprised by the opposition. "I think it is very difficult for people who work for the paper company to sit and vote whether they should sell the paper company," he says. If the Nemours Foundation were covered by the 1969 act, of course, it would already have had to prepare for divestiture of the paper company and been forced to increase its attention to charity substantially.

A trustee should act solely in the interest of the foundation and the further-ance of its charitable purposes. But if he is an officer, director, or stockholder of the allied company, or if he has an emotional or family tie to the donor of the foundation's stock, he may find it difficult to ignore the interests of the company, which may often be at variance with those of the foundation. Asked about the five individuals who are both officers or directors of Kellogg Co. and trustees of the Kellogg Foundation, foundation president Russell Mawby replies: "My experience is that the trustees act very responsibly and objectively and separate the two responsibilities very carefully. I see absolutely no conflict in their performance."

Yet, as in educational endowments, situations often arise in foundations that can subject the trustee with corporate affiliations to strains that he may feel compelled to resolve by favoring the company's management over the foundation's. Such situations include proxy fights and anti-management shareholder resolutions. It was recently reported, for instance, that a group of shareholders (including Frank Sinatra) was preparing a takeover fight against Del E. Webb Corp., an Arizona land developer and hotel-casino owner.[13] About 35 percent of the company's stock is held in the estate of Del E. Webb, who died in 1974. When Webb's estate is settled, the stock will go to the Del E. Webb Foundation. The executor of the estate and head of the foundation is Robert H. Johnson, the company's chief executive officer. According to *Business Week*, the company's "overall performance has been lackluster."[14] Yet it is difficult to believe that if a proxy fight developed, Johnson would decide it was in the best interests of the estate or the foundation to side with insurgents.

The most flagrant example of trustees favoring their own interests over those of the foundation is, of course, the failure of one-stock foundations to diversify. It is no coincidence that at virtually every foundation that keeps most of its assets in the shares of a single company, the board of trustees is closely linked to the company. Willingness to permit such a concentration of assets runs directly counter to long-accepted standards of prudent investment management.[15] Among all the portfolios in the United States over which professional investment managers have discretion, it is difficult to find a single one that is more than 25 percent invested in a single company. In the $500 billion universe of professionally managed assets, the one-stock portfolios so common among private foundations are an anomaly. Everywhere else prudence is synonymous with diversification.

Arguments against diversification, nonetheless, have been vigorously advanced by foundations such as Kellogg, whose shares have experienced substantial capital gains over the years. "We feel the general policy of holding Kellogg has served us well," says Russell Mawby. "The performance of the stock has been dramatic and has far exceeded the general market indicators. If the idea of a foundation is to maximize the resources available for educational and charitable purposes, then society's interests would have been less well served if we had invested in something else." Executives of other foundations that have invested heavily in a single growth leader, such as Johnson & Johnson and S. S. Kresge, might make the same statement.

Most other one-stock foundations, though, have had their portfolios committed to less successful issues. For many years the Grant Foundation, founded in 1936 by William T. Grant. was almost entirely invested in 1,294,000 common shares and 11,900 convertible perferred shares of W. T. Grant Co., the retail chain. In 1969, long before the company's troubles had become apparent, the foundation fortunately, reportedly in part at the urging of the New York State attorney general's office, began an active diversification policy and, by the time the company went bankrupt in 1975, had reduced its holdings to 400,000 shares and accumulated a diversified portfolio now worth nearly $50 million. The remaining 400,000 shares, worth $20 million at the end of 1969, are now carried on the foundation's books for a nominal value of $1.

Other one-stock foundations invested in nongrowth issues, such as the John A. Hartford Foundation, have made much less timely diversifications. Still others, such as the William Penn Foundation, have made negligible efforts at diversification despite the depreciation of their assets. The market value of the shares of Polaroid that company chairman Edwin Land and his family contributed to the Rowland Foundation, $94.2 million at the time of the gifts, was $33 million at the end of 1975. The Henry Luce Foundation's block of Time Inc. stock, most of which it received when Henry R. Luce died in 1967, at a cost basis of $68 million, was valued at $50 million at the end of 1975. The Moody Foundation's block of American National Financial Corp., valued at $103 million when the foundation received it, is now valued at only $85 million. Duke Power shares have been continously falling for the last decade; now they are selling for half the price that prevailed in the 1960s.

One-stock portfolios, moreover, are much more volatile than well-diversified ones. Between the end of 1974 and the end of 1975, when the market as a whole was up, the market value of the Lilly Endowment's holding of Eli Lilly and Co. dropped $216 million to $688 million. To meet payout obligations, holders of a diversified fund can either use dividends and interest income or dispose of the least attractive issues in their portfolios. But one-stock foundations, particularly if the stock has a low dividend, often must sell portions of their principal holding. The Lilly endowment, for example, might have had to sell Eli Lilly shares at a time, such as 1975, when their price was unusually depressed.

One-stock foundations, by definition, are committed to equities and thus the stock market. But during periods such as the early 1970s, which featured desultory stock performance and high interest rates, the best performing portfolios were those balanced between equities, debt securities, and money market or near-cash instruments. One-stock foundations cannot adjust to such shifts in the market.

The illiquidity of one-stock portfolios can present additional difficulties. In most cases these large holdings consist of stock that has not been registered for public sale with the SEC. Small amounts of such stock can be sold under SEC Rule 144, which generally permits sales over a six-month period of an amount equal to the lesser of 1 percent of the company's outstanding stock or the average weekly trading volume. Unregistered shares also can be disposed of through private placements or swaps with other institutions. But major disposals to the public usually require a registered secondary offering, which can be conducted only with the participation and approval of the company. When an unexpected crisis afflicts a company in which a foundation with a diversified portfolio has a position, the foundation usually can unload its shares quickly and limit its losses. If the foundation instead holds a very large unregistered block, the company may refuse to cooperate in a secondary offering that could exacerbate its financial troubles and depress its stock. The foundation then has no choice but to watch its endowment shrink. Even when the company agrees to a secondary, the process of drawing up a prospectus, obtaining approval from the SEC, and organizing and conducting the sale can take months. Meanwhile, the company's shares may be falling drastically.

Explaining why the Kresge Foundation began a diversification program in 1965, when he became president, William H. Baldwin says, "As a trustee, I felt we had too many eggs in one basket. In a way, I'm sorry we didn't keep all the stock. If we'd held it, we'd be up to a billion and a quarter dollars instead of three quarters of a billion. But though we would have had an enormous corpus, it would have been absolutely illiquid and immobile." The foundation, which once had 95 percent of its assets in Kresge stock, has reduced its Kresge holding to a quarter of its portfolio. In part because of the stock's superior performance, S. S. Kresge Co. has been very cooperative with the foundation in arranging secondaries.

Because it may force a foundation to sell pieces of its major holding so it can meet grant commitments and legal payout requirements, low yield is a particularly common and serious problem for one-stock foundations. In some cases low yield may simply be a reflection of the company's lackluster earnings record. Shares of Sun Co. and Eli Lilly and Co. are selling for roughly the same price as a decade ago and pay out only 3-4 percent. This low yield has resulted in continual erosion in the holdings of the Pew Memorial Trust and the Lilly Endowment. A foundation exclusively invested in a stock with no growth, which pays a dividend below the 5 percent minimum payout, must inevitably run out of money.

In some cases stocks have low yields because corporate managers prefer to use the company's income for other purposes. Unless they have reasons for behaving otherwise, corporate executives, spurred by, among other things, stock options and incentive bonuses, tend to be more interested in promoting capital growth than in paying generous dividends. They are inclined to increase dividends only when necessary to satisfy shareholders and attract buyers to their stock. The executives of a company that is largely or totally owned by a charitable foundation whose board or trustees is, in turn, controlled by the company are unlikely to feel pressure or to see reason to make large dividend payouts. As Julius Greenfield, then assistant attorney general of New York State, testified before Wright Patman's Subcommittee on Domestic Finance in 1973, "I don't think I have to tell this committee how easy it is for persons who administer foundations and who at the same time are interested in the closely held businesses themselves [owned by the foundations] to manipulate the closely held businesses so that there is little, if any, return to the foundation from those holdings of the foundation.''[16]

In some instances such niggardly payouts have come under attack, ironically, from members of the donor's family who still retain important shareholdings in the company, although they have lost control of the foundation to company executives. For example, the James Irvine Foundation until recently owned 54.5 percent of the stock of the Irvine Co., whose executives dominated the foundation. For years Joan Irvine Smith, who owned or controlled 22 percent of the company's stock, waged a running battle with its management, which she accused of deliberately and consistently understating the company's worth and earnings and paying out very stingy dividends.[17] Because nearly all the remaining stock was closely held by Irvine family members and the company's management, there was no public market for the stock; hence, its estimated value was usually derived from appraisals commissioned by the company and the foundation. By understating the value of its Irvine Co. holdings, of course, the foundation was able to reduce the amount of charitable benefits it is required to pay out under the 1969 act. In its annual report for the year ending March 31, 1976, the foundation valued its 4,590,000-share holding of Irvine Co. stock at $94,095,000, or $20.50 a share. If this valuation was correct, the company was paying the foundation a dividend of 3.5 percent. (Before Joan Irvine Smith began her campaign, the company had been paying out much less.) But an investor group including Smith and Henry Ford II recently acquired the company for $40.10 a share,[18] topping a $40 bid by Mobil Corp. If these offers fairly reflect the company's value, the foundation's actual yield from its Irvine Co. stock was less than 2 percent, and in that case its charitable payments were over $3.5 million a year less than the minimum required by the 1969 act.

Noble Affiliates, Inc., is an Oklahoma oil concern organized by the Samuel Roberts Noble Foundation. As of April 1976, the foundation owned 70.5 percent of the company's stock. Sam Noble, chairman of Noble Affiliates, is a trustee of the foundation, as is E. E. Noble, his brother. Although in 1975 the company had retained earnings of $71.8 million, cash and marketable securities worth $4 million, and profits of $11.6 million, Noble Affiliates saw fit to pay out only $700,000 in dividends to the foundation. The foundation's yield on its holding was about 1.5 percent. Noble Affiliates' officers and directors, meanwhile, paid themselves direct and indirect remuneration of over $550,000. Sam Noble received $125,000. According to foundation president John March, ''Their business needs a great deal of money for growth, and their growth is more important than increased dividends.'' However, in compliance with the 1969 act, the Noble Foundation will have to divest at least a portion of its stock in the company.

Many foundation executives argue that reinvesting earnings to promote growth instead of paying high dividends is in the best long-run interest of the foundation as well as the company. Growth companies such as Kellogg may have a modest current yield, but continuously rising earnings have permitted Kellogg to increase its dividend to keep pace with the rising price of its stock. On the Kellogg Foundation's original investment, thus, the current yield is very high. According to this argument, mandated payout minimums frustrate foundations with growth stocks. If the payout is higher than the current dividend yield, the foundation will have to invade its corpus regularly and to sell shares that may later appreciate in value and might otherwise eventually make possible much higher payments to charity. Of course, very few foundations that follow the policy of earnings reinvestment have been as successful as Kellogg. Still, several one-stock foundations used these arguments effectively in lobbying for a reduction in the required payout provisions of the 1969 act.[19] In 1975 the payout level required under the 1969 act was 6 percent. In 1976 it was to have varied in accordance with prevailing money market rates and investment yields, with the annual adjustment limited to 0.25 percent. But due to foundation lobbying, the Tax Reform Act of 1976 set the payout permanently at 5 percent.

James Abernathy, a frequent critic of foundation policy, comments:

It sounds like they're trying to do just what the 1969 act was trying to avoid, which is piling up money. Someone who donates stock to a foundation gets a tax advantage immediately. Other taxpayers have to make up for it immediately by paying higher taxes. But society doesn't receive any benefits from the foundation except over a long period of time, particularly if the dividend is low. What Congress wanted to do in passing the [1969] act was to make the return to society quicker.

Consider a hypothetical rich individual who gives $1 million worth of securities in his company to a foundation. If he is in the 70 percent tax bracket, the government immediately foregoes $700,000 in taxes as a result of his charitable contribution tax deduction. If he leaves the securities to a foundation upon his death, the government may lose an equivalent amount in estate taxes. If the stock given to the foundation yields 5 percent, it will just cover the foundation's current payout requirement. At that rate charity will have to wait fourteen years to obtain $700,000 in benefits from the gift, not counting the interest the government could have earned (or might not have had to pay on its debt) during that time by collecting the money in taxes the first year.

If the gift of stock declined in value during those fourteen years, charity would have to wait even longer. For example, Edwin Land gave $94 million worth of Polaroid stock to the Rowland Foundation. His current salary at Polaroid is $235,280; so he may have taken a $66 million deduction. In addition, Land may have saved another $25 million by avoiding the capital gains taxes he would have had to pay if he had sold those shares.

Polaroid's price drop over the past few years has sharply reduced the value of the foundation's assets; hence, in 1975 the foundation paid out less than $1 million in grants. At that rate charity will take a hundred years to reap the benefits of government's tax loss, again not counting interest. If the price of Polaroid's stock and thus the foundation's assets continue to fall, it could take even longer.

VIII • BANKERS AND BROKERS

"The very existence of a set of guidelines for the staff and board of a foundation serves to remind us from time to time of the possibility of conflict— or the appearance of conflict," says Irving Clark, a director of the Northwest Area Foundation in St. Paul, Minnesota. "Even though our intentions are good, it is helpful to be reminded."[1]

A couple of years ago, Clark drew up written conflict-of-interest guidelines for the foundation that, among other things, require foundation officers and trustees to disclose outside affiliations and to refrain from discussing and voting on matters in which they have a personal interest. Mostly as a result of the 1969 act, a number of other foundations, including Kellogg, Rockefeller, Ford, and Jerome, also have adopted formal conflict-of-interest rules. Other foundations, including Bush, Rosenberg, and Kresge, have informal policies. Lawrence Stifel, secretary of the Rockefeller Foundation, explains:

The discussions leading to the Tax Reform Act revealed a degree of ignorance and suspicion of private foundations which has not been fully perceived by the foundation community. The political reaction against foundations emphasized the need for foundations to make every effort possible to maintain the highest fiduciary responsibilities of trustees and officers.

None of these guidelines has much effect on tight foundation-company-donor relationships; apparently, few trustees view these relationships as a conflict-of-interest problem. The guidelines focus on conflict situations such as the affiliation of trustees or foundation officers with organizations applying for grants and organizations that supply the foundation with services.[2] But the effectiveness of the guidelines in dealing with these problems is questionable.

Despite the Northwest Area Foundation's policy, there is a clear conflict of interest on its own board of directors. Harry L. Holtz, director of the foundation, is chief executive officer and director of the First Trust Company of St. Paul. The chairman of the foundation's board is an advisory director of the bank. First Trust Company is the foundation's fiscal agent. It manages the portfolio and supplies the foundation with other banking services. The third largest holding in the foundation's portfolio is $4.3 million worth of stock, which the foundation received as a gift, in First Bank System, Inc., the bank holding company that owns First Trust Company. A large portion of the original gift has been sold over the years. Nevertheless, a trust company whose chairman is a trustee of a foundation manages the foundation's money and keeps the foundation heavily invested in the bank's own stock.

In its annual report, the Northwest Area Foundation discloses its relationship with the bank; this foundation is one of very few to disclose such information. The report also states that, in accordance with the foundation's written conflict-of-interest rules, the bank's chief executive officer "does not participate in or vote on board actions pertaining to the fiscal agent." Holtz makes it a practice of not being present when the board votes on actions pertaining to the fiscal agent. But whether this permits the other directors to vote their minds freely is very questionable.

Conflicts involving advisors, brokers, and bankers, nevertheless, seem to be less common at foundations than at college and university endowments. One main reason, of course, is the self-dealing section of the Tax Reform Act to 1969. Another is that, because many foundation portfolios are relatively committed to a single stock, they usually are managed internally by the treasurer. And because foundations are under much less pressure for performance, even those with more diversified portfolios tend to be less actively managed than college or university endowment funds and thus generate fewer brokerage commissions. Many foundation portfolios, in fact, have changed little since they were received from the donors. Because of the relative paucity of their securities transactions and the relative simplicity of their cash management, the banking and custodial needs of foundations also are relatively simple.

Among foundations that produce sizable brokerage, however, the temptation to channel commissions to interested parties and to generate excessive commissions is always present. In 1973 Julius Greenfield of New York's attorney general's office told the Patman subcommittee that his office had encountered several cases of churning. In one instance the foundation was under the control of a stockbroker who directed commissions to himself and unnecessarily traded the portfolio. Greenfield recovered the commissions and dissolved the foundation.[3]

Not all less-than-arm's length brokerage arrangements involving foundations violate the prohibition against self-dealing. For example, the Boettcher Foundation in Denver discloses—in one of the rare "transactions with related party" footnotes in foundation annual reports—that "an officer of the Foundation is a partner of Boettcher and Co., an investment banking firm that buys and sell [sic] investments and performs certain other services, including securities valuations for the Foundation." That officer is E. Warren Willard, president of the foundation. Boettcher & Co., a New York Stock Exchange member firm, was founded by the same family that started the foundation. Willard, for many years the firm's managing partner, is still a limited partner and owns an interest in the firm.

Under the 1969 act, Willard is a disqualified person. But the self-dealing rules do not prohibit Willard or Boettcher & Co. from performing personal services for the foundation, including brokerage, if the services are reasonable and necessary to enable the foundation to carry out its tax-exempt purposes and if the compensation is not excessive. The footnote to the foundation's annual report states that the foundation's business dealings with Boettcher & Co. ''are based on the prevailing rates and terms employed by Boettcher and Co. for similar customers.''

But commission discounts offered by brokerage houses vary widely, and officials at the Boettcher Foundation, which manages its portfolio internally, may well feel some inhibition, given Willard's tie with Boettcher & Co. and his senior position at the foundation, in exploring the possibility of lower rates elsewhere.

Most of the conflicts of interest that affect services supplied to foundations seem to involve banks. Many foundations have strong links with banks that might inhibit the foundation from seeking the best banking services at the lowest cost. One of the most incestuous relationships, apparently, is that of the six foundations created by the Pew family with the Glenmede Trust Co.[4] Athough very secretive, Glenmede Trust is known to be owned and controlled by the Pew family, which accounts for nearly all of its business. Among Glenmede's directors are several Pews, including R. Anderson Pew, president of Sun Co. subsidiary, and several longtime Pew loyalists, such as Robert G. Dunlop, retired chairman and still a director of the Sun Co. Glenmede acts as sole trustee for all six of the Pew foundations and is also fiduciary or cofiduciary for several other family trusts and estates. In all it has the power to vote 34.6 percent of the Sun Co.'s shares.

In establishing a fee level for Glenmede's services to the foundations, the Pew family is deciding, in effect, how much to pay itself. The foundation's tax returns suggest that the family's inclinations are toward generosity. In 1975, for instance, the Pew Memorial Trust, the largest of the six foundations, paid Glenmede $645,134 in fees. Precisely what Glenmede did for all that money is not known. But management of the foundation's portfolio cannot have consumed very much time. The portfolio consists of little more than shares of Sun Co. and a $222 million note from International Paper Co. received in return for the sale of shares in an oil company. (Glenmede received another $100,000 for computing the foundation's capital gain on the deal.) Unless Glenmede's fees can be proved to be excessive, the Pew family-Pew Memorial Trust-Glenmede relationship is in perfect compliance with the letter of federal law—even though the foundation is clearly a captive of the family that funded it and of the family's bank.

Other close associations between foundations and banks derive from the affiliation of the donor with the bank. For example, Karl Hoblitzelle, who created the Hoblitzelle Foundation in Dallas, was chairman of Republic National Bank of Dallas until shortly before his death eight years ago. Nearly all of his estate, including a sizable block of stock in the bank, went into the foundation. Today, the bank maintains a very close association with the foundation and with Karl Hoblitzelle's shares of Republic of Texas Corp., the holding company that owns Republic National. James W. Aston, chairman of Republic of Texas, is the president and a trustee of the foundation. Among the other trustees are James W. Keay, chairman of Republic National Bank, and two of Republic of Texas' other directors. All own stock in the bank. John M. Stemmons, a Dallas businessman on the bank's board, is the foundation's treasurer.

Republic National Bank manages the foundation's portfolio, the largest holding of which is Karl Hoblitzelle's old block, now $12.7 million worth of Republic of Texas Corp. Robert L. Harris, vice president of the foundation, reports that the IRS conducted an audit of the foundation and that "they showed some interest" in the Republic of Texas holdings (which the bank is free to sell) as well as in the $4.8 million that was invested in eight other local banks. He adds: "They went into it very thoroughly but were satisfied." It is not known how much the foundation paid the bank for its services. The bank's published schedule reports that its investment management fee for portfolios the size of the Hoblitzelle Foundation is negotiable. In arriving at a fee for handling the foundation's business, the bank more or less negotiates with itself.

The George Gund Foundation was established by the former chairman of the Cleveland Trust Co. Before his death in 1966, George Gund also had been the bank's largest individual shareholder. The president of the foundation's board of trustees is Frederick K. Cox, executive vice president of Cleveland Trust. George Gund's two sons are trustees of the foundation, directors of the bank, and owners of a total of $5 million worth of the bank's stock. Cleveland Trust is the foundation's custodian and the manager of its portfolio. In 1974 the bank was paid $44,657 for its services for the foundation. The portfolio's third largest holding is $1.9 million worth of CleveTrust Corp., the bank's holding company. Neither the George Gund Foundation nor the Hoblitzelle Foundation refers in its annual reports to its complex and close relationship with its bank.

The Mellon Bank, the largest in Pennsylvania, maintains similar relationships with the various Mellon-created foundations. The entire Mellon empire, in fact, is a dense thicket of corporate and family interconnections that often obscure the distinctions between business and charity. In recent years several important family leaders have died, and according to some reports, the current generation of Mellons is unable or unwilling to fill the leadership vacuum. In the absence of such leadership, the Mellon family may not exert the concerted financial power that it once did.[5] But the Mellon fortune, estimated at between $3 billion and $5 billion, remains an immense financial force.

The three principal Mellon foundations are the Andrew W. Mellon Foundation ($610 million in investments), the Richard King Mellon Foundation ($225 million), and the Sarah Scaife Foundation ($71 million).

The Mellons who created the foundations were members of the second and third generations. Richard King Mellon, the family's financial leader until his death in 1970, was president of the Mellon Bank. (His great-grandfather founded it.) Seward Prosser Mellon is his adopted son. Sarah Scaife, who died in 1965, was his sister. Richard Mellon Scaife is her son. Paul Mellon is the son of Andrew W. Mellon, who died in 1937, and is Richard King Mellon's cousin.

The Mellon Bank is investment manager for the Sarah Scaife Foundation. The Mellon family owns about 40 percent of Mellon National Corp., the holding company for the bank.

Paul Mellon, trustee of the Andrew W. Mellon Foundation, owns 14 percent of Mellon National Corp. Although the foundation, like all of the Mellon foundations, has been diversifying from its Mellon-related industrial holdings, it still holds $225 million in Mellon-related companies, mainly Gulf Oil Corp. (Mellons are usually represented on the boards of companies, such as Gulf, in which they have major shareholdings.) It owns $20.2 million worth of Mellon National Corp.

Seward Prosser Mellon, trustee and chairman of the executive committee of the Richard King Mellon Foundation, is a director and a major stockholder of Mellon National Corp. The foundation has two-thirds of its assets in Mellon-affiliated companies, such as Gulf Oil, General Reinsurance Corp., and Alcoa. It also owns $16.3 million in Mellon Bank certificates of deposit.

Richard M. Scaife, chairman and trustee of the Sarah Scaife Foundation, is a director of Mellon National Corp. and owns 6 percent of its stock. The foundation owns $49.4 million in Mellon-related investments, including positions in Gulf Oil and First Boston Corp., an investment banking house that underwrites most Mellon-related issues, and $5.8 million in Mellon Bank certificates of deposit.

On a smaller scale, Elliott Averett, chairman of the Bank of New York, is a director of the Josiah Macy Jr. Foundation ($44.2 million in investments). The Bank of New York is the foundation's investment advisor.

Morgan Guaranty Trust Co. seems to be especially active in maintaining trustee and advisory-custodial relationships with foundation clients. They include the John and Mary R. Markle Foundation ($31.5 million in investments), of which Daniel P. Davison, senior vice president of the bank, is a trustee, and the Alfred P. Sloan Foundation ($256 million in investments), of which Ellmore C. Patterson, chairman of the bank, is a trustee. The Alfred P. Sloan Foundation owns $4.7 million worth of stock in J. P. Morgan & Co. (the holding company for the bank) and the John and Mary R. Markle Foundation owns $1.2 million worth. [6]

Although these relationships are not necessarily sinister or excessively costly to the foundations involved, they do create conflicts of interest for trustees who are bankers. And they may deter foundation officials from seeking out the best banking services at the lowest cost or from complaining about the banks' practice of putting shares of the banks' own stock in the foundation portfolio.

IX • CONCLUSIONS

Foundation critic Waldemar Nielsen has referred to "the almost limitless capacity of foundations to resist adaptation and self-improvement."[1] Apart from such exceptions as Ford, Carnegie, Hartford, and Kresge, which have moved decisively in the direction of becoming independent, nonconflicted institutions, most foundations today conform to Nielsen's description:

> The reforms which foundations most need all run directly against the grain of the thinking of most of the people who control them. From the perspective of the typical donor, diversifying the board and the portfolio and professionalizing the staff would mean depersonalizing his foundation, diluting his influence, and frustrating his dynastic ambitions. From the perspective of most trustees, such reforms would mean the ending of collegiality, the intrusion of unfamiliar people and alien ideas, the sharing of authority with nonbusiness professionals and intellectuals, and the commitment of the foundation to open dialogue and dispute. Their natural inclination has been, and presumably will be, to stand pat.[2]

Foundations also are afflicted by the same "golden goose syndrome" that impedes reforms at college and university endowments. Foundations cannot exist without the time and expertise provided by trustees and the money provided by donors. Cumbersome and annoying restrictions on trustees and donors may frustrate or eliminate their charitable inclinations. "I'm torn between having the field invulnerable to attack on the one hand yet making sure it can attract new money," says a senior foundation executive. "If you make the rules too tough, I'm concerned that you will lose a lot of money for charity."

A senior official at a large foundation also fears that strict rules governing trustee behavior would discourage the best qualified individuals from accepting foundation board memberships. "In choosing trustees," he says, "you face a trade-off between purity and ignorance. You want people who are informed and knowledgeable, who are experienced and in the prime of their working lives. But such people always have a lot of outside relationships. That's what makes them very valuable board members."

Granted, conflict situations are inescapable. The presence of businessmen on a board creates conflicts involving the selection of portfolios, banks, brokers, and investment managers. Educators, journalists, other foundation executives, and other intellectuals may have conflicts involving grants. The latter conflicts, though, may be more amenable than the former to control by such easily facilitated mechanisms as written guidelines. And even uncontrolled, they are less potentially detrimental to a foundation's long-term financial health.

Businessmen trustees may initially resist guidelines because they often view business arrangements with a foundation as a *quid pro quo* for their willingness to serve on the board. Yet business from the foundation seldom is very important to the trustee's company. Approached tactfully on the matter, such trustees may be willing to agree to a prohibition on these arrangements in the best interests of the foundation. In any case most investment-related conflicts of interest involving foundations would be much less widespread if foundation boards included fewer businessmen and more individuals whose backgrounds qualify them to provide informed guidance on a foundation's charitable activities. Foundations, unlike educational endowments, do not depend on a continuing stream of gifts and therefore do not need to use board membership as a reward for important donor businessmen.

A number of foundation executives maintain that even existing controls on foundations imposed by the Tax Reform Act of 1969 have had a very repressive effect on foundations. They assert the act has reduced the birthrate of foundations and increased the death rate. However, the latest *Foundation Directory*, published by the Foundation Center, says: "We know the tax law tends to inhibit the birth of new foundations and encourages the dissolution of small ones, but thus far studies of birth and death rates have not revealed conclusive statistics for the whole field."[3] When he died in early 1979, John D. MacArthur, head of Bankers Life and Casualty Co, and probably the second richest man in America, created a new $750 million foundation that is the nation's fifth richest. If, in fact, old foundations have been dissolved and new foundations have not been created, the 1969 act may indeed be responsible. The purpose of the act was to deter unscrupulous donors from using foundations as a mechanism for corporate self-dealing or other questionable purposes. If, as a result of the act, this practice has become less common, then fewer foundations may be better than more, from the public's perspective. If the donor's purpose is solely to serve charitable causes—while, of course, still enjoying a nice tax deduction—there is nothing in the 1969 act to deter him.

The trouble with the 1969 act is not that it is too harsh and repressive but that it does not go far enough. It does not really touch the abuses that result from the still tight interconnections between many foundations, donor families, and companies. Conflicts at educational endowments tend to diminish over time, as financial and other pressures force trustees to realize that the old ways of management by crony are not serving the best interests of the school. But foundations do not confront the same pressures as educational endowments and are free to continue to pursue self-interested goals. Foundations would be well-advised to take many of the same voluntary steps recommended for educational endowments, such as the adoption of disclosure procedures beyond those required by the 1969 act.[4] But without the stimulus of new legislation, foundations almost certainly will not initiate such measures.

In April 1973, at the opening of hearings by his Subcommittee on Domestic Finance, Wright Patman remarked:

The recent happenings on Wall Street have shed light upon a major problem currently confronting the foundation community, that is, the fact that many foundations find themselves in a position where their entire portfolio is made up of the stock of one or two corporations. Thus, the foundation trustees and managers are placing the fate of their charitable beneficiaries in the hands of the managers and executives of these corporations.

This excessive concentration of investment unquestionably increases the risk of loss and places in jeopardy the fate of the charitable beneficiaries. The portfolio of a private foundation is no place for such imprudent investment policy.

There is considerable evidence that private foundations which have failed to diversify their portfolios have deprived their charitable beneficiaries of many millions of dollars.

Another major criticism of private foundations is that their governing boards fail to reflect in membership and philosophy the constituency they are intended to serve. The incestuous interlocking of the directors and trustees of private foundations with the family of the donor or with the officers and directors of the donor or foundation controlled corporation has served to perpetuate a group that in no way reflects the charitable beneficiaries it must serve.

If, in a sense, foundations are a "public trust," then the needs of the public must be placed above those of the alma mater.[5]

Patman had called these hearings to discuss two new pieces of reform legislation applicable to foundations. But the strong public sentiment for reform that had swept in the Tax Reform Act of 1969 was all but exhausted, and Patman's bills died, in part because of strong opposition from several major foundations. Today, the problems they were designed to solve are still with us. As a reasonable and nonstultifying approach to conflicts of interest at foundations, the proposed legislation deserves renewed consideration.

The bill that was labeled H.R. 5729 would have forced portfolio diversification by amending the definition of a jeopardizing charitable investment to include "nondiversified holdings." The bill defined a *nondiversified holding* as "the amount (if any) by which the value of a private foundation's holdings of stock and debt obligations of any corporation exceed 10 percent of the value of the total assets of the private foundation."[6] It would have given foundations five years after the bill became law to comply.

Such a law would substantially reduce—even destroy—the value of many essentially one-stock foundations to the businessmen who control them. Many of these businessmen might even resign from their trusteeships, creating opportunities for the recruitment of more philanthropically minded individuals to foundation boards. Foundations might then be able to increase their concentration on charity.

Patman's other bill, H.R. 5728, could also have far-ranging, if less dramatic, consequences. It would have funneled a major portion of the 4 percent excise tax collected from foundations by the IRS to state agencies, enabling them to increase their supervision to private foundations "to insure that such private foundations will promptly and properly use their funds for charitable purposes."[7] The IRS, whose regulatory efforts over foundations are regarded by many observers as lackluster and often ineffectual, is generally limited to taxation as an enforcement mechanism. State laws applicable to foundations are far broader and far more flexible, and officials of some states have been very aggressive in enforcing them. The state laws are usually based on the common law notion that, because it is virtually impossible for a particular individual to prove that he is the intended beneficiary of a foundation and thus has standing to take court action against the foundation, the state must serve as a representative of the public and enforce charitable dispositions for the public benefit. Many state laws give the attorney general the same standing as a director or officer of the foundation in effecting changes and make him a party to all court proceedings involving charitable distributions. In 1973, having peformed such functions in his capacity as assistant attorney general for New York, Julius Greenfield told the Patman committee:

The federal approach, the imposition of sanctions, certainly has a deterrent effect upon improper foundation administration. But it only goes part of the way. It does not provide, and there is some doubt that it can, for the various kinds of court and administrative actions that are available to the state attorney general. These would include imposition of personal responsibility on foundation managers for improper administration, removal of officers and directors and appointment or election of new officers and directors, dissolution of foundations and distribution of their assets to public charities and requiring a full judicial accounting of the activities of foundation administrators.[8]

Greenfield cited as an example of his office's enforcement a case when

. . . a very detailed investigation and examination of the foundation directors revealed extensive areas of self-dealing, waste, and failure to make the assets productive. The major holding of the foundation consisted of control holdings in several business corporations, in which the foundation managers were principal officers and directors. As such they received very handsome compensation. As a result of our efforts the following occurred: (1) the board of directors of the foundation was increased to include disinterested directors who would constitute a majority on the board; (2) the foundation was to be represented on the board of directors of the business corporations by one of the new directors; (3) the foundation would and has adopted a plan of dissolution and distribution of its assets to charitable institutions; and (4) this distribution, which may approximate $14,000,000, will be made to eligible charitable beneficiaries within a year.[9]

In Minnesota local officials, including the state attorney general, took the lead during the 1960s in totally overhauling and reforming the Bush Foundation, which was established by one of the leading figures in Minnesota Mining and Manufacturing and held nearly all of its assets in 3M stock.[10] The Bush family spent a number of years struggling with 3M executives for control of the foundation; during this period both sides participated in a number of dubious transactions. Finally, the attorney general and a state court reorganized the foundation's board of directors to include a majority of independent trustees, none of whom is permitted own more than a 5 percent interest in any profit-making corporation. With the aid of Brown Brothers Harriman & Co. and United States Trust Co. in New York and the Northern Trust Co. in Chicago, the foundation divested the 3M shares and invested the proceeds in a diversified portfolio now worth $125 million.

Not all states enforce their laws pertaining to charitable institutions with such vigor. But with federal financial assistance and encouragement from a law modeled after H.R. 5728, many more might make the effort.

Reform of foundation conflicts of interest will not come easily. The notion that foundations are not a public trust but the personal property of the donor, his family, or his company remains widespread. When asked, at a business luncheon a few years ago, why his foundation had never issued an annual report or any other report to the public, J. Howard Pew shouted, "I'm not telling anybody anything. It's my money, isn't it?"[11] Not until the still extensive interlocks between donors, companies, and foundations are broken for good can the nation's private foundations rid themselves of still common but avoidable conflicts of interest and devote themselves exclusively to charity.

NOTES

Author's Preface

[1] There are a few significant exceptions. For example, when he died in June 1976, J. Paul Getty left his 21.5 percent interest in the Getty Oil Co., now worth $750 million, to the J. Paul Getty Museum in Malibu, California. As a result, the endowment of this museum is probably larger than that of all the country's other museums put together.

[2] The New York Stock Exchange, *1976 Fact Book*, p. 53.

[3] (SEC), *Statistical Bulletin* 35, no. 5 (May 1976).

[4] Ibid.

I. Introduction, Educational Endowments

[1] *Ford Foundation Annual Report* (1966), p. 7.

[2] See Advisory Committee on Endowment Management, *Managing Educational Endowments: Report to the Ford Foundation*, 2nd ed., 1972.

[3] For an analysis of the changes in endowment fund policies after the Bundy statement, see Chris Welles, "University Endowments: Revolution Comes to the Ivory Tower," *Institutional Investor* (September 1967), p. 11.

[4] When no source is given for a quotation, it may be assumed that the statements were derived from interviews with the author between November 1976 and January 1977. When the quoted individual is not identified by name or institution, it is because the person would talk with the author only if his or her name was withheld, usually because of the sensitivity of the matter being discussed.

[5]J. A. Livingston, "How Howard Butcher Handled Sales of Penn Central Stock," Philadelphia *Evening Bulletin*, December 9, 1970, p. 1.

[6]The best sources of statistical data on the structure and policies of endowment fund management are: Louis Harris and Associates, Inc., *Managing Endowment Funds: A Survey of Endowed Institutions* (1971), which surveyed 660 nonprofit institutions including 214 colleges and universities; and National Association of College and University Business Officers, *Results of the 1975 NACUBO Comparative Performance Survey and Investment Questionnaire* (1975), which surveyed 157 pooled endowment funds. Additional data based on a survey of 383 colleges and universities are contained in William L. Cary and Craig B. Bright, *The Developing Law of Endowment Funds: "The Law and the Lore" Revisited* (New York: The Ford Foundation, 1974).

[7]The situation is discussed in detail in James Ridgeway, *The Closed Corporation* (New York: Random House, 1968). See also Richard J. Barber, *The American Corporation* (New York: E. P. Dutton & Co., 1970), pp. 99-107.

[8]"Colleges Go into Business to Make Ends Meet," *U.S. News & World Report* (January 27, 1975), pp. 33-34.

[9]Barber, *The American Corporation*, p. 105.

[10]For this study financial reports were obtained from ninety-three universities, colleges, and private schools. Only twenty-eight contained breakdowns of portfolio composition. After follow-up requests, several other institutions supplied portfolio data. But some did so only on the condition that the data not be released. Others refused to supply any further data.

[11]*Funds for the Future*, a background paper by J. Peter Williamson for the Twentieth Century Fund Task Force on College and University Endowment Policy (1975), p. 74.

[12]Harris, *Managing Endowment Funds*, p. 26.

[13]Charles C. Abbott, *Trusteeship in Profit Corporations and Non-Profit Organizations* (Cambridge, Mass.: The Cheswick Center, 1974), p. 19.

[14]*Stern et al. v. Lucy Webb Hayes National Training School for Deaconesses and Missionaries et al.*, 381 F. Supp. 1003 (D.C.D.C. 1974).

II. The Trustees

[1]Charles Ellis, *Institutional Investing* (Homewood, Ill., Dow Jones-Irwin, 1971), p. 188.

[2]Prefatory note to the Uniform Management of Institutional Funds Act drafted by the National Conference of Commissioners of Uniform State Laws, 1972, p. 4. Versions of this act have been passed by the legislatures of several states.

[3]*Blankenship v. Boyle*, 329 F. Supp. 1089, 1096 (D.C.D.C. 1971).

[4]Comment on Section 6 of the Uniform Management of Institutional Funds Act, p. 14.

[5]Like Hazel Sanger, many people use the term *conflict of interest* to signify an actual abuse. In this chapter that term refers to a situation in which an individual had two opposing interests, usually his obligations as a fiduciary and trustee and his private financial interests. Such a situation is not inherently improper. But a conflict of interest may lead to abuse when the individual does not keep his conflicting interests separate, when, for instance, he permits his private interests to interfere with his performance as a fiduciary, to the detriment of the institution involved.

III. The Portfolio

[1]Unless otherwise indicated, data on endowment holdings and trustee identifications were derived from the college or university's latest published financial report, supplemented, in cases where they were not part of the financial report, by schedules of portfolio investments supplied at the request of the author. Additional information about investment policies was obtained from interviews with treasurers and other individuals associated with or knowledgeable about the funds.

[2]California Institute of Technology, *The President's Report, 1975-1976* (November 1976), p. 123.

[3]See pp. 530-552.

[4]Statement of John G. Simon, Hearings on Private Foundations, Subcommittee on Foundations, U.S. Senate, October 2, 1973, p. 178.

[5]*Restatement of Trusts (Second)*, Sec. 228 (1957).

[6]Employee Retirement Income Security Act of 1974, Sec. 404 (a) (1) (C).

[7]Marion Fremont-Smith, *Foundations and Government* (New York: Russell Sage Foundation, 1965), p. 100.

IV. Investment Managers, Brokers, and Bankers

[1]A sampling of some of the major articles: "On the Average: More Pension Funds Try to Tie the Market Instead of Beating It," *The Wall Street Journal*, November 12, 1975, p. 1; "Much Ado About Index Funds," *Institutional Investor* (February 1976), p. 17; "Tieing Your Investments to the Indexes," *Money*, (May 1976), p. 87; "Index Funds—An Idea Whose Time Is Coming," *Fortune* (June 1976); "Queering Wall Street's 'Money Game,' " *The Nation* (March 12, 1977), pp. 300-304.

[2]Three recent books accessible to the laymen that describe efficient market theory: James H. Lorie and Mary T. Hamilton, *The Stock Market: Theories and Evidence* (Homewood, Ill.: Richard D. Irwin, 1973); Burton G. Malkiel, *A Random Walk Down Wall Street* (New York: W. W. Norton, 1973); Richard A. Brealey, *An Introduction to Risk and Return from Common Stock* (Cambridge: The M.I.T. Press, 1969).

[3]"Why Money Managers Like Index Funds," *Business Week* (December 20, 1976), p. 54.

[4]For a lucid study that discusses the difficulties presented by the efficient market thesis for endowment funds, see Burton G. Malkiel and Paul B. Firstenberg, *Managing Risk in an Uncertain Era: An Analysis for Endowed Institutions* (Princeton: Princeton University Press, 1976).

[5]*1975 NACUBO Comparative Performance Survey*, p. 5.

[6]See pp. 23-157, this volume.

[7]For a recent account of commission rate competition, see Chris Welles, "Discounting: Wall Street's Game of Nerves," *Institutional Investor* (November 1976), p. 27.

[8]*Funds for the Future*, p. 165.

[9]"A Fund to Prop Up Colleges," *Business Week* (January 20, 1975), p. 45.

V. Conclusions

[1]*Stern et al. v. Lucy Webb Hayes National Training School for Deaconesses and Missionaries et al.*, 381 F. Supp. 1003 (D.C.D.C. 1974). The case grew out of a newspaper article: Ronald Kessler, "Trustees' Banks Use Hospital Money," *Washington Post*, February 4, 1973, p. 1.

[2]Myles M. Mace, "Standards of Care for Trustees," *Harvard Business Review* (January-February 1976), p. 15.

[3]*Stern et al. v. Lucy Webb Hayes National Training School for Deaconesses and Missionaries et al.*, p. 1015.

[4]American Hospital Association, *Guidelines for Resolution of Conflicts of Interest in Health Care Institutions*, (1974).

[5]*Stern et al. v. Lucy Webb Hayes National Training School for Deaconesses and Missionaries et al.*, p. 1019.

[6]Mace, "Standards of Care for Trustees," p. 22.

[7]*Stern et al. v. Lucy Webb Hayes National Training School for Deaconesses and Missionaries et al.*, 367 F. Supp. 536 (D.C.D.C. 1973).

[8]Mace, "Standards of Care for Trustees," p. 28.

[9]Ibid., p. 148.

[10]*Stern et al.* v. *Lucy Webb Hayes National Training School for Deaconesses and Missionaries et al.*, 381 F. Supp. 1003 (D.C.D.C. 1974), p. 1016.

[11]William C. Porth, "Personal Liability of Trustees of Educational Institutions," *The Journal of College and University Law* 1 (Fall 1973), p. 88.

[12]*Giving in America: Toward a Stronger Voluntary Sector*, Report of the Commission on Private Philanthropy and Public Needs (1975), p. 175.

[13]Committee on College and University Accounting and Auditing, American Institute of Certified Public Accounts, Inc., *Industry Audit Guide: Audits of Colleges and Universities*, (1973), p. 9.

[14]For an analysis of current practices, see *Funds for the Future*, pp. 135-142.

[15]American Institute of Certified Public Accountants, Inc., "Related Party Transactions," *Statement on Auditing Standards* (July 1975), p. 2.

VI. Introduction, Foundations

[1]*Congressional Directory* (August 7, 1961), p. 13755.

[2]*The Foundation Directory* (New York: The Foundation Center, 1975), 5th ed., pp. xii-xiv.

[3]The Patmen reports are entitled *Tax Exempt Foundations and Charitable Trusts: Their Impact on Our Economy*, Subcommittee Chairman's Report to Subcommittee No. 1, Select Committee on Small Business, House Of Representatives. They are dated: December 31, 1962; October 16, 1963; March 20, 1964; December 21, 1966; April 28, 1967; March 26, 1968. Two additional reports were issued on June 30, 1969, and August 1972. In addition to these reports, useful accounts of the activities of foundations during this period are Waldemar A. Nielsen, *The Big Foundations*, A Twentieth Century Fund Study (New York: Columbia University Press, 1972); Joseph C. Goulden, *The Money Givers* (New York: Random House, 1971): Ferdinand Lundberg, *The Rich and the Super Rich* (New York: Lyle Stuart, 1968), pp. 465-530 (paperback); Ovid Demaris, *Dirty Business* (New York: Harper's Magazine Press, 1974), pp. 252-325; Ralph L. Nelson, *The Investment Policies of Foundations*, A Foundation Center Study (New York: Russell Sage Foundation, 1967).

[4]The foundation was forced to make this drastic reduction because Joan Irvine Smith, who was a disqualified person under the terms of the act, held 22 percent of the company's stock.

[5]Nielsen, *The Big Foundations*, p. 177.

[6]For an account of this period, see Eleanor Johnson Tracy, "How A&P Got Creamed," *Fortune* (January 1973), p. 103.

[7]Nielsen, *The Big Foundations*, p. 317.

VII. The Donors and Their Companies

[1]Most of the information that follows on foundation holdings, trustees, and corporate relationships derives from the latest available foundation annual reports, foundation income tax returns (both 990-AR and 990-PF), corporation annual reports and proxy statements, and interviews by the author with foundation executives. The author is also greatly indebted to *The Big Foundations* by Waldemar Nielsen (A Twentieth Century Fund Study published by Columbia University Press) for background information on most of the major foundations.

[2]Quoted in Nielsen, *The Big Foundations*, p. 240.

[3]*Tax Information for Private Foundations and Foundation Managers*, Internal Revenue Service, U.S. Department of the Treasury, September 1975, pp. 50-51.

[4]The Twentieth Century Fund has 14 percent of its $28 million portfolio in shares of Federated Department Stores, Inc., which were donated to the foundation by Edward A. Filene, who established the foundation. None of the foundation's officers or directors is a director or officer of Federated.

⁵See Demaris, *Dirty Business*, pp. 259-266.

⁶Wallace Turner, "Petition Could Validate a 'Lost' 1938 Hughes Will," *The New York Times,* January 13, 1977, p. 20; "Legal Dispute over Howard Hughes's Newly Profitable Empire Approaching a Climax," *The New York Times*, June 3, 1979, p. 14.

⁷For information on the Howard Hughes Medical Institute submitted by the institute to Congress, see Hearings on Tax Exempt Foundations and Charitable Trusts, Subcommittee on Domestic Finance, U.S. House of Representatives (April 5-6, 1973), pp. 140-170. See also Donald L. Barlett and James B. Steele, *Empire* (New York: W. W. Norton & Company, 1979).

⁸"The Secret World of Howard Hughes," *Newsweek* (April 19, 1976).

⁹See Rush Loving, Jr., "Ed Ball's Marvelous, Old-Style Money Machine," *Fortune* (December 1974), p. 170, and Phyllis Berman, "The Strange Case of Ed Ball," *Forbes* (February 15, 1977), pp. 63-66.

¹⁰Loving, op. cit., p. 171.

¹¹See a series of articles on the foundation by Curtis Wilkie in the *Wilmington (Del.) Evening News*, March 19 and March 29, 1974, reprinted in Hearings on Private Foundations, Subcommittee on Foundations, U.S. Senate (May 13, 14, and June 3, 1974), pp. 140-146.

¹²Robert D. Shaw, Jr., "Du Pont Trust: Where Will the Money Go?" *Miami Herald*, August 1, 1976, p. 1. See additional articles by Shaw in the *Miami Herald* on November 15 and 19, 1976.

¹³"Sinatra Wants More of the Webb Action," *Business Week* (April 11, 1977), pp. 30-31.

¹⁴Ibid., p. 30.

¹⁵See p. 512.

¹⁶Hearings on Tax Exempt Foundations and Charitable Trusts, Subcommittee on Domestic Finance, p. 200.

¹⁷For background on the Irvine Foundation, see Nielsen, *The Big Foundations*, pp. 126-134. For a recent statement on Joan Irvine Smith's allegations, see Hearings on Private Foundations, Subcommittee on Foundations, pp. 185-201. For a recent account of the Irvine Co., see Wyndham Robertson, "The Greening of the Irvine Co.," *Fortune* (December 1976), p. 84.

¹⁸*The Wall Street Journal*, May 23, 1977, p. 2.

¹⁹Eileen Shanahan, "House Tax Panel Eases Rule on Foundation Spending," *The New York Times*, October 14, 1971, reprinted in Hearings on Tax Exempt Foundations and Charitable Trusts, Subcommittee on Domestic Finance, pp. 21-22.

VIII. Bankers and Brokers

¹Much of the information on conflict-of-interest guidelines that follows is derived from Frederick Williams, "Are Written Guidelines Useful?" *Foundation News* (May-June 1977), p.51.

²For example, in 1973 the Danforth Foundation made a $60 million matching grant to Washington University. William H. Danforth, chairman of the board of trustees of the foundation, is chancellor of the university.

³Hearings on Tax Exempt Foundations and Charitable Trusts, Subcommittee on Domestic Finance, p. 182.

⁴For a background on the family, see Michael C. Jensen, "The Pews of Philadelphia," *The New York Times*, October 10, 1971, Sect. 3, p. 1.

⁵See Michael C. Jensen, "An Old Fortune Moves On," *The New York Times*, May 2, 1971, Sect. 3, p. 1.

⁶A number of banks hold very large—sometimes controlling—percentages of their own stock in trust department fiduciary accounts. For a large portion of these holdings, the banks have sole or partial voting power. The Cleveland Trust Co., for instance, holds 31.24 percent of CleveTrust Corp. stock in its trust department and has sole voting power over 11.93 percent. The Trust Company of Atlanta, Georgia, has 24.25 percent of Trust Company of Georgia stock in its trust department and has sole voting power over 12.61 percent.

IX. Conclusions

[1]Nielsen, *The Big Foundations*, p. 431.
[2]Ibid., p. 443.
[3]*The Foundation Directory*, pp. xiii-xiv.
[4]See pp. 534-36.
[5]Hearings on Tax Exempt Foundations and Charitable Trusts, Subcommittee on Domestic Finance, pp. 1-2.
[6]Ibid., p. 5.
[7]Ibid., p. 3.
[8]Ibid., p. 183.
[9]Ibid., p. 181.
[10]Nielsen, *The Big Foundations*, pp. 121-123.
[11]Ibid., p. 126.

Conclusions and Recommendations

by Roy A. Schotland

for the Steering Committee

I • INTRODUCTION

Conflicts, like death and taxes, are inevitable. And conflicts of interest are inherent in the handling of other people's money. The Twentieth Century Fund Steering Committee on Conflicts of Interest in the Securities Markets commissioned its studies to determine the extent and assess the harmfulness of such conflicts. Drawing on the findings of these studies and on other evidence, we have concluded that the functioning of the securities markets currently provides substantial opportunities for abuse of the fiduciary relationship.

Few of those who have these opportunities use them. Countervailing pressures such as individual integrity, concern for reputation, distaste for legal intervention, and competitive forces combine to prevent most conflicts from resulting in abuse. But additional safeguards are in order to strengthen public confidence in the securities markets and to promote the direct public participation that is essential for orderly, liquid markets. We believe that all participants in the securities markets will benefit if such safeguards are put into place with more than deliberate speed.

We are not under the illusion that conflicts can—or should—be eliminated entirely. Our aims are more modest. The recommendations that we propose are milder than some critics of the industry might favor but tougher than most of those in the securities industry might consider necessary.

Traditionally, the industry has suffered from a barn door syndrome, taking corrective action only after publicized and flagrant scandals. More recently, some parts of the marketplace have begun responding, when weaknesses have been called to their attention, by undertaking some useful voluntary improvements. It is our view that the industry should now take further steps on just such a voluntary basis. Those with fiduciary responsibilities are under an obligation to take action before trouble again erupts.

In some situations the establishment of safeguards to insure fairness seems to conflict with the goal of efficiency. But sound fiduciary practices generally promote efficiency. Standards of fairness and fidelity in continuing relationships, such as those between investment manager and beneficiary or between investment banker and issuer, encourage trust and thus facilitate the efficient division of labor. Standards of fairness and confidence in otherwise anonymous public markets promote efficient pricing and liquidity, which are essential for capital formation on the scale our economy requires. Hence, promoting sound fiduciary conduct should enhance willingness to engage in transactions and may lead to lower transaction costs.

The establishment—through legislation or other means—of safeguards against abuses of conflict of interest is not tantamount to legislating morality. We are aware that morality cannot be imposed by fiat and that fiduciary relationships ultimately rest on the integrity of the individuals involved. But integrity unaccompanied by judgment and experience does not necessarily enable an individual to deal with the complex challenges that many conflict situations present. Setting forth guidelines and insisting on standard practices simply save individuals from having to think through each situation *de novo* and increase the likelihood that decisions will be fair.

In a market dominated by long-established firms with limited turnover in personnel, word-of-mouth training and shared experience might suffice to maintain satisfactory standards of conduct. But our financial institutions are so large and in such flux, individuals in our society enjoy such career mobility, and new firms emerge so frequently, that many people with inadequate experience often find themselves charged with substantial fiduciary responsibilities. These conditions call for ''systems and procedures which fill the classic three-fold test of keeping temptation from the weak, opportunity from the venturesome, and suspicion from the innocent.''[1]

We cannot suggest specific procedures for each setting of each problem in the many areas of the securities industry. We have, instead, sought to indicate the types of safeguards and legal devices that can be used to support and stimulate the adoption of corrective steps. (In addition to the steering committee's general recommendations, which follow, each study in this volume concludes with more particularized recommendations provided by its author.[2])

II • STEPS TOWARD IMPROVEMENT

Legislators, regulators, individual investors, and financial institutions must face the inevitability of conflicts and the challenge of devising whatever specific safeguards are necessary to prevent their abuse. This caution may seem obvious, but it has often been ignored. In drafting the legislation that made possible the creation of real estate investment trusts, Congress failed to consider the danger of conflicts; as a result the legislation had features that virtually invited abuse. Clearly, legislators dealing with the securities field should be alert to potential conflicts and seek expert testimony and counsel on conflicts from regulators of securities markets and financial institutions, from attorneys, accountants, investment professionals, academics, and from others with knowledge and experience. Legislation drafted on such a basis may not eliminate the problem but is likely to minimize it.

In addition, regulators of financial institutions must recognize that both their long-standing—and primary—concern with financial soundness and their emerging concern with the consumer protection call for systematic review of the procedures used by regulated firms to handle conflict of interest. (In 1976 the Office of the Comptroller of the Currency revised its examinations to cover this issue.) The responsibility of regulators goes beyond merely determining whether a firm has policies and procedures that purport to serve as safeguards against conflicts. Unfortunately, individual firms, especially smaller ones, generally lack the resources and experience available to regulators for shaping appropriate policies and procedures. So regulators should take on the task of tailoring systems to the problems of individual firms. This approach to preventing abuses is preferable, if it can be made to work, to the imposition of general legal requirements or restrictions on the industry. It would be far less costly to implement and police and less likely to impose disproportionate burdens on smaller firms.

Voluntary Action

Ideally, individual firms would voluntarily adopt safeguards againt conflict abuse. But that route is slow, and too often those firms most in need of safeguards are the slowest—or most reluctant—to adopt them. Another course is collective self-regulation by associations of individual firms or not-for-profit organizations. Or course, we favor voluntary initiatives. But no effort at self-regulation can be effective or credible unless the safeguards are written and concrete and provide for implementation and oversight. Moreover, in some settings entirely voluntary action, collective or individual, may be mere facade. A better course might be to combine the flexibility and direct involvement of self-regulation with close oversight by a regulatory agency, like the SEC's supervision of the self-regulatory activities of stock exchanges and the over-the-counter markets.

Associations of firms and institutions can play a useful role by describing in detail how particular organizations treat particular problems; in this connection the American Bankers Association has published some exemplary reports on conflicts problems in commercial banking. Guidelines and models are needed on subjects such as treatment of inside information; allocation by investment managers of purchases for client accounts; due diligence procedures in underwriting; and for mergers and other battles for corporate control, the proper behavior of investment bankers, broker-dealers, and institutional investors.

Competition

Competition is enormously effective in enabling purchasers to select sellers who best serve their interests. As a means of resolving conflict problems, though, it has its limitations.

Many conflicts arise precisely when competition is likely to be ineffective or nonexistent. Transactions characterized by conflict occur only when an individual's or firm's judgment is playing a dual or multiple role; they differ from marketplace, arm's-length transactions in which the interested parties represent only themselves and from other transactions in which a disinterested person may make a decision objectively. Once the purchaser of fiduciary services has reposed trust—and power over his assets or affairs—in the hands of another, then, as the episodes described in our studies reveal, conflicts are bound to arise, and some result in abuses.

Many conflicts and even abuses go uncorrected. Only some of them come to light. Clients or beneficiaries may be unaware that a given practice is improper. And conflict situations are often tolerated because of the triviality of the abuse, the costs of seeking corrections, the benefits of another service provided by the fiduciary, or the difficulty of shifting to another fiduciary. In addition, certain laws and industry practices limit the effectiveness of competition as a resolver of conflicts. Legal restraints are often challenged on the basis of how much they reduce economic efficiency, but they also should be judged in terms of their tendencies to promote conflicts and even abuses.

Legal constraints on the choice of corporate trustees are an important example of restraints on competition that warrant legislative reconsideration and, in our view, revision. Many pension funds require and many individuals prefer having a corporate trustee. But under the laws of most states, only banks can serve as corporate trustees. Banks compete vigorously among themselves to serve as corporate trustees, but if general banking practice allows certain conflicts and even abuses (as it did for many years regarding uninvested cash or the use of brokerage), confining competition to banks only is not the way to reduce conflicts. Instead, banks must also compete with other types of firms, allowing the strengths of each competitor to come into play, with the result that purchasers will be offered better services, lower prices—and fewer conflicts.

Existing legislation prohibiting insurance companies, thrift institutions, investment counsellors, and broker-dealers from serving as corporate trustees is coming under attack. In 1976 a bill before the House Banking and Currency Committee proposed an expansion in authorization of institutions to exercise trust powers. In 1977 broker-dealer firms in New York and Ohio sought to secure corporate trustee powers. We recommend that the current barriers give way to freer entry with safeguards, such as suitable staffing and adequate capital or other security against liabilities, for nonbank corporate trustees.

Although laws impose a variety of restraints on competition, few such restraints can be deemed responsible today for aggravating conflicts problems. As recently as five years ago, competition was severely limited by the organization of the securities markets themselves, the position of the New York Stock Exchange, and the existence of fixed commission rates. The organization of the securities markets has since undergone profound and rapid change. Numerous participants and commentators are studying those changes and working out their intricacies. The steering committee applauds the replacement of restraints on competition with explicit pricing and, through the reduction of artificial limitations on who can service orders, on how services are priced, and on whether services can be unbundled.

Whether instigated by law or by industry practice, bundling, implicit charges, and other practices that obscure what services are being rendered and at what prices, tend to weaken competition. Explicit pricing not only facilitates competition indirectly but reduces conflicts directly. The easier it is to determine what services are being performed for what prices, the easier it will be to determine the effects of noneconomic or other external factors on transactions. Explicit pricing can help less sophisticated clients protect themselves through comparison, thereby enhancing effective competition.

The Role of Law

Total reliance on legal measures to resolve conflicts problems reduces flexibility and diversity. Drafting and administering a statutory system of safeguards is, at best, intricate and burdensome. Still, in some cases modest legal requirements may serve to stimulate effective competition. For example, competition alone cannot keep a firm from favoring its larger and more sophisticated clients in allocating scarce investment opportunities and giving them priority in the timing of orders. But buttressed by legislation requiring firms to disclose how they allocate the timing of orders or placement of limited investment opportunities, competition might work to keep firms from unduly favoring large clients. Although we recommend some legal prescriptions and proscriptions, we view the primary role of law in the area of conflicts as increasing awareness and accountability through, for another example, required disclosure of each firm's systems to safeguard against conflicts.

The "first line of defense" against abuses of conflicts is within each firm. If firms adopt sound systems; if their boards of directors exercise their oversight responsibility effectively; if clients, beneficiaries, investors, and the public routinely have the information to hold those boards accountable, we can expect both abuses and the burdens of protecting against abuses to be minimal.

The overall task of dealing with conflicts is to achieve the right mix of law with market forces and other private initiatives.

Structure of Firms

SEPARATION OF FUNCTIONS

Separating functions such as the broker's from the investment advisor's, or the broker-dealer's from the investment banker's, or the banker's from the trustee's seems to some people the simplest way to eliminate a major source of conflicts. We make no recommendation regarding such separation, not from reticence or any reluctance to raise politically sensitive issues but because separation goes far beyond conflicts as such. Any answer we might try to provide would rest either on preconceptions or on an artificial prominence we are unwilling to assign to conflicts. That is, we deem it useless to say: "All other things being equal, conflicts considerations warrant . . ."

Proposals to separate, for example, bank trust departments from their banks or their bank holding companies raise questions such as:

1. How would separation affect the cost of services and the conditions of competition in the investment management market? Traditionally, banks have used their trust departments to strengthen overall bank-customer relations. The trust departments themselves were generally unprofitable. Today, a few trust departments (among the largest in the industry) are profitable, but most still are not. Trust departments now manage over $500 billion, the bulk of institutionally managed assets in the nation. It would be irresponsible to recommend separation without analyses of impacts on cost.

2. Would the separation be limited to large trust departments? Banks with large trust departments tend to be intricately involved with many of the companies whose stock is held in trust department portfolios; also, these trust departments often have conflicting involvements as managers for such companies' pension accounts. The great size of major trust departments, their banks, and their corporate clients makes these conflicts especially important. Yet size also renders those departments particularly visible, forcing them to develop elaborate safeguards against abuse. These trust departments have resources to install safeguards that smaller trust departments do not have. Hence, for the large banks, mandated separation may be overkill.

3. Would the separation include even quite small trust departments? Many small trust departments are located in small communities. Separation of banking from trust functions might render the latter so uneconomic that such communities would be deprived of local investment management services; this deprivation would not only be inconvenient but also sacrifice relationships of personal trust and confidence. Yet small departments, and especially those in small communities, face numerous direct conflicts. The local bank is likely to be the lender for just those companies that have substantial blocks of stock in estates and trusts administered by the trust department; the professional staff of

many such banks include no one whose sole responsibility is on the trust side. And of course such banks lack the resources to implement substantial systems of safeguards.

4. Many people in the trust industry fear that the newly independent trust operations would be unable to secure adequate capital to reassure potential clients that they would be answerable for fiduciary breaches. Perhaps fiduciary insurance or bonding could eliminate the need for large amounts of capital. In practice, very few disputes regarding fiduciary breaches of departments have resulted in successful suits or settlements. Is the concern for capital or other protection unwarranted, or is the risk of fiduciary liability rising along with many of the other great changes in institutional investment?

Without answers to such questions, which go into a degree of detail beyond these studies, we believe it improper to support or oppose separation of trust and banking functions.

In some states legislative efforts are afoot to facilitate transfer of trust responsibilities to a separate subsidiary of the trustee bank's holding company. The purpose of this approach is less to eliminate conflicts than to improve the organization of bank holding companies generally. But such transfers may operate to reduce conflicts if legislators consider the issue of conflicts and include in their bills appropriate safeguards regarding, for example, the flow of research information within the holding company, and the use of uninvested cash.

As a result of the Pension Reform Act of 1974 and the Securities Acts Amendments of 1975, legislative and administrative consideration is now lively on whether to reverse any of the recent moves toward separating functions in the broker-dealer/investment manager sphere. This consideration involves questions of such intricacy and so many aspects apart from conflicts that here, too, we can only sound a plea for full focus on the implications of any proposed legislation for conflicts. This plea also applies to the issue of relations between banking and securities activities, which involves reconsideration of the Glass-Steagall Act of 1933.

"HIDDEN COMPENSATION FOR FIDUCIARIES"

Certainly unlawful in the case of all formal trusteeships and equally wrong in any fiduciary setting is the securing of hidden compensation over and above disclosed, agree-upon fees for fiduciary services. For example, banks with trust departments as well as broker-dealers and other firms that are obligated (but not necessarily operated) to make timely payments of clients' funds often gain by holding clients' idle cash without paying interest. Capturing hidden compensation is sometimes disguised as community service; members of the boards of nonprofit institutions have too often used their positions to secure captive accounts for banks or broker-dealers or investment managers. Such abuses are best controlled by mandated disclosure. But their pervasiveness calls for an explicit statement of a principle so fundamental that it ought not need stating: Fiduciaries are not entitled to profit from their relationships apart from disclosed, agreed-upon fees. Undisclosed extra compensation systems are unfair to less sophisticated clients. They give unwarranted and unfair competitive advantages to firms or industries that can charge what appear to be low fees precisely because they use subterfuges to extract additional compensation from their unsuspecting clients.

Governance: Boards of Directors

Conflicts can be minimized by external forces of disclosure and competition, structural changes and prohibitions. But ultimately, individuals within each firm decide whether a conflict will lead to abuse.

Few aspects of corporate structure, including that of not-for-profit organizations, have received as much attention recently as boards of directors. In the last decade, openness and representativeness have increased in government and universities, and business and not-for-profit organizations have been called upon—first by outside critics and more recently by bodies such as the SEC and the NYSE—to increase the extent to which their boards represent interests other than management. Some participants in this effort have sought to make boards more generally ''representative,'' substantially like political bodies. Other participants have sought to increase the independence, number, and role of nonmanagement directors, whether or not they represent any particular constituencies.

We believe that the board of directors is the vital private-sector mechanism for dealing with conflicts in a manner that is detached yet informed, and systematic yet geared to each firm's situation. We do not propose appointment of ''public'' directors or ''representative'' boards for business corporations. But we oppose boards that are wholly composed of or dominated by management or merely leavened by a few ''outside'' cronies of management. Appropriately constituted boards are an essential safeguard against conflict abuses in both business and not-for-profit organizations. We believe that no organization can be adequately protected against such abuses and consequent liability —or, possibly, even against wrongful liability resting only on unrebuttable suspicion—unless its board satisfies the following guidelines.

UNAFFILIATED DIRECTORS

Some observers believe that the contributions made by unaffiliated and ''independent'' directors of investment companies (and in the past few years, by the less independent directors of REITs and by the ''public'' directors of self-regulatory bodies like the NYSE) have been so limited that appointing such directors is at best cosmetic. We reject that skepticism, especially in light of recent experience in a number of large corporations. But such board composition must be viewed as merely one piece of a pattern of necessary safeguards; however, the role of the unaffiliated director must be strengthened. Recent evidence suggests that corporations have come to recognize the usefulness of strong, centrally involved, independent directors in sustaining their managements' claim to integrity, if that comes under question.

It is our belief that a majority of the directors of larger corporations and not-for-profit organizations should be unaffiliated. Smaller companies and organizations that have difficulty in securing the services of competent outsiders should have a minimum of three unaffiliated directors.

In corporations in which conflict abuses or related problems have come to light, we recommend requiring substantial majorities, or even all, of the board members to be unaffiliated, and we urge consideration of including this requirement among the panoply of sanctions authorized for illegal conduct. Recently, several institutions have been required to make unaffiliated individuals comprise a majority of their boards. In the late 1960s, the attorney general of the state of Minnesota imposed this requirement on the Bush Foundation (related to Minnesota Mining). Similarly, in 1975 a REIT, First Mortgage Investors, entered a consent decree with the SEC requiring that it add new unaffiliated trustees and maintain a majority of such trustees on its executive committee. (The settlements of private suits against substantial corporations such as Lockheed, Phillips Petroleum, and Northrup also involve such an arrangement.)

Who is "Unaffiliated?" No director can claim to be unaffiliated unless he is completely free from relationships that might reduce independence in dealing with the organization. Thus, in business organizations not only management but also its bankers and investment bankers, outside counsel, and customers and suppliers doing more than minimal business with the organization are disqualified from consideration as unaffiliated directors, although, of course, they may still become directors.

The board composition of not-for-profit institutions differs in several respects from that of business organizations. But clearly, compensated officers and employees, individuals who sell more than minimal services or goods to the organization or receive more than minimal benefits from it, and persons affiliated with some other organization whose interests potentially conflict with those of the not-for-profit institution (officers or directors of business corporations in which the nonprofit holds substantial blocks of shares) have relationships that might reduce their independence.

BOARDS OF NOT-FOR-PROFIT INSTITUTIONS AND PENSION FUNDS

Like large business corporations, large not-for-profit institutions should have a majority of unaffiliated directors. Too often, not-for-profit organizations get less fully focused scrutiny from their directors than business organizations get from theirs. In addition, not-for-profit organizations lack the discipline supplied by competition or the scrutiny provided by shareholders.

Hence, perhaps even more than business organizations, not-for-profit institutions need detached, close, and continuous oversight.

The purpose of exempting not-for-profit institutions and pension funds from taxation is to help them pursue stated objectives that are deemed to serve the public interest. Too often, the personal interests of trustees have prevailed over these institutional objectives. We regard the presence of trustees or directors who have no interests that conflict with the institution's as so important that we recommend making appropriate board composition a prerequisite for tax-exempt status.

Not-for-profit institutions have a cogent reason that business organizations lack to have "representative" boards; they enjoy tax exemption precisely because they are explicitly "affected with a public interest." Representative boards, however defined, have different and more complex implications for private corporations.

The need of pension funds—whether sponsored by business corporations, joint boards of employers and unions, or state and local governments—for representative boards is particularly clear. The proposition that certain funds shall be managed for the "exclusive benefit" of a defined group whose members are excluded from representation in the fund's management is absurd. The conflict abuses that have occurred in pension funds call for more thoroughgoing remedies than a provision that some or even a majority of trustees be "unaffiliated." To assure the use of assets exclusively to benefit employees and without in any way favoring some employees over others, we believe it essential that every pension board include:

1. Unaffiliated trustees, that is, individuals who have no other relation to either the sponsoring organization or the beneficiary group.

2. Representatives of the sponsoring organization, including, in the case of state and local funds, taxpayer representatives as well as public officials.

3. Representatives of the beneficiary group, including current employees with vested interests (a constituency now represented on many fund boards) and, separately, retired employees or their beneficiaries. (Several state pension funds now provide for separate representation of retirees. Such representation may not be necessary if retirees participate in selecting employee representatives, as they do in a few industrial unions.)

The boards of state and local pension funds have a special need for independence, given the pressures on them to allow ever more massive pension assets to be invested or managed for purposes other than the exclusive benefit of the beneficiaries. We urge state and local governments to provide their pension funds with fully representative boards possessing the same stature and independence enjoyed by most boards of regents or state university boards of trustees. For example, any appointive member of such boards should be confirmed by legislative advice and consent.

The boards of many foundations and endowments already are fairly representative of their various constituencies. Nevertheless, some observers believe that, in addition to requiring representativeness and an appropriate unaffiliated presence, not-for-profit institutions should impose a flat ban on directors with conflicting relationships. We consider such a ban feasible for large not-for-profit institutions, or even medium-sized ones in large communities. Such organizations can recruit board members easily from a fairly wide range of persons.

But smaller not-for-profit institutions often have difficulty in recruiting to their boards individuals with diverse backgrounds and appropriate experience. A flat ban may make it impossible for such organizations to secure the active, low-cost involvement of such individuals. Even in large not-for-profit institutions, a flat ban may interfere with personal or institutional arrangements of great value and low risk of conflict abuse. Instead of an absolute prohibition on directors with conflicting relationships in eleemosynary institutions, we recommend disclosure as a device that both preserves the benefits of free choice of board members and reduces the risk of abuse.

Composition of key board committees. Unaffiliated directors should constitute all of a board's audit committee and at least a majority of the committee on executive compensation. Audit committees are responsible for, among other things, establishing and implementing safeguards against conflict abuses. Not-for-profit institutions and pension funds that have representative boards also should make these committees as representative as is feasible.[1]

Selection of unaffiliated and representative directors. Initially, some boards may have to proceed through existing processes to select unaffiliated directors. Once unaffiliated directors are on the board, they should nominate (and in some organizations, even select) their successors.

Assuring representativeness in nonprofits and pension funds is a complex problem. Organizations, such as pension funds, that now serve organized constituencies, may have less difficulty than, say, foundations, in using an elective process, but the nonpolitical and relatively technical tasks of pension fund boards justify the use of appointment even when elections are possible.

Qualifications for unaffiliated directors. The qualities of independence and, where appropriate, representativeness, are not incompatible with financial sophistication. Many conflict abuses, especially within not-for-profit institutions, state and local pension funds, and "union" or jointly managed pension funds, take place apparently because although well-intentioned "watchdogs" are present, they do not adequately understand what they are watching. Being responsible for substantial assets, often quite liquid in form, trustees are inevitably favorite targets of those whose business it is to sell financial services. Even relatively unsophisticated boards will be able to screen out unscrupulous sales efforts. But conflicts are frequent in finance, and the unsophisticated are likely to have less awareness of what constitutes an abuse than the sophisticated. Such boards have a duty to acquire or to recruit members who possess adequate financial knowledge. Many vigorous retired people as well as active professionals have all the necessary qualifications for board membership and should be considered.

Rosters of unaffiliated directors. Unaffiliated (and representative) directors must be able to work with their board colleagues and not see their function as adversarial. However, experience suggests that conflict between affiliated and unaffiliated directors is far less common than the failure of directors selected through an "old boy" network to introduce independent or sincerely varied views.

The surest way to secure appropriately experienced as well as truly unaffiliated directors is to have interested persons qualify for a roster maintained by an organization for industry self-regulation, possibly a trade association or perhaps, preferably, a specialized organization that is independent in itself, such as the American Arbitration Association. (For jointly managed or "union" pension funds, the Federal Mediation and Conciliation Service, which maintains a roster of arbitrators, also should maintain a roster of pension fund trustees.)

Terms for unaffiliated directors. Since properly chosen unaffiliated board members will, by definition, lack other relationships with the organization and therefore will have only such support as their merit draws, it is imperative that their terms be at least as long as (and preferably longer than) the terms of other directors; otherwise, unaffiliated directors may be tempted to sacrifice some of their independence to retain their directorships.

Support for unaffiliated and representative directors. Unaffiliated and representative directors cannot be expected to serve more than a cosmetic function unless they receive adequate compensation and a budget with which to hire independent consultants for legal or accounting services, special advice, or other analysis pertinent to the board's tasks, whenever it is appropriate to do so.

Implementation. We recommend that the appropriate regulatory agencies consider and adopt the most effective measures—whether statutory amendment, rule, or statement of policy—to promote inclusion and strengthening of unaffiliated directors on corporate, pension, and not-for-profit boards. For example, we urge Congress to consider requiring all tax-exempt organizations (except religious ones) to meet specific guidelines for this purpose.

Regulation: Disclosure

In more than forty years of experience with federal securities regulation, disclosure has proved to be one of the most successful legal devices for the regulation of financial activity. Disclosure imposes no governmental impediment on lawful activity, however venturesome or even silly any particular proposition may be. Without reducing innovation, flexibility, or individuality, it maximizes the efficacy of market forces and individual judgments. Disclosure deters illegal and improper conduct and increases the probability that, if such conduct does occur, it will be corrected. Disclosure is an appropriate measure in situations in which it is believed that with adequate information, market forces will produce more acceptable or desirable results than would any governmental decision about what is acceptable or desirable.

Certainly, disclosure costs money. It may involve the publication of documents containing large amounts of complex information, such as prospectuses for the new issuance of securities. But in many situations the costs of disclosure are inconsequential. A firm might simply include in its normal merchandising material—distributed to every potential client—a description of the practices it follows to prevent unjustified favoring of some customers over others or to prevent improper use of inside information. Implementing the practices disclosed also costs money, but presumably these costs represent a lesser evil than the abuses that the practices are intended to prevent. The choice of disclosure represents a decision that safeguards against such abuses should exist, that different firms may properly choose varying types of safeguards, and that the least intrusive yet most effective way of assuring the implementation of safeguards is simply to require that every firm disclose what safeguards it does have.

Firms may minimize the costs of such disclosure by including reasonably complete summaries in material otherwise disseminated and by making full data available on request.

Most beneficiaries do not focus on such reports, unless an event or scandal gives the subject prominence. But the possibility that even a small number may read carefully and understand what they are reading helps preserve management's sense of accountability.

PERIODICAL DISCLOSURE OF FULL INVESTMENT PERFORMANCE DATA

The ultimate test of whether investment managers (such as trust departments and investment counsellors) or investment portfolios (such as pension funds and endowment funds) are performing disinterestedly and competently is how their results compare with those of funds that have similar objectives. Of course, total integrity is quite compatible with poor investment judgment or simply an unfavorable period, just as high ability or a run of good fortune are compatible with significant conflict abuses. But making adequate data on an account's investment results available to the relevant public—and no routine disclosure will draw as full attention as performance data—can be expected to put pressure on the account managers (and on the persons who select them) to avoid any abuse that might worsen the results. Continuously poor results invite scrutiny, and although readers knowledgeable about securities markets will accept occasional setbacks, and a few people may even tolerate continuous weak peformance, disclosure is bound to endanger the positions of managers whose selection had been influenced by a conflict of interest or who are not performing disinterestedly. Effective and full disclosure of performance data ranks as a major safeguard against conflict abuses.

We believe that every organization that provides investment management must disclose, at least once a year, its investment performance to the community of its beneficiaries. In the case of personal trust accounts, this practice is of long standing. But such data should be available to all of a pension fund's beneficiaries; to the public in the case of state and local government pension funds; to faculty, students, staff, and alumni of educational institutions; and to the various constituencies of foundations and similar eleemosynary institutions.

Although foundations are now required to make public major data on their financial affairs, not all foundations issue public reports, and not all the reports include the kinds of data we recommend. Educational endowments are not required to disclose such data (we believe they should be), and very few endowments provide investment information even when it is requested for research purposes. We urge the endowments to reconsider this position, which is particularly inappropriate for institutions devoted to full access to information and the pursuit of truth.

The performance data to be disclosed should include:

- Market valuations (at least for publicly traded securities) rather than mere cost data, as well as realized gains and losses and inflows and outflows.
- Measurement of relative riskiness.
- Comparison with a substantial sample of similar accounts.
- Comparison with other accounts under the same investment manager.

Currently, much performance reporting covers market valuations adequately. But only the more sophisticated presentations include mathematical measures of the degree of risk in each investment. The last decade has brought widespread understanding that a sound evaluation of the "total return"—income and capital gains or losses—of a given portfolio must reflect the amount of risk assumed to secure that return. A 5 percent total return from investments in insured savings accounts is superior to a 5 percent return from investments in particularly volatile securities. (Riskier investments can be justified only by higher returns.) Our use of the phrase *relative riskiness* is not meant to indicate a preference for any one of the various methods of measuring risk. But some measurement of risk is indispensable if disclosure of investment performance is to be complete.

Sound evaluation of performance also requires comparison with similar investment portfolios. Endowment accounts are frequently compared with broad market indices, such as the Standard & Poor's 500, but they must also be compared with other endowment accounts. In the past ten years, market analysts have developed data bases and methods of comparison so today a pension fund or endowment can evaluate its portfolio's performance relative to those of other similar funds.

Many investment portfolios have some unique features. When such features are present, disclosure of appropriate comparisons should be accompanied by a brief explanation. Thus, an endowment may have unusually high needs for current income or a pension fund may have unusually heavy inflows. It also is important to disclose investment objectives, because the performance of a portfolio cannot be evaluated properly without knowledge of its objectives. It is particularly likely to be misleading to compare one portfolio with any other single portfolio or with a small number of portfolios. (In one sector, foundations, even comparison with a large number may be misleading, because some portfolios are highly concentrated, and because many portfolios are still implementing the requirements of the Tax Reform Act of 1969.)

Such comparative data are now commonplace among sophisticated accounts. Only a handful of the most sophisticated—and usually exceptionally large—accounts, however, secure data showing how the performance of their portfolios compares with that of other accounts under the same investment management. Every investment manager has conflicts among its various accounts, and, of course, accounts have many differences that may affect performance. But if the account principals learn that their fund is in, say, the manager's bottom quartile, or below the median, they can make inquiries to protect their fund against abuses. Data of this type have come into use sufficiently that no one can claim inability to present such information (although managers are entitled to charge extra for it).

Comparison with other accounts under the same investment manager also may need a brief accompanying explanation.

PERIODIC DISCLOSURE ON SERVICE PROVIDERS

Because the financial affairs of a tax-exempt (nonreligious) institution are of public interest, the identities and compensation of those who provide financial services to the institution are appropriate subjects for public disclosure. With demonstrated frequency institutions secure such services on conflicted, improper bases instead of on the basis of competence. In corporate pension funds, the sponsoring corporation's interests may override concerns for the pension funds; in state and local government pension funds, political factors may affect such decisions; and in eleemosynary institutions personal relationships may determine the choice. Because the least expensive financial services are not necessarily the best bargain, we do not recommend requiring institutions to hire only lowest bidders. (Competitive bidding has many virtues, but it should not preclude the trustees from exercising their own professional judgment.)

Instead, we recommend requiring that the institution disclose (to the public in the case of state and local government funds, to the relevant community in case of other funds):

1. Whom it employs to provide financial services.
2. What general services were rendered by and what payments were made to each service provider for the period covered by the report.
3. To the extent it is possible to report more than boilerplate, what factors were considered in the selection of any service provider hired since the last report.
4. What, if any, other significant relations link the service providers with the organization, fund, or trustees.
5. If other significant relations do exist, and if 10 percent or more of the service provider's gross income from such goods or services comes from sales to the institution, the precise percentage should be given.

DISCLOSURE OF SYSTEMS TO PREVENT ABUSES OF CONFLICTS

Every conflict that is part of the ordinary operation of a firm involved in the securities markets should (unless specially regulated, for example, as investment companies must secure SEC approval before engaging in conflicted transactions) be surrounded by a system of safeguards that are fully disclosed to the firm's existing and potential customers. Such disclosure must be very specific. The statement of a bank trust department or broker-dealer firm that "we make every effort to keep uninvested cash balances at a minimum" or "we do not use material inside information in connection with any decision or recommendation to buy or sell securities" is no more than a pledge of compliance with the law, neither informing customers nor helping to assure that the firm both has established and actually implements safeguards against abuse. We can neither list all the subjects on which disclosure of safeguard systems should be required nor spell out every detail of the matters that we do note. The pertinent regulatory agencies (or trade associations if, as in the cases of endowments and REITs, no one agency is specifically charged with regulation) must assume the burden of supplying detailed specifications.

Allocation among customers. Every firm that manages more than one investment portfolio faces conflicts about which portfolio comes first in timing of orders, in allocation of limited-supply investments, and in allocation of managerial talent. A number of systems have proved effective in preventing or reducing abuse of the allocation conflict. For example, all accounts too small to warrant individualized focus may be invested in pooled funds; or discretionary accounts may routinely be placed ahead (chronologically) of non-discretionary accounts. But some systems in wide use appear to provide only partial safeguards. Many firms, for example, simply give all accounts pro rata participation in any investment move; this system works well if accounts are roughly equal in size and the firm is not too large. But most very large investment managers have accounts of diverse size and varied portfolios. Some investment transactions involve spreading orders over weeks and even months; hence, the accounts that are moved early may fare better than those that are moved later. If a large firm gives pro rata treatment to all accounts in stock X, an account with, say, forty thousand shares of IBM and another account with only four hundred shares may each be sold out of half their holdings at the same time. Some clients would be satisfied with such an arrangement; others would be outraged that the much smaller holding was not sold out early—giving priority to accounts with small holdings would benefit them vastly more than it would damage accounts with large holdings. But size of holdings or accounts is only one of the many considerations that should shape the choice of an allocation system. Of the commonly used solutions for the allocations problem, only two are clearly wrong: taking care of the larger (and therefore more remunerative) or more sophisticated (and therefore more mobile) accounts ahead of others and failing to disclose the precise system of allocation.

At present very few investment management firms disclose their allocation systems as part of the material regularly presented to potential clients. Many firms do not even have any written allocation systems. Each firm should disclose to current and potential clients these specifics:

1. How it allocates orders.
2. How it allocates limited supply investments.
3. How investment information flows within the firm.
4. Which individuals, with which positions in the firm's investment decision-making structure, are responsible for the account.
5. If the firm publishes investment advisory materials for distribution to other firms or to the public, how the timing of such publications relates to the timing of executions for accounts managed by the firm.

Material "inside" information. Few conflicts have received as much notoriety, as well as official and scholarly attention, as the misuse—and the possibility of liability even when actual misuse does not take place—of material "inside" information. Multiple-function firms, such as commercial banks with trust departments and investment bankers that also provide investment management or advice, inevitably face this problem. But single-function firms are not immune. An investment counsellor may be offered an opportunity to participate in a private placement and thus may receive nonpublic information about an issuer; or the investment manager of a large corporate pension account may learn material nonpublic information about the account principal's affairs; or a director interlock may be a steady source of inside information. A recent survey indicates that financial analysts find that proper handling of inside information is the most difficult of all conflicts problems.

It is unfortunate that the standard term for a safeguard against this conflict has become the *Chinese wall*; the connotations of imperviousness suggested by the term have demoralized investment professionals in their efforts to erect realistic safeguards and have led outsiders to view any protection short of total separation as mere propaganda.

A firm that may secure material nonpublic information about an issuer or about significant investment moves with respect to an issuer's securities risks abuse—and liability even without actual abuse—unless it has the following formal policies and procedures:[2]

1. What access, if any, to files and other research materials that may include material nonpublic information is shared by departments performing conflicting functions, such as banking and investment management?

2. What joint visits or other joint contacts, if any, with issuers are made by personnel in different departments at the firm? Are joint contacts, for example, limited to introductory efforts to develop new business?

3. What personnel, if any, are shared between departments performing conflicting functions? What precise roles do they perform? If the common personnel are involved with the banking or investment banking affairs of an issuer, what limits, if any, are imposed on their involvement with investment management decisions involving the issuer?

4. What personnel, if any (including directors), oversee departments in the performance of conflicting functions? What, precisely, is the normal role of such upper echelon personnel? When a firm in which the trust department holds a large investment position is also involved with, say, the banking side, in a negotiation so substantial that the matter rises to high echelons that supervise both departments, what procedure does the bank follow to prevent abuse? For example, the investment management department might freeze its decisions with respect to that issuer for the duration of the negotiations and a fixed interval after they conclude.

5. When individual officers are transferred from one department to another, what procedures does the bank use to prevent misuse of material inside information? For example, the individual might be barred from acting on certain accounts for a fixed interval after the transfer.

6. What special procedures are used to safeguard investment holdings in close corporations and other situations involving special relationships?

7. What is done in the case of common director or officer affiliations?

8. What is done if personnel accidentally (for example, during a visit with a issuer's officers to discuss the issuer's pension account) come upon material inside information? For example, does the officer involved notify, say, an attorney or compliance official in his firm? If so, what does the person notified do? (He might, for example, freeze trading in that issuer's securities while examining the situation and, if need be, for a longer period.)

9. If the firm publishes investment advisory materials for other firms or for the public, how is such publication handled when the firm is in possession of material inside information? For example, is publication delayed until the problem is resolved? What if the security in question is already on a "recommended positions" list?

The new set of conflicts in takeover situations—whether the conflicted participant is a bank, an investment banker, or a lawyer—is mainly a problem of handling confidential information. For example, a target company's lead bank or investment banker may well have information about the company's liquidity, access to external funds, relations with key stockholders, pending developments, and so forth. Such information may be critical to another company when deciding whether to embark upon a takeover, or how to price the offer, or, in the final result, how far to go if a contest breaks out. This set of conflicts of interest, which emerged after our studies had been done, must be examined in this chapter to establish a basis for our recommendations.

Conflicts of interest in takeovers are peculiarly important for two reasons: First, conflicted financial institutions that succumb to taking advantage of the conflict are likely to opt in favor of their larger customer, which more often than not will be the larger of the contesting companies. When such an external relationship influences the market for corporate control, it introduces an undesirable and avoidable bias in favor of big companies' acquiring smaller ones. Whether or not size should succeed in the struggle for corporate survival, conflicts of interest should not contribute to the result. Second, although contested takeovers are prodigious producers of litigation, thorough examination of the facts in dispute is difficult because even a slight delay may actually decide the whole contest for control.[3] Yet there is no avoiding close exploration of the facts—unless the courts decide to ignore claims of abusive conduct by conflicted participants—where there are neither guidelines nor systematic procedures. A brief review of three conflicted takeover situations reveals how acute the conflicts are, the difficulty of ignoring claims of abuse, and the lack of safeguard systems within the firms in queston.

The first known instance of a conflicted bank's participating in a contested takeover arose in 1976. Irving Trust had long been lead bank for both the would-be acquirer, General Cable (with whom the bank shared four common directors), and for the target company, Microdot. The bank received quarterly reports of Microdot's operations on a nonpublic divisional basis, as well as daily nonpublic statements of Microdot's cash position. The bank also provided most of the financing for General Cable's effort to take over Microdot. The only previous statement the bank had made about what it would do in such a conflicted takeover consisted of one officer's saying, at a seminar on takeovers a year before General Cable went after Microdot: "I can assure you that a responsible bank will remain loyal to its present customer and certainly wishes to avoid choosing sides." However questionable the Irving's position might be—and although they had no policy or systems to buttress their claim that they committed no abuse, it must be remembered that this was the first time the problem became visible—the facts do suggest that no abuse occurred: (1) General Cable was simply drawing on a preexisting general line of credit for more than the sum sought for the tender offer and allegedly did not consult the bank at all about the takeover; (2) there was no showing of how the Irving Trust's information about Microdot might have been useful to General Cable even if consultation had occurred; (3) Irving Trust may no longer have been Microdot's lead bank, since another large bank had secured a director interlock with Microdot, the Irving was furnishing only a minor fraction of Microdot's credit, and their relationship had been declining.

In a second situation, Morgan Stanley did furnish Johns-Manville, the would-be acquirer, with confidential information about its target, Olinkraft. Months earlier Olinkraft had given Morgan Stanley that information for use in another matter. When that other matter had terminated, Olinkraft requested return of the information and apparently believed that Morgan Stanley had complied with that request. Morgan Stanley justified giving Olinkraft's confidential earnings data to Johns-Manville by saying that they did so only after the Olinkraft board of directors had decided to accept a $51-per-share offer from a third company and only to help Olinkraft shareholders by assisting Johns-Manville in offering $57 per share.[4] Morgan Stanley alleged no safeguards or policy that might help assure its clients against the firm's using confidential information about them in unanticipated ways, except that the firm consulted its counsel before acting.

Another situation that reveals the inadequacy of existing safeguards and the resulting need for close factual inquiry: Joseph Flom of New York City is one of the two or three lawyers most sought after in takeover contests, working sometimes for a would-be acquirer, other times for the defense. Several years before Curtiss-Wright sought to take over Kennecott, Curtiss-Wright had entered a retainer arrangement with Flom for advice on defending itself against takeovers. In that connection Flom allegedly learned important facts about Curtiss-Wright's relations with the financial community. And pursuant to that retainer, Flom was still handling a Curtiss-Wright lawsuit when Kennecott hired him to help defend itself against Curtiss-Wright's takeover attempt. Several days after Flom was well into that Kennecott defense, he so informed Curtiss-Wright, which thereupon sued him for breach of duty. Curtiss-Wright lost at the trial level, and their appeal was dropped as part of an overall settlement when Curtiss-Wright secured several seats on Kennecott's board. Subsequently, Flom revised the terms of his retainer agreements in an effort to make clearer what his clients might expect him to do if two of them became involved in a takeover battle.

The vacuum of guidelines surrounding these conflicts (see also "Introduction," above) should be filled quickly.

Some firms (for example, Georgeson & Co., the leading proxy solicitation and investor relations firm) follow a simple policy that resolves most problems: whenever two clients are in a takeover contest, the firm goes with the defense, and all new clients are so informed.[5] Such a guideline may be less feasible at a bank that, for example, may have a general line of credit outstanding on which a would-be acquirer wishes to draw. On the other hand, for a bank to announce, as one has, the simple policy of staying out of contests where it has a "significant relationship with the target," but to refuse to say what is "significant," is to announce only a facade.

Any firm that may secure material nonpublic information about an issuer, who then may be called upon to participate in a takeover involving that issuer, risks abuse—and not only liability even without clear abuse but also the likelihood of causing avoidable judicial interference with the results of a takeover contest—unless the firm has adopted and disclosed to its clients its policies with respect to questions such as these:

1. Will the firm participate in a contested takeover involving two clients? Even if it will not, how does it determine early enough whether a proposed acquisition will be contested? (Perhaps it is feasible to have a bank condition the financing on the lack of opposition by the target company, but that condition seems operationally unrealistic and wholly unrealistic for an investment banker.)

2. If the firm will participate in contested takeovers involving two clients, will it automatically go with the defender or the acquirer?

3. If the firm does not automatically choose one side or the other, how does it choose? If the choice turns on the "significance of prior relations," what are the criteria of significance: for example, the volume of business from the client's point of view, or from the financial institution's? Is some dollar level the determinant of "significance"?

4. Will the financial institution participate if its involvement requires no consultation, for example, as by merely honoring a draw on a preexisting line of credit?

5. When if ever will the financial institution participate on behalf of a new client in a contest involving a preexisting client?

6. If the financial institution is involved in consultations about a contested takeover involving a preexisting client, what steps does it take to insure that material nonpublic information it has about that client is not used against that client's interests? For example, it is easy to establish a routine of notifying personnel handling both accounts to observe special precautions about files, and even discussions, during a contest.[6]

7. If a client asks a financial institution to return material nonpublic information, does the financial firm retain any copy of such data (as it may have proper reasons for doing) and, if so, for what purposes and with what system to safeguard against misuse?

Transactions and relationships that involve conflicts. Transactions that involve conflicts clearly should be disclosed to the appropriate public (unless unquestionably trivial in amount or nature). Corporations subject to SEC proxy regulation already are required to disclose such transactions. All other entities should be required to include in their annual reports brief notes on the nature and dimensions of such transactions.

Transactions that involve conflicts are the episodic outcroppings of conflicting relationships. Most such relationships (for example, common directorships or the fact that the new trustee of the university or of the state pension fund is a broker-dealer) are disclosed in the ordinary course of events. In addition to our recommendation that organizations, particularly not-for-profit institutions, that do not already disclose their investment holdings should do so, we urge full disclosure with respect to investment holdings that are themselves the result of transactions or relationships based on conflict. For example, one major trust department recently began disclosing on an annual basis its purchases and sales of the securities of all director-affiliated companies. We oppose prohibiting investment managers from holding securities in companies for which they are, say, the pension account managers or investment bankers (because we believe such a ban would be tantamount to forcing segregation of functions and breakup of firms along lines that, in our judgment, may produce inordinate inefficiencies). But to prevent the conflict from warping portfolio judgments, the manager should be required, as part of its routine reporting, to disclose all purchases or sales in such "specially related" companies, at least when the relationship is already disclosed publicly or when disclosure would not breach a legitimately confidential relationship.

In addition, managers or account principals should disclose conflicting holdings or transactions to the beneficiaries at least annually. For example, the identity of the investment manager of a pension fund covered by ERISA is public information; if that investment firm also holds substantial securities of the corporate sponsor of that pension fund, the firm should disclose its holdings, purchases, and sales. A similar procedure should be followed in investment banking relationships, for jointly managed or union pension fund portfolios that contain holdings in any corporation that is in the union's industry and geographic area, and for not-for-profit institutions that have holdings in a substantial contributor or trustee-related company.

Entities that vote shares in corporations with which they have conflicting relationships should make annual disclosure of their votes on all nonroutine matters, including executive compensation and any contests for directorships. Some investment management firms (especially bank trust departments) hold in their portfolios voting securities of the investment firm itself (or of its parent or any commonly owned affiliate). In such cases we believe that disclosure cannot adequately insure against self-serving use of the voting power.[7]

Other conflicting interests of directors and employees. To what extent should organizations be required to disclose conflicts that involve not matters of public information, such as directorships and employment positions, but nonpublic information about, say, a director's large personal ownership of stock in a firm with which the organization may do business?

We strongly favor boards that reflect detached and diverse judgments rooted in knowledge, and we believe that persons otherwise qualified and willing to serve ought not be excluded from doing so simply because they are unwilling to make their personal affairs public. In the post-Watergate period, public disclosure on a vast spectrum of matters has enjoyed almost unqualified approval. Yet it may well cease to do so as the public realizes that the values of disclosure sometimes compete with values of privacy, and that some disclosures bring fewer benefits than burdens. Disclosure of matters related to the organization (for example, a not-for-profit organization's trustee's large holding in a corporation with which the organization does business) is a necessary safeguard against conflict abuses; disclosure of broader matters (for example, the names or amounts of a trustee's holdings generally) is not. The burden of disclosure that the public is entitled to impose on persons assuming high governmental offices is different from that on trustees of not-for-profit institutions and directors of profit-making organizations. In addition, attitudes toward full disclosure may vary geographically, particularly as between major urban centers and smaller communities.

In this area we believe that each organization should decide to what extent it can implement public disclosure and to what extent it will instead implement internal reporting. Few persons otherwise willing to serve an organization would refuse to comply with the following guidelines:

1. Board members who have conflicting relationships that are not already substantially public information should disclose the relationships, at least annually, in appropriate detail, to the full board or a designated unaffiliated member of the board. (In addition, of course, the member with the conflict should excuse himself whenever the conflict bears on a matter before the board.) Officers and specified employees should report on their conflicting relationships to the general counsel or other designated person as well as to the board's audit committee.

2. Directors, officers, and specified employees with any role in investment management, even if limited to selecting the management firm or to receiving fuller and more immediate reports about investment decisions than are generally available to the community of beneficiaries, should report to a designated person, at least quarterly, on all investment moves (not merely ones they consider tinged by conflict) made for their personal portfolios or those of members of their immediate family. In addition, persons occupying roles significantly involved with the investment process, including those who have no role in investment decisions, might be subjected to special safeguards; for example, they might be prohibited from making investment moves for a set period after receiving any information about the organization's own moves or

recommendations, or required to accept minimal holding periods for any investments in small capitalization issuers that might also be considered for investment by the organization.

Self-dealing with managed accounts. In recent years the practice of allowing uninvested cash to lie idle and produce undisclosed extra income for investment managers has received considerable criticism, but it is merely one of several forms of self-dealing that are inevitable, at least in some degree, even with formal trust accounts. Transaction costs make it impossible to eliminate all idle uninvested cash. Similarly, some investment managers can use securities left on deposit with them to increase their total income from an account. Managers engaged in underwriting a security sometimes decide that it is an attractive investment for discretionary accounts they manage; but allowing such placements also enables managers to dump undesirable securities into captive accounts. And some managers, especially trust departments handling estates and positions in closely held companies, may need to decide whether to lend to or even buy from or sell to such accounts, or may have customer relationships or other affiliations with parties seeking to enter transactions with such accounts.

In all of these situations, managers should make advance disclosure of the specific transaction to the affected persons. In addition, they should disclose, in detail, their systems for dealing with continuing, routine conflicts, such as the handling of idle cash or securities. In some of these situations, we recommend substantive requirements to go beyond disclosure.[8]

A trustee should disclose its system for handling idle cash—including the minimum dollar amounts and time periods at which the benefits of moving the accumulation to income-producing cash equivalents outweigh transaction costs; trustees also should report to each account, periodically, its average daily noninterest-bearing deposit balance. (A nontrustee manager should make such information available upon request.)

Broker-dealers and a few other market participants have the opportunity to use securities on deposit for their own benefit. Requiring broker-dealers to report each actual use to each account would be costly, and changes that have taken place since the advent of negotiated commission rates are not yet fully understood. When bank trustees or other nonbroker-dealer managers (certainly in the capacity of trustees, who are entitled to no profit from managing the trust beyond the agreed-upon fees) use securities on deposit, they should make full disclosure of this use to beneficiaries. We urge that securities, banking, and insurance regulatory agencies and private groups such as the Investment Counsel Association examine the adequacy of existing assurances of fairness in this area.

Portfolio consideration by pension funds and nonprofit institutions of noninvestment criteria. Suggestions arise periodically that institutional investment portfolios should select investments not merely to maximize performance but also to promote other objectives, such as "corporate responsibility," aid to urban redevelopment or to in-state firms, or jobs in, say, a multiemployer fund's industry. Such objectives, however worthy in themselves, may conflict with the beneficiaries' interest in a sound fund.

We believe that employee retirement security and the preservation of independent not-for-profit institutions are themselves socially valid goals for investment portfolios. But funds that use noninvestment criteria for their portfolios should disclose, as part of their regular reporting on the portfolio, what the criteria are, how they are factored into investment decisions, and which investments were selected in part on the basis of these criteria.

Beyond Disclosure: Structural Changes in Markets and within Firms, and Legal Prohibitions

Disclosure has its limitations. It works well only if accompanied by incentives or mechanisms for action on the information disclosed. Although competition provides such incentives, competition operates sporadically and may have no effect at all on practices that involve only minor losses to each individual client. Therefore it is imperative to facilitate efforts to secure redress.

However, disclosure only inhibits the occurrence or abuse of conflicts that, in some instances, might be wholly eliminated by structural changes, such as paying broker-dealers not by commissions but by salaries, or separating the trust function from commercial banking. At the one pole, if a structural change can eliminate the temptation to abuse, there is no reason to settle for the mere inhibition of abuse through disclosure. At the other pole, if the structure cannot be changed but a practice fraught with potential for abuse can be isolated and carries no countervailing benefits, the practice should be barred outright rather than surrounded with inhibitions. But when structural changes removing conflicts and bars against conflicts have side effects of great complexity or undesirable impact, disclosure, although providing only modest correction, may be the preferred remedy.

Other Regulatory Prescriptions and Proscriptions

Governmental prescriptions regarding the operations of firms or the conduct of transactions and governmental proscriptions against particular conduct are intrusions into the private sector that require clearer justification than does disclosure. We strongly believe that regulatory intrusion is necessary in many cases to protect the public interest, including the interest in preserving vigorous competition to minimize the need for still further intrusion. But regulation of substantive conduct must be far more finely tailored to the enterprise than requirements for the governance structure of firms or for disclosure. Hence, our recommendations in this section are limited to a few illustrative examples.

Legitimate transactions that involve conflict. A broker-dealer who also acts as an underwriter or market maker may, for completely proper reasons, want to sell directly to a number of the investment accounts it manages. The fact is that investors often are eager to purchase newly offered securities, and market makers often are able to offer such securities at a better price than is available elsewhere. But if such transactions are permissible, some underwriters may dump weak or slow-selling securities into the accounts they manage, and some market makers may take advantage of the acute difficulty of retrospectively evaluating what purported to be "best execution."

This kind of problem arises in a great many investment management situations. A bank trustee may believe quite sincerely that the best purchaser for close corporation shares in one trust account would be another trust account, or that the bank itself is the lowest cost lender to a trust account, or that a private placement arranged by the trust department's commercial side is an excellent investment for several trust accounts. Other activities that may be legitimate despite the presence of conflict include a municipal pension fund's purchase of local mortgages, a multiemployer or union pension fund's purchase of the securities of one of the employer firms, or in the case of construction industry multiemployer funds, of mortgages on new construction in the locality.

All of these transactions involve investments without clearly established fair market values. In such situations efforts to find buyers or sellers without conflicts are obviously desirable; we are not sure whether requiring such efforts would reduce abuses or merely increase red tape, but we recommend that the relevant regulators and trade associations consider such a requirement. Certainly, as soon as the conflicted transaction is deemed a reasonable possibility, we recommend requiring full disclosure of the probable terms and prospective parties to the transaction. The *sine qua non* for such transactions should be independent appraisal and, in the case of formal trust relationships, court approval (unless all beneficiaries are sophisticated enough to give informed consent, and do so). Whenever possible the appraiser should be chosen by the beneficiaries, not the investment manager.

Even if they involve clear conflicts, transactions—with safeguards—may be permitted if they involve securities traded actively enough or, in the case of a new offering or a package or mortgages, are being purchased widely enough to establish a clear fair market value. Actively traded securities should be salable from one account to another under common management if (1) advance general consent is given; (2) such transactions demonstrably lower transaction costs and thereby benefit the accounts; and (3) the manager has established an objective, routine method of determining the market price that does not favor the buying account over the selling account or vice versa. (One such method might be to time-stamp the order before the market opens, for execution at the day's average price.) Similarly, investment managers should be free to sell their new offerings, private placements, packages of mortgages, and similar securities to the accounts they manage if (1) advance specific consent is secured; (2) the manager so places no more than a minor portion of its participation, say 10 percent or 20 percent (including any placement in the manager's own account); and (3) the remainder of such a manager's participation is sold on the same terms as those for its accounts.

We believe that self-dealing transactions involving conflicts can take place provided that the bulk of such an investment is made on the same terms by clearly independent purchasers. Such a provision can prevent abuse in numerous situations. If, say, a municipal pension fund wishes to purchase local mortgages, the risk of weak or unsound investments is removed if the fund acts not alone but as a minority participant with local financial institutions. Or a market-making firm that also manages accounts may sell directly to its own accounts, up to a fixed small fraction of its daily volume, on terms as good as the best given the same day.

Voting by investment managers of stock holdings in their own firms. It has long been recognized as inevitable that some voting shares in a bank (or bank's parent holding company) will come under the bank trust department's management as estates and other accounts deposit assets other than cash. Bank regulators and state statutes have attempted, by such means as removing the voting power from these shares, to reduce the conflict of interest.

The voting power inherent in common stock defies disinterested exercise by the management of the bank, publicly held broker-dealer firm, or corporate pension fund holding shares in the sponsoring corporation. Even if not voted at all, such holdings reduce management's accountability. We see no justification for failing to "pass through" such voting power to the principals or a representative of the beneficiaries, especially in institutional accounts. (Several major trust departments have endeavored, in recent years, to reduce their own voting power generally, not merely on conflicted securities.) Although beneficiaries of individual accounts may prefer to be free of any decisional role, they can appoint a neutral party to decide on proxy solicitations (unless the trust or estate instrument cannot easily be changed, in which case facilitating statutes are appropriate).

Similarly, the trustees of corporate pension funds (and multiemployer funds) with holdings of common stock of employer firms should appoint more disinterested beneficiary representatives to vote such stock.

Restraint on the size of holdings that involve conflict. A state or local government pension fund may, exercising the best investment judgment, choose to hold securities of local firms; a bank trust department may hold shares not only in its own bank but also in firms that are commercial customers of the bank.

We are unwilling either to bar such conflicts (which are not harmful enough to justify the inefficiencies that would result from a flat prohibition) or to rely solely on the other safeguards we have recommended. Instead, we urge that institutions limit the sizes of positions that involve significant conflicts. Thus, a major bank trust department should be free to maintain a large position in a major corporation with which the bank has a minor depository relationship, but not with a corporation to which the bank is the lead lender; in such cases the bank's trust department should keep its portfolio position modest both in relation to its other holdings and as a proportion of the issuer's outstanding shares.

We envision no flat requirement of such restraint, believing that regulatory watchfulness over such situations will prevent both abuse and suspicions of abuse.

Enforcement Mechanisms

Even independent boards must be kept accountable; the fruits of disclosure must be usable; and compliance with substantive requirements must be assured. Only modest adjustments are needed to strengthen the existing scheme of enforcement.

1. Many of the official examination processes covering financial institutions have recently been substantially modernized. At trivial additional costs, these processes can be extended so regulators can review regulated firms' safeguard systems and handling of specific conflicts problems. We particularly urge the SEC (in its oversight of broker-dealers, investment advisors, and investment companies), the bank regulators, and the insurance regulators to reexamine their examination or inspection processes to insure that they give adequate priority and thoroughness to conflicts questions.

2. State attorneys general are traditionally responsible for official oversight of nonprofit institutions; most such officials have given this responsibility a near-bottom priority. In the past twenty-five years, assets of nonprofits and especially of foundations have grown enormously. Overseeing the disposition of these assets demands higher priority and a larger share of the offices' budgets than sufficed generations ago.

Since the Tax Reform Act of 1969, the federal government has collected a 4 percent excise tax from foundations. We wholeheartedly endorse the recent proposals to channel back foundation tax revenue funds—with guidelines to insure against diversion—to the states to finance the efforts of state attorneys general to protect the public interest against fiduciary abuse in local nonprofit organizations.

3. The appropriateness of class actions and the award of attorneys' fees to plaintiffs who substantially prevail in vindicating interests that transcend the personal pocketbook is a hotly debated and intricate legal question. The answer to this question may involve a general approach to litigation or vary among substantive areas. But fiduciary obligation, as a special creation of the law, has a special claim on the concern of legislators and courts to facilitate institutional accountability. We hope that the principle of ERISA's provision for awarding attorneys' fees to beneficiaries who substantially prevail in suits will itself prevail in all analogous settings.

III • FURTHER STUDY

It is our hope that our recommendations, in addition to being implemented, will prompt responsible and interested persons in the industries we have studied, in the relevant government bodies, and in the universities to face conflicts problems more openly. We have not touched on all the matters that need action or study if equity and efficiency are to be preserved and "the level of conduct for fiduciaries kept at a level higher than that trodden by the crowd." But we believe that our analyses, comparisons of different problems, and suggested solutions may prove useful in other areas.

For example, for a number of years, officials, commentators, and directly affected persons have been engaged intensely in study of two critical issues:

1. The conflicts surrounding the role of the specialist have been so clearly apparent for so long that the SEC and others have studied them in detail, and today a web of safeguards surrounds every move of the specialist. But as the stock markets have evolved and continue to change dramatically, the roles of other market makers—particularly block traders and especially multiple-function firms that engaged in block trading—have become perhaps even more significant, and at least as conflict-ridden, as those of specialists. We urge full, open consideration of the conflicts of market makers before the new trading mechanisms build up their own resistance to change.

2. Few aspects of finance have received as much recent attention as pension fund liabilities, both in the pension plans of federal, state, and local governments and in the private sector. The federal government has recognized the presence of the conflicts of interest in determining and disclosing the extent of such liabilities; too many other pension fund sponsors have not.

Several state governments have recently made impressively thorough efforts to ascertain realistic pension liability estimates for their own and their municipalities' systems; a more limited congressional study has been attempted. Accountants and actuaries are struggling with the complexities of this issue, which goes beyond "honesty alone, or even the punctilio of an honor the most sensitive." We urge Congress to take an active and informed role in devising processes for the calculation and disclosure of pension liabilities, for this area is one in which we are the fiduciaries for future generations.

NOTES

I. Introduction

[1]FDIC, Manual of Examination Policies, §M: Management, p. 3 (1973).
[2]See pp. 120-28, 211-16, 259-62, 304-09, 355-61, 415-18, 489-94, 555-59.

II. Steps Toward Improvement

[1]In addition, large multiple-function firms, such as banks with trust departments or investment banking-brokerage firms, need some "outside audit committee" to review periodically the adequacy of fiduciary safeguards. Many banks already have such outside committees for specific branches or geographic areas; thus, a "fiduciary department visiting committee" would not be a departure from an accepted level of outside involvement.

[2]In 1976 Citibank's trust department sent a two-page letter to all its institutional investment customers, informing them of the bank's procedures for dealing with material inside information. A smaller investment manager would necessarily adopt different procedures, but banks of all sizes can devise appropriate procedures for this purpose. Financial institutions that fail to provide such written advice to their customers should expect their sincerity and the efficacy of their safeguards to be viewed with skepticism.

[3]In the one takeover contest in which a court did intervene to stop a conflicted bank's participation, the target company that sought that intervention used the delay it had won to secure a "friendly" merger with a third company, forcing the original would-be acquirer to drop its effort. *Washington Steel Corp.* v. *TW Corp.* (D.Ct. W.D. Penna., 1979).

[4]Apparently, Johns-Manville decided on July 17, 1978, to consider making an offer for more than $51 per share. But earlier, on July 14, the day after the other bidder had announced its $51 per share offer, Morgan Stanley's arbitrage department, "strictly in light of the announced discussions, without consulting with Morgan Stanley's merger and acquisition department," started acquiring 149,200 shares of Olinkraft. *The Wall Street Journal*, October 31, 1978, p. 12, and ibid., November 9, 1978, p. 28. See also Tim Metz, "Morgan Stanley's Rivals Lose Their Smirks Over Olinkraft as Fear of Crackdown Dawns," *The Wall Street Jounral*, March 5, 1979, p. 47.

[5]No simple policy can solve all the problems in complex situations. Presumably, when one Georgeson client goes after control of another, the firm restricts access to its own files on the offeror, while concentrating its efforts on behalf of the target company. But inevitably, a takeover contest may occur between two companies ordinarily handled by the same individual executive. Perhaps the only way of avoiding abuse in such situations is to stay out of the contest.

[6]Although the courts may have been correct in exonerating Continental Illinois Bank from any abuse when one of its customers, Humana, sought to take over another, American Medicorp, two troublesome aspects of the case could have been avoided easily: (1) the bank officer working on the loan to finance the tender offer, "flipped through" a fifteen-page summary of the bank's credit file on American Medicorp and extracted portions of it; (2) two other bank officers working on that loan had an informal discussion with two officers who worked on American Medicorp's account. "[T]he latter two officers were told that the [bank] was considering helping finance the Humana tender offer. The officers discussed the amount of business which the [bank] might lose from the plantiff [American Medicorp], specifically the amount of proposed loans to the plaintiff, but again, there is no showing that the information was used in deciding to make the Humana loan or transmit it to the officer primarily in charge of it." *American Medicorp Inc.* v. *Continental Illinois Bank and Trust Company* (No. 77-C-3865, N.D. Ill., December 30, 1977), p. 9.

[7]See Regulatory prescriptions and proscriptions, p. 591.

[8]See pp. 590-591.

Index